TRUCKERS'
handbook
2ND Edition

First published 2006
Reprinted 2007 (with amendments)
Second edition 2008

ISBN 978 1 84425 511 5

Haynes Publishing, Sparkford,
Yeovil, Somerset BA22 7JJ
Telephone: 01963 442030
Fax: 01963 440001
E-mail: sales@haynes.co.uk
Web site: www.haynes.co.uk

British Library Cataloguing in Publication Data
A catalogue record for this book is available from
the British Library

Printed by J. H. Haynes & Co. Ltd, Sparkford,
Yeovil, Somerset BA22 7JJ, UK

ABOUT THE AUTHOR

**Lisa Marie Melbourne became a van driver in 1992, took her Class II HGV (LGV Class C)
in 1997 and then her Class I HGV (LGV Class C+E) in 1998 – and has been trucking ever
since. Following a conversation with a friend about the lack of information for
truckers, she spent three years researching and compiling the invaluable data
contained in this book.**

TRUCKERS'
handbook
2ND Edition

LISA MARIE MELBOURNE
FOREWORD BY **SALLY TRAFFIC**

Contents

Foreword by Sally Traffic

Trucking can be a lonely business. There you are, out on the road at all times and in all types of weather, delivering everything imaginable from food to furniture, battling through ever increasing traffic jams and taken for granted by much of the population. These days, truck drivers are under more pressure than ever to deliver. Legislation, targets, fuel prices – all these things add stress to an already stressful job. I've learnt through my own job reporting on traffic jams throughout the UK that daily traffic chaos is almost normal, and this "Daily Battle of the Traffic" only adds to an already difficult and stressful job.

So this wonderful handbook is a Godsend. It takes the guesswork out of everything from where to eat, what's best to eat, legal matters, understanding your truck – in short, everything a trucker could possibly want to know.

The image of truckers has changed a lot over the years. No longer seen as "greasy Joes", the trucking business and those employed in the haulage industry in general are seen as total professionals who drive sometimes complicated and technologically advanced vehicles. Thus, conditions in the industry have gradually improved, along with drivers expectations of their day to day working environment. Truckstops across the country, for example, are now known for serving delicious, cheap and healthy food! And you'll find some of them here. In many drivers cabs, you'll find computers, televisions, microwaves – highly technical homes from home! As they make their way across the country these Knights of the Road survive in a different way than those who have gone before them and this book gives a modern, up-to-date look at facilities, the law, terminology and a host of other information that is relevant today. As they say, information is power!

This book will not only help each and every driver plan and improve their day, but it will also make their lives so much easier. I had no

idea, for example, that a Beaver Tail was the name of the up-and-down ramps at the rear of a flat bed trailer. I thought it meant something entirely different …

If every truck had this handbook in their cab, then you would never again ask a single truck-related question. It's all here, honest.

The only thing it can't do is tell you how busy the M25 is on a Friday night, clockwise, approaching the M1 … thank goodness there's still something I can help out with!

Sally

Sally Boazman

How to use this guide

This handbook is the ultimate companion for truck and coach drivers or anyone who lives life on the road.

The first part of the book provides invaluable information for new and experienced drivers alike. It advises on everything from how to operate your vehicle and its equipment to personal driver health and laws applicable to truckers, all presented with clear colour photographs and diagrams. There is also a glossary of slang and technical terms, lists of contact details useful to the driver, dealership addresses and a dictionary in six languages.

The second part of the book reviews in detail the most popular truckers' haunts, truck-friendly filling stations and fuel bunkers in the UK and Ireland. These are shown in an easy-to-read symbol format. Information provided in this section covers everything from canopy height, showers and fuel cards accepted to the price of a cup of tea. All entries can be located on the regional colour maps situated throughout this section of the book using the site identity code.

Your comments

Extensive research was carried out when compiling information for all the sites listed. However, please be aware that some site details and prices pay have changed since publication. If you have any comments or observations about any site, we'd greatly appreciate it if you could go to www.truckershandbook.co.uk, where you can enter details which will then be noted for the next reprint of the book.

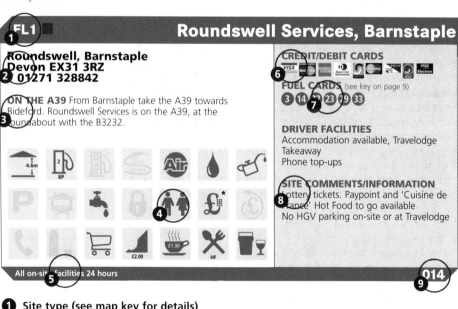

1 Site type (see map key for details)

2 Full name and address of site

3 Comprehensive directions

4 Easy-to-understand symbols for popular services and facilities – see p8 for details

5 Site opening times

6 List of credit/debit cards accepted by site

7 List of fuel cards accepted by site – see p9 for details

8 Listings of additional services and facilities

9 Identity code – cross-referenced on maps at back of book

KEY TO SYMBOLS

 LGV canopy height, shown in metres. If the box is not highlighted it means there is no LGV canopy

 Fuel available. May also list fuel supplier and number of pumps

 Red Diesel available (known as Green Diesel in Ireland)

 Card-operated automatic fuel bunker (where 'C/D' appears the bunker will also accept credit or debit cards)

 Air available for LGVs

 Forecourt water available for LGVs

 Oil available

 Parking details

 Site/parking/fuel accessible for abnormal loads (S, P or F letters may appear in symbol, indicating which is accessible; when phone symbol appears, drivers must telephone in advance)

 Standpipe

 Secure site

 A symbol that is faded out, as here, indicates that the facility is not available at this site

 Toilets

 Cashpoint machine (* = charge for use)

 Cashback facility

 Payphone

 Hot flask water available

 Shop

 Sandwiches, cold snacks available (price indicates average cost for sandwich)

 Tea, coffee, hot drinks available (price indicates average cost)

 Café or restaurant (CR), deli bar with seating available (DB), licensed restaurant (LR), or hot food without seating available (HF); initials may appear in the symbol indicating which type is available (price indicates average cost for breakfast)

 Pub/bar (PB), licensed restaurant (LR), off-licence (OL); these letters will appear indicating what type of refreshment facility is available

A Rough Guide to using your fuel card

The fuel card and network system is an extremely complicated one, even for those with a thorough understanding of how it works. Many companies who own fuel card networks have their own cards (such as Red and Keyfuels), others don't (as in the case of Routex and UK Fuels), and some allow other fuel card companies to use their networks as well as having their own. Then you have the fuel companies such as BP or Shell; some of these also have their own cards and even their own networks. And so the confusion goes on.

Opposite I have tabulated which networks and filling stations take which cards, but remember that this is only a rough guide and not set in stone. You may find that your card has more than one network logo on it (check the reverse), but you should always check that the site accepts your card before you fuel up.

NAME OF NETWORK	CARDS THAT USE THAT NETWORK
Keyfuels	Diesel Direct, Keyfuels, Eurodiesel, Abbey Easy Diesel, Dieseline, CSC UK
Red	Red (UK, Bunker and European), Morgan (Smart and UK use this network in the UK only)
Arval	Arval fuel card, BP Supercharge
Fastfuel	Fastfuel
Routemate	Routemate
Routex	OMV Eurotruck, Statoil Diesel, BP Plus (UK and Europa)
UK Fuels	Fastfuel, Ace, DCI
Emo	Emo and Emo Smart
DCI	DCI and DCI Smart, Nichols, Fuelwise Smart
CSC	CSC Ireland
IDS	IDS
Morgan	Morgan (Smart, UK, Ireland, Executive and Armagh GAA)
UTA	UTA
DKV	DKV
Eurotraffic	Eurotraffic, Eurodiesel

BRAND OF FILLING STATION	CARDS THAT CAN USE THAT FILLING STATION
Texaco	Fastfuel
Jet	Jetcard
Gleaner	Euroshell Fleetcard UK (selected stations only)
Shell	Euroshell Fleetcard UK, Euroshell CRT, Totalcard (selected stations only)
BP	BP Supercharge, BP Plus (UK and Europa), BP Bunker, (Motorway stations only), Totalcard (selected stations only)
Esso	Esso Europe, Esso UK, Euroshell Fleetcard UK (selected stations only)
Total	Totalcard, Dieseline, Euroshell Fleetcard UK (selected stations only)
Brobot	Keyfuels (Selected stations only)
Maxol	Fuelnet
Campus	QED
Top Oil	Top oil
Emo	Emo and Emo Smart
Statoil	Statoil Diesel, Routex
DCI	DCI and DCI Smart

KEY TO FUEL CARDS

1 Diesel Direct/Keyfuels cards and network
2 Red (formerly known as Fuelserve) card and network
3 Arval (formerly Overdrive, Allstar, Dial, PHH) card and network
4 Fastfuel card and network
5 IDS card and network
6 Morgan card and network
7 Routemate card and network
8 DKV card and network
9 CSC Ireland (formerly CSC Greencard) card and network
10 Eurotraffic card and network
11 Emo card and network
12 DCI card and network
13 UTA card and network
14 Routex network
15 Statoil Diesel card
16 Dieseline card
17 Fuelnet (formerly Maxol) card
18 Nicholls card
19 QED (formerly Stafford Oil) card
20 Fuelwise Smart card
21 Top Oil card
22 BP Plus (UK and Europa) cards
23 BP Supercharge card
24 Euroshell CRT card
25 Euroshell Fleet Card UK
26 Esso Europe card
27 Esso UK card
28 Total card
29 Eurodiesel card
30 Ace Fuel card
31 Abbey Easy Diesel card
32 OMV Eurotruck card
33 BP Bunker card
34 UK Fuels network
35 Other fuel cards

YOU AND THE LAW

HEALTH AND SAFETY

THE MANAGEMENT OF HEALTH AND SAFETY AT WORK (AMENDMENT) REGULATIONS 2006. STATUTORY INSTRUMENT 2006 NO 438

This is an enormous piece of legislation and too large to print in this book. The main legislation pertaining to general employment and self-employment can be accessed free via the Internet at www.opsi.gov. uk. Just enter the above title into their search panel, and from there you can buy a book, print a free copy or go to 'frequently asked questions'.

GENERAL HEALTH AND SAFETY TIPS

As a truck driver you may experience many hazards in the course of your day. It is important to remain alert, particularly in an unfamiliar environment such as a customer's premises. Any hazards, accidents or incidents you witness or encounter should be reported as soon as possible to someone in charge. Below are some general tips and advice about things to watch out for when you're out of the cab.

Warehouses
- Look out for forklift trucks manoeuvring on and off loading bays, as they may not easily see you.
- Keep to designated pathways within the warehouse wherever possible; these are designed with your safety in mind.
- Keep an eye out for wet floors and spillages and report any that are not marked up.
- Watch out for plastic strapping on the floor (pick it up and dispose of it safely) and report any other trip hazards you may come across.
- Look out for others carrying boxes or pushing wheeled cages or pallets as they may not be able to see you.
- Wear your protective clothing and use any other protective equipment that you have been provided with.
- Do not use any equipment that you have not been trained to use, or misuse any equipment that has been provided for your use.
- Be aware of the position of your nearest exit should you be required to leave the building quickly.

Inside the trailer
- Again, watch out for any goods that are being moved, particularly if your trailer is on a slope. You may find yourself getting 'run over'.
- Remain outside of the trailer or keep a safe distance whenever a forklift truck is inside.
- Take care when manoeuvring wheeled goods on and off the loading ramp as they may tip, 'separate' or fall off the edge of the ramp.
- Be careful when unstrapping, as your load may

TO CORRECTLY LIFT A LOAD, YOU SHOULD FOLLOW THESE STEPS:

Assess the load. If you believe it will be too heavy for you to lift on your own, get help.

STEP ONE

Place your feet shoulder-width apart (one slightly in front of the other) and bend your knees until you're at the level where you can grip the load from the base and about two-thirds of the way in from the edge nearest to you. Then raise your head and prepare to lift.

STEP TWO

tilt or fall if it has shifted during transit.
- If using a tail-lift take great care not to be pushed off the edge by your load.

Curtain-sided trailers
- Take care on windy days – flying straps and curtain poles can cause injury to yourself and others. Strap curtains back where possible and only open one curtain at a time.
- Stay well back when goods are being loaded onto the deck from the side with a forklift, as the load may fall and cause injury.
- Be careful when strapping your load, particularly if you're using a curtain-sider where the straps' 'anchor points' are in a guttering along the edge of the deck (this type of curtain-sider is the type designed to take wheeled cages). This may mean that you have to squeeze around the side of your goods on an open trailer with nothing to prevent you from over-balancing and falling off!

In the yard
- Again, give priority to forklifts and shunter vehicles manoeuvring in the yard.
- Look out for pedestrians not using designated walkways or walking behind you when you're reversing.
- Look out for trip hazards such as rubbish or strapping or slippery and muddy areas near to drains or a vehicle wash.

- Be aware of ground level or overhead obstructions when manoeuvring.
- Take care to avoid spilling diesel or oil in the refuelling areas and report any spillages that have occurred earlier, as spilled diesel is extremely slippery and can cause accidents, particularly when transferred by your shoes to your brake pedal!

MANUAL HANDLING

Manual handling isn't just about lifting and carrying. It also applies to lowering, pushing, pulling, moving, holding and restraining an object, animal or person, and covers the use of force to operate levers and handle power tools. Here is a list of the types of manual handling most likely to cause injury:
- Work that involves too much bending, reaching or twisting.
- Work that involves sudden, jerky, or hard to control movements.
- Work that involves long periods of time spent holding the same position.
- Work that is fast and repetitive.
- Work that involves the regular handling of heavy weights.
- Work where force is needed to carry out a task.
  So as you can see, that covers pretty much everything a lorry driver does. But there are steps you can take to avoid injury. Where provided,

Lift the load with your back straight. Straighten your knees slowly and pull the load towards you.

STEP THREE

Step forward to align your balance and hold the load close to your body as you carry it.

STEP FOUR

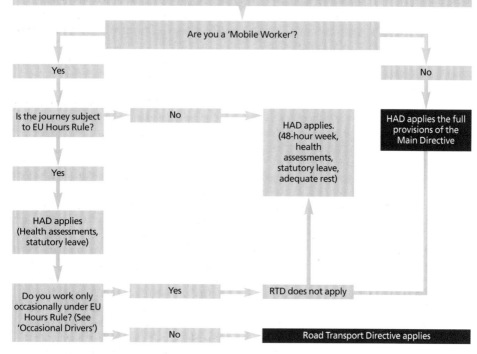

'Mobile Worker' is defined by HAD as any worker employed as a member of travelling personnel by a company that operates transport services for passengers or goods by road. This covers drivers and crew, apprentices and trainees of goods vehicles and includes own account operations.

Are you a 'Mobile Worker'?

Yes — Is the journey subject to EU Hours Rule?

No → HAD applies. (48-hour week, health assessments, statutory leave, adequate rest)

No → HAD applies the full provisions of the Main Directive

Yes — HAD applies (Health assessments, statutory leave)

Do you work only occasionally under EU Hours Rule? (See 'Occasional Drivers')

Yes → RTD does not apply

No → Road Transport Directive applies

---

use mechanical devices (cages, trolleys, wheels, sack trucks or pallet trucks) as often as possible. If something looks heavy, ask for assistance to move it – don't do it alone out of bravado and regret it later. And of course, always use correct manual handling techniques at all times.

Remember, it's your responsibility to yourself to lift things safely, and it's your employer's responsibility to provide you with help (mechanical or otherwise) to enable you to do this. On the previous page I've provided some diagrams depicting manual handling. For more information go to www.hse.gov.uk and select 'Manual Handling Operations Regulations 1992'.

SEAT BELTS

If your vehicle is fitted with seat belts, they must be worn by both driver and passenger. If they're not working, don't use the vehicle. Don't risk being fined up to £500. Remember that seat belts are there for a reason. They may be uncomfortable, but they could save your life in the event of an accident.

THE WORKING TIME DIRECTIVE

Introduction
Working time legislation in the road transport sector originates from three EU directives:
- **Main Directive** – introduced in the UK in 1998, but at the time the transport sector was temporarily excluded from the rules.
- **Horizontal Amending Directive (HAD)** – introduced in 2003 and amended the Main Directive by removing the exemption for the transport sector. It applied the full rules of the Main Directive to non-mobile workers and some of the rules to mobile workers.
- **Road Transport Directive (RTD)** – introduced in 2005, applied specific rules to mobile workers in the road transport sector (drivers and crew of vehicles subject to EU drivers' hours rules).

See the diagram above for details on which rules apply to which workers.

RTD (Road Transport Directive)
- The Working Week starts at 00:00 hours on Monday and ends at 24:00 hours on Sunday.

This is known as the 'fixed week'.
- The Maximum Average Working Week is 48 hours. This average is worked out over a period of 17–18 weeks (known as a 'Reference Period'). This Reference Period can be extended to a maximum of 26 weeks and set by calendar by individual companies with the consent of their workforce under what is known as a 'Collective or Workforce Agreement'. This means that different companies may all end up working to different Reference Periods. If you work for an agency *their* Reference Period will apply to you, not the Reference Period of the company you have been hired to work for.
- There is a Maximum Weekly Working Time of 60 hours. Remember that if you work 60 hours one week, some of your other working weeks within that Reference Period will have to consist of fewer than 48 hours in order to bring your Average Working Week back down to 48 hours.
- 'Working Time' does not include Breaks, Daily or Weekly Rest Periods, Periods of Availability (POA), voluntary or unpaid work (such as for charities) or evening classes or day release courses. Neither does it include work undertaken for the Territorial Army, Retained Fire-fighters or Special Constables. However, your company may request that you do inform them of any work undertaken for any of these latter three services. 'Working Time' does however include: Work meetings, training that is part of normal work and is part of the commercial operation, overtime and any other paid work undertaken for any other road transport employer. The latter must be declared by the driver and included in the calculation of working time.
- If time spent DRIVING on your shift does not amount to that which legally requires you to take a 'Tachograph Break' the RTD requires you to take a break after no more than six hours of work. You are required to take a total of 30 minutes break if your total working time is more than six but not more than nine hours, or a total of 45 minutes if total working time is over nine hours. Breaks must be taken during working time (in other words they may not be taken at the very start or very end of a shift) and may be split into separate periods of at least 15 minutes long.
- There is a Maximum Nightly Working Time of 10 hours. 'Night Time' is defined as the hours between midnight and 04:00 hours for crew of goods vehicles or 01:00 and 05:00 for crew of

passenger vehicles. If any of your shift encroaches on these hours, it will be deemed that you are a night worker for that shift. However, under a 'Collective or Workforce Agreement' the Maximum Nightly Working Time can be extended.
- All night workers must have medical check ups made available to them. These medicals are not compulsory though workers may be asked to sign a declaration to say that this has been offered to them.
- Periods Of Availability (POA) are periods of time when the driver is available for work, but not actually working, and is not required to remain at the workstation (for a driver this will usually be your vehicle). This does not mean that you MUST leave your vehicle if you do not wish to do so for whatever reason, but you should be free to do so if you should wish (unless you have to stay in the vehicle for reasons of safety or security). You must not undertake any other work during this time, but should be available to undertake work should you be requested to do so. The tachograph mode should then be re-set if this should occur. POA can include: Time spent waiting to be loaded and unloaded or queuing at depots, time spent with a broken down vehicle (provided you do not have to direct traffic or undertake any other work), time spent as second driver (though not driving), delays at customs or delays due to traffic prohibitions.
- For POA to be valid the period of availability and its forseeable duration must be known in advance. If you typically expect to be delayed for a specific period of time, this will qualify as being known in advance. Where delays extend beyond the expected or notified period, there is nothing to stop another period of availability being recorded after the first if you have sufficient information. For example, you arrive at an RDC and are told there will be a 30-minute delay when you arrive. If at the end of the 30 minutes you are then told there will be further 45-minute delay this second period can also be counted as a POA provided you are not going to do any work and are free to leave your vehicle (unless it is unsafe or unsecure to do so).
- POAs must be recorded on the tachograph using the square sign (or 'packing case' symbol.) If the driver is not in possession of a vehicle, the period must be recorded manually. Failure to record POA properly will mean that the time is likely to be classed as 'Working

Time'. This could result in the driver running out of working or driving hours. Ensure that everyone who requests or requires a copy of your tachograph chart or Record Of Work receives them every week.

- At the time of writing, every employee must have four weeks paid leave per year. This is known as 'Statutory Leave' and may include bank holidays. Any leave in excess of the statutory minimum is 'Contractual Holiday' and will vary from company to company.

- There are special rules that apply when you are absent due to: statutory annual leave; sick leave; maternity; paternity; adoption; or parental leave. When your employer calculates working time over the reference period, they must add in 48 hours for each fixed week of leave taken. When you have not been absent for a full fixed week, eight hours for each individual day is added.

- 'Occasional Workers' do not come under the jurisdiction of the RTD. An 'Occasional Worker' is one that drives or is a member of the vehicle crew of a vehicle in-scope of the EU drivers' hours rules on no more than 10 occasions in any Reference Period that is shorter than 26 weeks or 15 occasions in a reference period of at least 26 weeks. Occasional workers will be subject to the rules of the main directive and/or HAD. If the driver exceeds his restricted number of 'Driving Occasions' allowed within a Reference Period he becomes subject to the full RTD Rules.

- Self Employed Drivers are not covered by the RTD until 2009. However, the definition of Self Employed Driver is very tightly restricted. A Self Employed Driver is one whose main occupation is the transportation of goods or passengers for hire or reward, one who is not tied to any employer by any contract, one who is free to organise his own relevant working activities, one whose income depends directly on profits made and who is free to have commercial relations with several customers.

Main Directive – Non-mobile workers

- Employees cannot be made to work more than an average 48 hours per week over the reference period. However, at the time of writing, opt out agreements signed individually by each employee can be made available to those in operations not subject to EU Rule. The agreement can be cancelled with seven days notice. This opt out agreement system is likely to be reviewed by the European Commission.

- Reference Periods of 16 or 17 weeks are used to calculate the average weekly working time. An employee's total working time over the whole reference period is added up and an average is worked out. Under certain circumstances, the reference period can be extended to 26 or 52 weeks subject to a Collective or Workforce Agreement. This agreement allows for more flexible and varied working times.

- Working time includes meetings, working lunches, job training and work (including overtime). It does not include rest or breaks, travelling to and from work, college or university classes.

- Night time is the period between 23:00 and 06:00. This can be varied with a Collective or Workforce Agreement but it must be less than seven hours and include the period between midnight and 05:00. If one third of the employee's working time is spent working at night, he is classed as a night worker. Mobile workers in operations subject to EU Rule should refer to the RTD for information regarding Night Workers.

- Non-Mobile night workers are restricted to an average of eight hours in a 24-hour period. If the work is particularly strenuous workers may be restricted to eight hours only per 24 hours (rather than the average). In certain circumstances, the night limits may be dis-applied if a relevant agreement exists.

- Night workers must have annual medical check ups made available to them. These medicals are not compulsory though workers will be asked to sign a declaration to say that this has been offered to them.

- Non-Mobile workers should have 11 hours of rest in every 24-hour period. Mobile Workers not subject to EU Rule are entitled to 'adequate rest'. (Drivers should also see British Domestic Hour Rule.)

- Non-Mobile workers are entitled to one whole day off per week or two hours per fortnight in addition to paid annual leave. Mobile Workers not subject to EU Rule are entitled to 'adequate rest'. (Drivers should also see British Domestic Hour Rule.)

- Non Mobile Workers are entitled to a 20-minute break during six hours of work. This must not be taken at beginning or end.

- At the time of writing, every employee must have four weeks paid leave per year. This is known as 'Statutory Leave' and can include bank holidays. Employers can stipulate when Statutory Leave is taken.

DRIVING HOURS

EU Rules
Introduction
On 11th April 2007, Modified EU rules (set out below) came into force applying to all drivers operating within their jurisdiction. The EU rules have been 'simplified' to lessen confusion and to better 'mesh' with The Working Time Regulations. Maximum penalties for violations of these rules are a maximum fine of £2,500 per infringement. If a record is deemed to be deliberately falsified the maximim penalty increases to £5,000 or up to two years in prison

- As with the RTD, the fixed week begins 00:00 Monday and ends 24:00 Sunday.
- You can drive for a maximum of nine hours per day. This can be extended to 10 hours twice a week
- You must drive for no more than 56 hours in a week, and no more than 90 hours in a fortnight.
- After four-and-a-half hours of continuous or accumulated driving you must take a total of 45 minutes' break, unless beginning a daily or weekly rest period.
- Breaks can now be taken in TWO parts only (rather than three.) The first part can be taken at any time up until the time that a total of four-and-a-half hours of driving has been reached, the last part should be taken at the time (or just before the time) that the four-and-a-half hours is reached. The first part must now be a minimum of 15 minutes and the second part a minimum of 30 minutes. Do not set your tachograph to the square (packing case) symbol and record 'POA' in place of 'break'. You must be able show a visible record of your breaks and their times.
- Normally, Daily Rest Periods must consist of at least 11 consecutive hours taken within 24 hours from the end of your last daily or weekly rest. This may be shortened to nine hours no more than three times between any two weekly rests. Reductions in Daily Rest Periods no longer have to be 'paid back' in following weeks.
- Daily Rest Periods can additionally be split into two portions. If this is done, the first portion of Daily Rest must consist of a minimum of three hours, the second a minimum of nine hours. Making a total minimum of 12 hours of Daily Rest.
- There must be no more than six 24-hr periods (144 hrs) between weekly rests.
- Normally, Weekly Rest periods should consist of 45 consecutive hours, which can be reduced

to a minimum of 24 hours. (The driver no longer has to be away from base to do this.) In any two consecutive weeks, you must have at least two weekly rests and one of those must be at least 45 hours long. If weekly rest is reduced then the reduced amount must be paid back in one chunk by the end of the third week following the week in which it was taken.
- If at any time the journey involves driving partly off road (such as on a building site) the driver is no longer able to class this driving as 'Other Work'. It must now count towards driving hours.

Work for other employers
Your main employer should monitor any time you have spent in his employ doing 'Other (non driving) Work' or driving a vehicle exempt from EU Rule. However, the driver himself is responsible for declaring, monitoring, recording and providing information relating to all work done for other employers. You must record any other work undertaken during the week in which you work for any other employer on either a tachograph chart, a printout from a digital tachograph or as a manual entry using the data input facility on a digital tachograph. On any day that you drive or work for another employer you must have had your proper weekly rest for the previous week, daily rest for that day and weekly rest for that week and must ensure that you are compliant with whatever regulations apply to all work undertaken for all employers.

Multi-Manning
- Multi-Manning means that during each period of driving there are at least two drivers in the vehicle to do the driving (though for the first hour of the driving period, the presence of another driver is optional).
- Daily Tachograph and Working Time breaks can be taken by the 'second driver' on a moving vehicle, provided that he or she is not required to carry out any other work.
- Each driver must have a daily rest period of no less than nine hours in every 30-hour period. This rest must not be taken on a moving vehicle.
- The vehicle may be driven for up to 20 hours (maximum of 10 hours per driver) but the working day must not exceed 21 hours.

Ferries and Trains
On occasions when the driver is taking an 11-hour rest on a train or ferry, this rest may be interrupted

twice due to customs formalities. These interruptions must not exceed a total of 1 hour.

Emergencies

Provided road safety is not jeopardised a driver is permitted to exceed the rules in order to reach a safe stopping place to the extent necessary to ensure the safety of persons, vehicle and or its load. On arrival at the safe stopping place the driver must immediately indicate the reason manually on his tachograph chart or digital printout.

Operations exempt from EU Rule

Changes to Operations Exempt From EU Rule are due to be brought in on April 11th 2007. These changes involve limiting and amending those operations and allowing individual EU member states to adjust them according to their needs. Listed 1 to 11 below applies to operations in the UK, EU and internationally. 12 to 29 applies to operations within the UK only.

1. Vehicles or combinations of vehicle and trailer not exceeding 3.5 tonnes MGW that are used for the carriage of goods.
2. Vehicles with no more than nine seats (including the driver's seat) that are used for the carriage of passengers.
3. Vehicles used for the carriage of passengers on regular services with a route of not more than 50km.
4. Specialist vehicles used for medical purposes (such as screening units).
5. New or rebuilt vehicles not yet in service.
6. Vehicles undergoing road tests for repair, maintenance or technical development.
7. Vehicles not capable of exceeding 40kph.
8. Vehicles owned or hired without a driver by the armed services, civil defence, fire services and forces responsible for maintaining public order, when the carriage is a consequence of their assigned tasks and is under their control.
9. Emergency and rescue vehicles and those transporting humanitarian aid non-commercially.
10. Specialist breakdown vehicles operating within 100km radius of base.
11. Vehicles or combinations of vehicle not exceeding 7.5 tonnes being used for non-commercial carriage of goods.
12. Vehicles used in connection with flood, sewerage, water, gas, electricity maintenance services, highways maintenance and control, door to door household refuse collection and disposal,

telegraph and telephone services, radio and television broadcasting and detection of radio or television transmitters or receivers.
13. Specialist vehicles transporting circus and funfair equipment.
14. Vehicles being used for milk collection from farms or delivery to farms of milk containers or milk products intended for animal feed.
15. Vehicles used by agriculture, horticulture, forestry, farming or fisheries for the use of carrying goods as part of their own entrepreneurial activity within 100km radius of base.
16. Agricultural and forestry tractors being used within 100km of base.
17. Vehicles carrying animal carcasses or waste not intended for human consumption.
18. Vehicles used to carry livestock to markets or slaughterhouses and vice versa within a radius of up to 50km.
19. Certain historical or vintage vehicles not being used for the commercial carriage of goods or passengers or any vehicle manufactured before 1 January 1947. (The list of vehicles included in this category is very specific. Individuals may have to consult the Department for Transport for further clarification.)
20. Vehicles with between 10 and 17 seats (including the driver's seat) used exclusively for non-commercial carriage of passengers.
21. Vehicles used by a public authority to provide public services not in competition with professional road hauliers. This list is under revision though in the UK it currently includes:
    a. Ambulance service vehicles used to carry patients staff and medical supplies
    b. Vehicles employed to provide certain social services
    c. Coastguard, lighthouse and harbour authorities (within the limits of the harbour)
    d. Airport authorities within the perimeter of the airport
    e. Railways Authorities, Transport for London, passenger transport executives or local authorities for railway maintenance
    f. British Waterways Board for purposes of maintaining waterways.
22. Vehicles specially fitted as a 'mobile project vehicle' the primary purpose of which is use as an educational facility when stationary. This could include vehicles such as play buses and mobile libraries.
23. Vehicles or combination vehicles of not over

7.5 tonnes being used by the driver within 50km radius of base for carrying materials used in the course of his work and where driving does not constitute the driver's main activity.

24. Vehicles operating on an island not exceeding 2,300sq km and not connected to Great Britain by a bridge, ford or tunnel.

25. Gas or electrically propelled vehicles used for the carriage of goods not exceeding 7.5 tonnes operating within a 50km radius of base.

26. Vehicles being used for solely driving instruction and/or examination with a view to obtaining a driving licence or CPC.

27. Vehicles being used by the RNLI to haul lifeboats. (This is currently under revision.)

28. Any vehicle which is propelled by steam.

29. Vehicles used exclusively within hub facilities such as ports, airports and railway terminals.

British Domestic Hours Rules

British Domestic Hours Rules apply to drivers on journeys within the UK who are exempt or excluded from EU Rule. Drivers will be either expected to use a tachograph with which to record their hours or be asked to keep a 'Record Book'. Make sure you know how to use this if one is provided.

- Daily driving limit 10 hours in any 24-hour period
- Daily duty limit 11 hours in any 24-hour period. Any time spent on break, (known as 'meal relief') is not classed as duty time.
- Part time drivers should not exceed four hours of driving in any 24-hour period.
- There are currently no requirements for daily rest periods or meal relief breaks under British Domestic Hours Rule. However, breaks should be taken in accordance with the 'Horizontal Amending Directive' and any current health and any legislation applicable to the company you are working for. (You should ask your company for clarification of this.)
- Under British Domestic Hours Rules a Weekly Rest Period is not required. However, The Horizontal Amending Directive should be followed.
- The British Domestic Hours week begins at 00:00 Monday and ends 24:00 Sunday.

Emergencies

British Domestic Hours Rules Limits can be exceeded in the following circumstances: Events that cause or may cause:

- A danger to life or health of a person or animal

or where events are likely to cause damage to property in a way that immediate action must be taken.

- A serious interruption in water, gas, electricity, drainage, telecommunications, use of roads, railways, ports and airports.

Exemptions to British Domestic Hours Rules and EU Rule

- Drivers of vehicles used by the armed forces, police and fire brigades
- Drivers who always drive off the public road
- Private driving unconnected with any employment.

Light vans and dual-purpose vehicles

Drivers of vans not exceeding 3.5 tonnes MGW when engaged solely in the use of certain professional activities, i.e. such as those used by doctors, dentists, nurses, midwives, vets, sales reps, employees of the AA, RAC and RSAC and persons using their vehicles to assist in carrying out any service of inspection, cleaning, maintenance, repair, installation or fitting are subject to the 10-hour driving regulations stated opposite. Also included is cinematography, radio or television broadcasting staff.

Driving under mixed EU and British Domestic Rules

This occurs when a driver operates a vehicle covered by EU Rules and another covered by British Domestic Rules within the same day or the same week. He must be aware that:

- Driving time under the EU Rule does not count as off duty time under British Domestic Rules.
- Driving time under British Domestic Rules cannot count as Break or Rest Period under the EU Rules.
- Driving under the EU Rules counts towards driving and duty limits under the British Domestic Hour Rules.
- Mixed driving on the same day limits the driver to British Domestic Hour Rule Duty and Driving times. (10 hours Driving and 11 hours of Duty Time, though in Northern Ireland Duty Time limit is 14 hours.)
- When driving under EU Rules, the driver must observe EU Daily and Weekly Rest requirements.
- When driving under EU Rules, all driving done on the same day under British Domestic Hour rule should be marked on the tachograph chart as 'Other Work' by manual entry.

Examples of illegal Working Patterns

Here are a few examples of how it is possible to make mistakes in calculating your hours under EU regulations and the Road Transport Directive. All examples given here are for single manned vehicles only. I have tried to create as many scenarios as possible within 1 week and 1 day though I am sure you can think of many more. As you can see, there are a multitude of potential traps where a driver can find himself in difficulty and sometimes simply working it all out and keeping track of all hours and possible scenarios can be a real headache. Chances are your hours are unlikely to be any where near as long or as varied as the examples given here,

though it is wise to keep daily records of your start and finish times, daily driving hours, daily and weekly rest hours and times when you work beyond midnight. During the course of your day don't forget to keep track of when you need to take your breaks in accordance with the RTD and EU Regulations.

- ■ Split daily rest
- ▢ Weekly rest
- ▢ Daily rest
- ■ Breaks
- ■ POA
- ■ Other work
- ■ Driving

Monday

Illegal — Why?

1. Driver has not taken a 30-minute break at the end of or within his first 6 hours of working. In accordance with Road Transport Directive (RTD).
2. Forty five minutes of the shift occurred after midnight (see Tuesday) therefore breaking the '10 hour maximum shift' part of the night-time working regulation section of the RTD.

Tuesday

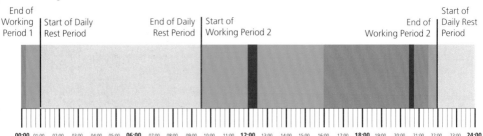

Illegal — Why?

1. Driver has started shift with less than 9 hours rest from the previous day.
2. Driver has taken 30-minute break in accordance with RTD but has then taken only 15 minutes break after 4 and a half hours of driving. This break should have been 45 minutes as break requirements for accumulated driving time and accumulated working time should be thought of as separate entities even though they can be taken at the same time (concurrently) where working patterns allow.

Wednesday

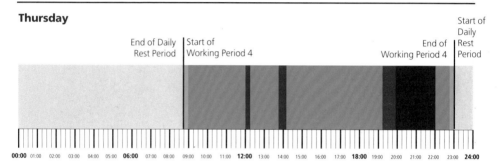

End of Daily Rest Period | Start of Working Period 3 | End of Working Period 3 | Start of Daily Rest Period

00:00 01:00 02:00 03:00 04:00 05:00 **06:00** 07:00 08:00 09:00 10:00 11:00 **12:00** 13:00 14:00 15:00 16:00 17:00 **18:00** 19:00 20:00 21:00 22:00 23:00 **24:00**

Illegal — Why?

1. Driver has taken 30 minute and 15 minute breaks in wrong order.
2. Driver has driven for more than 10 accumulated hours.
3. Driver is intending to follow a reduced daily rest pattern of 9 hours within the 24 hour time frame from where his last daily rest period has ended (which was 08:00 on Wednesday). This would not be attainable since his total shift pattern within this 24 hour time frame has exceeded 15 hours. Remember that breaks and POA cannot be counted towards daily rest. The driver would have been better advised to time his breaks and POA to enable him to adopt a 'Split Daily Rest' system for this period.

Thursday

End of Daily Rest Period | Start of Working Period 4 | End of Working Period 4 | Start of Daily Rest Period

00:00 01:00 02:00 03:00 04:00 05:00 **06:00** 07:00 08:00 09:00 10:00 11:00 **12:00** 13:00 14:00 15:00 16:00 17:00 **18:00** 19:00 20:00 21:00 22:00 23:00 **24:00**

Illegal — Why?

1. Driver's accumulated break after first 4 and a half hours of accumulated driving amounted to less than 45 minutes.
2. Driver has driven for more than 4 and a half hours before taking a break. This is only permitted in certain circumstances (see Driving Hours - EU Rules, section on emergencies).

Friday

End of Daily Rest Period | Start of Working Period 5 | End of Working Period 5 | Start of Daily Rest Period

00:00 01:00 02:00 03:00 04:00 05:00 **06:00** 07:00 08:00 09:00 10:00 11:00 **12:00** 13:00 14:00 15:00 16:00 17:00 **18:00** 19:00 20:00 21:00 22:00 23:00 **24:00**

Illegal — Why?

1. Driver has now exceeded his Reduced Daily Rest allowance of 3 occasions between any two Weekly Rest Periods.
2. Driver has driven for over 9 hours a day on more than 2 occasions in this Weekly Period.
3. Driver has interrupted Break Period before 15 minutes have elapsed thereby invalidating the first part of his 2nd break of the day. Even though both parts of the 2nd break added together amount to 45 minutes, the first part is invalid and cannot be counted. This means that the break is insufficient.

Saturday

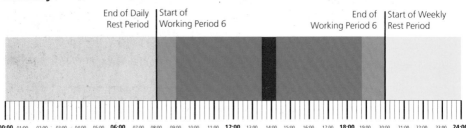

End of Daily Rest Period | Start of Working Period 6
End of Working Period 6 | Start of Weekly Rest Period

00:00 01:00 02:00 03:00 04:00 05:00 **06:00** 07:00 08:00 09:00 10:00 11:00 **12:00** 13:00 14:00 15:00 16:00 17:00 **18:00** 19:00 20:00 21:00 22:00 23:00 **24:00**

Illegal — Why?

1. By middle of shift, Driver's Maximum Weekly Working Time has exceeded 60 hours.

Sunday

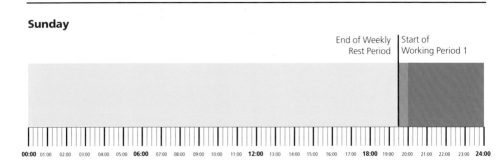

End of Weekly Rest Period | Start of Working Period 1

00:00 01:00 02:00 03:00 04:00 05:00 **06:00** 07:00 08:00 09:00 10:00 11:00 **12:00** 13:00 14:00 15:00 16:00 17:00 **18:00** 19:00 20:00 21:00 22:00 23:00 **24:00**

Monday

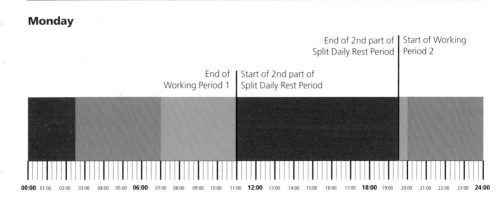

End of 2nd part of Split Daily Rest Period | Start of Working Period 2

End of Working Period 1 | Start of 2nd part of Split Daily Rest Period

00:00 01:00 02:00 03:00 04:00 05:00 **06:00** 07:00 08:00 09:00 10:00 11:00 **12:00** 13:00 14:00 15:00 16:00 17:00 **18:00** 19:00 20:00 21:00 22:00 23:00 **24:00**

Sunday / Monday: Illegal — Why?

1. Driver's Weekly Rest consisted of less than 24 hours
2. Driver's first section of Split Daily Rest consisted of less than three hours and the second less than nine, making a total of less than 12 hours of split daily rest. The split daily rest scenario is sometimes used when the driver has used up (or is likely to use up) his legal weekly quota of reduced daily rests but due to his shift pattern for that week is able to take a split daily rest.
3. Part of working period 1 has occurred between midnight and 04:00 therefore breaking the 10 hour maximum working time rule of the night-time working regulation section of the RTD.

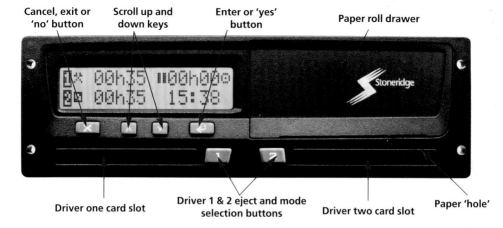

Cancel, exit or 'no' button — Scroll up and down keys — Enter or 'yes' button — Paper roll drawer

Driver one card slot — Driver 1 & 2 eject and mode selection buttons — Driver two card slot — Paper 'hole'

DIGITAL TACHOGRAPHS

Introduction

Digital Tachographs are fitted to all vehicles first used on or after 1 May 2006. Although there is no general requirement to fit older vehicles with the digital equipment, these will have to be fitted to *most* PCVs and LGVs should the analogue tachograph unit have to be replaced in the event of its complete failure. (There are specific rules and exemptions regarding this matter.)

The Digital Tachograph (known as the VU or Vehicle Unit) looks a little like the old analogue tachographs. It has two slots for insertion of the Smart Cards and a slot where the printer paper comes out. It also has an LED display and various mode and menu buttons.

Information is entered into the VU by the driver (such as mode and starting location) and other information is copied from the inserted card into the VU. Different types of information are stored both within the VU and the Drivers' Card(s). (There are four types of card, but we will come to those later.)

Information can later be accessed from the VU and from the cards using external 'plug in equipment' or 'card reading' equipment owned by the fleet holder. The driver may also need to create a printout of his working period each day, this printout (like with the analogue tachograph chart) may be a legal document and should be stored in a cool dry place along with any analogue charts for that day away from heat and sunlight to prevent degradation.

If you would like more information about the Stoneridge digital tachograph, type this link into your address bar (this part of the Stoneridge website provides a mini training video and enables you to download a quick user guide): http://www.stoneridgeelectronics.co.uk/digital_tacho_2.aspx

For more about the Siemens digital tachograph, type this link into your address bar (this takes you straight to an abbreviated instruction booklet): http://dtco.siemensvdo.co.uk/NR/rdonlyres/3A52146F-10FC-4659-9D71-5B842FD1076C/0/DTCOshortoperatinginstructions4.pdf

Operating the Stoneridge Vehicle Unit

1. Inserting your card
- Turn on your ignition first.
- Choose your driver slot ('1' for main driver or '2' for 2nd driver) and press the numbered button for 3 seconds.
- The drawer will pop open. Place your finger below the draw and gently pull it all the way out.
- Place your card on the tray so that it lays flat with the chip facing upwards and furthest away from you.
- Gently push the drawer closed.

2. Manual Entries (and what to do next)
- The display will ask you to select your country. Use the scroll buttons to find the UK (if you are in the UK) and press ◄┘
- The display will then ask you if you 'wish to perform manual entries'.
- If you wish to make a manual entry, use your scroll keys to select ✔ then press ◄┘ to enter. If you do not wish to make a manual entry select and enter 'no' and the main menu screen will appear.
- If you are making a manual entry, select the mode for your manual entry – such as the ⌐ symbol for daily rest or the ⊘ symbol for POA (if for example if you have been available for work but without a vehicle up until this point) then press ◄┘ to enter.

- Next select the ⬕ symbol to enter the start times of your manual entry and the ⬕ symbol to enter the finish times of your manual entry.
- When you have finished making manual entries, select ✔ for 'modified entries' and press ◀┘ The display will then read 'saving entries' and return itself to the main screen.

3. Multi-manning
- If there are 2 drivers in the vehicle you must now insert the driver 2 card into the number 2 slot and make any nessesary manual entries as previously instructed up until this point.

4. Using the menu
- Changing the mode can only be done when the vehicle is stationary using the '1' & '2' buttons. (Press once, do not press and hold.)
- When the vehicle is moving 'driving mode' is automatically selected for driver one and POA is automatically selected for driver two.
- It is important to note that if you have to interrupt your break, the tachograph mode will automatically default to 'other work'. Once stationary, you will manually have to return the mode to 'break' once again.
- To access the advanced menu, first press◀┘ and then use the ⌄⌃ keys to move up and down through the five different displays. This can be done when the vehicle is either moving or stationary.
a) Display 1 (from top left to top right) shows driver one, activity mode of driver one, duration of that mode and accumulative break for this period. The line below shows driver two, activity mode of the driver, duration of that mode and in the far lower right corner; the local time.
b) Display 2 (from top left to top right) shows driver one, activity mode for driver one and odometer reading. The line below shows driver two, activity mode for driver two, current speed, and local time.
c) Display 3 shows UTC and the local time written below it. Then top right indicates the card type and bottom right shows the current date.
d) Display 4 (from top left to top right) shows driver one, driving symbol, cumulative driving time for current period and cumulative break time for that driving period. The line below is a repeat of the line above but for driver two.
e) The last display shows (from top left to top

right) driver one, driving symbol, and cumulative driving time for that driver for the last 14 days. The line below is a repeat of the line above but for driver two.

- By pressing and holding the **X** for three seconds you can exit these displays or by pressing ◀┘ you can move onto a sub menu. (This sub menu is only available when the vehicle is stationary.)

5) Making a printout
- To get a printout, press the ◀┘ button twice. This will take you to a choice of six legal printouts that you can access using the up and down scroll buttons. From either of these you can also access a sub-menu of other printout display options though I have only listed the six main ones here.
a) Shows the last 24 hours' activities from the driver card (this is the one you will use most often).
b) Last 24 hours' activities of the VU.
c) Warnings from the driver card.
d) Warnings from the VU.
e) Technical data.
f) Data on overspeeding.

6) Removing the card
- Press and hold the number '1' or '2' button for three seconds.
- The display will ask you for your 'end country'.
- Use the scroll buttons to find the correct country and press ◀┘
- The drawer will pop open. Pull the drawer all the way out by putting a finger below the drawer and pulling it towards you.
- Take the card and close the drawer.

7) Changing the printer roll
- You should normally find a small piece of paper sticking out of the printer roll door. This usually indicates that you have paper. It is a legal requirement that you have paper in your VU at all times. If you cannot see any paper you may need to insert a fresh roll.
- To insert a fresh roll, open the roll door by pushing on the upper half of the printer door. Pull out the printer cartridge by holding onto the lower section of the door and pulling towards you. The whole assembly will come out.
- Insert printer roll paper so that the paper is curling backwards and upwards away from the

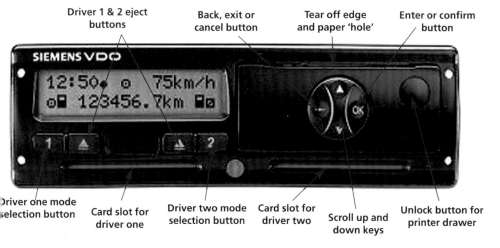

Driver 1 & 2 eject buttons

Back, exit or cancel button

Tear off edge and paper 'hole'

Enter or confirm button

Driver one mode selection button

Card slot for driver one

Driver two mode selection button

Card slot for driver two

Scroll up and down keys

Unlock button for printer drawer

printer door then round and underneath so that when you reinsert the cartridge a little bit of paper will be sticking out through the bottom of the door.

- Once cartridge is reinserted, push the door closed.

8) Changing Local Time

- Turn on ignition (make sure card is removed).
- Press the 'enter' button once. The display should now read 'print menu'.
- Press the 'scroll down' button 4 times. Display should now read 'setting menu'.
- Press the 'enter' button once.
- Press the 'scroll down' button once. Display should now read 'settings and local time'.
- Press 'enter' button once. Display should show local time.
- Press 'scroll up or down' buttons to alter time by half hour increments.
- Press 'enter' button to confirm.
- Press 'X' button twice to return to normal display.

Operating the Siemens VDO Vehicle Unit

1. Inserting your card

- Switch on your ignition.
- Push the driver card into the chosen driver slot ('1' for main driver or '2' for second driver) with the chip facing upwards and furthest away from you.
- You may have to push quite firmly before the VU will take the card in.

2. Manual Entries (and what to do next)

- The display will then show a welcome

greeting. The local time will then appear in the lower left corner with a black circle next to it. The UTC time will appear on the right with 'UTC' next to it. This lasts for about 3 seconds.

- The next display will show the driver's name with a 'progress bar' showing that the card is being read. This will last about 10 seconds.
- The next display shows date and time of previous card withdrawal shown in UTC time. This will last about 4 seconds.
- The display will then read 'M entry addition?'. Use the scroll keys to select 'yes' or 'no' then press **OK** to enter.
- If you select 'no' to a 'manual entry addition' the display will then ask you to enter your start country. Use the scroll keys to find UK and press **OK** to enter.
- If you select 'yes' to a 'manual entry addition' it will display the date (in the left hand corner) and the time in UTC that your card was last in a VU. It will then ask 'end of shift?' if this is correct, scroll to yes and press **OK**
- If this was not the case, use the 'scroll up' and

'scroll down' keys to select the time that your first unrecorded event occurred (such as where you had some period doing 'other work' at the end of your shift and you were unable to leave your card in your vehicle due to it being given to another driver).

- When you have correctly entered these times by pressing **OK** you will then be asked what mode applies to that particular manual entry (such as break/daily/weekly rest, POA, driving or other work). Use the scroll buttons to select the correct one and press **OK**.
- You will then be asked 'end of shift?' If this is still not the case you can continue to add other manual entries for that day in the same way.
- When you have made all of your manual entries and selected 'yes' for 'end of shift?' and **OK** it will then ask, 'end country?' Select the correct country and press **OK**.
- Once this is done it will state your start date and time for your current shift. If this is correct and you do not need to make any manual entries for the start of your current shift press **OK**.
- The display will then ask you for your start country of your current shift. Scroll to select the country and press **OK**.
- If you have at this time selected to make a manual entry for the start of your shift (such as some time as POA spent waiting to be given a vehicle) use the instructions already stated to add manual entries to the start of your current shift.
- The display will then ask you to confirm your manual entries. If you are satisfied that they are correct, select 'yes' and press **OK**.

3. Multi-manning

- If there are two drivers in the vehicle you must now insert the driver two card into the number '2' slot and follow the same directions as outlined above.
- When multi-manning, cards must be re-positioned in the VU in order to record rest for driver number two, as rest mode cannot be selected for driver 2 when the vehicle is in motion.

4. Using the mode button

- Changing the mode, by using the '1' and '2' buttons, can only be done when the vehicle is stationary.
- When the vehicle is moving 'driving mode' is automatically selected for driver one and POA is automatically selected for driver two. When

stationary, the tachograph automatically switches to 'other work' for driver one and POA for driver two.

5. Logging off and removing the card

- Turn on the vehicle ignition.
- Use the mode button to switch to ⊢ symbol.
- Press eject button for driver slot card '1' (card '2' has to be removed last).
- Driver's name will appear on the display along with the 'progress bar'.
- Select correct country for the end of the shift and press **OK**.
- Display shows continuing 'progress bar'.
- Display then reads '24hr day'. If you require a printout, select 'yes' at this point and press **OK**. Otherwise select 'no' and **OK**.
- The display will then indicate that the printout has started and shows a continuing 'progress bar'.
- Card is released and printout can be torn off. Standard display then appears.

6. Changing the printer roll

- You should normally find a small piece of paper sticking out of the printer roll hole. This usually indicates that you have paper. It is a legal requirement that you have paper in your VU at all times. If you cannot see any paper you may need to insert a fresh roll.
- Press the unlock button for the printer roll drawer. The drawer should open towards you.
- Insert the roll so that the end of the paper is facing upwards and towards you. When you close the draw by simply pushing it shut, the end of the paper should be sticking out through the hole.

7) Changing local time.

- Turn on ignition (make sure card is removed).
- Press **OK** button. Display should read 'printout' and 'driver 1' (this should be flashing).
- Press 'scroll up' button five times. Display

should now read 'entry' and 'vehicle' (this should be flashing).

- Press **OK** button once.
- Press 'scroll up' button twice. Display should now read 'vehicle' and 'local time' (this should be flashing).
- Press **OK** button once. Display should show UTC and date. Bottom left corner should display current local time and bottom right should also show local time but this will be flashing.
- Press 'scroll up' or 'scroll down' buttons to alter time by half hour increments.
- Once new correct time is reached, press **OK** and then the 'back/exit' button until you return to the main display.

VU display and Printout Pictograms

There are 38 pictograms that can be found on your printout or LED display, in addition to which there can also be 46 combinations of pictograms. Below are listed the most common. You should familiarise yourself with these.

▢	Available	⊕	Clock
○	Drive	▢	Display
h	Rest	⊥	External storage
✕	Work	÷	Power supply
❚❚	Break	▼	Printer/Printout
?	Unknown	⊓	Sensor
24h	Daily	▲	Vehicle/Vehicle Unit
I	Weekly	✕	Fault
II	Two	◆	Location
✚	From or To	⊟	Security
1	Driver slot	⊙	Time
2	Co-driver slot	Σ	Total/Summary
▯	Card		

Note: Additional pictograms may be specific to the VU manufacturer.

Creating a manual entry on your printout

If you turn your printout over, you will find several lines above or below a manual completion chart. The manual completion chart is similar to what you would find on the rear face of an analogue tachograph, except that with a digital printout it runs in a straight line along the length whereas in an analogue tachograph it follows the circumference of the disc.

You mark out your day using a normal ballpoint pen and simple straight lines ending with a short cross-line to indicate the start and end of each mode (you do not need to colour in the sections as with the analogue tachograph).

Country Codes

These are Start and End locations and must be entered manually into the VU when requested.

A	Austria	MC	Monaco
AL	Albania	MD	Republic of
AND	Andorra		Moldova
ARM	Armenia	MK	Macedonia
AZ	Azerbaijan	N	Norway
B	Belgium	NL	The
BG	Bulgaria		Netherlands
BIH	Bosnia and	P	Portugal
	Herzegovina	PL	Poland
BY	Belarus	RO	Romania
CH	Switzerland	RSM	San Marino
CY	Cyprus	RUS	Russian
CZ	Czech Republic		Federation
D	Germany	S	Sweden
DK	Denmark	SK	Slovakia
E	Spain	SLO	Slovenia
EST	Estonia	TM	Turkmenistan
F	France	TR	Turkey
FIN	Finland	UA	Ukraine
FL	Liechtenstein	UK	United
FR	Faeroe Islands		Kingdom,
GE	Georgia		Alderney,
GR	Greece		Guernsey,
H	Hungary		Jersey, Isle of
HR	Croatia		Man, Gibraltar
I	Italy	V	Vatican City
IRL	Ireland	YU	Yugoslavia
IS	Iceland	UNK	Unknown
KZ	Kazakhstan	EC	European
L	Luxembourg		Community
LT	Lithuania	EUR	Rest of Europe
LV	Latvia	WLD	Rest of the
M	Malta		world

Note: UK may be found under G for GB even though is displayed as UK

Spanish Regions

AN	Andalucia	EXT	Extremadura
AR	Aragón	G	Galicia
AST	Asturias	IB	Baleares
C	Cantabria	IC	Canarias
CAT	Cataluña	LR	La Rioja
CL	Castilla-León	M	Madrid
CM	Castilla-La-	MU	Murcia
	Mancha	NA	Navarra
CV	Valencia	PV	Pais Vasco

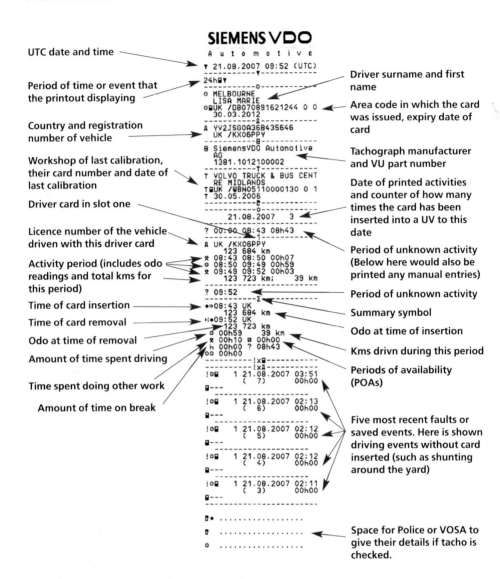

To record your personal details such as start place and name etc you use the lines provided above or below the manual completion chart. The Siemens chart asks for more information than the Stoneridge chart and you should write the information in as follows:

Line 1: Driver's name.
Line 2: Digital card number (this is number 5b on the front of your card).
Line 3: Vehicle registration (no fleet codes).
Line 4: Start location.
Line 5: Finish Location.
Line 6: Finish odometer reading.
Line 7: Start odometer reading.
Line 8: Total kilometres.
Line 9: Date.
Line 10: Signature.

VU Warnings

Your VU may provide you with warning notices that you will have to acknowledge by pressing the OK/Enter button. These are some of the warnings it will give you.

- **Break! 4 hrs 15 mins drive** (This means a break is due within the next 15 minutes)
- **Break! 4 hrs 30 mins drive** (This means you must take a break now!)
- **Stop for break** (repeats every 15 mins showing current drive total – Seimens only)
- **Overspeeding** (When your vehicle's set speed limiter is exceeded for longer than 60 seconds)
- **Driving without card** (If you are driving with no card)
- **No Data** (This occurs when you request a printout from the VU with no card inserted)

- **Wrong card type** (Check you haven't inserted your bank card by mistake!)
- **No paper**
- **Printout not possible** (Check ignition is on)
- **Please enter** (OK/Enter has not been pressed during manual entry procedure)

UTC (Universal Time Co-ordinated) and Local Time in the UK and Ireland
Converting Local Time to UTC:
During Winter Time:
UTC = Local Time
During Summer Time:
UTC = Local time minus 1 hour
Converting UTC to Local Time:
During Winter Time:
Local time = UTC Time
During Summer Time:
Local time = UTC Time plus 1 hour

Golden Rules and helpful information regarding Digital Tachographs
- Keep digital printouts and analogue tachograph discs produced on the same day *together* and hand them in together.
- Remember that when you're making manual entries, check your watch to see whether or not your display is showing local time or UTC time and make your entries accordingly. If you're using your digital printout to work out your start and finish times when you write out your timesheets, don't let UTC catch you out.
- Do not move your vehicle while making manual entries or the procedure will terminate. This also happens if the card is removed, no keys are pressed for one minute, or a long press of the cancel button occurs on the Stoneridge VU.
- If you forget to make manual entries at the start of your day you must make them manually on the back of the printout at the end of your day. (See instructions for this.)
- If you're using both analogue and digital tachographs during your week, you don't *need* to record manually on a digital card or printout any recordings that have already been made using an analogue tachograph. This includes any daily or weekly rest indicated on the analogue tachograph chart by the drawing of the 'finish' and 'start' lines.
- When displayed on a digital tachograph local time is always accompanied by a solid black

circle. UTC time is always displayed with the initials 'UTC'.
- If you move your vehicle during a rest period, your mode will automatically revert to 'other work' mode. Remember to switch it back if continuing your break. Wrong mode selection must be recorded on the rear of the tachograph printout.
- You can drive with a malfunctioning VU under certain specified circumstances, but if you have a problem you should notify your manager as soon as possible to ensure that it's rectified as soon as circumstances permit.
- If you overspeed or if your VU develops a fault a small light may appear in the corner of the speedometer. Any overspeeding events must be acknowledged by pressing the 'enter' or 'OK' button before the light will clear.
- Your card will store approximately 28 days of activities. The VU will store approximately a year of activities.
- Information stored within the VU includes distance travelled, speed and overspeeding, dates and times of driving, modes used, driver cards used and dates used, times when no card is used, countries, faults in VU and on cards, workshop data, information regarding VU downloads, adjustments of times, and multi-manning information.

Cards:
Cards are available from the DVLA at a cost of £38 for a new card or £19 for a replacement or renewal card. You can apply using the dedicated phone line 0870 8501074 or by completing an Application form (D779B) available from the DVLA, DVLA Local Offices and VOSA Testing Stations. The completed form along with any relevant documentation and the fee should be sent to DVLA, Swansea, SA99 1ST. For more information and notes on applying for a Driver Card go to www.dvla.gov.uk, then 'Driver information' and scroll down to 'Digital Tacho Card Issuing and Company Cards'.

Driver Card (White in colour)
Owned by the driver
- Identifies the driver by his photograph, full name, date and birthplace, driving licence number, home address and signature. It also shows the issuing Authority, Country, dates of validity and serial number. This data is also stored within the card's chip.
- The driver card is valid for no more than 5 years.

Lost stolen or damaged driver cards

The driver must make a printout at the start and end of his journey. He must manually record details of any activity during his daily working period (i.e. between rests) on these printouts. He must also manually record on each printout enough detail to enable him to be identified (such as driver card number, name, driving licence number) then the driver must sign the printout. Loss or theft should be reported to DVLA as soon as possible and within seven working days. They will issue a replacement within five days. If the card was lost or stolen abroad, the driver must also report it to the 'competent authority' within that country.

Drivers may continue to drive without a card for a maximum of 15 calendar days or longer if necessary to return the vehicle to its premises. During this period, drivers must produce two daily printouts as detailed above.

Drivers' Responsibilities

1. Ensure you have a valid Driver Card and carry it with you even when you are using an analogue tachograph. Failure to bring your card to work may mean that you will not be able to drive on that day!
2. You should have only one card at any time. Do not let anyone else use your card and keep it safe. Your company may offer to keep your card for you, but it is best that you take responsibility for it yourself
3. You must produce your card to the police or VOSA if requested and sign any printouts you are requested to sign
4. You must allow your employer to download from your card
5. You must report lost, stolen, damaged and malfunctioning cards and apply for replacement
6. You should understand how to enter all data and how the unit and printer works
7. You should understand the pictograms (see above) and data produced on the printout
8. You should always carry spare print rolls
9. You should keep 15 calendar days (prior to the current week) tacho printouts and/or analogue tachograph charts on you and be in possession of any tachos or printouts for that current week. This is due to be changed to the current day plus 28 days' tachograph charts and/or printouts on 1 January 2008

The card currently stores approximately 28 days worth of information at any given time, this includes:

1. Vehicles used by the driver, date and time of last use and vehicle odometer readings at that time
2. Driver activity data and modes selected
3. Start and finish places
4. Card faults and VU faults experienced
5. Data regarding any recent information downloads and printouts made. (This way any printouts cannot be 'discarded' by the driver since evidence that printouts have been made is stored on the card)
6. Dates and times card has been inserted.

The VU reads from the card when inserted information necessary for it to:

1. Identify card type, holder, previously used vehicle date and time of last usage and mode selected at the time
2. Check that the last 'session' was properly closed
3. Add up the driver's continuous driving time, cumulative break and driving times for previous and current week
4. Create a printout if one is requested
5. Download information into 'plug in' or 'external equipment'.

Note that in case of a reading error, the VU will try 3 times before declaring the card faulty and invalid.

10. Agency drivers should ensure that their agency is regularly supplied with photocopies of printouts and tachographs.

Company Card (Yellow in colour)

Owned by fleet operators

Valid for five years. Coupled with 'plug in equipment' and 'card readers', Company Cards enable fleet owners to download, display and print the information stored within the VU and recording equipment

Workshop Card (Red in colour)

Owned by workshops and fitters

Issued to recording equipment manufacturers, vehicle manufacturers and qualified fitters in a VOSA approved workshop. The workshop card enables the cardholder to test, calibrate and download information from the VU. It is valid for one year. Each fitter should own one and a pin number is required to operate the card.

Control Card (Blue in colour)

Owned by enforcement authorities (such as police, DVLA and VOSA)

Valid for two years, the Control Card identifies the official body and cardholder and allows them access to data stored in the VU or in the recording equipment enabling printouts to be made.

ANALOGUE TACHOGRAPHS

How to correctly complete an analogue tachograph chart

- Surname and first name must be entered in full. Initials and/or abbreviations are not acceptable.
- Recognisable start and finish journey place-names (such as a town or village) must be entered on the front and rear of the tachograph chart. The rear face should be completed in exactly the same way as the front for this particular part of the field.
- Date and place where the use of the chart starts and ends must both be entered, as date, month and year. If you use more than one vehicle, times of vehicle changes should also be entered if space is provided for this on the back of the tachograph chart.
- The full vehicle registration for each vehicle driven must be entered. Any fleet codes are not acceptable.
- Enter full odometer figures for the start and finish of a journey in each vehicle, with the total for each vehicle in the space beneath.
- Start of working period and end of working period should be clearly marked with a straight line. Take care not to mark the tachograph chart trace. To be on the safe side, mark your line at some point between 5 and 15 minutes before and after the start and end of the trace. If you are completing a manual trace, a straight line will not be necessary.
- At no time should the writing spill out from the central field so that it interferes with any written information or cover any part of a tachograph chart trace. This is a tachograph offence.

Remember that different companies or agencies may have different tachograph chart completion requirements. Make sure you know how your company or agency likes to have its tachograph charts presented before you begin driving for them.

You must record every period of activity during your shift that isn't shown and recorded by the tachograph. As demonstrated in the examples below, you should either manually trace on the rear of the tachodisc, or use two small lines on the edge of the front of the tachodisc and write between them words such as 'Rest' or 'OWP' (other work period) to indicate the type of work or rest undertaken. But ask first what's required of you.

Only one tachograph chart should be used for each driving period within a time frame of 24 hours. Exceptions are as follows:

- If the tachograph chart is damaged either in or out of the vehicle and another is required to continue recording the working or driving period. In instances such as these, the replacement

tachograph chart should be clipped to and handed in along with the damaged one.
- If you're driving more vehicles than your tachograph chart will allow to record details of on the reverse or on vehicles where the chart is not compatible with both tachographs. Again, they should be clipped together and both handed in.

Other rules you should be aware of
- You must not use a chart to record more than 24 hours' worth of information
- You are required to be able to produce at the roadside charts and printouts or manual records for the current day and the previous 28 calendar

TACHOGRAPH CHART [MANUAL TRACE]

Note: Example shown here was created under EU Rule.

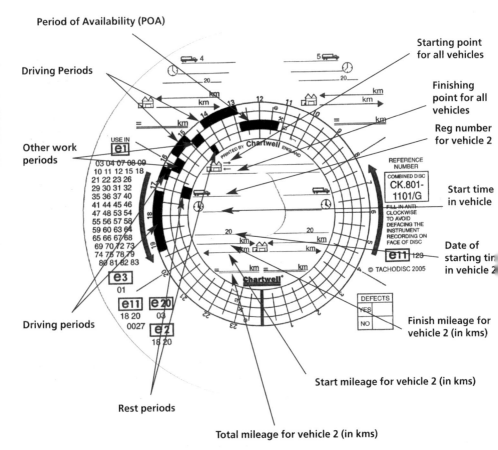

days together with your drivers' tachograph card if you hold one.

- Charts and printouts should be returned to your employer within 42 days of completion.
- A tachograph chart is a legal document. Look after it and buy a tachograph chart pouch, available from all good truckstops and truckers' shops.
- You should not remove a tachograph chart from the tachograph to check driving times without writing a note in the comments box on the reverse of the disc.
- If you are stopped by the police, ensure that they sign your tachograph chart after checking it.
- If a tachograph develops a fault indicated by a 'v' on the tachograph display or a red light at the bottom of the odometer face (not to be confused with the 'maximum speed reached' light) this should be noted on the rear of the tachograph chart in the comments or defects box, and the defect reported immediately to your depot manager.
- If your tachograph becomes faulty or has been reported as faulty before leaving the yard and a trace is not visible on the front of the tachograph chart, a manual trace of your working day must be made on the back. Keep a note of your driving, resting, POAs and loading times in order for you to be able to complete this accurately at the end of your day.

TACHOGRAPH CHART [FRONT FACE]

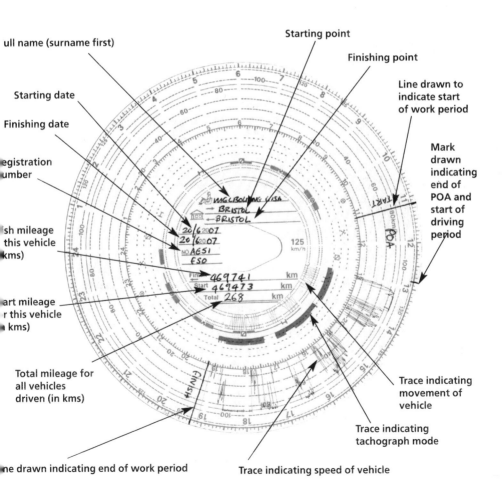

ull name (surname first)

Starting date

Finishing date

egistration umber

sh mileage this vehicle kms)

art mileage r this vehicle kms)

Total mileage for all vehicles driven (in kms)

ne drawn indicating end of work period

Starting point

Finishing point

Line drawn to indicate start of work period

Mark drawn indicating end of POA and start of driving period

Trace indicating movement of vehicle

Trace indicating tachograph mode

Trace indicating speed of vehicle

HOW TO RECORD YOUR DAY CORRECTLY

DRIVING	This mode is automatically selected when your vehicle moves. If your tachograph does not show this symbol, use the cross hammers symbol. The actual driving times will record on the tachograph chart.
REST OR BREAK	1 Break from driving in accordance with regulations (eg 45 minutes after 4 and a half hours of driving). 2 Daily or weekly rest in accordance with regulations.
PERIOD OF AVAILABILITY	1 Delays due to traffic prohibitions (including queues on site). 2 Waiting for someone else to load or unload a vehicle where the driver does not have to be in attendance and is free to use his time as and where he wishes. Expected delay time must be reported and recorded by your depot. 3 Delays at customs where the driver does not have to be in attendance and is free to use his time as and where he wishes. Again expected delay time must be reported and recorded by your depot. Once you go beyond that estimated time, it is classed as normal other work time. 4 Time spent with a broken-down vehicle at the roadside awaiting repairs or recovery. Expected delay time must be reported and the driver should not undertake any other duties during this time.
OTHER WORK	1 Walk round vehicle checks. 2 Cleaning and maintenance of a vehicle. 3 Securing the load. 4 Livestock attendance. 5 Driving a forklift. 6 Administration duties. 7 Any other work away from driving that you are required to do.

ALSO:

1 Where the driver knows the likely duration of the delay in advance, but it is safer to remain inside the cab, this will not disqualify them from being able to record this time as a period of availability. Only if the driver is required to stay with the vehicle, should he have to record it as normal working time.

2 Time that satisfies the definition of 'period of availability' can instead be used towards taking breaks from driving or working time requirements.

MOBILE PHONES

It is now illegal to make calls or to text using your hand-held mobile phone whilst driving, *unless you are using it to make a 999 call*, in which case you are permitted to do so if you are unable to stop. In order to make and receive any other type of call or to text using the handset, *you must be stationary, parked in a safe place (not the hard shoulder of a motorway) with the engine switched off.* However, there are things you can do or which are permitted, and here is a list of them:

• You may have a phone on 'silent' or switched off, with a voicemail system in place to pick up calls for you.

• You can use a voice-activated headset (non-cordless or cordless such as Bluetooth) to make calls, and a 'button on the headset' activated device to receive calls, *but if you have to actually pick up the phone to do either of these things, you are breaking the law.*

• You are permitted to use phone systems that are built into the vehicle or ones where you sit your phone in a cradle on the dashboard.

If the company you work for offers you a phone for use in your work and it is not compatible, do not use it whilst driving. The penalty points for doing so include 6 points on your licence and fines which start from £60 and rise to £2,500 (for drivers of lorries or buses) if contested. You can also face prosecution for failing to be in proper control of a vehicle (even whilst using hands-free equipment) and careless, dangerous or reckless driving – with penalties ranging from a fine to a ban and imprisonment – if using a phone affects your control of your vehicle. (See fines and endorsements section.)

Your company can also be prosecuted under health and safety laws and face unlimited fines and charges of individual or corporate manslaughter if you flout the law.

VEHICLE SIZE AND BRIDGES

The law regarding oversized vehicles
If your LGV and its load are over a certain size, special conditions apply. This may mean having to fit markers, carry an attendant, and notify the police. These conditions may apply if:
• Your load is more than 2.9 metres (or 9ft 6in) wide.
• If any part of your load projects more than 305mm (12in) on either side.
• If your load projects by more than 1m (3ft 3in) from the rear of your vehicle.
• If your vehicle and load have a combined rigid length of more than 18.65m (61ft 2in).

You must comply with the requirements of the Special Types Order if your vehicle and load fall within the following description:
• If your vehicle is more than 2.55m wide (8ft 4.5in) or together with its load either:
• Exceeds the gross vehicle weight or gross train weight allowed by the Construction And Use Regulations or Authorised Weight Regulations for ordinary lorries and/or the vehicle and its load are more than 4.3m (14ft 1in) wide.

You must apply to the Department for Transport for permission to move your vehicle if:
• The weight of the vehicle and its load exceed 150 tons (147.6 tonnes).

• Its width is more than 5m (16ft 5in).
• Its rigid length is more than 27.4m (89ft 11in).

The address to write to is: Department for Transport, VSE5 Zone 2/01, Great Minister House, 76 Marsham Street, London, SW1P 4DR.

If your vehicle is over 16ft 6in high you'll need to make Special Routing Arrangements with regard to the clearance of overhead power cables and bridges. These arrangements will have to be made with:
• Each local highways agency
• British Telecom (if over 17ft 6in)
• The National Grid plc
• Scottish Power
• Scottish Hydro Electric Power.

The law regarding bridges
If you hit or even scrape a bridge, you are legally required to stop. Failure to do so is an offence and could result in a heavy fine for you and a weakened bridge that becomes a danger to life.

Look for a sign mounted on the outside of the bridge or near it. This should show the exact location and a telephone number to contact. You should also immediately dial 999 and inform the police of the bridge strike. Do not leave the scene. Wait for the correct authorities to arrive and only leave when you have been given permission to do so.

If you approach a bridge that is lower than the height of your vehicle, you are legally required to stop. If you are unable to turn your vehicle, phone the local police authority of that area for advice or assistance. (See under 'Government Bodies' in the index.)

Advice regarding bridges
Every year hundreds of rail bridges are hit by truck drivers who are lost or don't know their vehicle height. Here are a few points to note so that you can avoid this happening to you:
• It is a legal requirement that every truck over 3m (9ft 6in) tall should display a sign stating vehicle height in the cab. If you get into a truck and this is not displayed, make it known and ask for the height of the vehicle before you leave the yard. If it is displayed only in either feet or metres, check the Imperial to Metric conversion table overleaf for the missing figures.
• Buy and use a trucker's atlas to plan your route. These are obtainable from any good book store, and these days also from most motorway service stations.

VEHICLE HEIGHTS, WEIGHTS AND DIMENSIONS

Height

The normal travelling height of your vehicle should be clearly marked. If you're driving a rigid without drawbar trailer, this height should be a fixed height and displayed prominently in the cab. It's normally somewhere between 9ft 6in and 14ft. If you're driving a solo unit the height will normally be between 13ft and 14ft 6in.

Trailer heights when coupled may vary wildly, between 14ft and around 16ft, though they should not exceed 16ft 5in.

You should always check the height of your vehicle and its trailer before you leave the yard.

Maximum weight of Class C1 rigid vehicles

- 7.5 tonnes MGW.

Maximum weight of Class C1+E vehicles (Combination of C1 rigid vehicle and drawbar trailer)

- 12 tonnes MGW.

Weight of Class C rigid vehicles

- Two axles: 18 tonnes MGW
- Three axles: 26 tonnes MGW
- Four or more axles: 32 tonnes MGW.

Weight of Class C+E vehicles

- Three axle artic: 26 tonnes MGW
- Four axle artic: 38 tonnes MGW
- Four axle rigid and drawbar trailer combination: 36 tonnes MGW
- Five axle artic/rigid and drawbar trailer combination: 40 tonnes MGW
- Six axle artic/rigid and drawbar trailer combination: 44 tonnes MGW.

Please note that weights given above are a general guideline and not a hard and fast rule. Specialist vehicle dimensions may vary from these guidelines. For the correct legal maximum load weight for your vehicle or for the unladen weight of your vehicle, you should check the MoT (Vehicle Inspectorate) plate or your trailer's manufacturer's plate. For more information on this see 'Know your cab – MoT (Vehicle Inspectorate) plate'.

Length

- Class C1: Minimum 5 metres
- Class C1 + E: Combined length of between 8 and 12 metres
- Class C: Between 8 and 12 metres
- Class C+E Rigid and drawbar trailer combinations: 18.75 metres maximum
- Class C+E Artic and unit combination: 16.5 metres maximum
- Trailers with 4 or more axles being drawn by vehicle of over 7.5 tonnes MGW: 12 metres maximum length
- All other drawbar trailers: 7 metres maximum length

Width

- Unit and trailer/rigid and drawbar trailer combination: 2.55 metres maximum
- Refrigerated trailer/rigid and drawbar trailer combination: 2.6 metres maximum
- Trailer drawn by 3.5 tonne rigid: 2.3 metres maximum.

METRIC / IMPERIAL CONVERSION TABLE

To Convert	Multiply by	To Convert	Multiply by
Inches to Centimetres	2.5400	Cu Feet to Cu Metres	0.0283
Centimetres to Inches	0.3937	Cu Metres to Cu Feet	35.3100
Feet to Metres	0.3048	Cu Yards to Cu Metres	0.7646
Metres to Feet	3.2810	Cu Metres to Cu Yards	1.3080
Yards to Metres	0.9144	Cu Inches to Litres	0.0163
Metres to Yards	1.0940	Litres to Cu Inches	61.0300
Miles to Kilometres	1.6090	Gallons to Litres	4.4560
Kilometres to Miles	0.6214	Litres to Gallons	0.2200
Sq Inches to Sq Centimetres	6.4520	Grains to Grams	0.0648
Sq Centimetres to Sq Inches	0.1550	Grams to Grains	15.4300
Sq Metres to Sq Feet	10.760	Ounces to Grams	28.3500
Sq Feet to Sq Metres	0.0929	Grams to Ounces	0.0352
Sq Yards to Sq Metres	0.8361	Pounds to Grams	453.600
Sq Metres to Sq Yards	1.1960	Grams to Pounds	0.0022
Sq Miles to Sq Kilometres	2.5900	Pounds to Kilograms	0.4536
Sq Kilometres to Sq Miles	0.3861	Kilograms to Pounds	2.2050
Acres to Hectares	0.4047	Tons to Kilograms	1016.00
Hectares to Acres	2.4710	Kilograms to Tons	0.0009
Cu Inches to Cu Centimetres	16.3900	Fahrenheit to Centigrade	(°F -32) x 0.56
Cu Centimetres to Cu Inches	0.0610	Centigrade to Fahrenheit	(°C x 1.8) +32

- Remember that any bridge with a clearance height of over 5.03m (16ft 6in) is unsigned and you will be able to drive safely under it, provided you are not driving an over-height vehicle.
- Avoid using unnumbered roads, as any low bridges will not be marked on your trucker's atlas.
- The heights of arched bridges are displayed in a triangle warning sign to advise of the safe clearance height for LGVs. You may also find white lines painted on the road to guide your passage through. Wait until it's safe for you to go – don't try to squeeze through alongside other traffic. Take your time and use all the space in the middle of the road.
- When picking up a trailer, check your trailer height. The height may or may not be written on the trailer. When it is, the height given is that which it would be if coupled to an average height 5th wheel. Afterwards you should adjust your height indicator in the cab if necessary.

COLLISIONS WITH OTHER ROAD-USERS, PEDESTRIANS, DOMESTIC ANIMALS OR PROPERTY

The law regarding accidents

The law states that if you become involved in an accident where other road-users, pedestrians or domestic animals are injured or property damaged you must do each of the following:
- Stop.
- Give your own name and address and the name and address of the vehicle owner or company that owns the vehicle, plus the registration number of the vehicle to those persons who would require it.
- If you do not do this at the time of the accident – say, for example, you were in a collision with

an unknown domestic animal – you must report the accident to the police immediately. You are allowed only 24 hours in which to do this, but must do it as soon as possible. Domestic animals include: horses, donkeys, cows, sheep, goats, deer, pigs, chickens, ostriches and dogs.

• In cases where other persons are injured you must also produce your insurance certificate to the police at the scene. If this is not possible you will be given a producer and asked to present all documents to your local police station within seven days.

Advice regarding accidents
If you're involved in an accident or stop to assist others you should:

• Use your hazard warning lights.
• Turn off your engine and ask others to do the same.
• Use the emergency telephones on the motorway or your mobile phone to contact the emergency services that you require. Use the marker posts placed every 100yd on a motorway to pinpoint your exact location. Don't forget to inform the emergency services of the nature of the accident and the condition of any casualties.
• Move uninjured persons as far away from the carriageway and hard shoulder as possible.
• Do not move any casualties from their vehicles unless they are in danger from fire or explosion.
• Do not remove a motorcyclist's helmet unless in an emergency (say, for example, in order to resuscitate the individual if you're otherwise

unable to reach the mouth). If you do have to remove the helmet, this should be done with great care and the neck should be supported at all times.
• Administer First Aid wherever possible.
• Stay at the scene until the emergency services arrive.
• If you have a camera or camera phone, take photographs. These can be of great use to any insurer. Also note the exact time and location of the accident, the position of any vehicles involved, the conditions of the road, and visibility. Take the names of any witnesses and the personal and/or insurance details of any persons involved. This will help you later if you need to complete any paperwork regarding the accident.

Accidents involving dangerous goods vehicles
Vehicles carrying dangerous goods will be displaying plain orange reflective plates. Vehicles carrying tanks full of dangerous goods will be displaying hazard-warning plates which state the nature of their contents. If you or anyone else is involved in an accident with a vehicle carrying dangerous goods you should also:

• Switch off engines and extinguish all cigarettes.
• Do not use a mobile phone in close proximity to the vehicle.
• Do not be tempted to rescue casualties as you yourself could become one.
• Call the emergency services and give as much information as you can about the labels and markings on the vehicle.

SPEED LIMITS

Type Of Vehicle	Built Up Area	Single Carriageway	Dual Carriageway	Motorway
Cars and Motorcycles	30	60	70	70
Cars towing Caravans or Trailers	30	50	60	60
Buses and Coaches	30	50	60	70*
Goods Vehicles not exceeding three and a half tonnes	30	50	60	70
Goods Vehicles exceeding three and a half tonnes	30	40	50	60**

*restricted to 62   **restricted to 56 (may not apply to 3.5–7.5-tonne vehicles registered before October 2001)

BREAKDOWNS ON THE MOTORWAY

For more information regarding breakdowns, see the section 'Troubleshooting, and what to do when things go wrong' on p.109. If your vehicle breaks down:

- Attempt to leave at the next exit or service area.
- If this is not possible, pull onto the far left-hand side of the hard shoulder and turn your wheels towards the verge.
- Try to stop close to an emergency phone (placed at one-mile intervals along the hard shoulder).
- Use your lights and hazard warning lights to alert other drivers.
- Leave the vehicle by the passenger door.
- Any horses or livestock must remain in the vehicle, except in an emergency, when they should be properly controlled on the verge.
- Do not attempt to repair your vehicle by the roadside.

- Contact the local motorway police from the emergency phone, stating the nature of the breakdown.
- Contact the transport department of the company you are driving for, or ask the motorway police to do so.
- Return and wait – behind the barrier, away from the vehicle – for the breakdown services to arrive.

ALCOHOL

As a professional driver, you should not be drinking and driving and here's why. The penalties listed below are pretty much the final nail in the coffin lid for any LGV driver. Any employment agency or haulage company is highly unlikely to employ a driver with these types of endorsement on their licence.

Failing to provide a roadside breath test (Code DR70)
Penalty: Fine up to Level 3 (£1,000), four penalty points on your licence. Disqualification is at the discretion of the Court.

Driving/Attempting to drive with excess alcohol (DR10)
Penalty: Fine up to Level 5 (£5,000) and/or up to six months' imprisonment. Mandatory disqualification for at least 12 months for first offence. Mandatory disqualification for at least three years for second offence within ten years.

Being in charge of a motor vehicle with excess alcohol (DR40)
Penalty: Fine up to Level 4 (£2,500) and/or up to three months' imprisonment. Ten penalty points on your licence. Disqualification is at the discretion of the Court.

After Driving/Attempting to drive refusing to provide samples for analysis (DR30)
Penalty: Fine up to Level 5 (£5,000) and/or six months' imprisonment. Mandatory disqualification for at least 12 months for first offence (18 months tends to be the norm, as you are considered to have been trying to avoid being found guilty). Mandatory disqualification for at least three years for second offence within ten years.

After being in charge of a motor vehicle refusing to provide samples for analysis (DR60)
Penalty: Fine up to Level 4 (£2,500) and/or three months' imprisonment. Ten penalty points on your licence. Disqualification is at the discretion of the Court.

The police can request a breath test or sample from anyone who is believed to have been involved in an accident or who is driving, attempting to drive, *or in charge of any motor vehicle parked in a public place*, including car parks and lorry parks. So having a few pints before you bunk-up for the night can result in disaster.

It's worth remembering that:
- One pint of normal strength beer will take approximately two hours to work through the body.
- A single whisky or half a pint of beer will take one hour to work through.
- Smaller men and women are more greatly affected by alcohol, as their body's water content is lower.
- Nothing can be used, taken or done to eliminate alcohol from the blood faster than its normal rate. Four pints of beer will take eight hours regardless of how much coffee you drink or how many cold showers you take.

And for the technically minded here are the legal alcohol driving limits in scientific terms:
- 35 micrograms of alcohol per 100 millilitres of breath.
- 80 milligrams of alcohol per 100 millilitres of blood.
- 107 milligrams of alcohol per 100 millilitres of urine.

It is usually considered that approximately 2 pints of normal strength beer equate to the examples given above. But this is not the same for everyone and it would be far safer not to drink at all.

It is worth remembering that the recommended number of alcohol units per week for women is 14 and men it is 21. A glass of wine, champagne, a single measure of spirits or a normal strength beer all equate to 1 unit each. Cocktails equate to 2 units.

DRUGS
Penalties for drugs are the same as those for alcohol (see endorsements list), though the methods for testing are different. Skin, blood and urine samples are used for this, and although you may think you'll get away with it because drug taking is not easily detected by smelling it on the breath, you can still be asked for a sample at almost any time if you're in charge of a vehicle or if you've been involved in an accident. Remember that some drugs remain in the blood for up to 28 days. My advice is simple, if you value your licence and your life, DON'T DO IT!

LOW EMISSION ZONE FOR GREATER LONDON (LEZ)
This is a new regulation that came into force on 4 February 2008 to help improve the air quality of Greater London. It means that the most polluting diesel-engined trucks, buses, coaches, minibuses and large vans will be required to meet specific emissions standards before being allowed to enter the Low Emission Zone in Greater London.

Older vehicles not compliant with Euro 3 emissions regulations (for tractor units this usually means anything built before

October 2001) will have to be modified or replaced before entering the zone or else pay a daily charge.

In July 2008 the same regulations come into force for all rigid vehicles over 3.5 tonnes and from October 2010 this will also apply to vans. By January 2012 both tractor units and rigids must be Euro 4 compliant before being permitted to enter the LEZ.

If you are asked to enter the LEZ and are unsure whether or not your vehicle is compliant, ask your manager before leaving the yard.

For further detailed information on the law and best practice in road transport see the Freight Transport Association's web site (www.fta.co.uk) or their Driver's Handbook available by calling 08717 11 11 11.

FINES AND ENDORSEMENTS

Offence	Imprisonment	Fine	Disqualification	Penalty points
Causing death by dangerous driving	14 years	Unlimited	Obligatory, minimum of 2 years	3–11 points (if exceptionally not disqualified)
Dangerous driving	2 years	Unlimited	Obligatory	3–11 points (if exceptionally not disqualified)
Causing death by careless driving under the influence of drink or drugs	14 years	Unlimited	Obligatory, minimum of 2 years	3–11 points (if exceptionally not disqualified)
Careless or inconsiderate driving		£2,500	Discretionary	3–9 points
Driving while unfit through drink or drugs or with excess alcohol; or failing to provide a specimen	6 months	£5,000	Obligatory	3–11 points (if exceptionally not disqualified)
Failing to stop after an accident or failing to report an accident	6 months	£5,000	Discretionary	5–10 points
Driving while disqualified	6–12 months	£5,000	Discretionary	6 points
Driving after refusal or revocation of licence upon medical grounds	6 months	£5,000	Discretionary	3–6 points
Driving without insurance		£5,000	Discretionary	6–8 points
Driving otherwise than in accordance with licence		£1,000	Discretionary	3–6 points
Speeding		£1,000–£2,500 for motorway offences, or fixed penalty	Discretionary	3–6 points
Traffic light offences		£1,000	Discretionary	3 points
No MoT Certificate		£1,000		
Seat belt offences		£500		
Dangerous cycling		£2,500		
Careless cycling		£1,000		
Cycling on pavement		£500		
Failing to identify driver of a vehicle		£1,000	Discretionary	3 points

THE TRUCK

Walk-round vehicle check

There are certain things on a truck that need to be checked every day to ensure its roadworthiness and legality. Do not rely on the previous driver – he may not have looked either! Here is a list of the checks:

- **Fuel:** Make sure that you have enough to get you to your destination and back again (if required). It would be wise to remove the cap on the tank and check the level manually. Older vehicles may have unreliable fuel gauges. Remember that if you are driving a refrigerated vehicle or trailer, the fuel level for this will also need to be checked.

- **Oil:** The dipstick is usually found under the front grille or behind the driver's cab, though in many modern vehicles the oil level can only be checked using the 'dashboard diagnostics' before the engine has been started. The diagnostics can be accessed using buttons on the stalk, a push in dial or buttons on the dashboard. The 'hardware' may vary though all you need to find are the methods of 'scrolling', 'entering' and 'exiting' through the menu. Oil level will be in there somewhere.

- **Fluid in Radiator:** The radiator is almost always located under the front grille. Grilles are usually opened from the front using a couple of latches just under the lip, but some simply pull straight up and out, without having latches.

- **Washer water:** Either under the front grille or in the driver or passenger stairwell leading up to the cab.

- **Lights:** Make sure all of them work, including those on the trailer. You'll need help to check the brake lights on unit and trailer. Don't forget to also check the marker lights down the side and at the top corners of your trailer and unit. All lights should be clean and not obstructed.

- **Curtains:** Check that they close, open, and strap down correctly.

- **Doors and retainers:** Make sure they can be correctly secured.

- **Tail-lifts:** Make sure that they're correctly stowed away.

- **Load:** Check that it is secure before you pull away.

- **Tyres and wheels:** Look out for any excessive or uneven wear (your tread depth should be no less than 1mm for vehicles over 3.5 tonnes (1.6 for less than 3.5 tonnes) and should apply to three quarters of the width of the tyre and all around the circumference). Look for scrubbing, bald patches, punctures, peeling or cracking of the tyre wall or any dents in the wheel rims. If any of your vehicle's axles have two tyres on one wheel, look at them from behind and check that the tyres are not 'kissing'.

- **Windscreen:** Check for cracks and chips. Severe cracks may require immediate attention. Make sure that the screen is clean inside and out.

- **Mirrors:** See that they're clean and undamaged.

- **Wheel nuts:** Most have yellow fluorescent markers that should all be pointing opposite each other. Check for any that are missing or damaged and look for rust marks around the nuts, this could indicate that they may be loose.

- **Brakes:** When you're hooked up to your trailer, listen for any hissing sounds, as this could indicate a

Many drivers would be unaware of how many pounds per square inch their vehicle's tyres should have and with good reason. Many companies do not not display the PSI requirements for their vehicles' tyres anywhere on the vehicles or trailers themselves. Also, the correct PSI for tyre pressures may vary enormously from vehicle to vehicle. Below is an APPROXIMATE guide of what your tyres should be. This guide should only be used if you have no other information regarding your tyre pressures available to you.

Type of Vehicle	Front Tyres	Middle Tyres	Rear Tyres
Tractor Unit	95	105	100
Trailer for Tractor Unit	95–115	95–115	95–115
26 Tonne Rigid	125	100	100
17 Tonne Rigid	120	N/A	100
7.5 Tonne Rigid	95	N/A	100

serious air leak. If your ABS is working correctly, a light (usually green) should come on – provided it's working – at the bottom driver's side corner of your trailer when you press the brake pedal.

- **Number plates:** Ensure that your unit has two (front and rear) and your trailer has one, and that they're undamaged, clean, and visible.
- **Service leads and fittings on unit and trailer:** Check that they're not damaged, split, or leaking.

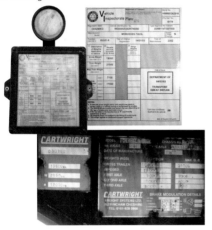

- **MoT (Vehicle Inspectorate) plate:** Check the one on the trailer (on the trailer body, beneath the floor) and the one in the cab. Make sure they are the right one for the vehicle or trailer you are operating and check that the date of the round MoT disc on the trailer has not expired. If your trailer is less than one year old, it will not have an MoT plate. Look for the manufacturer's plate (a silver or blue metal plate beneath the trailer body) to check the year of manufacture.
- **Tax and O licence:** Displayed in the windscreen of the cab. Check the dates.

- **Fire extinguisher, spill kit, eye kit, First Aid kit:** If it's required that you carry these, check that they contain the items they should and that they appear to be in working order. With fire extinguishers check that they haven't been used and not replaced.
- **Height indicator:** Check that your vehicle has one and that it is correct for the type of trailer you are pulling. Your trailer height (when coupled to an average 5th wheel

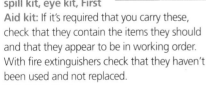

height) should be displayed somewhere on the trailer (usually at the front). If your cab is not displaying the correct height, adjust the indicator (so you don't forget what it is). If your cab is not displaying a height indicator at all, report it as a defect.

- **Wiper blades:** Make sure they aren't split, cracked, or bent.
- **Seat belt:** If one is provided, make sure that it's undamaged and working correctly.
- **Horn:** Check that it works.
- **Tachograph:** If you have an analogue tachograh, check that it's set on the right time and isn't showing any obvious faults or fault lights. Don't forget to make sure that if you only have one tachograph chart inserted you should switch the second driver mode to 'Break'. If you have a digital tachograph check for any pictograms showing a fault with the unit.
- **Odometer:** If your vehicle has an electronic odometer, check that it is set on km and not miles since all odometer readings should be written in kilometres on your tachograph chart. If in doubt check the readings on the tachograph itself (if it has an LED display) as these are always shown in km.
- **Interior:** Look for anything broken, damaged, or missing and notify your manager.
- **Dashboard diagnostics:** If, when you turn on the ignition, your vehicle diagnostics tell you that there's a problem with the vehicle or trailer, check it manually. Remember that after you've just coupled up to a new trailer, or if the vehicle has been sitting for a while, the air pressure will be low and will take some time to reach normal levels. If after a few minutes of idling or a few yards of driving your diagnostics system is still showing red lights, or if the red lights return or are intermittent, stop and get the vehicle looked at immediately. Don't drive on red lights! If the diagnostics system shows an orange ABS light for the trailer this may be due to a fault within the unit's or trailer's ABS system, or the ABS service lead may need replacing. Check with your company's workshop, as driving with faulty ABS systems can cause damage to the tyres when cornering or cause the vehicle to skid when braking. If your braking system is working correctly a green light will usually illuminate in the bottom corner of the front of your trailer when you brake, but remember that this light may not be working even if your ABS is.

Your vehicle's equipment

Using a pallet truck

For first-time users, pallet trucks can be pretty awkward things. If you push the handle to the right the forks move left, and vice versa, so manoeuvring them can take a little getting used to. Here are a few tips on how best to use one:

- To check if your pallet truck is working correctly, run your finger around the 'neck' of the handle where it joins the base of the forks. If this is wet and leaking oil profusely, the pallet truck is faulty and shouldn't be used. If it appears to be only slightly greasy, push the pumping lever down and away from you and pump the handle up and down. If it rises quickly and falls swiftly when you pull the pumping lever towards you, then it's in good working order. Check that the wheel and fork rollers are clear of debris in order to ensure free movement.

- If you're struggling to get the forks through the base of the pallet, push down on the handle as you push the forks through. This will lift the front end of the forks up and clear of any obstructions. Ensure that the forks are fully 'let down' before you attempt this.

- A pallet truck is much easier to control if the handle is pointing towards chest level. Any lower or higher and the forks will be harder to direct, forcing your load to wobble around all over the place.

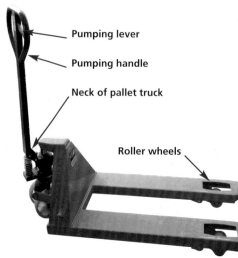

Pumping lever

Pumping handle

Neck of pallet truck

Roller wheels

- Some pallet trucks have a brake lever. This is usually situated on the opposite side or next to the pumping lever. It is a rare but useful addition, enabling you to stop the progress of the load without having to pull in the pumping lever and drop it onto the deck.

- Some pallet trucks have a lever near the bottom of the neck and next to the spring. This is a 'let down' lever that lowers the pallet truck and its load. In this case, the pumping lever (which normally acts as the let down lever) becomes only a 'mode changing' lever that you push away from you in order to ready the pallet truck for 'pumping up'.

- A pallet truck cannot be used over kerbs, on cobbles, or on gravel, untarmacked, or uneven surfaces. Nor should it be used on sloping ground without assistance. Steep slopes should be avoided at all costs. The load should be broken down and taken into the premises piece by piece.

- The back of the trailer should be swept clean regularly. Even small chips of wood can abruptly halt the progress of a loaded pallet truck.

- If you're off-loading on a slope, use your tractor unit and trailer suspension to 'level out' the angle of the trailer and/or tail-lift. This should help to avoid instances of back injury through trying to pull a load uphill, and should help prevent accidents caused by being swept off your feet by a loaded, runaway pallet truck.

- To secure your pallet truck in transit, place the forks through the base of a loaded pallet or a pile of empty ones and pump the handle until the forks touch the pallet. Do not lift the pallet itself. This should be enough to hold the pallet truck in place on your journey. To ensure absolute security, run a strap through the handle and secure tightly to either side of the trailer. If you have no strap and no pallets, turn the pallet truck upside-down on the floor of the trailer. This should only be done as a last resort, as it will weaken the hydraulic seals in the pumping mechanism.

- You may come across pallets that can only be approached from two sides, the openings on the other two being too narrow to push the forks through. These types of pallets are often oddly shaped. If they're narrower than the length of the forks, you shouldn't push the forks all the way through and out the other side – you may end up picking up the next pallet in line and damaging it in the process. Also, narrow pallets have their cross-members in different places to what you would expect. If you start pumping up the pallet truck when the roller is resting on one of these cross-members, you'll split the pallet. If in doubt, a quick glance underneath should tell you where your rollers are.

Shrink-wrapping and securing pallets

Pallets should be wrapped from the base upwards. Pull out a length of shrink-wrap and twist it. Tie the twisted length in a knot around a chock at the base of the pallet. Beginning with the base, circle the load several times holding both ends of the shrink-wrap. Work upwards gradually towards the top of the load. This will make you dizzy, but persevere. Keep the wrap as taught as possible and use liberally – it's better to over-wrap a pallet than under-wrap it. To break shrink-wrap, use a knife or your nails – don't pull it, as it will only stretch and not break.

Handballing goods

Handballing – the manual handling of goods – is becoming less frequent as more companies become aware of the safety implications and the time wasted in removing goods from a vehicle by hand. The sort of places that you are most likely to encounter goods that need to be handballed are bakeries and those places where deliveries are made to the front of a shop. Even then, such goods will often be in cages or on wheels these days.

If you're delivering goods in stacks of plastic tubs or trays they can be moved fairly efficiently using a 'pulling bar'. This is a metal bar with a hook at one end and a handle at the other. The hook is positioned under the lip of the lid on the tray or tub. Using this method a whole stack can be moved at a time. However, great care should be taken to avoid twisting your body. If you have to do any lifting, manual handling techniques and guidelines must be followed.

Using cages

These are wire containers on wheels, used for transporting loose goods. Many supermarkets use them. They should be moved carefully and stored well. Don't off-load cages on a slope, and be sure to strap them in well during transit. Curtain-sided vehicles should never be used to transport cages unless they have been specially designed to do so. If your cages have foot brakes or braking bars, use them.

Using wheeled platforms

Many bakeries use these to move tall stacks of trays containing bread. Trays or tubs are placed on them and secured inside box trailers by means of retaining bars. However, stacks of goods on wheeled platforms are very unstable and should be manoeuvred carefully, as they have a tendency to topple over or separate. If moving a wheeled stack over a lip or gap, a foot should be placed on the bottom of the stack close to the wheeled platform in order to stabilise it.

Using retaining bars

Spring-loaded bars can be a little awkward to use and are not always very secure, as the sides of the trailer move and flex during transit, so if you have straps use them as well. You'll find most of them have handles to make for easier insertion. First place the spring-loaded end in one of the holes on the side of the trailer, then pull back towards the side forcing the spring-loaded section to compress. This will enable you to insert the other end into one of the holes on the other side. When using bars, try to make them as straight across as possible and do not set them at an angle.

A superior system that can withstand much abuse is the 'cup and bar'. To fit the 'cups' which carry the bar, tilt the end of the cup nearest to you upward, and it should slot into the hole and drop into place. Do the same with the cup on the other side (make sure they're as accurately opposite each other as possible). The ends of the bar simply fall into the cups and a small retaining clip pops over the top to stop them falling out in transit. If the clip is missing, don't use that cup.

'Clipped bars' are very difficult to use and are unreliable when they become old and bent. To use them, first drop the lip of the end of the bar into the slot on the wall of the trailer. Lift the other end of the bar upwards and do the same. The retaining clips should flick forward to hold the bar in place. If they don't, choose another bar or try another slot. Unfortunately this system often jams when weight is pressed against it. If this occurs, close the back of the trailer, then drive forward a few feet slowly and brake hard. This should throw your load forward enough to release the bar.

Using chocks, blocks and stillages

Very large goods are often placed on the deck of the trailer using blocks. These are long thick planks of wood placed widthways across the trailer, which the goods sit on top of. This keeps them off the deck and allows forks to go underneath to lift them off.

Chocks are triangular-shaped blocks often used in the securing of very large cylindrical loads, such as reels of paper for printing works. The chocks are placed either side of the cylinders to prevent movement.

When not in use, chocks and blocks should be stored at the front of the trailer or in a locker along the side of the trailer body if provided.

Stillages are large metal containers on legs used to transport loose items. They come in all shapes and sizes but can often be stacked two or more high. They should, however, always be securely strapped down.

Using internal and external straps

Additional internal or external straps should be used with all load carriers and retainers to ensure the security of the load. Be sure that you are using the correct type and number of straps to hold the weight of your load. Remember, it is always better to use too many rather than too few.

Ratchet straps

These are used to secure loads likely to move in transit. The strap itself threads through a spindle in the ratchet mechanism. Each part of the strap (one short piece attached to the ratchet and one long piece) has a hook at either end which fits into any number of holes along the sides of the trailer. If the strap is being used as an 'over the top' external strap on a curtain-sided vehicle, the hooks should be clamped beneath the body of the trailer. To move the ratchet mechanism, pull the clip towards you to release it. Keep hold of the threaded strap and move the ratchet back and forth to tighten the strap into place. Remember that ratchet straps are extremely powerful and can bow the sides of a trailer inward if tightened too greatly. If you're using your ratchet straps to secure over the top and down the sides of a load, the easiest way to get them over the top (without climbing over the load) is to separate the two parts of each strap and wind the long end into a snail-like coil. Keeping hold of a free 3ft length of it, throw the remainder of the coil over the top of the load (make sure no-one is standing on the other side

when you do this) and then fasten it under the body of the trailer on either side.

External straps

Similar to ratchet straps, these are normally used to secure loads inside a box trailer. You may find that some are attached to the walls of the trailer itself (as shown here). This helps to prevent theft, but also means that when a strap is damaged it isn't always replaced. Check that the ones you are intending to use are in full working order. Also be careful not to trap your straps behind or below your load. You will find that most of these fixed straps will be attached to the wall of your trailer using a 'ring and running wire' system; others may be attached to the trailer using a 'runner' screwed to the wall and a system where you have to pull out a knob at the end of the cord leading to the strap in order to

move the strap up and down the length of the vehicle. Remember that these often get knocked and damaged, so check that they are working first. External straps are tightened in a similar way to ratchet straps but don't have a ratchet mechanism. Stronger types are secured with a clip whereas others just fold over. Remember with all box-sided trailer strapping that the straps should be clipped to the walls a foot or so in front of the back end of the load. This will hold the load more securely.

Internal straps

Internal straps are used on curtain-sided vehicles, where they hang either from a bar across the roof of the trailer or, in the case of curtain-sided trailers designed for wheeled cages, from a dozen or so side-bars down the length of the trailer. In both cases they can be used to prevent sideways or backward movement.

Straps that are attached to the roof bar should hang vertically down either side of the part of the load that you wish to hold in place, and be secured by clipping the strap beneath the body of the trailer (usually where the curtain straps go). Movement of the strap along the top

ring is only prevented by the tightness of the strap and its inability to move along the body of the trailer by being 'hemmed in' by the curtain straps. To prevent rear movement of the load, the straps should again hang down in line with the back end of the load and diagonally outwards towards the edges of the trailer (if possible threaded through the base of the pallets) and then be fastened beneath the body of the trailer.

Straps that are attached to the dozen or so side-bars in trailers designed to take wheeled cages should be permanently fastened to a loop on the bars close to the top, using an unusually-shaped pointed 'dog clip' end. Two straps on opposing sides can then be run over the top of the load diagonally in an X formation and fastened just behind the rear end of each section of the load.

There are so many bars and straps that this can be done with every block of four or eight (if stacked two-high) pallets or stillages. The straps are fastened at the base to specially designed anchor-points that run along a guttering on the outer edge of the trailer floor. If you're transporting cages the straps should remain as before at their high anchor-point on the bar, but this time you run the strap halfway down the length of the bar and through a U-shaped piece of metal.

From this point the strap runs backwards towards the rear and across the rear end of your load in the conventional manner (as it would if

you were strapping in a box trailer) and then attaches to the U-shaped piece of metal on the bar opposite. The raised guttering on each side of the trailer floor also prevents the wheeled cages from escaping through the closed curtain when in transit.

Balancing the load

There are many instances where you have to pick up sealed trailers with no opportunity to check the load, but whenever you load it yourself try to ensure that the heaviest items are over and between the axles – that is, about 6 ft from the front of the trailer and about 6–9ft from the back doors (see diagram). If you load extremely heavy items onto the front section of your trailer you may actually cause your front axles or the axles of your tractor unit to be overweight, even though your overall gross weight may be well within the limits for your vehicle. Extremely heavy items on the very front and very rear of your vehicle will also cause it to become unstable and place unnecessary strain on individual axles. If you're pulling a

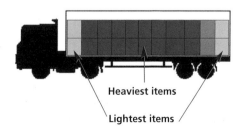

Heaviest items

Lightest items

double-deck trailer, make sure that the heaviest items are placed on the lower deck. Also try to ensure that the load is evenly balanced from one side to the other. Do not place all the light items on one side and all the heavy items on the other, or be tempted to place the load on the rear of the trailer for easy removal. Both these actions will make the vehicle very unstable around corners.

Door seals

Electronic seals consist of a panel on the rear of the doors (usually covered by a protective plastic flap) with a thick wire running from it through the door handle and back to the panel. The panel has an LED display and a plastic lever with a red button on it. The plastic lever is used to hold the wire securely in place, and the red button, when pressed, gives you your seal number.

Plastic seals consist of a simple red tag that has to be pulled hard to be broken. A number is printed on the seal, which should be recorded on your paperwork.

Metal seals can be very difficult to remove, although they are very secure. To remove, pull

height- or width-restricted road. The consequences of this are obvious: stuck drivers and damaged low bridges!

But help is at hand. Many sat-nav companies are recognising the need to cater for truck drivers and a trickle of new LGV sat-navs has recently begun to appear on the market. Just type 'sat-nav for trucks' into any search engine or check out www.nav-now.co.uk and type 'truck' into their search panel.

Sat-navs are fully portable and are powered by an adaptor which you plug into the truck's cigarette lighter. However, the LGV ones are still very expensive, with a price tag of around £400–£500, so unless you're willing to spend the cash, get a Truckers Atlas and stick to the A-roads!

You also need to know that recent legislation regarding sat-navs states that it is illegal to pick up or program your sat-nav whilst driving. You can also be prosecuted for using one of these systems legally if it is found that you were not in proper control of your vehicle at the time. Penalties for this are similar to those covering the use of mobile phones.

downwards on the seal and wiggle the joining point up and down until it snaps. Don't try to twist off a metal seal, or you'll be there for a very long time!

Note that inbound and outbound seal numbers to and from all your destinations should always be recorded on your paperwork. Some shops and warehouses insist on removing the seal themselves, so this shouldn't be attempted until you've been given permission.

Satellite navigation systems

There are many horror stories regarding trucks and sat-nav – I'm sure you've heard them all. As I'm also sure you're aware, most sat-nav systems aren't designed for LGVs and do not indicate to the driver that he is approaching a weight-,

Anatomy of a truck

Getting into the back of your vehicle

This isn't always as easy as it may seem, and if you have no tail-lift it can be a bit of a struggle. Inside your trailer or at the rear of your rigid there should be a handle on the right- or left-hand corner strut, about 2ft up from the deck. It may be either a cord strap or a metal handle. Place your foot on the T-bar beneath the rear lights, grip the handle, and haul yourself up. You should also check beneath the rear of the trailer, as some of them have built-in pull-out ladders. If you use this ensure that it's fully stowed before you drive off. If you are driving a vehicle with a column tail-lift, and don't wish to drop the whole platform, look for toe holes or drop-down steps on the rear of the tail-lift.

close to the tail-lift control box. Not all trailers have them, and in those that do they often don't work. With some interior lights, the vehicle headlights may have to be switched on in order for them to work.

INTERIOR LIGHT SWITCH

Tail-lifts

These vary enormously from brand to brand and vehicle to vehicle. If you're unsure of yours, ask someone to show you how to use it before you leave the yard. Be aware that some tail-lifts have an isolator switch either on the dashboard in the cab or on the tail-lift control box. If a key is required to operate the tail-lift or to open the control box, make sure you have it before you leave! Some tail-lifts also require you to keep a button pushed in on the control box while you're using the lift from outside the trailer. These complications are all designed to confuse and deter potential thieves (as well as the driver) so make sure you secure your tail-lift if you're parking in a public place overnight.

It's also important to remember that all tail-lifts have a series of buttons inside the trailer

Trailer interior light

Some newer trailers have interior lights. The switch usually comes in the form of a grey pad situated either outside or inside the trailer,

TAIL-LIFT CONTROLS

	Moves up and under tail-lift out from its stored position
	Moves up and under tail-lift back into its stored position
	Moves tail-lift up
	Moves tail-lift down
	Tilts tail-lift when used in conjunction with up or down arrow
	This button needs to be held in when using tail-lift outside of the trailer
	This is representing a red push-in lock often found near tail-lift control panels. If you have to use this, be sure you have the key.

with a 'mode' switch that controls the inside and outside operation. Don't forget to push this switch back across after operating the tail-lift from inside the trailer, otherwise once you've got out and shut the back doors you'll be unable to stow your tail-lift without opening the doors again.

Some tail-lifts have a three-pronged lead that looks a little like a service lead and connects to the trailer in a similar way, which provides an electric feed to the lift. But most tail-lifts rely on an Anderson lead, a two-pronged double-ended lead which is fixed on the service lead frame and clips into a housing on the front of the trailer. Note that Anderson Clips come in more than

one size. Check that your lead fits into both ends correctly. Another similar type is called the Cow Bell. This again is a lead attached to the service lead frame that clips into a housing on the front of the trailer, and is held in place by a pull-down lever. When not being used both these leads should either be removed and stowed in the cab or tied around the service lead cradle.

entirety and require no more unfolding (apart from the ramp stoppers).

To store your up-and-under, simply repeat the process in reverse, ensuring that the tail-lift is fully tucked under as far as it will go before you drive away. You may also find (though these are rare) that your particular up-and-under tail-lift has an additional feature that allows it to be operated using two rubber buttons on the tail-lift itself. These can be a little awkward if moving large loads on and off the tail-lift as the load itself can get in the way and accidentally activate the buttons.

When your tail-lift is in operation remember to keep your hands and feet well clear of the moving parts and the platform, and don't allow inexperienced persons into the back of your trailer or onto the tail-lift except in an emergency.

The cantilever tail-lift

This type is fairly large and sits flat against the

The up-and-under tail-lift

With its multitude of buttons this can be pretty complicated to use, but the rules are fairly simple. Move the tail-lift down about 6in before you move it out. When it's at is fullest extension it will make a 'straining' noise. From here, operation varies. Some up-and-unders will automatically flip the rest of the tail-lift out, some require you to use the tilt buttons to make the rest of the tail-lift present itself, and others need to be folded out manually (these can be quite heavy, so take care). However, most up-and-unders fit beneath the trailer in their

back of the trailer doors. It is fairly simple to use and requires no manual handling. Firstly, you should check whether or not it has any additional safety features, such as a pull-out lever on the side of the lift which holds it in place and stops it from flopping down should the hydraulics fail. Pull this lever out, then press the 'down' and 'tilt' buttons at the same time until the lift is at right-angles to the back of the trailer. Then lower, lift, and tilt it as desired. To store, raise the tail-lift to its fullest height and press the 'up' and 'tilt' buttons at the same time until the lift is flat against the back doors.

The column tail-lift

same time pull the top edge of the tail-lift down and outwards. When it reaches right angles with the back of the trailer, a small wedge at the base of the lift's nearside hinge should pop into place and hold it at that angle. You then just use the up and down buttons to operate the lift. To store, push down on the floor of the tail-lift and pull up the handle or flip the wedge at the base of the hinge. The floor should try to spring upwards into its stored position. Push it all the way up until it clips securely into place. Press the up button until it stops moving. A retainer at the top will prevent it from falling down in transit.

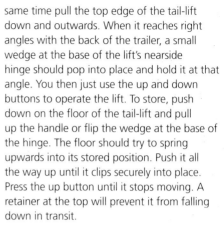

Again, a very simple tail-lift with usually only two buttons to worry about. Press the down button until the bottom of the tail-lift reaches just above knee-height. Check the edge of the lift and you should find a release clip or latch. Undo this and at the

The insider tail-lift
These are found on double-deck trailers and bread delivery trucks. The tail-lift is incorporated inside the trailer itself, acting as part of the floor when in the fully up position. It generally uses only up and down buttons and there may not be any externally accessed control panel.

Using a tail-lift on a slope
You should make efforts to avoid having to do this, but it is occasionally necessary. If your

vehicle is facing an uphill slope, lower the cab suspension and lift the trailer suspension. This should make things a little more even. If you're facing a downhill slope you should lift the cab and lower the trailer. If you're driving a rigid or an artic with no adjustable suspension don't attempt to off-load if the cab is facing an uphill slope, particularly if you're off-loading wheeled goods or palletised goods – a runaway pallet truck accident is not a pretty sight!

Take care to ensure that your goods remain on the floor of the tail-lift and don't slide backwards or forwards off it and under the rear of the truck, or out into the street, as you begin raising it.

Using a tail-lift around pedestrians

If you make deliveries to the front of a shop, be very aware of pedestrian complacency. I've seen people walk beneath, into and over tail-lifts, and even, in a drunken fit of bravado, attempt to climb onto them. If you drive onto pedestrian precincts take great care. You'd be surprised how unconcerned your average man in the street can be about seeing a 38-tonne truck trundling towards him.

Be sure always to use stoppers and safety rails if you have them. If possible, when off-loading make it difficult for pedestrians to walk close to your tail-lift. Block the surrounding area with boxes, tubs, cones, or anything else you have to hand. You'll normally be provided with some assistance if you're delivering to the front of a shop, and you should make good use of this second pair of eyes: ask them to watch out for any miscreants acting foolishly or dangerously around your tail-lift.

Stoppers and safety rails

Stoppers and rails are there to help you and prevent accidents. If provided, they should be used, particularly if you're off-loading wheeled goods. A stopper is a retainer of some description on the widest outside edge of the tail-lift that stops goods from sliding off when the tail-lift is in use. Some tail-lifts provide stoppers on all three edges or additional rails. Here is a description of those most commonly used and a few tips on how to operate them:

Folding ramps

The most common type of stopper. When folded out they provide an upright barrier on the edge or edges of the tail-lift. To use them as

ramps, they should be lifted upwards and outwards until they drop down towards the floor. If your tail-lift has three ramps, take care when stowing as they need to fall in a certain order to sit flush on the floor of the lift.

Flaps

These sit at the outer edge of the tail-lift and are normally flush against the floor. To activate them you most often have to apply weight on one side of each, which will tip them upright. Other flap stoppers are activated by pushing across a lever in the floor (next to the stopper itself) with your foot, which springs them upright. To close, simply stand on the stopper.

Removable safety rails

Some tail-lifts contain holes in the floor at the two short edges. These are for holding removable safety rails which prevent goods (and drivers) from falling off the edge. If your tail-lift has these, look in the back of the trailer or a side locker for the rails. If you're unloading wheeled goods, these can be a real lifesaver.

Trailer door security

Barn doors

'Barn doors' comprise two large doors at the back of the trailer that open outwards, secured by two or four vertical bars that fasten at the top and bottom. They're secured in place by twisting two or four levers, located at head height, towards the outer edges of the trailer. This turns the clips at either end of the bars into locking mechanisms at top and bottom. The levers are

Fridge doors

These are usually barn doors secured using flat door clips that have a 'push-in' bit in the centre of the handle to release the door. Remember that fridge doors are airtight and often difficult to open and close, so be certain they're secure before you drive off.

then positioned in clips on the door to hold them in place. Such doors can often be very stiff, but it's important to ensure that the clips at both top and bottom are fully secured and that the levers are fully seated within their clips.

Roller shutter doors

These normally use one of two types of lock. The first is the swing-over latch, which is a bar at the back of the trailer that rotates from left to right in order to secure the door and pushes a clip through a hole in the floor. Be sure to check that the door is fully down before you swing the latch across, otherwise it won't clip down. To be certain it's secure, try to pull the door upwards after you've secured it. If it won't budge, it's safe. If it has a Yale lock on the back, also remember to check that you have the keys before you leave the yard.

The other type of lock is a swinging catch. To secure this, simply pull the handle around to the right, which pushes the clip into a hole in the floor. Keep pulling the handle round till it comes up hard against a stopper. A securing latch should then pop in over the top of the handle. If it doesn't do this, it isn't secure.

Types of door retainers

When a door is open it's important to use retaining clips at all times, as a swinging barn door is an accident waiting to happen. You'll find your retainers about 3ft from the back of the trailer, just under the floor. Some are metal bars on springs which pull out and hold back the open door, some are looped wires which clip through a loop on the bottom of the barn door catches. With box trailers you may find that they're attached to the side of the trailer itself and hook onto catches on the backs of the doors. If you're using a curtain-sided vehicle and the retaining clips are broken, pull out the curtain strap second from the end and wrap it around the lever on the back of the door before clipping it back under the trailer body. Most of the time this should be enough to hold the door in place while you off-load.

Adjusting the height of a trailer or unit

Adjustable suspension

Most modern trailers have this. It is usually in the form of a black or silver handle found at the rear passenger side of a trailer. It can be swung upwards to the left or right to raise or lower the suspension. With the modern black-handled version, the lever must be pulled outwards to level the ride height. With older versions, the lever must simply be placed centrally. To adjust the suspension in your unit you'll find an adjustment panel inside the cab, near the floor

to the right of the driver. If this is of the small square type, the top centre button activates the panel, the up and down keys raise and lower the suspension, and a button with an arrow pointing forwards (or in some cases a green button with arrows facing towards each other) returns you to ride height. If it's of the large rectangular type, both switches should be in the central position to return you to ride height.

Dump valves

A dump valve is used to release all the air from the trailer suspension. Dump valve buttons are usually black and are sometimes located in the same place as the trailer brake (don't mistake them for the trailer brake!) or else at the front of the trailer. Occasionally you'll find them at the back, but they're almost always on the passenger side. A prolonged release of air is usually heard when the dump valve is used.

If you have no air suspension on your trailer

This only occurs with very old trailers. If you're attempting to couple up to a trailer that's too low for your unit and you're unable to adjust your cab suspension so that you can fit beneath it, you must raise the trailer manually. This is achieved by pushing in your leg-winding lever. This changes the gearing on the winder and allows you to very slowly raise the trailer. You can also use this technique if your trailer feet

seem to be stuck in the floor and you're unable to raise them in the conventional way.

Trailer brakes

Most trailers have brakes that are fairly easy to locate. They're normally one-third of the way from the front of the passenger side of the trailer. Sometimes they're located in a little rectangular box mounted onto the body under the trailer floor. Trailer brake buttons are normally red, though this isn't always the case. A sharp release of air is normally heard when you engage a trailer brake. Don't confuse the trailer brake with the shunt button, which is usually (though not always) blue.

Lift axles on units, rigids and trailers

Some tractor units and trailers have lift axles. This is where one axle of a three-axled unit or trailer can be lifted clear of the ground. Axles should only be lifted when the vehicle is not fully loaded. Lifting axles will save on wear and tear of the tyres but will make the vehicle unstable if it's carrying a full load, and places enormous strain on the other axles. To lift a tractor unit or rigid axle, look for a button in the cab that resembles a couple of off-set zeros (see 'Know your cab instrumentation and equipment'). You should ensure that your vehicle's systems are full of air and that your engine is running or the ignition is on.

Automatic lift axles on a trailer are controlled by a sensor within the trailer's ABS system and will automatically rise when the trailer is empty, and lower when the trailer is around half loaded. If this doesn't occur, there may be a fault with the ABS system. Get it checked.

The functions of service leads

You usually have five, or occasionally six, types of service lead running from the tractor unit to the trailer. Each performs a different function:

- **Red air lead:** This provides all the air to the unit and trailer systems, including brakes, suspension, clutch, driver's seat, and so on.
- **Yellow air lead:** The purpose of this lead is a little hard to define but the best analogy I can give is that if you imagine the red air lead as a tap that lets water into a sink (the 'sink' being the trailer and unit air tanks), then the yellow air lead is the valve that increases and restricts the flow of the water in accordance with requirements.
- **Black electric leads:** There are two of these, providing lights for the trailer.
- **ABS (anti-lock braking system) lead:** This

provides anti-lock braking for the trailer, to help prevent skidding. It is black in colour and has a clip on it which is used to secure the coupling. If your trailer does not have an ABS coupling but your unit has an ABS lead, the lead should be either removed and stored in the cab, wound around the service lead cradle, or stored coupled into a dummy holder.
- **Tail-lift lead:** Some units and trailers have permanently attached tail-lift leads that look a little like service leads but only have three pins. Unlike Anderson leads or Cow Bells, these do not need to be removed or securely stored when the vehicle is in transit.

Battery isolator switch

This is a small red switch located at thigh height

on the passenger side just behind the cab. Not all units have one. It is used to help prevent load or vehicle theft and also to prevent drainage of the battery on cold nights. Note that when this switch is employed all power to the vehicle's systems from the battery is cut.

Cab lockers

Cab lockers are to be found outside the cab near the driver's and passenger's doors. They may be heavily disguised as part of the bodywork but are often full of useful items such as spare gloves, straps and air-leads. To access the lockers, look for a small cable with a ring-pull just inside the door near the rear of the seat, or a lever built into the top of the wheel arch beneath where the door sits.

Know your cab

Adjusting your driving position

You'll find all of your seat adjusters on the right-hand side and front of your seat. Those at the front (usually consisting of pull-up or slide-across bars) adjust the seat backwards and forwards, while those at the side control height, angle, suspension, and lumbar. The most comfortable driving position you can attain is one where the seat is tilted slightly backwards. Avoid using too much lumbar support as this can tire the muscles in the lower back. To avoid having to stretch as you turn it, bring the steering wheel as close as is comfortable. It is often better to have your knees either side of the steering column rather than behind them, and position your height so that you can see out of the windscreen clearly yet still reach the pedals comfortably. Avoid putting too much 'bounce' on the seat. If you are of small build, this will throw you into the cab roof! The controls perform the following functions:

 Lumbar support: Provides support for the lower back and in some cases also for the sides of the body.

 Seat suspension: Brings the seat up to the ride height you've selected or drops it to the floor.

 Seat-back adjuster: Adjusts the back of the seat from laid-back to bolt upright.

 Heated seat: Unfortunately not all seats have this, but on cold winter days it's a blessing (even if it does make you feel as though you've just wet yourself!).

 Seat tilt: Tilts the front of the seat up or down. Instead of a button at the side of the seat, this can sometimes be found in the form of a paddle at the front edge of the seat.

 Seat height adjuster: Adjusts the height of the seat.

Seat springiness adjuster: Allows you to adjust the suspension according to your weight and personal preference. If you're light, you should have this set to minimum.

Steering wheel

It's important to get the position of your steering wheel correct and comfortable. If it's too far away, this will cause a strain on your arms, shoulders, and lower back, and if it's too close it may impair your ability to turn the wheel rapidly. Most are fully adjustable, with about four different types of adjusters:

- **The wheels:** There are two wheels, one on either side of the steering column, that you have to undo. Once loosened, one will pull the steering wheel towards you and the other will lift it up and down. These adjusters are often very stiff, as they have to be tightened firmly to stop the steering wheel moving in transit.
- **The lever:** This is found either on the front of the steering column close to the driver's knees, or at the side at knee height. It can be a push-in button, a lift-up button, a lift-up lever, or a twist-back-and-forth lever. The steering wheel can be adjusted in all directions when applied.
- **The floor button:** This is to be found either in the centre of the floor or on the right-hand side close to the base of the seat. The driver has to push it in with his heel in order to adjust the steering wheel. Not to be confused with an exhaust brake.
- **The pedal:** Situated above the accelerator or clutch pedal, this looks like a miniature brake pedal. When pushed in, the steering wheel can be fully adjusted.

Dashboard buttons, lights and dials

The symbols found on your dashboard will vary greatly from vehicle to vehicle. However, I've provided diagrams and explanations of the most popular ones that you're likely to encounter in the course of your working day:

 Overhead lighting and/or isolator switch for trailer lights: This provides lighting for the cab and may also be used as a symbol for a dashboard isolator switch for the trailer interior lights. Should not be turned on whilst driving.

Overhead red nightlight: Provides the driver with dim, red illumination inside the cab. This can be used whilst driving.

 Headlight adjuster: Raises and lowers the angle of the headlights. Only to be used to lower the headlights when the vehicle is fully loaded.

 Rear and front fog lights: Apply only when visibility is considerably reduced. On some vehicles you may have to pull out the dipped headlight switch to activate fog lights.

 Inspection light: This allows you to couple and uncouple more easily in the dark. It may sometimes be necessary for your vehicle's head or sidelights to be on in order for the inspection light to work.

Dashboard light brightness switch: This is usually a dimmer switch type dial. It enables the driver to see his dashboard dials and buttons better in the dark.

 Exhaust brake: May need to be used along with a lower gear when descending a steep hill. The exhaust brake may come in the form of a button on the dashboard, a flat button on the floor, or a feature on one of the steering column stalks, when it is usually displayed as a circle with a dotted crescent around each side. Make sure this is not stuck on when you're accelerating, as you'll not get anywhere fast!

 Cruise control: This may be featured on one of the steering column stalks or on the steering wheel itself. You may have several options: an on/off switch, an option to reduce or increase speed in cruise control, and one to resume cruise control. These options may be displayed using many different symbols and may employ many different means of activation, including pulling the stalk in various directions. However, all cruise control systems are deactivated by braking.

 Dif lock: Only to be used to move the vehicle if it is momentarily unable to grip the road or surface. It must be turned off immediately the moment it has served its purpose.

 Loss of traction warning light: This (or something like it) will appear on the LED display if your tyres are momentarily unable to grip. This sometimes occurs when pulling away on a steep hill or in wet or icy weather.

 Reverse warning alarm: This silences the reverse warning alarm and should only be used between 23:00–07:00 hours.

 Tank bleeder: If your vehicle runs out of diesel, the system will need to be bled of air. Very few vehicles have a tank-bleeding switch, so try to avoid running out of fuel! The alternative is a costly breakdown bill.

 Tank heater: In this country you're unlikely to ever require this. Under extremely low temperatures it's possible for diesel to freeze, and a tank heater will prevent this from happening.

 ABS light: This is a light on your dashboard that may appear orange if your ABS lead is faulty or if the ABS systems of your truck or trailer are faulty. In the case of an ABS lead, this can often be caused by nothing more than a bent pin within the lead's couplings. Get this checked. Failure to do so may result in wheel-locking and tyre-scuffing when you brake. It will light up red if you have a serious fault with your ABS system. If this happens while you're driving, stop. If it appears when you're in the yard and doesn't turn off after you've driven a few yards, don't leave.

 EBS light: EBS is a system that works through the ABS lead to reduce general brake wear and braking distance in an emergency. It can also assist in trailer stability and improve compatibility between trailer and unit. If this light shows on your LED display, your ABS lead or the EBS system on your trailer may be at fault. Get it checked before you leave the yard. Remember, yellow lights require attention, red lights mean you should stop immediately.

 Brake light: This will appear in red if you have your handbrake on or if you don't have enough air in the system, in which case you won't be able to move. If it comes on when you're driving, stop immediately (though you may not have much choice in this, as the brakes will automatically be applied anyway).

Raise lift axles: This button raises and lowers your unit or rigid's lift axles. A similar button showing the circles set at the same level, lowers it again.

Air pressure dials: These tell you how much air you have in your vehicle's brake, clutch and suspension tanks. If the needle falls within the red section of the dial on either tank you won't be able to move the vehicle, as the pressure is too low.

Fontaine 2 sliding fifth wheel release button: This button must be pressed and held in order to move the Fontaine 2 sliding fifth wheel (this is a non-manual type of sliding fifth wheel, not to be confused with the manual type).

Hill-start button: Specific to automatic and tiptronic gearboxes, this aids smoother acceleration and can be used when manoeuvring slowly on a steep hill. Should be switched off immediately after use.

AdBlue dial: You will find this on any vehicle built after 2006. It is incorporated into the dashboard and indicates levels of AdBlue in your AdBlue tank.

Phone: Many newer trucks have been designed with the current mobile phone laws in mind, incorporating phone menu controls into the dashboard or onto the steering wheel. These will allow you to answer the built-in phone and select a phone number from the phone book's memory. Some will also show the number that's calling on the truck's main LED display.

Trailer battery warning light: If your trailer has its own battery supply, your unit or rigid will be fitted with a three-pin suzie lead for charging the battery in transit. If this is connected but not charging, this warning light may show.

● **Tacho overspeed/fault light:** If your vehicle has a digital tachograph you may find a small orange circle with a 'T' at the bottom of you speedometer face. This indicates a tachograph fault or incidents of overspeeding.

MoT (Vehicle Inspectorate) plates

MoT plates are positioned both in the cab and on the trailer. These will tell you the make of your vehicle and registration, the maximum gross weight, year of manufacture, and in the case of rigid and drawbar combinations its train weight – this is its maximum gross weight when connected to a trailer. When looking for your particular vehicle or trailer's maximum gross weight you should refer to the figures written below where it states 'Weights not to be exceeded', not in the figures below 'Design Weights'. The figures in 'Weights not to be exceeded' refer to the vehicle or trailer's taxation class, while those in the 'Design Weights' column refer to the maximum weight that the vehicle or trailer could take if it were taxed to that limit. Below the 'Weights not to be exceeded' column you will also find figures stating the maximum permitted weights of each axle when loaded. This is extremely useful when weighing your vehicle using a weighbridge.

Trailers less than one year old will not have an MoT plate. Check the manufacturer's plate for this information. The trailer MoT plate also has a round disc attached or nearby. This tells you when its next inspection is due. In the cab the MoT plate is usually found behind the driver or passenger seat, on the dashboard, or on the rear wall. On a trailer it can be found attached to the chassis below the floor or at the front near the service leads. Manufacturer's plates are usually to be found below the floor of the trailer close to the legs. See also 'Walk round vehicle check'.

Tax and O licence

This is displayed in the windscreen of every vehicle. It shows your company's operators' licence number, the vehicle registration, and the expiry date.

Fuses

Usually found where you'd expect to find the glove box on a car. Fuses often blow following a power surge or a short-out (such as a bulb blowing). Inside the lid of the fuse box there's normally a diagram stating which fuse does what. This also shows you where the spare fuses are kept.

Broms Brake

Only found in Volvos, this is a secondary brake – situated below the normal handbrake – that automatically comes on when the unit is very low on air, and will remain on until released manually. To release the brake, push the knob inwards.

Cab heaters

These are used to warm the cab in cold weather when the engine isn't running. I wouldn't advise

using these while you sleep, as they're powered by diesel from your tank and can dry the air so much that you could find yourself waking up with an awful headache. It's also worth remembering that there's a delay between turning on or adjusting a heater and it actually doing what you just asked it to do. This makes it difficult to be sure exactly what your heater's doing.

Most cab heaters have a timer switch that you can adjust using arrow keys, enabling you to set it to come on at a certain time. They also have a dial switch to control the 'fan', and many have a temperature switch. The more sophisticated even have an alarm clock built in. (Also look out for an isolator switch on the dashboard – this must be employed before the cab heater will work.) However, all cab heaters are different, so you may have to play with it to find out what yours does. (At least it gives you something to do before bedtime.)

Uncomfortable seat belts

With older vehicles you'll often find that the seat belts are secured very high up on the side of the

cab, and if you're small you may find that the belt will cut right across your neck. However, there is a solution: pull the seat belt out across your chest, longer than is needed, twist the end round and round several times to alter its position across your body, and then clip it in.

Remember that if a seat belt is provided in the cab, you must wear it.

Positioning your mirrors to maximise your vision

Normal mirrors should be positioned so that you can see a small proportion of the trailer, three-quarters ground level, and one-quarter sky. Wide-angled mirrors should be positioned so that slightly more of the trailer is visible. This will help to reduce the size of any blind spots. Kerb mirrors (the ones that hang over the top of the passenger door) should be positioned so that they point straight down without being angled towards the front or rear. Only a small part of the side of the cab should be visible.

The worst blind spots for a truck are the area extending approximately 25ft from the rear of the trailer, the area just behind and beside the passenger door, and a smaller area below and behind the driver's door. There's also another area that extends approximately 5ft in front of the cab. The mirrors themselves also obstruct your view when approaching a roundabout or crossroads, so be aware of this and check the area several times before you pull away.

Different types of analogue tachograph

Type 1

This is the conventional type of tachograph. It is built in as part of the speedometer and is opened by turning a key above the speedometer dial and pulling it towards you. The tachograph will fold out on a hinge. Tachograph charts should be placed in this type of tachograph with the trace facing upwards. The tachograph mode selectors are found at the bottom of the speedometer, close to the hinge. Always ensure that this type of tachograph is fully closed afterwards. If it isn't, a tiny red warning light should appear at the bottom corner of the speedometer when you're stationary. To

adjust to British Summer Time, turn the white cogwheel inside the tachograph until you reach the correct time.

Type 2

Fairly uncommon but usually found in older Volvos. This type of tachograph is hidden behind a panel in the top edge of the dashboard that's opened by twisting a lever found between the mode selectors above the speedometer. The tachograph chart should be placed facing towards you so that its edge falls into the green slot at the bottom. The lever should then be twisted back so that the whole mechanism is hidden again.

Type 3

Popular in newer vehicles before the advent of the Digital Tachograph. You could be forgiven for mistaking this type of tachograph for a radio, as it is normally placed above the driver's head. To open it, turn on your ignition and press the button that looks like an eject button. The front should flop open after about five seconds. If this doesn't happen, push it in, as it may be on a spring catch. Pull the open tray towards you and down and insert your tachograph chart facing upwards. Ensure that it is seated below the guide on the top left-hand side of the tray. To close, push the tray upwards and in until it clicks. You then select your mode using the '1' button (if

you're the only driver) and watch the LED display for the various mode symbols. Remember to select the correct mode before you drive off. With this type of tachograph it is impossible to know which mode you are in once the vehicle is moving. If 'break mode' was last selected and you later become stuck in traffic, your tachograph chart will show readings of hundreds of 'mini breaks' taken. This is a tachograph offence and will be noticed.

When adjusting to British Summer Time, all tachograph discs must be removed. This includes the 'lining' disc usually kept in the 'second driver' tray. Remove this by lifting the flap. Close the tray and press and hold the 'M' and minus buttons at the same time for around 30 seconds. When you release them, a different LED display will appear.

Use the plus and minus keys to alter the time then press and hold the 'M' button for around three seconds. Your new time will be entered and the display will return to its normal screen.

Type 4
Specific to the Mercedes Actros, this type of tachograph consists of two slots below the speedometer (one for each driver). To use, turn on the ignition and simply insert your prepared disc into slot one in the same way you'd insert a CD into an in-car stereo system, with the trace side facing upwards. The tachograph will do everything else for you; all you have to do is select your mode. Note that this type of tachograph uses a 120 type of tachograph chart as opposed to a 125 used by most other tachographs.

Understanding your gearbox

Manual

Straight 5 or 6 (with or without splitter), rigids only

This is basically much like a car gearbox. It has no high or low ratio gears, though it may have a splitter providing half gears. Those with splitters are usually found on rigids used for towing trailers. With the old type of Iveco gearboxes these can occasionally jump out of gear when going over a bump.

Four over four

The most common type of gearbox. Contains four low ratio forward gears and four high ratio forward gears. This type of gearbox may or may not contain a splitter providing half gears.

Three over three

Same as a four over four, but with only three low and three high ratio gears.

Four beside four

Sometimes known as 'eight with a gate'. Most commonly found in Ivecos and Renault Premiums, this contains four forward gears on the left-hand side of the box. The driver then has to push the gearstick through a gate in the middle to reach the other four higher ratio gears. This can be a very fast gearbox and may or may not contain a splitter providing half gears. It can also be a very stiff and awkward gearbox. The trick is not to attempt to force it into submission. Allow the gearlever to find its way from neutral into the correct gear with the maximum amount of guidance and minimum amount of force. Note that this type of gearbox can be very easily, accidentally put into reverse. If possible, try to choose your start off gear before you have fully stopped at a junction.

Crash

Eaton Twin Splitter
Every new driver's worst nightmare, the Eaton Twin Splitter is rarely seen these days and usually found only in older ERFs, Fodens and DAFs. Some informal training may be required in order to operate one of these.

The configuration is 12 gears in a four over four type of configuration. Each of the four gearstick positions contains three gears that are selected using a three-position splitter lever (towards the driver, in the middle, and away from the driver). When changing gear using the splitter lever only, or changing up through the gearbox using a combination of the splitter and the gearstick, it isn't necessary to use the clutch. It's vital that, whatever you're doing, your revs are within the green band or the gearbox won't select the gear. Down changes made while the vehicle is still travelling should be made gear by gear, though if you've stopped or almost stopped you can block change.

The changing-up technique from standstill goes something like this: pre-select splitter position, put in clutch, rev engine into the green band and move gearstick: the gearbox will select the gear. Pull away. When revs are at the top of the green band, pre-select next higher splitter gear, take your foot off the accelerator, change the gearstick position (if necessary) and while revs are in the green band the gearbox will select the gear. It's the same for changing down, though you'll often find yourself braking then clutching and revving in order to get the box to select a gear. The Eaton Twin Splitter has a lot of power in the lower gears, and unless carrying a heavy load you're unlikely to need to pull away in any gear lower than fifth or sixth. Once fully proficient, a driver can change up and down the box hardly using the clutch at all.

Fuller Road Ranger

This behaves similarly to the Eaton Twin Splitter in that the revs must be within a certain range in order to change gear. The gear configuration is the same as that of a four over four gearbox

with a high and low splitter lever. The main difference between the behaviour of these two gearboxes is that with the Fuller you must use the clutch until you've become fully proficient as it doesn't pop into gear as easily as the Eaton. It also has the added scary function of a 'clutch brake'. This means that if you push the clutch all the way to the floor you won't be able to change gear. This gearbox is now considered to be very archaic, therefore you're unlikely to come across it.

Automatic and Tiptronic

Keypad (mostly found in refuse trucks)

This type of gearbox is almost idiot proof. The gear-changing system consists of a keypad situated in the centre console with one drive gear (represented by 'D'), a first and second gear for slow forward motion, a neutral gear (represented by 'N'), a gear for when the vehicle is parked (represented by 'P'), and a reverse gear (represented by 'R'). It's important to note that with this type of gearbox, when the vehicle is placed in any forward or reverse gear the engine is engaged automatically and the vehicle will begin to move. There isn't a clutch, so when not moving neutral or park should be selected.

Actros Automatic

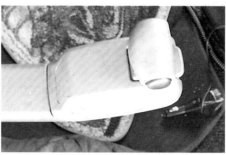

A clutchless gearbox, specific to the Mercedes Actros. In newer models the gearstick is situated on the end of the armrest, while in older models it's attached to the side of the seat. Unlike the Keypad gearbox, the vehicle won't pull forward when a drive or reverse gear is selected. Instead, the vehicle will behave as though it's in neutral, so brakes must be applied – it will only move when you press the accelerator. Be aware that because of the nature of this gearbox moving backwards on a slope can be a buttock-clenching experience, since you have no clutch to regulate your vehicle's movement.

This gearbox may or may not have an A/M (automatic/manual) switch. If it doesn't, it's manual. This means that you will have to select each gear yourself by pushing the gearknob forward and backward to change up and down the box. If, however, automatic mode is available, once a forward gear is selected the gearbox does the rest. With both the manual and automatic modes, to select a forward gear when you're in neutral you have to press in the right-hand button at the same time as pushing forward on the gear knob. If you wish to change into a lower gear than that selected by the 'box, you should push down on the lever attached to the neck of the gear knob. This will put you into the next lowest gear. If you wish to select the next highest gear, pull this lever upwards. To select neutral press the button on the left of the gear knob, and to select reverse push the button on the right of the gear knob and pull back on the stick at the same time.

DAF AS-Tronic

Also a clutchless gearbox, the DAF AS-Tronic comes as two different options: dashboard switch or central console. With the former, the automatic controls are accessed via a round switch on the dashboard while the manual options are accessed using the specially designed column stalk. With the central console option, the automatic controls are accessed using the dial at the rear of the base of the gearstick and the manual options are accessed via the gearstick itself.

As with most tiptronics, the gearbox behaves as though in neutral until the accelerator is pressed. Be aware, though, that with the AS you must apply pressure on the accelerator very gently, as aggressive use may launch you forward in a most undignified fashion. This is useful for 'quick getaways', but not for movement in slow traffic.

With both dashboard and console options, the switch positions left to right are: slow

reverse (indicated by the picture of a tortoise), normal reverse (R), neutral (N), drive (D) and slow drive (also indicated by a tortoise but this time on a different coloured background).

With both options, the round switch is what you'll use if you wish to remain in automatic mode. Simply switch from neutral to drive and pull away.

With the central console option, however, if you're in automatic mode and wish to switch to manual move the gear stick over to the far left, to the 'M/A' position. To select the next (or first) forward gear, move the gearstick one position forward. If you wish to block change up, push the gearstick forward as far as it will go. For single and block changes down, pull the gearstick backward. If you wish to get the gearbox to select the best gear for you push the stick over to the right ('S' position). To re-select automatic again, push the gearstick back over to

the left; 'A' for automatic should appear on your dashboard LED display.

If your AS is the dashboard switch version, your manual options are on your right-hand steering column stalk. To switch from automatic to manual simply press the button at the end of the stalk. To change up and down the gears, push the stalk either towards you or towards the windscreen.

When using the exhaust brake the AS will automatically change down a gear or two. Also, if you leave the vehicle or open the doors without selecting neutral an alarm will sound. It is good practice to select neutral and handbrake whenever stationary.

Iveco Stralis

A clutchless gearbox specific to the Iveco Stralis. So far there have been no modifications to this gearbox. It can be operated in either automatic or semi-automatic mode, which are selected by using the right-hand button on the top of the gear stick. The LED display will tell you which mode and gear you're in. If automatic is selected

you'll only need to push the stick forward once, to take the vehicle out of neutral – the gearbox will decide everything else for you. As with the Actros Automatic, the vehicle won't move in either direction until you press the accelerator. If semi-automatic is selected you'll need to push the stick forwards and backwards in order to change up and down. To select neutral, press the button on the left of the gear stick, and to select reverse pull up on the collar at the base of the gearstick while at the same time pulling the 'stick backwards.

MAN AS-Tronic

This clutchless box is fully automatic with an option for partial manual. The gearshift is to be found in the form of a dial in the central console and displays five positions. From right to left these are: slow reverse (RM), standard reverse (R), neutral (N), drive (D) and slow drive (DM). To select an automatic forward gear, simply turn the dial to 'D', release the handbrake, press the accelerator and pull away. To select manual option (say, for example, you wanted to be in a lower or higher gear than the gearbox selected for you) pull the stalk either towards you (to go up the box) or away from you (to go down). Holding the stalk either towards or away from you for several seconds will allow you to block change. This is an extremely intelligent box and if it doesn't like what you've chosen it will select for you. It will also return you to auto mode automatically once you've finished your manual manoeuvres.

As with most other new tiptronic boxes, the MAN has a 'kickdown' facility allowing you to pull away rapidly or apply more power if desired by pushing down hard on the accelerator.

Renault Opti 2

A clutchless gearbox found in the old Renault Magnum. This is quite unlike most other gearboxes and not easy to understand by sight alone. To select manual or automatic modes, push the gearstick to the left. To select neutral, push the gearstick hard to the right. To remove from neutral hold down the button on the right-hand side of the gear knob at the same time as pulling the gearstick back across to the left. If in manual mode push the gearstick forward or backward to change up and down the 'box, and if in automatic mode simply push forward once and the gearbox will select the appropriate gear. As with other automatics, the vehicle will not move until you press the accelerator and behaves as though in neutral. To select reverse hold in the button at the front and pull the gearstick backwards.

Renault Optidriver 2

With the new Renault Magnum, this clutchless gearshift is to be found on the right-hand steering column stalk. The stalk has two collars and a 'minus/plus' symbol at the end which indicates how you select manual gears. When in neutral the 'N' and the white square on the first collar should line up, and the two squares on the outer collar should be in line with each other. If you wish to select an automatic forward gear, simply turn the inner collar so that the white square lines up with the 'D', release the handbrake, press the accelerator and drive away. To select reverse, with the first collar still aligning with 'D' turn the outer collar so that the white square on the collar itself lines up with the 'R'. The gearbox will automatically select the slowest reverse gear. But you can then use the '+' and '–' to select higher and lower gears. To return to an automatic forward gear, simply return the

outer collar to its middle 'resting' position and pull the whole stalk towards you.

If you wish to select manual, pull the stalk towards you and select lower and higher manual gears by pushing the end of the stalk upward and downwards. You can block change one, two or three gears at a time depending on how far you push. If you wish to select crawler gears for slow forward manoeuvring, turn the outer collar to 'C'. Whenever you're moving, and in whichever direction, 'D' should be selected. Your dashboard LED display will clearly indicate what gear you are in. As with the DAF AS-Tronic, there is a 'kickdown' facility that allows for quick getaways by pushing 'pedal to metal'. Take care not to activate this accidentally.

Scania Opticruise

This is another driver-friendly tiptronic, with many additional features – so pay attention!

Unlike many tiptronic's this gearbox actually has a clutch. You only use the clutch to select a gear for pulling away in when stationary and when stopping.

Gear selectors are all to be found on the right-hand steering column stalk. There is a twistable collar which you use to select drive (D), neutral (N), reverse (R), or hill mode (H), but more about that one later. There is also a button at the end that allows you to switch between manual and automatic gears. Manual mode can be selected at any time and at any speed. Once manual mode is selected you use the stalk to change up and down through the box. Pull it towards you to change up and away from you to change down. The box selects gears only one at a time but you can block change up and down by pulling or pushing twice in quick succession.

To start off in automatic mode turn the collar from 'N' to 'D' and depress the clutch. Your first forward gear is now selected and you can pull away; the gearbox will do everything else for you. This gearbox is designed so that you can crawl along in very slow-moving traffic without the need to depress the clutch; you only need to use it again when you're just about to stop.

To select a reverse gear from neutral, first push the collar inwards towards the steering wheel, then twist to select 'R'. This takes you to 'high reverse'. To select 'low reverse' for slow manoeuvring pull the whole stalk towards you once.

The Opticruise has the added feature of a 'hill mode' (H.) This should only be selected for extremely steep hills and should not be selected once stationary. When approaching the gradient simply twist the collar to 'H'. Once you've ascended or descended the hill, return the gearbox to 'D' mode immediately.

As with most tiptronics, the Opticruise has a 'kickdown' facility that facilitates rapid gear change and fast manoeuvring and gives you that little bit of extra power on a gentle gradient.

Volvo Automatic

A clutchless gearbox similar in appearance to what you would find in a car. This makes it instantly familiar. To change your mode, pull the button under the gearstick and select either reverse, neutral, automatic, manual or low (indicated by 'R', 'N', 'A', 'M' and 'L'). The appropriate letter will appear on the LED screen on your dashboard indicating your selected gear. Be aware that this gearstick isn't illuminated at night and it is very easy to select the wrong gear. If you select manual you change gear using the buttons at the sides of the top of the

use and great for city work. It has a clutch used in the conventional way when the gear is actually changed. The gear 'stick' consists of a box in the centre console. On top of the box is a forward and backward handle, attached to which there is a lever with a button on either side at the top.

To begin the gear changing process you push the handle forward (without having the clutch pushed in at the time). The onboard computer block-changes for you and usually selects second or third gear if you're stationary on level ground. You then push the clutch in to actually engage the gear. To change down gears pull the handle backwards instead of forwards. To select neutral press in the button on the top left-hand side of the handle, and to select reverse push in the button on the top right-hand side of the handle at the same time as pulling the lever backwards. For both neutral and reverse you should be stationary and have the clutch pushed in. If you wish to select a lower gear than the one the computer has chosen, push down on the lever attached to the handle and then push the clutch in again (you won't often need to do this). If, however, an alarm sounds when you attempt this you've selected too low a gear. Don't let the clutch out – instead, alter your selection and try again. Occasionally, the gearbox may throw you into neutral. To resolve this push the clutch in and the lever forward at the same time. The computer should then select the correct gear.

gearstick. If you select automatic you simply press the accelerator to go. The gearstick will also fold out of the way for easier access to the passenger side of the vehicle. Press 'Fold' on the top of the gearstick and push it down.

Semi-automatic

EPS 1
Specific only to Mercedes, the EPS 1 is the earliest type of EPS gearbox. Its main difference from the EPS 2 is that there's no lever with which to manually select a lower or higher gear because, unlike the EPS 2, the computer won't automatically calculate and block change for you. Instead it will only select the next higher or lower gear to the one you're in. To block change up or down, you must push the lever backwards or forwards more than once before you engage the clutch.

EPS 2
Specific only to the Mercedes Actros, the EPS 2 semi-automatic is an excellent gearbox, easy to

Comfort Shift
Usually found in old MANs, the Comfort Shift, also known as the Tipmatic gearbox, looks and behaves like a normal four over four gearbox with one difference: it has two  clutches! The conventional one is where you'd expect it to be, while the other takes the form of a thumb-operated button on the top right-hand side of the gear knob. This means that as you begin to change gear, you press in the button at the same time instead of pushing the clutch down. However, you shouldn't leave either the button or the clutch pushed in for any length of time (say, for instance, if you're sitting in traffic), as this will use air and will momentarily disable the clutch.

Fuelling up

FUELLING UP

Automated card bunkering systems

These are used at unmanned fuel bunkers and many truck stops. Some garages also provide a bunkering system out of hours. Here are a few basic tips on how to use one:

• Check that the card you have is accepted at the pump (search the guide in the front half of this book or look on both sides of your card for any logos matching those displayed at the bunker).
• Pull up to the pump and undo fuel cap.
• Look for an electronic machine on a stand next to either of the pumps (it'll look a little bit like an oversized intercom system with a keypad on the front).
• Find the slot where the card goes. This is sometimes hidden under a flap.
• Insert card in the manner indicated on the machine.
• The machine will ask you for your pin number (be sure that you've been given this by your company).
• The machine will then ask you for information regarding your vehicle, such as odometer reading and registration number. If necessary you should write these down before getting out of the cab, as the machine will only wait a short while before 'timing you out': you'll then have to reinsert your card and start again.
• The machine will next ask you to choose your pump. Numbers are usually clearly marked on the sides of bunker pumps.
• You should now be free to draw fuel. Be careful not to overfill. Only fill to just below the neck, not the top of it.
• When complete, the machine may ask if you'd like a receipt (this is usually an additional option). Press 'enter' or 'yes' and a receipt should emerge.
• You should now be free to remove your card if the machine hasn't already instructed you to.

On-site key systems

Many large distribution centres provide a fuel pump for drivers using their vehicles. Check your

key ring for any strange-looking plastic keys or fobs – these are used to draw fuel from this type of system. If you're driving a hire vehicle you may have to ask for a key from the transport division.

• Pull up to the pump and undo the fuel cap.
• Look for the electronic machine on a stand next to either of the pumps.
• Find the hole where the key goes. This may be under a flap.
• Insert key into the hole or press against the electronic reader. Keys will often only fit in a certain way and those that actually look like real keys often have to be turned to the right after insertion.
• The machine will then ask you for information regarding your vehicle, such as odometer reading and registration number.
• The machine will next ask you to choose your pump, and either re-show your fob or remove your key.
• You should now be free to draw fuel. Be careful not to overfill. Only fill to just below the neck, not the top of it.

Red diesel/Green diesel/Gasoil

Be very careful when choosing your pump if you're working for a company that transports refrigerated good, as they may have a red diesel pump on site. Don't put red diesel into your tractor unit tank – this is a very serious offence and your company can be prosecuted for it. Red diesel, known as 'Green diesel' in Ireland, (or gas oil) must only be used in the fuel tanks of refrigerated trailers or shunter vehicles. If you've been provided with one of these, be sure to fill it up at the end of the day. White

AdBlue and the new Euro 4 and 5 Legislation

European legislation to reduce vehicle emissions and consumption began in 1990 with 'Euro 0' regulations. In October 2006 we reached 'Euro 4.' This legislation is ongoing and Euro 5 comes out in 2008. In order for trucks to be able to meet the Euro 4 legislation, two new systems of reducing emission and consumption have been created. One of these is known as the SCR (Selective Catalytic Reduction) system and uses a liquid called AdBlue. The liquid itself is clear, non-toxic, non-hazardous and non-flammable. AdBlue is the product name so you may see it advertised under other trademarks such as Air1. If you are given a new vehicle, ask if it uses AdBlue. If in doubt, check around the vehicle. You should clearly see an additional tank near the fuel tank. This will be marked AdBlue. Inside the vehicle you will also find gauges telling you how full the AdBlue tank is. You should always keep your AdBlue tank topped up, failure to do so could result in expensive damage to the vehicle's catalytic converter. AdBlue will be available at the pumps in most truck stops, dealerships and LGV-friendly petrol stations. It is also available in 10 litre cans (which will enable you to drive approx 600km) or most haulage firms are supplying it at the pumps in their depots.

Where this is the case you may find that the 'container' is a large, clear, square plastic receptacle with a pump sticking out of a hole in the top. Look for a push button on this pump. When switched on you should be able to draw Adblue from the 'tap nozzle' at the other end of the hose.

Do not put AdBlue in your diesel tank or vice versa. There should be safeguards in place to prevent this happening (such as different sized nozzles and tank necks) but be very careful not to get them mixed up!

The other system of reducing emissions is being used by MAN and *most* Scanias. This is known as the EGR (Exhaust Gas Re-circulation) System and requires no action from the driver.

(normal) diesel can also be used to run refrigerated trailers if red isn't available, but red is preferred as it's much less expensive.

Top ten tips to fuel efficiency

1. Drive smoothly – avoid harsh acceleration and heavy braking wherever possible; pulling away too fast uses 60 per cent more fuel.

2. Drive defensively – look ahead and anticipate the road conditions and the actions of others; you'll be less likely to have an accident and will reduce fuel consumption.

3. Use the gearbox more efficiently – changing to a higher gear as soon as possible can reduce fuel consumption by 15 per cent.

4. Don't leave the engine running – idling to heat the engine from cold wastes fuel and causes rapid engine wear; never leave the engine running when the vehicle is left unattended.

5. Don't over-rev the engine – don't pump the accelerator or rev the engine unnecessarily, it simply wastes fuel.

6. Keep your speed low – driving at 50mph in a car or van uses 25 per cent less fuel than at 70mph.

7. Check your tyre pressures – under-inflated tyres wear out more quickly and can increase fuel consumption by up to 3 per cent.

8. If you're stuck in a jam, switch off – turning off the engine after two minutes (if it's safe to do so) will save fuel and cut emissions.

9. Use the right-sized vehicle – try and encourage your company to choose the best vehicle for the load you'll be carrying.

10. Don't use the tail-lift with the engine running – you'll save fuel and prevent exhaust fumes entering the loading dock; for double-deck trailers, use electronic hook-ups instead wherever they're provided.

Coupling a unit and trailer

1 Check that your tractor unit is roadworthy, legal, and in full working order. Check the fluid levels in your unit before you move it. (See 'Walk-round vehicle check'.)

2 Reverse the back of the unit up to the front of the trailer. Arrange the unit and trailer so that they're both pointing at the same angle and are perfectly lined up.

3 Apply the parking brake and get out of the unit to check the trailer over. If it isn't in a bay, check that the back doors are closed and secure (if not still being loaded). Check that the trailer is roadworthy and has a valid licence (you should find this beneath the body of the trailer on the passenger side, about three-quarters of the way towards the back, or at the front of the trailer).

If the curtains are open, close and fasten them securely (provided it is not required that the load be re-checked before leaving the yard).

4 Notify anyone loading the trailer that you're about to reverse under it. Many sites will not allow you to reverse under a trailer whilst it is being loaded, so check first that it is OK for you to do this.

5 Check that the trailer brake has been applied; if not, apply it. Remember, pull to park.

6 Check the height of the unit and ensure that the fifth wheel plate will fit beneath the trailer. If the unit is too high or low, adjust the air suspension in the cab. If your cab has no air suspension you'll need to adjust the trailer height manually. (See 'Adjusting the height of a trailer or unit' on p.58).)

Also take a good look at your fifth wheel plate. If it appears to be almost greaseless it may be a Teflon-coated fifth wheel. Take great care with these. Make sure your unit's suspension is very low as you begin to reverse part-way under. These plates are fragile and can easily break.

7 Reverse part of the way beneath the trailer.

8 Apply the parking brake, get out of the cab and check the height again.

The fifth wheel plate should be flat and pushed hard up against the bottom of the trailer. If it is not, adjust the suspension.

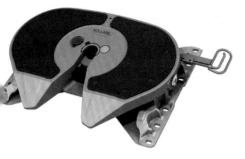

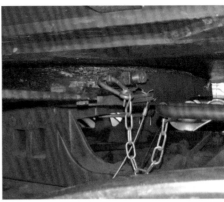

Remember that if your cab suspension is too low or your trailer is too high, the fifth wheel may miss the pin altogether and you will find yourself reversing the back of your cab into the front of the trailer. This is a very costly mistake, so it is imperative that you get this right.

9 If you know that the unit and trailer are so close coupled that you'll be unable to squeeze in between in order to put the service (Suzie) leads on, you can do that at this point, though I'd not recommend it unless you have no other choice. If the trailer brake has been applied, it shouldn't move. However, it is wise to exercise great caution when doing this. Do not attempt it on a slope. Be sure that the trailer legs are not off the ground while executing this technique and ensure that you insert the yellow air lead first.

10 Reverse carefully under the trailer until you hear a loud click. This is the sound of the pin on the trailer slotting into place and being secured.

11 Put the vehicle into a low forward gear and try to pull away. You shouldn't be able to go anywhere. Try this several times. If you are able to move the unit out from under the trailer then the pin has not been caught. If you are lining the trailer and unit correctly and you have positioned the unit and trailer at the correct height but this continues to happen, it may be that the spring in the catch has gone. Line up, and reverse back under the trailer until you can reverse no more. Put the unit into park and get out of the cab. Pull the fifth wheel lever across to your left – it may spring inward into place. Get back into the cab and try to pull forward. If you are unable to, then you know you've correctly picked up the trailer. You should, however, remember to report this fault as a defect as soon as possible.

12 Apply the parking brake and get out of the cab. Go under the driver's side of the trailer near the fifth wheel plate and attach the safety catch from the fifth wheel lever. This is of vital importance and is your  insurance that you've correctly coupled the unit to the trailer. Your unit may also, or instead, have a metal retainer that pops down over part of the fifth wheel lever when the trailer has been securely coupled to the unit. If this metal retainer is not in place then the unit and trailer haven't been properly coupled. Some of these types of retainers don't have a conventional safety clip on a chain, the fifth wheel handle being released by pulling on the wire attached to the retainer at the same time as pulling the lever to the right. If you're unable to pull the lever across to the right or out, your trailer is securely coupled. Alternatively, if your fifth wheel handle looks a little like the one above it may be an air-assisted handle. If you are unable to pull the lever across to the right or out without pulling on the 'loop' inside the handle, you should be OK. If in doubt, ask!

13 Fold back any wind deflectors at the side of the unit (some pull out and towards you, some pull out and forward).

Use the steps at the side of the unit to mount the footplate. Attach the leads furthest from you first. This will prevent the spread of fifth wheel grease over your clothing. If you struggle with the yellow and red air leads, attach them first. This may involve some interesting acrobatics in order to keep yourself

clean; however, you can stand on the service leads to keep them from brushing against you, though you may just end up with the grease all over your boots instead. If you find the leads particularly tough, get right behind them and find something to rest your foot on, then grip the leads, wedge your elbow against your knee and push hard, this should be enough to insert them. Alternatively you can push against any other bony part of your anatomy such as your hips or your chest (depending on the height of your couplings) in order to push the air leads in.

If you're still having difficulty, turn off your engine (if it's running) and pump the foot brake for a short while. This will expel air from the system and make insertion easier. If your leads have been left looking like a mass of spaghetti, stand on the floor and pull them all across the footplate towards one side and stretch them out. This is by far the best way to untangle them.

If your leads have been stowed in 'dummy holders' at the back of the unit, this can be a little confusing for a new driver, who may not be able to tell which is the dummy and which is the genuine clip. Remember that the dummy holder will have no leads running to it at the back. It is important to note that when inserting your electric couplings into the headstock on the trailer, you should always ensure that the spring-loaded flap covering the couplings falls back over the top of them. Failure to do this may result in your leads popping out in transit. The two electric couplings should go easily into their corresponding sockets. If not, do not force them, you may be trying to insert the wrong coupling into the wrong socket or you may have them incorrectly lined up. It is important to note also that if you are driving a fully automatic tractor unit, it may be wise to couple up your air leads with the engine running as many of the vehicle's systems on an automatic are linked to the air supply and a massive loss of air from the unit to the trailer as the vehicle attempts to fill the trailer's tanks and systems may result in an inability to even so much as start the tractor unit after coupling up. Once you have fully coupled-up your leads, dismount from the footplate backwards and walk back to the cab.

14 Turn on ignition, lights, and hazard lights. Check all of these are working on the trailer and report any defects. Note that it is not wise to do this before connecting your trailer's electric couplings as this may cause bulbs or fuses to blow.

15 Go to the leg-winding handle on the passenger side of the trailer. Occasionally you may find this on the driver's side). Detach the

handle from its housing. You use your foot to do this if it's stiff. If the winding handle appears to be wedged firm within its holding clip, and if you have air suspension, raise the suspension until the trailer legs are off the ground. This should free the handle. Now wind the handle forwards towards the unit (forwards to go,

backwards to stay). You may occasionally find that this action is reversed. If the handle won't budge, turn the ignition and raise the cab suspension, then try again. If you don't have air suspension on your cab, you'll have to alter the gearing on the winding handle (see 'Adjusting the height of a trailer or unit' on p.58), and free the feet of the winding legs bit by bit manually. Wind the legs up as far as they'll go – usually so that you can no longer see the oily or rusty parts of the legs. Stow the handle correctly, don't leave it dangling. If there is no safe way of stowing it, secure it to the body or cross-member using cable ties or string.

16 Check that your vehicle brake is on and release the trailer brake.

17 Check the back of your vehicle if you're in a loading bay and make sure that your load is

secure and that it's safe for you to pull out. If you have roller shutter doors, close them securely before you pull out of the bay.

18 If your trailer is carrying a drop-box, check that the twist locks are in the correct position. The red handle should be pointing up and down the length of the vehicle, not out towards the side (see 'Changing boxes on a rigid and drawbar trailer' on p.95).

19 If you have barn doors, pull forward so that you have enough room to securely close them.

20 Affix any seals required.

21 Affix number plate to the back of the trailer. If the number plate is missing, report it and have one made up. Do not leave the yard without a number plate of some sort.

22 If you were in a loading bay and were unable to check the rear lights before, turn on the ignition and do it now.

Uncoupling a unit and trailer

1 If your trailer has barn doors and you're reversing into a loading bay, open them first and use the retainers to hold them back.

2 Remove the number plate and stow it in the cab.

3 Reverse carefully into your allocated bay or parking space.

4 Apply the parking brake and get out of the cab. Walk to the side of the trailer and apply the trailer brake. Some sites prefer you not to leave the trailer brake on after you have uncoupled, but always apply it anyway in order to do this.

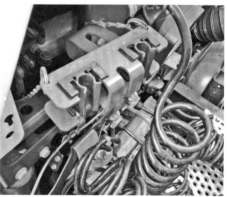

side of the footplate and stretch them out. When done, stow them safely using the 'dummy clips' if provided, or, if not, tie them as securely as possible over the back of the service lead frame.

5 Mount the footplate and, starting with those nearest to you, remove the leads from their clips on the trailer. Take great care with the red and yellow air lines, as these will spit back at you. If the lines have become tangled and you have room to untangle them, pull them to the

6 Wind down the legs using the winding handle. Extend them until they are sitting about 1 inch above the ground and re-stow the handle.

7 Undo the safety clip and pull the fifth wheel plate handle across to the right and out, then across to the right again until it slots into its open position. If your fifth wheel handle looks a little like the one in this photograph, it may be an air-assisted handle and is unlikely to have a safety clip. To release, simply pull on the 'loop' inside the handle and pull the handle towards you in the conventional manner.  The 'air assistance' will do the rest. With some manual units you may also have to pull on a wire that opens a little retainer at the same time as pulling the handle across and out. With older units (these usually have shorter, less accessible handles) you may have to pull the handle out first then across. If you have difficulty pulling out the handle, get back into the cab and reverse the unit against the trailer; this technique should enable you to then pull out the handle. If this doesn't work, try a forward gear instead and pull away from the trailer. You should then be able to pull out the handle. If neither of these techniques work, seek help.

8 Once uncoupled, drive forward slowly, part of the way out from under the trailer. Stop and apply the parking brake. Lower the unit suspension all the way down before commencing full exit from under the trailer. This prevents damage to the trailer legs and wheel covers on the back of the unit. If your unit has a Teflon fifth wheel fitted, careful uncoupling will also prevent damage to this.

9 Raise the unit back to normal ride height before parking up or refuelling.

Moving a sliding fifth wheel

There are four types of fifth wheel: fixed, manual sliding, Fontaine 2 sliding and Teflon-coated (these can be fixed or adjustable). You may find that from time to time you need to adjust your fifth wheel plate, particularly when coupling-up to trailers of different sizes and types. If your fifth wheel is too far forward for your trailer, the front of your trailer may be too close to the back of your cab, resulting in damage to the rear of the cab and/or your suzie leads as you manoeuvre around corners. If your

It is wise to note, however, that trailers with refrigerated units on the front are designed to sit quite close to the rear of the cab – if in doubt check underneath. If your unit has a sliding fifth wheel and it is back as far as it will go, you know you should be OK. Another good rule is to check how far the trailer couplings are from the cab couplings. Much less than three-

quarters of an arm's length is too close. If in doubt, ask for advice.

Fixed fifth wheels cannot be adjusted. They're easily spotted even beneath a trailer, as they're firmly bolted down and not fixed to runners. They have no adjustment handle and are usually used by companies with large fleets who don't often use rented trailers or those from other haulage firms.

Manual Sliding Fifth Wheel

Manual sliding fifth wheels are attached to greased runners and have an adjustment handle

fifth wheel plate is too far backwards your combination of cab and trailer may be illegally too long and/or you may pull your leads out of their sockets as you go around corners.

adjacent to the fifth wheel handle that looks like a smaller, shorter version of it.

- It is preferable to adjust a manual sliding fifth wheel while detached from your trailer. To do this you should undo the safety clip and pull out the adjustment handle in the same manner as you'd pull out a fifth wheel handle; you may then be able to move the fifth wheel to the desired position. If this isn't possible, reposition the adjustment handle back to the closed position and couple your unit to the trailer in the conventional manner.
- When reversing the unit onto the trailer, check regularly that the front of your trailer and rear of your cab are not so close as to be likely to collide. Don't attach any air or electric leads and don't raise the trailer legs. Ensure that your trailer brake is engaged and that your fifth wheel safety clip is attached.
- Again, pull out your adjustment handle. If this is particularly difficult you may have to take the weight off the fifth wheel by lowering the cab suspension a little, allowing the trailer legs to take some of the weight. You should now be able to pull out the adjustment handle.
- Adjust your sliding fifth wheel to the desired position by driving your cab slowly forward in a low gear to widen the gap between cab and trailer, or slowly backwards to reduce the gap.
- Once you have attained the desired gap, reposition the adjustment handle back to its closed position. Get back into the cab and attempt to pull forward and reverse a couple of times in low gear (this acts as a 'pull test').
- Replace the safety clip on the adjustment handle and continue with your coupling procedure.

Fontaine 2 Position Sliding Fifth Wheel

This type of fifth wheel is a fairly recent innovation and allows you to adjust the position of the fifth wheel (with little effort) to aid ease of coupling only, and to avoid the need for 'split coupling'. However, it doesn't allow you to leave the fifth wheel in anything but its 'normal' travelling position.

- Check your fifth wheel. If it is attached to greased runners but appears to have no adjustment handle, check the cab dashboard for a button that has a symbol that looks a little bit like this – this is the slider release button.

- Reverse your unit onto the trailer. Do not attach any air or electric leads at this point and do not raise the trailer legs. Ensure that your trailer brake is engaged and that your fifth wheel safety clip is attached.
- Get back into your cab and press and hold the slider release button. At the same time, release your handbrake (yes, as well as holding the steering wheel!) and drive forward to increase the gap.
- Once you're close to attaining the desired position, release the slider button and the fifth wheel should lock into place.
- Attach your leads, but leave the trailer legs down and the parking brake engaged.
- Get back into your cab and press the slider release button again. Reverse slowly and release the button. The slider should lock into place.
- Perform a forward/reverse pull test to ensure that this is so and continue with your coupling procedure.

Note that the Fontaine 2 is fitted with a sensor which restricts the speed of the vehicle to about 10mph if you've failed to re-close the gap or lock the slider back into its 'travelling' position. This sensor also prevents accidental activation of the slider if the vehicle is in transit.

Coupling a rigid and drawbar trailer

the safe-T-bar supports towards the rear of the trailer so that they're in the open position. Then lift the safety bar upwards and reposition the levers in the closed position. Safe-T-bars can be very heavy, so you may require assistance to do this.

1 Check that your rigid is roadworthy, legal, and in full working order. Check the fluid levels in your rigid before you move it. (See 'Walk-round vehicle check' on p.44).

2 Reverse the back of the rigid up to the front of the trailer. Arrange the rigid and trailer so that they're both pointing at the same angle and are perfectly lined up.

3 Apply the parking brake and get out of the unit to check the trailer over. If it isn't in a bay, check that the back doors are closed and secure (if not still being loaded). Check that the trailer is roadworthy and has a valid licence (you should find this beneath the body of the trailer on the passenger side, about three-quarters of the way towards the back, or at the front of the trailer). If the curtains are open, close and fasten them securely (provided it is not required that the load be re-checked before leaving the yard).

4 Notify anyone loading the trailer that you are about to reverse up to it. Check first that it is OK for you to do this.

5 Check the trailer brake has been applied; if not, apply it. Remember, if your trailer has an air brake it's pull to park. If your trailer has a ratchet brake, pull it back and forth until it becomes stiff. You may also find at this point that your safe-T-bar has to be raised to enable you to couple your rigid to your trailer. You should do this by pulling the levers halfway up

6 Check the height of the rigid and ensure that the drawbar eye of the trailer is lined up with the 'guide funnel' (cup) of the rigid. If the rigid is too high or too low, adjust the air suspension in the cab. If your cab has no air suspension you'll need to adjust the height of the trailer manually. (See 'Adjusting the height of a trailer or unit on p.58).

7 You will notice that your rigid can be fitted with a coupling which is either manually opened or have a partially or fully air-activated system that operates the pin. You will also find that your vehicle will have one of three different types of operating mechanism. These are described in detail below.

For all of these types of coupling, the pin should be in the raised position before coupling can commence.

The manual lever type

If you are facing the 'guide funnel' of the coupling mechanism, you will see on its top, left-hand side a small lever. Lift the lever until the coupling pin is raised into the latched

open position, a small red indicator button just in front of the lever will pop out. This shows that the pin is up and the mechanism is ready for coupling.

The plunger and handle type

Take a look along the side of the rigid, near the back and you will find an exposed valve box which has a handle and a black plunger knob on top.

To open the coupling pull the plunger knob upwards and at the same time turn the handle through 90° to lift the pin.

The control box type

Again, in roughly the same sort of place as you would normally find the 'plunger and handle type' you should instead see a small

box with a hinged lid. Inside this box will be found a red air tap and located beside it is a yellow control valve. Fold the valve handle down and press on the spring part beneath it. At the same time turn the handle anticlockwise through 90° to open the coupling.

Do not touch the red lever within the box. This is for the use of mechanics only.

Check the 'guide funnel.' If you see any debris inside, remove it as this could prevent the pin from dropping completely. (Use a stick for this don't under any circumstances use your hands.) Check the eye of the drawbar trailer for excessive wear or damage. Faults such as a worn eye or wear pad, debris or grease in the guide funnel are some of the primary reasons why coupling can be made difficult and why trailers can detach themselves in transit. (You don't want this happening to you!) If you find grease on the coupling or eye, either clean it off or defect the vehicle. (Couplings should be maintained using oil, not grease as this is too thick.) Check

for damage and air leaks in and around the coupling, control box or behind the plunger and handle (you should be able to hear these).

8 If you have a rear camera monitor in the cab, turn it on. Reverse the vehicle so that the drawbar eye is inside the guide funnel. The pin should automatically drop down into place.

9 Get out of the cab and walk to the coupling.
If you have the manual lever type, look at the lock indicator button. If it's flush with its housing and not exposed the coupling is locked. If the red button is exposed, carry out the uncoupling procedure and then try to re-couple. If the red indicator button will not sit flush with its housing even after a few attempts at re-coupling, defect the vehicle. You should not drive the rigid or tow the drawbar trailer. Neither should you use the release handle as an indicator that it is coupled up as it could be fitted in the wrong position on the cross shaft.
If you have a 'plunger and handle type' make sure that the plunger is down and the lever is pointing towards the floor. Check that the handle is functioning correctly and that excessive

play is not present. If you suspect a fault, do not drive the vehicle or tow the drawbar trailer.

If you have a 'control box type' put the yellow lever back in its closed position inside the box. If you cannot close the control box lid and the yellow valve is not folded and stowed properly, then you are not properly coupled up. Carry out the uncoupling procedure and try again. If you are still unable to stow the yellow handle and close the control box, there is a fault. Do not drive the vehicle or tow the drawbar trailer.

With all of these mechanisms do not use a pull test to find out whether you are properly coupled up or not. If the pin hasn't dropped properly you will damage the coupling!

10 Attach the air/electric service lines from the rigid to the trailer. If at any time the trailer is not being used the service leads should be either unclipped from the trailer and stored in the cab, or, if the couplings are similar to these shown here, simply drape them over the underbody of the trailer so that they don't touch the ground and become wet or damaged. To couple the electrics, simply lift the black flap and push in the 'plug'. For the airlines, pull down on the silver handle and then push the airlines into the open housing. If you find that when you attach the leads from the rigid to the trailer they drag on the ground, use a piece of string and tie a loose loop around the drawbar encircling the leads to hold them away from the floor.

Do not allow your leads when uncoupled to drop onto the ground. The ends could become damaged and debris or water could get into the system.

11 Turn on ignition, lights, and hazard lights. Check all of these are working on the trailer. Report and correct any defects.

12 Go to the leg-winding handle and detach the handle from its housing (you can use your foot to do this if it's stiff). Wind the handle forwards towards the rigid (forwards to go, backwards to stay). Remember that occasionally you may find this action is reversed. If the handle won't budge, turn the ignition and raise the rigid's

rear suspension, then try again. If you don't have air suspension on your rigid, you'll have to alter the gearing on the winding handle (see 'Adjusting the height of a trailer or unit' on p.58), and free the feet of the winding legs bit by bit manually. Wind the legs up as far as they'll go – usually so that you can no longer see the oily or rusty parts of the legs. Stow the handle correctly, don't leave it dangling. If there is no safe way of stowing it, secure it to the body or cross-member using cable ties or string. Occasionally your trailer may have more than one support leg. Make sure that all of them are fully raised.

13 Check that your vehicle brake is on and release the trailer brake.

14 Check that all twist locks holding the box to the chassis are in the correct position and not pointing outwards away from the centre of the vehicle. (This means they are undone.)

15 Check the back of your vehicle if you're in a loading bay and make sure that your load is secure and that it's safe for you to pull out. If you have roller shutter doors, close them securely before you pull out of the bay.

16 If you have barn doors, pull forward so that you have enough room to securely close them.

17 Affix any seals required.

18 Affix number plate to the back of the trailer. If the number plate is missing, report it and have one made up. Do not leave the yard without a number plate of some sort.

19 If you were in a loading bay and were unable to check the rear lights before, turn on the ignition and do it now. If your trailer usually has a Moffat forklift on the back but is not carrying one now, make sure that the lights are in the driving position, not stored to one side. To bring lights to the driving position, pull up the pin on the hinge, swing the lights towards the rear of the trailer and replace the pin.

20 Check that the suspension on your rigid and trailer is in the 'ride height' position before pulling away. On trailers with air suspension this means that the adjustment handle is pointing down.

NEW MULTI-FUNCTION COUPLING COMING SOON FROM VBG

This new type of coupling created by VBG (a company that makes many of our rigid and drawbar couplings in the UK) will become available in the Swedish and Danish markets in 2008 and will eventually be available right across Europe. Presently it has only been developed for turntable-type trailers (A-frame) and not centre-axle types (the most common variety in the UK). This new innovation allows the driver to completely couple up without even leaving the cab!

What it looks like

On the dashboard sits a display screen which when in operation during reversing has a target point and a series of red lights that guide the driver into the correct position. On the trailer end is an arrow-shaped piece that has sensors built into it, and it is these sensors that relay information to the cab display panel. Behind the arrow-shaped part is a hook-type ball coupling that acts in a similar way to the universal joint on a prop shaft.

Coupling

The driver reverses towards the trailer and a hinged flap door opens automatically, which opens the receiver part fitted to the truck. This is set to open when the truck reaches a pre-set distance from the trailer. The driver can steer the truck into the correct position simply by looking at the cab display and using the red lights on the screen to keep the 'arrow' in the target zone.

The arrow part enters the receiver and the wedge action ensures its correct alignment. Now two air-locking bolts travel down inside the receiver and lock the two parts together. Seconds later the air and electrics are engaged. This is the clever bit, as the connections are on the side of the arrow-shaped part and the air connections are 'face'-type sealing while the electrics are of the 'blade' type. You can even connect hydraulics (ie for a trailer-mounted crane) in this way.

As previously stated this new innovation isn't available in the UK yet, but watch out for in the coming years. We shall keep you posted with more information describing hands-on experience as it comes our way!

Uncoupling a rigid and drawbar trailer

1 If your trailer has barn doors and you are reversing into a loading bay, open them first and use the retainers to hold them back.

2 Remove the number plate and stow it in the cab.

3 Reverse carefully into your allocated bay or parking space. Remember that it is always easier to 'pick up' a trailer on level ground, so always try to avoid dropping a trailer on an uneven surface.

4 Apply the parking brake and get out of the cab. Walk to the side of the trailer and apply the trailer air or ratchet brake. Some sites prefer you not to leave the trailer brake on after you have uncoupled, but always apply it anyway in order to do this.

5 Remove leads from their clips. If you're not hitching up to another trailer, either remove the leads from the trailer and stow them in the cab or, if they're similar to those shown here, uncouple the electrics by lifting the black flap and pulling on the 'plug'. Uncouple the air leads by pulling down the silver handle. Once disconnected, simply drape them over the underbody of the trailer. Do not allow

your leads when uncoupled to drop onto the ground. The ends could become damaged and debris or water could get into the system.

6 Wind down the leg(s) (check that your trailer doesn't have more than one) using the winding handle(s). Extend all the way to the ground and re-stow the handle(s).

7 Raise the pin using one of these three methods:

The manual lever type
If you are facing the 'guide funnel' of the coupling mechanism, you will see on its top, left-hand side a small lever. Lift the lever until the coupling pin is raised into the latched open position, a small red indicator button just in front of the lever will pop out. This shows that the pin is up and the mechanism is ready for uncoupling.

The plunger and handle type
Take a look along the side of the rigid, near the back and you will find an exposed valve box which has a handle and a black plunger knob on top. To open the coupling pull the plunger knob upwards and at the same time turn the handle through 90° to lift the pin.

The control box type
Again, in roughly the same sort of place as you would normally find the 'plunger and handle type' you should instead see a small box with a

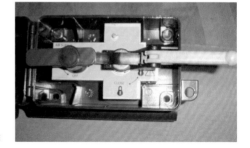

hinged lid. Inside this box will be found a red air tap and located beside it is a yellow control valve. Fold the valve handle down and press on the spring part beneath it. At the same time turn the handle anticlockwise through 90° to open the coupling.

Do not touch the red lever within the box. This is for the use of mechanics only.

8 Once uncoupled, drive forward slowly.

9 Lower the pin within the coupling, using one of the three methods shown in paragraph 9 of coupling a rigid and drawbar trailer, though in the case of the 'manual lever type' the pin should automatically drop down. If it does not, this could indicate a fault. Report the defect and do not drive the vehicle.
It is vitally important always to drive with the pin down. This keeps the area around the pin clear of rust and debris.

10 If your safe-T-bar is in the raised position, and you are not coupling to another trailer, pull the levers on the safe-T-bar supports towards the rear of the trailer one at a time. Do not position yourself below the safe-T-bar when you do this, as the bar will drop with some considerable force. When the bar has been lowered, push the levers forward into the closed position. Similarly, if your lights are folded outwards move them back into the driving position before you pull away.

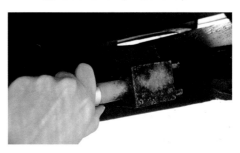

Opening and closing curtains

Opening curtains

1 Only undo one curtain at a time. If you open both and it's windy, the wind will blow straight across the trailer and make it very difficult to close the curtains again.

2 Release the straps. There are three different types, one that you push up (strap type 1), another where you pull down on the strap to release the clip (strap type 2), and a simple fold-down type usually only found on rigid vehicles. The last is not very strong and should be done up extremely tightly.

3 Once the clip is released, remove the hook of the strap from beneath the body.

4 Release the curtain ratchet. In type one (found at the front of curtain-sided trailers) you'll find a handle that you pull towards you. This releases the ratchet and allows the pole to move freely. In type two you'll need to pull on the shorter handle to release the ratchet. (These are often held in place with a clip.)

5 Pull the curtain hard and it should unwind from the pole.

6 When fully unwound, lift the pole upwards and off of the ratchet spindle.

7 Go to the other end of the trailer and pull on the curtain straps. Continue pulling back every sixth strap or so (less if on a rigid), working towards the freed pole, until the entire curtain is folded at one end.

8 Fold the pole backward. Pull out some of the folds from behind it and fold them around in front. This will better secure the pole and stop it swinging in the wind while the forklift driver unloads your vehicle. You may find some lengths of strapping attached to the inside struts of your curtain sides. These are for pulling out and around the curtain to secure it to the outside door latches. This will hold the curtain in place while unattended.

Moving the central bar

Type 1: This bar is the older and most common type on conventional curtain-sided trailers. It is released by pulling a catch across to the right and swinging the bar outward. This way, goods can be easily placed behind the bar with a forklift when the curtains are open. To close simply reverse the procedure, ensuring that the catch is fully pushed home.

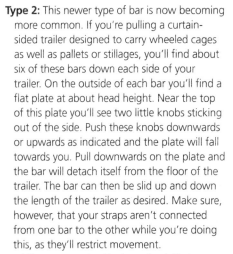

two little knobs or indents on the runners at the top to show where this is).

Check that the bottom is also in the marked zone (you may find that the edge of the trailer is painted a different colour to indicate where this is). Fix the bottom of the bar plate beneath the floor of the trailer and push upwards hard on the plate with a flat hand (do not grip the sides, as you will catch your fingers). The plate should then click into place.

Type 2: This newer type of bar is now becoming more common. If you're pulling a curtain-sided trailer designed to carry wheeled cages as well as pallets or stillages, you'll find about six of these bars down each side of your trailer. On the outside of each bar you'll find a flat plate at about head height. Near the top of this plate you'll see two little knobs sticking out of the side. Push these knobs downwards or upwards as indicated and the plate will fall towards you. Pull downwards on the plate and the bar will detach itself from the floor of the trailer. The bar can then be slid up and down the length of the trailer as desired. Make sure, however, that your straps aren't connected from one bar to the other while you're doing this, as they'll restrict movement.

When re-securing the bars check that they're hanging straight and vertical, and that the top is within the marked zone (you'll see

Closing curtains

1 Pull on the straps at the free end of the curtain. Keep going until the curtain is taut along the length of the trailer.

2 Angle the pole downwards and into the groove. Push it up the groove until it slots in at the top.

3 Continue lifting the pole upwards and drop it onto the spindle above the curtain ratchet.

4 With type 1, the curtain is tightened as you push on the ratchet. With type 2, the short lever should be secured against the body of

the trailer and the curtain is tightened as you pull on the ratchet. Continue working the ratchet until the curtain is as tight as you can get it.

5 Secure the strap hooks beneath the body of the trailer. If they won't reach, loosen the straps.

6 Pull on the loose end of the strap and work the strap clip up and down a couple of times in order to tighten it before you clip it down. Remember that if it's too tight you'll be unable to clip it. It will also be difficult if there are any bits of strap in the way. If your straps are tucked up under the clip and you're finding it difficult to fasten the clip, untuck the straps before fastening.

7 Tuck the loose end behind the rest of the strap to hold it in place and stop the ends fraying.

Pulling a double-deck trailer

Handling
Depending on the type of tractor unit you're using (different units cope differently with double-deck trailers) you may or may not notice a significant difference in the handling of your vehicle. Generally if the trailer is fully loaded it will be wobbly on corners and roundabouts and be quite unstable in high crosswinds. It will also run away with you even on gentle slopes, so watch your speed. Take care and don't rush if you're unused to a double-deck trailer.

Dangers of raising the suspension
When the suspension of any trailer is raised, the airbags inflate. Because a double-deck trailer sits so low this means that the airbags almost touch the ground. Therefore such trailers should not be moved more than a few feet with the suspension in the raised position due to the risk of scraping the airbags on uneven ground.

Reversing a double-deck trailer
Most double deck trailers have steering rear axles. This makes forward turning easier as the trailer doesn't cut across corners as much, but it makes reversing harder. Your trailer may have a rear-axle steering lock (usually situated near the couplings on the trailer). This should only be applied when the trailer and unit are in a direct straight line with each other. When used, it makes reversing easier as it prevents the trailer's rear wheels from going all over the place.

Loading the trailer
A double-deck trailer should be loaded with the heaviest goods on the bottom deck over and between the axles. Top-heavy loading will result in the trailer being extremely unstable. Don't allow anyone inside the trailer when raising and lowering the deck – though incidents of deck collapse are rare, they have been known to happen. All double-deck trailers have been created with 'safety stoppers' that prevent the top deck from falling all the way to the floor;

however, the 'survival space' that these provide is only about 18in high, so make sure you stand outside the deck when you use the control keys. Remember that the top deck of a double-deck trailer is slightly narrower than a standard trailer – take this into account when loading goods and position them accordingly. You may find that your trailer has a 'swan neck' (a raised area) at the front. This can usually only be utilised with the help of a pallet truck. Where a swan neck is present you'll also find a security gate, which prevents the goods on it from toppling down onto goods in the area below. Make sure you secure this gate whenever the swan neck is in use.

Goods stored on the top deck should be made very secure. Your upper deck may have a set of stoppers at the end near the door which should be raised to prevent goods from falling off. If your upper deck does not have this, use plenty of retaining bars and straps to prevent movement.

If travelling with an empty double-deck trailer,

the deck should be left in the raised position. This tightens the chains that hold the upper deck and prevents them from slapping against the sides of the trailer whilst in transit.

Charging the battery

Your double-deck trailer may or may not have its own power supply. Where this is not the case, power to the upper deck, trailer interior lights and suspension is supplied in the usual way using an Anderson lead, three-pin plug or cowbell attachment from your tractor unit to the trailer. Where the trailer does have its own power source this can usually be found in the form of a battery situated in a compartment near to the couplings, accessed from the outside by a door.

Make sure that when you're driving the vehicle the battery is in the correct mode to be charged by the truck engine. (If in doubt, ask how to do this.) If your trailer has

a power jack plug just inside the rear of the trailer (this often resembles an Anderson lead plug), and if the loading bay you're using is specially designed for double-deck trailers, you may find you're able to prevent draining your trailer battery by plugging into one of their own specially designed power supplies.

When you park your trailer up for the night, look for designated double-deck spaces with electrical hook-up points. Again check that your battery is in the correct mode for charging, plug in to the trailer and switch on the power supply. Don't forget to remove the lead in the morning, safely stow it, and put the battery back into 'charging from the engine' mode.

Control panel

These will vary from trailer to trailer, and because of this each button is usually clearly marked with its function. You will find 'deck raising and lowering' buttons and may also find a 'deck isolator switch/power' button, an 'emergency stop' button, a button that must be continuously pressed when operating any of the other buttons, a button to provide internal lighting, and a button to raise or lower the suspension of the trailer and return it to ride-height. These particular buttons are sometimes

POWER CONNECTOR

DECK RAISE
DON-BUR
DECK LOWER

EMERG STOP

INTERIOR LIGHTS
DON-BUR

AUDIBLE WARNING MUTE

RAISE
DON-BUR
RESET
SUSPENSION CONTROL
LOWER

located outside below the level of the deck close to the back doors, and may only be operational when connected to an external power source such as by an Anderson lead from the tractor unit. If this is the case you should check the ride-height is correct before you disconnect the Anderson lead from the trailer. If your trailer also has a tail-lift (though these are rare) you'll find that your control panel also contains buttons for this. The panel itself may be positioned just inside the trailer or be on a separate 'portable' box for easy access.

Pulling a refrigerated trailer

Checking fuel

First of all check the fuel tank of your trailer. You'll find this in a round tank beneath the body of the trailer. On the side of this tank is a fuel gauge – check that it is at least three-quarters full. If it's empty, fill it with red diesel/gasoil/green diesel, if this is available. If not, normal diesel is fine. If you're driving a rigid, your refrigerated motor may not have an additional tank and may take its fuel supply from the normal diesel tank.

Electric charging

Check your fridge unit for an electric hook-up. If a lead is attached and the fridge motor appears to be running quietly then turn off the electric power at the mains and on the fridge unit control panel and unplug the lead,

stowing it safely before starting up the motor to run from diesel.

Start-up and setting-up procedure
Control panels for refrigerated units vary widely, so if in doubt ask for help. With rigids the control panel is usually inside the cab, either above the driver's head or in the centre of the dashboard.

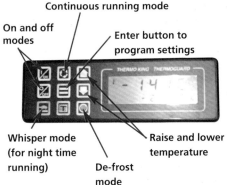

Continuous running mode

On and off modes

Enter button to program settings

Whisper mode (for night time running)

De-frost mode

Raise and lower temperature

With trailers, it's usually on the front of the trailer at about head height. You may find that your trailer will have this as well as (or instead of) a round-faced dial. This is usually found on older trailers. Your control panel should illuminate at night for easy use.

First of all, check your paperwork and see how many compartments are being used and what type

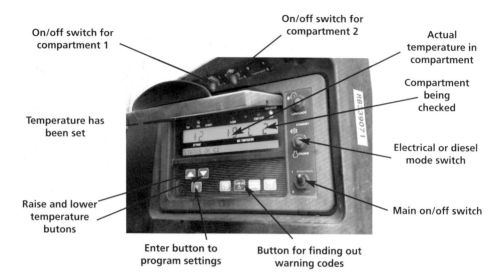

On/off switch for
compartment 1

On/off switch for
compartment 2

Actual
temperature in
compartment

Compartment
being
checked

Temperature has
been set

Electrical or diesel
mode switch

Raise and lower
temperature
butons

Main on/off switch

Enter button to
program settings

Button for finding out
warning codes

of goods are being carried. Some fridge trailers may have up to three compartments divided by insulated 'doors' so that frozen, chilled and ambient goods can be transported together in one trailer. Rigids usually have one or two compartments – three is unusual.

Now look at the control panel. If your goods are being stored at three different temperatures, turn on the switches for all of your compartments. (Remember that you may not have a temperature controlled area for ambient.) If only one type of goods is being transported and no insulated dividers are being used, turn on your temperature control for only one compartment. This is because switching on two fridge motors to cool one area will force the fridges to compete against each other and actually make them less efficient.

Next turn on the main power switch to your fridge motor. You may then hear some clicking and buzzing noises as the fridge motor attempts to start up. If these noises continue for more than about 20 seconds without the motor starting, there may be a fault; get it checked. If there is a fault, an alarm may sound or a red light may come on somewhere in the control panel. Press the fault-finding button (usually red) and the display should show a fault code.

Once your fridge motor has started, check the temperature settings against your paperwork. Compartment 1 is at the front of your trailer, compartment 2 is behind it, and compartment 3 is at the rear, closest to the doors. Set your temperatures accordingly. Frozen should be set for –25°, Chilled at +2° and ambient at +15°. To alter and set the temperatures, wait until your display is checking the compartment you wish to

change then use the up and down keys to select the correct temperature. Next press the enter key to set it and do the same for the other compartments.

Before you leave the yard, and at regular intervals thereafter, check that your actual compartment temperatures correspond with the temperatures that have been set. For frozen, the acceptable level is –18° to –30° (though these may vary according to the type of food you're carrying), for chilled it's 0° to +5°. For ambient it's 'room temperature' so strict levels aren't required, though +15° is the ideal.

Don't be alarmed if on occasion your fridge motor seems to be running extremely fast and loud. This is defrost mode, a method used by all fridge motors to maintain a constant temperature and prevent the compartments becoming too cold. You only need to worry when you can't hear it at all!

Managing the load

Before entering the back of any refrigerated trailer or rigid you should switch off the fridge motor using the main power switch. This is a health and safety matter, as the floor can become very slippery and the atmosphere difficult to breathe. Many stores or distribution centres may wish to check your temperatures before you do this, so give them the opportunity to do so.

Inside the compartments you may find that your goods are extremely cold, so always wear gloves and adequate warm clothing.

To raise the dividing insulated doors, pull at the strap on each edge until they fold back, then grip the strap at the bottom of the divider and raise it like an up-and-over garage door. The dividers can be moved up and down the length of the trailer on runners and secured open by means of straps that you'll find hanging from the roof. Don't use dividers as a solid restraint. Always secure your goods using a strap or a retaining bar behind and/or in front of the load.

If you collect any empty cages or pallets, you should store these in the ambient area.

Printouts

You may occasionally be required to provide a printout of your fridge unit's temperatures. If you open the printer unit (usually found halfway inside the trailer, below the floor in a lockable box) you'll see two main buttons. The right-

hand button provides a printout of your temperatures at that moment. The left-hand button if pressed once provides details of temperatures during your journey, if pressed twice it gives a printout for the whole day, and if pressed three times it gives a printout for the whole week. Beneath these buttons is another panel that includes a red cancel button – useful if you've just pressed the wrong one!

Driving a rigid and drawbar trailer

A rigid and drawbar is a very different animal to a unit and trailer. Besides the ride being a bumpier one you'll also find that the manoeuvring capabilities are vastly different. It follows around corners more tightly, making city driving a joy, but if you're used to a unit and trailer you'll find that reversing a wagon and drag requires the patience of a saint. Its trailer whips round more quickly and you need much more space at the front of your lorry, as the turning circle of a rigid is significantly larger.

Changing boxes on a rigid and drawbar trailer

Dropping a box (straight lift system)
1 Ensure that you're on very level ground before you attempt to drop a box.

2 Raise the suspension height of the front and rear of the vehicle. This is done by using the

keypad inside the cab to raise the height of the rear, and the right-hand side pull-in-and-out button (situated behind the cab) to raise the height of the front.

3 Lift the latch holding the front legs in place and pull them towards you. They may be quite stiff if they're not used often. When the legs are fully pulled out they should drop towards the ground.

4 If the legs aren't hanging straight down, they're not fixed. To be sure they're secure, try to kick the legs forwards towards the cab or backwards towards the rear of the vehicle. They shouldn't move. If the legs haven't dropped all the way down, raise the suspension a little more. If you're still unable to secure the legs you may have to stow them away briefly and move the vehicle to more level ground.

6 Move the twist locks holding the box to the chassis so that the red handles are pointing out towards the sides of the vehicle.

5 If your rear legs are similar to those shown in the photographs, you'll need to pull the lever towards the floor. The legs should drop down. You may have to lift them up a little in order to position the lever into one of the notch holes on the leg. Wherever possible try to put it into the last notch hole, and push the lever skyward to secure the legs in place.

7 Lower the front and rear suspension of the vehicle. The body should come away from the chassis and be held up by the legs.

8 Check that the legs are securely supporting the box and that it is free of the chassis, and slowly drive the vehicle out from beneath it. Return the vehicle to normal ride height.

Picking up a box

1 Lower the front and rear suspension of your vehicle.

2 Reverse the chassis slowly beneath the box, making sure that the V-shaped grooves are either side of the ridge of the chassis. You should get out and check this several times as you're reversing. When you're all the way under, the box will hit the front of the chassis and you'll be able to go no further.

3 Raise the chassis at the front and rear so that the box legs lift off the ground.

4 Secure the twist locks so that the red handles are lying flush against the centre of the chassis and pointing forwards and backwards, not out towards the sides.

5 Lift up the handle on the sides of the front legs and lift the legs upwards. Push them in towards the vehicle and flip the clip over to secure them in their stowed position.

6 Do the same for the rear legs and ensure that they're correctly stowed and secure.

7 Return the vehicle to normal ride height.

Acting as a banksman

How to be safe and remain visible

Everyone needs a banksman at times, even the most experienced drivers. It's always courteous to offer if you can see that a driver is struggling.

Wear your high visibility vest and make sure you can see the driver in his mirrors at all times: if he's reversing in the conventional manner, then he'll have difficulty seeing the whole of the nearside of his trailer and unit, and the front and rear offside corner. If he's reversing blindside he'll experience trouble seeing just about everything!

Many different signalling methods are employed by different companies to direct their drivers. However, some are universal. Whatever hand signals are used, they should be clear and easily seen from a distance.

• **Move towards me:** This is an exaggerated beckoning motion with both arms.

• **Stop:** Hold up one hand high and shout stop!

• **Your trailer needs to go to the right:** This is a continuous jabbing motion to the right.

• **Move away from me:** This is a continuous jabbing forward motion with both hands.

• **Your trailer needs to go to the left:** This is a continuous jabbing motion to the left.

Parking: against a kerb

When parking tight against the side of a road, a manoeuvre called a 'swan neck' is used. This involves driving your cab towards, then away from, then towards and level with the side of the road. This should enable you to pull your trailer in level.

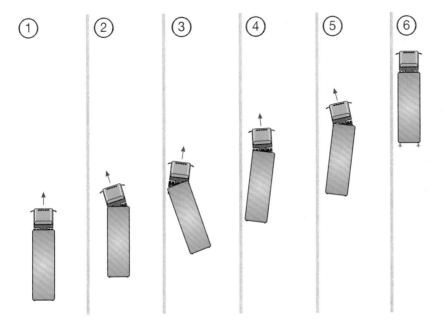

Parking: reverse parallel

This is a difficult manoeuvre that shouldn't be attempted by an inexperienced driver without the aid of a banksman. However, this type of reversing is often necessary if attempting to park in a designated loading area on the side of a road. Take your time and don't let anyone rush you. Mistakes can be costly if there are other vehicles nearby. First you should assess the space, to ensure there's plenty of room. Drive forwards, inwards, and out, then position the front of the cab at an angle pointing slightly towards the kerb before you attempt the manoeuvre.

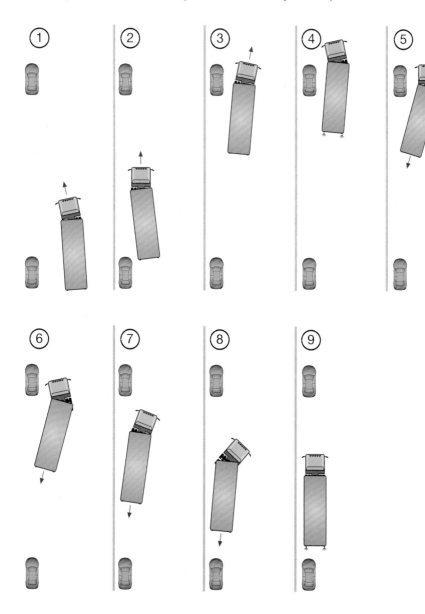

U-turns and tight corners

The dangers of U-turns and tight turns

U-turns and sharp corners are fine manoeuvres to make in a yard, where you have plenty of room, but there are certain things you should be aware of, particularly while executing them on a public highway.

- If you're turning in an extremely tight circle of 180°, your trailer will actually go into reverse. This can place you in something of a predicament if you haven't allowed space for it. Also, the trailer corner opposite to the direction in which you're turning will swing out wildly. Be very aware of this if you're turning a tight corner at a junction or roundabout, and close the lanes down on approach by straddling two of them. This should allow you more room to manoeuvre and prevent any unsuspecting car drivers from being squashed.
- If your leads are particularly tangled, the extreme action of a 180° turn can actually pull them out, particularly if you have anything on the front of your trailer that they can catch on (such as a cow-bell housing). If you can, it's best to stop and check afterwards.
- If you have to do a right-hand U-turn at a road junction, shut down as much of the junction as possible. If it's a dual carriageway cut a slightly diagonal swathe across as many lanes as you can with your cab pointing slightly towards the left. Don't let anyone get on the inside or outside of you. If necessary wait until all other traffic near you has gone. Take the angle wide first, then hard right, making sure that you allow enough space for the back of the trailer to clear the central reservation. This should get you round. Remember that U-turns on public roads are fraught with danger and should be avoided if at all possible. If one has to be attempted, don't try it if there are any 'No U-Turn' signs on the traffic lights or central reservation.

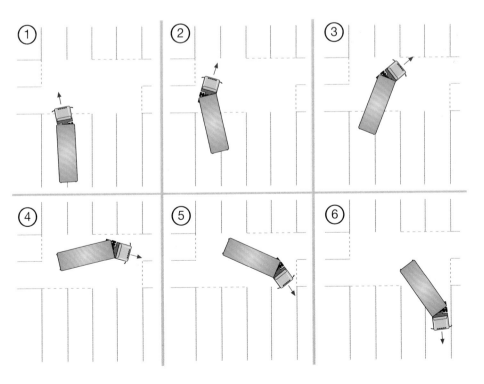

Reversing into loading bay

Check the area

If entering a yard that's unknown to you, it's wise to check the area before you drive in – if you're an inexperienced driver, this could help you to avoid getting yourself into a situation you're unable to get out of. If it looks tight, ask the staff how other drivers normally manoeuvre in. Check the width and length available to you. Make a note of any height restrictions and obstacles and be sure that you can actually fit into the space. Use all the room available, ask for assistance if you're unsure about reversing. Stop if you hear any noises you are unsure about or feel any 'resistance' to your momentum. Don't allow others to rush you and take it slowly – you'll do less damage if you hit something at a low speed! Some loading bays have guiding lines or metal lining-up posts on

the floor to help you aim in the right direction. Most loading bays have large rectangular blocks of hard rubber screwed to the wall to prevent damage to both the back of the trailer and the loading bay. You should also have rubber blocks on the rear of your trailer or unit. When reversing you should aim the rear of your trailer centrally between the rubber blocks on the loading bay

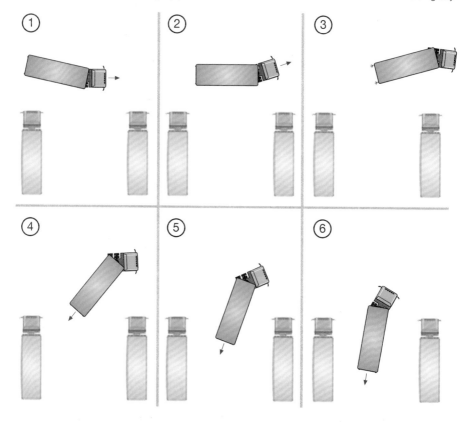

wall. Once hard up against the rubbers, pull forward an inch or two to prevent damage to your vehicle as it rises and falls during off-loading. If your vehicle or trailer has a cantilever tail-lift, check the loading bay. You may find a rectangular hole in the bottom of the loading bay. This is for your cantilever tail-lift. First line up your vehicle before lowering your tail-lift so that it sits about 1ft off the floor before completing your reverse manoeuvre.

It is also vital to note that if at any point you are not in attendance of your vehicle while it is being off-loaded be sure to check that your door is fully closed and your load is secure before you leave the yard.

Reversing blindside

Reversing blindside is an extremely difficult manoeuvre even for an experienced driver, because your view in your nearside mirror is obscured by the trailer once it goes beyond a certain angle with the tractor unit.

Wherever possible you should approach a loading area from its right-hand side so that you can clearly see the offside (driver's side) of your trailer as you manoeuvre backwards, even if this means driving past the loading area and turning your vehicle around.

If you have no other choice but to reverse in blindside, position your nearside (passenger side) wide-angled mirror outwards a little and pull back the curtain covering your cab's rear window (if you have one). This should give you an improved view of the side of your trailer and the area you're reversing into.

Check the area within which you have to manoeuvre, and make a note of the distances between you and any potential obstructions. Get help, even if only from a passer-by: ask them to stand in a safe place and shout if you're about to hit anything behind or to either side of you. Wind down your windows and move very slowly. If you're using a banksman, stop if he disappears from your view.

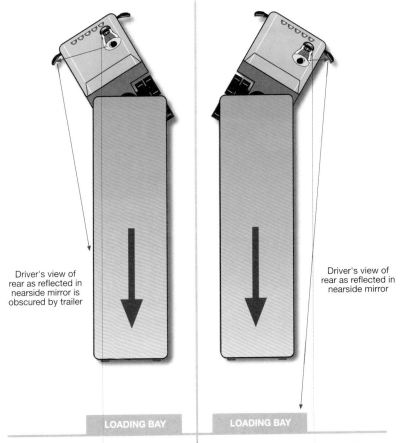

Driver's view of rear as reflected in nearside mirror is obscured by trailer

Driver's view of rear as reflected in nearside mirror

LOADING BAY

LOADING BAY

BLINDSIDE REVERSING MANOEUVRE

NORMAL REVERSING MANOEUVRE

Using dock levellers or loading ramps

There are several types of loading areas. Some companies may have nothing more than a large door that you reverse the rear of your vehicle up to, and goods are taken off using a forklift and a pallet truck. However, you are increasingly more likely to come across loading bays that employ several different methods of operation in order to load and unload goods from your vehicle. Here is a brief description of some of them.

The most basic is a raised area which you reverse up to and goods are taken off using either your own raised or partially raised tail-lift, or a metal ramp lifted into place to bridge the gap between the loading area and the rear of your vehicle.

The second is a scissor lift. This is a large platform, surrounded by railings, which you raise to the height of your trailer. The goods are wheeled off across a ramp that folds out from the scissor lift; the ramp is then retracted, the scissor lift lowered and the goods wheeled away into the loading area.

The controls for scissor lifts are similar to those for a conventional loading ramp or dock leveller (the most popular form of loading/unloading bay). Instructions for dock levellers are as follows:

- First check that it is safe to reverse your vehicle on to the loading bay in the conventional manner. Make sure that the loading bay door is closed, and if the bay employs a green and red light system check that the green light is on.

- Once reversed into position on the loading bay, engage the handbrake and walk around to the rear of your vehicle. Check that you're positioned correctly on the loading bay and that the sides of the loading ramp or dock leveller will actually fit inside the rear door of your vehicle.

- Turn off your ignition and lock your vehicle (if desired). Hand in your keys or hang them up on the hook provided near to the bays.

- Open the door to the loading bay (if there is one). You may find this door will be manually operated, in which case look for a lifting handle on the rear of the door or a chain pulley system used to raise the door. If the door is not manually operated, look to either side of the door for a control panel. At least one of the buttons will be for raising and lowering the bay door.

- Open the bay door and then the rear door of your vehicle.

- Go back to the control panel and look for a button that indicates it's used to operate the ramp. It may say 'raise leveller' or simply show a picture of the loading ramp in extended position. If there appears not to be a button for the ramp, look closely at the ramp. It may have a hole in the edge about an inch in diameter; this is for a leverage pole, which is placed into it. The pole is then levered backwards and the ramp opens out.

- If your leveller is not a manual type, press the ramp button. The ramp will then raise and the lip may automatically extend outwards. If it doesn't, check the panel again for a button that says 'extend lip'; once pressed, the ramp should drop down and fit smoothly onto the deck of the vehicle. If it doesn't, either raise the ramp and retract or extend the lip a little. If this isn't possible you may have to move your vehicle slightly forwards or backwards.

- Once you've completed loading/offloading, follow these procedures in reverse. If you have difficulty fully retracting an automatic-type dock leveller you may have to press the leveller button several times in short sharp bursts before the ramp will fold back into place.
- Close the bay door, collect your keys, check that the traffic-light system (if there is one) is on green, and pull slowly away from the bay.

Using a weighbridge

Many sites will provide their own weighbridge. There are two types; the simpler and most common type consists of a metal strip that the driver manoeuvres the vehicle over. This weighs each axle individually, though it should be noted that you have to drive over it very slowly indeed.

The second type works like a huge set of scales where all the vehicle's axles need to be simultaneously situated upon a weighing platform for an accurate reading. With both types a control panel is used to enter and retrieve information, as follows:

- Firstly, check that the display reads zero. If it doesn't, check for obstructions on the weighbridge, and if the control panel has a 'clear' button press it.
- Drive onto the weighbridge or over the metal strip (depending on type). When you've completed this manoeuvre, get out of the vehicle and go to the control panel.
- The panel may ask you for your registration details, which you should enter.
- Press print, and you should receive a printout stating your overall MGW and the weight over each axle. This is very important, as having one axle overweight (even though you are within overall weight limits for your vehicle) could still land you with a fine.
- Check your results against your vehicle and/or trailers' MoT (Vehicle Inspection) plate to see that you're within the MGW limits for your vehicle and/or trailer. If your trailer is less than one year old, check underneath for a silver or blue Manufacturer's Plate. This should provide the information you need. (For further information on weights see section on Vehicle Heights, Weights and Dimensions.)

Adverse driving conditions and hazards

Night driving
Some drivers love it and others hate it. Of course, the advantages are obvious – less traffic and fewer hazards than day driving. However, it can take a toll on your eyes. The human body isn't designed to function in low light levels, so it's important to have regular eye-tests and take plenty of Vitamin A. Avoid staring directly at oncoming traffic and try instead to focus on the full extent of the area illuminated by your lights and beyond. Watch out for nocturnal animals and cats when driving through rural areas or along residential streets. Make sure the headlights are clean and bright. If they seem too dim, get them checked. Remember, you should never drive using sidelights – they're only designed for use when parked or stopped on unlit streets.

Narrow roads
For new drivers these can be very unnerving, and only experience will help you overcome this. Just bear in mind that all A-roads are designed to take two trucks side by side in most places. If the road is about to narrow so that this isn't possible, you'll be warned – look out for triangular road narrowing signs or any indication of tight bends up ahead, and slow down. You may have more room than you realise anyway: check your nearside mirror regularly – you may be surprised how much space there is.

Residential streets and parked cars
The hazards are obvious: children and animals running out from between cars, pedestrians crossing, and car drivers opening doors. Take great care when driving through residential areas. Drive below the speed limit and keep your wits about you. Turn off the stereo and wind down the window. If you have to pass pedestrians or cyclists on the side of the road, give them plenty of room and check your nearside mirror as you pass. Don't be rushed or hurried into any manoeuvre – take your time and drive carefully.

Snow
Hopefully you'll never have to do this, but in regularly snowbound parts of the country your company may supply you with snow chains. Make sure you're trained on how to fit them correctly. Failing that, take great care to ensure that your tyres are in good condition. It can take a truck almost ten times the normal distance to stop safely on a snow-covered road. Avoid braking sharply. Drive very slowly, and if you have traction control or a dif lock, switch it on when required.

Fog
In reduced visibility, use rear fog lights and front fog lights if you have them. Don't forget to turn them off when visibility returns to normal. Slow down and maintain a safe distance. Don't 'hang on the lights' of the vehicle in front of you. If driving in built-up areas, wind down the window and listen for oncoming traffic at junctions, or children playing nearby.

Cold or icy conditions
Before leaving the yard ensure that your screen and mirrors are entirely clear of ice and aren't misted up. If you don't possess a windscreen scraper climb up the front of the cab and use the edge of cassette box or unused credit/loyalty card to scrape off the ice. Don't use the windscreen wipers until the screen has fully cleared, as this will damage them. If you have heated mirrors, use them. Run the engine until the cab heats up and you can clearly see ahead of you before you drive off. Remember to keep a safe distance between you and the vehicle in front.

Heavy rain
Turn on your lights and wipers. Slow down and maintain a good distance from the vehicle in front. Try to stay out of the spray of other vehicles, avoid overtaking, and don't tailgate.

Steep hills
When descending a steep hill, slow down at the top, change into a lower gear and use your exhaust brake if your vehicle has one. On a more gentle slope, drop down one or two gears and again use the exhaust brake. If approaching a steep incline, change down one gear before starting – you should lose power less quickly:

don't wait until the engine is straining before you change down through each gear or you'll struggle before you reach the top. If you have to stop on a steep incline, choose your first lowest gear or crawler gear to move off in. If you lose traction, switch on the dif lock. This should be enough to get you up the hill. Don't forget to turn it off at the top.

High winds

Many a curtain-sided vehicle has been blown over in high winds while driving across exposed parts of the country. Take particular care if you're pulling a double-deck trailer. If the trailer is empty, pull back the curtains and secure them well to the rear of the trailer using any external straps that you have available. Internal straps should be folded back and secured along with the curtains so that they don't flap or fly about in the wind. Safely stow anything loose in the trailer, such as blocks or chocks. If the trailer is full, try to stick to low ground and roads that aren't so exposed.

Other obstructions or hazards you may encounter

Horses

Take particular care around horses. Keep your revs low and even, keep well back until the opportunity to overtake presents itself, and pass slow and wide. A spooked horse can kill itself, its rider, and possibly even you.

Overhead obstructions

Be aware of overhead cables, low canopies, hanging branches (particularly after a storm), and overhanging wall signs on pedestrianised streets. These can all take the top off your cab's wind deflector or trailer.

Ground-level obstructions

Watch out for bollards, posts, high kerbs, low walls, and holes in the ground. If you're in a pedestrianised area, everything from litter-bins to trees can be a problem, so remember to get out of the cab and take a good look around before reversing.

Tramlines

These are indentations in the road (usually the first lane of a motorway) that the wheels of a truck often fall into (sometimes with alarming ferocity). They can even be capable of pulling the steering wheel clean out of the driver's hand.

Contraflows and Roadworks

You may encounter many different types of hazard within roadwork's or contraflows, so it is vital that you stay alert, avoid changing lanes and stick to any temporary speed limits imposed. These hazards may include: Road maintenance staff crossing the carriageway, uneven or loose road surfaces, ramps, uneven cambers, poor lighting, inconsistent road markings, missing barriers and very narrow lanes. If in doubt, slow down and don't be rushed.

Gritter Lorries

On a motorway, these vehicles will normally occupy the middle lane in order to spread grit more evenly. Pass slowly and give the vehicle

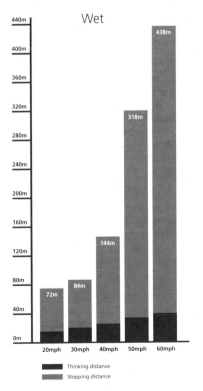

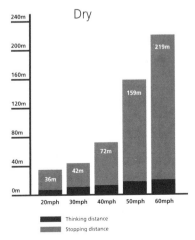

plenty of room. Remember motorbikes and cyclists will be trying to give any gritter lorries a wide birth. Be prepared for them slowing down or moving further away than you expect.

Abnormal Loads

On a motorway, an abnormal load may be too large to fit into one lane and will straddle the first two. In these instances it is acceptable for an LGV driver to pass in the third lane. If the vehicle is gingerly occupying the first lane only, pass slowly and allow him plenty of room, straddling lanes two and three if you feel it is necessary.

When You Can Use the Third Lane of a Motorway

- If you're driving a vehicle of 7.5 MGW or less.
- If the first lane has become a slip road.
- If the motorway has more than three lanes.
- If the motorway does not have a third lane you can use the lane closest to the central reservation.
- If there is an obstruction on the first and second lanes.
- If roadworks or contraflows dictate that you use the third lane.
- If directed to use the third lane by someone controlling traffic.
- When there is a wide slow vehicle occupying the first and second lanes.
- When overtaking a gritter lorry that is situated in the middle lane you can use the third lane, but during busy times it is better to 'undertake' in the first lane. Both are permitted under these circumstances.

AVOIDING LOAD THEFT, DAMAGE, AND PERSONAL ATTACKS

- Where possible use truck stops, transport cafés and motorway services stations, preferably with CCTV, floodlights, and/or security guards. Keep to well-lit areas and avoid parking overnight in lay-bys.
- If your trailer is empty, or if you're carrying unmovable goods (such as sheet steel), open a back door and fasten it securely. This will deter thieves from slashing open your curtains just to get a look at your load.
- Even on extremely hot nights, it's not wise to leave your window open. A determined thief may break in and assault you in order to steal your load. Other tactics include using ether to knock out the sleeping driver, or gassing him using carbon monoxide from a car exhaust attached to a pipe pushed through the cab window. Instead of leaving a window ajar, open

the sunroof if you have one. You should find anyway that once the sun goes down, the inside temperature of the cab will drop dramatically. If it's a particularly warm day try to park your cab in the shade of a wall or hedge. This should cool the cab more quickly.

- If you have a locking fuel cap on your tank, make sure it's locked before you park up for the night. A truck holds many hundreds of pounds-worth of fuel. In some parts of the country siphoning is common. I've even heard of instances where the entire fuel tank was removed during the night!
- Don't leave valuables in plain sight. Remove from the dashboard anything that can be seen from outside.
- When delivering in public places (at the back or front of a shop, for instance) lock the vehicle and keep mobile phones and CDs hidden. This rule should be observed even when using a filling station or bunker. Remember that thieves fuel up too.
- Women in particular should take great care when parking overnight. Don't park alone. Make yourself known to your male neighbours in the lorry park and remove anything on or in your vehicle that singles you out as being female.

PARKING UP FOR THE NIGHT

- Avoid parking on a slope wherever possible – this can make your night a very uncomfortable one. If it can't be avoided, sleep with your head at the highest end and your back sloped into the wall of the cab. Choose a quiet, traffic-free spot away from entrances or exits and as far from refrigerated lorries as possible (unless you're used to that sort of thing).
- With most truck stops you pay on entry. With most motorway services, a warden is normally in attendance somewhere on the premises (usually in a little yellow hut). If you can't find anywhere to pay, ask in the shop or café; they should be able to point you in the right direction. You'll find that you can purchase two types of ticket, one for parking only and one for parking plus a meal voucher. Don't forget to get a receipt or your company may not be able to reimburse you.
- Before you pay to park, check out the facilities and make sure that everything is working. It isn't much fun to find out in the morning that there's no working shower or hot water.

Troubleshooting, and what to do when things go wrong

'I've released the handbrake but the vehicle won't pull away.'
- Check trailer brake isn't on.
- Check that there's enough air in the braking system (you'll find dials for this on the dashboard: they should display how much air should be present). Normally an alarm will sound when the air is particularly low. Gently increasing the engine revs will enable the system to fill with air more rapidly.
- Make sure that the air leads are correctly coupled and listen for sounds of escaping air. If you have an air leak, you won't be able to pull away.
- If you're driving a Volvo, look for a Broms Brake (a push in/pull out knob) close to the handbrake on the dashboard. This must be pushed in before the vehicle can pull away.

'I can't push the clutch in.'
- Again, check that you have enough air in the system, as the clutch is also air assisted.
- Check for any obstructions beneath the pedal.
- If driving an old Iveco, be aware that their clutches are particularly stiff.

'The gear lever won't move.'
- If your engine is cold, be gentle with it. A truck has a very large gearbox and a cold one takes a little time before it is moving smoothly and fluidly. Run the engine for a short while before putting it into gear and moving off.
- If the gearbox feels jammed, put the lever into neutral position and shift it into high then low ratio a couple of times (with the clutch in of course) this usually frees a stuck box.
- If your gearlever is completely floppy, it may have become disengaged or its linkage broken. Seek help from a mechanic or fitter.

'I can't adjust the seat.'
- Once again, if height is the problem, check that there's enough air in the system, as seats too are air assisted. If, however, you are driving a DAF push the seat backwards a little as the tube supplying the air to the seat occasionally gets trapped. Once the seat is at its correct height you can pull it forward again.
- If you're unable to move it back and forth, use your weight and use lots of force. Also make sure you have the lever fully pulled up.

'I can't pull out the lever to release the pin from the fifth wheel.'
- Check that your lever isn't a pull out, pull across type. This variety usually has a shorter, less accessible handle.
- Reverse the unit towards the trailer. If this doesn't work put the unit into first and try to pull forward. Either of these motions should free a stuck lever and enable you to pull it out. (Be sure that the trailer brake is on before you attempt this.) If neither of these methods is successful, try pulling out the lever after the cab suspension has been raised or lowered, occasionally this does work. If all of these things fail, seek help.

'I can't push the air leads in.'
- Check you have the collar pulled back and/or the notch lined up.
- Rest your foot on something and push, bracing your elbow against your knee. Or use some solid bony part of your body (such as your hip-bone or chest) to put your elbow into and push against.
- If there isn't enough room for you to squeeze in, refer to the 'How to couple and uncouple a unit and trailer' section on p.74–81.
- If all of these fail, switch off the engine and pump the footbrake to release air from the system.

'My mirrors keep dirtying in the rain and I can't see behind me.'
- Switch on your heated mirrors if you have them. If you're unsure where the switch is, see the 'Know your cab instrumentation and equipment' section on p.60.
- If you have no heated mirrors, or if they're not working, tie a small strip of cloth around the stanchion above the top of the mirror. The movement of the air around the cloth will flick it over the mirror, constantly wiping it.

'The trailer is too low to reverse under and I have no adjustable cab suspension.'
- You'll have to manually adjust your trailer height. See the section on 'Adjusting the height of a trailer or unit' on p.58.

'The lights don't work on my trailer.'
- If there's more than one light not working, check that your trailer electrics are correctly

coupled to your trailer and that the leads and couplings don't appear to be damaged.

- If there's one defective light, tap it gently and see if it comes back on. If it does, you may have a loose connection behind the light. If not, then it may be a blown bulb or defective couplings.
- Check fuses to make sure none have blown.

'My tail-lift isn't doing anything when I press the buttons.'

- Check that the electric feed for your tail-lift is undamaged and fully clipped in.
- Look for a tail-lift isolator switch in the cab. This is normally a very obvious 'added on' switch on the dashboard.
- Check there's not an additional switch at the rear of the trailer near to or inside the control box, which you must keep pressed in order for the tail-lift to work.
- Check your key ring or the control box for any weird-looking keys or bits of plastic. These could be tail-lift isolator keys.

'I can't open/close the trailer doors.'

- If you're opening or closing refrigerated trailer doors, these are airtight and require some considerable force. Make sure you're attempting to close or open them in the correct sequence. The one with the overlapping rubber strip closes last.
- With barn doors, unclip and open in the correct sequence, one at a time. When closing check that the clips top and bottom are fully seated correctly. If your trailer is fully loaded, ensure that you are on level ground. An uneven surface will cause the trailer frame to twist. This will make it more difficult to open and close the barn doors.
- With roller shutter doors, check the wires that run up and down the side of the door about one foot in from either edge. If these are slack or appear to be off kilter, the door may be broken. Remember that some roller shutter doors are also very stiff when old and/or if they have a few rollers missing. If your door appears to be broken, get help to open it and/or defect the vehicle or trailer if necessary (see Glossary). Check that the door rope (the strip of cord you pull on to close the shutter) isn't caught in anything.
- As with all doors, check there are no obstructions preventing you from opening or closing them (such as chips of wood, door ropes, or parts of your load).

'Help! I've hit something.'

- Don't panic. Follow the advice set out in the section on 'Collisions with other road-users, pedestrians, domestic animals or property' on p.37.
- If you've hit a domestic, non-domestic or wild animal such as a pet cat or a badger, stop. If the pet has an address tag, use it to contact the owner. Don't leave any injured animal to suffer. Call the RSPCA's 24-hour Cruelty and Advice Line number found in the 'Useful contacts' list.
- If an animal is dead it won't be breathing, its gums will turn pale very rapidly, and there'll be no reflex response if you tap the inside corner of its eye. Even an unconscious animal gives this response. If the animal is alive, resuscitation techniques can be followed in the same way as for a human, with the exception that you close the mouth and administer rescue breaths down the nose. For very small animals the infant technique should be followed. Many animals (with the exception of birds) don't survive a collision with a vehicle and die within a few minutes from shock. If this doesn't happen, attempts should be made to keep the animal alive until the RSPCA arrive or until the animal can be driven to a veterinary clinic.
- A dead animal should be moved away from the road, but not out of sight. Badgers are the exception to this rule. If you're able, move a badger well out of sight of the road. Though illegal, badger baiting still occurs in this country, and a baiter can trace a whole family from one dead badger.
- If you have hit a non-wild animal, you may also wish to register it with Petsearch. This is an organisation run by volunteers who keep an online database of all lost and found pets. (Both dead and live animals can be registered.) Their details can also be found in the 'Useful contacts' list.

'I've broken down on an A-road.'

- Move the vehicle out of the way of passing traffic as much as possible.
- Put on your lights and hazard warning lights. If you have a warning triangle, use that too.
- Get out of the cab on the passenger side and take with you your mobile phone (if you have one), high visibility vest, phone number of your transport department, and any warm clothing you have.
- If you're causing a serious obstruction hazardous to other road-users, call the police immediately. Put on your high visibility jacket and walk up the road the way you came. Find a safe place from which to warn other drivers of the obstruction.
- Call the 24-hour phone number for your transport division and/or the breakdown number if one is displayed in the cab, and let them know the nature of the breakdown and your exact location. If you're not provided with a breakdown number, your company may give you a number to call, or will get their breakdown assistance provider to call you. If you don't have a mobile you should walk to the nearest house or business with a light on, or attempt to flag down a passer-by.
- Stay out of the cab. Remain in a safe place on the roadside verge (even if it's raining) until assistance arrives.

'I've broken down on a motorway.'

- For motorway breakdown rules see the section on 'Breakdowns on the motorway' on p.39.

'I'm at a filling station and I don't have the fuel cap keys.'

- Call your transport division and let them know what's happened. They may advise you to attempt to return to your transport yard. If the orange fuel light comes on, contact them again for further instructions.
- If they are sending someone out to you with the keys, drive out of the way of the pumps to a place where you can't cause an obstruction and wait for them to arrive.
- If it appears the keys have been lost, your transport division may send a breakdown service out to you.
- Under no circumstances should you attempt to remove the fuel cap yourself unless you've been expressly given permission by someone in authority.
- To remove a fuel cap, you either need to damage the lock or prise off the cap using a screwdriver and hammer (or heavy solid object). There's every chance that parts of the cap may fall into the fuel tank. If this happens, the workshop should be notified.
- Take great care not to damage the neck of the tank whilst doing this. A damaged neck means replacement of the whole tank.
- When you've removed the now damaged fuel cap and filled up you'll need to seal the tank again. Place the damaged fuel cap back onto the neck and place a latex or surgical glove over the top and secure under the lip of the tank's neck with a cable tie.

'An orange light has appeared on my dashboard.'

- Stop at the next service station or lay-by and ring your transport division. They should be able to advise you what to do. Note that a few makes of truck use an orange light to tell you that it is checking the air tanks. These lights will feature close to the air tank gauge and will alternate continuously between the two tanks to demonstrate which one is being checked. If you are unsure that this is what you are observing, ask.

'A red light has appeared on my dashboard.'

- Stop immediately and ring your transport division. Continuing to drive when a red light is present may cause significant damage to the vehicle. Note, however, that some vehicles have a few interesting quirks when it comes to diagnostics systems. If you have not long switched off your vehicle and everything was fine but now it is giving you every warning light under the sun, switch it off again and leave it for about 30 seconds. This re-sets the diagnostics back to normal.

'There's no clip to hold my number plate in place.'

- Use whatever you can – string, a bulldog clip, several cable ties or rubber bands. Don't leave the yard without a number plate on your trailer.

'My truck wont start.'

- Check your key fob for any unusual looking items that could possible act as an immobiliser key then check your dashboard for a 'lock' to put it into. Immobilisers' 'locks' often come with a little flashing light above them that change colour when deactivated by pushing the key into them for about 3–5 seconds.
- If your vehicle does not have an immobiliser, check that you are not in gear and/or do not have the clutch pushed in when you are trying to start the vehicle. Some vehicles have a safety mechanism built in that prevents you from starting it in gear.
- Check that the battery isolator switch is not en-gaged. This is usually a red 'twist around' knob located outside of the cab near the battery cover.
- If all these fail, turn the key so the ignition is on and check that you have headlights and a horn. If you have neither of these, it is quite likely that your battery is flat.

'There's a dangerous obstruction in the road. What do I do?'

- If you're on a motorway, do not attempt to remove the obstruction yourself. Chances are you'll be a long way past it before you're able to stop anyway. Obstructions on a motorway are extremely dangerous, particularly to motorcyclists, so pull over at the nearest opportunity and call either the highways agency on 0845 302148 or the police on 999 or 112 (from a mobile), giving the exact location and nature of the obstruction.
- If you're on an A-road or dual carriageway, you may wish to attempt to remove the obstruction yourself. Wear your high visibility clothing and take extreme care. If the obstruction is too large to remove, call either of the numbers listed above and walk a little way back along the road in order to try to warn traffic of the obstruction ahead until help arrives.

'I'm stuck on a level crossing.'

If you're on a level crossing and an incident occurs or if your vehicle becomes grounded or breaks down, you should follow these steps:
- Get out of the vehicle immediately.
- Use the railway telephone next to the crossing to tell the signal operator. Follow any instructions you are given.
- Move the vehicle clear of the crossing if you're able to or if there's time before a train arrives. If the alarm sounds or if the amber light comes on, leave the vehicle and get clear of the crossing immediately.

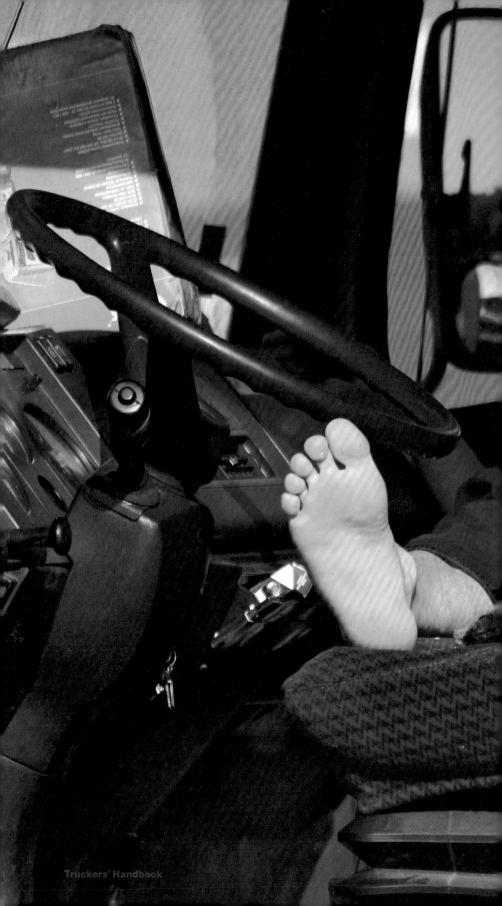

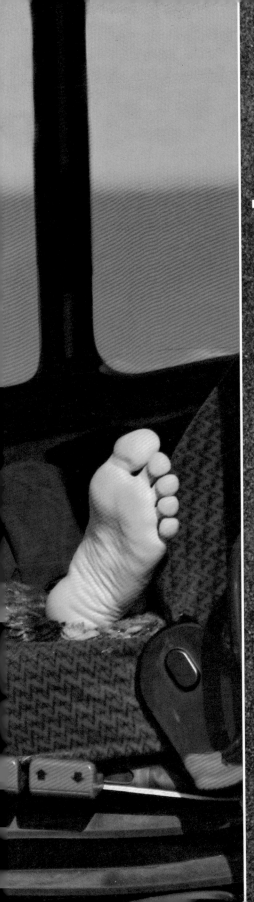

THE DRIVER

Your personal health

WHAT YOU SHOULD AND SHOULD NOT EAT

Well, we all know what these are, even if we don't always follow the advice. But just so you can be certain of what's recommended, here's a list of the *average* Guideline Daily Amounts (GDAs) for adults:

A: Adult males: recommended daily amount for the moderately active (30 minutes exercise, 3–5 times per week)
B: Adult females: recommended daily amount for the moderately active (30 minutes exercise, 3–5 times per week)

	A	B
Calories	2400–2800 (reduce by 500 calories if dieting)	2000–2200 (reduce by 500 calories if dieting)
Carbohydrates	300g (can reduce by up to 80g if dieting)	230g (can reduce by up to 80g if dieting)
– of which sugars	120g	90g
Fats	95g (can reduce by 35g if dieting)	70g (can reduce by 35g if dieting)
– of which saturates	30g	20g
Salt	6g	6g
Protein	55g	45g
Fibre	24g	24g

- Though maximum recommended salt levels listed here appear very low, recent salt reductions in our everyday foods have made this guideline amount very realistic and easy to keep to.
- The GDA for fibre (essential for bowel health and regularity) is far harder to attain and involves considerable consumption of high fibre cereals and/or wholemeal bread. The GDA listed here is what you should be consuming every day, though it can be raised above this amount as there is no upper limit for fibre.
- Protein (for building and maintaining muscle) is also difficult to attain without raising the level of saturated and non-saturated fats

accordingly. You can cheat, however, by buying protein powder, which can be added to soya milk and made into a shake. Fat levels can then safely be lowered, if dieting, in favour of complex carbohydrates, without compromising the GDA for protein.

- Carbohydrates (vital for mental and physical energy) come in two forms – complex, such as those found in cereals and wholemeal bread; and simple, such as those found in sweets, cakes, soft drinks, pasta and anything containing white flour or refined sugar. The GDA for simple carbohydrates (sugar) is extremely low with good reason. Too much sugar in our diet causes our energy levels to peak and crash, it also creates cravings for more simple (sugary) carbohydrates. To avoid this, keep to slow-burning (complex) carbohydrates such as those found in nuts, vegetables, fruit, wholemeal bread and cereals. The GDA levels shown here are very easy to adhere to within a healthy diet; however, carbohydrates should never be reduced by more than 80g or a person will become very weak and confused.

To summarise, these are the steps you should be taking to help towards a healthier diet:

- Cut down on refined sugar (that's anything containing cane or beet sugar – these cause the pancreas to work overtime and can lead to Type 2 diabetes in later life).
- Keep fats to a minimum and grill rather than fry. If you have to fry or use additional fats stick to high quality oils.
- Buy smaller, leaner cuts of meat.
- Eat fresh fruit and vegetables whenever possible.
- Supplement with fruit rather than sugary snacks.
- Avoid sugary drinks and replace with water or a tumbler-sized glass of fresh (no added sugar) fruit juice.
- Stay away from processed foods and ready meals whenever possible and plump for freshly prepared food.
- Buy organic whenever you can.

- Reduce cholesterol by opting for soya-based dairy and meat alternatives.
- Cut down on salt where possible and use sea salt rather than rock salt. It tastes nicer and contains more useful minerals.
- Don't eat anything you can't identify.

I'd personally recommend supplementing any diet with vitamins. However, some 'supermarket' and mass-produced vitamins aren't all they appear to be: rather than coming from Mother Nature's fair hand many are made in a lab using artificial ingredients. The best types to buy are natural vitamins and chelated minerals, which can be found in all good health food stores, or try www.gandgvitamins.co.uk, their 'daily packs' are particularly good.

DRINKING FLUIDS

This is something that truck drivers don't do enough of. Let me tell you a little story from my own personal experience to demonstrate how dangerous this can be.

Several years ago I was making a delivery late in the afternoon on a very hot day, to a site on private land which had just closed up for the night. I'd been provided with a key and told where to make the delivery. This involved taking palletised goods off a tail-lift while perched precariously on a steep slope and moving them downhill across an uneven surface to the front of the shop. This took a long while and was exhausting. I had no water with me, as I'd run out some hours before, and as I delivered the last pallet I fainted in the doorway from dehydration. Fortunately I wasn't injured in the fall and came to fairly quickly. I spent the next half-hour lying in front of their mineral water fridge with the door open. Fortunately, as I left I found someone at home in an on-site residence and was able to get a drink. It took *three pints* before I felt normal again!

Water is vital to the health of our bodies, and when I say water I mean *water*. Not tea, juice, squash or anything else. Without it our urinary tract becomes infected, our kidneys cease to function, and major organ failure will ensue. You should be drinking at least eight glasses of water (which equates to just under 2 litres) per day and in hot temperatures or when exercising you can almost double that figure. For those particularly susceptible to urinary infections I can highly recommend cranberry juice capsules,

which can be purchased from any health food shop. For those drivers who handball in high outdoor temperatures I'd also recommend tissue salt and potassium capsules. Don't try eating spoonfuls of pure salt – you'll just vomit!

About tea and coffee

Other than the obvious fact that tea and coffee (even decaffeinated brands) contain a certain amount of caffeine, there are other things you should know about these beverages.

Although both have many beneficial properties (tea contains flavanoids, documented as beneficial in the fight against heart disease, while coffee contains ingredients believed to help lower the risk of liver cirrhosis), there's one inescapable fact common to these popular national institutions: they're diuretics – that's to say, that they make you urinate far more than you've consumed by taking fluid out of the body where it's needed and flushing it through the bladder. Aside from the obvious inconvenience to a truck driver, this also increases the likelihood of dehydration in hot weather and may in turn increase the risk of urinary tract infections. Tea has also been known to affect the absorption of iron into the body and it's believed that some types of coffee can increase blood cholesterol.

So, although tea and coffee is greatly enjoyed and consumed by many drivers (including myself) the dangers of over-consumption are obvious and should be taken into consideration. One or two cups a day is more than adequate.

There are, however, many alternatives to your average cuppa. If you're looking for naturally caffeine-free, try Rooibos or Red-bush tea. This is also high in antioxidants and can be found in many flavours. Some supermarkets and most health food shops now stock it in its basic form, but for more unusual varieties check out www.bluemoontea.com. If you feel very adventurous you could opt for the fruit or herb teas found in most major supermarkets. These are an acquired taste but contain none of the previously mentioned harmful substances.

GETTING ENOUGH SLEEP

Doctors recommend at least eight hours of sleep per night with good reason. The consequences of sleep depravation are a horrific catalogue of unwanted symptoms. These can include:
- Reduced life expectancy
- Heart palpitations

- High blood pressure
- Increased risk of organ failure
- Irritability
- Irrationality
- And for professional drivers, the possibility of falling asleep at the wheel.

Solutions to insomnia

I wouldn't personally recommend any drugs, over the counter or otherwise, and the reason becomes clear if you read the packaging. They're potentially dangerous for you, as a person and as a driver, with side effects that include not only drowsiness but also depression, heart palpitations, increased blood pressure, headaches, nausea and vomiting.

However, there are alternative solutions. These include:

Taking a walk a couple of hours before bedtime

A walk around a local park or an area where there are people and/or interesting things to look at will distract you from whatever's going on in your mind. It's also good exercise and should help you sleep more restfully.

Avoiding caffeine and other stimulants

All drugs, including caffeine, behave in the same way. A little bit will stimulate, a lot will sedate, and too much will kill (though in the case of liquids containing caffeine, the amount would be undrinkably vast!). Even when decaffeinated, tea, coffee and some soft drinks contain a certain amount of caffeine unless they're naturally caffeine free. It's important to avoid even decaffeinated drinks for several hours before you sleep. The same applies to alcohol and drugs. In the case of these, if you consume a generous amount you'll become sedated, but as they work through your system you'll become re-stimulated and artificially 'woken up'. You'll also use vitamin B1 more rapidly if you take any kind of stimulant. This can result in nightmares, restless sleep, and terrible headaches.

Food before bedtime

Avoid eating a large meal any time within three hours of going to bed, as this won't settle easily in the stomach and can cause trapped wind or indigestion. It may also produce an uncomfortable bloated sensation and make sleep more difficult. Very light snacks are OK, but try to have nothing more substantial than a biscuit or a piece of fruit.

Taking control of your environment

To reduce the chances of being disturbed, ensure you're sleeping in an area which is quiet and away from the noise of traffic. Ensure that the curtains in your cab go all the way round, and cover any gaps by draping a towel or used clothing inside the window. Ensure that the temperature is not too hot or cold: 17–20° Celsius is recommended. Keep a thermometer in the cab if necessary.

I wouldn't recommend using a cab heater all through the night. They're good for heating the cab before bedtime and for half-an-hour before you get up (if you can figure out how to work the timer), but many of them are noisy, use diesel to power up, and dry the air in the cab so that it becomes very stuffy very quickly. They also cause dramatic fluctuations in the warmth of the cab. I'd instead recommend a very high quality sleeping bag and/or large duvet.

Smells can act as mild stimulants and produce headaches and/or a sense of unease, so avoid the use of scented washing powders and softeners on your bedding and night things – I'd personally recommend Ecover liquid and softener. Don't ever use air fresheners in your bedroom or cab, for the same reason.

Personal equipment

Earplugs (foam are the best) and eye masks are essential to shut out light and noise. Both take a little getting used to and feel strange at first, but persevere. You'll find the advantages well worth the initial discomfort. To avoid infections, they should be washed on a regular basis, and earplugs should be replaced once every six months.

In extreme weather conditions remember that you lose the majority of your body heat through your extremities. A woolly hat and bedsocks may look strange but they'll keep you warm if the weather is particularly chilly.

Taking vitamins and minerals before bed

It is well documented that the use of B Complex vitamins before bedtime can aid restful sleep. Look for a B complex where the major B vitamins are between 25 and 50ml (no more than this or you will become very alert).

A drink of Cal-mag (calcium and magnesium powder mixed with an edible acid) can also be very beneficial. Both of these can be purchased from any health food store.

But do not take either on a completely empty stomach. If Cal-mag is unobtainable you can instead use hot milk (this contains high levels of both calcium and magnesium) or make a drink of Horlicks. (The modern variety can be made with boiling water instead of hot milk.)

HOW TO AVOID FALLING ASLEEP AT THE WHEEL

When you should stop
Other than when you are legally required to, if you're on a long journey or didn't sleep well the night before you should stop at the next available opportunity if you notice these things occurring:

- An increased difficulty focusing.
- An inability to keep looking straight ahead for more than five minutes.
- Itchy, sweaty or clammy skin.
- A slight feeling of nausea.
- A feeling of fogginess or lack of concentration.

These are all symptoms of sleep depravation and of the body preparing to shut down. Night drivers are particularly susceptible, as they have to fool their bodies into staying awake at times when their senses, metabolism and hormones are telling them to sleep.

If you have the opportunity to stop safely, you should sleep. Even 20 minutes can help, while a good two-hour nap makes quite a difference. In a cab without a bunk this should be attempted by tilting the seat back as far as it'll go. If you're really sleepy you may nod off quite quickly. Afterwards it's important to get out of the cab and walk around for 10 or 15 minutes. This should wake you up again. Remember to set an alarm (use your mobile phone if you have one), or ask your base to ring and wake you after a certain time. Failure to do either may result in you sleeping for longer than intended.

Where you can stop and sleep in an emergency
Of course, it's always best to get yourself to a service station or truck stop, but if that's not possible without running the risk of falling asleep at the wheel there are other places where you're allowed to stop if in dire need:

- Lay-bys: The obvious choice for many, but be aware that the law requires sidelights to remain on if you park in a lay-by. This is particularly important if you park in one that has no kerb or verge separating it from the road.
- At the top of a motorway slip road: Provided you've passed the 'motorway start and end' sign, this is legal though not ideal. If you're not taking a legally required break, you can be moved on. Try and choose a quiet and seldom-used junction, with a wide roundabout at the top. Again, leave your sidelights on – and remember, don't do this on a 'motorway regulations still apply' junction.
- Any road that isn't a red route and doesn't have double yellows or other parking restrictions – but use your common sense. Don't stop on the sides of dual carriageways or along unlit roads (except in lay-bys), where you'll cause an obstruction and possibly an accident. Avoid residential roads if possible and head for industrial estates where signposted. And remember, it's illegal to park on the wrong side of the road at night, since your rear reflectors will be facing the wrong way and won't be seen by approaching traffic.

HOW TO PREVENT BOREDOM ON LONG JOURNEYS

Audio books
Though the very nature of the job involves staring straight ahead when you're driving on a motorway, try to take a look about you as you go along, since the mind is a highly sophisticated mechanism and gets bored pretty quickly. For the professional driver, being behind the wheel of a truck for four-and-a-half hours in a straight line doesn't take up too much attention, so I'd recommend listening to tape or CD 'audio books' to help the journey pass more quickly. You can borrow these from any library for around three weeks at a time. Some are abridged versions whereas others are presented in their entirety. Choose the same sort of books that you'd normally enjoy reading. Alternatively go to www.audible.co.uk, where for a monthly membership fee you can download audio books off the Internet.

Radio
Some music has the effect of lulling us to a sleep, so I'd advise sticking to radio stations that consist mostly of talking. This tends to keep you alert and involved in what's being discussed. Radio 4 and Steve Wright's afternoon slot on

Radio 2 are good examples. Avoid aggressive music as this can have an antagonising effect, and if you're sleepy avoid music that's too relaxing. Agency drivers should take their own personal stereos or MP3 players as they tend to get given vehicles with no stereos on a regular basis.

METABOLISM

Regardless of whether you're a day walker or a night stalker, the body's metabolism is affected by daylight! The hours of daylight, and particularly the first half of the day, are when our bodies burn energy fastest. Even if you work nights and sleep until 2pm your body will demand most of its energy in the few hours before nightfall. This is why a hearty breakfast is so important. A good rule of thumb is: breakfast like a king, lunch like a prince, and supper like a pauper.

EXERCISE IN AND OUT OF THE CAB

The recommended daily requirement for adults is half an hour of cardio-vascular exercise per day. This can be anything from a very brisk walk to a fast run. Basically, anything that gets you slightly out of breath for 20 minutes or more will help towards maintaining a healthy heart. Even taking the dog for a walk, jogging to the shops, or cycling to work can make a difference. The benefits of exercise are more than just strengthening your heart, circulation and cardiovascular system. It also increases energy levels and endurance, lowers blood pressure, improves muscle tone, strengthens bones, reduces anxiety levels, improves sleep and boosts self-esteem.

There are a couple of exercises you can perform while driving, to reduce the possibility of aching shoulders and deep vein thrombosis (blood clots forming in the legs due to long periods of inactivity), though I'd only advise that you attempt these on a motorway:

Shoulder shrugs
Keeping your back straight, lift your shoulders up and forward towards your ears. Release your shoulders down and back in a smooth circular motion five times. Repeat the action in the opposite direction a further five times.

Ankle circles
If you have room in the foot-well, point the toe of your left foot towards the floor then upwards and circle the foot in an anticlockwise motion five times, then repeat the action in the opposite direction five times. If you have cruise control you can do this with the right foot too.

SMOKING

By now everyone knows the dangers of smoking. Not only does it seriously damage the health and life expectancy of the smoker, but it is also a highly anti-social habit which affects the immediate and long-term quality of life of all those in the vicinity of the smoker and since July 2007 is now illegal if partaken in the 'workplace' of the cab of a truck. The list of diseases, disorders and cancers that can result from tobacco addiction is too long and well-known to need repeating here, but note that most of these conditions can impact particularly severely on the working-life of a truck driver, who gets little exercise.

There are many ways of giving the habit up and you probably know them all. Patches, gum and cold turkey all have their success stories. Just type 'smoking' into any computer search engine – there's a lot of help out there. Check out www.gosmokefree.co.uk or see your GP for more advice.

COMMON COMPLAINTS AND AILMENTS OF TRUCKERS

Foot problems

Chilblains
The symptoms of chilblains include itching, redness and skin on the toes that is often swollen and painful to touch. Chilblains are caused by exposure to cold conditions and then rapid re-heating of the affected area. It is exacerbated by poor circulation (something drivers do suffer from greatly).

Preventing Chilblains can be difficult once at least one attack has occurred, however, a change of diet to include healthier, fresher foods can help, so can regular exercise and the use of warmer socks containing natural fibres. When the feet have become chilled try to resist heating them too rapidly. Choose a warm footbath rather than sticking them on the radiator for half an hour. Avoid rubbing and scratching the affected area, as this will create an infection under the skin that may require treatment from your GP.

Athlete's Foot

Extremely common among wearers of trainers or steel toe capped boots, athlete's foot appears as a creamy white and slightly cheesy smelling covering between the toes that can spread to other areas of the foot. Athlete's foot is a fungus that grows in warm damp conditions and therefore easily treatable when mild. When severe it can show up as blistering in other areas and cracking and swelling on the soles of the foot. This can be extremely painful and is usually the sign of a secondary infection within the skin that will require treatment. Avoiding athlete's foot entirely though may prove very difficult, particularly if your toes are set very close together. Regularly washing your feet and changing your socks and shoes can help as can ensuring that whenever your feet become wet, that you dry very thoroughly between each toe. Try wearing sandals in the summer and walking barefoot whenever possible this should help to allow the skin to breathe and 'drying out' to occur.

Toenail Fungi

If you have athlete's foot, chances are that your toenails will also become infected. This looks thoroughly unpleasant and causes the nails to turn white, yellow or black (in severe cases.) They may also appear distorted, thick or crumbly. This infection spreads quickly across the nails so get it treated.

Foot Eczema

A less common condition than athlete's foot, foot eczema is also worsened by warm damp conditions such as those found in trainers, steel toe capped or rubber boots. Visible symptoms can include tiny blisters, though more often than not it begins with dry itchy skin that becomes red, swollen and infected after it has gone hard, cracked and bled. Once this has happened, treatment may be required from your GP.

Prevention is the same for that of athlete's foot with the addition that keeping the feet quite cold really does seem to help. Moisturise the skin where possible using a simple unperfumed cream that contains few chemicals. This should help to prevent cracking and blistering.

Dry skin, eczema and acne

Driving trucks plays havoc with the skin, with constant exposure to the elements and pollution inside and outside the cab. Taking care of the skin on your face and hands is therefore important, so here are some useful tips for combating problems you're likely to encounter.

- Carry a lip balm. Harsh weather will cause lips to dry, crack, bleed and peel.
- Use intensive hand cream daily to avoid cracked, sore and bleeding hands.
- Try to bathe, rather than shower, once a week. Bathing is better for the skin and helps to prevent it flaking and itching.
- Use a natural moisturiser on any affected parts of the face or body.
- Switch to a nylon/cotton glove with textured rubber hand grip. These will allow the skin to breathe more easily.
- Avoid directing the warm air vents of the truck at any affected area, as this will heat up and dry out the skin.

If you suffer from mild or irritant eczema or acne, avoid using chemicals or heavily perfumed products (look at the 'ingredients' on the back of any bottle of shampoo or shower gel to see the long list).

- Buy your toiletries from your local health food shop. Try Dead Sea Salt products or check out www.organicguys.com and www.greenpeople.co.uk
- Replace household cleaners, washing powders and washing up liquids with an 'eco-friendly' type, which will avoid chemicals.

Urinary tract infections

Whether we like it or not, many of us (particularly women) are prone to these. If you do a job – such as driving a truck – which involves having to remain seated for much of your day or regularly having to 'hold it in' you may find you are more likely to suffer. Symptoms will include:

- Increased desire to urinate
- Increased difficulty passing water
- Only being able to pass small amounts each time
- Eye-watering levels of discomfort when you make the attempts.

Possible methods of prevention include: Drinking more water, more often, wearing looser underwear made with natural fibres, urinating and washing after intercourse (though not too vigorously or using a strong soap) and learning to spot the warning signs so that over the counter medicines can be used to solve the problem. If left unchecked they can result in more serious conditions such as kidney infections. If you're suffering from any of these symptoms, seek medical help as soon as possible (preferably within 24 hours). Urinary tract infections can worsen rapidly and cause excruciating abdominal pain.

Headaches
Something of an occupational hazard for truck drivers, headaches are at best an irritation and at worst can lead to nausea and an inability to sleep, concentrate or think rationally. The usual causes of headaches include dehydration, poor diet, allergies, lack of vitamin B1, lack of sleep, confusion, anxiety or simply trying to remember too much. (The solution to the latter is to simply write things down.)

If you're alone, an excellent drug-free therapy is to get out of the cab and take a walk. Look at things (near and far) in great detail and enjoy them. You may find that your headache will lift. If you have friends who're particularly good at cracking jokes, ring them up. Or if you have a portable DVD player in your cab, take some good comedy DVDs with you and watch them when you park up for the night. Laughter is a wonderful cure. As I've mentioned previously, smells can also stimulate a headache, so avoid aftershaves and scented toiletries, air fresheners, and scented washing powder or softener.

Backache
This too is something that many drivers suffer from, due to long periods of inactivity followed by short bouts of strenuous activity. To help prevent the possibility of injury, exercise well and often. Yoga in particular will help to keep the body strong and supple. Other aids I'd recommend are a hot-water bottle or hot wheat pack applied to the affected area. These can both be purchased from any major chemist.

It's best to try and sleep flat on your back at night, with a low but supportive pillow for the neck and head. When driving during the day, position your seat to tilt slightly backwards. This will push you further into the seat and provide more support to your lower back.

Coughs, colds and flu
Anyone regularly stepping out of a warm environment into a cold one is likely to suffer from coughs, colds and flu. Although this action in itself will not cause even so much as a cold, it does make a person more miserable and lowers their sense of well being, in turn making them more likely to pick up a virus. Prevention is the best cure. I personally believe that if you eat and sleep well, supplement with vitamins, and don't smoke, you shouldn't suffer too greatly. Take bed rest when you have flu and avoid contact with children or the elderly. (Remember that flu is often accompanied by extreme tiredness and nausea and isn't just 'a very bad cold'.) If you have a cold or a sore throat, get lots of rest and allow fresh air into the room while you sleep – this should relieve a stuffy nose. For both of these ailments take plenty of vitamin C and drink lots of water.

Constipation
Another occupational hazard for truckers caused by a diet lacking in fibre and long periods of physical inactivity. Since the body requires physical movement to keep the digestive system operating correctly, regular daily exercise can help remedy this. If you particularly suffer from this complaint try switching to high fibre bread or cereals and eating fresh fruit and veg whenever possible. If you can stomach it, prunes or prune juice can be highly effective. Failing that 'Ortisan Fruit Cubes' from your local health food shop are an excellent alternative and can be used every night before bedtime without any of the harmful side affects that laxatives bring. However, do not exceed the stated dose or your constipation may be relieved more rapidly than you would hope for!

About medicines and painkillers
Be aware that all painkillers – even paracetamol and aspirin – reduce a person's level of awareness to some degree. Even mild, over-the-counter drugs can induce a sense of fogginess, making the person more susceptible to accidents and mishaps and lowering their sense of well-being. Stronger prescription painkillers are definitely out of bounds for truck drivers. Many of them carry explicit warnings that they 'May cause drowsiness. If affected, do not drive or operate machinery.' It's worth noting that even seemingly innocuous drugs such as cold and flu remedies and antihistamines may have similar warnings printed on their packets or in the information leaflets that come with them. Always check! Never just assume that yours will be OK.

DRESSING FOR THE JOB

Footwear

Probably one of the most important items of clothing you'll ever own is a pair of steel toecap boots. Anyone who's experienced that terrifying moment of having a forklift truck roll over their feet will understand what I mean. Don't be tempted to go to work in trainers on a hot day – the risks aren't worth it. If you really suffer in warm weather then purchase a pair of steel toecap shoes (rather than boots or trainers), obtainable from most good work-wear shops. Check out www.arco.co.uk for a large selection of styles. For vegetarian steel toecaps see www.heavenlysoles.com and www.veganline.com. Both of these suppliers provide shoes in men's and women's sizes.

Gloves

Again, essential for the job, not just for protection but also as a barrier against dirt and grease. Many truckers prefer leather or a suede-and-cloth mix glove, which are fine – until they get wet. There's nothing worse than putting on wet gloves! Even drying them off on the dashboard isn't always possible if they're particularly wet and you're making several drops. Personally, I prefer a reinforced rubber type with a cloth cuff, for many reasons:

• They're completely waterproof.
• You can buy textured varieties which offer more grip.
• They're fully washable (though you must turn them partly inside out and hang them upside down in order to dry them).
• They provide adequate protection whilst still allowing some feeling in the fingers.

Their only disadvantage is that when they're new they shed bits inside the glove, and your hands will sweat and smell in them before they've been washed. They can also cause mild skin disorders in those prone to such things.

High-visibility clothing

Every driver should personally own and wear a high-visibility vest at all times. This should incorporate both a fluorescent colour and grey light-reflective strips. Such vests can be purchased from all good work-wear stores and suppliers. If you're provided with additional high visibility garments, wear them! They're for your

protection. Remember that transport yards and even warehouses can be dark, dingy places, and no one wants to run over their staff or colleagues in a truck or forklift.

Other protective equipment

Different sites have different requirements. You may be asked to wear (and be provided with) additional protective items including safety hats, ear protectors and eye protectors (which should fit over any prescription glasses). Make sure they fit and use them. You may feel like a prat, but they're provided for a reason. Don't forget to return them when you leave.

KEEPING WARM AND DRY

Hell hath no fury like a cold, wet lorry driver! But you can take simple steps to avoid this. Wear layers of thinner clothing closer to the body, and tuck in T-shirts or polo shirts so they're close to the skin and trap air. If you can find thin polo-neck tops these are even better. Wear at least one close-fitting thick layer on top and always carry a hooded waterproof jacket that falls below the groin. (In the autumn or spring months you can substitute this for a pac-a-mac.) In particularly bad weather you could also benefit from wearing waterproof leggings over your trousers.

Jeans are great, but they don't retain body heat when they get wet. Corduroy, army combat trousers, or men's work-wear trousers are better. Some have the added advantages of extra pockets.

To keep shoes and boots waterproof, coat them in wax. Many types can be bought from any outdoors store, but the best ones are those which are easy to apply.

Socks are also important. Thermal ones may be necessary at times. You can also purchase thermal undergarments and long johns for men and women. I'd highly recommend these for drivers who spend much of their time out of the cab in all weathers. Try your local outdoors store or check out www.millets.co.uk, though their thermal supplies may be limited during the summer months. You can, however, find these all year round by typing 'thermal clothing' into any computer search engine.

And of course, a woolly hat is essential! A great deal of our body heat is lost through the head, particularly if you don't have much hair, and you may be surprised the difference that a hat can make.

The truckers' code of conduct

1   **Keep to site speed limits and observe pedestrian walkways and crossing points.**
Follow any and all regulations on the site, including use of protective headgear, high visibility vests, ear protectors and eye protectors. Hand in your keys if required and don't use any equipment you're not authorised to.

2   **Assist other drivers to reverse or manoeuvre if they're having difficulties.**
Don't wait to be asked, just do it unless site restrictions expressly forbid it.

3   **Be courteous.**
If anyone offers you assistance, thank them and return the favour where possible. Be polite and well-mannered. Don't moan and whinge about being kept waiting – remember, a well-liked driver is a well-respected driver.

4   **Always offer to assist in the loading and off-loading of your vehicle.**
Even it you know your help is not likely to be required, your offer will be appreciated. If for any medical reason you're unable to do this, ensure that your employer is made aware.

5   **Always ensure that you park considerately**.
Don't block entrances or thoroughfares.

Avoid creating an obstruction to road-users or pedestrians by parking either on the kerb or too far away from it.

6   **Fuel up your vehicle at the end of the day.**
No one likes to get halfway to their destination and find that they have an empty tank.

7   **Keep your vehicle clean.**
Even if it's filthy, isn't yours, and you have it for only one day, remove any rubbish and don't add to the dirt inside. If it's required that you clean it, don't grumble. No one likes to get into a dirty vehicle. Maintain high standards. It won't go unnoticed.

8   **Do not drive an unroadworthy vehicle.**
If the vehicle you've been given has what you'd consider to be a serious fault or defect, do not drive it. Remember, it's your licence that will be revoked as well as the operators' licence of the company you're working for. There are instances where vehicles develop faults within their own diagnostics systems, so if in doubt get help to check manually. A vehicle with any obvious major defect like faulty brakes and damaged tyres, or a huge oil leak, should be taken off road.

9   **'Flash in' other drivers.**
This includes coach drivers and towing vehicles on motorways and dual carriageways when it's

safe for them to pull across into your lane. This is particularly important in low visibility conditions or at night, as it's more difficult to judge the length of a trailer. Avoid using the flash for other purposes except to warn oncoming drivers of a hazard ahead of them (if it is daylight give the oncoming driver the 'thumbs down' sign at the same time). You can also use a flash of your lights to beckon someone through a small gap. If you are 'flashed in' from behind, use your own judgement to decide whether it's safe to pull across or not and don't forget to acknowledge. This is usually done with one blip to either side with your indicator.

10 Warn traffic behind you of difficulties in front of you.
Use your hazard lights to warn of heavily braking vehicles ahead. Remember, you're in a position to help prevent accidents.

11 If you see an accident happening in front of you, stop and offer assistance.
If no one has been hurt leave your name and contact details so that you can be reached. If there are injured parties, don't be afraid to take control. Use the First Aid advice in this book. Call the emergency services immediately and remain until they arrive. If there's a possibility that persons could have been injured in an accident that seems to have happened a little while ago but the emergency services are not yet in attendance, call them anyway. They'd rather have more than one genuine call than none.

12 If you see an injured animal, stop and help.
Call the RSPCA for assistance if required (see the list of 'Useful contacts' on p.159 and the section headed 'Help! I've hit something').

13 If you come across a large obstruction in the road, remove it if possible.
If this is too dangerous – say, for example, if the obstruction is on a motorway or fast-moving dual carriageway – stop as soon as you can and call either 999 if there's a risk to life, or the local constabulary if there's no immediate danger. (You'll find their numbers in the 'Government bodies' section.) Remember to state the exact location and nature of the obstruction.

14 Maintain a safe environment.
If you see or experience a potential hazard, report it and/or (if possible) remove it. In doing so, you will help to keep your environment safe for yourself and your colleagues.

15 Keep to the LGV speed limits.
Take particular care in built-up areas where there may be children and other hazards. Avoid cutting through towns and villages. No one likes to have a truck rumbling past their window.

16 Maintain good communication with your transport division or agency.
If anything goes wrong with you, your vehicle, load or delivery point, they're your first point of contact. Keep their phone number with you at all times.

17 Always do your vehicle checks.
Even if you're pushed for time, this is of vital importance. Any defects or damage should be noted, since no one wants to be blamed for something they haven't done. Levels are particularly important to the correct running of the vehicle and any problems should be rectified and/or reported before you leave the yard.

18 Be green!
Block change where possible, keep your revs in the green band, use cruise control and your exhaust brake where safe and appropriate to do so, pull away in the correct gear and make sure your vehicle is well maintained. All these pointers will help cut down on fuel consumption and save your company money.

19 Set a good example.
Turn up for work on time and leave only when you've been given permission. Take your breaks, remain legal and alert, but don't waste time. Remember that people are relying on you to make your deliveries. Be patient when you're kept waiting, be productive when you're working. Help others whenever you can and retain a cheerful outlook. Maintain your integrity and don't be taken advantage of. If you commit yourself to a task, follow it through, or don't commit yourself in the first place. Remember that you're a professional in your field – act like one!

First Aid for motorists

A road traffic collision could be one of the most traumatic situations that you'll ever experience, and potentially one of the most dangerous. The following information is a guide to dealing with an accident scene safely and efficiently. In all the actions that you take at the scene of an accident, remember that your own safety is paramount. You should never put yourself at risk.

These tips are no substitute for a thorough knowledge of First Aid. St John Ambulance holds First Aid courses throughout the country. To contact your local St John Ambulance County Headquarters, call 08700 10 49 50 or visit www.sja.org.uk.

This section is the copyright of St John Ambulance 2005. It provides guidance on initial care and treatment but must not be regarded as a substitute for medical advice. Every effort has been made to ensure that the material reflects the relevant guidance from informed authoritative sources, which is current at the time of publication. First Aiders are advised to keep up to date with developments and to obtain First Aid training from a qualified trainer.

ASSESS THE SITUATION

- Survey the scene. Do not approach the scene of an accident unless it's safe to do so.
- Check for hazards – what could prove a potential danger? Look for leaking fuel, smoke or fire, hazardous chemicals, etc.
- Find out what happened. Are there any witnesses? Try to gather as much information as you can. This is important because it highlights what action you should take and will give you the information you need to pass on to the emergency services.
- How many casualties are there, and what type of injuries do they have? Check for 'wandering wounded' or for motorcycle pillions who may have been thrown well clear of the scene. Rear foot pegs down on a motorcycle may indicate the presence of a passenger.

QUESTIONS TO ASK ON THE SCENE

- **Location:** What type of road, motorway or country lane? Different road types require different actions.
- **Position of vehicles:** Are they in a dangerous position? Do they present a risk?
- **Casualties:** How many are there? Where are they and what is the nature of their injuries?
- **Communication:** If you don't have a mobile where is the nearest phone?
- **Bystanders and witnesses:** How can they help?
- **Getting help:** Which emergency services are required and what information can you give them?

MAKING SAFE

- Look after yourself – don't put yourself at risk.
- Warn approaching traffic. If there are others at the scene, send them in both directions to warn oncoming traffic.
- At night or in poor visibility, if possible use lights on undamaged bikes or vehicles to illuminate the accident scene.
- Avoid chemical or fuel spillages.
- Battery acid may also be a hazard at the scene. It will cause burns.
- Apart from being an indicator of a potential fire, smoke at the scene of an accident may contain noxious or poisonous fumes. Minimise your exposure to smoke wherever possible.
- If there's a fire, keep clear. Fuel tanks are an obvious risk, but gas struts, shocks and suspension units can also explode in a fire.
- Take care around damaged vehicles, watch out for sharp edges, broken glass, etc.
- Airbags and seat belt pre-tensioners can go off at any time, causing additional injury. Avoid leaning into a vehicle where the airbag has not obviously been activated.
- Don't climb on or into unstable vehicles.
- Wherever possible leave as much vehicle

debris as you find it. If you need to move it make a mental note of where it was.

- Often police don't get the contact details of the person who performed First Aid. To help the emergency services, make sure you give your details to the police.
- If you're taking charge of the scene, ask bystanders to call the emergency services by dialling 999 or 112. Always ask for the police. Information provided will help the operator to advise other emergency services.
- Calling 999 or 112 from a mobile doesn't necessarily put you through to your local operator. The operator may not have local knowledge so will require precise details of your location.
- **REMEMBER** – Wherever possible do not leave a casualty. If you're on your own at the scene of an accident, and you don't have a mobile phone, it may be necessary to leave the scene to call for assistance. Alerting the emergency services will be your priority in these circumstances.

INFORMATION FOR EMERGENCY SERVICES

- Location of the incident.
- Type and seriousness of the incident.
- Number and type of casualties.
- Any specific hazards which may be present at the scene.
- Any specific care needs (pregnancy, infants, elderly).
- Consider the route – is it blocked?

It is a legal requirement for anyone involved in the accident to remain at the scene. If you're aware of any vehicle leaving the scene try to make a note of any details.

CASUALTIES

- Don't do too much. You can't effectively treat all the casualties at once.
- Assess the needs of the casualties. This will help decide your priorities – such as a casualty needing immediate resuscitation.
- Use disposable gloves if you have them. They'll protect you and your casualty from infection.
- Quickly assess the casualty or casualties.
- Give emergency aid.

If there's more than one casualty, treat in the following order:

1 Unconscious – carry out the resuscitation sequence ('DRABC' – see below).
2 Serious bleeding.
3 Fractures.
4 Other injuries.

Only move casualties if they're in immediate danger as a result of their current position, eg in the middle of the road, near a fire or chemical hazard.

- When moving casualties be aware of possible neck or back injuries. Don't give a casualty anything to eat or drink, or allow them to smoke.
- Get help. Use bystanders to call for help – get them to dial 999 and give the following information:

1 Full address or location of the accident, as clearly and precisely as possible.
2 Describe what has happened.
3 Describe the injuries found.

THE RESUSCITATION SEQUENCE

Remember the mnemonic **DRABC**:
Danger – check for danger.
Response – check response.
Airway – check airway.
Breathing – check for breathing.
Circulation – check for signs of circulation.

If the casualty is

Conscious and breathing
- Check circulation (including a check for severe bleeding).
- Treat any injuries.
- Get help if necessary.

Unconscious and breathing
- Place the casualty in the recovery position.
- Check circulation (including a check for severe bleeding).
- Treat any life-threatening conditions.
- Call for an ambulance.

Unconscious and not breathing
Circulation is present, and the condition is due to injury, drowning or choking:
- Give ten rescue breaths.
- Call an ambulance, return to casualty and follow resuscitation sequence again, acting on your findings.

Circulation is present, and the condition is not due to injury, drowning or choking:
- Call for an ambulance, then continue to give rescue breaths until help arrives.
- Check for circulation after every ten breaths.

Circulation is absent, and the condition is due to injury, drowning or choking:
- Perform CPR for one minute.
- Call an ambulance, then return to casualty and follow resuscitation sequence again, acting on your findings.

Circulation is absent, and the condition is not due to injury, drowning or choking:
- Call for an ambulance, then continue to perform CPR until help arrives.

DIFFERENCES FOR INFANTS AND CHILDREN

(For the purposes of these instructions an infant is considered to be less than one year old and a child one to seven years inclusive.)

If the infant or child is

Conscious and breathing
- Check circulation (including a check for severe bleeding).
- Treat any injuries.
- Get help if necessary.

Unconscious but breathing
- Place infant/child in the recovery position.
- Check circulation (including a check for severe bleeding).
- Treat any life-threatening conditions.
- Call an ambulance.

Unconscious, not breathing but has circulation
- Give 20 rescue breaths.
- If the infant or child is small enough, carry them to the telephone and call for an ambulance.
- If you've left the infant or child to call an ambulance, follow the resuscitation sequence again on your return.
- If the infant or child is still unconscious and not breathing, continue to give rescue breaths until help arrives.
- Check for circulation after every 20 breaths.

Unconscious, not breathing and has no circulation
- Perform CPR for one minute.
- If the infant or child is small enough, carry them to the telephone and call for an ambulance.
- If you've left the infant or child to call an ambulance, follow the resuscitation sequence again on your return.
- If the infant or child is still unconscious, not breathing and has no circulation, continue to perform CPR until help arrives.

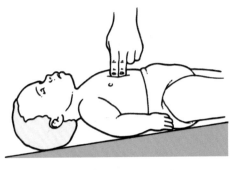

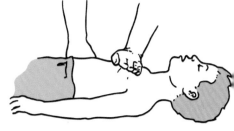

UNCONSCIOUS CASUALTIES

Recovery position – adult

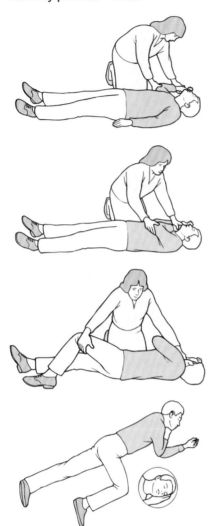

Jaw thrust technique

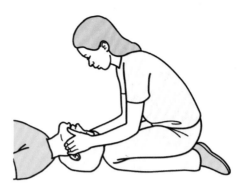

1 Kneel behind the casualty and support their head in a neutral position.
2 Place your hands either side of the casualty's head, fingertips at the jaw.
3 Gently lift and support the jaw taking care not to move the head.
4 Monitor breathing and circulation constantly. If breathing stops follow the resuscitation sequence DRABC (see above).
5 Keep a close eye on a casualty who's sustained a head injury for the next 24 hours, and if you're at all worried seek medical advice.

Recovery position – infant

1 Cradle the infant in your arms, with his head tilted downwards.
2 Monitor breathing, level of response and pulse until medical help arrives.
3 For children over one year old, the adult recovery position should be used.

An unconscious casualty who is breathing and has no other life-threatening conditions should be placed in the recovery position.
1 Turn casualty onto their side.
2 Lift chin forward in open airway position and adjust hand under the cheek as necessary.
3 Check casualty cannot roll forwards or backwards.
4 Monitor breathing and pulse continuously.
5 If injuries allow, turn the casualty onto other side after 30 minutes.
Note: *if you suspect spinal injury, use the jaw thrust technique described below to maintain an open airway.*

HEAD INJURIES

If the casualty has fallen and knocked their head and is not unconscious, treat any external injury first by applying firm, even pressure to the wound with a clean pad if you have one; otherwise use your fingers. If there are any loose flaps of skin gently replace them. Once the bleeding has stopped, secure the pad with a bandage.

With a head injury there may be things you can see, or there may be no clue as to how bad the injury is – so check the casualty's level of response by asking simple questions. If the responses seem impaired for more than three minutes, dial 999 for an ambulance. Check breathing and circulation every ten minutes.

Whether you think the injury is serious or not, get the casualty to lie down for a short while with the head supported in a neutral position. If they lose consciousness, follow the resuscitation sequence DRABC (see above) using the jaw thrust technique.

If the casualty is breathing, use the jaw thrust technique to maintain the open airway.

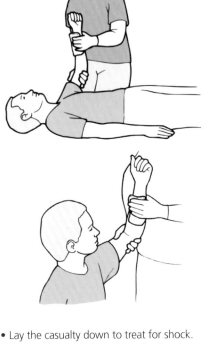

BLEEDING

Minor cuts, scratches and grazes
Treatment
- Wash and dry your own hands.
- Cover any cuts on your own hands and put on disposable gloves.
- If dirty, clean the cut under running water. Pat dry with a sterile dressing or clean lint-free material. If possible, raise affected area above the heart.
- Cover the cut temporarily while you clean the surrounding skin with soap and water and pat the surrounding skin dry. Cover the cut completely with a sterile dressing or plaster.

Severe bleeding
Treatment
- Put on disposable gloves.
- Apply direct pressure to the wound with a pad (eg a clean cloth) or fingers until a sterile dressing is available.
- Raise and support the injured limb. Take particular care if you suspect a bone has been broken.

- Lay the casualty down to treat for shock.
- Bandage the pad or dressing firmly to control bleeding, but not so tightly that it stops the circulation to fingers or toes. If bleeding seeps through first bandage, cover with a second bandage. If bleeding continues to seep through bandage, remove it and reapply.
- Treat for shock.
- Dial 999 for an ambulance.

Remember
- Protect yourself from infection by wearing disposable gloves and covering any wounds on your hands.
- If blood comes through the dressing do not remove it – place another bandage over the original.
- If blood seeps through both dressings, remove them both and replace with a fresh dressing, applying pressure over the site of bleeding.

Objects in wounds
Where possible, swab or wash small objects out of the wound with clean water. If there's a large object embedded:

Treatment
- Leave it in place.
- Apply firm pressure on either side of the object.

- Raise and support the wounded limb or part.
- Lay the casualty down to treat for shock.
- Gently cover the wound and object with a sterile dressing.
- Build up padding around the object until the padding is higher than the object, then bandage over the object without pressing on it.
- Depending on the severity of the bleeding, dial 999 for an ambulance or take the casualty to hospital.

Fractures
Treatment
- Give lots of comfort and reassurance and persuade them to stay still.
- Do not move the casualty unless you have to.
- Steady and support the injured limb with your hands to stop any movement.
- If there's bleeding, press a clean pad over the wound to control the flow of blood. Then bandage on and around the wound.
- If you suspect a broken leg, put padding between the knees and ankles. Form a splint (to immobilise the leg further) by gently, but firmly, bandaging the good leg to the bad one at the knees and ankles, then above and below the injury. If it's an arm that's broken, improvise a sling to support the arm close to the body.
- Dial 999 for an ambulance.
- If it doesn't distress the casualty too much, raise and support the injured limb.
- Don't give the casualty anything to eat or drink in case an operation is necessary.
- Watch out for signs of shock.
- If the casualty becomes unconscious, follow the resuscitation sequence DRABC (see above).

BURNS AND SCALDS

Severe burns
Treatment
- Start cooling the burn immediately under running water for at least ten minutes.
- Dial 999 for an ambulance.
- Make the casualty as comfortable as possible. Lie them down.
- Continue to pour copious amounts of cold water over the burn for at least ten minutes or until the pain is relieved.
- Whilst wearing disposable gloves, remove jewellery, watch or clothing from the affected area – unless it is sticking to the skin.

- Cover the burn with clean, non-fluffy material to protect from infection. Cloth, a clean plastic bag or kitchen film all make good dressings.
- Treat for shock.

Minor burns
Treatment
- For minor burns, hold the affected area under cold water for at least ten minutes or until the pain subsides. Remove jewellery etc and cover the burn as detailed above.
- If a minor burn is larger than a postage stamp it requires medical attention. All deep burns of any size require urgent hospital treatment.

Clothing on fire
Treatment
- Stop the casualty panicking or running – any movement or breeze will fan the flames.
- Drop the casualty to the ground.
- If possible, wrap the casualty tightly in a coat, curtain or blanket (not the nylon or cellular type), rug, or other heavy-duty fabric. The best fabric is wool.
- Roll the casualty along the ground until the flames have been smothered.

On ALL burns DO NOT
Use lotions, ointments and creams.
Use adhesive dressings.
Break blisters.

SHOCK

In the case of a serious accident, once you've treated any obvious injuries and called an ambulance watch for signs of shock:
- Pale face.
- Cold, clammy skin.
- Fast, shallow breathing.
- Rapid, weak pulse.
- Yawning.
- Sighing.
- In extreme cases, unconsciousness.

Treatment
- Lay the casualty down and support their legs.
- Use a coat or blanket to keep them warm – but not smothered.
- Don't give them anything to eat or drink.
- Check breathing and pulse frequently. If breathing stops, follow the resuscitation sequence DRABC (see above).
- Give lots of comfort and reassurance.

What every driver should wear or carry

WEAR
- Steel toecap boots.
- High visibility vest or jacket.
- Any other protective clothing if required.
- A strong pair of trousers that will offer some protection.
- Clothing suitable to the weather conditions.

CARRY
- A good strong bag, preferably a rucksack.
- Gloves.
- Any equipment required for the job, such as a pulling hook.
- Cash, cashpoint card or credit card.
- Phone.
- Hands-free kit and phone charger (if necessary).
- MP3 player or personal stereo and CDs or tapes of your choice.
- Reading material (if long waiting times are likely).
- Licence (both parts).
- Timesheets.
- Maps, your own and any that are provided by the company you're working for.
- The phone number of your agency and a 24-hr number for the company you're working for.
- Fuel card if required.
- All keys required for the vehicle.
- Any paperwork or export documents.
- A disposable camera or camera phone (provides evidence in the event of an accident or incident).
- Food and water.
- Several very thin strips of rag to tie to the tops of your mirrors (as they move in the wind they'll wipe rain from the surface).
- Disposable surgical gloves (even untangling Suzie leads can be pretty messy).
- Cable ties.
- Mini roll of Duct Tape.
- A screwdriver or two.
- Bulldog clip (to secure a number plate if the clip is missing).
- A small pair of pliers.
- A packet of tissues.
- Tachograph charts and pouch.
- Driver Card for digital tachographs.
- Print rolls for digital tachographs.
- Pens and notepaper.
- Stanley knife (to rip shrink wrap).
- Waterproof mac or, in colder weather, a waterproof coat with a hood.
- Waterproof leggings for extremely wet weather (if you spend much of your day outside off-loading).
- Plasters.
- A digital watch or timer to count the amount of accumulated time you've been driving.
- At least one item of clothing that can be rolled up and used as a pillow or spread over you and used as a cover.
- A tie-back if you have long hair.
- Ice scraper (in cold weather).
- Sunglasses (in sunny weather).
- A miniature screwdriver and spare screws if you wear glasses, in case the screw that holds in the lens pops out (this has happened to me on many occasions).
- Felt-tip pen (for drawing manual traces if required).
- A mini torch.
- A calculator (to calculate total kilometres on tachograph chart).
- Tyre depth gauge and tyre pressure gauge.

IF YOU DO OVERNIGHT WORK OR TRAMPING
- Sleeping bag, duvet and pillow.
- Hand cream.
- Food and drink.
- Personal washing equipment, towel.
- Sleepwear, earplugs and eye mask.
- Alarm clock (or use mobile phone).
- Cab shoes (for in the cab or the washrooms).
- Thermometer (if required).
- Nailbrush, nail clippers, scissors.
- Cab cleaning equipment.
- Large water container (if you're likely to be stuck overnight without washing facilities).
- Small washing-up bowl (useful for many purposes).
- A bottle of tea-tree oil lotion (to cleanse cuts or to disinfect when diluted in water).
- At least two bin liners.
- A shovel, if driving in snowy conditions.

Qualifications and training

TAKING YOUR TESTS

Having the right entitlements

One of the first steps you should take on the road to becoming an LGV or PSV driver is applying for provisional entitlement to drive the categories of vehicle you wish to take a test for. Check the back of your licence against the tables provided on the following page, to make sure you don't already possess the entitlement you wish to gain.

The driving test and licensing system has been designed so that drivers learn the ropes and gain considerable experience in smaller vehicles before being allowed to 'upgrade', so if you took your car test after 1997 and are under 21 years of age, not in the armed forces or a member of a young driver scheme it may be some time before you're entitled to jump into a 44-tonne artic and take it for a spin!

First you would have to take your B test, then C1, then C and eventually C+E. If, however, you have a B licence and you're over 21, or if you've held your B licence since before 1997, you should be able to apply for provisional entitlement to jump straight to C and then onto C+E. An LGV driver with full C+E entitlement is also immediately granted the right to drive D1 and D1+E (though not for hire or reward), but D and D+E drivers are not automatically given the right to drive C1 and C1+E vehicles.

Taking a medical

You will need to pass a medical in order to be allowed to drive any LGV or PSV for which you have not been granted automatic entitlement. The medical tests your eyesight and hearing and asks questions about your health and lifestyle. It also checks for any medical history or conditions that may affect your ability to operate your vehicle safely. Medicals can be obtained through your GP or through any company specialising in medicals for drivers (check the Internet for those in

your area). If you're already in contact with a driving school they may be able to recommend someone. However, medicals can be expensive. Prices range from around £50 upwards. During your medical the doctor will complete a D4 form which you'll need to send to the DVLA in order to gain your provisional entitlements.

Applying for provisional entitlements

You should apply for your provisional entitlements by completing the D2 form you'll find in any major post office. They are also available from the DVLA ordering service online at www.dvla.gov.uk (go to 'online services' and click on 'online form ordering'). If you're already in contact with a driving school they may offer to help you book a theory test and supply you with the forms that you need.

If you already have a photo-card licence the DVLA will require that you supply them with both parts of your licence and your medical form. There will be no fee for obtaining your provisional entitlement. If, however, you don't have a photo-card licence you'll need to order one of these as well. The D1 form is available from any major post office and from the DVLA ordering service. You will be required to supply a signed photograph, your paper licence and a fee of around £22.

Booking a theory test

Before you undertake any practical driving lessons you'll need to pass a theory test. This will be undertaken either at your nearest test centre or in a building or training school used by the Driving Standards Agency (DSA) for this purpose. The test environment will be similar to that of a school exam (separate tables, timed, and horribly quiet).

The test will be supervised by DSA-approved examiners, and though you may be able to raise your hand and ask for help they may or may not be able to answer any questions that you ask.

To book your test you can either go to your nearest test centre personally (you should be able to find one in Yellow Pages), or if you're

DRIVING LICENCE CATEGORIES

Route	Current Classification	Old Classification and/or Common description	Category	Minimum age and entitlement
Universal Step 1 for LGV and PCV route	B	Car or van with or without small trailer	Car or van of less than 3.5 M.G.W. with no more than 8 passenger seats plus entitlement to tow trailer up to 750 kilos M.G.W.	17 16 if in receipt of higher rate Disability Living Allowance
Optional addition to step 1 for those under 21	BE - Also known as B+E	Car or van with large trailer	Car or van of less than 3.5 tonne M.G.W. with no more than 8 passenger seats plus trailer over 750 kilos M.G.W	17 (Automatic entitlement if holder of category B before 1997)
Step 2 for those under 21 wishing to drive 7.5 tonne LGV before the age of 21	C1	7.5 tonne lorry	Rigid vehicle of between 3.5 and 7.5 tonne M.G.W. with entitlement to tow trailer up to 750 kilos M.G.W.	18 (Automatic entitlement if holder of category B before 1997)
Optional addition to Step 2 for those under 21 (restricted to 8.25 tonnes train weight for those who passed category B after 1997)	C1E - Also known as C1+E	7.5 tonne lorry plus trailer	Rigid vehicle of between 3.5 and 7.5 tonne M.G.W. and trailer combination with total train weight of up to 12 tonnes. (M.G.W. of trailer must not exceed unladen weight of towing vehicle)	21 18 if train weight is less than 7.5 tonnes (Automatic entitlement to current holders of category C or if holder of category B before 1997)
Step 3 for those who have already followed step 1 and 2, or step 2 for those already over 21 and those who took Class B before 1997	C	Class II	Rigid vehicle usually of between 7.5 and 32 tonnes M.G.W (though this category can apply to any rigid vehicle over 3.5 tonnes) with entitlement to tow trailer up to 750 kilos M.G.W.	21 17 if member of the armed forces 18 if member of a young drivers scheme
Final step for those pursuing LGV licence	CE - Also known as C+E	Class I	Rigid vehicle usually of between 7.5 and 32 tonnes M.G.W (though this category can apply to any rigid vehicle over 3.5 tonnes) with trailer above 750 kilos M.G.W.	21 17 if member of the armed forces, 18 if member of a young drivers scheme
Step 2 for those pursuing PCV licence who passed class B after 1997	D1	Minibus	Passenger vehicles of between 9-16 passenger seats plus entitlement to tow trailer up to 750 kilos M.G.W.	21 17 if member of the armed forces 18 if taking test or if after passing test your route does not exceed 50km. 18 If driving PCV constructed to carry less than 16 passengers or if the vehicle is operated under a public service (PSV) operators licence or permit. (Automatic entitlement if holder of category B before 1997 though entitlement cannot be used for hire or reward)
Optional addition to step 2 for those pursuing PCV licence who passed class B after 1997	D1+E - Also known as D1+E	Minibus and Trailer	Vehicles between 9-16 passenger seats plus trailer over 750 kilos (provided train weight does not exceed 12 tonnes and the M.G.W. of trailer does not exceed the unladen weight of towing vehicle)	21 17 if member of the armed forces (Automatic entitlement if holder of category B before 1997 though entitlement cannot be used for hire or reward)
Step 3 for those pursuing PCV licence who passed class B after 1997. Step 2 those who took Class B before 1997	D	PSV (Bus or Coach)	Passenger vehicle of more than 8 passenger seats plus entitlement to tow trailer up to 750 kilos M.G.W.	21 17 if member of the armed forces
Optional additional to category D	DE - Also known as D+E	PSV (Bus or Coach) with trailer	Passenger vehicle of more than 8 passenger seats plus trailer over 750 kilos M.G.W.	21

already in contact with a driving school ask them if they can arrange to book a test for you. You can also book online at www.dsa.gov.uk, where you can purchase theory test books and find out everything you ever needed to know about taking your test and what it will be like. However, as always the best defence is to be prepared and to revise diligently.

Finding a driving school

If you haven't already done so, the best place to find your driving school is through Yellow Pages or online using Google or a similar search engine. Choose a school close to your home or place of work and if you wish to check if your instructor is DSA-qualified (though this is not yet a legal requirement) you can do this through their website at www.dsa.gov.uk. Costs for training vary greatly, from around £150 per half day (four hours) to around £200. Most people require at least five or six lessons, perhaps more depending on their ability. And in spite of what anyone says there is no such thing as a guaranteed pass!

Credit options are available with some companies, who charge a set amount per week over a period of ten months to a year (though they also usually charge interest). Some haulage companies will offer you your lessons for free provided that you sign a contract to work for them for a set period of time. So shop around to see what sort of deal is best for you.

Information Codes on Your Driving Licence

Code	Description
1	eyesight correction
2	hearing/communication aid
10	modified transmission
15	modified clutch
20	modified braking systems
25	modified accelerator systems
30	combined braking and accelerator systems
35	modified control layouts
40	modified steering
42	modified rear-view mirror(s)
43	modified driving seats
44	modifications to motorcycles
45	motorcycle only with sidecar
70	exchange of licence
71	duplicate of licence
78	restricted to vehicles with automatic transmission
79	restricted to vehicles in conformity with the specifications stated in brackets

101	not for hire or reward
102	drawbar trailers only
103	subject to certificate of competence
105	not more than 5.5m long
106	restricted to vehicles with automatic transmission
107	not more than 8250kg
108	subject to minimum age requirements
110	limited to invalid carriages
111	limited to 16 passenger seats
113	limited to 16 passenger seats except for automatics
114	with any special controls required for safe driving
115	organ donor
118	start date is for earliest entitlement
119	weight limit does not apply
120	complies with health standard for category D1
121	restricted to conditions specified in the Secretary of State's notice
122	valid on successful completion: Basic Moped Training Course

DRIVER CPC (CERTIFICATE OF PROFESSIONAL COMPETENCY)

Regulations

The Driver CPC regulation (not the same as a normal CPC, usually held by owner-drivers) comes into force in September 2008 for PCV licence holders and in September 2009 for LGV licence holders. It is primarily designed to enable new and old drivers alike to keep up to date with new technologies and regulations within the transport industry.

The actual application of the Driver CPC regulations will vary from driver to driver according to the type of licence they currently hold or wish to take, though it affects anyone with or wishing to acquire the following entitlement codes on their licence: C, C+E, C1, C1+E, D, D+E and D1+E. Generally, nearly all drivers with these entitlements will eventually have to undertake 35 hours' worth of training over each period of five years (that's one day per year, though you can take all or several days' worth of your training in one week if you wish). There are a few notable exemptions to the Driver CPC and these include:

• Drivers only operating vehicles with a maximum speed not exceeding 45kmph.

Licence currently held

- Armed forces, civil defence, fire services or those maintaining law and order.
- Those using a vehicle in a state of emergency or who are on rescue missions.
- Those undertaking the non-commercial carriage of goods or passengers.
- Anyone using a vehicle for training purposes.
- Anyone transporting materials used in the course of their work, provided that driving is not their principal activity.

Drivers currently holding a full LGV licence must have completed their training before September 2014, or September 2013 for PCV drivers. New drivers taking their test before September 2008 (for PCV) or 2009 (for LGV) will find that some of their CPC training will be incorporated into a more rigorous theory test before they embark on their five-year periodic training cycle.

Any driver holding both a full LGV and PCV licence will not have to take two Driver CPCs.

Training

The training itself is more of a course of development and will not include a 'pass or fail' element. The courses must be at least seven hours long. Each will be tailored to suit individual drivers' needs, and will cover three main areas:

- Safe and efficient driving
- Legal requirements
- Health and safety

These will also include:
- Customer service
- Social environment

Courses must be approved by the Driving Standards Agency (DSA) and undertaken only at approved centres. These can include commercial training organisations, driving schools, local colleges and haulage companies. Though individual trainers themselves don't have to be approved they must be registered as being suitably competent and experienced.

A stamped and dated receipt will be issued to each course participant as proof of their attendance. The driver will then receive a plastic card (credit card size) on which is stated his level of training. Training centres and the DSA themselves will also maintain records of who they have trained, in case the driver should lose his card or receipt. Some companies may offer to pay for driver training, though in other cases it may be up to the drivers themselves to pay. For more information go to: www.transportoffice.gov.uk/cpc.

BECOMING AN LGV DRIVING INSTRUCTOR

Currently there are no additional qualifications or training prerequisites required to become an LGV instructor. However, you must have held the licence for the categories you wish to teach for at least three years. This is all about to change though in 2009–10 when additional qualifications will become mandatory.

The new DSA Instructors' Licence will be valid for four years, though you'll have to take your re-test to renew it before the fourth year is up. The test comes in three parts:

- Part 1: Theory and hazard perception test. After passing this you must take the other two parts within two years or you'll have to take part one again.
- Part 2: One-hour practical driving test. A pass is five or fewer minor marks.
- Part 3: One-hour instructional test. This is where the examiner takes the role of the student learning to drive.

Most training schools have already begun putting their own instructors through this rigorous test. If you're currently an LGV driver and wish to gain this extra qualification, any good driving school with DSA-qualified instructors should be able to organise everything for you.

HAZARDOUS FREIGHT QUALIFICATIONS (ADR)

All drivers required to move hazardous substances by road in tanks, tank containers and packages must hold a valid ADR licence. The licence is valid for a maximum period of five years, and you can take a course covering any one of nine different groups of Hazardous Freight. This may include radioactive material, explosives, flammable goods, etc. Courses must be taken to obtain this licence. You must pass exams to ensure that:

- You have sufficient knowledge and information to enable you to operate safely, respond to and deal effectively with emergency situations.
- To ensure you know and understand the current legislation and how the legislation impacts upon you.

Refresher courses must be taken before the end of each 5 year licence expiry period.

HI-AB (LORRY LOADER OR MOBILE CRANE)

Drivers required to lift goods using a mobile crane or lorry loader on the back of their vehicle must complete a Hi-Ab or lorry loader course. General contents of the course are as follows:

- Health and safety.
- Types of lifting gear.
- Inspection of lifting gear and loader.
- Hand signals.
- Practical training on loader including inspection of area.

- Setting vehicle up for loading/unloading.
- Written and practical test.

Refresher courses must be taken before the end of each 5 year licence expiry period.

FORKLIFT LICENCE

Anyone required to operate a forklift must hold a valid licence for the type of forklift they're operating. This can be one of the following types:
- Counterbalance.
- Reach truck.
- Ride on pallet truck.
- Side-loading forklift truck.
- Moffat (Quap licence).

Training includes both practical and theory exams and covers all aspects of health and safety regarding the use of forklift trucks. You also require specialist training to operate an EPT (electric pallet truck).

Refresher courses must be taken before the end of each 5 year licence expiry period.

IPAS (POWERED ACCESS LICENCE)

Trains the individual to operate scissor lifts and cherry pickers. This licence has to be renewed every four years. The two-day course includes:
- Written and practical exams.
- Health and safety training.

Refresher courses must be taken before the end of each licence expiry period.

CPC (FREIGHT) CERTIFICATE OF PROFESSIONAL COMPETENCE

Everyone involved in road transport who operates vehicles for hire and reward must demonstrate evidence of professional competence, in compliance with the Goods Vehicle (Licensing of Operators) act 1995. To sit a CPC exam the law first requires that:

- You are professionally competent
- You are of good repute
- You have appropriate financial standing

The certificate itself requires that you sit and pass exams regarding issues such as:

- Employment law • Transport Law
- Vehicle law • Financial management
- Marketing • Safe transportation of goods
- Documentation • Advertising
- Man management

Types of work

INTRODUCTION

LGV driving is not the same the world over. There are many different types of work that can be undertaken and you'll often find that some types suit you whereas others you'll dislike intensely. When you first start out, agency work is a good option. Not only will it help you gain a good deal of experience and teach you many new skills, but it may also help you find your niche.

Wages for LGV work also vary greatly, as you will find from reading this section. Not only do the wages for different types of work vary but there are also a great many regional variations. The greatest pockets of high earning potential are usually to be found in or around towns or cities with large industrial areas (such as Bristol, Swindon, Reading, Coventry, Northampton etc). These are regions in which LGV drivers are in large demand and short supply. By contrast, the earning potential in rural areas can be extremely low. I have even been offered less per hour for C+E work than our local MacDonald's was willing to pay for flipping burgers!

You'll also find that most companies and agencies offer an increased rate of between approximately 5–15 per cent for work undertaken before 06:00 and after 18:00, or any work of over eight hours per day (as an example). Saturday work is also usually offered at an increase of around 25 per cent, while for Sundays and bank holidays the additional rate can increase to around 50 per cent. Christmas Day, and Boxing Day often carry huge premiums of about 50–150 per cent extra, so choose your work carefully and you can do very well.

Many agencies will also allow some drivers to be self-employed. If done correctly, the earning potential can be much higher than for drivers on PAYE. You'll find details of self-employment at the end of this section.

Female drivers should be particularly aware of possible wage discrimination. They should always check with their male colleagues what **their** rate of pay is and approximately what they receive every week. Although illegal, this type of discrimination is rife within the transport industry. Don't think it wont happen to you. Always make sure you're being treated fairly and equally to your male colleagues.

AGENCY WORK

Requirements
Must be reliable, polite, well presented and responsible. Must be willing to work flexible hours.

Nature of work
Agency workers may be asked to work for almost anyone and drive and deliver almost anything within their realm of experience. Agencies may keep individual drivers on certain long-term placements or place the driver with a different company every day. Some agencies even have a temp-to-permanent arrangement with a few of their clients. Agency work is ideal for new drivers, as they'll acquire a great deal of experience quickly. Most agencies are willing to take on new drivers or those with some points on their licence. This type of work would also suit experienced drivers looking for part-time work or flexible hours. Some smaller agencies are willing to offer work to self-employed drivers.

FLATBED WORK

Requirements
Experience and informal training on roping and sheeting and beaver-tailed trailers (if required). Driver must be fit and physically strong. If using a low-loader trailer the driver may also need additional qualifications that allow him to transport abnormal loads or plant vehicles.

Nature of work
You may be asked to transport almost anything from caravans to aircraft parts. This type of work should only be undertaken by an experienced

driver, as they must know the correct methods of securing and covering a whole variety of cargoes. This type of work is hard, physical, and often very dirty.

TANKER (MILK) WORK

Requirements
Informal training on the 'fixtures and fittings' of a milk tanker, competency as a driver, and (if collecting from farms in a class C vehicle) a strong stomach. Drivers should also be aware of the Domestic Hours Regulations regarding the collection of milk from farms.

Nature of work
If collecting from farms you'll be required to reverse in and out of small awkward spaces. You should be provided with protective clothing, as farms are not the cleanest of places. Milk collection is messy, smelly work, often involving long hours and many collections. If delivering milk in an artic from dairy to dairy be aware that your safe stopping distance is less than a conventional lorry, as your liquid load will hit you hard from behind when braking.

TANKER (HAZARDOUS SUBSTANCES) WORK

Requirements
A valid ADR licence. Ideally, drivers should also be very experienced and used to transporting liquid loads. Drivers should not possess a dislike of strong smells if transporting fuel.

Nature of work
If delivering fuel to garages, this type of work often involves reversing in and out of awkward spaces and can be rather dirty. However, it is extremely well paid and the hours are not usually particularly long. The vehicles used are normally new (though sometimes a little fragrant).

TRADEPLATING

Requirements
A good deal of experience driving many different types of vehicle. Drivers must be polite, intelligent, clean, well presented and good communicators. They must also possess an uncanny sense of both direction and adventure.

Nature of work
This is a driving job like no other. The driver must be willing to hitch-hike all over the country (and be good at it), collecting vehicles (as opposed to cargo) and delivering them as and where required. He must be prepared to sleep out and carry his whole life in a rucksack on his back. The hours are long and the wages not outstanding by comparison, but you won't find any other job like it anywhere.

GENERAL HAULAGE

Requirements
A fairly good level of experience of securing loads and using curtain-sided vehicles, a good general knowledge of the UK, and a willingness to work nights if required.

Nature of work
You'll be asked to collect and deliver almost anything to and from anywhere. Most general haulage involves the use of curtain-sided vehicles, though in some instances flatbed trailers are used. This is almost always artic work. The hours are long, the pay is good to average, and the work can be hard and a little dirty. You may also often be asked to wait for long periods of time in order to off-load.

HI-AB (LORRY LOADER) WORK:

Requirements
A valid Hi-Ab licence. Drivers must be fit and strong, willing to work outside in all weathers, and have good general knowledge of safely securing loads on a flatbed trailer.

Nature of work
Much Hi-Ab work involves delivering and collecting to building sites or builders' suppliers and merchants. The work is not usually long distance but it's physical and dirty.

SUPERMARKET DELIVERIES

Requirements
Most supermarkets (though not all) require that you've held your C+E licence for at least two years. You should have good knowledge of transporting both ambient and refrigerated goods and be a well-presented, polite, patient and competent driver. An induction course and assessment is usually given.

Nature of work
Delivering to stores and dealing with paperwork. You may have to reverse in and out of some very awkward loading bays (depending on whether you're working for a large or small supermarket chain). The goods are usually palletised or caged. Minimal effort is required and sometimes you won't even be expected to off-load yourself. Supermarket work is some of the cleanest and easiest of all lorry-driving work, though you may often be asked to wait for long periods of time. The vehicles provided are normally clean and new, the work is well paid, and the hours are average.

SHOP DELIVERIES

Requirements
Good knowledge of tail-lifts and wheeled, caged and palletised goods. The driver should be polite, diplomatic, well-presented, patient, capable of directing others, safety conscious and able to take control of a vehicle and its load in a public thoroughfare.

Nature of work
More like that of a company representative than a lorry driver. Shop deliveries can be very physical, the pay is average to good, and the hours are long (particularly if delivering in a class C vehicle).

Deliveries are sometimes made at the front of the shop during opening hours, and drivers have to be prepared to handle every type of possible scenario which may arise from this.

REFRIGERATED VEHICLE OR TRAILER WORK

Requirements
Some informal training is required. Drivers should be competent, safety conscious, intelligent and hard-working. They shouldn't suffer from poor circulation of the hands or feet and should have good working knowledge of tail-lifts and delivering palletised goods.

Nature of work
This type of work involves spending time in the back of a vehicle with a temperature of anything from −5° to −30°. (In the winter this is no joke!) The work usually involves delivering to supermarkets, food manufacturers and shops and can involve reversing into and out of any number of tight spaces. It is fairly clean work and not particularly physical, the pay is good to average, but the hours in a class C can be long.

BAKERY DELIVERIES

Requirements
Drivers should be extremely fit and strong and have good working knowledge of tail-lifts, retaining bars, and wheeled goods.

Nature of work
You'll often be required to manoeuvre stacks of bread weighing anything up to 20 stone (that's about 130kg), so this type of work shouldn't be undertaken by anyone with a previous back injury. You'll often be required to drive older types of vehicles, though the work itself is not too dirty. The hours, however, can be long, and the pay is good to average. There may be a degree of waiting time involved at depots. On the plus side, bakery workers are usually a cheery bunch and very helpful to a new driver.

TRUNKING

Requirements
Good knowledge of the UK and of coupling and uncoupling many different kinds of trailers. The driver must also be fairly experienced and willing to work nights if required.

Nature of work

Almost always class C+E, trunking is by far the easiest of all lorry-driving work. It mostly consists of one or two long-distance drops, rarely involves any off-loading (normally you just swap trailers), and is usually undertaken at night. The work is not normally too dirty, the vehicles are fairly new and clean, the pay is good to average, but the hours are long.

SKIP WORK

Requirements

Some informal training is required. The driver should be diplomatic, capable of handling cash, and very safety conscious, particularly since it's been known for people to be found asleep inside skips.

Nature of work

Skip work is extremely dirty and often involves driving a class C vehicle into all sorts of places. The driver will be required to deliver to anywhere, from a building site to a school. You'll often be required to collect cash from private addresses and to understand how to secure your skip and its contents correctly. The work is physical, dirty, and not particularly well paid.

TIPPER WORK

Requirements

Some training is required. The driver should be competent and fairly experienced. He must

also be extremely good at finding his way around.

Nature of work

Tippers come in all shapes, sizes and types. The work is fairly dirty, particularly if delivering building or resurfacing materials. Delivering feed or grain, however, is usually cleaner, unless delivering to farms. Hours are average to long and pay is average to good. You'll sometimes be expected to deliver to places that aren't even on a map, so a good knowledge of the area would be an advantage.

TRANS-CONTINENTAL WORK

Requirements

Only to be attempted by highly experienced drivers. Multilingual capabilities would be a great advantage, as would excellent map-reading skills. You may also be expected to drive a left-hand-drive vehicle.

Nature of work

You'll be expected to drive a vehicle on the wrong side of the road in countries with alien road systems and inconsiderate drivers. Although facilities for truck drivers in Western European countries are better than those in Britain, the further east you go the more alien the customs and 'ways of the road' become. In colder countries you'll be expected to cope with extreme weather and difficult border crossings. You'll find yourself very much on your own. The hours are long and lonely, and although the wages can be very rewarding forget having any kind of home life.

BIN LORRY WORK

Requirements
You should be a skilled and confident class C driver. You must be very safety conscious and extremely social. You should be happy with early starts and not be bothered by strong smells.

Nature of work
You'll be expected to drive and reverse your vehicle into impossibly tight spaces with ease. You need to enjoy the company of your loaders and work happily as part of a team. Bin work is extremely dirty, and even though you'll be sitting at the wheel the whole time your companions will make for very fragrant, grubby company. The hours are fairly short, though the pay is not good and the smell can be terrible!

CAR TRANSPORTERS

Requirements
Drivers should be experienced, but will receive thorough informal training. They should be safety conscious and prepared to work nights.

Nature of work
You'll often be required to deliver on the roadside, and to drive vehicles safely up and down ramps and secure them correctly. Mistakes are extremely costly and you and your load are always at risk from theft and attack. The work can be fairly well paid though physical, and the hours are long.

SHUNTER WORK

Requirements
You should be a competent driver and great at reversing. You should have an LGV C+E or Shunter licence. You should not mind being out in all weathers and getting covered in fifth wheel grease. Training on specialised shunter vehicles would be an advantage.

Nature of work
Shunter work can be very tedious, as you don't actually get to go anywhere. As long as you don't leave the private property of your yard you can acquire a shunter licence without having an LGV licence, though the shunter licence is specific only to the yard you're working from. Shunter work is very much a love it or hate it kind of job. The pay is average, hours can be long, and the work is very dirty indeed.

SELF-EMPLOYMENT AND LIMITED COMPANY STATUS

Before you register
As a truck driver you have several options that may apply to your employment status. Most drivers are employed by one haulage company or agency on a PAYE basis. A few drivers (and these days it is only a few) work for themselves, supplying their own vehicle and running their own business. Doing this involves keeping your own records of billing and purchasing, completing all tax forms, keeping tacho records, providing your own insurance, organising your own work and having your own O-licence and CPC – a daunting concept for anyone!

If, however, you work through one or several agencies you may have the option to work as a limited company, although setting yourself up as a limited company is not always a straightforward process.

There is strict legislation regarding the eligibility of an individual or group to set themselves up as a limited company. This legislation is known as the IR35. The first step you should take is to go to www.hmrc.gov.uk/ir35/ and look through the following links:

- Supplying services through a limited company or partnership – a general guide.
- The circumstances in which legislation applies.
- Link to general guide on employed or self-employment.

You should also go to 'business and corporations', click on 'excise and other tax information and guides' and read the regulations regarding 'money laundering'.

If you are sure that your form of employment could satisfy the parameters set out in these guidelines, you would do well to seek out a good accountant. Some accountants specialise in offering a complete service to truck drivers and will take care of almost everything for you, dealing with the setting-up of your registration at Companies House, with the HMRC and even with a bank. They will also complete your tax return forms on your behalf and keep track of your expenses and income. A good accountant will offer consultation and advice for free. Charges for services vary greatly according to how much you would like your accountant to do for you, though it can be well worth it for the amount of money that a good accountant will save you in tax payments.

If you wish to go ahead without the help of an accountant (though I wouldn't recommend it), the following is a step-by-step guide giving you some idea of what you'll have to do.

Registering as a limited company

1. Decide on a name for your company and register it at Companies House via their recommended agency, known as Duport, at www.duport.co.uk.
2. If you wish to register it yourself without the help of an agency, go to the Companies House website at www.companieshouse.gov.uk/ and click on 'forms'. Scroll to 'download paper forms here' and click on forms '288a', '10', '12', and '88(2)'. You will need these in order to complete your registration.
3. You will have to appoint a company director (this can be yourself) and a company secretary, using form '288a'. One person cannot be both secretary and director, though if you're using an accountant you'll be able to appoint them or their corporate entity as your company secretary. A director should not have a criminal record, particularly for any offences regarding money laundering or offences under the terrorism act. They should not be a non-discharged bankrupt or have any IVAs (Individual Voluntary Arrangements) outstanding against them, as this may make it very difficult for them to get a company bank account.
4. Form '10' asks you to provide the address of the company's registered office. This is the place where most of your business will be carried out. This can be your home address, but if you're using an accountant as your secretary they may suggest that you use their business premises as the registered office.
5. Form '12' is your declaration upon application stating the identity of the secretary and director.
6. Form '88(2)' is the 'allotment of shares'. Every limited company is issued with 1,000 shares valued at £1 each that it can use as it wishes. You don't have to buy all of your shares from Companies House, though every director should be allocated at least one.

7. You should receive your 'Certificate of Incorporation' through the post within a week or two.
8. Once you have registered your company, Her Majesty's Customs and Excise (HMCE) will send you a 'CT41G' form, which you must complete, giving your new company details. This enables them to issue you with a Corporation Tax Reference Number.
9. Your next step is to open a company bank account. You may wish to use your own bank for this as it makes payments and transfers between company and personal bank accounts much easier. Your bank will need to see your Certificate of Incorporation, your passport and your driving licence. They will then do a company search to make sure that the company has been properly formed and a personal search on the director and secretary for records of un-discharged bankruptcy or IVAs.

Responsibilities of the Company Directory

As a company director you will also be responsible for the following:

- Keeping track of driving hours undertaken.
- Returning tachographs to your agency (or agencies) or each company where the tachograph was produced.
- Providing the company secretary with records of invoices to clients (such as the haulage companies or agencies you do work for), supplier purchase orders connected with business (such as company phones or equipment) and receipts for items such as stationery and clothing.
- Providing the company secretary with a record of bank statements, business mileage records and payments you have received from the clients you've worked for.

So as you can see, setting up as a limited company is not a step to be taken lightly. A good accountant will take most of the headache out of it by completing forms on your behalf and chasing up any discrepancies between what you have invoiced your clients for and what they have paid you. However, you're still responsible for everything listed above, so you'll have to be of an organised nature and be able to dedicate at least one hour a week towards administrative duties.

Truck dealerships, service centres and fitters

DAF TRUCKS UK, Eastern Bypass, Thame, Oxfordshire, OX9 3FB
Tel: 00 (44) 1844 261111, Fax: 00 (44) 1844 217111, www.daftrucks.co.uk
DafAid UK: 0800 919395

Aberdeenshire: Norscot Truck and Van Ltd, Norscot House, The Parkway, Bridge of Don, Aberdeen, AB23 8JZ	01224 824444
Anglesea: Holyhead Truck Services, The Garage, Llanfaethlu, Holyhead, LL65 4NW	01407 730759
Angus: Norscot Truck & Van Ltd, Block 9, Nobel Rd, West Gourdie Industrial Estate, Dundee, DD2 4UH	01382 611166
Ayrshire: Ian Gordon Commercials, Schawkirk Garage, On the B730, Ayr, KA5 5JA	01292 591764
Grant Welsh Commercials, Unit B12, Olympic Business Park, Drybridge Road, Dundonald, KA2 9BE	01563 851015
Barr Truck Services, Braehead, Girvan, KA26 0QR	014658 21300
Bedfordshire: Brian Currie, Chesney Wold, Bleak Hall, Milton Keynes, MK6 1LH	01908 665379
Brian Currie, Brunel Road, Barkers Lane Industrial Estate, Bedford, MK41 9TL	01234 211241
Luton DAF, 166 Camford Way, Sundon Park, Luton, LU3 3AN	01582 505464
Belfast: TBF Thompson DAF Trucks, 19 Michelin Road, Hydepark Industrial Estate, Mallusk, Newtown Abbey, BT36 8PT, N Ireland	02890 342001
Berkshire: Barnes DAF, Station Road, Theale, Reading, RG7 4AG	01189 300900
Heathrow DAF, Spedtion Park, Lakeside Industrial Estate, Bath Road, Colnbrook, Slough, SL3 0ED	01753 681818
Berwickshire: J E Douglas and Sons, Station Road Industrial Estate, Duns, TD11 3HS	01361 883411
Buckinghamshire: Ring Road Garage, Gawcott Road, Buckingham, MK18 1DR	01280 814741
Euroway DAF, Central Workshops, Unit B, Lincoln Road, Cressex, High Wycombe, HP12 3RH	01494 465464
Camarthenshire: Swansea DAF Truck Centre, Unit 43, Cwmdu Business Centre, Fforestfach, Swansea, SA5 8LG	01792 582255
Wynne Phillips Truck Centre, Station Road, Whitland, SA34 0QE	01994 240820
Cambridgeshire: Universal Garage DAF, 67 Hall Barn Road, Isleham, Ely, CB7 5QZ	01638 780642
Ford & Slater DAF, Newark Road, Eastern Industrial Estate, Peterborough, PE1 5YD	01733 295000
Ford & Slater Ltd, Commercial House, Algores Way, Wisbech, PE13 2TQ	01945 461316
Marshall Motor Group Ltd, Airport Garage, Newmarket Road, Cambridge, CB5 8SQ	01223 377900
Cheshire: MCA Commercials, Dockyard Road, Ellesmere Port, CH65 4EG	0151 355 1076
A M Bell (Garage) Ltd, Hawkshead Quarry, Leek Old Road, Sutton, Macclesfield, SK11 0JB	01260 253232
North West Trucks, Griffiths Road, Lostock Gralam, Northwich, CW9 7NU	01606 818088
JDS Trucks, Broadgate, Broadway Business Park, Chaderton, Oldham, OL9 9NL	0161 947 1400
Euroway DAF, Geodis House, Holmsfield Road, Farrel Street Industrial Estate, Warrington, WA1 2DR	01925 629116
Clwyd: Imperial Commercials Ltd, Wrexham Road, Rhostyllen, Wrexham, LL14 4DP	01978 346100
Conwy: Parrys Commercials Ltd, Craig Road, Glan Conwy, LL28 5RA	01492 580303
Cornwall: Cawsey Commercials Ltd, Unit 11, Newport Industrial Estate, Launceston, PL15 8EX	01566 772805
County Cavan: Interparts Ltd, Dublin Road, Cavan, Ireland	00353 (0) 494361277
County Cork: DAF Truck Services Ltd, Mallow Road, Cork, Ireland	00353 (0) 214301444
County Donegal: Letterkenny 4X4 & Commercials Ltd, Drumkeen, Lifford, Ireland	00353 (0) 749124196
County Dublin: DAF Distributors Ireland Ltd, Baldonnell Business Park, Baldonnell, Dublin 22, Ireland	00353 (0) 14591864
North Dublin Commercials Ltd, Knocknagin, Balbriggan, Ireland	00353 (0) 18411815
County Durham: Chatfields, Drum Barley Mow, Birtley, DH3 2AF	0191 492 1155
Chatfields, Teesway, North Tees Industrial Estate, Stockton on Tees, TS18 2RS	01642 637660
County Galway: Galway Truck Centre Ltd, Syulan, Headford Road, Galway, Ireland	00353 (0) 91755224
County Tipperary: Guilfoyle Truck Sales Ltd, Carrig, Limerick Road, Roscrea, Ireland	00353 (0) 50521849
County Waterford: Rolor Commercials Ltd,Grannagh, Waterford, Ireland	00353 (0) 51872866
County Wicklow: Jimmy Healy & Sons, Commercials, Kilmartin, Ashford, Ireland	00353 (0) 12819576
County Kilkenny: Kilkenny Truck Centre, Callan Road, Kilkenny, Ireland	00353 (0) 567722657
County Wicklow: Grove Motors Ltd, Main Street, Newtown Mount Kennedy, Ireland	00353 (0) 12819803
County Limerick: Limerick Parts Depot, Clondrinagh Industrial Estate, Ennis Road, Limerick, Ireland	00353 (0) 61451193
Craigavon: TBF Thompson, Diviny Drive, Carn Industrial Estate, Portadown, BT63 5WE, Northern Ireland	02838 393300
Cumbria: Solway DAF, Kingstown Broadway, Kingstown Industrial Estate, Carlisle, CA3 0HD	01228 539394
Solway DAF, Gillwilly Lane, Gillwilly Industrial Estate, Penrith, CA11 9BN	01768 892938
Solway DAF, 6G Reedlands Road, Solway Road, Clay Flatts, Workington, CA14 3YF	01900 66927
Derbyshire: Imperial Commercials Ltd, 35 Ashbourne Rd, Mackworth, Derby, DE22 4NB	01332 824371
H W Martin, Fordbridge Lane, Blackwell, Alfreton, DE55 5JY	01773 813313
Chatfields, 7 Orgreave Drive, Handsworth, Sheffield, S13 9NR	01142 548854
A Herring Ltd, Toc H Yard, Old Road, Chesterfield, S40 2RG	01246 234213
Devon: Wessex DAF, 1 Roundhead Road, Heathfield Industrial Estate, Newton Abbot, TQ12 6UE	01626 833737
Saltash DAF, HMG House, Channon Road, Moorlands Industrial Estate, , Plymouth, PL12 6LX	01752 848359
Dorset: Adams Morey Ltd, Yeomans Way, Yeomans Industrial Estate, Bournemouth, BH8 0BJ	01202 524422

Dumfriesshire: Solway DAF, Lochside Industrial Estate, Irongray Rd, Dumfries, DG2 0JE — 01387 720820
Dyfed: Aberystwyth Automotive Services, Unit 3, Glan Yr Afon Industrial Estate, Aberystwyth, SY23 3JQ — 01970 631090
East Sussex: Brewers DAF, Hammonds Drive, , Eastbourne, BN23 6PW — 01323 745700
Essex: Harris DAF, 601 London Road, West Thurrock, Grays, RM20 4AU — 01708 864426
Ontime (Service Garage) Rescue & Recovery Ltd, Cranes Close, Cranes Farm Road, Basildon, SS14 3JB — 01268 290680
Harris DAF, 5 Wheaton Road, Witham, CM8 3UJ — 01376 533680
Fife: Drummond Motor Co Ltd, Ferrard Road, , Kirkcaldy, KY1 2YX — 01592 201555
Glamorgan: DAF Truck Centre, Leckwith Industrial Estate, Whittle Road, Cardiff, CF1 8AT — 02920 308595
Gloucestershire: Watts Truck Centre Ltd, Mercia Road, Gloucester, GL1 2SQ — 01452 508700
Gloucestershire (South): Watts Truck Centre, Dean Road, Yate, BS37 5ND — 01454 333370
Guernsey: Rabeys Garage Ltd, PO Box 507, Vale Industrial Estate, North Side, Vale, GY1 6DP, Guernsey — 01481 244551
Gwent: Fairwood Truck Centre, Afon Ebbw Road, Rogerstone Park, Risca, Newport, NP10 9HZ — 01633 891991
Hampshire: Adams Morey Ltd, The Causeway, Redbridge, Southampton, SO15 0DR — 02380 663000
Basingstoke Commercials, Whitney Road, Daneshill Industrial Estate, Basingstoke, RG24 8NS — 01256 811414
Adams Morey Ltd, Burrfields Road, Portsmouth, PO3 5NN — 02392 691122
Herefordshire: Watts Truck & Van Centre, Unit F, Moreton Park, , Moreton On Lugg, HR4 8DS — 01432 763900
CCS, Masters Yard, Railway Terrace, Kings Langley, WD4 8JA — 01923 262199
Foulger's (CVS) Ltd, Melda Farm, Bury Lane, Melbourn, Royston, SG8 6DF — 01763 262826
Harris DAF, 1 Station Approach, Waltham Cross, EN8 7NA — 01992 651155
Humberside (South): Imperial Commericals Ltd, Estate Rd No 2, South Humberside Industrial Estate, , Grimsby, DN31 2TG — 01472 362929
Imperial Commercials Ltd, Midland Industrial Estate, Kettering Rd, , Scunthorpe, DN16 1UW — 01724 282444
Invernesshire: Sheriffmill Motor Co Ltd, Sheriffmill Road, Elgin, IV30 6UH — 01343 547121
Norscot Truck & Van Ltd, The Truck Centre, 52 Sleaford Road, Inverness, IV1 1SG — 01463 712000
Isle of Man: Wade's Truck Services, Bath Lane Industrial Estate, Ballasalla, IM9 2AQ, Isle of Man 01624 825559
Isle of Wight: Adams Morey Ltd, 1-2 Riverway Industrial Estate, Newport, PO30 5UY, Isle of Wight — 01983 522552
Jersey: Rabeys, La Grande Route de St Martin, Five Oaks, St Saviour, JE2 7GR, Jersey — 01534 852304
Kent: Channel Commercials PLC, Brunswick Road, Cobbs Wood Estate, Ashford, TN23 1EH — 01233 629272
Channel Commercials PLC, Unit 18, Cooting Road, Aylesham, Canterbury, CT3 3EP — 01304 841111
Morgan Elliott DAF, Crabree Manor Way North, Belvedere, DA17 6BT — 0208 319 7801
Channel Commercials PLC, North Downs Business Park, Pilgrims Way, Dunton Gr, Sevenoaks, TN13 2TL — 01732 469469
Channel Commercials PLC, Whitehall Road, Medway City Industrial Estate, Strood, ME2 4DZ — 01634 296686
Lanarkshire: Imperial Commercials Ltd , 8, South Wardpark Court, Wardpark South, , Cumbernauld, G67 3HE — 0123 672 7771
Trucktec, Clark Way, Bellshill Industrial Estate, , Bellshill, ML4 3NX — 01698 339090
Lancashire: Lancashire DAF, Unit 223-224, Walton Summit Centre, Bamber Bridge, Preston, PR5 8BW — 01772 338111
Lynch Truck Services Ltd, Barnfield Way, Altham Business Park, Altham, Accrington, BB5 5YT — 01282 773377
Lakeland Trucks Ltd, Carnforth Industrial Estate, Lodge Quarry, , Carnforth, LA5 9DW — 01524 734544
Simmons Commercials, Clarke Street, Poulton Le Fylde, FY6 8JR — 01253 884521
Woodwards Truck & Van Centre, Stephens Way, Warrington Rd Industrial Estate, Wigan, WN3 6PQ — 01942 230026
Chatfields, Mellors Road, Trafford Park, Manchester, M17 1PB — 0161 877 2519
Leicestershire: Ford & Slater DAF, Hazel Drive, Narborough Road South, Leicester, LE3 2JG — 01162 632900
Lincolnshire: Ford & Slater DAF, Sleaford Road, Bracebridge Heath, Lincoln, LN4 2NQ — 01522 518170
R Eastment & Son, Newark Road, Torksey, LN1 2EJ — 01427 718638
Ford & Slater DAF, 58 Station Road, Donington, Spalding, PE11 3ZN — 01775 715680
Londonderry: TBF Thompson DAF Trucks, 6-10 Killyvally Road, Garvagh, Coleraine, BT51 5JZ, Northern Ireland — 028295 58353
Manchester (Greater): Chatfields, 40 Ashton Old Road, Macclesfield, M12 6NA — 0161 273 7351
Merseyside: North West Trucks, Huyton Industrial Estate, Wilson Road, Huyton, Liverpool, L36 6AJ — 0151 480 0098
MTC Northwest Ltd, Gores Rd, Knowsley Industrial Park, Liverpool, L33 7XS — 0151 545 4750
Mid Lothian: Lothian DAF, Pentland Industrial Estate, Loanhead, Edinburgh, EH20 9QH — 0131 440 4100
Norfolk: Ford & Slater DAF, William Frost Way, Longwater Business Park, New Costessey, Norwich, NR5 0JS — 01603 731600
Ford & Slater DAF, Maple Road, , Kings Lynn, PE34 3AH — 01553 764466
Perfect Engineering, Harfreys Rd, Harfreys Industrial Estate, , Great Yarmouth, NR31 0JL — 01493 657131
Northamptonshire: F W Abbott Ltd, Unit 10, Orion Way, Kettering Business Park, Pytch, Kettering, NN15 6NL — 01536 517704
Brian Currie, Gayton Road, Northampton, NN7 3AB — 01604 858810
Ford & Slater DAF, Gretton Brook Road, Corby, NN17 4BA — 01536 207980
North Yorkshire: Pelican DAF, Rhine Park Industrial Estate, Altofts Lane, Castleford, WF10 5UB — 01924 227722
Kettlewell Commercials, Station Depot, Melmerby, Ripon, HG4 5EX — 01765 640913
Cayton Commercials, 1 Main Street, Scarborough, YO11 3RU — 01723 582697
Nottinghamshire: Charnwood Truck Services, Hillside, Gotham Rd, , Kingston on Soar, NG11 0DF — 01159 830093
Ford & Slater DAF, Unit 12, Newark Storage Co, Bowbridge Road, , Newark, NG24 4EQ — 01636 674441
Imperial Commercials Ltd, 2, Padge Rd, Boulevard Industrial Park, Beeston, Nottingham, NG9 2JR — 01159 677077
Imperial Commercials Ltd, Fulwood Rd South, Fulwood Ind Est, , Sutton in Ashfield, NG17 2JZ — 01623 516735
Oxfordshire: R P Cherry & Son Ltd, Thrupp Lane, Radley, Abingdon, OX14 3NG — 01235 531004
GB Fleetcare Ltd, Fine Lady Bakeries, Southam Road, Banbury, OX16 2RR — 01295 270072
Barnes DAF, 18 Pony Road, Horsepath Trading Estate, Cowley, Oxford, OX4 2SA — 01865 749899
Windrush DAF, Burford Road, Minster Lovell, Witney, OX29 0RB — 01993 702131
Perthshire: Norscot Truck & Van Ltd, Shore Road, Perth, PH2 8BH — 01738 626688

Renfrewshire: Imperial Commercials Ltd, 131 Bogmoor Rd, Glasgow, G51 4TH — 0141 425 1530
Shropshire: Greenhous DAF, March Way, Battlefield Enterprise Park, Harlescott, Shrewsbury, SY1 3JE — 01743 467904
 Halesfield Truck & Van Ltd, Halesfield 9, Telford, TF7 4QW — 01952 586454
Somerset: Taunton DAF, 148 Priorswood Road, Taunton, TA2 8DW — 01823 331275
 Imperial Commercials Ltd, Unit 12, Moore Acres, Marston Trading Estate, Manor Furlong, Frome, BA11 2FD — 01373 464524
 Imperial Commercials Ltd, Days Road, St Phillips, Bristol, BS2 0QP — 01179 557755
South Yorkshire: Imperial Commercials Ltd, Brooklands Rd, Aldwick Le Street, Doncaster, DN6 7BA — 01302 727040
 Fishlake Commercials Ltd, Jubilee Bridge Works, Selby Rd, Thorne, Doncaster, DN8 4JD — 01405 740086
 Imperial Commercials Ltd, Auster Road, York, YO30 4XD — 01904 692909
Staffordshire: Imperial Commercials Ltd, Leek New Road, Hanley, Stoke On Trent, ST6 2DE — 01782 276600
Stirlingshire: Imperial Commercials Ltd, 17 Main St, Polmont, Falkirk, Grangemouth, FK3 8EB — 01324 473700
Suffolk: Chassis-Cab Truck Centre, Addison Way, Great Blakenham, Ipswich, IP6 0RL — 01473 833003
 Chassis-Cab Truck Centre, Northern Way, Bury St Edmunds, IP32 6NL — 01284 768570
Surrey: Morgan Elliott DAF, 93 Beddington Lane, Croydon, CR0 4TD — 0208 683 6200
 Barnes DAF, Slyfield Industrial Estate, Woking Road, Guildford, GU1 1RT — 01483 594900
Warwickshire: Noden Truck Centre, 3 Avon Industrial Estate, Butlers Leap, , Rugby, CV21 3UY — 01788 579535
 Imperial Commercials Ltd, Unit 1, 15, Lock Lane, Warwick, CV34 5HE — 01926 479197
West Midlands: Imperial Commercials Ltd, Park Road, Halesown, B63 2RL — 01384 424500
 Greenhous DAF, Neachells Lane, , Willenhall, WV13 3SF — 01902 305090
 Commercial Fleet Services, Richmond House, Wainright Street, The Heartlands, Birmingham, DAF B6 5TJ — 0121 326 6985
 Imperial Commercials Ltd, Bannerley Road, , Birmingham, B33 0SL — 0121 784 4023
 Ford & Slater DAF, Rowley Road, Coventry, CV3 4FL — 02476 302856
West Sussex: Barnes DAF, 44 Dolphin Road, Shoreham, BN43 6PB — 01273 454887
 GB DAF Gatwick , Fleming Way, , Crawley, RH10 9NS — 01293 537520
West Yorkshire: F & G Commercials (Huddersfield) Ltd, Leeds Road, Kirklees, Huddersfield, HD2 1UR — 01484 300500
 Chatfields, Grangefield Industrial Estate, Pudsey, Leeds, LS28 6SD — 0113 2 571701
 F & G Commercials Ltd, Unit 2, Barkston Road, Carlton Industrial Estate, Carlton, Barnsley, S71 3HU — 01226 731870
 Imperial Commercials Ltd, Heddon Road, Hull, HU9 5PJ — 01482 795111
Wiltshire: Adams Morey Ltd, Stephenson Road, Churchfield Industrial Estate, Salisbury, SP2 7NP — 01722 412171
 Imperial Commercials Ltd, Radway Road, Stratton St Margaret, Swindon, SN3 4ND — 01793 835200
Worcestershire: Watts Truck & Van Centre, Bath Road, Broomhall, Worcester, WR5 3HR — 01905 829800

FODEN, Foden Trucks (Head Office), Moss lane, Sandbach, Cheshire, CW11 3YW
Tel: 01270 758400, Fax: 01270 762758, www.foden.com,
FODEN ASSIST (FROM A LANDLINE): 0800 591101 FODEN ASSIST (FROM A MOBILE): 01922 646136

Aberdeenshire: Norscot Foden, Norscot House, The Parkway, Bridge of Don, Aberdeen, AB23 8JZ — 01224 826096
Ayrshire: John Maitland & Sons, Trabboch, Mauchline, KA5 5HT — 01292 592001
Bedfordshire: Brian Currie Bedford, 3 Brunel Road, Bedford, MK41 9TL — 01234 360804
 Osborn Transport Services, 35A Stanbridge Road, Leighton Buzzard, LU7 4PZ — 01525 852385
 Foden Luton, 166 Camford Way, Sundon Park, Luton, LU3 3AN — 01582 505679
Berkshire: Foden Heathrow, Spedition Park, Lakeside Industrial Estate, Bath Road, Colnbrook, Slough, SL3 0ED — 01753 683901
Cambridgeshire: Ford and Slater Ltd., Newark Road, Peterborough, PE1 5YD — 01733 295010
Carmarthenshire: Swansea Truck Centre Ltd., Unit 43, Cwmdu Business Centre, Fforestfach, Swansea, SA5 8LG — 01792 579895
Cleveland: Parsons Truck Centre, Brenda Road, Hartlepool, TS25 2BJ — 01429 860838
Coleraine: TBF Thompson (Garvagh) Ltd., 6 -10 Killyvalley Road, Garvagh, BT51 5JZ — 028 2955 7957
Craigavon: TBF Thompson Truck & Van Centre, Diviny Drive, Carn Industrial Estate, Portadown, BT63 5RH, N. Ireland — 028 3839 1710
Cumbria: Cumbria Truck Centre Ltd., Leabank Road, Kingstown, Carlisle, CA3 0HB — 01228 590300
Denbighshire: Imperial Commercials, Wrexham Road, Rhostyllen, Wrexham, LL14 4DP — 01978 346118
Derbyshire: H.W. Martin (Plant) Ltd., Fordbridge Lane, Blackwell, Alfreton, DE55 5JY — 01773 813305
Devon: Wessex Foden, 1 Roundhead Road, Heathfield Industrial Estate, Newton Abbot, TQ12 6UE — 01626 837878
Dublin: Foden Ireland, Baldonnel Business Park, Baldonnel, Dublin 22, Ireland — 00353 (0) 1403 4100
Essex: Harris Truck & Van Ltd., 5 Wheaton Road, Witham, CM8 3UJ — 01376 533686
Gloucestershire: Joseph Rice Truck Services Ltd., 26A Hempsted Lane, Gloucester, GL2 5FH — 01452 300456
 Watts Truck & Van Centre, Mercia Road, Gloucester, GL1 2SQ — 01452 508708
Gwent: Fairwood Truck Centre, Afon Ebbw Road, Rogerstone Park, Risca, Newport, NP10 9HZ — 01633 894700
Hampshire: Adams Morey Foden, Burrfields Road, Portsmouth, PO3 5NN — 02392 694022
Hertfordshire: Valley Trucks Ltd., Bingley Road, Hoddesdon, EN11 0NX — 01992 451105
 Foulgers Garage, Melda Farm, Elliot Drive, Melbourn, Royston, SG8 6DF — 01763 262668
Kent: Acorn Truck Sales Ltd., Acorn Ind. Park, Crayford Road, Crayford, DA1 4AL — 01322 550403
Lancashire: Lancashire DAF, Four Oaks Road, Walton Summit Centre, Bamber Bridge, PR5 8BW — 01772 332667
Lanarkshire: Imperial Commercials, 131 Bogmoor Road, Govan, Glasgow, G51 4TH — 0141 425 1840
Leicestershire: Ford & Slater Leicester, Hazel Drive, Narborough Road South, Leicester, LE3 2JG — 0116 263 0042
 Midland Commercial Services Ltd., Hazel Way, Barwell, Leicester, LE9 8GP — 01455 847105
Lincolnshire: Ford & Slater Donington, 58 Station Street, Donington, Spalding, PE11 4UJ — 01775 821715
 Gallows Wood Service Station Ltd., Barnetby, DN38 6DW — 01652 680796
 R. Eastment & Son, The Garage, Newark Road, Torksey, Lincoln, LN1 2EJ — 01427 718465

Manchester (Greater): Chatfields, Mellors Road, Trafford Park, Manchester, M17 1PB — 0161 877 3735
Merseyside: MTC Northwest Ltd., Gores Road, Knowsley Industrial Park, Kirkby, Liverpool, L33 7XS — 0151 545 4760
Midlothian: Lothian DAF, Pentland Industrial Estate, Loanhead, EH20 9QH — 0131 448 2070
Morayshire: Baillie Brothers (Truck Services) Ltd., Linkwood Place, Linkwood Industrial Estate, Elgin, IV30 1HZ — 01343 555310
Newtownabbey: TBF Thompson, 19 Michelin Road, Hydepark Industrial Estate, Mallusk, Newtownabbey, BT36 4PT, N Ireland — 028 9083 5466
Norfolk: Carrow Commercials (Wymondham), South Side, Ayton Road, Wymondham, NR18 0RA — 01953 607090
Ford & Slater King's Lynn, Marple Road, King's Lynn, PE34 3AH — 01553 764612
Northamptonshire: Brian Currie Northampton, Milton Trading Estate, Gayton Road, Milton Malsor, Northampton, NN7 3AB — 01604 859995
North Lanarkshire: Imperial Commercials, 8 South Wardpark Court, Wardpark South, Cumbernauld, G67 3EH — 0123 672 0883
Nottinghamshire: Charnwood Truck Services, Hillside, Gotham Road, Kingston-on-Soar, Nottingham, NG11 0DF — 0115 983 0072
Oxfordshire: R.P. Cherry & Son Ltd., Thrupp Lane, Abingdon, OX14 3NG — 01235 524810
Shropshire: T.J. Parry & Sons, Wattlesborough Heath Garage, Halfway House, Shrewsbury, SY5 9EG — 01743 885019
Staffordshire: Imperial Commercials, Leek New Road, Cobridge, Stoke-on-Trent, ST6 2DE — 01782 276629
H & H Commercial Truck Services Ltd., Nevada Close, Sneyd Industrial Estate, Burslem, Stoke-on-Trent, ST6 2NT — 01782 812913
Somerset: Imperial Commercials, Days Road, St. Phillips, Bristol, BS2 0QP — 0117 304 2826
Imperial Commercials, Unit 12, Marston Trading Estate, Frome, BA11 4RL — 01373 468535
Tyne & Wear: Albany Motors, Saltmeadows Road, Gateshead, NE8 3AH — 0191 4770848
West Midlands: Greenhous Commercials Ltd., Neachells Lane, Willenhall, WV13 3SF — 01902 864551
West Yorkshire: Pelican Engineering Co. Ltd., Rhine Park Industrial Estate, Altofts Lane, Wakefield Europort, Castleford, WF10 5UB — 01924 227723

IVECO/SEDDON ATKINSON, Iveco Ltd, Iveco House, Station Road, Watford, Hertfordshire, WD17 1SR
Tel: 01923 246400, Fax: 01923 240574, Iveco Non-Stop 0800 590509 in the UK or 00800 82747368 if abroad
www.iveco.co.uk

Aberdeenshire: AM Phillip Limited, 218 Auchmill Road, Bucksburn, Aberdeen, AB21 9NB — 01244 714716
Anglesey: Holyhead Truck Services, The Garage (A5025), Lanfaethlu, Holyhead, LL65 4NW, Anglesey — 01407 73004
Angus: AM Phillip Limited, Camperdown Industrial Park, Dryburg Industrial Estate, Dundee, DD2 3SN — 01382 832520
Bedfordshire: Evans Halshaw, 3 Ronald Close, Woburn Road Industrial Estate, Bedford, MK42 7SH — 01234 363931
Stormont Truck & Van Limited, 23 Eastern Avenue, Dunstable, LU5 4JY — 01582 884522
Berkshire: Grays Truck & Van, Unit 8, Arrowhead Road, Reading, RG7 4AZ — 0118 9304458
Buckinghamshire: EW Smith, Unit 1, Chepping Park, Lincoln Road, Cressex Industrial Estate, High Wycombe, HP12 3RB — 01494 533220
Cambridgeshire: TC Harrison, Unit One, Ely Road, Waterbeach, Cambridge, CB5 9PG — 01223 441892
TC Harrison, Oxney Road, Eastern Industrial Estate, Peterborough, PE1 5YN — 01733 425647
Carmarthenshire: CEM Day Limited, The Truck Centre, Beaufort Road, Morriston, Swansea, SA6 8HR — 01792 616213
Cheshire: Chatfields Truck & Van, Taylor Road, Trafford Park, Urmston, Manchester, M41 7JQ — 0161 7461904
Kenwood Commercial Vehicle Services, Kenwood Road, Off Station Road, Reddish, Stockport, SK5 6PH — 0161 4319804
Chatfields Truck & Van, Unit 12, Clayton Road, Risley, Warrington, WA3 6PH — 01925 284413
Bowers Threeways Garage Ltd, Road Three, Winsford Industrial Estate, Winsford, CS7 3DP — 01606 554198
Clwyd: Parry Commercials Ltd, Graig, Glan Conwy, LL28 5RA — 01492 596980
Cornwall: Vospers Commercial Services, Victoria Business Park, Roche, St Austell, PL26 8LQ — 01726 892105
County Antrim: Eakin Brothers Ltd, 48 Main Street, Claudy, Londonderry, BT47 7HR, Northern Ireland — 02871 338890
Hilltop Garage, 22 Cranagh Road, Coleraine, BT51 3NN, Northern Ireland — 02870 356709
6 Carn Court Industrial Estate, Portadown, BT63 5YX, Northern Ireland — 02838 399774
County Cork: D. Dennehy Ltd, Carrigtwohill, Cork, Ireland — 00353 (0) 4883654
Mallow Commercials, Lower Quatertown, Mallow, Cork, Ireland — 00353 (0) 2221614
County Donegal: BOD Vehicle Support Services, Letterkenny, Donegal, Ireland — 00353 (0) 872554970
County Dublin: BOD Vehicle Support Services, Naas Road, Dublin, 12, Ireland — 00353 (0) 872554970
Truck Dealers International, Naas Road, Dublin 12, Ireland — 00353 (0) 14194592
Euro Commercials, U1 Feltrim Industrial Estate, Swords, Ireland — 00353 (0) 18624415
County Galway: Excelsior Garages Ltd, Tuam Road, Galway, Ireland — 00353 (0) 91751671
County Kilkenny: Kilkenny Truck Centre, Callan Road, Kilkenny, Ireland — 00353 (0) 56776845
Minogues Garage, Dublin Road, Kilkenny, Ireland — 00353 (0) 568838711
County Limerick: BOD Vehicle Support Services, Dock Road, Limerick, Ireland — 00353 (0) 872554970
County Louth: Kearns & Murtagh, Mooretown Road, Dundalk, Ireland — 00353 (0) 429322139
County Monaghan: Declan Treanor Commercials Ltd, Drumfurrer, Carrickrowe, Ireland — 00353 (0) 872593132
County Offaly: Jennings Truck Centre, Kilbeggin Road, Tullamore, Ireland — 00353 (0) 50652494
County Waterford: Pat Macarthy Car Sales, Killure Road, Waterford, Ireland — 00353 (0) 51853285
County Wicklow: Derek Burton Sales Ltd, Kilpedder, Wicklow, Ireland — 00353 (0) 12810955
County Wexford: Gethings Garage Ltd, Moyne Park Industrial Estate, Enniscorthy, Ireland — 00353 (0) 5439737
Cumbria: North East Truck & Van Ltd, 49 Parkhill Road, Kingstown Industrial Estate, Carlisle, CA3 0EX — 01228 596556
Derbyshire: Sherwood Commercial Vehicles Ltd, Berristow Lane, Blackwell, Alfreton, DE55 5HP — 01773 864019
Jeffreys Vehicle Services Ltd, Swadlincote Road, Woodville, Swadlincote, Burton On Trent, DE11 8DD — 01283 817345
Devon: Hendy Van & Truck, Grace Road Central, Marsh Barton Trading Estate, Exeter, EX2 8QA — 01392 423394
Vospers Commercial Services, Valley Road, Plympton, Plymouth, PL7 1RS — 01752 206820
Dorset: Hendy Van & Truck, Whitney Road, Nuffield Industrial Estate, Poole, BH17 0GH — 0121 677701
East Ayrshire: Kerr & Smith, Riverside Garage, Ayr Road, Cumnock, KA18 1BJ — 01290 420555

Essex: Dagenham Motors, 51 River Road, Barking, IG11 0SW — 020 8477 4020
Dagenham Motors, Cuton Hall Lane, Springfield, Chelmsford, CM2 6PB — 01245 235420
Dovercourt Motor Company Ltd, 4 Newcomen Way, Severalls Business Park, Colchester, CO4 9YR — 01206 222242
Fife: AM Phillip Limited, Blackwood Way, Bankhead Industrial Estate, Glenrothes, KY7 6JF — 01592 770739
Flintshire: Evans Halshaw, Chester Road, Bretton, Chester, CH4 0DS — 01224 661460
Gloucestershire: Bristol Street Commercials, Bristol Road, Gloucester, GL2 5YB — 01452 314909
Guernsey: Bougourd Ford, Les Grange, PO Box 168, St Peter Port, GY1 3LB, Guernsey — 01481 727894
Hampshire: Pitter Commercials Ltd, Botley Road, West End, Southampton, SO30 3HA — 023 8047 4283
Hendy Van & Truck, School Lane, Chandlers Ford Industrial Estate, Chandlers Ford, Southampton, SO53 4DG — 023 8057 9815
Hendy Van & Truck, Quartremaine Road, Portsmouth, PO3 5QH — 02392 696929
Herefordshire: Truckcare, Unit 3, Perseverance Road, Hereford, HR4 9SD — 01432 265414
Invernesshire: DMR, 35 Henderson Drive, Inverness, IV1 1TR — 01463 233283
Isle of Man: Wades Truck Services, Unit 2, Balthane Industrial Estate, Ballasalla, IM9 2AQ, Isle of Man — 01624 825708
Isle of Wight: Southern Vectis Commercials, Nelson Road, Newport, PO30 1RD, Isle of Whight — 01983 524146
Jersey: La Motte Ford, 14 Rue Des Pres Trading Estate, St Saviour, JE4 8UR, Jersey — 01534 636688
Kent: Haynes Trucks, 73-74 Ellingham Way, Ashford, TN23 6JU — 01233 667501
Haynes Trucks, Vauxhall Industrial Road, Canterbury, CT1 1HD — 01277 783479
Haynes Trucks, 23 Ashford Road, Maidstone, ME14 5DQ — 01622 753038
Stormont Truck & Van Limited, London Road, Hildenborough, Tonbridge, TN11 8NN — 01732 838072
Lanarkshire: Kerr & Smith (Glasgow) Ltd, 10, Springhill Parkway, Glasgow Business Park, Bailleston, Glasgow, G69 6GA — 0141 773 5250
Lancashire: Pye Motors Limited, Ovangle Road, Morecambe, LA3 3PF — 01524 844367
Concept Truck, Europa Park, Stoneclough Road, Radcliffe, Manchester, M26 1GG — 01204 799542
Chatfields Truck & Van, Ashton Old Road, Ardwick, Manchester, M12 6JD — 0161 2744814
Walton Summit Truck Centre Ltd, Unit 211, Walton Summit Road, Bamber Bridge, Preston, PR5 8AQ — 01772 629602
Leicestershire: Paynes Garages, Watling Street, Hinckley, LE10 3ED — 01455 237757
Chatfields, 302 Melton Road, Leicester, LE4 7SL — 0116 266 7607
Chatfields Truck & Van, Unit C, Belton Road, Chrisie Bradford Industrial Estate, Loughborough, LE11 0XH — 01509 240863
Lincolnshire: North East Truck & Van Ltd, Manby Road, Immingham, DN40 2LJ — 01469 571490
TC Harrison, Riverside Industrial Estate, Marsh Lane, Boston, PE21 7RP — 01205 367947
North East Truck & Van Ltd, Westminster Road, North Hykeham, Lincoln, LN6 3QY — 01522 812819
Merseyside: Chatfields Truck & Van, Bridle Road, Bootle, Liverpool, L30 4UG — 0151 524 3902
Middlesex: Norfolk Trucks Ltd, Mollison Avenue, Brimsdown, Enfield, EN3 7NE — 020 8970 2022
Dagenham Motors, Dawley Road, Hayes, UB3 1EH — 020 8606 1533
Mid Glamorgan: Glenside Commercials, Trecenydd Industrial Estate, Caerphilly, CF83 2RZ — 02920 858009
Dragon Truck & Van, Unit 22, Merthyr Tydfil Industrial Park, Pentrebach, Merthyr Tydfil, CF48 4DR — 01443 693162
Northamptonshire: Stormont Truck & Van Limited, Jackdaw Close, Crow Lane Industrial Estate, Great Billing, Northampton, NN3 9ER — 01604 417119
Norfolk: ARM Truck Repairs, Garage Lane Industrial Estate, Setchey, Kings Lynn, PE33 0BE — 01553 810145
Norfolk Trucks Limited, School Lane, Sprowston, Norwich, NR7 8TL — 01603 253343
North Yorkshire: North East Truck & Van Ltd, Cowpen Bewley Road, Haverton Hill, Billingham, TS23 4EX — 01642 375223
North East Truck & Van, Auster Road, Clifton Moor, York, YO30 4XA — 01904 476059
Nottinghamshire: Heage Road Vehicle Services, Newlink Business Park, Newark, NG24 2NZ — 01636 594081
Sherwood Commercial Vehicles Ltd, 522 Derby Road, Lenton, Nottingham, NG7 2GX — 0115 942 9647
Oxfordshire: Wasties Motors, A40 Northern Bypass, Eynsham, Oxford, OX29 4EF — 01865 883376
Renfrewshire: McKinnon & Forbes Ltd, 48-58 Clark Street, Paisley, PA3 1RB — 0141 889 5804
Ross-shire: AM Phillip Limited, Leanaig Road, Conon Bridge, Dingwall, IV7 8BE — 01349 866020
Shropshire: Furrows Commercial Vehicles Ltd, Halesfield 21, Telford, TF7 4NX — 01952 683517
Somerset: 9 Oxford Road, Pen Mill Industrial Estate, Yeovil, BA21 5HR — 01935 432035
Bristol Street Commercials, Cabot Park, Poplar Way West, Avonmouth, Bristol, BS11 0YW — 01179 381064
JR Harding, Handlemaker Road, Marston Trading Estate, Frome, BA11 4RJ — 01373 456411
South Glamorgan: Dragon Truck & Van Limited, Coaster Place, Rover Way, Cardiff Docks, Cardiff, CF10 4XZ — 02920 449677
South Humberside: Direct Commercial Vehicle Services, Island Car Industrial Estate, Brigg, DN20 8PD — 01652 650386
North East Truck & Van Ltd, 44 Newdown Road, South Park Industrial Estate, Bottisford, Scunthorpe, DN17 2TX — 01724 858925
South Yorkshire: Fishlake Commercials Ltd, Jubilee Bridge Works, Selby Road, Thorne, Doncaster, DN8 4JD — 01405 740931
Sherwood Commercial Vehicles Ltd, Highfield Lane, Sheffield, SL13 9DB — 01142 693338
Staffordshire: Sherwood Commercial Vehicles Ltd, Etruria Old Road, Stoke On Trent, ST1 5PE — 01782 265918
Suffolk: Brand of Beccles, Common Lane North, Beccles, NR34 9BN — 01502 717156
Norfolk Trucks Limited, Lodge Lane, Great Blakenham, Ipswich, IP6 0LB — 01473 834201
Surrey: Grays Truck & Van, 37 - 39 Imperial Way, Purley Way, Croydon, CR0 4RR — 0208 680 0678
Grays Truck & Van, Slyfield Industrial Estate, Woking Road, Guildford, GU1 1RY — 01483 546430
Sussex: Stormont Truck & Van Limited, Ellen Street, Portslade, Brighton, BN41 1DW — 01273 430891
Tyne & Wear: North East Truck & Van Ltd, Chainbridge Road, Blaydon-on-Tyne, Newcastle, NE21 5TR — 0191 4140850
Warwickshire: Guest Trucks, Kingswood Close, Holbrook, Coventry, CV6 4BJ — 02476 584 486
Malen Ltd, Sydenham Drive, Leamington Spa, CV31 1PH — 01926 430625
West Lothian: AM Phillip Limited, Simpson Road, East Mains Industrial Estate, Broxburn, EH52 5NP — 01506 865005
West Midlands: Guest Trucks, 31 Shefford Road, Aston, Birmingham, B6 4PQ — 0121 359 3337
Guest Trucks, Kenrick Way, West Bromwich, B70 6BY — 0121 5536482

Guest Trucks, 55 Willenhall Road, Wolverhampton, WV1 2HL	01902 351779
West Sussex: Lifestyle Ford, 53-55 Bishopric, Horsham, RH12 1QJ	01403 249481
North East Truck & Van, Staithes Road, Hedon Road, Horsham, HU12 8DX	01482 895858
West Yorkshire: Northern Commercials (Mirfield) Ltd, Armytage Road, Brighouse, HD6 1PG	01484 380444
Knottingley Trucks Limited, Altofts Lane, Wakefield Europort, Castleford, WF10 5UB	01924 227778
Northern Commercials, Albert Road, Morley, Leeds, LS27 8TT	0113 238 1707
Wiltshire: Chambers Engineering Limited, Warmstone Works, Warmstone Road, Waddesdon, Aylesbury, HP18 0NF	01296 651498
Edwards Commercials, Stephenson Road, Churchfield Industrial Estate, Salisbury, SP2 7NP	01722 328602
Bristol Street Commercials, Marshgate Trading Estate, Stratton Road, Swindon, SN1 2PA	01793 421601
Worcestershire: Brooklyn Ford Redditch, Battens Drive, Redditch, B98 0LJ	01527 405051
Worcester Truck Services, Unit 16a, Blackpole East, Blackpole Road, Worcester, WR3 8SG	01905 753206

MAN/ERF, Frankland Road, Blagrove, Swindon, Wiltshire, SN5 8YU
Tel: 01793 448000, Fax: 01793 448265 www.man.co.uk
EUROSERVICE 24 (MAN): Freefone 0800 0287728 or 01793 448044
EUROSERVICE 24 (ERF): Freefone 0800 424333 or 01793 448044

Aberdeenshire: Aberdeen MAN ERF, Minto Road, Altens Industrial Estate, Aberdeen, AB12 3LU	01224 895968
Elgin Truck & Van Centre Ltd, Grampian Road, Elgin, IV30 1XN	01343 552277
Bedfordshire: John Arnold Commercials, Kenneth Way, Wilstead Industrial Park, Bedford, MK45 3PD	01234 743090
Imperial Commercials Ltd, Unit 10, Finway, Dallow Road Industrial Estate, Luton, LU1 1TR	01582 481720
Buckinghamshire: Ring Road Garage, Gawcott Road, Buckingham, MK18 1DR	01280 815684
Cambridgeshire: Welch Group (Commercial), Granta Terrace, Stapleford, Cambridge, CB2 5DL	01223 847021
Imperial Commercials Ltd, Fengate, Peterborough, PE1 5XG	01733 891122
Carmarthenshire: W G Davies (Landore) Ltd, Unit 11, St, David's Road, Morriston Enterprise Park, Morriston, Swansea, SA6 8QL	01792 797823
Cheshire: P & K Truck Centre, Catalyst Trade Park, Waterloo Road, Widnes, WA8 0WG	0151 420 4638
Cleveland: Stockton MAN ERF, Bowesfield Lane, Stockton on Tees, TS18 3HJ	01642 618430
Beech's Garage (1983) Ltd, Shelton New Road, Cliffe Vale, Stoke-on-Trent, ST4 7DL	01782 844200
Clwyd: A N Richards, The Garage, Froncysyllte, Llangollen, Wrexham, LL20 7RA	01691 774201
Cornwall: Patrick Uren Commercials (Fraddon), Moorlands Road, Indian Queens, St Columb, TR9 6HN	01726 860717
Patrick Uren Commercials, 17 Jon Davey Drive, Treleigh Industrial Estate, Redruth, TR16 4AX	01209 313399
County Antrim: R K Trucks Centre Ltd, Edgar Road, Comber Road, Carryduff, Belfast, BT8 8NB, Northern Ireland	028 9081 4115
County Tyrone: R K Trucks Centre Ltd, 126 Tamnamore Road, Dungannon, BT71 6HW, Northern Ireland	028 8772 7393
Cumbria: North East Truck and Van Limited, 49 Park Hill Road, Kingstown Industrial Estate, Carlisle, CA3 0EX	01228 596555
Derbyshire: Jeffrey's Vehicle Services, Swadlincote Road, Woodville, Swadlincote, DE11 8DD	01283 817345
Imperial Commercials Ltd, Ashbourne Road, Mackworth, Derby, DE22 4NB	01332 824114
HRVS Group, Heage Road Industrial Estate, Heage Road, Ripley, DE5 3GH	01773 741599
Devon: S A Trucks Ltd, Peamore Truck Centre, Alphington, Exeter, EX2 9SL	01392 832909
S A Trucks Ltd (c/o Shell Workshops), Cattedown Road, Cattedown Wharf, Plymouth, PL4 0RW	01752 256793
Dorset: E T S Trucks Ltd, Unit H3, Dawkins Road Industrial Estate, Hamworthy, Poole, BH15 4JP	01202 669918
Essex: Colchester MAN ERF, Westside Centre, London Road, Stanway, Colchester, CO3 5PB	01206 213444
Purfleet Commercials Ltd, 520 London Road, West Thurrock, Grays, RM20 3BE	01708 868226
Falkirk: Grangemouth MAN ERF, Dalgrain Industrial Estate, Grangemouth, FK3 8EB	01324 665323
Gloucestershire: Richard Read (Commercials) Ltd, Monmouth Road, Longhope, Gloucester, GL17 0QG	01452 831422
Greater London: Enfield MAN ERF, Crown Road, Off Southbury Road, Enfield, EN1 1TH	020 8443 3838
Allied Commercials, 4 Atcost Road, Off River Road, Creekmouth, IG11 0EQ	020 8594 7608
Gwent: Commercial Motors, Frederick Street, Newport, NP20 2DR	01633 220543
Hampshire: Harwoods Truck Centre Ltd, Majestic Road, Nursling Industrial Estate, Southampton, SO16 0YT	023 8074 0442
Harwoods Truck Centre Ltd, Nutsey Lane, Southampton, SO40 3NB	023 8066 6284
Kent: Aylesford MV Trucks, New Hythe Lane, Aylesford, ME20 7PW	01622 790249
Lanarkshire: Bellshill MAN ERF, Clark Way, Motherwell Food Park, Bellshill, ML4 3NX	01698 327894
Glasgow MAN ERF, 30 Clydesmill Drive, Clydesmill Industrial Estate, Cambuslang, Glasgow, G32 8RG	0141 641 0493
Lancashire: Steadplan Limited, Salthill Industrial Estate, Lincoln Way, Clitheroe, BB7 1QL	01200 422719
Manchester MAN ERF, Irlam Wharf Road, Northbank Industrial Estate, Manchester, M44 5PN	0161 776 7720
Manchester MAN ERF, Trafford Park Road, Trafford Park, Manchester, M17 1NJ	0161 872 8334
Preston ERF, 69 Walton Summit Road, Walton Summit, Preston, PR5 8AQ	01772 313216
Lincolnshire: R & A Scott Autoservices Ltd, 5 Sandars Road, Heapham Road Industrial Estate, Gainsborough, DN21 1RZ	01427 614255
DSV Commercials Ltd, Estate Road Number 2, South Humberside Industrial Estate, Grimsby, DN31 2TG	01472 250995
Merseyside: P & K Service Centre, Yew Tree Trading Estate, Kilbuck Lane, Haydock, St Helens, WA11 9UX	01942 274589
Middlesex: Cordwallis Group, Great South West Road, Bedfont, TW14 8ND	020 8582 6031
Northamptonshire: Northampton MAN ERF, 14 Gambrel Road, Westgate Industrial Estate, Weedon Road, Northampton, NN5 5BB	01604 587040
North Humberside: East Yorkshireman Trucks Ltd, 67 Gillett Street, Witty Street, Hull, HU3 4JF	01482 321233
Chatfields, Littlefair Road (off Hedon Road), Hull, HU9 5LP	01482 790877
North Yorkshire: Fishlake Commercial Motors Ltd, Jubilee Bridge Works, Selby Road, Thorne, Doncaster, DN8 4JD	01405 740931
North Yorkshire Commercials, Dalton Industrial Estate, Dalton, Thirsk, YO7 3HE	01845 577586
Nottinghamshire: M V Trucks, Salfords Industrial Estate, Salford, Redhill, RH1 5ES	01293 786379
HRVS Group, Newlink Business Park, Newark, NG24 2NA	01636 594081

Norfolk: Imperial Commercials Ltd, Barnard Road, Bowthorpe, Norwich, NR5 9JB	01603 741742
Oxfordshire: Cordwallis Group, Oakfield Industrial Estate, Stanton Harcourt Road, Eynsham, Oxford, OX29 4TH	01865 882012
Perth & Kinross: Fife MAN ERF, Cross Gate Road, Halbeath, Fife, KY11 7EG	01383 625217
Somerset: SMV Commercials, Lynx West Trading Estate, Yeovil, BA20 2HP	01935 432353
South Glamorgan: W G Davies, Newlands Road, Wentloog Corporate Park, Cardiff, CF3 2EU	029 2079 6423
South Gloucestershire: S A Trucks, Third Way, Avonmouth, Bristol, BS11 9YS	0117 916 0497
South Humberside: Scunthorpe MAN ERF, Ermine Street, Brigg, Nr Broughton, Scunthorpe, DN20 0AQ	01652 658659
South Yorkshire: Sheffield MAN ERF, Shepcote Lane, Sheffield, S9 1TX	0114 256 0145
Suffolk: Felixstow MAN ERF, Bryon Avenue, Felixstowe, IP11 8HZ	01394 675618
Tyne and Wear: Gateshead MAN ERF, Earlsway, Team Valley Trading Estate, Gateshead, NE11 0RQ	0191 421 5098
Warwickshire: Nuneaton MAN ERF, Harrington Way, Bermuda Park, Nuneaton, CV10 7SA	024 7635 7810
West Lothian: Broxburn Man Erf, Westerton Road, East Mains Industrial Estate, Broxburn, EH52 5DE	01506 857332
West Midlands: Aquila Truck Centres Ltd, Chimney Road, Great Bridge, Tipton, DY4 7BY	0121 520 1800
Aquila Truck Centres Ltd, Westgate, Aldridge, Walsall, WS9 8EZ	01922 743356
West Yorkshire: Croft Fleet Maintenance (Leeds) Ltd, 126 Gelderd Close, Gelderd Road, Leeds, LS12 6DS	0113 279 3911
Chatfields, Royds Farm Road, Gelderd Road, Leeds, LS12 6DX	0113 238 9998
Wiltshire: Cordwallis Group, Frankland Road, Blagrove, Swindon, SN5 8YU	01793 614360
S A Trucks Ltd, 24 Headquarters Road, West Wilts Trading Estate Westbury, BA13 4JR	01373 858656
Worcestershire: Worcester Truck Services, Blackpole Trading Estate, Worcester, WR3 8SG	01905 753206

Mercedes-Benz, Charter Way, Burystead Court, Caldecotte Lake Drive, Caldecotte, Milton Keynes, MK7 8ND
Tel: 0870 840500, Fax: 0870 8409000, www.mercedes-benz.com
Mercedes 24 Hour: 00800 17777777

Aberdeenshire: John R Weir Truck & Van Centre, Hareness Road, Aberdeen, AB12 3LE	01224 894848
Angus: John R Weir Dundee, Kings Cross Road, Dundee, DD2 3PT	01382 576601
Ayrshire: Caledonian Trucks, Whitfield Drive, Ayr, KA8 9RX	01292 611170
Berkshire: Rygor Commercials Wokingham, Molly Millars Lane, Wokingham, RG41 2RX	0118 9772605
Buckinghamshire: Hughes of Aylesbury, Bicester Road, Aylesbury, HP19 8BL	01296 392310
Intercounty Truck & Van (M Keynes), 8 Fingle Drive, Milton Keynes, MK13 0AY	01908 228201
Cambridgeshire: Intercounty Truck & Van (P'borough), Broadway Business Park, Peterborough, PE7 3EN	01733 244734
Fengate Commercials Mercedes-Benz Authorised Repairer, Bretton Way, Peterborough, PE3 8YQ	01733 263232
Carmarthenshire: Euro Commercials Swansea, Viking Way, Swansea, SA1 7DA	01792 526527
Cheshire: Enza Motors Warrington, Leacroft Road, Risley, WA3 6NN	01925 838628
Cleveland: Bell Truck Sales Billingham, Macklin Avenue, Billingham, TS23 4BY	01642 561999
Clwyd: Road Range Commercials (Deeside), Link 56 Weighbridge Road, Deeside, CH5 2LL	01244 288916
Cornwall: Commercial Motors (South West) Ltd, Bucklers Lane, St Austell, PL25 3JL	01726 874210
County Antrim: Mercedes-Benz Truck and Van (NI), 45-47 Mallusk Road, Newtownabbey, BT36 4PJ, Northern Ireland	02890 831977
County Durham: Bell Truck Sales Birtley, Portobello Road, Birtley, DH3 2SH	0191 4109138
Bell Truck Sales Spennymoor, Coulson Street, Spennymoor, DL16 7RS	01388 810943
County Tyrone: Trevor Haydock Limited, 104 Bush Road, Dungannon, BT71 6QG, Northern Ireland	02887 752111
Cumbria: Ciceley Commercials Carlisle, Peterfield Road, Carlisle, CA3 0EY	01228 546720
Devon: Commercial Motors South West (Exeter), Heron Road, Exeter, EX2 7LL	01392 211730
Western Truck Rental, Roundswell Industrial Estate, Barnstaple, EX31 3NL	01271 344661
Dorset: Pentagon Poole, Cabot Lane - Brunel Way, Poole, BH17 7BX	01202 658183
Dumfrieshire: Ciceley Commercials Dumfries, Brownrigg Loaning, Dumfries, DG1 3JU	01387 250622
East Sussex: Rossetts Commercials Eastbourne, 7 Birch Road, Eastbourne, BN23 6PD	01323 761235
Essex: Orwell Truck & Van - Colchester, Heckworth Close, Brunel Way, Colchester, CO4 9TB	01206 751552
S & B Commercials - West Thurrock, Central Avenue, West Thurrock, RM20 3WD	01708 892555
Gloucester: Mudie-Bond (Tewkesbury), Newtown Trading Estate, Tewkesbury, GL20 8JG	01684 850616
Greater London: S G Smith (Motors) Forest Hill Ltd, 812 Old Kent Road, London, SE15 1NH	0207 6394956
Gwent: Euro Commercials Newport, Traston Garage, Newport, NP19 4RD	01633 284939
Hampshire: Pentagon Andover, Scott Close, Andover, SP10 5NU	01264 332817
Pentagon Fareham, Standard Way, Fareham, PO16 8XL	01329 823432
Pentagon Southampton (MBCV After Sales), Unit A, Andes Road, Southampton, SO16 0Y2	02380 735021
Rossetts Commercials Aldershot, Unit 1, Aldershot, GU12 4TD	01252 245522
Rygor Newbury, Unit 13 Hambridge Lane, Newbury, RG14 5TU	01635 528140
Hertfordshire: S & B Commercials Stansted, Start Hill, Bishop's Stortford, CM22 7DW	01279 712260
S & B Commercials, Travellers Close, Hatfield, AL9 7JL	01707 274546
Invernesshire: John R Weir Inverness, Longman Road, Inverness, IV1 1RY	01463 230613
Kent: Sparshatts Kent (Dartford), Unit H Acorn Industrial Estate, Dartford, DA1 4FL	01322 520039
Sparshatts of Kent Ltd (Ashford), Leacon Road, Ashford, TN23 4TU	01233 610401
Sparshatts of Kent Ltd (Sittingbourne), Unit 10, Sittingbourne, ME10 3RN	01795 428976
Sparshatts of Kent Ltd (Tonbridge Wells), Longfield Road, Tunbridge Wells, TN2 3EY	01892 531813
Lanarkshire: Western Commercial Bellshill, Site C1 Melford Road, Bellshill, Glasgow, ML4 3LR	01698 498998
Western Commercial Glasgow, 260 Broomloan Road, Govan, Glasgow, G51 2JQ	0141 2725001
Lancashire: Ciceley Commercials Blackburn, Commercial Road, Darwen, BB3 0DB	01254 870980

Ciceley Commercials Preston, Mercedes Benz House, Preston, PR1 4HH	01772 201423
Ciceley Truck & Van Centre, Weston Street, Bolton, BL3 2BZ	01204 380382
Enza Motors Salford, 207 - 221 Bury New Road, Manchester, M8 8DU	0161 7080521
Enza Motors Trafford Park, 117 Trafford Park Road, Manchester, M17 1HG	0161 8737067
North Manchester Commercials Mercedes-Benz Authorised Repairer, Briscoe Lane, Manchester, M40 2NL	0161 2306801
Lincolnshire: H & L Garages Boston, Lealand Way, Boston, PE21 7FW	01205 311277
H & L Garages Lincoln, Wrightsway, Lincoln, LN2 4JY	01522 524777
Merseyside: Road Range Commercials (Liverpool), Rathbone Road, Liverpool, L13 1BA	0151 2828800
Middlesex: Rygor Commercials Heathrow, Stanwell Road, Feltham, TW14 8NW	0208 8903031
Mid Glamorgan: Euro Commercials Bridgend, Brynmenyn Industrial Estate, Bridgend, CF32 9TD	01656 304305
Norfolk: Orwell Truck & Van - Norwich, 39 Hurricane Way, Norwich, NR6 6HE	01603 428038
Northamptonshire: Intercounty Truck and Van Limited, Finedon Road Industrial Estate, Wellingborough, NN8 4TR	01933 232601
North Humberside: H & L Garages Hull, Henry Boot Way, Hull, HU4 7DY	01482 577799
North Somerset: Commercial Motors South West (Bristol), 12 Vale Lane, Bristol, BS3 5RU	01179 669902
North Yorkshire: H & L Garages York, Outgang Lane, York, YO19 5UP	01904 427634
Oxfordshire: Mudie-Bond (Oxford), Eynsham Road, Oxford, OX29 4DD	01865 880577
Somerset: Commercial Motors South West (Yeovil), Oxford Road, Yeovil, BA21 5HR	01935 426801
Mercedes-Benz of Weston-super-Mare, Bridge Road, Weston super Mare, BS23 3NE	01934 641717
South Glamorgan: Euro Commercials Cardiff, Ipswich Road, Cardiff, CF23 9AQ	02920 310311
South Gloucestershire: Commercial Motors South West (Avonmouth), Kings Weston Lane, Avonmouth, BS11 9BY	01179 825685
South Humberside: H & L Garages Immingham, Humber Road, Immingham, DN40 3DL	01469 571774
H & L Garages Scunthorpe, Grange Lane North, Scunthorpe, DN16 1BT	01724 868493
South Yorkshire: Northside Truck & Van Ltd (Doncaster), Balby Carr Bank, Doncaster, DN4 8DE	01302 368972
Northside Truck and Van Ltd Sheffield, Amberley Street, Sheffield, S9 2LU	01142 617354
Staffordshire: Enza Motors Stoke, Chemical Lane, Stoke-on-Trent, ST6 4PB	01782 575574
Suffolk: Orwell Truck & Van - Ipswich, 28 Betts Avenue, Ipswich, IP5 3RH	01473 610631
Orwell Truck & Van - Newmarket, Fordham Road, Newmarket, CB8 7LG	01638 721405
Surrey: S G Smith CV Croydon, Unit 2 Beddington Cross, Beddington, CR0 4XH	0208 6650011
Rossetts Commercials Crawley, Unit 1 Manor Gate, Crawley, RH10 9SX	01293 652564
Rossetts Commercials Guildford, Unit 1a, Guildford, GU2 7YB	01252 345522
Tyne & Wear: Bell Truck Sales, North East Fruit & Veg Market, Gateshead, NE11 0QY	0191 4971161
Bell Truck Sales Longbenton, Bellway Industrial Estate, Longbenton, Newcastle-upon-Tyne, NE12 9SW	0191 2664780
West Lothian: Western Commercial Edinburgh, 8 Simpson Road, Broxburn, EH52 5NP	01506 208091
West Midlands: Gerard Mann Birmingham, 2 Lichfield Road, Birmingham, B6 5SU	0121 3264330
Gerard Mann Coventry, Wheler Road, Coventry, CV3 4LA	024 76305231
Gerard Mann Wolverhampton, Neachells Lane, Wolverhampton, WV13 3RP	01902 602818
West Sussex: Rossetts Commercials Worthing, Meadow Road Industrial Estate, Worthing, BN11 2RU	01903 223404
West Yorkshire: Northside Truck and Van Ltd Bradford, Legrams Lane, Bradford, BD7 2HR	01274 521256
Northside Truck and Van Ltd Leeds, Elland Way, Leeds, LS11 0EY	0113 2760068
Wiltshire: Rygor Commercials Swindon, Hunts Rise, Swindon, SN3 4TG	01793 821822
Rygor Commercials Westbury, The Broadway, Westbury, BA13 4JX	01373 855535
Worcestershire: Mudie-Bond (Kidderminster), No 3 Road, Kidderminster, DY10 1HY	01562 756235

RENAULT, Boscombe Road, Dunstable, Bedfordshire, LU5 4LX
Tel: 01582 471122, www.renault-trucks.com
RENAULT TRUCKS 24/24: 0800 626541

Aberdeenshire: Alex Aiken And Son Limited (Aberdeen), Greenbank Crescent, East Tullos Industrial Estate, Aberdeen, AB12 3BG	01224 891465
Alex Aiken And Son Limited (Peterhead), Damhead Way, Peterhead, AB42 3GY	01779 481030
Argyll & Bute: John Allan Motors Ltd, Lockavullin Industrial Estate, Oban, PA34 4SE	01631 571158
Bedfordshire: Renault Trucks Chiltern, Luton Road, Dunstable, LU5 4QF	01582 478250
Fleet Commercial Services Ltd, Units 5 & 6, Greenend Industrial Estate, Gamblingay, Sandy, SG19 3LB	01767 654100
Berkshire: Renault Trucks South (Reading), Bennet Road, Reading, RG2 0QX	0118 931 3040
Cambridgeshire: Manchetts Commercials, 1 Ness Road, Burwell, CB5 0AA	01638 742966
Welch Group (Cambridge), Granta Terrace, Stapleford, CB2 5DL	01223 847021
Fengate Commercial Services Ltd, Bretton Way, North Bretton, Peterborough, PE3 8YQ	01733 336451
County Antrim: Coulter Truck & Van (Newtownabbey), Commercial Way, Mallusk, Newtownabbey, BT36 8UB	02890 842237
County Armagh: Coulter Truck & Van Portadown, 11 Vicarage Road, Portadown, BT62 4HF, Northern Ireland	02838 398779
County Cork: Transport Services (Ballyvolane) Ltd, Sarsfield Court Industrial Estate, Glanmire, Ireland	00353 2148 23309
County Tipperary: Surehaul Commercials, Ballylynch, Carrick-on-Suir, Ireland,	00353 5164 0429
Cumbria: Border Trucks Ltd, 20b Millbrook Road, Kingstown Industrial Estate, Carlisle, CA3 0EU	01228 590365
Deeside: Imperial Commercials Ltd, Factory Road, Engineers Park, Sandycroft, CH5 2QJ	01244 520834
Devon: Renault Trucks South West (Exeter), Dunns Business Centre, Trusham Road, Marsh Barton, Exeter, EX2 8RL	01392 422116
Plymstock Commercials, Unit 14, Central Avenue, Lee Mill Industrial Estate, Ivybridge, PL21 9ER	01752 201591
Dorset: W Belben Commercials Ltd, 73 Ringwood Road, Parkstone, Poole, BH14 0RG	01202 740055
Dublin: Setanta Vehicle Sales Ltd, Unit 19-21, Parkmoor Industrial Estate, Long Mile Road, Dublin 12, Ireland	00353 1403 4599

East Sussex: Mick Gould Commercials Ltd, The Royal Oak Garage, London Road, Flimwell, TN5 7PJ — 01580 879377
  MV Trucks (Brighton), 53 Victoria Road, Portslade, Brighton, BN41 1XP — 01273 424160
Essex: Renault Trucks Essex, Weston Avenue, Waterglade Industrial Estate, West Thurrock, RM20 3FZ — 01708 681375
Greater London: MV Trucks (Croydon), 1-2 Felnex Industrial Estate, 190 London Road, Hackbridge, SM6 7EL
Greater Manchester: JDS Trucks (Manchester), Broadway, Salford Quays, Salford, M50 2UW — 0161 786 8155
Guernsey: Rabeys Commercial Vehicles, PO Box 507, Vale Industrial Estate, North Side, Vale, GY1 6DP, Guernsey — 01481 248825
Hampshire: Sparks Commercials (Portsmouth) Ltd, Quartermaine Road, Copnor, Portsmouth, PO3 5QG — 02392 699501
  Renault Trucks South (Southampton), North Road, Marchwood Industrial Park, Marchwood, — 023 8066 0567
  Southampton, SO40 4BL
Hertfordshire: Valley Trucks Ltd, Bingley Road, Hoddesdon, EN11 0NX — 01992 470669
Jersey: Rabeys Universal Ltd, La Grande Route de St Martin, Five Oaks, St Saviour, JE2 7GR, Jersey — 01534 862549
Kent: KTS Trucks Ltd, East Kent International Freight Terminal, Dargate, Faversham, ME13 9EN — 01227 751515
  MV Trucks (Maidstone), New Hythe Lane, Aylesford, Maidstone, ME20 7PW — 01622 711094
Lancashire: Coulters Truck & Van (Haydock), Unit H1, Haydock Cross Industrial Estate, Kilbuck Lane, St Helens, WA11 9UX — 01942 290008
  Woodwards Truck and Van Centre, Stephens Way, Warrington Road Industrial Estate, Goose Green, Wigan, WN3 6PQ — 01942 826026
  JDS Trucks (Blackburn), Forrest Street, Furthergate Business Park, Blackburn, BB1 3BB — 01254 297255
  JDS Trucks (Oldham), Broadgate, Broadway Business Park, Chadderton, Oldham, OL9 9NL — 0161 947 1455
Leeds: JDS Trucks (Leeds), Howley Park Road, Howley Park Ind. Estate, Morley, LS27 0BN — 0113 393 6755
Lincolnshire: Clugston Distribution Ltd, Brigg Road, Scunthorpe, DN16 1BB — 01724 281714
  Thompson Commercials (Boston), Baythorpe, Boston Road, Swineshead, PE20 3HB — 01205 821577
  Thompson Commercials (Grimsby), Estate Road No 5, South Humberside Ind Est, Grimsby, DN31 2TG — 01472 241502
London: Renault Trucks London, 37/43 Gorst Road, Park Royal, NW10 6LA — 020 8961 8590
Middlesex: MTHL Fleet Services, 391 Viscount Way, Heathrow Airport, Hatton, TW6 2JD — 0208 8972346
Midlothian: David Philp Commercials Ltd, Camps Industrial Estate, Kirknewton, EH27 8DF — 01506 882197
Morayshire: Baillie Bros.(Truck Services), Linkwood Industrial Estate, Elgin, IV30 1HZ — 01343 555310
Newtownabbey: Coulter Truck & Van Mallusk, Commercial Way, Mallusk, BT36 8UB , Northern Ireland — 02890 842237
Nottinghamshire: Truck & Trailer Care UK Ltd, Unit L, Lodge Lane Industrial Estate, Lodge Lane, Tuxford, NG22 0NL — 01777 870033
Norfolk: Kenny Commercials, Unit 4 Rollesby Road, Hardwick Industrial Estate, King's Lynn, PE30 4LS — 01553 660448
Northamptonshire: Renault Trucks Wellingborough, Ise Valley Industrial Estate, Finedon Road, Wellingborough, NN8 4BJ — 01933 271961
  Gerald White Group, Banbury Road, Kislingbury, Northampton, NN7 4AW — 01604 833000
  Shires Vee and Inline Ltd, Royal Oak Way North, Royal Oak Industrial Estate, Daventry, NN11 8PQ — 01327 703281
Northern Ireland: Coulter Truck & Van (Portadown), 11 Vicarage Road, Portadown, BT62 4HF — 02838 398779
North Humberside: Thompson Commercials (Hull), Salvesen Way, Clive Sullivan Way, Hull, HU3 4UQ — 01482 322449
North Lanarkshire: Scot Truck Limited (Bellshill), James Street, Righead Industrial Estate, Glasgow, ML4 3LU — 0845 241 1301
North Yorkshire: Thompson Commercials (Teeside), Nuffield Road, Cowpen Lane Ind Estate, Billingham, Cleveland, TS23 4DA — 01642 565520
  Thompson Commercials (Boroughbridge), Clay Pit Lane, Roecliffe, Boroughbridge, YO51 9LS — 01423 320800
  Ebor Trucks, Brockett Industrial Estate, Acaster Airfield, Acaster Malbis Way, York, YO2 1VY — 01904 708373
Nottinghamshire: RH Commercial Vehicles Ltd, Lenton Lane, Nottingham, NG7 2NR — 0115 943 8056
Oxfordshire: Bicester Commercial Garages Ltd, Unit 40, Murdock Road, Bicester, OX26 4PP — 01869 321064
  Wootton Trucks Ltd, Unit 28, Nuffield Way, Ashville Trading Estate, Abingdon, OX14 1XZ — 01235 531835
Renfrewshire: Scot Truck Limited (Glasgow), Penilee Road, Hillington Ind Est, Bellshill, Glasgow, G52 4UW — 0141 810 5193
Shropshire: Perry's Of Gobowen, Ifton Industrial Estate, Colliery Road, St Martins, Oswestry, SY11 3DA — 01691 770399
Somerset: A.E.George & Sons, Ltd, Brewham Road Depot, Bruton, BA10 0JH — 01749 812321
South Glamorgan: Englands Truck Care, Hadfield Road, Cardiff, CF11 8AQ — 029 2023 1411
South Gloucestershire: Renault Trucks South West (Bristol), Fifth Way, Avonmouth, Bristol, BS11 8DT — 0117 923 5323
South Yorkshire: Thompson Commercials (Sheffield), Hydra Business Park, Nether Lane, Ecclesfield, Sheffield, S35 9ZX — 0114 240 1600
Staffordshire: Staffordshire C V, Bute Street, Fenton, Stoke-On-Trent, ST4 3PS — 01782 598674
  Allports Truck Centre, Westhill Road, Fradley Park, Lichfield, WS13 8NG — 01543 420122
Suffolk: Renault Trucks Felixstowe, Sub Station Road, Felixstowe, IP11 3JB — 01394 673911
  Roy Humphrey Car & Commercial, A140 Ipswich Road, Eye, IP23 8AW — 01379 871333
Tyne and Wear: Thompson Commercials (Tyneside), Wesley Way, Benton Square Industrial Estate, Newcastle upon Tyne, NE12 9TA — 0191 2702990
Warwickshire: Malen Ltd, Soans Site, Sydenham Drive, Leamington Spa, CV31 1PH — 01926 468696
West Midlands: Renault Trucks Midlands (Tipton), Power Way, Black Country New Road, Tipton, DY4 0PW — 0121 505 0333
Wiltshire: Complete Trucks, 15 Hunts Rise, South Marston Park, Swindon, SN3 4TE — 01793 832600

SCANIA, Scania GB Ltd, Delaware Drive, Tongwell, Milton Keynes, MK15 8HB
Tel: 01908 210210, Fax: 01908 215040, www.scania.co.uk
SCANIA ASSISTANCE: 0800 800 660 (IF IN UK), 0044 127 430 1260 (IF ABROAD)

Aberdeenshire: Scania Ltd, Blackness Road, Altens Industrial Estate, Aberdeen, AB12 3LH — 44(0)1224 896312
Angus: Scania Ltd, Maryfields Goods Yard, 96 Clepington Road, Dundee, DD4 7DF — 01382 455556
Bedfordshire: Pip Bayleys Ltd, Unit 5, The Ridgeway, Blunham, MK44 3DE — 01767 641111
Berkshire: Scania Ltd, Daytona Drive, Colthrop, Thatcham, RG19 4ZD — 01635 87 11 57
Buckinghamshire: TruckEast Ltd, Chesney Wold, Bleak Hall, Milton Keynes, MK6 1LP — 01908 242448
Cambridgeshire: TruckEast Ltd, 42 Lancaster Way, Lancaster Way Business Park, Ely, CB6 3NW — 01353 66 65 03
  TruckEast Ltd, Forty Acre Road, Boongate, Peterborough, PE1 5PS — 01733 55 52 33

TruckEast Ltd, Hamlin Way, Hardwick Narrows, Kings Lynn, PE30 4NG	01553 77 18 77
Cheshire: Scania Ltd, North Road , Ellesmere Port, CH65 1BW	0151 355 0199
West Pennine Trucks Ltd, 140 Moss Lane, Macclesfield, SK11 7YT	01625 869208
Clwyd: Deeside Truck Service, Pinfold Lane, Alltami, Mold, CH7 6NY	01244 547202
Cornwall: Scania Ltd, Jon Davey Drive, Treleigh Industrial Estate, Redruth, TR16 4AX	01209 310090 Parts: 0845 600605
County Antrim: Road Trucks Ltd, Circular Road, Larne, BT40 3AB , Northern Ireland	028 2827 9611
County Down: Granco, 26 Downshire Road, Newry, BT34 1EE , Northern Ireland	028 302 66335
County Durham: Scania Ltd, Whessoe Road, Darlington, DL3 0XE	01325 480713
County Tyrone: Road Trucks Ltd, Gortrush Ind Est, Great Northern Road, Omagh, BT78 5LU, Northern Ireland	028 8225 9198
Cumbria: Graham Commercials Ltd, Kingstown Broadway, Kingstown Industrial Estate, Carlisle, CA3 0HA	01228 529149
Devon: Scania Ltd, Unit E, Denbury Court, Off Silverton Road, Matford Business Park, Marsh Barton, Exeter, EX2 8NB	01392 824474
Dorset: Scania Ltd, 543 Wallisdown Road, Poole, BH12 5AD	01202 53 39 78
Dumfriesshire: Scania Ltd, Heathhall Industrial. Estate, Dumfries, DG1 3PH	01387 25 05 02
Dyfed: Silurian Scania, Cross Hands Business Park, Cross Hands, Llanelli, SA14 6RB	01269 844855
East Sussex: Scania Ltd, 28 Cliffe Industrial Estate, Lewes, BN8 6JL	01273 479123
Essex: French Marine Motors, 61/65 Waterside, Brightlingsea, CO7 0AX	01206 302 133
Scania Ltd, Ensign Estate, Arterial Road, Purfleet, RM16 1TB	01708 257400
TruckEast Ltd, Unit 5, Moss Road, Witham Industrial Estate, Witham, CM8 3UQ	01376 50 30 03
Gloucestershire: Keltruck Ltd, Golden Valley, Gloucester Road, Cheltenham, GL51 0TT	01242 252 140 Parts: 01242 582 111
Gwent: Silurian Scania, Unit 55, Symonds Cliffe Way, Severn Bridge Industrial Estate, Caldicot, NP26 5PT	01291 431715
Hampshire: Apas Engineering, Unit 4, Shamrock Quay-William St, Wolsten, Southampton, SO14 5QL	01703 632 558
Golden Arrow Marine Ltd, Saxon Wharf, Lower York Street, Northam, SO14 5QF	02380 710 371
Scania Ltd, 9 Whittle Avenue, Segensworth West, Fareham, PO15 5SH	01489 886800
Scania Ltd, Unit C, Andes Road, Nursling Ind. Est, Southampton, SO16 0YZ	02380 734455
Hertfordshire: Scania Ltd, Bignell's Corner, St. Albans Road, South Mimms, EN6 3NG	01707 64 99 55
Scania Ltd, Goodrich , Ross-on-Wye, HR9 6EG	01600 891257
Scania Ltd, Unit B, Stansted Distribution Centre, Start Hill, Great Hallingbury, Bishop's Stortford, CM22 7DG	01279 758088
Invernesshire: Scania Ltd, Unit 1a, Henderson Road, Longman Ind Est, Inverness, IV1 1SN	01463 729400
Kent: Scania Ltd, 15a Eurolink Industrial Estate, Sittingbourne, ME10 3RN	01795 430 304
Scania Ltd, Pike Road Industrial Estate, Pike Road, Tilmanstone, Dover, CT15 4ND	Workshop: 01304 831730
Lanarkshire: Scania Ltd, Melford Road, Righead Ind. Est. , Bellshill, ML4 3LF	01698 841288
Lancashire: Halebank Scania, Pickerings Road,Halebank Ind Est, Halebank, WA8 8XW	0151 423 8601
Haydock Commercial Vehicles Ltd, Haydock Cross, Kilbuck Lane, Haydock, WA11 9XW	01942 71 41 03
Preston Scania, Four Oaks Road, Walton Summit Centre, Bamber Bridge, PR5 8BW	01772 69 88 11
SJB Sales & Service, T.N.T. Garage, Hornby Road, Caton, LA2 9JA	01524 77 04 39
West Pennine Trucks Ltd, Unit 1, Circle South, John Gilbert Way, Trafford Park, Manchester, M17 1NF	0161 877 77 08
West Pennine Trucks Ltd, Stakehill Industrial Park , Middleton, M24 2RW	0161 653 97 00
Leicestershire: Keltruck Ltd, Bilton Way, Lutterworth, LE17 4JA	01455 550740
Keltruck Ltd, Midland Distribution Centre, Markfield Road, Groby, LE6 0FS	01530 24 31 33
Lincolnshire: Scania Ltd, Main Road , Wigtoft, PE20 2NX	01205 46 08 41
Scania Ltd, Plot 5, Whisby Way, Whisby Road Industrial Estate, Lincoln, LN6 3LQ	01522 681222
Scania Ltd, Wardentree Lane, Pinchbeck, Spalding, PE11 3UG	01775 713707 Truck Rental: 01775 717461
Merseyside: James Troop & Co Ltd, Pleasant Hill Street, Liverpool, L8 5SZ	01517 090 581
Middlesex: Scania Ltd, Crane Road, off Bedfont Road, Stanwell, Staines, TW19 7LY	01784 24 07 77
Norfolk: M&K Commercials Ltd, 11-13 Morgan Way, Bowthorpe Industrial Estate, Norwich, NR5 9JJ	01603 74 89 95
TruckEast Ltd, Unit 8, Mundford Road Trading Estate, Thetford, IP24 1NB	01842 763400
Northamptonshire: TruckEast Ltd, Darwin Road, Willowbrook East Industrial Estate, Corby, NN17 5XZ	01536 443883
TruckEast Ltd, Eldon Way, Crick, NN6 7SL	01788 823930
TruckEast Ltd, Kilvey Road, Brackmills Industrial Estate, Northampton, NN4 7BQ	01604 874747
TruckEast Ltd, Stewarts Road, Finedon Road Ind Est, Wellingborough, NN8 4RJ	01933 303303
Northumberside: Scania Ltd, Priory Park East, Kingston Upon Hull, HU4 7DY	01482 626880
North Yorkshire: Scania Ltd, Skipton Rock Quarry, Harrogate Road, Skipton, BD23 6AB	01756 79 71 97
Scania Ltd, Thirsk Industrial Park, York Road, Thirsk, YO7 3AA	01845 57 35 00
Nottinghamshire: Keltruck Ltd, Brunel Drive, Newark Ind Est, Newark, NG24 2EG	01636 700203
Keltruck Ltd, Rennie Hogg Road, Riverside Industrial Estate, Nottingham, NG2 1RX	0115 986 51 21
Keltruck Ltd, Unit 2, Fullwood Road South, Sutton-in Ashfield, NG17 2JZ	01623 55 95 59
Oxfordshire: Scania Ltd, 178a Milton Park, Didcot, OX14 4SE	01235 834933
Scania Ltd, Unit 5, Wildmere Park, 10 Wildmere Road, Banbury, OX16 3JU	01295 272857
Powys: West Pennine Trucks Ltd, Station Road, Knighton, LD7 1DR	01547 52 86 00
Renfrewshire: Scania Ltd, Clyde Street , Renfrew, PA4 8SL	0141 886 56 33
Shropshire: West Pennine Trucks Ltd, Halesfield 17, Telford, TF7 4PW	01952 587 222
West Pennine Trucks Ltd, Unit 19, Mile Oak Industrial Estate, Maesbury Road, Oswestry, SY10 8HA	01691 67 15 00
Somerset: Scania Ltd, Unit 14, Dunball Ind. Park, Dunball, TA6 4TP	01278 68 50 60
Scania Ltd, Waterlip, Shepton Mallet, BA4 4RN	01749 880088
South Glamorgan: Silurian Scania, Penarth Road, Cardiff, CF11 8UT	02920 224671
South Gloucestershire: Scania Ltd, Avonmouth Way, Avonmouth, BS11 8DB	01179 37 98 00

South Humberside: Scania Ltd, Estate Road One, South Humberside Industrial Estate, Pyewipe, Grimsby, DN31 2TA — 01472 34 69 13
Scania Ltd, Grange Lane North, Scunthorpe, DN16 1BT — 01724289088
South Yorkshire: Keltruck Ltd, Old Manton Colliery, Retford Road, Worksop, S80 2RZ — 01909 500595
Scania Ltd, Claylands Avenue, Worksop, S81 7DJ — 01909 50 08 22
Scania Ltd, Don Road, Sheffield, S9 2TL — 0114 262 6700
Staffordshire: Keltruck Ltd, 3rd Avenue, Centrum 100, Burton-on-Trent, DE14 2WD — 01283 510011
Keltruck Ltd, Watling Street, Dordon, Tamworth, B78 1TS — 01827 33 01 00
West Pennine Trucks Ltd, Cross Street, off Chemical Lane, Longport, ST6 4PU — 01782 57 79 55
Stirlingshire: Scania Ltd, Thronebridge Yard, Lauriston Road, Grangemouth, FK3 8XX — 01324 620620/01324 612112
Suffolk: TruckEast Ltd, 6 Hodgkinson Road, Felixstowe, IP11 3QT — 01394 67 66 25
TruckEast Ltd, Violet Hill Road, Stowmarket, IP14 1NN — 01449 61 35 53
Surrey: Diesel Power, Unit 5, Autumn Park Industrial Estate, Dysart Road, Grantham, NG31 7OD — 020 864 800 41
Scania Ltd, Unit 53a, Hobbs Industrial Estate, Newchapel, Lingfield, RH7 6HN — 01342 837373
Tyne & Wear: Scania Ltd, Mandarin Way, Pattinson Ind Est, District 15, Washington, NE38 8QG — 0191 418 8500 — Parts: 0191 418 8518
Scania Ltd, Mylord Crescent, Camperdown Industrial Estate, Killingworth, NE12 5UW — 0191 256 1910 — Days: 07971 154423
West Midlands: Keltruck Ltd, Kenrick Way, West Bromwich, B71 4JW — 0121 524 1800
Warwickshire: Keltruck Ltd, Unit 8, Glebe Farm Road, Glebe Farm Industrial Estate, Rugby, CV21.1GQ — 01788 571959
West Midlands: Keltruck Ltd, 7a&7b Paragon Way, Zone 4a, Bayton Road Ind. Estate, Exhall, Coventry, CV7 9QS — 02476 644 664
Keltruck Ltd, Vinculum Way (off Armstrong Way), Willenhall, WV13 2RG — 01902637777
West Lothian: Scania Ltd: Newbridge Industrial Estate , Newbridge, EH28 8PJ — 0131 333 4200
West Yorkshire: Scania Ltd, Ripley Drive, Normanton Ind. Est., Normanton, WF6 1QT — 01924 228800
Scania Ltd, Royds Farm Road, Beeston Royds Ind Est, Leeds, LS12 6DX — 0113 231 14 11
Wiltshire: Scania Ltd, Faraday Road, Dorcan Ind Est, Swindon, SN3 5PA — 01793 715100 — Sales: 01793 645290
Worcestershire: Keltruck Ltd, Unit 28c, North Bank, Berry Hill Ind. Est. , Droitwich, WR9 9AU — 01905 77 70 60

VOLVO, Group UK Limited t/a Volvo Trucks (Head Office)
Wegnock Lane, Warwick, CV34 5YA
Tel: 01926 401777, www.volvo.com/trucks/uk-market/en-gb/
EMERGENCY BREAKDOWN NUMBER: 0800 929292

Ayrshire: Volvo Truck and Bus Centre Scotland, Highfield Business Park, St Quinox, Ayr, KA6 5HQ — 01292-613383
Bedfordshire: Volvo Truck and Bus Centre London, Wolseley Road, Woburn Industrial Estate, Kempston, Bedford, MK42 7SE — 01234-853877
Cambridgeshire: Volvo Truck and Bus Centre East Anglia, Club Way, Cygnet Park, Hampton, Peterborough, PE7 8JA — 01733-894940
Volvo Truck and Bus Centre East Anglia, 101 Lancaster Way Business Park, Ely, CB6 3NX — 01353 772200
Carmarthenshire: Volvo Truck and Bus Centre Wales & West, 21 Viking Way, Winchwen Industrial Estate,
Swansea Enterprise Park, Swansea, SA1 7DA — 01792-795462
Cheshire: Thomas Hardie Commercials Ltd., Bredbury Parkway, Bredbury, Stockport, SK6 2SN — 0161-9356100
Thomas Hardie Commercials Ltd., Road Beta, Brooks Lane Industrial Estate, Middlewich, CW10 0QF — 01606-830130
Cornwall: Stuarts Truck & Bus, Drump Road, Redruth, TR15 1SP — 01209-314496
County Antrim: Dennison Commercials Ltd., 37 Hillhead Road, Ballyclare, BT39 9DS, Northern Ireland — 028-93352827
County Cork: McCarthy Commercials, Danville Business Park, Ring Road, Kilkenny, Ireland — 00353 (0) 56 7734200
McCarthy Commercials, Watergrass Hill, Cork, Ireland — 00353 (0) 21 4889700
County Durham: Volvo Truck and Bus Centre North, Lingfield Way, Yarm Road Business Park, Darlington, DL1 4PY — 01325-355161
Volvo Truck and Bus Centre North, Lingfield Way, Yarm Road Business Park, Darlington, DL1 4PY — 01325-355161
County Kildare: Irish Commercials Ltd, Naas Industrial Estate, Naas, Ireland, 00353 (0) 45879881 — 045-875462
County Londonderry: Dennison Commercials Ltd., Loguestown Industrial Estate, Bushmills Rd, Coleraine, BT52 2NS — 028-70321155
County Monaghan: McDonnell Commercials (Monaghan) Ltd, Urblekirk, Dunraymond, Ireland — 00353 (0) 47 83588/00353 (0) 47 84121
County Tyrone: Dennison Commercials Ltd., Derrycreevy Lane, Stangmore, Dungannon, BT71 6SA, Northern Ireland — 028-87722220
Cumbria: Volvo Truck and Bus Centre North, Kingstown Broadway, Kingstown Industrial Estate, Carlisle, CA3 0HA — 01228-529262
Devon: Stuarts Truck & Bus, Hill Barton Business Park, Sidmouth Road, Clyst St. Mary, Exeter, EX5 1DR — 01395-232800
Stuarts Truck & Bus, Crown Hill, Plymouth, PL6 5JS — 01752-752233
Dorset: M C Truck & Bus Ltd., Shaftesbury Road, Blandford, DT11 7FB — 01258-480404
M C Truck & Bus Ltd., Shaftesbury Road, Blandford, DT11 7FB — 01258-480404
Dumfries and Galloway: Volvo Truck and Bus Centre North, Lockerbie Road, Dumfries, DG1 3PG — 01387-262646
East Yorkshire: Crossroads Truck & Bus Ltd, Valletta Street, Heddon Road, Hull, HU9 5NP — 01482 781831
Essex: M C Truck & Bus Ltd., Barclay Way, Waterglade Industrial Park, West Thurrock, RM20 3FB — 01708-868956
Volvo Truck and Bus Centre London, Longreach Road, Barking, IG11 0JR — 020 8477 4486
Volvo Truck and Bus Centre London, c/o Sainsbury's VMU, Fleming, Waltham, Waltham Abbey, EN9 3DZ — 01992-766118
Flintshire: Thomas Hardie Commercials Ltd., 23 Fourth Avenue, Deeside Industrial Park, Deeside, CH5 2NR — 01244-281004
Gloucestershire: Volvo Truck and Bus Centre Wales & West, Burcott Road 9, Severnside Trading Estate, Avonmouth, BS11 8AP — 01179-823741
Volvo Truck and Bus Centre Wales & West, Tuffley Mill, Lower Tuffley Lane, Gloucester, GL2 5DP — 01452-560010
Gwent: Volvo Truck and Bus Centre Wales & West, Spytty Road, Lee Way Ind. Estate, Newport, NP9 OQU — 01633-290929
Hampshire: M C Truck & Bus Ltd., Test Lane, Nursling, Southampton, SO16 9JX — 023 80-663500
M C Truck & Bus Ltd., Dundas Spur, Dundas Lane, Copnor, Portsmouth, PO3 5NY — 023 92-662187
Volvo Truck and Bus Centre London, Knight Park Road, Basingstoke, RG21 6XE — 01256-340509
Hertfordshire: Volvo Truck and Bus Centre London, 4 Old Parkbury Lane, Colnet Street, Radlett, AL2 2DZ — 01923-852950
Invernesshire: Volvo Truck and Bus Centre Scotland, Longman Drive, Inverness, IV1 1SU — 01463-221177

Kent: M C Truck & Bus Ltd., The Link Park, Hythe, CT21 4LR — 01303-266864
  M C Truck & Bus Ltd., Beddow Way, Aylesford North, Maidstone, ME20 7BT — 01622-710811
Lancashire: Volvo Truck and Bus Centre North, Newgate, White Lund Industrial Estate, Morecambe, LA3 3PT — 01524-62866
  Thomas Hardie Commercials Ltd., Unit 4 Millennium City Park, Millennium Road, Ribbleton, Preston, PR2 5BL — 01772-799000
  Thomas Hardie Commercials Ltd., Lockett Road, Bryn, Ashton-in-Makerfield, Wigan, WN4 8DE — 01942-505100
  Thomas Hardie Commercials Ltd., Fifth Avenue, Trafford Park, Manchester, M17 1TR — 0161-9354100
Lanarkshire: Volvo Truck and Bus Centre Scotland, Fifty Pitches Place, Cardonald Business Park, Glasgow, G51 4GA — 0141-8102777
Leicestershire: Volvo Truck and Bus Centre East Anglia, Station Road, Stoney Stanton, LE9 6LJ — 01455-273260
  Volvo Coach Sales, Brisco Avenue, Loughborough, LE11 0HP — 01509-217777
  Volvo Truck and Bus Centre East Anglia, Station Road, Stoney Stanton, LE9 6LJ
Lincolnshire: Crossroads Truck & Bus Ltd, Freeman Road Ind. Est., North Hykeham, Lincoln, LN6 9AP — 01522-684496
  A Culpin & Son, Northgate Garage, Pinchbeck, Spalding, PE11 3SE — 01775-725038/9
  Crossroads Truck & Bus Ltd, Freeman Road Ind. Est., North Hykeham, Lincoln, LN6 9AP — 01522-684496
Merseyside: Thomas Hardie Commercials Ltd., Lea Green District Centre, Lea Green Road, Lea Green, WA9 5HX — 07744-833083
  Thomas Hardie Commercials Ltd., Newstet Road, Knowsley Industrial Park, Liverpool, L33 7TJ — 0151-5493000
Middlesex: Volvo Truck and Bus Centre London, Mollison Avenue, Brimsdown, Enfield, EN3 7NJ — 0208-3443700
  Volvo Truck and Bus Centre London, The Bulls Bridge Centre, North Hyde Gardens, Hayes, UB3 4QQ — 0208-6245100
Mid Glamorgan: Volvo Truck and Bus Centre Wales & West, Unit C, Gellihirion Industrial Estate, Pontypridd, CF37 5SX — 01443-844088
Norfolk: Volvo Truck and Bus Centre East Anglia, Saddlerbow Road, Kings Lynn, PE30 5BN — 01553-816460
  Volvo Truck and Bus Centre East Anglia, 24-28 Frensham Road, Sweet Briar Industrial Estate, Norwich, NR3 2BT — 01603-785100
  Volvo Truck and Bus Centre East Anglia, Gapton Hall Road, Norfolk, Great Yarmouth, NR31 ONL — 01493-443001
  Volvo Truck and Bus Centre East Anglia, 34 Howlett Way, Thetford, IP24 1HZ — 01842-855900
Northamptonshire: Volvo Truck and Bus Centre East Anglia, Pytchley Road Industrial Estate, Kettering, NN15 6JJ — 01536-516311
  Volvo Truck and Bus Centre East Anglia, C/O Comet NDC, Longcroft Rd, Corby, CV3 4SJ — 01536-740775
  Volvo Truck and Bus Centre East Anglia, Wellingborough, NN8 6GR — 01933-401933
  Volvo Truck and Bus Centre London, Delaware Drive, Tongwell, Milton Keynes, MK15 8JH — 01908-210525
North East Lincolnshire: Crossroads Truck & Bus Ltd, Redwood Industrial Park, Kiln Lane, Stallingborough, DN41 8DL — 01469-556930
North Lincolnshire: Crossroads Truck & Bus Ltd, Kendale Road, Off Grange Lane North, Scunthorpe, DN16 1BY — 01724-280724
Northumberland: Volvo Truck and Bus Centre North, Ennerdale Road, Kitty Brewster Industrial Estate, Blyth, NE24 4RT — 01670-359999
  Volvo Truck and Bus Centre North, Ennerdale Road,, Kitty Brewster Industrial Estate, Blyth, NE24 4RT — 01670-359999
North Yorkshire: Crossroads Truck & Bus Ltd, c/o Coors Brewery, Wetherby Road, Tadcaster, LS24 9SD
  Crossroads Truck & Bus Ltd, Unit 6, Becklands Close, Roecliffe Lane, Buroughbridge, YO51 9NR — 01423 320220
  Crossroads Truck & Bus Ltd, 7 James Street, York, YO1 3DW — 01904-883041
Oxfordshire: Volvo Truck and Bus Centre London, Hawksworth, Southmead Industrial Estate, Didcot, OX11 7EN — 01235-519179
  Volvo Truck and Bus Centre London, Hawksworth, Southmead Industrial Estate, Didcot, OX11 7EN — 01235-519179
  Volvo Truck and Bus Centre London, Souldern Gate Garage, Banbury Road, Souldern, Bicester, OX27 7HT — 01869-345151
  Volvo Truck and Bus Centre London, Souldern Gate Garage, Banbury Road, Souldern, Nr Bicester, OX27 7HT — 01869-345151
Pembrokeshire: Mansel Davies & Son (Garages) Ltd., Station Yard, Llanfyrnach, SA35 0BZ — 01239-831631
Perth & Kinross: Volvo Truck and Bus Centre Scotland, Ruthvenfield Way, Inveralmond Industrial Estate, Perth, PH1 3UF — 01738-637256/7
  Volvo Truck and Bus Centre Scotland (Kingdom of Fife Parts Centre), Lyneburn Ind Est, Dunfermline, KY11 4JT — 01383-625594
Shropshire: Hartshorne (Shrewsbury) Ltd., Ainsdale Drive, Harlescott Industrial Estate, Shrewsbury, SY1 3TL — 01743-444555
Staffordshire: Hartshorne (Potteries) Ltd., Pasturefields, Great Hayward, Stafford, ST18 0RB — 01889-270600
  Hartshorne (Potteries) Ltd., Hammond Road, Parkhouse Industrial Estate, Chesterton, Newcastle-Under-Lyme, ST5 7RX — 01782-568600
  Hartshorne (East Midlands) Ltd., Derby Street, Burton-On-Trent, DE14 2LG — 01283-515777
  Hartshorne (Potteries) Ltd., Hammond Road, Parkhouse Industrial Estate, Chesterton, Newcastle-Under-Lyme, ST5 7RX — 01782-568600
Somerset: Volvo Truck and Bus Centre Wales & West, Gurney Slade, Nr Bath, BA3 4TQ — 01749-840777
South Yorkshire: Crossroads Truck & Bus Ltd, Canklow Meadows Ind Est, West Bawtry Road, Rotherham, S60 2XL — 01709-365566
Suffolk: Volvo Truck and Bus Centre East Anglia, Bury Road, Chedburgh, Bury St Edmunds, IP29 4UQ — 01284-850418
  Volvo Truck and Bus Centre East Anglia, The Exchange, Ransomes Euro Park, Ipswich, IP3 9RT — 01473-718223
  Volvo Truck and Bus Centre East Anglia, Unit H4 Foxtail Road, Ransomes Europark, Ipswich, IP3 9RT — 01473 273211
  Volvo Truck and Bus Centre East Anglia, Bryon Avenue (Off Walton Avenue), Felixstowe, IP11 8HZ — 01394-674711
Surrey: Volvo Truck and Bus Centre London, Beddington Farm Road, Croydon, CR0 4XB — 0208-6655775
Tyne and Wear: Volvo Truck and Bus Centre North, Crowther Road Industrial Estate (District 3), Washington, NE38 0AQ — 0191-4151111
  Volvo Truck and Bus Centre North, Crowther Road Ind. Est (District 3), Washington, NE38 0AQ — 0191-4151111
West Lothian: Volvo Truck and Bus Centre Scotland, Drover's Road, East Mains Industrial Estate, Broxburn, Edinburgh, EH52 5ND — 01506-856892
Warwickshire: Hartshorne Motor Services Ltd., Riversdale Rd, Carlyon Road Industrial Estate, Atherstone, CV9 1LP
  Hartshorne Motor Services Ltd., Riversdale Rd, Carlyon Road Industrial Estata, Atherstone, CV9 1LP
West Midlands: Hartshorne Motor Services Ltd, Blk A Unt 1, Willenhall Trading Estate, Midacre, Willenhall, WV13 2JW — 01902-635489
  Hartshorne Motor Services Ltd., Bentley Mill Close, Walsall, WS2 0BN — 01922-704600
  Hartshorne Motor Services Ltd., Hanover Drive, Gravelly Industrial Park, Birmingham, B24 8HZ — 0121-3801950
  Hartshorne Motor Services Ltd., Dandy Bank Rd, Pesnett Trading Estate, Kingswinford, DY6 7TD — 01384-402333
West Sussex: M C Truck & Bus Ltd., Unt1, Braybon Bus Park, Consort Way, Victoria Gardens, Burgess Hill, RH15 9ND — 01444-230700
West Yorkshire: Crossroads Truck & Bus Ltd, Pheasant Drive, Birstall, Batley, WF17 9LR — 01924 425000
  Crossroads Truck & Bus Ltd, Aftofts Lane, Wakefield Europort, Normanton, WF10 5UB — 01924-894001
  Crossroads Truck & Bus Ltd, C/O First Bus Garage, Bradford, BD4 8SP — 01274-734833
Wiltshire: Volvo Truck and Bus Centre Wales & West, Clark Avenue, Porte Marsh Industrial Estate., Calne, SN11 9PZ — 01249-817345

Fuel & bunker card contacts

Ace Fuel Cards & Abbey Fuel Cards
Ace Fuelcards Ltd
Abbey House
Stirlings Road
Wantage
Oxfordshire
OX12 7BB
Tel: 0845 6301312
www.ace-fuelcards.co.uk
www.discountdiesel.co.uk

ARVAL
Arval UK Ltd
Arval Centre
Windmill Hill
Swindon
SN5 6PE
Tel: 0870 419 7000
Fax: 0870 419 4502
www.arval.co.uk

BP Plus (UK, Europa, Supercharge & Bunker)
BP Oil UK Ltd
Witan Gate House
500–600 Witan Gate
Central Milton Keynes
Bedfordshire
MK9 1ES
Tel: 0800 585104
Fax: 0870 2430077
www.bp.com

DCI, DCI Smart & Nicholls
DCI Ltd
176 Clooney Road
Greysteel
Londonderry
County Derry
Northern Ireland
BT47 3DY
Tel: 02871 812121
Fax: 02871 812180
www.dcicard.ie

Diesel Direct/Key Fuels/C H Jones
Keyfuels
Premier Business Park
Queen Street
Walsall
West Midlands
WS2 9PB
Tel: 01922 704455
Fax: 01922 704456
www.fuel-cards.net

Dieseline
Total Butler
County House
Bayshill Road
Cheltenham
Gloucestershire GL50 3BA
Tel: 01242 222999
Fax: 01242 229498
www.total.co.uk

DKV
DKV Euro Service Ltd
Premier Business Park
Queen Street
Walsall
West Midlands WS2 9PB
Tel: 0800 1973960
www.dkv-euroservice.com

Emo & Emo Smart
Emo Oil Ltd
Clonminam Industrial Estate
Portlaoise
County Laois
Ireland
Tel: 00353 (0) 578674700
Fax: 00353 (0) 578674750
www.emo.ie

Esso Europe & Esso UK
ExxonMobil
The Cornerstone
The Broadway
Woking
Surrey GU21 5AN
Tel: 01483 774200
Fax: 01483 774201
www.exxonmobil.co.uk

Euroshell CRT International & Euroshell Fleet Card UK
Shell UK Oil Products Ltd
Rowlandsway House
Rowlandsway
Manchester M22 5SB
Tel: 0161 4994000
www.shell.com

Eurotraffic & Total Card
Total UK
40 Clarendon Road
Watford
Hertfordshire
WD17 1TQ
Tel: 01923 694000
Fax: 01923 694400
www.total.co.uk

Fastfuel
UK Fuels Ltd
Windermere House
4–5 Macon Court
Herald Drive
Crewe
Cheshire CW1 6EA
Tel: 01270 655600
www.fastfuel.co.uk

Fuelnet
Maxol Direct (NI) Ltd
48 Trench Road
Mallusk
Newtownabbey
County Antrim
Northern Ireland BT36 4TY
Tel: 028 9084 8586
www.maxoldirect.com

Fuelwise Smart
Fuelwise Network Ltd
8 Brook Street, Coleraine
Northern Ireland BT52 1PW
Tel: 0845 0099117
www.fuelwise.ie

IDS
IDS, Kuwait Petroleum
International
Ground Floor
Duke's Court
Duke Street, Woking
Surrey G21 5BH
Tel: 01483 737177
Emergency tel: 00800 565656 / 0032 (0) 2772 0117
Fax: 08702 384640
www.ids.q8.com

Morgan (Smart, UK, Ireland, Executive, Armagh GAA)
Morgan Fuel Direct
(UK Office)
Armagh House
214d Hagley Road
Birmingham B16 9PH
Tel: 0121 4562300
www.morganfuels.com

OMV Eurotruck
OMV (UK) Ltd
14 Ryder Street
LondonSW1Y 6QB
Tel: 0207 3331600
Fax: 0207 3331610
www.omv.com

QED
Campus Oil
4 Bracken Business Park
Bracken Road
Sandyford
Dublin 18
Ireland
Tel: 00353 (0) 12915500
Fax: 00353 (0) 12915510
www.campusoil.ie

Red
Red Fuel Cards Europe Ltd
Red House
Sproughton Road
Ipswich
Suffolk IP1 5AN
Tel: 01473 466666
Fax: 01473 749706
www.redfuelcards.com

Routemate
Route Mate
Osbourne House
Sandbeck Way
Wetherby
West Yorks
LS22 7DN
Tel: 0870 7777880
Fax: 0870 7777879
www.routemate.co.uk

Statoil Diesel
Statoil
Statoil Card Centre
Claregalway Road
Oranmore
County Galway, Ireland
Tel: 00353 (0) 91788116
Fax: 00353 (0) 91795777
www.statoilcard.ie

Top Oil
Tedcastles Oil Products
Promenade Road
Dublin 3
Ireland
Tel: 00353 (0) 18198000
www.top.ie

UTA (Full Service & Mercedes Service)
UTA
Mainparkstrasse 2–4
63801 Kleinostheim
Germany
www.uta.com

Government bodies

Companies Registration Office
Companies House, Crown Way
Maindy
Cardiff CF14 3UZ
Tel: 0870 3333636
www.companieshouse.gov.uk
The main functions of Companies House are to incorporate and dissolve limited companies, examine and store company information delivered under the Companies Act and related legislation and to make this information available to the public.

Department for Business, Enterprise and Regulatory Reform (formerly D.T.I.)
Ministerial Correspondence Unit
Department for Business, Enterprise and Regulatory Reform
1 Victoria Street
London SW1H 0ET
Tel: 020 72155000
Fax: 020 72150105
enquiries@berr.gsi.gov.uk
www.berr.gov.uk
Formally the DTI, the Department for Business, Enterprise and Regulatory Reform works to create successful British business and industry, helps companies to become more productive and protects the rights of working people and consumers.

Department for Transport
Great Minster House
76 Marsham Street
London SW1P 4DR
Tel: 020 79448300
www.dft.gov.uk
The DFT oversees the delivery of a reliable, safe and secure transport system whilst safeguarding our environment.

Department of Work and Pensions
www.dwp.gov.uk
The Department for Work and Pensions promotes opportunity and independence for all through modern, customer-focused services. It helps people to achieve their potential through employment, so that they are able to provide for their children and to work and save for secure retirement.

DirectGov
www.direct.gov.uk
A website facility that brings together the widest range of public service information and services online and provides links to all government bodies in the UK.

Driving Standards Agency
Stanley House
56 Talbot Street
Nottingham
NG1 5GU
Tel: 0115 901 2500
Fax: 0115 901 2510
www.dsa.gov.uk
The DSA is responsible for driving standards, testing car drivers, truckers, motorcyclists and driving instructors. You can even book your test online at their website.

Duport
www.duport.co.uk
An agency recommended by Companies House to enable individuals and groups to register themselves as having Limited Company status.

DVLA
Longview Road
Morriston
Swansea
SA6 7JL
Tel: 01792 782341
www.dvla.gov.uk
The DVLA maintain registers of drivers and vehicles and collect road tax.

European Parliament
Correspondence with Citizens
GOL03A012
L-2929 Luxembourg
Fax: (352) 430027072
www.europarl.eu.int
For written publications covering parliament's plenary sessions fax the above contact number or search the website for latest truck and driver legislation.

HM Revenue and Customs (formerly HM Customs & Excise)
Tel: 0845 0109000
www.hmrc.gov.uk
HM Revenue and Customs is the new name for the amalgamated forces of HM Customs and Excise and the Inland Revenue. It is a government department with the responsibility for collecting tax, VAT and customs duties. It also has a front-line role in protecting us from the illegal import of drugs, alcohol and tobacco and combatting tax fraud.

Health and Safety Executive
Tel: 0845 3450055
www.hse.gov.uk
The Health and Safety Commission (HSC) and the Health and Safety Executive (HSE) are responsible for the regulation of almost all the risks to health and safety arising from work activity in Britain.

Highways Agency
Tel: 0845 7504030
ha_info@highways.gsi.gov.uk
www.highways.gov.uk
The Highways Agency is an executive agency of the Department for Transport (DFT), and is responsible for operating, maintaining and improving the strategic road network in England on behalf of the Secretary of State for Transport.

Identity and Passport Service (formerly UK Passport Service)
Tel: 0870 521 0410
www.ips.gov.uk
You can use this number for any passport enquiries or to report a lost or stolen passport. Go online to find out more about different types of passports or the other services offered by the Identity and Passport Service.

Jobcentre Plus
Jobseeker Direct Helpline: 0845 6060234
www.jobcentreplus.gov.uk
Jobcentre Plus offices provide a fully integrated work and benefit service.

Learning and Skills Council
Cheylesmore House
Quinton Road
Coventry
CV1 2WT
Tel: 0870 900 6800
info@lsc.gov.uk
www.lsc.gov.uk
The LSC exists to make England better skilled and more competitive. It is responsible for planning and funding high-quality vocational education and training for everyone.

Office of Employment Tribunals
www.employmenttribunals.gov.uk
Tel: 08457 959775
The Office of Employment Tribunals hears claims about matters to do with employment. These include unfair dismissal, redundancy payments and discrimination. It also deals with a range of claims relating to wages and other payments.

Police
Anti-terrorist hotline Tel: 0800 789 321

British Transport Police
(Public Rail Systems) Tel: 0800 405040

Crimestoppers Tel: 0800 555111

National Non-emergency Number: 101 (comes into force across the UK in 2008)

101 is a new 24-hour number provided by your police and local council to deal with community safety issues, including certain non-emergency crime, policing and anti-social behaviour. 101 is currently in use across five areas of the UK and goes live across the whole of the UK in 2008. www.101.gov.uk

Dial 999 from a landline or 112 from a mobile if:

A. There is a danger to life or risk of injury being caused, such as a serious road accident or assault.

B. A crime is in progress, such as a robbery, burglary or theft, and the offender is still on the scene or has just left the area.

C. The immediate attendance of the police is necessary – such as someone acting suspiciously and obviously about to commit a crime.

Local constabulary contact numbers
Avon and Somerset: 0845 4567000
Bedfordshire Police: 01234 841212
Cambridgeshire Constabulary: 0845 4564564
Central Scotland Police: 01786 456000
Cheshire Constabulary: 0845 4580000
City of London: 020 7601222
Cleveland Constabulary: 01642 301207
Cumbria Constabulary: 0845 3300247
Derbyshire Constabulary: 0845 1233333
Devon and Cornwall Constabulary: 0845 2777444
Dorset Police: 01202 222222
Dumfries and Galloway Constabulary: 0845 6005701
Durham Constabulary: 0845 6060365
Dyfed Powys Police: 0845 3302000
Essex Police: 01245 491491
Fife Constabulary: 0845 6005702
Gloucestershire Constabulary: 0845 0901234
Grampian Police: 0845 60057000
Greater Manchester Police: 0161 8725050
Gwent Police/Heddlu Gwent: 01633 838111
Hampshire Constabulary: 101 (new 24 hour non emergency number)
Hertfordshire Constabulary: 0845 3300222
Humberside Police: 0845 6060222
Kent Police: 01622 690690
Lancashire Constabulary: 0845 1253545
Leicestershire Constabulary: 0116 2222222
Lincolnshire Police: 01522 532222
Lothian and Borders Police: 0131 3113131
Merseyside Police: 0151 7096010
Metropolitan Police Service: 020 72301212
Norfolk Constabulary: 0845 4564567
North Wales Police: 0845 6071002
North Yorkshire Police: 0845 6060247
Northamptonshire Police: 08453 700700
Northern Constabulary: 08456 033388
Northumbria Police: 08456 043043
Nottinghamshire Police: 0115 9670999

Police Service of Northern Ireland:
  0845 6008000
South Wales Police: 01656 655555
South Yorkshire Police: 0114 2202020
Staffordshire Police: 08453 302010
Strathclyde Police: 0141 5322000
Suffolk Constabulary: 01473 613500
Surrey Police: 0845 1252222
Sussex Police: 0845 6070999
Tayside Police: 01382 223200
Thames Valley Police: 0845 8505505
Warwickshire Police: 01926 415000
West Mercia Constabulary: 08457 444888
West Midlands Police: 0845 1135000
West Yorkshire Police: 0845 6060606
Wiltshire Constabulary: 0845 4087000

ROSPA
Edgbaston Park
353 Bristol Road
Edgbaston
Birmingham
B5 7ST
Tel: 0121 2482000
Fax: 0121 2482001
www.rospa.co.uk
Provides up-to-the-minute advice and information on safety issues and law.

Traffic Scotland
Transport Scotland
8th Floor (North Wing)
Buchanan House, 58 Dundas Street
Glasgow G4 OHF
Tel: 0131 2447510
www.trafficscotland.org
Provides up-to-the-minute information about Scotland's road conditions, traffic and weather.

Vehicle and Operator Services Agency (VOSA)
Tel: 0870 6060440
www.vosa.gov.uk
VOSA aims to improve road safety and the environment and enforce compliance with commercial operator licensing requirements. It also has the authority to stop and spot-check HGVs.

Vehicle Certification Agency
VCA Bristol
1 The Eastgate Office Centre, Eastgate Road
Bristol B55 6XX
Tel: 0117 9515151
www.vca.gov.uk
The VCA is responsible for national approval and policy formulation with regard to the enforcement of vehicle safety and environmental standards.

Useful contacts

AA
The AA
Contact Centre
Lambert House
Stockport Road
Cheadle
SK8 2DY
AA Roadwatch Tel: 09003
401100
www.theaa.com
*AA Roadwatch will send texts or
email the latest traffic info to
your phone and provide
personalised routes and
interactive maps for an
annual fee. Find out more
online.*

ALLMI Training
Second Floor Suite
9 Avon Reach
Monkton Hill
Chippenham
Wiltshire
SN15 1EE
Tel: 01249 659150
Fax: 01249 464675
www.allmitraining.co.uk
*ALLMI Training Ltd is the
independent training
accreditation service and
standards body for the
Association of Lorry Loader
Manufacturers and Importers
of Great Britain (ALLMI).
ALLMI is the UK's only trade
association devoted exclusively
to advancing safety and
standards in the lorry loader
industry.*

Drivers Helpline
7 Sinclair Court
Scarborough
Yorkshire
YO12 7DS
Tel: 01723 351425
Mobile: 07791 601307
email: dneale@aol.com
www.drivershelpline.co.uk
*A service offering advice and
support for drivers, or the
families of drivers who have
been arrested abroad. The
helpline is a free service and is
available 24 hours a day, seven
days a week.*

European Shippers Council
ESC Brussels
Park Leopold
Rue Wiertz 50
B-1050 Brussels
Belgium
Tel: (322) 230 21 13
www.europeanshippers.com
*The ESC looks after the interests
of companies represented by 15
national transport user
organisations and a number of
European commodity trade
associations.*

FERRIES

Brittany Ferries
Tel: 0870 9076103
www.brittanyferries.co.uk

DFDS Seaways
Tel: 0871 8820881
www.dfds.co.uk

Fjord Line
Tel: 0047 81533500
www.fjordline.co.uk

Irish Ferries
Tel: 09705 171717
www.irishferries.com

LD Ferries
www.ldlines.co.uk
Tel: 0844 5768836

Norfolk Line
Tel: 0870 8701020
www.norfolkline.com

P&O Ferries
Tel: 08705 980333
www.poferries.com

SeaFrance Ferries
Tel: 0871 6632546
www.seafrance.com

Stena Line
Tel: 08705 707070
www.stenaline.co.uk

P&O Irish Sea
Tel: 0870 2424777
www.poirishsea.com

Swansea Cork Ferries
Tel: 01792 456116
www.swanseacorkferries.com

Caledonian MacBrayne
Tel: 08000 665000
www.calmac.co.uk

**Northlink Orkney &
Shetland Ferries**
Tel: 0845 6000449
www.northlinkferries.co.uk

Orkney Ferries
Tel: 01856 872044
www.orkneyferries.co.uk

Freight Transport Association
Tel: 08171 112222 (Member
Service Centre number)
www.fta.co.uk
*The Freight Transport
Association represents the
transport interests of companies
moving goods by road, rail, sea
and air. Its members range from
small and medium size
enterprises to multinational
public companies and are
involved in all modes of
transport. FTA members operate
over 200,000 goods vehicles –
almost half the UK fleet.*

Garage Watch
FPS Forecourt Division
6 Royal Court
Tatton Street, Knutsford
Cheshire WA16 6EN
Tel: 01565 631313
Fax: 01565 631314
www.garage-watch.co.uk
*Representative body for the
UK's 45,000 independent
garages.*

Lady Truckers Club
7 Sinclair Court, Scarborough
Yorkshire YO12 7DS
Tel: 01723 351425
Mobile: 07791 601307
email: dneale@aol.com
www.ladytruckersclub.co.uk
*A club aimed exclusively at
female truck and coach drivers,
addressing the particular issues
faced by girls on the road.*

**London Congestion Charge
Customer service enquiries
Congestion Charging**
PO Box 2985
Coventry
CV7 8ZR
Penalty charge enquiries
Congestion Charging
PO Box 2984
Coventry
CV7 8YR
Tel: 0845 900 1234
www.cclondon.com

M6 Toll
(Midland Expressway Ltd)
Midland Expressway Ltd
Freepost
NAT 9069
Weeford
Lichfield
WS14 0PQ
Tel: 0870 850 6262
Fax: 01543 267001
www.m6toll.co.uk
*Call or go online to find out
about tags and charges.*

Network Rail
Network Rail
40 Melton Street
London
NW1 2EE
Tel: 020 7557 800
Fax: 020 7557 9000

National Rail Enquiries
Tel: 08457 484950

Network Rail Helpline
Tel: 08457 114141
www.networkrail.co.uk
*Network Rail is an engineering
company formed to
revitalise Britain's railways. It
maintains, improves and
upgrades every aspect of
the rail infrastructure including
tracks, signalling systems,
bridges, viaducts, tunnels,
level crossings and
stations.*

Petsearch
Tel: 01889 562907 (national
number)
www.ukpetsearch.freeuk.com
*Provides a free service, run
and funded by volunteers, to
reunite owners with their lost
pets. You can also register any
pets found by the road (dead,
injured or alive) online or via
your local petsearch phone
operator (a list of phone
numbers is given on the
website).*

RAC
RAC Motoring Services
Great Park Road
Bradley Stoke
Bristol
BS32 4QN
Tel: 01922 727313
www.rac.co.uk
*Gives information about mobile
phone law, traffic, weather and
route planning for an annual
fee. Alternatively gain instant
access to the latest traffic by
dialling 1740 from any mobile.*

**Recruitment and
Employment Confederation**
15 Welbeck Street
London
W1G 9XT
Tel: 020 7009 2100
Fax: 020 7935 4112
www.rec.uk.com
*The Recruitment and
Employment Confederation is
the body representing the
private recruitment industry in
the UK. It offers services to
employers, jobseekers and
industry observers.*

Road Haulage Association
www.rha.net

**Scotland and Northern
Ireland**
Roadway House
The Rural Centre
Ingliston
Newbridge
EH28 8NZ
Tel: 0131 4724180
Fax: 0131 4724179
scotland-
northernireland@rha.net

Northern Region
Roadway House
Little Wood Drive
West 26 Industrial Estate
Ckeckheaton
BD19 4TA
Tel: 01274 863100
Fax: 01274 865855
northern@rha.net

**Midlands and Western
Region**
Roadway House
Cribbs Causeway
Bristol
BS10 7TU
Tel: 01179 503600
Fax: 01179 505647
midlands-western@rha.net

**Southern and Eastern
Region**
Roadway House
Bretton Way
Bretton
Peterborough PE3 8DD
Tel: 01733 261131
Fax: 01733 332349
southern-eastern@rha.net

RHA Weybridge (Head Office)
Roadway House
35 Monument Hill, Weybridge
Surrey KT13 8RN
Tel: 01932 841515
Fax: 01932 852516
weybridge@rha.net
The Road Haulage Association
provides dedicated
campaigning, advice,
information and business
services specially tailored to the
haulage industry.

RSPCA
Cruelty and advice line (24-
hour) Tel: 0300 1234999
www.rspca.org.uk
Call this number anywhere in
the UK to report a distressed or
injured animal (wild or
domestic). An operator will
advise you on what to do, direct
you to the nearest RSPCA centre
or send an officer to your
location.

Skills for Logistics
14 Warren Yard
Warren Farm Office Village
Stratford Road
Milton Keynes MK12 5NW
Tel: 01908 313360
www.skillsforlogistics.org
Skills for Logistics is an
independent UK-wide
organisation that helps
employers tackle the skills and
productivity needs of the
logistics sector.

T&G
Transport & General Workers
Union
Central Office
Transport House
128 Theobald's Road, Holborn
London WC1X 8TN
Tel: 0207 6112500
www.tgwu.org.uk
With over 900,000 members in
every type of workplace, the
T&G is the UK's biggest general
union, and has a long and
proud tradition of representing
members in the workplace.

International Dialling Codes

Note: International Dialling Codes provided below are only those likely to be reached by a truck. For more information on International Dialling codes, go to: www.homephonechoices.co.uk

Country	Access code dialling from	Access code dialling to
Albania	00	355
Armenia	8*10	374
Austria	00	43
Azerbaijan	00	994
Bahrain	00	973
Belarus	8*10	375
Belgium	00	32
Bonsnia and Herzegovina	00	387
Bulgaria	00	359
Croatia	00	385
Cyprus	00	357
Czech Republic	00	420
Denmark	00	45
Estonia	00	372
Finland	00	358
France	00	33
Georgia	8*10	995
Germany	00	49
Gibraltar	00	350
Greece	00	30
Hungary	00	36
Iceland	00	354
Iran	00	98
Iraq	00	964
Ireland	00	353
Israel	00	972
Italy	00	39
Jordan	00	962
Kazakhstan	8*10	7
Kuwait	00	965
Kyrgyzstan	00	996
Latvia	00	371
Lebanon	00	961
Lithuania	8*10	370
Luxembourg	00	352
Malta	00	356
Monaco	00	377
Netherlands	00	31
Netherlands Antilles	00	599
Norway	00	47
Oman	00	968
Poland	00	48
Portugal	00	351
Quatarr	00	974
Romania	00	40
Russian Federation	8*10	7
Saudi Arabia	00	966
Slovakia	00	421
Slovenia	00	386
Spain	00	34
Sweden	00	46
Switzerland	00	41
Syrian Arab Republic	00	963
Turkey	00	90
Ukraine	8*10	380
United Arab Emirates	00	971
United Kingdom	00	44
Uzbekistan	8*10	998
Vatican City	00	39 379
Yemen	00	967
Yugoslavia (Serbia and Montenegro)	99	381

Example: To call the U.K from Uzbekistan dial 81044. (810 is the international access code from Uzbekistan and 44 is the country or 'destination' code for the U.K.)

To call Uzbekistan from the U.K. dial 00998. (00 is the international access code from the UK and 998 is the country or 'destination' code for Uzbekistan.)

Glossary

Abnormal load: Any load that's heavier than 42 tonnes, or wider, longer or taller than the normal size of an articulated vehicle trailer. See 'Vehicle size and bridges' on p.34.

AdBlue: A liquid placed within a separate tank (close to the fuel tank) that reduces emissions in new vehicles. Also see AdBlue p.73.

A-frame: A drawbar trailer with a steering front axle.

Activity mode: The type of mode being recorded on a tachograph, such as 'break' or 'POA'. See 'Driving hours'.

ADR (Hazardous Goods): A type of licence required by drivers who have to transport hazardous goods by road. See section on 'Additional qualifications and training'.

Agency: A company which provides drivers with temporary employment and employers with a temporary workforce.

Aggregated: Usually used to refer to a total amount of time spent on your various modes of activity through out the day (such as total – aggregated – amount of time spent driving, or total – aggregated – amount of time spent on break). See 'Driving hours'.

Air brakes: Used to efficiently stop a large vehicle by providing a circuit of air through pipes and valves on the rigid, tractor unit and/or trailer. If the air ceases to flow due to leakage or closure of a valve (such as that operated by braking) the brakes will immediately be applied.

Air suspension (adjustable): Used for adjusting the height or angle of the trailer, unit, or rigid vehicle.

Ambient goods: Transported goods that require no refrigeration or freezing (such as household cleaners and tinned food).

Anderson lead and clip: An electric lead used to carry current from the tractor unit to the trailer with a male and female clip at opposite ends. Only to be applied when tail-lift is in use.

Articulated vehicle (artic): Any vehicle comprised of two coupled independent and separable parts. 'Artic' is usually a term used to describe a tractor unit and trailer of at least 26 tonnes maximum gross weight.

Banksman: Any person (in an official capacity or otherwise) who assists a driver to safely reverse their vehicle.

Barn doors: Two large doors on the back of a trailer that open outwards.

Beaver tail: Two huge fold-up-and-down ramps on the rear of a flatbed trailer that enable vehicles to be driven on and off.

Block change: Changing gears without going through every single gear or half gear in the 'box. See section on 'How to understand your gearbox' on p.66.

Blocks: Long thick blocks of wood placed beneath large goods to provide a gap through which forks can be inserted to lift the goods from the deck of the trailer.

Bonded goods: Cigarettes and alcohol are the two main ones. These goods come strictly and separately sealed, and deliveries are often timed. Rigid codes of conduct surround bonded warehouses – be aware of this if you have to collect or deliver from or to one.

Bouncing: An action used to describe driving a solo unit without a trailer. See 'Running Bobtail' and 'Running Solo'.

Box trailer: A trailer with hard sides and top.

Break: A standard tachograph break is 45 minutes, following four-and-a-half accumulated hours of driving. See section on 'Laws regarding driving hours' on p.17.

British Domestic Hours Rule: A type of driving hours configuration that applies only to drivers working for certain types of operations. See 'British Domestic Hours Rule' on p.19 and 'Operations Exempt From EU Rule' on p.18.

Broms Brake: A secondary parking brake on Volvo tractor units, situated close to the normal parking brake on the dashboard. It's described as a round pull-out knob. This should be pushed in before driving can commence.

Bunker (fuel): A no-frills fuelling site designed for LGVs. Fuel/Bunkering Cards and their pin numbers are required in order to draw fuel, as many of these sites are unmanned.

Burns kit: Usually provided by companies whose drivers transport hazardous chemicals. The kits are usually kept in the cab. Training is given on their use and application.

Cab heater: Used for heating the cab when the engine is switched off.

Cages: Upright wire containers on wheels used for transporting loose goods. They're awkward to move and often come without brakes. Some can be collapsed for ease of storage.

Canopy: The cover over a filling station or loading bay designed to protect those below it from the elements. Be sure to make certain your vehicle is low enough to get under it.

Cantilever tail-lift: A large type of tail-lift that folds flat against the rear doors of the trailer. See 'Tail-lifts' section on p.54.

Catwalk: Term sometimes used to describe the footplate at the rear of a tractor unit that you stand on when coupling to your trailer.

Central bar (curtain-sided trailer): The posts that run from deck to roof in a curtain-sided vehicle. These can be unclipped and swivelled or swung out so that goods can be more effectively placed behind them.

Centre axle trailer: A drawbar trailer with one or more fixed axles situated in the centre of the trailer.

Certificate of Incorporation: A certificate issued by Companies House stating (among other things) the name of the limited company.

Cherry picker: A vehicle with a platform located at the rear that's raised and lowered on an hydraulic arm. This type of vehicle is used for (amongst other things) repairing streetlights.

Chest compressions: A procedure used in resuscitation of unconscious persons. See section on 'First Aid for motorists'.

Chocks: Triangular pieces of wood inserted under each side of a large object to prevent its movement in transit. Also used to prevent movement of vehicles and/or trailers.

Close coupled: Term used to describe a tractor unit and trailer that are joined close together, providing little room for the driver to couple or uncouple the service leads.

Collective or Workforce/Workplace Agreement: Any agreement regarding working hours and times that is drawn up between an employer and his or her employees. By signing, employees agree to the terms stated.

Column tail-lift: Type of tail-lift that folds up against the back doors of the trailer. See 'Tail-lifts' section on p.55.

Construction And Use Regulations: See section on 'Vehicle size and bridges' on p.34.

Contraflow: A traffic directing system created using cones and temporary cat's eyes that directs traffic away from roadworks.

Corporation Tax: A government tax payable by all Limited Companies.

COSHH (Control of Substances Hazardous to Health): Regulations and advice regarding the storage and handling of hazardous substances.

Cow bells: An electric lead used to carry current from a tractor unit to a trailer. This lead has a large, square, bell-like attachment at one end which secures into a housing on the trailer. This should only be connected when the tail-lift is in use.

CPC: A qualification which confirms an individual has the training and authority to run a transport department.

CPC (Driver): A new test for truck and bus drivers that becomes compulsory in 2008–9, designed to enable new and old drivers alike to stay up to date with new technologies and regulations within the transport industry. See page 133.

CPCS: A qualification that allows an individual to move and operate plant machinery and to work on a construction site.

Crash box: Any gearbox without a synchromesh, where the driver can only change gear at a certain point on the rev counter. This includes Fuller Road Ranger and Eaton Twin Splitter gearboxes. See section on 'How to understand your gearbox' on p.66.

Cross-members (pallet): The three wooden struts across the base of a pallet.

Cross-members (trailer legs): The diagonal supports that hold the trailer legs in place.

Cruise control: A feature that allows a driver to maintain his speed without using the accelerator.

Cup and Bar: A type of load retaining bar. See page 47.

Curtain-sider or tautliner: A trailer with strong plastic sides that can be folded back like a curtain to allow goods to be loaded.

Daily driving limit/time: The accumulated hours that anyone is allowed to drive within a 24-hour period. See 'Driving Hours' on p.17 and Working Time Regulations on p.14.

Daily duty limit: The number of hours that a driver is allowed to be on duty in any 24-hour period. See 'British Domestic Hours Rule'.

Daily rest period: The number of hours during which a mobile worker has to rest between in two 24-hour periods. See 'Driving Hours' on p.17 and Working Time Regulations on p.14.

Deck: The inside floor of the trailer.

Defect: Term used to describe any fault on a vehicle unit or trailer. Also used to describe the action of writing a report about a particular defect in order to have the vehicle repaired – eg 'I defected that vehicle last week,' meaning 'I wrote a defect report on that vehicle.'

Demountable body: See 'Drop-box trailer'.

Design weight: The weight that a vehicle or unit is manufactured to be able to carry. This may be higher than the weight it is legally allowed to carry according to its class of vehicle tax.

DFT (Department for Transport): See section on 'Government bodies'.

Diagnostics system: The tractor unit's onboard computer that tells you if there's something wrong with the braking system, lights or fluid levels. Some systems can be very complex and comprehensive. With some newer vehicles you may only be able to check the truck's condition using the diagnostics system. The menus are usually accessed using the right-hand stalk that branches off from the steering column, or a button/dial on the dashboard.

Dif lock: Allows axles to turn at different speeds, giving grip to one axle if the other is unable to grip in snow or extreme conditions.

Dog clip: See 'Safety Catch'.

Dollies: See 'Wheeled Platforms'.

Domestic hours: See section on 'British Domestic Hours Rule' on p.19.

Door retainers: Clips and bars that hold open trailer doors securely and prevent movement.

Double-deck trailer: A type of trailer with two internal floors and an tail-lift that services both levels. These types of trailer have small wheels and sit very low to the ground. They are also extremely tall.

Doubling the clutch: A procedure used to change gear in a vehicle with a crash gearbox. See section on 'How to understand your gearbox' on p.66.

Drawbar Eye: The coupling attachment on a drawbar trailer. Also see: 'Coupling a rigid and drawbar trailer'

Drop-box: A changeable box or boxes on a rigid or trailer that can be removed, put on legs, stored, or placed on another chassis.

Drop-box trailer: A rigid or articulated vehicle trailer with a system designed so that the body or box of the trailer can be removed from the chassis and stored separately. See 'Driving a rigid and drawbar' on p.95.

DSA (Driving Standards Agency): See section on 'Government bodies'.

DTI (Department of Industry): Now known as BERR – Department for Business enterprise and Regulatory Reform. See 'Government bodies'.

Dummy holders/clips: Clips attached to the service lead bar used to safely store and hold service leads and couplings while not being used.

Dump valve: A pull/push lever or handle-type combination (on adjustable suspensions) that releases the air from the trailer suspension in order to lower it.

DVLA (Driver and Vehicle Licensing Agency): See section on 'Government bodies'.

EBS: A braking system that creates greater braking efficiency and safer braking during emergencies. It also improves trailer stability and compatibility between unit and trailer.

Engine retarder: Similar to an exhaust brake and operated by the driver in the same way.

ESC (European Shippers Council): See 'Useful contacts' list.

Exhaust brake: Used instead of or in addition to conventional brakes to slow a vehicle on steep or long hills. Some vehicles feature an automatic exhaust brake which is applied when you decelerate.

External straps: Straps (usually removable) used to secure the load. Can be used around the back of a load in order to push it hard up against the front of a trailer, or over and around the top and sides of a load in curtain-sided vehicles to prevent movement in any direction.

Eye kit: Provided in vehicles that carry hazardous chemicals. Used to wash out the eyes should they come into contact with harmful substances.

Fifth wheel: The large upside-down U-shaped plate on the back of a tractor unit that the trailer rests and swivels on.

Fifth wheel grease: Lubrication grease applied to the fifth wheel plate. This is horrible stuff, very difficult to remove from skin and clothing, but not harmful.

Fifth wheel lever/handle: The handle or lever that has to be pulled in order to release the trailer pin from the fifth wheel.

Flatbed trailer: An open-backed trailer used for transporting large, heavy or abnormal loads.

Fleet codes: Unique code numbers applied by some large companies to their vehicles in order to identify each vehicle within their fleet.

Footplate (see also 'catwalk'): The flat area of the chassis at the rear of the cab next to the fuel tank. Designed for standing on while inserting service leads.

Fork rollers: The roller wheels at the front of the forks of a pallet truck.

Forklift truck: A machine used to mechanically load a vehicle. Stand-on and ride-on forklift trucks all require special licences. See section on 'Additional qualifications and training'.

Fortnightly driving limit: The number of hours that a driver is allowed to drive in a 14-day period. See 'Driving Hours' on p.17 and Working Time Regulations on p.14.

FTA (Freight Transport Association): See 'Useful contacts' list.

Gantry: The structure above a motorway on which signs are displayed.

Gas oil: See 'Red diesel' in Glossary and section on 'Fuelling up' on p.72.

General haulage: A type of work where you may be asked to transport almost any type of goods. General haulage usually involves several drops in a day, covering long distances, and working long hours. Deliveries and collections are often assigned ad hoc.

Green diesel: The Irish version of red diesel or gas oil.

Guide Funnel: The coupling attachment on a rigid that the 'Drawbar Eye' slots into. Also see: 'Coupling a rigid and drawbar trailer'

Guide posts: Low-level metal posts concreted into the floor of a loading bay to help guide you into the correct position.

Handballing: See 'Manual handling' in Glossary and section on 'Manual handling' on p.13.

Headstock: The area of the front external wall of a trailer to which the service leads are coupled.

Height indicator: A legal requirement for any vehicle over 9ft 6in or 2.9m. It tells you the height of your vehicle or any normal height trailer it might be coupled to. It is normally situated on the dashboard or behind the sun visor.

HGV (heavy goods vehicle): The old title used to describe any vehicle over 7.5 tonnes.

HGV Class 1: The old title used to describe any articulated tractor unit and trailer combination. Also used to describe the licence entitlement to drive that class of vehicle.

HGV Class 2: The old title used to describe any rigid vehicle above 17 tonnes. Also used to describe the licence entitlement to drive that class of vehicle.

HGV Class 3: The old title use to describe any rigid vehicle between 7.5 tonnes and 17 tonnes. Also used to describe the licence entitlement to drive that class of vehicle.

Hi-Ab: A type of licence required by anyone loading and unloading a vehicle using a crane attached to its rear. See section on 'Additional qualifications and training'.

High visibility clothing: Normally consists of at least a jacket or vest that fits over the top of your outer garments. It usually displays a fluorescent colour and at least one light-reflective strip. This is a site requirement within most yards, distribution centres, and warehouses.

Highways Agency: A government agency responsible for operating, maintaining and improving the road network throughout the UK.

Hill start option: Particular to tiptronic gearboxes, the 'hill start' option or button is used to aid manoeuvring on steep hills.

Hitching up: A slang term meaning to couple up a unit or rigid to a trailer.

HMSO (Her Majesty's Stationery Office): Now known as OPSI – Office of Public Sector Information. Publishes and distributes government books and pamphlets such as the Highway Code, Theory Test Books, and others pertaining to transport and employment law.

Horizontal Amending Directive (HAD): See p.19.

HSE (Health and Safety Executive): See section on 'Government bodies'.

HSW (Health and Safety at Work): Legislation and advice on the health and safety of employees in the workplace.

Imperial: Old style of measurement still widely used by lorry drivers. Common imperial measurements include feet and inches, yards and miles, gallons and fluid ounces, pounds, stones, hundredweights and tons. See 'Metric to Imperial conversion table' on p.37.

Insider: Type of enclosed tail-lift most commonly found on bread delivery vehicles. When not in use the tail-lift acts as part of the floor. See 'Tail-lifts' section on p.52.

Internal straps: Fixed load-restraining straps used in curtain-sided trailers. See section on 'Using internal and external straps' on p.48.

Inspection Light: A light at the rear of the cab that enables the driver to couple and uncouple in the dark.

IPAS (Powered Access Licence): A licence that allows an individual to operate cherry pickers and scissor lifts.

IR35: Legislation regarding self-employment. (See 'Self-employment and Limited Company status.)

Isolator switch (battery): A red switch usually found on the passenger side of the tractor unit at thigh height, just behind the cab. This switch cuts power to the battery and prevents overnight draining in cold conditions.

Isolator switch (tail-lift): A switch normally found inside the cab or within the tail-lift control box at the rear of the vehicle. The tail-lift cannot be used if this switch is not employed.

Kerb mirror: The mirror that hangs over the passenger side door and gives the driver a view of the nearside kerb area.

Kickdown: The surge of power experienced by pushing the accelerator that little bit further into the floor than it normally goes. On vehicles with tiptronic gearboxes this is known as the 'kickdown facility'.

Kissing (Tyres): Where a wheel has more than one tyre on it, and those tyres are touching because the gap between them is too narrow.

Legger (4/6/8): Slang term indicating the number of axles on a unit, rigid or trailer, eg a 'four legger' has two axles, a 'six legger' has three axles and so on.

Leg winding handle: Used to raise and lower the legs of a trailer. See section on 'How to couple and uncouple a unit and trailer' on p.82–87.

Legs (trailer and box): The supporting legs used to hold a trailer or a drop-box away from the ground when it's not being pulled by a unit or rigid.

LEZ (Low Emissions Zone for Greater London): Regulations regarding the types of LGVs and PCVs allowed into London in accordance with the amount of emissions their engines produce.

LGV C: A rigid vehicle with a maximum gross weight of between 7.5 and 32 tonnes. Also used to describe the licence entitlement to drive that class of vehicle.

LGV C1: A rigid vehicle with a maximum gross weight of between 3.5 tonnes and 7.5 tonnes. Also used to describe the licence entitlement to drive that class of vehicle.

LGV C+E: Any articulated vehicle with a combined maximum gross weight usually between 12 and 44 tonnes. Also used to describe the licence entitlement to drive that class of vehicle.

Lift axles: Axles on a trailer, unit, or rigid which allow you to raise and lower the wheels when you're not carrying a load. This is employed to save on tyre wear.

Loading ramp or Dock Leveller: The ramp used to close the gap between the rear of the trailer and the loading bay floor. Can be manual or mechanical.

Low-loader: A flatbed trailer which sits close to the ground and normally has more than the usual quota of axles. These types of trailer are often used to transport plant machinery.

LSC (Learning and Skills Council): See section on 'Government bodies'.

MAM (maximum authorised mass): This means the vehicle and/or trailer plus its maximum load weight in accordance with what is allowed by the vehicle's class and/or taxation class.

Manual handling: Lifting, pulling or pushing any item or animal without mechanical assistance. See section on 'Manual handling' on p.13.

Manual entry: A way of recording your working day if a tachograph unit is unavailable or not working. See 'Digital and analogue tachographs' sections.

Manufacturer's plate: A metal silver or blue plate indicating date of manufacture, MGW and axle weights. See 'Know your cab'.

Matrix Signs: Electronic signs on a motorway that display information.

Maximum Average Working Week: The maximum average number of hours that an employee can work over a reference period. Also see 'Working Time Regulations' on p.14.

Maximum gross weight: The sum total weight of a vehicle and its load – for example, a 7.5 tonne vehicle would comprise the vehicle itself, weighing about 4.5 tonnes, plus its load of three tonnes.

Maximum Weekly Working Time: The maximum number of hours that any employee can work in one week. Also see 'Working time Regulations' on p.14.

Mobile worker: Drivers, driver's mates or apprentices and some types of warehouse staff are classed as 'Mobile Workers.' Also see 'Working Time Regulations' on p.14.

Moffat: A brand of forklift truck, designed to ride 'piggyback' on the rear of a trailer or rigid vehicle when not in use.

MoT: An annual test of roadworthiness for all engine-propelled and towed vehicles (excluding car trailers below a certain weight).

MoT Plate (Vehicle Inspectorate Plate): A plate displayed within the cab and underneath the trailer that shows the driver (among other things) the MAM and/or train weight of the vehicle or trailer. See 'Know your cab instrumentation and equipment' section on p.60.

Nearside: The passenger side of a vehicle, the side which is nearest the kerb.

O Licence (Operators' Licence): The licence owned by any transport company that transports goods for payment. See 'Know your cab instrumentation and equipment' section on p.60.

Occasional Drivers: One who drives on no more than 10 or 15 occasions in a reference period. Also see HAD on p.19 for full clarification.

Odometer: Records the speed of a vehicle in miles and kilometres, and in an LGV the distance travelled in kilometres rather than miles.

Offside: The driver's side of a vehicle, the side which is furthest from the kerb.

Operations Exempt From EU Rule: See p.18.

Overspeeding: Travelling at more than your vehicle's limited speed so that it is recorded by the digital tachograph or VU as an overspeeding event. See 'Digital tachographs'.

Pallet truck (pump truck): A hydraulic, manual (and sometimes battery-operated) device used to manoeuvre palletised goods on flat ground.

Pallets: A raised wooden platform to which goods are secured for ease of transportation and storage. Though they come in any number of shapes, sizes and strengths, the most common type is the square blue pallet.

Part Time Drivers: Drivers working under British Domestic Hour Rule who do not exceed four hours of driving in any 24-hour period.

PAYE: The basis under which most people are employed, where your employer deducts your tax and national insurance for you.

Payload: Total weight of the goods being carried.

Period of availability (POA): See 'Driving Hours' on p.17 and Working Time Regulations on p.14.

Permission to move your vehicle: See 'Vehicle size and bridges' on p.34.

Pictograms: Symbols used by digital tachographs that are shown both on the LED display and on any printout made. These symbols can represent and show anything from breaks taken, speeding events and power failures. Also see 'Digital Tachographs' on p.23.

Pin: Tapered cylindrical metal object beneath the floor of the trailer that is secured between the jaws of the fifth wheel plate when connected to the tractor unit.

Pin (Rigid and Drawbar): The drop down pin which secures a drawbar trailer into the coupling guide funnel. Also see: 'Coupling a rigid and drawbar trailer' on p.82.

Plated weight: This is the description for the weight or weights that are written on the MoT plate attached to each vehicle or trailer. These are usually the MAM or the train weight.

Prime mover: A rigid vehicle designed for towing a trailer. Such vehicles often have splitter gearboxes.

Producer: A ticket given to a driver by the police which demands that he take it and any documents requested to a police station of his choice within seven days.

PTPS (Personal Track Safety): A training qualification that allows the individual to collect and deliver railway trackside machinery and equipment.

Pull Test: A method of placing a coupled tractor unit in a low gear and trying to pull forward while the trailer brake is on. This is used to check if a unit is correctly coupled to the trailer. Not to be used on a rigid and drawbar trailer combination.

Pumping handle: See pictures in section on 'Using a pallet truck' on p.46.

Pumping lever: In order to pump up the forks of a pallet truck, this lever should first be pushed away from the user until it clicks before pumping can commence. When pulled towards the user, the pallet truck forks will be released and dropped to the ground. See pictures in section on 'Using a pallet truck' on p.46.

Ratchet: The mechanism used to tighten and loosen the curtains on a curtain-sided trailer. Consists of a spindle which the curtain pole sits upon, and levers which loosen and tighten the curtains.

Ratchet brake: Usually found on a trailer, and comes in the form of a long handle that looks a little like a handbrake in a car. To operate, you pull it back and forth on the handle to tighten the cable and apply the trailer brakes. See 'Coupling a rigid and drawbar trailer'.

Ratchet straps: Strong, thick cord straps with metal attachments used to secure movable goods in place during transit. Can be fastened very tightly indeed without too much effort. See section on 'Using internal and external straps' on p.48.

Record Book: A daily log completed by the driver and used by operations exempt from EU rule to keep track of working and driving hours.

Record Of Work: A log kept by drivers working under EU regulations. This is completed by the driver and shows all driving time, working time, rest, breaks and POA.

Recovery position: A position used in resuscitation techniques to prevent a breathing but unconscious casualty from blocking their own airway or choking before they regain consciousness. See section on 'First Aid for motorists'.

Red diesel: Diesel that is of the same quality as white (normal) diesel but for which there is no tax duty to be paid. Red diesel can only be used in vehicles not driven on the public highway. It can also be used to power the generators of refrigerated trailers. A red dye is added to the fuel to stain the tank and internal workings of an engine in order to easily detect misuse. Note that 'Red diesel' is know as 'Green diesel' in Ireland.

Reference period: A period of 17–18 weeks during which a company or agency measures the average working time of its mobile staff. A company can ask for the period to be extended for up to 26 or 52 weeks. See 'Driving Hours' on p.17 and 'Working Time Regulations' on p.14.

Rescue breaths: A method of resuscitating an unconscious person who has stopped breathing. See section on 'First Aid for motorists'.

Retaining bars: Metal bars placed widthways across a trailer to prevent forward or rearward movement of a load. See section on 'Using retaining bars' on p.47.

Reverse parallel parking: The process of reversing a vehicle into a space at the side of a kerb (usually in between two parked vehicles or obstructions). See section on 'How to park against a kerb' on p.99.

Reversing blindside: The process of reversing a vehicle into a space or loading bay from its left-hand side. This is an extremely difficult manoeuvre as the trailer obstructs the driver's view in the nearside mirror. See section on 'Reversing blindside' on p.103.

RHA (Road Haulage Association): See 'Useful contacts' list.

Riding shotgun: A slang term meaning to travel in a truck as a passenger or second driver.

Rigid: A term usually used to describe a non-articulated vehicle of more than 7.5 tonnes, though it can apply to any non-articulated vehicle.

Rigid and drawbar trailer: A rigid vehicle with a trailer attached.

Road Transport Directive (RTD): Regulations applicable to all mobile workers with regards to their working hours. See 'Driving hours'.

Rollerbed trailer: A specialised type of trailer used for transporting goods that can't be loaded using conventional means. These are normally used for transporting airfreight containers and require some training in their proper use.

Roll-on roll-off: A type of vehicle that can tilt and roll containers onto its chassis from ground level using a hydraulic arm and/or winch.

Roller shutter doors: The rear doors of a trailer that consist of slats held together with hinges and wires and open upwards and inwards on rollers which run along a gutter inside the trailer. See section on 'Trailer door security' on p.56.

Rope and sheet: A process used to cover and protect a large load on the back of a flatbed trailer or low-loader. Training is required for this process.

ROSPA (Royal Society for the Prevention of Accidents): See section on 'Government bodies'.

RSPCA (Royal Society for the Prevention of Cruelty to Animals): See section on 'Government bodies'.

Rubbers (loading bay): Most loading bays have large rectangular blocks of hard rubber screwed to the wall to prevent damage to both the back of the trailer and the loading bay. See section on 'Reversing safely into a loading bay' on p.102.

Rubbers (trailer): Some trailers have strips of rubber on the rear, just below the doors, to help prevent damage to the trailer when it's reversed into a loading bay.

Running bent: Driving or operating a vehicle when you're out of driving or working hours.

Running bobtail: Driving a tractor unit without a trailer attached. Also known as 'running solo'.

Running solo: See 'Running bobtail' above.

Sack truck: A small upright trolley on two wheels, upon which you can stack a small number of items to be taken over rough ground from the vehicle to their delivery point. Can be used up or down a small number of steps, up kerbs, and over gravel and cobbles.

Safe-T-bar: The shin-high horizontal bar at the rear of a trailer or rigid vehicle that prevents cars from sliding under your rear wheels in an accident.

Safety catch: The catch inserted into a hole on the fifth wheel plate handle which ensures that the trailer pin is properly secured within the jaws of the fifth wheel plate. If you're unable to insert the catch, the trailer is not secured correctly.

Safety clip retainer: A metal retainer that pops down over part of the fifth wheel handle when the trailer has been securely coupled to the unit.

Safety rails: Slotted into holes at the edges of a tail-lift in order to prevent goods from rolling off the edge when it's in use.

Satellite navigation systems: Hand-held devices that can be fitted into a vehicle using a power attachment to the cigarette lighter, that direct the driver which way to go using an on-screen mapping system.

Scissor lift: Similar to a cherry picker, a scissor lift has a platform which raises and lowers, allowing a person to gain access to streetlights and cables.

Scissor lift 2: Installed where a raised loading bay is not possible, it is a type of platform that the vehicle's load is placed upon. The platform is then mechanically lifted to the same level as the rear of the trailer and the goods loaded on and off.

Self Employed Drivers: See 'Working Time Regulations' on p.14.

Self-employed drivers or Limited Company status: See 'Types of work' section for more information.

Service lead fittings/couplings: Service leads that run from the tractor unit to the trailer using metal couplings and housings at either end, providing an electric feed to the lights and air to the brakes and suspension.

Shrink-wrap: A thin plastic film like a stronger version of cling film. Used to secure goods to a pallet.

Shunt button: A pull out/push in button situated next to the parking brake. Usually blue in colour, though not always. This is used only by mechanics, and should not be used by the driver.

Shunters: Vehicles used to move trailers around a yard. These can be old tractor units or specially designed vehicles. The same term is also applied to the drivers of such vehicles.

Siemens: Brand name of a type of digital tachograph or VU. See 'Digital tachographs'.

Skids: The two ramps mounted on the rear of a tractor unit, which lift a trailer into place and guide it towards the fifth wheel when coupling up.

Special conditions: See 'Vehicle size and bridges' on p.34.

Special routing arrangements: See 'Vehicle size and bridges' on p.34.

Special types order: See 'Vehicle size and bridges' on p.34.

Spill kit: Usually carried by vehicles transporting chemicals, petrol, or oil. Used to mop up and render any spillages harmless.

Split coupling: A term used to describe the technique of coupling the service leads to a trailer before the pin is secured to the fifth wheel plate. This is a risky technique fraught with potential hazards and should only be used when a trailer is close-coupled to its unit owing to a deep pin (one that's set far back from the front of the trailer).

Split daily rest period: The period of rest that a driver must complete between two 24-hour periods, split into two or more parts. See 'Driving Hours' on p.17 and 'Working Time Regulations' on p.14.

Splitter box: Any gearbox with low and high range gears within the same configuration, or half gears within the same configuration. See section on 'How to understand your gearbox' on p.66.

Steering rear axles: Usually found on very long or very short trailers. They allow the driver to take tighter corners without cutting across.

Statutory leave: Compulsory leave that all employees must be granted each year. In the UK this is 20 days and can include bank holidays.

Stillages: Large metal wire containers used to hold loose goods. Only used on curtain-sided vehicles or flatbed trailers and removed using a forklift truck. Can be stacked several high.

Stoneridge: Brand name of a type of digital tachograph or VU. See 'Digital tachographs'.

Stoppers: Barriers designed to prevent a load from falling off the edge of a tail-lift. See section on 'Stoppers and safety rails' on p.56.

Suspension: Most modern units, trailers, and rigids have adjustable air suspension designed to raise and lower the height of the vehicle and trailer. See section on 'Adjusting the height of a trailer or unit' on p.58.

Suzies: See 'Service lead fittings/couplings' in Glossary.

Swan neck (manoeuvre): A manoeuvre used to bring a trailer and unit tight up against and level with the kerb. See section on 'How to park against a kerb' on p.99.

Swan neck (trailer): The part of a low-loader, flatbed, or double-deck trailer above where the fifth wheel plate is coupled to the unit. It is stepped up above the main level of the deck.

Tare: The empty weight of a container.

T-bar: The bar at the rear of a trailer or rigid below the lights, designed to prevent cars from sliding beneath the vehicle in an accident.

T&G (Transport and General Workers Union): See 'Useful contacts' list.

Tachograph chart – analogue: A disc of wax-coated paper used to record movement and speed of a vehicle and the working modes of the driver. See 'Know your cab instrumentation and equipment' section on p.60 and 'Tachographs' on p.31.

Tachograph printout – digital: A piece of paper about the size of a till receipt that displays all the details of a driver's working day.

Tachograph – analogue: The recording unit into which the tachograph chart fits. See 'Know your cab instrumentation and equipment' section on p.63.

Tachograph – Digital: A recording unit (also known as a VU or Vehicle unit) into which the driver's card fits enabling him to record his working day. See digital tachographs on p.23.

Tail-lift mode switch: A switch on a panel within the back of a trailer that enables the controls to be accessed from either inside or outside.

Thinking distance: The distance travelled before a driver reacts to an emergency.

Timed out: A phrase used to describe being locked out of an automated bunkering machine for taking too long to enter your details.

Tiptronic: A type of automatic gearbox with options for manual. See 'Understanding your gearbox'.

Tradeplate drivers: Drivers (often with LGV licences) who hitch-hike around the country collecting and delivering vehicles going on or off hire. They also deliver new, unregistered vehicles out of the factory or showroom, take vehicles to port to be exported, and move vehicles to and from repair shops. The tradeplates themselves are white with red lettering and border. They license the driver to move a roadworthy vehicle without tax, MoT, or a conventional type of insurance.

Trailer brake: Used to hold the trailer in one place. This is usually (though not always) a red pull-out knob situated beneath the floor of or at the front of the trailer. Not to be confused with the shunt button, which is usually (though not always) blue.

Train weight: This is the maximum authorised mass of the vehicle plus the MAM of any additional trailer it may be pulling (such as in the case of a rigid and drawbar trailer).

Tram lines: Worn ruts in a road (usually the first lane of a motorway) that an LGV's wheels are often pulled into.

Tramping: Work that involves living and sleeping in your lorry for most of the week.

Trans-continental: Work that involves driving an LGV abroad.

Trolleys: See 'Wheeled platforms'.

Trunking: Long-distance driving that usually involves delivering only one load or swapping trailers.

Twist locks: Locks controlled by a handle beneath the body of a drop-box or container, that hold the box to the chassis.

U-formation: A method of using straps so that they are fastened slightly in front of the load, run around the back of the load and fasten in a similar way on the opposite side. See 'Your vehicle's equipment'.

Universal Time Co-ordinated: The time that all digital tachographs are set to. UTC is Greenwich Mean Time without the British Summer Time variation.

Up-and-under: A type of tail-lift that tucks up and under the rear of the trailer. See 'Tail-lifts' section on p.52.

Urbie: Nickname given to an urban trailer, which is a 32–35ft trailer designed for city and town deliveries. Usually has only one rear axle. Some have a steering rear axle for getting around tight corners.

VCA (Vehicle Certification Agency): See section on 'Government bodies'.

Vehicle Licence (Road Tax): An annual duty paid by any company or individual who owns a vehicle. See 'Know your cab instrumentation and equipment' section on p.60.

VOSA (Vehicle and Operator Services Agency): See section on 'Government bodies'.

Vehicle Unit (VU): Also known as a Digital Tachograph. Also see 'Digital Tachographs' on p.23.

Wagon: A slang term for a truck.

Wagon and drag: Slang term for a combination of a rigid and drawbar trailer.

Walking floor: A specialist type of trailer that allows bulk loads that can't easily be palletised (such as paper or textiles) to be moved more easily. This system works by literally 'walking' the load out of the back of the trailer using a mechanism which moves the metal floorboards against one another in an alternating motion using hydraulic pistons below the floor.

Waybill: Part of a driver's paperwork giving (amongst other things) details of the goods being carried.

Weekly rest period: The legally required period of time that a driver has to rest after no more than six consecutive working days. See section on 'Laws regarding driving hours' on p.17.

Weighbridge: A flat platform laid into the ground that weighs a vehicle and its load. In simple terms the equivalent of a giant set of scales.

Wheeled platforms: Small platforms with a wheel at each corner used to transport stacks of tubs or trays.

Wind deflectors: Plastic body modifications made to a vehicle to improve its aerodynamic properties. Wind deflectors can be found on the roof of the unit and at the sides and rear of the cab.

Working Time Directive. See p.14.

Workshop: An on-site facility within most transport yards to provide repair support to the fleet.

X-formation: A method of using straps so that they are fastened slightly in front of the load, run around the back of the load in a diagonal fashion (two straps forming a cross) and fasten lower down on the opposite side. See 'Your vehicle's equipment'.

Yard marshall: An individual employed to direct vehicles in a busy yard. They may also be employed to keep records of the location of all parked, loading and offloading vehicles.

Foreign dictionaries

Polish/English pronounciation

ENGLISH	GERMAN	FRENCH	ITALIAN	DUTCH	SPANISH	POLISH	Polish/English pronounciation
a	ein/eine	un	un/uno/una	een	un/una	to	ej, a
abnormal load	Schwertransport/Sondertransport	convoi exceptionnel	carico anormale	abnormale lading	carga anómala	nieprawidłowy ładunek	abnormal lold
accident	Unfall	accident	incidente	ongeval	accidente	wypadek	akcident
accommodation/bed and breakfast	Unterkunft/Bed&Breakfast	chambre d'hôte	alloggio	onderdak/pension	habitación	zakwaterowanie	akommodejszyn/bed and brejkfest
address	Adresse	adresse	indirizzo	adres	dirección	adres	adres
air pressure	Luftdruck	pression d'air	pneumatici	luchtdruk	presión atmosférica	ciśnienie atmosferyczne	er preszer
airport	Flughafen	aéroport	aeroporto	luchthaven	aeropuerto	lotnisko	erport
alternator	Generator	alternateur	alternatore	dynamo	alternador	prądnica, alternator	alternejte
ambulance	Krankenwagen	ambulance	ambulanza	ambulance	ambulancia	karetka	ambiulans
ample room for manoeuvring	ausreichend Platz zum Manövrieren	assez de place pour faire la manoeuvre	piazzola di manovra	ruim voldoende ruimte om te maneouvreren	sala amplia de maniobras	wygodny pokój	ampyl rum for manuvrin
and	und	et	e	en	y	i	and
animal	Tier	animal	animale	dier	animal	zwierzę	animal
arcade machine	Spielautomat	jeux électroniques	macchina da gioco	fruitmachine	videojuego	automaty do gier	arkejd maszin
area	Bereich/Gebiet/Fläche/Gegend/Stelle	aire	zona	gebied	zona	teren, obszar	arija
articulated vehicle/artic	Gelenkfahrzeug	tracteur trailer/semi-remorque	veicolo articolato	voertuig met aangekoppelde oplegger	camión articulado	samochód ciężarowy przegubowy	artikulejtet vejkal/artik
attack	Angriff	attaque	attacco	aanval	ataque	zaatakowany	atak
bank	Bank	banque	banca	bank	banco	bank	bank
banksman	Einweiser	banksman (une personne qui vous aide renverse votre camion)	manovratore	iemand die aanwijzingen geeft bij het achteruitrijden	banksman (una persona que ayuda para invertir un camión)	pracownik banku	banksman
bar	Stange	barre	sbarra	stang	barra	bar	bar
barrier	Absperrung/hindernis	barrière	barriera	barrière	barrera	ogrodzenie, barierka	barier
battery	Batterie	batterie	batteria	accu	batería	bateria	bateri

bend	Kurve	virage	curva	curva	bocht	zakręt	bend
bollard	Poller	cônes de signalisation	colonnina	baliza	verkeerszuiltje	pachołek	bolard
bottom	Unterseite	fond	fondo	fondo	bodem	dno, spód	botum
box	Barton/Kasten/Schachtel	boîte	scatola	caja	kist	pudełko	boks
brake	Bremse	frein	freni	freno	rem	hamulec	brejk
break	Pause	break	pausa	pausa	pauze	przerwa	brejk
breakdown	Ausfall/Betriebsstörung	en panne	guasto	avería	storing	awaria, niepowodzenie	brejkdałn
breakfast	Frühstück	petit déjeuner	prima colazione	desayuno	ontbijt	śniadanie	brejkfest
British	britisch	Britannique	britannico/britannica	británico	Brits	brytyjski	Britisz
bureau de change/Euro's accepted	Geldwechsel/Euroannahme	bureau de change/accepte les euros	la ufficio de cambio/accettata eurodollaro	la oficina de cambio/aceptar eurodivisa	wisselkantoor/ook euro's	kantor wymiany/walut	biuro de sząsz/juroł's akseptet
bus	Bus	bus	autobus	autobús	bus	autobus	bas
business park	Gewerbegebiet	business center	parco commerciale	parque industrial	industrieterrein	teren przemysłowy, handlowy	busines pak
button	Knopf/Taste	bouton	bottone	botón	knop	przycisk	baton
cab	Fahrerkabine	cabine / tracteur	cabina	cabina	cabine	szoferka	kab
café	Café	café	caffe	café	café	kawiarnia	kafe
cage	Käfig	cage	gabbia	jaula	kooi	klatka	kejdż
canopy	Baldachin	vache	cappa	toldo	overhuiving	zadaszenie, baldachim, sklepienie	kanapi
car	Auto	voiture	macchina	coche	auto	samochód	kar
caravan	Wohnwagen	caravane	roulotte	caravana	caravan	przyczepa mieszkalna	karavan
cashpoint machine	Geldautomat	distributeur d'argent	cassa automatica	cajero automático	pinautomaat	bankomat	kaszpoint maszin
caution	Vorsicht	attention	prudenza	precaución	let op	uwaga	koszion
central reservation	Mittelstreifen	terre-plein	banchina spartitraffico	mediana	middenberm	linia pomiedzy pasami ruchu	sentral reserwejszon
charge	Fracht, Gebühr, Anklage, Aufladung, Honorar, Kosten	tarif	tariffa	tarifa	tarief	opata	czardż
city centre	Stadtmitte	centre ville	centro citta	centro de la ciudad	stadscentrum	centrum miasta	sity senter
clean	reinigen	propre	pulire	lavado	reinigen	posprzątać	klin
clip	Klammer	pince	fermaglio	grapa	klem	spinacz, uchwyt, zacisk	klip
closed	geschlossen	fermé	chiuso/a	cerrado	dicht	zamknięty	klost
clothing	Kleidung	vêtements	vestiti	ropa	kleding	ubrania	klotin
coach	Reisebus	autocar	pullman	autobús	autobus	autobus	kołcz
coffee	Kaffee	café	caffe	café	koffie	kawa	kofi
congestion	Verkehrsstauung	circulation difficile	congestione	congestión	verkeersopstopping	przeciążenie	kondzeszczion
congestion charge	City-maut	péage pour rentrer dans le centre-ville de Londres	tarifa per congestione a Londra	tarifa por congestión en Londres	verkeerstarief in centrum van Londen	oplata od każdego samochodu do zapłacenia w centralnym Londynie	kondzeszczion czardż

ENGLISH	GERMAN	FRENCH	ITALIAN	DUTCH	SPANISH	POLISH	Polish/English pronounciation
couple up	ankoppeln	accrocher	agganciare/attaccare	aankoppelen	acoplar	połączyć, podłączyć	kopyl ap
crossing	Fußgängerstreifen	passage piétons	passaggio pedonale	oversteekplaats	paso de peatones	pasy	krosin
crossroads	Kreuzung	carrefour	incrocio	kruising	cruce	skrzyżowanie	krosrolds
curtain sided trailer	Anhänger mit plane	remorque a rideaux	rimorchio con lati a tenda	met zeildoek afgesloten aanhänger	camión con cortina	firanka, zasłona	kurtejn sajdet czrejler
customs	Zoll	douane	dogana	douane	aduana	celnik	kustoms
cycle	Fahrrad	vélo/bicyclette	bicicletta	fiets	bicicleta	jechać na rowerze	cajkl
danger	Gefahr	danger	pericolo	gevaar	peligro	niebezpieczeństwo	dendzer
dashboard	Armaturenbrett	tableau de bord	cruscotto	dashboard	salpicadero	błotnik	daszbord
dealership	Händler	concessionnaire	concessionario	dealerbedrijf	representación	sprzedawca samochodów i części	dilerszip
delay	Verzögerung	délai	ritardo	vertraging	demora	opóźniać, wstrzymywać	dilej
diagnostic system	Diagnosesystem	système diagnostic	sistemi diagnostico	diagnostisch systeem	sistema diagnóstico	przegląd, system diagnostyczny w ciężarowce	dajagnostik system
diesel	Diesel	diesel	gasolio	diesel	gasoil	diesel	disel
dispatch department	Versandabteilung	département pour les envois	reparto de spedizione	verzendafdeling	departamento de expedición	oddział wysyłek	dispacz dipartment
diversion	Umleitung	déviation	deviazione	omleiding	desviación	odwrócenie, zmiana kierunku	dajverszion
document	Dokument	document	documenti	document	documento	dokument	dokjument
door	Tür	porte	porta	deur	puerta	drzwi	dor
double yellow lines	durchgezogene gelbe fahrbahnmarkierung	double ligne jaune (route non stop)	doppia giallo linea (sosta vietata)	dubbele gele streep, niet parkeren	doble línea amarilla (prohibido aparcar/estacionarse)	podwójna żółta linia na której nie można parkować	dabyl jelol lajns
down	abwärts/nach unten	en bas	giu'	omlaag	abajo	dół	dałn
driver	Fahrer	conducteur	camionista	chauffeur	camionero/a	kierowca	drajwer
drivers washroom	Sanitäräume für fahrer	WC pour camionneurs	bagno per camionista	wasruimte voor chauffeurs	baño para conductor/a	łazienka dla kierowców	drajwers toszrum
driving licence	Fahrervorschriften	permis de conduire	patente	rijbewijs	permiso de conducir	prawo jazdy	drajwin lisens
driving regulations	Führerschein	règlements de conduite	regolamento per camionista	verkeersregels	normas de conducción	kodeks pracy dla kierowców	drajin regiulejszyn
dual carriageway	zweispurige Straße	deux voies	doppia corsia	tweebaansweg	carretera de doble sentido	droga dwukierunkowa	dulal kariadżej
Dutch		néerlandais		Nederlands			
east	Ost/Osten	est	est	het oosten	este	wschód	ist
engine	Motor	moteur	motore	motor	motor	silnik	endzin
entertainment	Unterhaltung	spectacle	intrattenimento	amusement	diversión	rozrywka, przedstawienie	entetejnment
entrance	Auffahrt/Eingang	entrée	entrata	ingang	entrada	wejście	entrens
exit	Ausfahrt/Ausgang	sortie	uscita	uitgang	salida	wyjście	eksit

English	German	French	Italian	Dutch	Spanish	Polish	Pronunciation
factory	Fabrik	usine	fabbrica	fabriek	fabrica	fabryka	faktori
fax/photocopy facility	Fax-/Kopiermöglichkeit	fax / photocopie	servizio copisteria	Fax/fotokopieermachine	instalación telefax/fotocopiadora	fax, kseropia	faks/fotokopi fesiliti
female	Frau	femelle	femmina	vrouw	femenino	kobieta	fimejl
ferry	Fähre	ferry	traghetto	veerdienst	trasbordador	przeprawiać	feri
fifth wheel	Sattelkupplung	sellette d'attelage	piattaforma d'innesto	koppelschotel	rueda de repuesto	siodło	fift fil
fire service	Feuerwehr	pompier	vigili del fuoco	brandweer	bomberos	straż pożarna	fajer servis
flood	Flut/Überflutung	inonder	inondazione	overstroming	inundación	powódź	flod
floor	Stockwerk	sol	pavimento	vloer	suelo	podłoga	flor
fog	Nebel	brouillard	nebbia	mist	niebla	mgła	fog
food	Essen	nourriture	cibo	voedsel	comida	żywność	fud
foot (ft)	Fuß (ft)	pied (mesure Britannique)	piede (Británico misure)	Britse voet (0,3048 m)	pie (Británico medida)	stopa	fut (ft)
for	für	pour	per	voor	para/por	za, dla	for
fork lift truck	Gabelstapler	chariot élévateur	carrello elevatore	vorkheftruck	carretilla elevadora	wózek widłowy	fork lift czrak
France		France					
free	kostenlos	libre	gratis	gratis	gratuito/gratis	bezpłatny	fri
French		Français					
fuel bunker	Treibstofftank	station service	pompa di gasolio automatica	branstofreservoir	fuel búnker	miejsce tankowania paliwa	fuel bankier
fuse	Sicherung	fusible	fusibile	zekering	fusible	zapalnik, bezpiecznik	fuse
fusebox	Sicherungskasten	boîte à fusibles	scatola dei fusibili	zekeringdoos	caja de fusibles	skrzynka bezpiecznikowa	fiuseboks
garage	Autowerkstatt/Garage	garage	officina	garage	taller	garaż	garedz
gearbox	Getriebe	boîte de vitesses	scatola del cambio	versnellingsbak	caja de cambios	skrzynia biegów	girboks
gentlemen	Herren	homme	signori/uomini	heren	caballeros	pan	dżentlemen
german	deutsch	allemand					
Germany	Deutschland	Allemagne					
give way (yield)	Vorfahrt gewähren	céder le passage	dare la precedenza	voorrang verlenen	ceder el paso	ustąp pierszeństwa	giv łej/jild
go	gehen/fahren	aller	avanti	gaan	ir	iść, poruszać się, jechać	goł
goodbye	Auf Wiedersehen	au revoir	arrivederci	tot ziens	adiós	do wiedzenia, żegnajcie	gudbaj
goods inward	Wareneingang	réception de marchandises	articoli in entrata	goederen in	entrada de mercancías	przyjęcie towaru	guds inłord
Great Britain	Großbritannien	grande Bretagne	Gran Bretagna	Groot-Brittannië	Gran Bretaña	Wielka Brytania	Grejt Brytyn
gymnasium/gym	Fitnessstudio	gym	la palestra	gymnastieklokaal	gimnasio	szkoła średnia, gimnazium	dżimnasium/dżim
hard shoulder	Standstreifen	accotement/bande d'arrêt d'urgence	corsia di emergenza	vluchtstrook	andén	pobocze	hard szolder
hazardous goods	Gefahrengüter	matières dangereuses	oggetti pericolosi	gevaarlijke goederen	mercancías peligrosas	substancje niebezpieczne	hazardos guds
he	er	lui	lui	hij	él	on	hi
healthy food menu	gesundes Essen	nourriture saine	menu di cibi sani	gezond menu	menú orgánico	zdrowa żywność	helti fud meniu
heater	Heizer	chauffage	riscaldamento	verwarming	calentador	grzejnik, podgrzewacz, grzałka	hiter
height	Höhe	hauteur	altezza	lengte	altura	wysokość	hajt

Polish/English pronounciation

ENGLISH	GERMAN	FRENCH	ITALIAN	DUTCH	SPANISH	POLISH	Polish/English pronounciation
hello	hallo	bonjour	ciao	hallo	hola	cześć	hello
help!	Hilfe!	au secours	aiuto!	help!	¡ayuda!	pomocy	help!
HGV/LGV (heavy/large goods vehicle)	LKW	poids lourd	veicolo per trasporti pesanti	vrachtwagen	vehículo pesado	ciężarówka, naczepa	hevi/lardz guds vejkal
high winds	starker Wind	vent fort	grande vento	harde wind	vientos fuertes	silne wiatry	haj lindz
hill	Hügel	colline	collina	heuvel	colina	wzgórze, górka	hil
Holland		pays bas		Nederland			
hospital	Krankenhaus	hôpital	hospital	ziekenhuis	hospital	szpital	hospital
hotel	Hotel	hôtel	albergo	hotel	hotel	hotel	hotel
how	wie	comment	come	hoe	cómo	jak?	hał
hungry	hungrig	faim	fame	honger	hambriento	głodny	hangri
I	ich	je	io	ik	yo	ja	aj
ice	Eis	verglas	ghiaccio	ijs	hielo	lód	ajs
identification	Identifikation	identification	documento d'identità	identificatie	identificación	identyfikacja, rozpoznanie, stwierdzenie tożsamości	ajdentifikejszyn
inch (")	Zoll (")	pouce (mesure Britannique)	pollice (Britanico misure)	Engelse duim (2,54 cm)	pulgada (Britanico medida)	cal (=2,54 cm)	incz
indicator	Kontrollleuchte	clignotant	indicatore di direzione	richtingaanwijzer	indicador	żółte światło sygnalizacyjne w samochodzie	indikejtor
industrial estate	Industriegebiet	zone industrielle	zona industriale	industrieterein	zona industrial	teren przemysłowy, magazyny	industrial estejt
information	Information	information	informazioni	informatie	información	informacja	informejszyn
inn	Gasthof	auberge	locanda	herberg	hostal	zajazd, gospoda	in
international newspapers	internationale Zeitungen	journal international	giornale internazionale	buitenlandse kranten	diarios internacionales	gazety międzynarodowe	internaszional niuspejpers
internet	Internet	accès internet	internet	internet	Internet	internet	internet
Italian		italien	italiano/italiana				
Italy		Italie	Italia				
jacuzzi	Whirlpool	jacuzzi	jacuzzi	jacuzzi	jacuzzi	jacuzzi	dżakuzi
junction/exit	Anschlussstelle/Ausfahrt	carrefour / sortie	incrocio/uscire	knooppunt/afslag	cruce/salida	zjazd z drogi	dżankszyn/eksit
keys	Schlüssel	clefs	chiavi	sleutels	llaves	klucze	kijs
kilometre	Kilometer	kilomètre	chilometro	kilometer	kilómetro	kilometr	kilometr
ladies	Damen	femmes	signore/donne	dames	señoras	panie	lejdis
laundry/launderette	Waschsalon	blanchisserie	lavanderia	wasserij/wasserette	lavandería	pralnia	londri/londrete
left	links	gauche	sinistra	links	izquierda	lewo	left
legs	Anhängerständer	jambes	gambe	benen	piernas	nogi, na których stoi naczepa	legs

level crossing	Bahnübergang	passage a niveau	passaggio a livello	gelijkvloerse overweg	paso a nivel	przejazd kolejowy	level krosin
lever	Hebel	levier	leva	hendel	palanca	dźwignia, lewar	liver
lights	Lichter/Leuchten	lumières	luci	lichten	luces	światła	lajts
loading bay	Ladebucht	quai	piazzola di carico	laadruimte	área de carga y descarga	miejsce załadunku	loldin bej
long stay parking	Dauerparkplatz	parking longue durée	parcheggio a lungo termine	lang parkeren	aparcamiento prolongado	parking długiego postoju	long stej parkin
lorry	Lastwagen	camion	camion	vrachtwagen	camión	ciężarówka	lori
lorry park	LKW-Raststätte	parking pour camion	parcheggio per camion	voorzieningen voor chauffeurs	aparcamiento para camiones	parking dla ciężarówek z udogodnieniami dla kierowców	lori park
low bridge	niedrige Brücke	hauteur limitée	ponte basso	lage brug	puente bajo	niski most	lol bridż
lower	Senken/Herablassen/Herabsetzen	plus bas	piu basso	laten zakken	bajar	opuszczać, zniżać, zmniejszać	loter
Madam	Frau	Madame	Signora	Mevrouw	Señora	pani	Madam
male	Mann	male	maschio	man	hombre	mężczyzna	mejl
maximum	Maximum	maximum	massimo	maximum	máximo	największy, maksymalny	maksimum
meal voucher	Essensgutschein	ticket restaurant	buono pasto	maaltijdbon	vale de comida	kupon rabatowy na posiłek	mil volčzer
mechanic	Mechaniker	mécanique	meccanico	monteur	mecánico	mechanik	mechanik
meter	Parkuhr	compteur	parchimetro	meter	parquímetro	miernik	miter
MGW (maximum gross weight)	MBG (maximales Bruttogewicht)	poids maximum	peso massimo lordo	maximum brutogewicht	Peso total máximo	waga maksymalna	maksimum gros wejt
mile (m)	Meile	mile (mesure Britannique)	miglio (Britanico misure)	mijl (1,60934 km)	milla (Británico medida)	mila (=1609,31 m)	majel
miles per hour (MPH)	Meilen pro Stunde (MPH)	mile a l'heure (mesure Britannique)	miglia all'ora (Britanico misure)	mijl per uur (1,60934 km/u)	millas por hora (Británico medida)	wskaźnik mil na godzinę	majels per aler
minimum	Minimum	minimum	minimo	minimum	mínimo	najmniejszy	minimum
mirror	Spiegel	miroir	specchio	spiegel	espejo	lustro	miror
Miss	Frau	Mademoiselle	Signorina	Mejufrouw	Señorita	panienka	Mys
Mister	Herr	Monsieur	Signor	Mijnheer	Señor	pan	Myster
mobile phone	Mobiltelefon	téléphone portable	telefono cellulare	mobiele telefoon	teléfono móvil	telefon komórkowy	mobajl fołn
money	Geld	argent	soldi	geld	dinero	pieniądze	mani
MoT plate/certificate	TÜV-Plakette	contrôle technique	certificato di revisione	Bewijs van verplichte jaarlijkse keuring	inspección placa/certificado	potwierdzenie sprawności pojazdu (tablica na naczepie i przedniej szybie)	em ot ti plejt,sertifikat
motorcycle	Motorrad	moto	motocicletta	motorfiets	motocicleta	motocykl	motocajkyl
motorway	Autobahn	autoroute	autostrada	snelweg	autopista	autostrada	motorłej
nearby	in der Nähe	près	vicino	dichtbij	cercano	pobliski	nirbaj
no	nein	non	no/non	nee	no	nie	noł
no entry	keine Einfahrt	sens interdit / défense d'entrer	senso vietato	verboden toegang	prohibido el paso	brak wjazdu	not enczri
north	Nord/Norden	nord	nord	het noorden	norte	północ	nort
number plate	Kennzeichen	plaque d'immatriculation	targa	nummerbord	placa de matrícula	tablica rejestracyjna	nambe plejt

ENGLISH	GERMAN	FRENCH	ITALIAN	DUTCH	SPANISH	POLISH	Polish/English pronunciation
oil	Öl	huile	olio	olie	aceite	olej (oil change -zmiana oleju)	ojl
okay	okay	ok	ok	in orde	OK	w porządku	okej
on site	vor Ort	sur le site	su luogo	op het terrein	en su sitio	na miejscu, na terenie (site-teren,położenie,okolica)	on sajt
one	eins/eine/ennen	un	uno/una	een	un/uno/una	jeden	łan
one way street	Einbahnstraße	sens unique	senso unico	straat met eenrichtingsverkeer	calle de sentido unico	ulica jednokierunkowa	łan wej strit
open	öffnen	ouvert	aperto/a	open	abierto	otwarte	ołpen
opening times	Öffnungszeiten	heures d'ouverture	orario di apertura	openingstijden	hora de abertura	godziny otwarcia	ołpenin tajms
over	über	au-dessus	sopra	over	encima	nad, po, w	ołver
overhead	Oberleitungen	au-dessus	sospeso in aria	bovenhoofds	arriba	na górze	ołverhed
overnight	über nacht	pour la nuit	durante la notte	nachtelijk	durante la noche	całonocny	ołvernajt
pain	Schmerzen	douleur	dolore	pijn	dolor	ból	pejn
pallet	Palette	palette	paletta	pallet	palet	paleta	palet
pallet truck	Gabelstapler	chariot elevateur (Equiptment a utilisé pour déplacer de palettes)	carrello elevatore - muletto	pallettruck	carretilla (equiptment para mover paleta)	paleciak	palet czak
pardon?	Wie bitte?	pardon?	scusa	pardon?	¿cómo?	słucham?	pardon?
parking space	Parkplatz	place de parking	posto per la macchina	Parkeerplaats	sitio para aparcar	miejsce parkingowe	parkin spejs
passport	Pass	passeport	passaporto	pasport	pasaporte	paszport	pasport
pavement	Bürgersteig	trottoir	marciapiede	trottoir	acera	nawiezchnia drogi	pejwment
pedestrian	Fußgänger	piéton	pedoni	voetganger	peatón	pieszy	pedesczian
petrol station	Tankstelle	station d'essence	stazione de servizio	benzinestation	estación de servicio	stacja benzynowa	pecztrol stejszyn
please	bitte	s'il vous plait	per favore	a.u.b.	por favor	proszę	plise
Poland		Pologne				Polska	Poland
police	Polizei	police	polizia	politie	policia	policja	polisz
Polish		polonais				polski	polis
port/harbour	Hafen	port	porto	haven	puerto	port	port/harbor
post office	Postamt	bureau de poste	ufficio postale	postkantoor	correos	poczta	połst ofis
priority to the right	rechts vor links	priorité à droite	dare la precedenza adestra	rechts gaat voor	dar la prioridad a la derecha	pierszeństwo w prawo	prijoriti tu de rajt
problem	Problem	problème	problema	probleem	problema	problem	problem
pub	Pub	pub	birreria	café	pub	pub	pab
pull	ziehen	tirer	tirare	trekken	tirar	pociągnąć	pul
pump	Pumpe	pompe	pompa	pomp	bomba	pompka	pamp

English	German	French	Italian	Dutch	Spanish	Polish	
puncture	Reifenpanne	crever, crevaison	gomma forata	lekke band	pinchazo	złapać gumę	pankczer
push	drücken/schieben	pousser	spingere	duwen	empujar	pchać	pusz
quarry	Steinbruch	carrière	cava	steengroeve	cantera	kopalnia, kamieniołom	klari
queue	Schlange	file	fila	rij	cola	kolejka	kju
quiet	ruhig	calme/tranquille	silenzioso	stil	silencioso	cisza, spokój	klajet
radio	Radio	radio	radio	radio	radio	radio	rejdiol
rain	Regen	pluie	pioggia	regen	lluvia	deszcz	rejn
raise	heben	soulever	sollevare	heffen	levantar	podnosić, ustawiać	rajz
red diesel	Roter Diesel/Heizöl	gas oil rouge (Diesel pour les véhicules agricoles)	gasolio rosso (gasolio per veicoli agrari)	rode diesel	gasoil teñido (gasóleo por agricultura vehículo)	paliwo do ciężarówek nieopodatkowane	red disel
red route	absolutes Halteverbot	Route rouge (route non stop)	itinerario rosso (divieto di sosta)	route met stopverbod	rojo ruta (prohibido aparcar/estacionarse)	miejsce, na którym wzbronione jest zatrzymywanie pod groźbą wysokiej kary pieniężnej	red rut
refrigerated goods/trailer	Kühlwaren/Anhänger	camion frigorifique	camion frigo	gekoelde goederen/aanhanger	mercancías refrigeradas/remolque	towary mrożone, przyczepa chłodnia	refridzerated guds/czrejler
repair	reparieren	réparation	riparazioni	repareren	reparación	naprawiać	riper
restaurant	Restaurant	restaurant	ristorante	restaurant	restaurante	restauracja	restafrant
restriction	Einschränkung	restriction	limitazione	beperkende bepaling	limitado	ograniczenie	restrikszion
reverse	Umdrehen/Wenden/Rückwärtsgang einlegen	marche arrière	inverso	achteruitrijden	inverso	odwracać	riverse
right	rechts	droite	destra	rechts	derecha	prawo	rajt
rigid and trailer/wagon and drag	Zugmaschine und Anhänger	train routier	camion e rimorchio	vrachtwagen met aanhanger	camión y remolque	ciężarówka	ridzit and czrejler/laon and dzrag
ring road	Umgehungsstraße	périphérique	cironvallazione	ringweg	circunvalación	obwodnica	ring rold
road	Straße	route	strada	weg	carretera	droga	rold
roadworks	Bauarbeiten	travaux	lavori in corso	wegwerkzaamheden	obras	robory drogowe	roldrorks
room	Zimmer	chambre	camera	kamer	alojamiento	pokój	rum
roundabout/island	Kreisverkehr/Verkehrsinsel	rond point	rotatoria	rotonde	glorieta	rondo	rándabaut/ajlend
route	Route	itinéraire	itinerario	route	ruta	trasa	rut
sandwich	Sandwich	sandwich	sandwich	boterham	bocadillo	kanapka	santicz
sauna	Sauna	sauna	sauna	sauna	sauna	sauna	sona
seal	Verriegelung	sceau	sigillo	zegel	sellar	pląba, pieczęć	sil
seat	Sitz	chaise	posto	stoel	asiento	siedzenie, miejsce	sit
seat belt	Sicherheitsgurt	ceinture de sécurité	cinture di sicurezza	veiligheidsgordel	cinturón de seguridad	pas bezpieczeństwa	sit belt
secure	sicher	ferme	sicuro	vast	firme	zabezpieczony, zamknięty	sekiur
security guard	Sicherheitswachmann	gardien	guardia giurata	bewaker	guardia de seguridad	strażnik	sekiurti gard
service leads/suzies	Anschlussleitungen	accouplement électrique	attacci dell'aria e corrente	verbindingskabels	parejas eléctricas	kable pomiędzy kabiną ciężarówki a naczepą	servis lids/suzis

ENGLISH	GERMAN	FRENCH	ITALIAN	DUTCH	SPANISH	POLISH	Polish/English pronounciation
services	Tank- und Raststätten	station service	area di servizio	stopplaats met winkels aan de snelweg	servicios	serwis na autostradzie (jedzenie,toalety,parking)	servysys
she	sie	elle	lei	zij	ella	ona	szi
shop	Laden	boutique	negozio	winkel	tienda	sklep	szop
shopping centre/mall	Einkaufszentrum	galerie marchande	centro commerciale	Winkelcentrum	centro comercial	centrum handlowe	szopin center/mall
short term parking	Kurzparkplatz	parking courte durée	parcheggio a orario limitato	kort parkeren	aparcamiento carga y descarga	parking krótkiego postoju	szort term parkin
shower	Dusche	douche	doccia	douche	ducha	prysznic	szaler
shrink wrap	Schrumpffolienverpackung	filmer	incelofanare	krimpverpakking	empaquetar en envase termoretráctil	folia	sznink rap
shunter vehicle	Rangierfahrzeuge	véhicule pour détourner de remorque	motrice rimorchio	rangeerwagen	vehiculo para maniobras	samochód używany do przestawiania naczep	syanter wejkal
single carriageway	einspurige Straße	voie simple	solo carreggiata	eenbaansweg	carretera de un solo sentido	pas ruchu	singyl karydżlej
sink	Handwaschbecken	lavabo	lavandino	gootsteen	fregadero	umywalka	synk
site	Standort	site	luogo	terrein	ubicación	miejsce	sajt
slow	langsam	lentement	lento/rallentare	langzaam	decelerar	powoli	slol
snack bar	Imbiss	snack bar	snack bar	snackbar	cafetería	bar	snack bar
snow	Schnee	neige	neve	sneeuw	nieve	śnieg	snol
south	Süd/Süden	sud	sud	het zuiden	sur	poludnie	saft
Spain		Espagne			España		
Spanish		espagnol			Español		
speed camera	Blitzgerät	radar	autovelox	snelheidscamera	radar	aparat robiący zdjęcia samochodom jadącym z niedozwoloną prędkością	spid kamra
speed limit	Geschwindigkeitsbegrenzung	limitation de vitesse	limite di velocità	maximumsnelheid	limite de velocidad	ograniczenie prędkości	spid lymit
spray	Spritzwasser	éclaboussure	spray	stuivend water	spray	woda tłapiąca spod kól samochodu	sprej
standpipe	Standrohr	fontaine	rubinetto pubblico	standpijp	tubo vertical	postój z wodą	standpajp
stay in lane	kein Fahrbahnwechsel	rester dans sa voie	tenere la corsia	baan aanhouden	quedarse en el camino	nie zmieniaj pasu ruchu	staj in lejn
steering wheel	Lenkrad	volant	volante	stuur	volante	kierownica	stiring fil
stop	anhalten	stop	alt	stop	alto	stop	stop
straight ahead	geradeaus	tout droit	sempre dritto	rechtdoor	siga recto	prosto	strajt ehed
strap	Riemen	sangle	tracolla	riem	correa	pas	strap
supermarket	Supermarkt	supermarché	supermercato	supermarkt	supermercado	supermarket	siupermarket
suspension	Aufhängung	suspension	sospensione	vering	suspensión	zawieszenie	sespens:ion

English	German	French	Italian	Spanish	Dutch	Polish	(pronunciation)
tacho disk	Tacho disk	tachydisque	tachidisk	disco diagrama de tacógrafo	tacho disk	tarza	takodisk/takograf czart
tachograph	Fahrtenschreiber	tachygraphe	tachigrafo	tacógrafo	tachograaf	tachograf	takograf
tail lift	Hebebühne	monte charge	pedana solevatore	plataforma elevadora	autolaadklep	winda na końcu naczepy	tejl lift
take-away	Imbiss zum Mitnehmen	à emporter	piatti pronti	comida para llevar	afhaalmaaltijd	na wynos	tejk-e tej
tank	Tank	réservoir	serbatoio	depósito	tank	zbiornik	tank
tank cleaning facilities	Tankreinigungsanlage	lavage pour camion-citerne	lavaggio per camion cisterna	lavado para camión cisterna	reiniger voor in tanks	myjnia dla cystern i zbiorników (od wewnątrz)	tank klinin fesilites
tea	Tee	thé	tè	té	thee	herbata	ti
telephone	Telefon	téléphone	telefono	teléfono	telefoon	telefon	telefołn
thank you	Danke	merci	grazie	gracias	dank u	dziękuję	tank ju
the	der/die/das	le, la	la/lo/il/le	los/las/lo	de/het	ten, ta, to	de
theft	Diebstahl	vol	furto	robo	diefstal	kradzież	teft
they	sie	ils, elles	loro	ellos/ellas	zij	oni	tej
thirsty	durstig	soif	assetato/aver sete	sediento	dorst	spragniony, chcący się napić	tersti
ticket	Ticket	ticket	biglietto	billete	kaartje	bilet	tiket
tired	müde	fatigué	stanco	cansado	moe	zmęczony	tajerd
t-junction	T-Kreuzung	intersection	incrocio a T	cruce en T	T-kruising	skrzyżowanie w kształcie litery T	ti-dzankszon
today	heute	aujourd'hui	oggi	hoy	vandaag	dzisiaj	tudej
toilet	Toilette	toilette	toilette	sanitario/aseos/servicios	toilet	toaleta	toilet
toll	Maut/Gebühr/Zoll	péage	pedaggio	peaje	tol	opłata, cło	toll
tomorrow	morgen	demain	domani	mañana	morgen	jutro	tumarol
tonnes/tons (British measurement)	Tonnen	tonnes/tons (mesure Britannique)	tonnellata/tonnellata (Britanico misure)	tonelada/toneladas (medida británica)	Engelse ton (1016 kg)	tona	tons
top	Oberseite/Spitze	dessus	cima	cima	bovenkant	na górze	top
town	Stadt	ville	città	ciudad	stad	miasto	tałn
tractor unit	Sattelschlepper	tracteur	motrice	tractor	tractor	ciągnik siodłowy, ciągnik do naczepy	czraktor junit
traffic lights	Ampel	feux	semaforo	semáforo	stoplichten	światła sygnalizacyjne	czrafik lajts
trailer	Anhänger	remorque	rimorchio	remolque	aanhanger	naczepa	czrejler
train	Zug	train	treno	tren	trein	pociąg	czrejn
tram	Straßenbahn	tram	tram	tranvía	tram	tramwaj	tram
transport department	Transportministerium	département de transport	reparto di trasporto	sección de transporte	transportafdeling	wydział transportu	czransport dipartment
truck	Lastwagen	camion	camion	camión	vrachtwagen	samochód ciężarowy	czrak
truckers accessories	Lastwagenzubehör	accessoires pour les camionneurs	accessorio per camionista	accesorios para camioneros	accessoires voor vrachtwagens en chauffeurs	akcesoria samochodowe	czrakers aksesoris
truckstop	LKW-Raststätte	parking pour camions	area di servizio per camion	parada de camioneros	chauffeurscafé	miejsce postoju z udogodnieniami dla kierowców	czrakstop
truckwash	LKW-Waschanlage	station lavage pour camions	lavaggio per camion	lavado de camiones	wasplaats voor vrachtwagens	myjnia dla ciężarówek	czraktosz

ENGLISH	GERMAN	FRENCH	ITALIAN	DUTCH	SPANISH	POLISH	Polish/English pronounciation
tunnel	Tunnel	tunnel	tunnel	tunnel	túnel	tunel	tanel
turn	Kurve	tourne	girare	draai	girar	obracać	tern
tyre	Reifen	pneu	gomma	band	neumáticos	opona	tajer
under	unter	dessous	sotto	onder	debajo	pod	ander
up	auf	vers le haut	su	op	arriba	nad	ap
van	Transporter	camionnette	furgone	bestelwagen	furgoneta	van, furgonetka	van
vehicle and operator services agency (VOSA)	VOSA (britischer TÜV)	VOSA (Le véhicule de gouvernement vérifie l'agence)	polizia stradale	controlebureau voor voertuigen	VOSA (Agencia de vehículo de gobierno)	służby kontroli pojazdów	vehjal and operejtor servisys ajdzensi
wait	warten	attendre	aspettare	wachten	espera	czekać	łejt
warehouse	Lager	entrepôt	magazzino	magazijn	almacén	magazyn	łerhałs
water	Wasser	eau	acqua	water	agua	woda	łoter
waybill	Wiegekarte	lettre de voiture	scontrino bilancia	vrachtbrief	conocimiento de embarque	kwit potwierdzający wagę pojazdu	wejbil
we	wir	nous	noi	wij	nosotros/as	my	łi
weak bridge	schwache Brücke	pont faible	ponte debole	zwakke brug	puente débil	słaby most, ograniczenie wjazdu ciężkim naczepom	łik bridż
weighbridge	Brückenwaage	pont-bascule	bascula	weegbrug	puente basculante	waga samochodowa	wejbridż
west	West/Westen	ouest	ovest	het westen	oeste	zachód	łest
wheel	Rad	roue	la ruota	wiel	rueda	koło	łil
when	wann	quand	quando	wanneer	cuándo	kiedy?	łen
where	wohin	où	dove	waar	dónde	gdzie?	łer
why	warum	pourquoi	perché	waarom	por qué	dlaczego?	łaj
wide load	Schwertransport	convoi exceptionnel	carico largo	brede lading	carga ancha	duzy załadunek	łajd lołd
windscreen	Windschutzscheibe	pare-brise	parabrezza	voorruit	parabrisas	przednia szyba	łindskrin
windscreen wipers	Scheibenwischer	essuie-glace	tergicristallo	ruitenwissers	limpiaparabrisas	wycierazki	łindskrinłajpez
with	mit	avec	con	met	con	z	łit
working	funktioniert	travail	funziona	werkt	operacional	działać, pracować	łorkin
workshop	Werkstatt	atelier	laboratorio	werkplaats	taller	warsztat	łorkszop
yard	Hof	dépôt/chantier	depósito	depot	depósito	miejsce postoju	jard
yard (yd)	Yard	yard (mesure Britannique)	iarda (Britanico misure)	0,914 meter	yarda (Británico medida)	jard (=0,914 m)	jard
yard marshal	Hofaufsicht	chef de chantier	ufficiale per deposito	rangeermeester	Oficial del depósito	osoba kierująca ruchem ciężarówek (nie jest to policjant)	jard marszal
yes	ja	oui	sì	ja	sí	tak	jes
you	du/Sie	vous	tu	u	tú	nie	ju

ENGLISH PHRASE	GERMAN PHRASE	FRENCH PHRASE	ITALIAN PHRASE	DUTCH PHRASE	SPANISH PHRASE	POLISH PHRASE	POLISH/ENGLISH PRONOUCIATION
Where is ___?	Wo ist ___?	où est ___?	dov'è ___?	Waar is ___?	¿Dónde está ___?	Gdzie jest?	ter is ___?
I would like ___	Ich möchte ___	je voudrais	Vorrei	Ik wil graag	Quiero	Chciałbym... Poprosze...	Aj łud lajk
Do you have ___?	Haben Sie ___?	avez-vous ___?	Ha ___?	Heeft u ___?	¿Tiene ___?	Czy macie ...?	Du ju hev ___?
I understand	Ich verstehe	je comprends	Capisco	Ik begrijp het	Entiendo	Zrozumiałem	Aj anderstand
I do not understand	Ich verstehe nicht	je ne comprends pas	Non capisco	Ik begrijp het niet	No entiendo	Nie zrozumiełem	Aj du not understand
Do you speak ___?	Sprechen Sie ___?	parlez vous ___?	Parli ___?	Spreekt u ___?	¿Habla usted ___?	Czy mówisz po...?	Du ju spik ___?
I do not know	Ich weiß nicht	je ne sais pas	Non lo so	Ik weet het niet	No sé	Nie wiem	Aj du not nol
Excuse me	Entschuldigen Sie	excuse-moi	Mi scusi	Pardon	Oiga, por favor	Przepraszam	Ekskjus mi
Excuse me	Entschuldigung	Pardon	Mi dispiace	Pardon	Perdone	" " "	" " "
I do not speak English	Ich spreche kein Englisch	je ne parle pas anglais	Non parli inglese	Ik spreek geen Engels	No hablo inglés	Nie mówię po angielsku	Aj du not spik inglisz
There has been an accident	Es gab einen Unfall	il y a un accident	C'e stato un incidente	Er is een ongeluk gebeurd	Ha habido un accidente	Zdazyl się wypadek	Ter has bin an aksident
I have ___	Ich habe ___	j'ai ___	Ho questo	Ik heb ___	Tengo	Mam ...	Aj hev ___
Can you help me?	Können Sie mir helfen?	pouvez-vous m'aider?	Può aiutarmi?	Kunt u mij helpen?	¿Me puede ayudar?	Czy mógłbyś/mogłabyś mi pomóc?	Ken ju help mi?
I have a problem with ___	Ich habe ein Problem mit ___	j'ai un problème avec ___	Ho un problema con ___	Ik heb een probleem met ___	Tengo el problema con ___	Mam problem z ...	Aj hev a problem wit ___
What is it?	Was ist es?	qu'est-ce que c'est?	Che cosa è questo?	Wat is het?	¿Qué es?	Co to jest?	łot is it?
How much is it?	Wie viel kostet es?	combien cela coûte?	Qunato costa ?	Hoeveel is het?	¿Cuánto es?	Ile to kosztuje? Ile place?	hał macz is it?
I am ___	Ich bin ___	je suis ___	Sono ___	Ik ben ___	Estoy/soy	Jestem/nazywam się...	Aj em ___
Can you give me a receipt?	Können Sie mir eine Quittung geben?	pouvez vous me donner un reçu?	Può darmi una ricevuta ?	Kunt u mij een bonnetje geven?	¿Puede darme un recibo, por favor?	Paragon poproszę	Ken ju giv mi a resit?
The bill please	Die Rechnung bitte	l'addition s'il vous plaît	Il conto, per favore	De rekening a.u.b.	La cuenta, por favor	Rachunek poproszę	Te bil plise

SITE REVIEWS

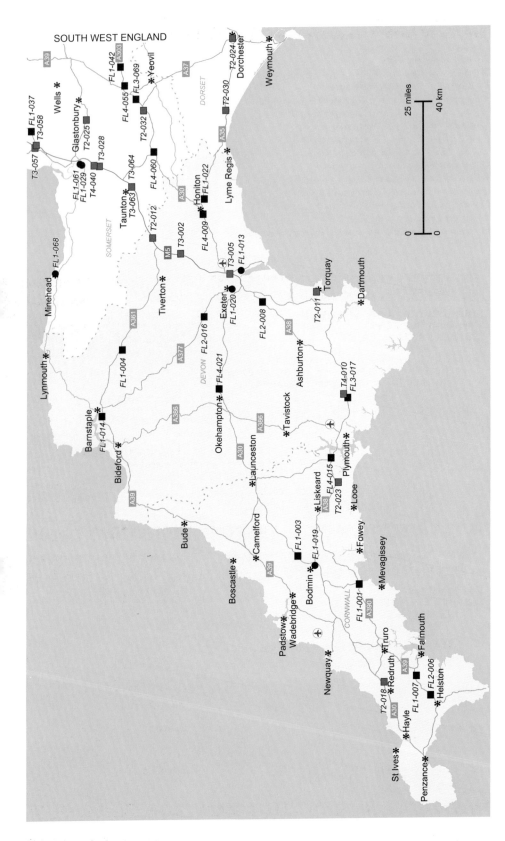

SOUTH WEST ENGLAND

Devon & Cornwall

- ■ *Cafe - Layby parking (FD1)*
- ■ *Cafe - No overnight parking (FD2)*
- ■ *Filling Station - No overnight parking/cafe (FL1)*
- ● *Bunkering Site - No overnight parking/cafe (FL1)*
- ■ *Filling Station - Nearby overnight parking no cafe (FL2)*
- ● *Bunkering Site - Nearby overnight parking no cafe (FL2)*
- ■ *Filling Station - Cafe no onsite overnight parking (FL3)*
- ■ *Filling Station - Onsite overnight parking (FL4)*
- ● *Bunkering Site - Onsite overnight parking (FL4)*
- ● *Bunkering Site - Cafe & onsite overnight parking (FL5)*
- ■ *Lorry Park - Onsite overnight parking no cafe or fuel (T1)*
- ■ *Truck Stop/Cafe - Onsite overnight parking (T2)*
- ■ *Motorway Service Station (T3)*
- ■ *Truck Stop - Bunker fuel/showers/cafe/onsite overnight parking (T4)*

For key to site symbols see page 8

FL1 ■   By Pass Filling Station, St Austell

Southbourne Road, St Austell
Cornwall PL25 4RS
T 01726 73274

ON THE A390 From the A30, follow the A391 towards St Austell. Turn right at the T-junction with the A390 signposted towards Truro. The By Pass Filling Station is on the left after the roundabout with Woodland Road.

CREDIT/DEBIT CARDS

FUEL CARDS (see key on page 9)
 ❸

TRUCK FACILITIES
Truck dealership nearby

DRIVER FACILITIES
Takeaway food

SITE COMMENTS/INFORMATION
Helpful, friendly staff

All on-site facilities 07:00-23:00 Mon-Sun.   **001**

T3   Cullompton MSA Services Ltd

Cullompton
Devon EX15 1NS
T 01884 38054

M5 JUNCTION 28
On the M5 at junction 28. Head for Cullompton. Services are a few yards on the left.

CREDIT/DEBIT CARDS

FUEL CARDS (see key on page 9)
㉒

TRUCK FACILITIES
P
Quiet area
Ample room for manoeuvring

DRIVER FACILITIES
Takeaway food
Truckers' accessories

SITE COMMENTS/INFORMATION
This site offers exceptional high quality, value for money, food

Parking, fuel, shop and some food accessible 24 hours. Restaurant accessible 07:00-23:00   **002**

Darcroft Garage & MoT Centre, Bodmin — FL1

Fourwinds, Bodmin, Cornwall PL30 4HH
T 01208 821238

ON THE A30 Darcroft Garage is on the A30 about 3 miles from Bodmin, just after the turning for Blisland if heading north-westbound towards Launceston. It is situated just after the dual carriageway becomes a single carriageway and is accessible from both directions.

CREDIT/DEBIT CARDS
FUEL CARDS (see key on page 9)

All on-site facilities 08:30-19:00 Mon-Fri   **003**

Southlea Service Station, South Molton — FL1

Devon 4x4 Centre Ltd
Bish Mill, South Molton
Devon EX36 3QU
T 01769 550900

ON THE A361 Devon 4X4 is on the main A361 Tiverton to Barnstaple road. If heading towards Tiverton it is on the left-hand side just after the turnings for South Molton.

CREDIT/DEBIT CARDS
FUEL CARDS (see key on page 9)

All on-site facilities 07:00-21:00   **004**

Exeter Services — T3

Moto Ltd
Sandygate, Exeter
Devon EX2 7HF
T 01392 436266 www.moto-way.com

M5 JUNCTION 30

CREDIT/DEBIT CARDS
FUEL CARDS (see key on page 9)

DRIVER FACILITIES
Accommodation on-site, Travelodge
Takeaway food, Train nearby

Full site details not available at time of going to press. For more information please contact site.

All on-site facilities accessible 24 hours   **005**

FL2 ■ Gables Service Station, Helston

Trevenen, Helston
Cornwall TR13 0NE
T 01326 572593

ON THE A394 From Helston take the A394 towards Falmouth. Gables Service Station is on the right-hand side 1 mile after the turning for Gweek.

CREDIT/DEBIT CARDS

FUEL CARDS (see key on page 9)
① ㉘

TRUCK FACILITIES
Overnight parking next door, free
Quiet area

DRIVER FACILITIES
Accommodation available nearby, next door, B&B
Post Office

SITE COMMENTS/INFORMATION
Easy access for LGVs

Nearby overnight parking 24 hours. All other on-site facilities 07:00-21:00   **006**

FL1 ■ Gulf Service Station Longdowns, Penryn

Longdowns, Penryn
Cornwall TR10 9DL
T 01209 860073

ON THE A394 Take the A394 from Helston to Falmouth. Gulf Service Station Longdowns is on the right, 100 yards before the first turning for Mabe Burnthouse village and 5 miles from the centre of Falmouth.

CREDIT/DEBIT CARDS

FUEL CARDS (see key on page 9)
① ③ ㉓

All on-site facilities 07:00-22:00   **007**

FL2 ■ Harcombe Cross Service Station, Chudleigh

Harcombe Cross, Chudleigh
Newton Abbot, Devon TQ13 0DF
T 01626 854033

ON THE A38 From the end of the M5 continue onto the A38 towards Plymouth. Go up the steep hill and Harcombe Cross Service Station is on the south-westbound carriageway, on the downward slope.

CREDIT/DEBIT CARDS

FUEL CARDS (see key on page 9)
③ ⑭ ㉓ ㉘

TRUCK FACILITIES
Overnight parking in lay-by

DRIVER FACILITIES
Phone top-ups

All on-site facilities 07:00-22:00   **008**

Heathpark Service Station   FL4 ■

Heathpark Way, Heathpark, Honiton
Devon EX14 1SF
T 01404 47325

ON THE A30 If heading west, exit the A30 where it is signposted Heathpark Industrial Estate. Turn left at the bottom of the sliproad and next right onto the A35. Head back towards the A30 and the service station is on the left before the A30 entrance sliproad.

CREDIT/DEBIT CARDS

FUEL CARDS (see key on page 9)
① ② ③ ④ ⑦ ⑭ ㉒ ㉓ ㉘ ㉝ ㉞

TRUCK FACILITIES
P free, Coach parking available, shared with LGV, Ample room for manoeuvring Truck washing facilities, Windscreen repairs, LGV tyre repairs nearby and LGV slales/dealer nearby

DRIVER FACILITIES
Drivers' washroom, Accommodation 200 yards away at Honiton Motel, Truckers' accessories, Takeaway food nearby Clothing for sale nearby

SITE COMMENTS/INFORMATION
Only one LGV pump not restricted by canopy

Parking 24 hours. Other on-site facilities 06:30-23:00   **009**

Lee Mills Truckstop & Transport Café   T4 ■

Lee Mills Bridge, Lee Mills, Ivybridge
Devon PL21 9EE
T 01752 202167

OFF THE A38 Signposted from the A38. If heading south, 1 mile beyond Ivybridge and if heading north, 1 and a half miles from the outskirts of Plymouth.

CREDIT/DEBIT CARDS

FUEL CARDS (see key on page 9)
① ② ③ ④ ⑦ ⑯ ⑱ ㉞

TRUCK FACILITIES
P
Coach parking available, shared with LGV
Quiet area, Adblue at pumps
Ample room for manoeuvring
Truck dealership/workshop nearby
Credit/debit cards accepted at bunker

DRIVER FACILITIES
Showers – 3 unisex. washroom, TV, phone top-ups/accessories, clothing for sale, truckers' accessories, takeaway food Post Office nearby

Parking and bunker fuel 24 hours. Other on-site facilities 06:30-19:30 Mon-Fri, 07:00-17:30 Sat   **010**

Lymington Road Coach & Lorry Park   T2 ■

Lymington Road, Torquay Devon TQ1 4BD
T 01803 201201/207694 Torbay DC

OFF THE A3022 Take the A3022 into the town centre. At the junction with the A379, turn left into Hele Road. Where the A379 turns sharp left, go right into Teignmouth road then next left into Lymington Road. Follow bend to the right and lorry park is on the right.

CREDIT/DEBIT CARDS NEARBY

TRUCK FACILITIES
Coach parking available, shared with LGV, Ample room to manoeuvre, Fridges, CCTV, Quiet area, Truck dealership/workshop

DRIVER FACILITIES
Shower, Accommodation half mile in various hotels
Clothing, Takeaway food, Vegetarian meals, Healthy meals, Post Office, Phone accessories, Phone top-ups, Truckers accessories, International papers, Taxi and Train nearby

Parking, toilets and showers accessible 24 hours   **011**

T2 — Morgans Transport Cafe

Burlescombe, Tiverton, Devon, EX16 7JX
T 01823 672273

ON THE A38 Exit M5 at junction 27 and follow A38 towards Wellington. Morgans is 3 miles along on the left.

TRUCK FACILITIES
P Free, Coaches overnight, shared with LGV, Fridge parking

DRIVER FACILITIES
Takeaway, Drivers' rest area

SITE COMMENTS
Traditional truckstop for the last 60 years with home cooked food, friendly staff and a welcoming atmosphere

Open 07.30-14:00 Mon-Fri. 07.30-10.30 Saturdays. Closed Sunday and Bank Holidays **012**

FL1 — O J Williams

Darts Business Park, Marsh Barton Farm
Clyst St George, Exeter, Devon EX3 0QH
T 01392 876880

OFF THE A376 From the M5, exit at junction 30 and take the A376 towards Exmouth. After 2 miles turn right towards the village of Topsham and O J Williams is 400 yards on the left.

CREDIT/DEBIT CARDS

FUEL CARDS (see key on page 9)
① ④ ㉞

DRIVER FACILITIES
Accommodation nearby, 600 yards, Ebford House Hotel

All on-site facilities 24 hours **013**

FL1 — Roundswell Services, Barnstaple

Roundswell, Barnstaple
Devon EX31 3RZ
T 01271 328842

ON THE A39 From Barnstaple take the A39 towards Bideford. Roundswell Services is on the A39, at the roundabout with the B3232.

CREDIT/DEBIT CARDS

FUEL CARDS (see key on page 9)
③ ⑭ ㉒ ㉓ ㉙ ㉝

DRIVER FACILITIES
Accommodation available, Travelodge
Takeaway
Phone top-ups

SITE COMMENTS/INFORMATION
Lottery tickets. Paypoint and 'Cuisine de France' Hot Food to go available
No HGV parking on-site or at Travelodge

All on-site facilities 24 hours **014**

Saltash Services

FL4

Moto Ltd, Callington Road, Carkeel
nr Saltash, Cornwall PL12 6LF
T 01752 845404

OFF THE A388 Take the A38 from Plymouth across the Tamar Bridge towards Liskeard. At the next roundabout, turn right taking the road signposted A388 Callington. Entrance to Saltash Services is a few yards on the left at the next roundabout.

CREDIT/DEBIT CARDS

FUEL CARDS (see key on page 9)

3 23 27 34

TRUCK FACILITIES
Coach parking available (6 spaces)

DRIVER FACILITIES
Shower
Travelodge on-site
Takeaway food
Payphone nearby
Phone top-ups
Clothing, Truckers' accessories
CB sales/repairs

Parking, shop and fuel 24 hours. Other on-site facilities 06:00-22:00

015

Shell Crediton

FL2

Exeter Road, Crediton
Devon EX17 3BN
T 01363 778910

ON THE A377 Take the A377 out of Crediton towards Exeter. Shell Crediton is on the right-hand side, just past the train station.

CREDIT/DEBIT CARDS

FUEL CARDS (see key on page 9)

3 25 27

TRUCK FACILITIES
Overnight parking in train station car park, free

DRIVER FACILITIES
Train nearby

SITE COMMENTS/INFORMATION
Easy to find
Easy access for LGVs

All on-site facilities 06:30-22:00

016

Smithaleigh Services & Little Chef

FL2

Plympton, Plymouth
Devon PL7 5AX
T 01752 893003

ON THE A38 WESTBOUND Go past exit for Lee Mills, take next exit to Smithaleigh and the filling station is on the left.

CREDIT/DEBIT CARDS

FUEL CARDS (see key on page 9)

3 14 22 25 33

TRUCK FACILITIES
Overnight parking in lay-by/Picnic area

All on-site facilities 06:00-22:00 Mon-Fri, Sat-Sun 07:00-22:00. Nearby overnight parking unknown

017

T2 Smokey Joe's Café & Truckstop

Blackwater, nr Scorrier, Redruth
Cornwall TR16 5BJ
T 01209 821810

OFF THE A30 A3047 INTERSECTION If heading south-west on A30, take 3rd exit for Blackwater at the A390 roundabout. Go through Blackwater for 1 mile. Smokey Joe's is on right. If heading north-east on A30, take the A3047 exit, turn right at roundabout. Continue 1mile and it's on the left

TRUCK FACILITIES
P
Voucher value – shower, meal and bottomless tea or coffee
Coach parking available, shared with LGV
Ample room for manoeuvring
Quiet area. Floodlighting
Truck dealership/workshop nearby

DRIVER FACILITIES
Shower – 1 unisex, washroom, TV
Takeaway food
Post Office and CB repairs/sales nearby

SITE COMMENTS/INFORMATION
Last orders for food 1 hour before closing

07:00-22:00 Mon-Thur, 07:00-20:00 Fri, 08:00-20:00 Sat, 10:00-20:00 Sun   **018**

FL1 ● Total Butler, Bodmin

Total Butler Ltd, 10 Lucknow Road
Walker Lines Industrial Estate
Bodmin, Cornwall PL31 1EZ
T 01208 72551

OFF THE A30 If heading south-west on A30, take 1st Bodmin exit onto A38. Remain on A38 for 1 mile. At roundabout with the A30, turn right onto Carminow Road. 600 yards turn right into Normandy Way then right into Lucknow Road to the end.

CREDIT/DEBIT CARDS

FUEL CARDS (see key on page 9)
① ② ④ ⑦ ⑯ ㉞

DRIVER FACILITIES
Showers available

All on-site facilities 09:00-17:00 Mon-Fri   **019**

FL1 ● Total Butler, Exeter

Total Butler Ltd, Marsh Green Road North
Marsh Barton Trading Est.,
Marsh Barton, Exeter, Devon EX2 8PB
T 01363 82643

OFF THE A377 Exit M5 junction 31, A30 towards Okehampton. After 1 mile take exit for A377. Continue past junction with B3123 and Sainsburys, turn right into Marsh Barton Road. Follow road round left into Marsh Green Road North and it's on the left.

CREDIT/DEBIT CARDS

FUEL CARDS (see key on page 9)
① ④ ⑦ ㉞

DRIVER FACILITIES
Takeaway food nearby

Bunker fuel 24 hours   **020**

Whitehouse Services

FL4

Exeter Road, Tongue End, Okehampton,
Devon EX20 1QJ
T 01837 840101

ON THE A30 Whitehouse Services is located on the Westbound carraigeway of the A30 at Okehampton, the site can be accessed Westbound and Eastbound.

CREDIT/DEBIT CARDS

FUEL CARDS (see key on page 9)

3 14 22 23 33

TRUCK FACILITIES
Coaches overnight, shared with LGV, free, Floodlights, CCTV, Room to manoeuvre, Fridge parking

DRIVER FACILITIES
Vegetarian/Healthy meals, Takeaway, Phone accessories/top-ups

All on-site facilities accessible 24 hours

021

Windmill Garage, Honiton

FL1

Offwell, Honiton
Devon EX14 9RP
T 01404 831228

ON THE A35 Take the A35 from Honiton to Axminster and Windmill Garage is on your right-hand side, about a mile and a half outside of the town of Honiton, just beyond the turning for Offwell.

CREDIT/DEBIT CARDS

FUEL CARDS (see key on page 9)

1 4

DRIVER FACILITIES
Takeaway food

SITE COMMENTS/INFORMATION
Easy access from A35 for LGVs

All on-site facilities 06:00-22:00

022

Windy Ridge Eating House

T2

Torpoint Road, Trerulefoot, Saltash
Cornwall PL12 5BJ
T 01752 841344

OFF THE A38 This site is situated on the A374 Torpoint Road close to the roundabout with the main A38 Liskeard to Plymouth road.

CREDIT/DEBIT CARDS

TRUCK FACILITIES
P
Coach parking (20 spaces)
Ample room for manoeuvring
Fridge parking, Quiet area

DRIVER FACILITIES
Shower – 1 unisex (£1.00), rest area, TV, internet access, Takeaway food, Vegetarian meals

SITE COMMENTS/INFORMATION
This site is renowned for its excellent breakfasts.

Nearby fuel, shop and on-site parking accessible 24hrs. Food available 07.30-18.30 (earlier on request.)

023

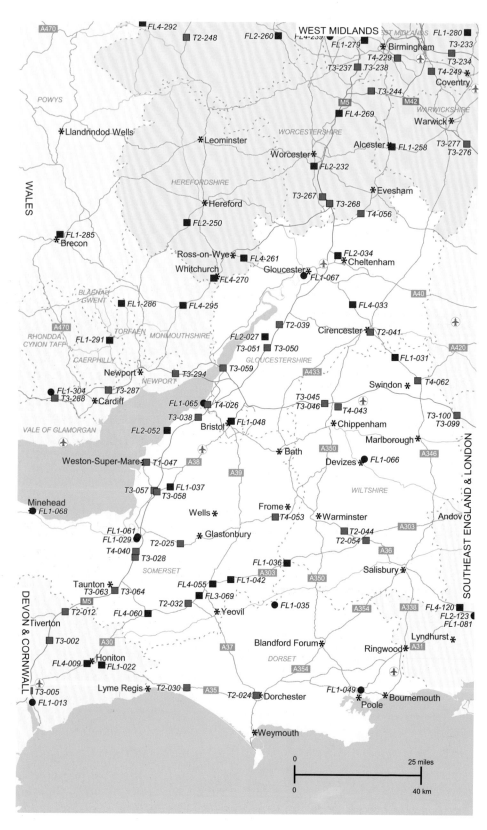

South West England

■ Cafe - Layby parking (FD1)
■ Cafe - No overnight parking (FD2)
■ Filling Station - No overnight parking/cafe (FL1)
● Bunkering Site - No overnight parking/cafe (FL1)
■ Filling Station - Nearby overnight parking no cafe (FL2)
● Bunkering Site - Nearby overnight parking no cafe (FL2)
■ Filling Station - Cafe no onsite overnight parking (FL3)
■ Filling Station - Onsite overnight parking (FL4)
● Bunkering Site - Onsite overnight parking (FL4)
● Bunkering Site - Cafe & onsite overnight parking (FL5)
■ Lorry Park - Onsite overnight parking no cafe or fuel (T1)
■ Truck Stop/Cafe - Onsite overnight parking (T2)
■ Motorway Service Station (T3)
■ Truck Stop - Bunker fuel/showers/cafe/onsite overnight parking (T4)

For key to site symbols see page 8

T2 — A35 Café

Top of Town Car Park, Bridport Road
Dorchester, Dorset DT1 1XT
T 01305 269199

ON THE B3150 From the A37 and A35 Dorchester Ring Road, take the B3150 into the town. Remain on the B3150 for 500 more yards after the junction with the B3144. The Military Keep is on your left and Top of Town Car Park is on the same side just past it.

TRUCK FACILITIES
P £2.50 overnight, £1.00 for 1 hour
Coach parking available, shared with LGV
Ample room for manoeuvring
Quiet area. Truck dealership/workshop
Tyre repair/sales, truckwash and
windscreen repair nearby, CCTV, Fridge
parking, Adblue in containers

DRIVER FACILITIES
Accommodation nearby, Truckers'
accessories. Takeaway food, Vegetarian
meals, Post Office, phone top-ups/
accessories and clothing for sale nearby

SITE COMMENTS/INFORMATION
Town centre location

Parking and nearby fuel accessible 24 hours. Café accessible 06:45-19:00. Other on-site times may vary   **024**

T2 — The Albion Inn & Truckstop

14 Bath Road, Ashcott, Bridgwater
Somerset TA7 9QT
T 01458 210281

ON THE A39 From junction 23 of the M5, head towards Glastonbury on the A39. The Albion Inn is on your right, 8 and a half miles from the motorway, just after the turning for Pedwell and just before you get into the village of Ashcott.

TRUCK FACILITIES
P With voucher £10.00 Voucher £5.00
Coach parking available (2 spaces)
Quiet, Floodlights, Ample room for
manoeuvring, Fridge lorry area (Switch
off at 22:00)

DRIVER FACILITIES
Accommodation, Showers, 1 m, 1 f
(charge £1 if not park overnight),
washroom, rest area, TV, truckers'
accessories, Takeaway food,
Vegetarian/healthy meals, TV, Arcade
mach., Euros, Post Office nearby

SITE COMMENTS/INFORMATION
Small, friendly site where drivers receive
a warm welcome and personal attention

Showers and parking accessible 24 hours. Other on-site facilities accessible 07:00-20:00 Mon-Thur, 07:00-15:00 Fri. Cafe open
07.00 -20.00 Mon-Thurs, 07.00-15.00 Fri & Sat, 10.00-15.00 Sun. Bar open 19:00 til late Mon-Sun.   **025**

The Avon Lodge Truckstop   T4 ■

Third Way, Avonmouth, Bristol
South Gloucestershire BS11 9YP
T 0117 9827706

M5 JUNCTION 18 OFF THE A4 From Junction 18 of the
M5 keep to the far right-hand lane off the sliproad, following
signs to Avonmouth and industrial estates. At the
roundabout turn right onto Avonmouth Way, then next left
onto Third Way. The Truckstop is round the bend on the left.

FUEL CARDS (see key on page 9)
① ② ④ ㉞

TRUCK FACILITIES
P
Quiet area. Ample room for manoeuvring
Truck washing facilities
Truck dealership/workshop
Tyre repair/sales nearby

DRIVER FACILITIES
Accommodation on-site, Showers, rest
area, TV, phone top-ups/accessories,
clothing for sale, truckers' accessories, CB
repairs/sales, Takeaway food. Train nearby

Bunker fuel 24 hours. Parking 07:00-21:30 Mon, 06:00-21:30, 06:00-21:30 Tues-Fri, 06:00-23:30 Sat, closed
Sun Café 07:00-20:00 Mon, 06:00-20:00 Tues-Fri, 06:00-11:00 Sat   **026**

Berkeley Heath Motors, Berkeley Heath   FL2

Gloucester Road, Berkeley Heath
Gloucestershire GL13 9ET
T 01453 511500

ON THE A38 Berkeley Heath is on the A38 and accessible
from both junctions 13 and 14 of the M5. If heading north
Berkeley Heath Motors is on the left-hand side, just after the
turning for Berkeley village.

CREDIT/DEBIT CARDS
VISA MasterCard 🅢 Maestro ▨ ◨ VISA Electron

FUEL CARDS (see key on page 9)
① ② ③ ④ ㉞

TRUCK FACILITIES
Overnight parking in lay-by

DRIVER FACILITIES
Phone top-ups

Toilets 24 hrs. All other on-site facilities 07:00-21:00 Mon-Sat, 08:00-21:00 Sun. Nearby parking 24 hrs in lay-by   **027**

Bridgwater Services   T3 ■

Moto Ltd
Huntsworth Business Park, Bridgwater
Somerset TA6 6TS
T 01278 456800 www.moto-way.com

M5 JUNCTION 24 On the M5 at junction 24 on the A38.

CREDIT/DEBIT CARDS
VISA MasterCard 🅢 Maestro ▨

FUEL CARDS (see key on page 9)
⑭

DRIVER FACILITIES
Takeaway food

Full site details not available at time of going to
press. For more information please contact site.

All on-site facilities accessible 24 hours   **028**

FL1 — British Benzol, Bridgwater

British Benzol Ltd, Unit 12
Wylds Road Industrial Estate
Bridgwater, Somerset TA6 4DH
T 01278 426464

OFF THE A38 Junction 23 of M5, take A38 towards Bridgwater for about 1 and a half miles. Turn right into Wylds Road (about 800 yards before the junction with the A39) and follow the road around to the left. British Benzol is 200 yards on the left.

CREDIT/DEBIT CARDS

FUEL CARDS (see key on page 9)
❶

TRUCK FACILITIES
Truck dealership/workshop

DRIVER FACILITIES
Takeaway food nearby

All on-site facilities 06:00-18:00. Mon-Fri

029

T2 — Café Royal

Tannery Road, off West Street, Bridport
Dorset DT6 1QX
T 01308 422012

OFF THE A35 From Charmouth on the A35, take the B3162 towards Bridport and Tannery Road is about 1 mile along on the left. Or from Beaminster on the A3066, turn right at the junction with the A35 onto the B3162. Tannery Road is 600 yards on the left.

CREDIT/DEBIT CARDS

FUEL CARDS (see key on page 9)

TRUCK FACILITIES
Coach parking available (15 spaces)
Ample room for manoeuvring
Quiet area

DRIVER FACILITIES
Washroom, TV
Phone top-ups/accessories nearby

SITE COMMENTS/INFORMATION
Situated in the bus station complex, very close to the town centre. Play area for kids and pool table on-site. Nearby seaside walks

Parking accessibility times unknown. All other on-site facilities accessible 07:00-23:00

030

FL1 — Calcutt Service Station, Swindon

Calcutt, Cricklade, Swindon
Wiltshire SN6 6JR
T 01793 752272

ON THE A419 This site is located on the left-hand side of the A419 Swindon to Cirencester road. If heading towards Cirencester it's just before the exit for Cricklade.

CREDIT/DEBIT CARDS

FUEL CARDS (see key on page 9)
❸ ㉗

SITE COMMENTS/INFORMATION
Friendly helpful staff
Always fresh food available

All on-site facilities 24 hours

031

Cartgate Diner

T2 ∎

Cartgate Service Area
Cartgate roundabout, Tintinhull
nr Yeovil, Somerset BA22 8
T 07976 949404

ON THE A303 If heading from Ilminster to Yeovil on the A303, Cartgate Service Area is on the left-hand side at the roundabout with the A3088.

CREDIT/DEBIT CARDS

FUEL CARDS (see key on page 9)

TRUCK FACILITIES
P
Coach parking. Quiet area. Fridge lorry area
Ample room for manoeuvring

DRIVER FACILITIES
Shower – 1 unisex (charge), washroom, TV, truckers' accessories
Takeaway food

SITE COMMENTS/INFORMATION
Site run by truck owners. Provides huge portions of food for the hungriest of men! Discounts and loyalty cards available. Recently refurbished site

All on-site facilities accessible 24 hours

032

Centurion Services

FL4

Gloucester Road, Dutisbourne Abbots,
Cirencester, Gloucestershire GL7 7RJ
T 01285 821878

ON THE A417 SOUTHBOUND If heading south, Centurion Services is located just off the southbound carriageway of the A417 Gloucester to Cirencester road, approximately 5 Miles from Cirencester and just after the exits to the villages of Winstone and Elkstone.

CREDIT/DEBIT CARDS

FUEL CARDS (see key on page 9)
① ② ③ ④ ⑥ ㉞

TRUCK FACILITIES
P £10.00
Coach parking available, shared with LGV
Ample room for manoeuvring
Overnight parking in designated spaces and on dead-end road adjacent to site

DRIVER FACILITIES
Drivers' washroom, Showers, male (2), unisex (1)
Truckers' accessories
Takeaway, Phone top-ups

On-site and nearby parking 24 hours. Other on-site facilities 05:00-21:30 Mon-Sun

033

Cheltenham Filling Station, Cheltenham

FL2

Tewkesbury Road, Cheltenham
Gloucestershire GL51 9SG
T 01242 257256

ON THE A4019 From the M5 southbound, exit at junction 10 and take the A4019 towards Cheltenham. Cheltenham Filling Station is 1 mile further on, on the left opposite Sainsburys and Gallager Retail Park.

CREDIT/DEBIT CARDS

FUEL CARDS (see key on page 9)
③ ⑭ ㉒ ㉓ ㉘ ㉝

TRUCK FACILITIES
Overnight parking in lay-by or on roadside of nearby Retail Park

DRIVER FACILITIES
Accommodation available nearby, 200 yards, Travel Inn
Truckers' accessories
Fax/copier
Gym nearby
Phone top-ups
Post Office nearby

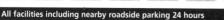

All facilities including nearby roadside parking 24 hours

034

FL1 — Ford Fuels

**Ford Fuels Ltd, Gibbs Marsh Trading Estate
Stalbridge, Sturminster Newton
Dorset DT10 2RU
T 01963 363014**

OFF THE A30 From the A30 Sherbourne to Shaftesbury road (if heading towards Shaftesbury) go straight on at the junction with the A357. Continue for about 1 mile, turn right at signs for Gibbs Marsh, left at T-junction, and then 2nd right onto the estate.

CREDIT/DEBIT CARDS

FUEL CARDS (see key on page 9)
① ② ④ ㉞

TRUCK FACILITIES
Adblue in containers

All on-site facilities 24 hours

035

FL1 — Forge Garages, Bourton

**Bourton, near Gillingham
Dorset SP8 5BD
T 01747 822409/840552**

OFF THE A303 From the A303 eastbound, go past the Wincanton exit and take the exit B3081 Gillingham, and head for Bourton. Forge Garages is in the middle of the village. The A303 can be rejoined by continuing through the village.

CREDIT/DEBIT CARDS

FUEL CARDS (see key on page 9)
① ③ ④ ⑦ ㉓

DRIVER FACILITIES
Truckers' accessories
Post Office
Phone top-ups

OTHER INFORMATION
LGVs must use pump next to jetwash
not pump beneath canopy due to height
restrictions

All on-site facilities accessible Mon-Sat, 07:30-19:00, Sun, 08:30-19:00

036

FL1 — G H Lunn & Sons, Axbridge

**New Road Garage, Lower Weare,
Axbridge, Somerset BS26 2JE
T 01934 732254**

ON THE A38 M5 exit at junction 22 and take the A38 to Cheddar for 7 miles. G H Lunn is on the right-hand side at Lower Weare, just past the turning for Compton Bishop.

CREDIT/DEBIT CARDS

FUEL CARDS (see key on page 9)
⑭ ㉒ ㉓ ㉝

On-site facilities 08:00-20:00

037

Gordano Services
T3

Welcome Break Ltd
Portbury, Nr Bristol
North Somerset BS20 7TW
T 01275 375885

M5 JUNCTION 19

CREDIT/DEBIT CARDS

FUEL CARDS (see key on page 9)
25

DRIVER FACILITIES
Accommodation, Welcome Lodge
Takeaway food
Showers

Full site details not available at time of going to press. For more information please contact site.

All on-site facilities accessible 24 hours
038

Gossington Truckstop
T2

Bristol Road, Cam, Nr Dursley, South Gloucestershire, GL11 5JA
T 01453 890927 www.gossington-truckstop.co.uk

ON THE A38 Situated on the A38 midway between Bristol and Gloucester. This road runs parallel to the M5 and can be accessed via junction 13 or 14.

CREDIT/DEBIT CARDS

TRUCK FACILITIES
P £15.00 voucher value £2.50, Coaches overnight, (shared with LGV), LGV tyre repairs/sales, 24 hour security, Secure fencing, Floodlights, CCTV, Fridge parking, Quiet parking
DRIVER FACILITIES
Showers, male 4, female 1 (£2.50 free with overnight parking), Accommodation nearby, Rest area, Vegetarian/Healthy meals, Takeaway, Evening entertainment, TV, Arcade mach., Games room, Internet, Fax/copier, Euros
SITE COMMENTS/INFORMATION
Abnormal loads park in layby outside site. Fridge lorries switch off 23:00. Weekend parking available. Fuel pumps coming soon!

Toilets: 24 hour, Cafe: 05:00- 21:00, Bar: 16:00-23:00. Showers and Shop: 05:00-23:00. Main gates locked from 23:00-06:00 for security. Drivers must contact security to exit durng these times.
039

Grahams Transport Stop & Woods Filling Station
T4

Taunton Road, North Petherton
Bridgwater, Somerset TA6 6PR
T 01278 663052/663076

ON THE A38 From the M5 junction 24 follow signs for A38 North Petherton and Taunton. Grahams/Woods is about 500 yards from the M5 roundabout on your left-hand side.

CREDIT/DEBIT CARDS

FUEL CARDS (see key on page 9)
1 2 4 5 34

TRUCK FACILITIES
P £5.00
Ample room for manoeuvring
Quiet area

DRIVER FACILITIES
Showers – 2 unisex (charge), washroom, TV, truckers' accessories
Takeaway food available

SITE COMMENTS/INFORMATION
Good home cooked food, good value for money, friendly atmosphere, family run business

Parking and bunker fuel 24 hours. Other on-site facilities 06:00-20:00 Mon-Thurs, 06:30-17:00 Fri, 07:00-23:00 Sat
040

T2 — Greasy Joe's Café

**The Lorry Park, King's Meadow Services,
Old Swindon Road, Cirencester
Gloucestershire GL7 1NP
T 01285 640275**
OFF THE A419 From Swindon take the A419 towards Cirencester. At the Tesco roundabout on the outskirts of the town, turn left and Greasy Joes is on your right. look out for sign's for Kings Meadow services

CREDIT/DEBIT CARDS

FUEL CARDS (see key on page 9)

TRUCK FACILITIES
P £6, Ample room for manoeuvring
Truck dealership/workshop
Tyre repair/sales nearby, Floodlights,
Fridge parking, Coach parking

DRIVER FACILITIES
Accommodation on-site, Shower – 1 unisex (deposit), washroom, TV, Phone top-ups/accessories, Takeaway food, Vegetarian meals, TV, Arcade machines, Internet, Fax/copier nearby, Evening entertainment nearby, Truckers' accessories nearby, Clothing nearby,

Parking 24 hr, Showers/washroom/toilets 06:00-18:00. Facs, Mon/Tues 06:00-14:00, Wed-Sat 06:00-16:00. **041**

FL1 — Hazelgrove Services, Yeovil

**Sparkford, Nr Yeovil,
Somerset BA22 7JE
T 01935 850697**

ON THE A303 Hazelgrove can be found just outside of Sparkford on the roundabout of the A303 and A359, and is easily accessible from all directions.

CREDIT/DEBIT CARDS

FUEL CARDS (see key on page 9)

TRUCK FACILITIES
Short-term coach parking (4 spaces, shared with LGV)

DRIVER FACILITIES
Hot drinks free with £100 fuel
Truckers' accessories
Takeaway food
Phone top-ups

SITE COMMENTS/INFORMATION
Large Spar shop

Toilets 05:30-23:00. Other on-site facilities 24 hours **042**

T4 — Hideaway Truckstop (Silvey's)

**Silvey Oils Ltd, Oakleigh Acres
Draycott Cerne, Chippenham
Wiltshire SN15 5LH T 01249 750645**
www.chippenhamtruckstop.co.uk

M4 JUNCTION 17 ON THE B4122 From the M4, exit at junction 17 and take the B4122 towards Sutton Benger. Silvey's Truckstop is about half a mile on the right-hand side.

CREDIT/DEBIT CARDS

FUEL CARDS (see key on page 9)

TRUCK FACILITIES
P with voucher   Voucher value
£12.50   £4.00
Manoeuvring room, Coach parking, shared with LGV, Quiet, Fridge parking (off 22:00), Truck dealership/workshop, Floodlights, CCTV, Adblue at pumps/in containers

DRIVER FACILITIES
Showers – 4 m, 1 f (£1), washroom, rest area, TV, phone top-ups/accessories, clothing, truckers' accessories, Takeaway food, Vegetarian/Healthy meals, Arcade mach., Internet, CB sales/repairs

Fuel 24hrs. Showers 06:00 to 23:30. Site open Mon 06:00 to Sat 11:00. Restaurant 06:00-23.00 Mon-Fri, 06.00-11.00 Sat. Internet Cafe and Meeting Room 06:00 to 23:00 **043**

Hillside Café   T2 ▪

**Salisbury Road, Codford, Warminster
Wiltshire BA12 0JZ
T 01985 850712**

ON THE A36 The Hillside Café can be found on the right-hand side of the A36 Salisbury to Bath road just after the village of Codford and 3 miles beyond the junction with the A303 if heading north.

FUEL CARDS (for nearby fuel)
❶ Nearby

TRUCK FACILITIES
P only £7.00
Ample room for manoeuvring, Quiet area, CCTV, Truck dealership/workshop nearby, Fridge lorries switch off at 21:00

DRIVER FACILITIES
Washroom, rest area
Takeaway food, Vegetarian/healthy meals, Post Office nearby, Phone top-ups nearby

SITE COMMENTS/INFORMATION
Clean and friendly site. Home cooked food

Parking accessible 24 hours. Nearby fuels accessible 05:00-20:00. Other on-site facilities accessible 06:00-19:00 Mon-Thurs, 06:00-17:00 Fri, 06:00-11:30 Sat.   **044**

Leigh Delamere Services eastbound   T3 ▪

**Moto Ltd
Leigh Delamere, nr Chippenham
Wiltshire SN14 6LB
T 01666 837691** www.moto-way.com

M4 EASTBOUND BETWEEN JUNCTIONS 17 AND 18

CREDIT/DEBIT CARDS

FUEL CARDS (see key on page 9)
❸ ㉓ ㉗

TRUCK FACILITIES
P with voucher   P only   Voucher value
£18.00   £16.00   £8.00
Coach parking available (28 spaces)
Room for manoeuvre, Fridge parking, Quiet area, Abnormal loads bay situated in entry to LGV Park

DRIVER FACILITIES
Accommodation Travelodge, Shower, male (2), female (2), washroom, Rest area, Seating area, Phone top-ups/accessories, Truckers' accessories
Takeaway food, Vegetarian meals
Clothing, Arcade mach., Internet

Restaurant, WH Smith, Forecourt 24hrs. Cafe Ritazza & Upper Crust 07.30-19:00, BK 10.00-22.00, M&S Simply Food 07.00-22.00   **045**

Leigh Delamere Services westbound   T3 ▪

**Moto Ltd
Leigh Delamere, nr Chippenham
Wiltshire SN14 6LB
T 01666 837691** www.moto-way.com

M4 WESTBOUND BETWEEN JUNCTIONS 17 AND 18

CREDIT/DEBIT CARDS

FUEL CARDS (see key on page 9)
㉗

DRIVER FACILITIES
Drivers' rest area
Takeaway food, Vegetarian/healthy meals
Phone top-ups/accessories
Truckers' accessories
Showers, male (2), female (1), washroom
Accommodation nearby, Travelodge
Arcade machines, Fax/copier

All on-site facilities accessible 24 hours   **046**

T1 ▪ Locking Road Coach & Lorry Park

Francis Fox Road, Weston-super-Mare
North Somerset BS23 3DE
T 01934 417117/888888 NSDC ext 257

OFF THE A371 From junction 21 of the M5, take the A371 dual carriageway into Weston-Super-Mare and follow signs to town centre. At roundabout with the A3033, go straight across over bridge and turn right at next roundabout, 4th exit at next roundabout (Back on yourself) then immediate left into lorry park.

CREDIT/DEBIT CARDS NEARBY

TRUCK FACILITIES
P £5.00
Coach parking available, shared with LGV
Quiet area, Truck dealership/workshop nearby, Floodlighting, CCTV, Fridges, LGV tyre repairs

DRIVER FACILITIES
Accommodation half mile Grand Atlantic & Royal Hotels £25.00 per night app
Takeaway food, evening ent., games room nearby, Phone top-ups/accessories
Laundry service, Internet, Post Office, Clothing for sale and Train nearby

SITE COMMENTS/INFORMATION
Cash only pay/display. Max width 5m

Open as a lorry park from 18:00 daily. Coaches 24 hrs **047**

FL1 ▪ Malthurst M32 Services

Silvey Oils Ltd, Newfoundland Road,
Bristol, South Gloucestershire BS2 9LU
T 0117 9351310

ON THE A4032 From the centre of Bristol's inner ring road follow signs for the A4032 and M32. Silveys is on the north-eastbound carriageway of the A4032 just before the start of the M32.

CREDIT/DEBIT CARDS

FUEL CARDS (see key on page 9)
②③⑦㉕

DRIVER FACILITIES
Accommodation nearby, half a mile, various hotels
Takeaway food

SITE COMMENTS/INFORMATION
Also note that exiting from this site should be done with great care as it can be a bit tight

Toilets 06:00-22:00. Hot food counter 07:00-14:00. Shop and fuel 24 hours **048**

FL1 ▪ M F Oils

5 Willis Way, Fleets Industrial Estate
Poole, Dorset BH15 3SS
T 01202 676263 www.mfoils.co.uk

OFF THE A349 From the A35, A3049, A350 roundabout take the A350 directly towards Poole town centre. Turn left at the next roundabout onto A349, take the next right into Willis Way. Take next 2 available right turns then left, left, and right. MF Oils is on the left.

CREDIT/DEBIT CARDS

FUEL CARDS (see key on page 9)
①②④⑤㉞

DRIVER FACILITIES
Accommodation nearby, half mile,
Travel Inn
Takeaway food nearby

All on-site facilities 24hrs **049**

Michaelwood Services northbound
T3

**Welcome Break Ltd
Lower Wick, Dursley
Gloucestershire GL11 6DD
T 01454 260631**

M5 NORTHBOUND BETWEEN JUNCTIONS 13 AND 14

CREDIT/DEBIT CARDS

FUEL CARDS (see key on page 9)
⑭ ㉒

DRIVER FACILITIES
Takeaway food

Full site details not available at time of going to press. For more information please contact site.

All on-site facilities accessible 24 hours

050

Michaelwood Services southbound
T3

**Welcome Break Ltd
Lower Wick, Dursley
Gloucestershire GL11 6DD
T 01454 260631**

M5 SOUTHBOUND BETWEEN JUNCTIONS 13 AND 14

CREDIT/DEBIT CARDS

FUEL CARDS (see key on page 9)
⑭ ㉒

DRIVER FACILITIES
Takeaway food

Full site details not available at time of going to press. For more information please contact site.

All on-site facilities accessible 24 hours

051

Morrisons Filling Station, Clevedon
FL2

**Morrisons Supermarkets Ltd
145 Old Church Road, Clevedon
North Somerset BS21 7TU
T 01275 875055**

OFF THE M5 JUNCTION 20 Exit M5 junction 20 for Clevedon. At the next roundabout go straight ahead towards town. At the small roundabout go straight ahead then turn left at the T-junction, continue half a mile, filling station is on the right.

CREDIT/DEBIT CARDS

FUEL CARDS (see key on page 9)
① ② ④ ㉞

TRUCK FACILITIES
Overnight parking on roadside only, 1 mile away on industrial estate

DRIVER FACILITIES
Truckers' accessories
Takeaway food nearby
Clothing for sale nearby

All on-site facilities 06:00-21:00. Nearby overnight parking PM only

052

T4 ▪ Nunney Catch Café, Truckstop and Ford Fuels

**Ford Fuels Ltd, Nunney Road, Nunney Catch
nr Frome, Somerset BA11 4NZ
T 01373 836331**

ON THE A361 Take the A361 from Shepton Mallet towards
Frome. Nunney Catch Café is on your left at the roundabout
with the A359, 3 miles before the town of Frome.

CREDIT/DEBIT CARDS

FUEL CARDS (see key on page 9)
① ② ④ ⑦ ㉞

TRUCK FACILITIES
P
Coach parking available, shared with LGV
Floodlighting, CCTV. Quiet area
Ample room for manoeuvring
Truck dealership/workshop nearby
Tyre repair/sales nearby
Windscreen repair nearby

DRIVER FACILITIES
Showers, washroom, TV, takeaway food

Parking and bunker fuel 24 hours. All other on-site facilities 07:00-19:30 Mon-Thur, 07:00-16:30 Fri, 07:30-13:00 Sat **053**

T2 ▪ The Old Willoughby Hedge Cafe

**West Knoyle, Nr Salisbury, Wiltshire
BA12 0QF
T 01747 830803**

ON THE A303 3 miles East of Mere on A303 & 800 yards
west of B3089/A303 Junction

CREDIT/DEBIT CARDS

TRUCK FACILITIES
Coaches overnight, shared with LGV
Manoeuvre room, Fridge parking, Quiet
area, Parking in layby only

DRIVER FACILITIES
Healthy menu, Takeaway

Open 08:00-17:00 during Winter weekdays 08:00-18:00 in Summer (20:00 friday) 08:00-16:00
Winter Sats, 10:00-16:00 Winter Suns 08:00-18:00 Summer Sats, 09:00-18:00 Summer Suns **054**

FL4 Podimore Services

**Podimore, Yeovil
Somerset BA22 8JG
T 01935 841717**

ON THE A303 Podimore Services is 6 miles from Yeovil on
the A303 at the roundabout with the A37 and A372.

CREDIT/DEBIT CARDS

FUEL CARDS (see key on page 9)
① ② ⑩

TRUCK FACILITIES
P
Coach parking available, shared with LGV
Ample room for manoeuvring
Quiet area
Truck dealership/workshop nearby

DRIVER FACILITIES
Travelodge on-site (£45 per night)
Takeaway food
Truckers' accessories

Parking, toilets, fuel and shop 24 hours **055**

'Route 46 (Vale Truckstop)   T4 ▪

**Formerly Vale Truckstop, Cheltenham Road
Ashton Under Hill, nr Evesham
Worcestershire WR11 7QP
T 01386 882 685**

ON THE A46 From junction 9 of the M5, take the A46 towards Evesham. Continue for 3 miles after the junction with the A435. Route 46 is on the right hand side.

FUEL CARDS (see key on page 9)

④ ㉒ ㉓ ㉙ ㉝ ㉞

TRUCK FACILITIES
P with voucher £13.00. Without voucher £9.00 Voucher value £7.00 Coaches overnight, shared with LGV (10 spaces), Night security, Quiet, Floodlights, CCTV, Adblue at pumps/in containers, Fridge parking on road by car park (switch off 21:00)

DRIVER FACILITIES
Accommodation £20.00
Showers m 5, 1 f, (free if parking overnight), rest area, TV, takeaway food, Vegetarian/healthy meals, Phone top-ups, Clothing, Truckers' accessories, Int. papers

SITE COMMENTS/INFORMATION
Cash only accepted at truckstop and cafe

Parking/adjoining shop & fuel facilities 24hrs. Other facilities 07:00-21:00 Mon-Fri, 08:30-16:00 Sat & Sun   **056**

Sedgemoor Services northbound   T3 ▪

**Welcome Break Ltd
Rooksbridge, Axbridge, Nr Weston-super-Mare, Somerset BS24 0JL
T 01934 750659**

M5 NORTHBOUND BETWEEN JUNCTIONS 21 AND 22

CREDIT/DEBIT CARDS

FUEL CARDS (see key on page 9)
㉕

TRUCK FACILITIES
P with voucher   P only   Voucher value
£15.00   £13.00   £6.00
Coach overnight (25)
Floodlights, Room for manoeuvre, Quiet area

DRIVER FACILITIES
Accommodation, Welcome Lodge
Takeaway food

Forecourt and Retail Shop open 24hrs. Toilet and shower block currently under reconstruction   **057**

Sedgemoor Services southbound   T3 ▪

**Roadchef Ltd
Rooksbridge, Axbridge
Somerset BS26 2UF
T 01934 750888**

M5 SOUTHBOUND BETWEEN JUNCTIONS 21 AND 22

The LGV, Caravan & coach areas are behind main building. Please follow signs carefully. Parking discount schemes available on request. Fridge lorries should park on right hand side and switch off PM during holidays.

CREDIT/DEBIT CARDS

FUEL CARDS (see key on page 9)
① ② ③ ④ ⑧ ⑩ ㉗

TRUCK FACILITIES
P with voucher   P only   Voucher value
£17.00   £14.00   £7.50
Coach parking available (8 spaces)
Floodlighting, Fridge parking (pm switch off), LGV & coach parking behind main building, Quiet area, Truck dealership/workshop

DRIVER FACILITIES
Shower, unisex (1), female (1), washroom
Truckers' accessories. Takeaway food, Vegetarian/healthy meals, Internet access, phone top-ups/accessories and CB sales/repairs nearby, Arcade machines, Euros

All on-site facilities accessible 24 hours   **058**

T3 ▪   Severn View Services

Moto Ltd
Aust, Bristol
South Gloucestershire BS35 4BH
T 01454 632855 www.moto-way.com

M48 AT JUNCTION 1 on the English side of the old Severn
Bridge.

CREDIT/DEBIT CARDS

FUEL CARDS (see key on page 9)
①⑦⑩⑭㉒㉔㉕

DRIVER FACILITIES
Accommodation, Welcome Lodge
Takeaway food

*Full site details not available at time of going to
press. For more information please contact site.*

All on-site facilities accessible 24 hours   **059**

FL4 ▪   Shell Ilminster

Horton Cross, Ilminster
Somerset TA19 9PT
T 01460 256000

ON THE A358 Shell Ilminster can be found where the A358
Taunton to Chard road and the A303 Ilminster to Honiton
road intersect. To access this site take the Chard road from
the roundabout and turn immediately right after a few yards.

CREDIT/DEBIT CARDS

FUEL CARDS (see key on page 9)
③㉓㉕㉖㉗

TRUCK FACILITIES
P free
Ample room for manoeuvring

DRIVER FACILITIES
Hot drinks free with 100 litres of fuel
Travelodge nearby (£50 per night)
Takeaway food

SITE COMMENTS/INFORMATION
Friendly helpful staff. Well stocked site

Little Chef restaurant 07:00-22:00. Other on-site facilities 24 hours   **060**

FL1 ●   Silvey Oils, Bridgwater

Silvey Oils Ltd, Bristol Road, Bridgwater
Somerset TA6 4BJ
T 0845 6644664 www.silvey.co.uk

ON THE A38 From the M5, exit at junction 23 and follow
the A38 into Bridgwater for 1 and a half miles. Silvey Oils is
on the right, 800 yards before the roundabout with the A39.

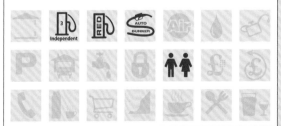

CREDIT/DEBIT CARDS

FUEL CARDS (see key on page 9)
①②④⑥㉞

TRUCK FACILITIES
Adblue at the pumps

Toilets 08:30-17:00 Mon-Fri. Other on-site facilities 24 hours   **061**

Swindon Truckstop   T4 ■

**Oxford Road, Stratton St Margaret
Swindon, Wiltshire SN3 4ER
T 01793 824812**
www.swindontruckstop.co.uk

ON THE A420 From M4 junction 15 continue along the A419 for several miles. Take A420 towards Oxford. Turn right at the next roundabout, continue past Sainsburys onto the service access road into Swindon Truckstop's lorry park.

CREDIT/DEBIT CARDS

FUEL CARDS (see key on page 9)

TRUCK FACILITIES
P
Coach parking. Quiet area
Fridge lorry area – electric hook-ups avail.
Ample room for manoeuvring
Truck dealership/workshop, tyre repair/sales and windscreen repair nearby
DRIVER FACILITIES
Accommodation nearby, 600 yards, Madison Inn
Showers, TV, truckers' accessories, takeaway food
Phone top-ups/accessories nearby

Parking 24 hours. Other on-site facilities 06:00-22:00 Mon-Fri, 06:00-12:00 Sat   **062**

Taunton Deane Services northbound   T3 ■

**Roadchef Ltd
Taunton
Somerset TA3 7PF
T 01823 271111**

M5 NORTHBOUND BETWEEN JUNCTIONS 25 AND 26

CREDIT/DEBIT CARDS

FUEL CARDS (see key on page 9)

TRUCK FACILITIES
P *with voucher*   P *only*   *Voucher value*
£17.00   £14.00   £7.50
Coach parking available (30 spaces)
Ample room for manoeuvring
Quiet area

DRIVER FACILITIES
Accommodation, Premier Inn (£54.00)
Takeaway food, Vegetarian/healthy meals
Phone top-ups/accessories, Arcade machines, Internet, Truckers' accessories
Clothing for sale

All on-site facilities accessible 24 hours   **063**

Taunton Deane Services southbound   T3 ■

**Roadchef Ltd
Taunton
Somerset TA3 7PF
T 01823 271111**

M5 SOUTHBOUND BETWEEN JUNCTIONS 25 AND 26

CREDIT/DEBIT CARDS

FUEL CARDS (see key on page 9)

TRUCK FACILITIES
P *with voucher*   P *only*   *Voucher value*
£17.00   £14.00   £7.50
Coach parking available (30 spaces)
Ample room for manoeuvring
Quiet area

DRIVER FACILITIES
Accommodation (£47.95 pn)
Takeaway food
Phone top-ups/accessories
Truckers' accessories
Clothing for sale

All on-site facilities accessible 24 hours   **064**

FL1   Total Butler, Avonmouth

**Total Butler Ltd, Royal Edward Dock
Avonmouth, Bristol, South Glos. BS11 9BB
T 0117 9822524/9824711**

OFF THE A4 From the M5 Junction 18, follow signs for
Avonmouth docks. Straight over 2 roundabouts and through
dock gates. Turn right opp Sims Metals, past Castle Cement, go
over railway, then 1st left. Continue 200 yards bear right,
continue 75 yards and bear right.

CREDIT/DEBIT CARDS

FUEL CARDS (see key on page 9)

DRIVER FACILITIES
Showers available
Train nearby

All on-site facilities 08:30-17:00   **065**

FL1   Total Butler, Devizes

**Total Butler Ltd, London Road
Devizes, Wiltshire SN10 2EP
T 01380 728564**

ON THE A361 Take the A361 out of Devizes towards the
M4. Total Butler is on the left on the outskirts of the town,
just after the turning for Windsor Drive which is on the right.

CREDIT/DEBIT CARDS

FUEL CARDS (see key on page 9)

All on-site and nearby facilities opening times unknown   **066**

FL1   Total Butler, Gloucester

**Total Butler Ltd, Hempstead Lane
Hempstead, Gloucester,
Gloucestershire GL2 5HU T 01452 523095**

OFF THE A430 From the M5 junction 12, take the A38 then
the A430 towards Gloucester town centre. Take the next left
past the BP garage on your right. Take 2nd right into
Secunda Way continue to roundabout. Go across into
Hempstead Lane and it's on the right.

CREDIT/DEBIT CARDS

FUEL CARDS (see key on page 9)

DRIVER FACILITIES
Takeaway food nearby

Toilets 07:00-17:00. All other on-site facilities 24 hours   **067**

◄ SOUTH WEST ENGLAND ►

Total Butler, Minehead   FL1

**Total Butler Ltd, Mart Road, Minehead
Somerset TA24 5BJ
T 01643 706091**

OFF THE A39 Take the A39 towards Minehead. At the first
roundabout turn right onto Seaward Way towards
Aquasplash and West Somerset Railway. Left at Aquasplash
into Vulcan Road, left at the end into Mart Road and it's
immediately on the left.

CREDIT/DEBIT CARDS

FUEL CARDS (see key on page 9)

DRIVER FACILITIES
Takeaway food nearby

All on-site facilities 08:00-17:00   **068**

Townsend Garage   FL3

**On the A303, Tintinhull, Nr Yeovil,
Somerset, BA22 8PF
T 01935 822636**

ON THE A303 This site is on the Easbound side of the
A303, halfway between the junctions with the A3088 and
A37.

CREDIT/DEBIT CARDS

FUEL CARDS (see key on page 9)

TRUCK FACILITIES
Short-term parking (2) coach (2), CCTV,
Floodlights

DRIVER FACILITIES
Vegetarian meals, Phone top-ups

Open: 09:00-16:00   **069**

212 | Trucker's Handbook

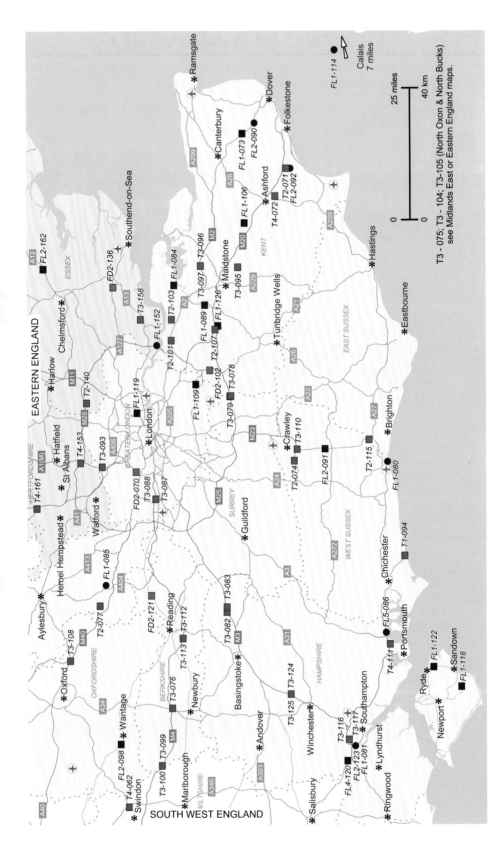

T3 - 075; T3 - 104; T3-105 (North Oxon & North Bucks)
see Midlands East or Eastern England maps.

25 miles
40 km

Calais
7 miles

FL1-114

* Ramsgate

* Canterbury
FL1-073   FL2-090

* Dover
* Folkestone
FL2-071 FL2-092
FL1-106   Ashford
T4-072

M2
* Maidstone
T3-096
T3-097
* Hastings
FL1-089
FL1-126
FL2-107
T2-102   FD2-102   T3-078
T2-101   FL1-109   T3-079   T3-078

* Tunbridge Wells

* Eastbourne

A259
A229
A21
A26
A22
A27

KENT
EAST SUSSEX

* Southend-on-Sea
FL2-162
FD2-136
T3-158
FL1-152
T2-103 FL1-084
A12
A13
A2

ESSEX
EASTERN ENGLAND

* Chelmsford
* Harlow
M11
T2-140
A127
GREATER LONDON

* Hatfield
* St Albans
* Watford
* Hemel Hempstead
FL1-085
* Aylesbury
T3-108
M40
T2-077
T4-161
A1(M)
T4-153
T3-093
A406
FD2-070
T3-088
T3-087
A41
A404
HERTFORDSHIRE

* London
FL1-119
A205

M25
M25

* Crawley
T3-110
T2-074
FL2-091
T2-115
* Brighton
FL1-080
M23
A24
A23

* Guildford
SURREY

* Chichester
T1-094
* FL5-086
* Portsmouth
T4-111
* Ryde
FL1-122
* Sandown
FL1-118
* Newport
A272
WEST SUSSEX

A3
A31
HAMPSHIRE

* Reading
FD2-121
T3-112
T3-113
T3-082   T3-083
T3-076
* Newbury
* Basingstoke
T3-124
T3-125
* Andover
* Winchester
T3-116 T3-117
* Southampton
* Lyndhurst
FL4-120
FL2-123
FL1-081
* Ringwood
M3
M4
A34
BERKSHIRE

* Oxford
OXFORDSHIRE
* Wantage
FL2-098
T3-099   T3-100
* Swindon
T4-062
* Marlborough
A346
A303
WILTSHIRE
* Salisbury
A40

214 | Truckers' Handbook

South East & London

■ *Cafe - Layby parking (FD1)*
■ *Cafe - No overnight parking (FD2)*
■ *Filling Station - No overnight parking/cafe (FL1)*
● *Bunkering Site - No overnight parking/cafe (FL1)*
■ *Filling Station - Nearby overnight parking no cafe (FL2)*
● *Bunkering Site - Nearby overnight parking no cafe (FL2)*
■ *Filling Station - Cafe no onsite overnight parking (FL3)*
■ *Filling Station - Onsite overnight parking (FL4)*
● *Bunkering Site - Onsite overnight parking (FL4)*
● *Bunkering Site - Cafe & onsite overnight parking (FL5)*
■ *Lorry Park - Onsite overnight parking no cafe or fuel (T1)*
■ *Truck Stop/Cafe - Onsite overnight parking (T2)*
■ *Motorway Service Station (T3)*
■ *Truck Stop - Bunker fuel/showers/cafe/onsite overnight parking (T4)*

For key to site symbols see page 8

FD2 ■   Ace Café, London

Ace Corner, Old North Circular Road
Stonebridge, London NW10 7UD
T 0208 9611000 www.ace-cafe-london.com

OFF THE A406 The Ace Café is on Ace Corner which is the junction of Beresford Avenue and the Old North Circular Road. This runs parallel with the New North Circular Road (A406.) The Ace Café is in the section between the A404 Harrow Road and the A40.

CREDIT/DEBIT CARDS

FUEL CARDS (for nearby fuel)
㉗

TRUCK FACILITIES
Coach parking available nearby (roadside only), shared with LGV, Quiet area, CCTV, Ample room to manoeuvre, Truck dealership/ workshop, tyre repair/sales, truckwash and windscreen repair nearby

DRIVER FACILITIES
Accommodation nearby, Abbey Point B&B, Rest area, TV, internet access, Euros changed/accepted, clothing for sale, Takeaway food, Vegetarian meals, Phone top-ups/accessories nearby, Arcade machines, Train nearby

Most on-site facilities 07:00-23:00. Parking not accessible 24 hours. Fuel accessible 24 hours nearby   **070**

T2 ■   Airport Café

Main Road, Sellindge, nr Lymne
Kent TN25 6DA
☎ 01303 813185

ON THE A20 If heading west along the M20 exit at junction 11 and take the A20 to Sellindge. Continue for 2 and a half miles and Airport Café is on the right about 1 mile before the village of Sellindge.

TRUCK FACILITIES
Coach parking available, shared with LGV
Ample room to manoeuvre
Quiet area

Parking accessible 24 hours. All other on-site facilities accessible 08:00-15:00 Mon-Fri, 08:00-12:00 Sat   **071**

Ashford Truckstop (formerly Eurotunnel Lorry Park) T4 ■

(formerly known as Eurotunnel)
GSE Waterbrook Ltd, Waterbrook Avenue
Sevington, nr Ashford, Kent TN24 0LH
T 01233 502919 www.ashfordtruckstop.co.uk
M20 JUNCTION 10 ON THE A2070 From M20, junction 10,
follow signs to Lorry park. Take A2070 towards Orlestone onto
Bad Munstereifel Road. Continue for a quarter of a mile and
Waterbrook Avenue is on the left at the next roundabout.

CREDIT/DEBIT CARDS

FUEL CARDS (see key on page 9)
① ② ③ ④ ⑤ 23 28 34

TRUCK FACILITIES
P *with voucher* £18.50, *voucher* = £5.00
Coach parking. Fridge lorry/quiet area. Full
security, Adblue, Truck washing, Tyre
repair/sales
DRIVER FACILITIES
Accommodation £30.00 inc b'fast/park
Showers (free) m8, f3, rest area, TV, internet,
Euros, phone top-ups/ accessories, clothing,
truckers' accessories, CB repairs/sales,
takeaway food, Vegetarian meals,
Entertainment, Games room, Laundry, Int.
papers
SITE COMMENTS/INFORMATION
Livestock not permitted onsite

All on-site facilities accessible 24 Hours. Travelex Travel Money part time   **072**

Barham Services, Canterbury FL1 ■

Folkstone Road, Barham, Canterbury
Kent CT4 6EX
T 01227 831356 www.arterbros.co.uk

ON THE A260 Barham is on the A260 between Folkestone and
the A2. If heading towards Dover on the A2, exit at the B2046
Aylesham and A260 Folkestone exits. Head for Folkestone, and
Barham Services is half a mile along on the right.

CREDIT/DEBIT CARDS

FUEL CARDS (see key on page 9)
① ③

TRUCK FACILITIES
NOT ACCESSIBLE FOR ARTICS

All on-site facilities 06:30-20:00 Mon-Sat, 08:00-20:00 Sun   **073**

The Cabin Café T2 ■

Crawley Road, Faygate, Horsham
West Sussex RH12 4SE
T 01293 851575

ON THE A264 From the M23, exit at junction 11 (Pease
Pottage) and take the A264 towards Horsham. Straight
across first roundabout, left at the second and The Cabin is a
mile further on the right.

TRUCK FACILITIES
P
Ample room for manoeuvring

DRIVER FACILITIES
Shower – 1 unisex (charge), washroom,
rest area, TV, clothing for sale, Train
nearby

Parking 24 hours. Other on-site facilities 06:00-19:00 Mon-Thurs, 06:00-13:00 Fri, 07:00-12:00 Sat   **074**

T3 ■ Cherwell Valley Services, Moto M&S Ltd

Moto Ltd
Northampton Road, Bicester
Oxfordshire OX6 9RD
T 01869 346060 www.moto-way.com

M40 JUNCTION 10

CREDIT/DEBIT CARDS

FUEL CARDS (see key on page 9)
(27)

TRUCK FACILITIES
P with voucher   **P** only   Voucher value
£20.00   £14.00   £7.50
Overnight coach parking (25)
Plenty of room to manoeuvre,
Quiet parking

DRIVER FACILITIES
Accommodation on-site, Travelodge
Showers, male (6), female (1)
Takeaway food, Vegetarian/healthy
meals, Phone top-ups/accessories,
Truckers' accessories, Arcade machines
Internet

All on-site facilties accessible 24 hours   **075**

T3 ■ Chieveley Services

Moto Ltd
Oxford Road, Thatcham, nr Newbury
Berkshire RG18 9XX
T 01635 248024
www.moto-way.com

M4 JUNCTION 13 Leave M4 at Junction 13. Access from
North and Southbound A34.

CREDIT/DEBIT CARDS

FUEL CARDS (see key on page 9)
(2)(3)(14)(25)

TRUCK FACILITIES
P with voucher   **P** only
£18.00   £16.00
Coach parking available (10 spaces)
Ample room for manoeuvring
DRIVER FACILITIES
Accommodation nearby, Travelodge &
  Hilton Newbury North
Showers, 2 m, 1 f (free), TV, truckers'/phone
accessories, Clothing, Takeaway food,
Vegetarian meals, Arcade mach. P top-ups
SITE COMMENTS/INFORMATION
Exit from site past filling station difficult
for wide loads

M&S Simply Food 07:00-22:00, Burger King 10:00-22:00 Tue-Thu & Sun 08:00-22:00. All other 24hrs   **076**

T2 ■ Chris's Café & Motel

Wycombe Road, Studley Green
Stokenchurch, Buckinghamshire HP14 3XB
T 01494 482121
ON THE A40 From M40 junction 5, take the A40 through
Stokenchurch and continue for 1 mile from the outskirts.
Chris's Café is on the left. From M40 junction 4, take the
A4010 to the A40. Turn left onto A40 and continue for 2
miles. Chris's Café is on the right.

CREDIT/DEBIT CARDS

FUEL CARDS (see key on page 9)

TRUCK FACILITIES
P
Quiet area
Ample room for manoeuvring

DRIVER FACILITIES
Accommodation B&B and evening meal
Shower, 1 m, washroom, rest area, TV
Takeaway food

SITE COMMENTS/INFORMATION
Home cooked food and pleasant
atmosphere. Cheques accepted

Parking and showers 24 hours. Other on-site facilities 06:00-19:00 Mon-Thu, 06:00-14:00 Fri, 06:30-12:00 Sat   **077**

Clacket Lane Services, eastbound　　　T3 ■

Roadchef Ltd
Westerham, nr Limpsfield
Kent TN16 2NR
T 01959 565577

M25 EASTBOUND BETWEEN JUNCTIONS 5 AND 6
M25 anti-clockwise.

CREDIT/DEBIT CARDS

FUEL CARDS (see key on page 9)
① ② ③ ⑧ ㉘

TRUCK FACILITIES
P with voucher　**P** only　Voucher value
£25.00　　　£20.00　£10.00
Coach parking available (30 spaces)
Quiet area, CCTV, Truck washing
Truck dealership/workshop
Ample room for manoeuvring

DRIVER FACILITIES
Accommodation on-site (£62.00 pn)
Showers, 2 male, 2 female (free),
washroom, phone top-ups/accessories
Takeaway food, Vegetarian/healthy meals
TV, Arcade mach., Clothing for sale,
Truckers' accessories

On-site accommodation Premier Travel Inn 24hrs. All other on-site facilities accessible 24 hours　　**078**

Clacket Lane Services, westbound　　　T3 ■

Roadchef Ltd
Westerham, nr Limpsfield
Kent TN16 2ER
T 01959 565577

M25 WESTBOUND BETWEEN JUNCTIONS 5 AND 6
M25 clockwise.

CREDIT/DEBIT CARDS

FUEL CARDS (see key on page 9)
① ② ㉘

TRUCK FACILITIES
P with voucher　**P** only　Voucher value
£25.00　　　£20.00　£10.00
Coach parking available (32 spaces)
Quiet area. Truck dealership/workshop
Ample room for manoeuvring, CCTV

DRIVER FACILITIES
Accomm. on-site, Premier Travel Inn
(£62.00 pn), Showers, 2 m, 2 f (free),
washroom, rest area, internet access, phone
top-ups/accessories and truckers' accessories
Takeaway food, Vegetarian/healthy meals
Clothing for sale

All on-site facilities accessible 24 hours　　**079**

Corralls Shoreham by Sea (CPL Petroleum Ltd) FL1 ●

CPL Petroleum Ltd, 33 Brighton Road
Shoreham by Sea, West Sussex BN43 6SA
T 01273 455511

ON THE A259 From the A27 Shoreham by-pass take the
A283 exit and head towards Shoreham town. At the
roundabout with the A259 follow signs to Brighton for half a
mile. Corralls is on the right just past McDonalds.

CREDIT/DEBIT CARDS
This site no longer accepts IDS cards

FUEL CARDS (see key on page 9)
① ② ④ ⑦ ㉞

TRUCK FACILITIES
Ample room for manoeuvring

DRIVER FACILITIES
Phone top-ups/accessories
Clothing for sale
Takeaway food nearby
Train nearby

SITE COMMENTS/INFORMATION
Lubrication oil can be paid for in cash
only. This site is within half a mile of the
town centre. Please note that this site no
longer accepts IDS cards

Bunker fuel 24 hours. Red diesel 08:30-14:00. This site is manned from 08:30-17:00　　**080**

FL1 ● Deben Transport Ltd

Oyster House, Andes Road
Nursling Industrial Estate
Southampton, Hampshire SO16 0YZ
T 02380 735566

OFF THE M271 From the M27, take the M271 towards Southampton. Exit at the next junction and turn right towards Nursling Industrial Estate. Take 2nd exit at next roundabout. Deben is 20 yards on the left.

CREDIT/DEBIT CARDS

FUEL CARDS (see key on page 9)
❶❷

TRUCK FACILITIES
Truck washing facilities
Truck dealership/workshop
Adblue at the pumps

DRIVER FACILITIES
Accommodation nearby, half mile,
Holiday Inn Express

All on-site facilities 24 hours **081**

T3 ■ Fleet Services north-eastbound

Welcome Break Ltd
Hartley Wintney, Basingstoke
Hampshire GU51 1AA
T 01252 628539/01252 621656
www.welcomebreak.co.uk

M3 NORTH-EASTBOUND BETWEEN
JUNCTIONS 4A AND 5

CREDIT/DEBIT CARDS

FUEL CARDS (see key on page 9)
㉕

TRUCK FACILITIES
P *with voucher*   **P** *only*   *Voucher value*
£20.00   £17.50   £7.00

DRIVER FACILITIES
Takeaway food

All on-site facilities accessible 24 hours **082**

T3 ■ Fleet Services south-westbound

Welcome Break Ltd
Hartley Wintney, Basingstoke
Hampshire GU51 1AA
T 01252 627205/01252 621656
www.welcomebreak.co.uk

M3 SOUTH-WESTBOUND BETWEEN
JUNCTIONS 4A AND 5

CREDIT/DEBIT CARDS

FUEL CARDS (see key on page 9)
㉕

TRUCK FACILITIES
P *with voucher*   **P** *only*   *Voucher value*
£20.00   £17.50   £7.00
Plenty of room for manoeuvre,
Overnight coach parking

DRIVER FACILITIES
Accommodation on-site, Days Inn
Takeaway food
Showers, unisex (3), Washroom
Arcade machines, Euros, Phone top-ups
Train nearby

All on-site facilities accessible 24 hours **083**

Four Elms Service Station North, Rochester   FL1 ■

**Main Road, Chattenden, Rochester
Kent ME3 8LL
T 01634 250445**

ON THE A228 Four Elms is in the village of Chattenden on the main A228 grain road, on the north-east bound carriageway.

CREDIT/DEBIT CARDS

FUEL CARDS (see key on page 9)
① ② ④ ⑦ ㉞

All on-site facilities 06:00-21:00   **084**

G E Stevens Fuels   FL1 ●

**Ruskin Buildings, 4 Oakridge Road
High Wycombe, Buckinghamshire HP11 2PE
T 01494 522782**

OFF THE A40 From the M40 exit at junction 4 and take the A404 into High Wycombe. At the Roundabout with the A40 turn left onto the A40 towards West Wycombe. After 800 yards turn left into Oakridge Road. G E Stevens is 40 yards on the left.

CREDIT/DEBIT CARDS

FUEL CARDS (see key on page 9)
① ② ④ ⑧ ㉞

TRUCK FACILITIES
Adblue in containers

All on-site facilities 07:00-17:00   **085**

Havant Lorry Park   FL1 ●

**C H Jones Ltd, Southmoor Lane
Havant, Hampshire PO9 1JW
T 02392 481001**
OFF THE A27 From A27 westbound - junction signed A3 London. First exit left (Broadmarsh) at light controlled roundabout at top of slip then 400m to small roundabout, third exit and immediate right into site.

FUEL CARDS (see key on page 9)
① ② ④

TRUCK FACILITIES
Overnight coach parking shared with HGV, Quiet parking

DRIVER FACILITIES
Takeaway food available
Trolley nearby, Vegetarian meals
Takeaway nearby, Laundry nearby
Phone top-ups nearby
Train nearby

SITE COMMENTS/INFORMATION
Development of new cafe building and drivers' showers planned

Bunker fuel and parking 24 hours. Café open 07:00-13:00   **086**

T3 ◼ Heston Services eastbound

Moto Ltd
North Hyde Lane, Hounslow
Middlesex TW5 9NB
T 0208 5802104 www.moto-way.com

M4 EASTBOUND BETWEEN JUNCTIONS 2 AND 3

CREDIT/DEBIT CARDS

FUEL CARDS (see key on page 9)
(14) (22)

DRIVER FACILITIES
Takeaway food

Full site details not available at time of going to press. For more information please contact site.

All on-site facilities accessible 24 hours

087

T3 ◼ Heston Services westbound

Moto Ltd
Phoenix Way, Hounslow
Middlesex TW5 9NB
T 0208 5802104 www.moto-way.com

M4 WESTBOUND BETWEEN JUNCTIONS 2 AND 3

CREDIT/DEBIT CARDS

FUEL CARDS (see key on page 9)
(14) (22)

DRIVER FACILITIES
Accommodation, Travelodge
Takeaway food

Full site details not available at time of going to press. For more information please contact site.

All on-site facilities accessible 24 hours

088

FL1 ◼ Holborough Services, Snodland

Holborough Road, Snodland
Kent ME6 5PH
T 01634 245083

ON THE A228 From the M20, exit at junction 4 and take the A228 northbound towards Chatham. By-pass Snodland, and Holborough Services is on the left-hand side on the roundabout at the far north end of Snodland.

CREDIT/DEBIT CARDS

FUEL CARDS (see key on page 9)
(1) (2) (4) (7) (34)

DRIVER FACILITIES
Train nearby

All on-site facilities 06:00-22:00.

089

Husk UK Ltd   FL2 ●

**The Freight Terminal, Lydden Hill
Dover, Kent CT15 7JW
T 01304 831222**

OFF THE A2 From Canterbury, take the A2 towards Dover. Continue for 3 miles beyond the turning for the A260. Take the first turning across the carriageway for Ewell Minnis and Temple Ewell. Husk is immediately on your right.

CREDIT/DEBIT CARDS

FUEL CARDS (see key on page 9)
① ② ④ ⑤ ㉞

TRUCK FACILITIES
P can be paid for in cash only
Quiet area
Truck washing facilities
Truck dealership/workshop
Ample room for manoeuvring

DRIVER FACILITIES
Truckers' accessories, showers
Takeaway food, clothes shop, phone
top-ups/accessories and internet nearby

SITE COMMENTS/INFORMATION
Very basic shop on-site

Parking, fuel and toilets 24 hours. Other on-site facilities and nearby shop 08:00-18:00   **090**

Jeremy's Corner Star Service Station, Bolney   FL2 ■

**London Road, Bolney
Haywards Heath, West Sussex RH17 5QD
T 01444 880100**

ON THE OLD A23 If heading northbound on the A23, go past Hickstead and over the junction with the A272. Take the next sliproad to Bolney village. Turn right at the roundabout and continue for half a mile. Jeremy's is 300 yards past the pub on the right.

CREDIT/DEBIT CARDS

FUEL CARDS (see key on page 9)
① ② ③ ④ ⑦

TRUCK FACILITIES
Overnight parking 50 yards away
Quiet area nearby

SITE COMMENTS/INFORMATION
Very friendly site offering an excellent service to all customers

Nearby parking 24 hours. All on-site facilties 06:00-22:00   **091**

The Link Park–Benfleet Container Services   FL2 ●

**Lympne Ind. Park, Otterpool Lane,
Lympne, Hythe, Kent CT21 4LR
T 01303 230030**

OFF THE JUNCTION 11 OF M20 From M20 junction 11, take the A20 towards Lympne. At the junction with the A261 turn right and continue along the A20 until the B2067. Turn left onto this and The Link Park is on the left opposite the Zoo and near Spicers.

CREDIT/DEBIT CARDS

FUEL CARDS (see key on page 9)
① ② ④ ⑤ ⑦ ⑩ ㉞

TRUCK FACILITIES
Nearby overnight parking not directly on road
Truck washing facilities
CCTV

Nearby parking, bunker fuel and standpipe 24 hours   **092**

T3 ■ London Gateway Services

Welcome Break Ltd
Mill Hill, Greater London, NW7 3HU
T 0208 9060611

M1 JUNCTION 3

CREDIT/DEBIT CARDS

FUEL CARDS (see key on page 9)
25

TRUCK FACILITIES
P *with voucher* P *only* *Voucher value*
£15.00   £13.50   £6.00
Coach overnight parking (34)
Room for manoeuvre, Quiet parking

DRIVER FACILITIES
Accommodation Days Hotel, Days Inn
Takeaway food, Showers, male (1),
female (1), Phone accessories/top-ups,
Vegetarian meals, Arcade machines,
Euros

WH Smiths Filling Station + all other facilities open 24 hrs. Hot Food from 06:00-22:00, BK 11:00-22:00 **093**

T1 ■ London Road Lorry Park

Upper Bognor Road, Bognor Regis
West Sussex PO22 8
T 01903 737500 Arun District Council

ON THE A259 If heading from Littlehampton to Chichester,
London Road Lorry Park is on the A259 on the left-hand side,
just after the entrance to Butlins and beyond Hotham Park
but just before you reach the junction with the A29.

TRUCK FACILITIES
P Free
Quiet area

DRIVER FACILITIES
Takeaway food nearby
Train nearby

Parking 24 hours. Toilets 08:00-20:00 summer, 08:00-17:00 winter **094**

T3 ■ Maidstone Services, Roadchef MSA

Hollingbourne, Maidstone, Kent,
ME17 1SS
T 01622 631100

ON THE M20 JUNCTION 8 If heading west, exit M62 at
junction 31, turn right at roundabout, go under motorway
then 1st exit at next roundabout. Exelby is 500 Yds on the
left.

CREDIT/DEBIT CARDS

FUEL CARDS (see key on page ??)
3 23 24 26 27

TRUCK FACILITIES
P £25.00 with voucher, £20.00 without
voucher Voucher value £10.00,
Floodlights, Coaches overnight (12),
Manoeuvring room, Fridge parking,
Quiet parking

DRIVER FACILITIES
Showers, male (1), female (1),
Accommodation £55.00,
Vegetarian/Healthy meals, Takeaway,
Arcade machines, Internet, Euros, Phone
top-ups, Clothing, Truckers' accessories

All on-site facilities accessible 24 Hours **095**

Medway Services Eastbound, Moto Hospitality Ltd T3 ■

Moto Ltd
Gillingham
Kent ME8 8PQ
T 01634 236900 www.moto-way.com

M2 EASTBOUND JUNCTION 4–5

CREDIT/DEBIT CARDS

FUEL CARDS (see key on page 9)
③ ⑬ ⑭ ㉒ ㉓ ㉘ ㉝

TRUCK FACILITIES
P *with voucher*   **P** *only*   *Voucher value*
£18.00   £16.00   £7.50
Room for manoeuvre

DRIVER FACILITIES
Takeaway food, Vegetarian meals, Showers, male (1), female (1), Accommodation nearby, Travelodge Phone top-ups, Clothing, Truckers' accessories, Arcade machines, Bureau de Change, Fax/copier

All on-site facilities accessible 24 hours   **096**

Medway Services Westbound, Moto Hospitality Ltd T3 ■

Moto Ltd
Gillingham
Kent ME8 8PQ
T 01634 236900 www.moto-way.com

M2 WESTBOUND JUNCTION 4–5

CREDIT/DEBIT CARDS

FUEL CARDS (see key on page 9)
③ ⑬ ⑭ ㉒ ㉓ ㉘ ㉝

TRUCK FACILITIES
P *with voucher*   **P** *only*   *Voucher value*
£18.00   £16.00   £7.50
Room for manoeuvre

DRIVER FACILITIES
Accommodation on-site, Travelodge Takeaway food
Showers, male (1), female (1)
Internet, Post Office, Phone accessories/top-ups and Clothing nearby

All on-site facilities accessible 24 hours   **097**

Mellors of Challow Ltd   FL2 ■

Faringdon Road, East Challow
Wantage, Oxfordshire OX12 9TE
T 01235 760606

ON THE A417 Take the A417 out of Wrantage towards Faringdon. Mellors of Challow is on the right-hand side, 1 mile beyond East Challow and just before the turning for West Challow.

CREDIT/DEBIT CARDS

FUEL CARDS (see key on page 9)
① ② ③ ⑥ ⑦ ㉓ ㉕ ㉖ ㉗

TRUCK FACILITIES
Overnight parking on roadside within industrial estate.
Truck dealership/workshop
Windscreen repair facility
Tyre repair/sales

DRIVER FACILITIES
Drivers' washroom
Takeaway food
Truckers' accessories

All on-site facilities 07:00–19:00   **098**

T3 ■ Membury Services eastbound

Welcome Break Ltd
Lambourn, Hungerford
Berkshire RG17 7TZ
T 01488 674360

M4 EASTBOUND BETWEEN JUNCTIONS 14 AND 15

CREDIT/DEBIT CARDS

FUEL CARDS (see key on page 9)
(14)

DRIVER FACILITIES
Takeaway food

Full site details not available at time of going to press. For more information please contact site.

All on-site facilities accessible 24 hours

099

T3 ■ Membury Services westbound

Welcome Break Ltd
Lambourn, Hungerford
Berkshire RG17 7TZ
T 01488 674360

M4 WESTBOUND BETWEEN JUNCTIONS 14 AND 15

CREDIT/DEBIT CARDS

FUEL CARDS (see key on page 9)
(14)

TRUCK FACILITIES
P with voucher   **P** only   Voucher value
£17.50   £11.50   £6.00
Coach overnight parking (20)
Floodlights, Room for manoeuvre
Fridge parking
DRIVER FACILITIES
Accommodation on-site, Days Inn £54.95
Takeaway food, Vegetarian/healthy meals
Showers, male (2), female (1), Phone
accesssories/top-ups, Clothing, Truckers'
accessories, TV, Arcade machines,
Internet, Euros

All on-site facilities accessible 24 hours

100

T2 ■ The Merrychest Café

Watling Street, Bean, nr Dartford
Kent DA2 8AH
T 01474 832371

ON THE A296 From the M25, exit at junction 2 and take
the A2 towards Gravesend. After 1 and a half miles take the
B225 towards Bluewater Shopping Centre then take the
A296 sliproad heading eastbound back onto the A2. The
Merrychest is on that sliproad on the right.

TRUCK FACILITIES
P
Ample room for manoeuvring
Quiet area

DRIVER FACILITIES
Rest area, phone top-ups/accessories

SITE COMMENTS/INFORMATION
Friendly, family run business

Parking 24 hours. Other on-site facilities 06:30-17:00 Mon-Fri, 06:30-12:00 Sat

101

Michaels Café
FD2 ▦

**London Road, Polhill, Halstead
Sevenoaks, Kent TN14 7AA
T 01959 534284**

ON THE A224 Exit the M25 at junction 4 and take the A224 towards Dunton Green. Continue for 1 mile and Michaels is on the left.

CREDIT/DEBIT CARDS

FUEL CARDS (see key on page 9)

DRIVER FACILITIES
Accommodation on-site, £22.95 pn
Vegetarian/Healthy meals, Take away, TV

On-site facilities accessible 07:00-15:00 Mon-Fri, 08:00-15:00 Sat

102

Nell's Café & Truckstop
T2 ▦

**Watling Street, Gravesend East
Gravesend, Kent DA12 5PU
T 01474 362457**

ON THE A2 From the A2 if heading eastbound. Continue past the A227 exit, the Premier Lodge and Manor Hotel and take the Gravesend East exit immediately afterwards into Valley Drive. Follow the sliproad round and take the very next right. Nell's is in front of you.

TRUCK FACILITIES
P Coach parking available (10 spaces)
Ample room for manoeuver
Quiet area nearby

DRIVER FACILITIES
Accommodation nearby, half mile,
Manor Hotel & Premier Lodge
Showers – 2 m, washroom, TV, truckers' accessories, takeaway food

SITE COMMENTS/INFORMATION
Excellent location, easy to find site,
home cooked food

Nearby and on-site parking and fuel 24 hours. Other on-site facilities 0:630-20:00

103

Newport Pagnell Services northbound
T3 ▦

**Welcome Break Ltd
Newport Pagnell
Buckinghamshire MK16 8DS
T 01908 217722**

M1 NORTHBOUND BETWEEN JUNCTIONS 14 AND 15

CREDIT/DEBIT CARDS

FUEL CARDS (see key on page 9)
③ ⑩ ㉕

DRIVER FACILITIES
Accommodation, Welcome Lodge
Takeaway food

Full site details not available at time of going to press. For more information please contact site.

All on-site facilities accessible 24 hours

104

T3 ▪ Newport Pagnell Services southbound

**Welcome Break Ltd
Newport Pagnell
Bedfordshire MK16 8DS
T 01908 217722**

M1 SOUTHBOUND BETWEEN JUNCTIONS 14 AND 15

CREDIT/DEBIT CARDS

FUEL CARDS (see key on page 9)
(10)(24)(25)(27)

DRIVER FACILITIES
Takeaway food

Full site details not available at time of going to press. For more information please contact site.

All on-site facilities accessible 24 hours — **105**

FL1 ▪ Northdown Service Station, Ashford

**Maidstone Road, Charing, Ashford
Kent TN27 0JS
T 01233 712375**

ON THE A20 From the M20, exit at junction 8 and follow the A20 towards Harrietsham and Charing. North Down Service Station is on the right, a few hundred yards before the roundabout with the A252, and can also be accessed from junction 9 of the M20.

CREDIT/DEBIT CARDS

FUEL CARDS (see key on page 9)
(1)(2)(3)(7)

DRIVER FACILITIES
Train nearby

All on-site facilities 06:00-21:00. — **106**

T2 ▪ Oakdene Café

**London Road, Wrotham, Sevenoaks
Kent TN15 7RR
T 01732 884873**

ON THE A20 From M20, exit at junction 2 and follow A20 towards M26 and Wrotham Heath. Oakdene is on the left 200 yards from M26. From M26, exit at junction 2A and take A20 towards Wrotham. Oakdene is 200 yards on the right.

CREDIT/DEBIT CARDS

FUEL CARDS (for nearby fuel)
(28)

TRUCK FACILITIES
P £5.00
Ample room for manoeuvring
Quiet area

DRIVER FACILITIES
Accommodation nearby, half mile, Travel Inn £40.00, Washroom, phone top-ups/accessories, Takeaway food, Vegetarian/Healthy meals

SITE COMMENTS/INFORMATION
This site provides hot, fresh cooked food

Parking, nearby fuel and shop 24 hours. Other on-site facilities 06:00-06:30 Mon-Fri, 06:00-17:00 Sat & Sun — **107**

Oxford Services

T3 ■

Welcome Break Ltd
Thame Road, Waterstock, Oxford
Oxfordshire OX33 1LJ
T 01865 876372

M40 JUNCTION 8A

CREDIT/DEBIT CARDS

FUEL CARDS (see key on page 9)
③ ⑩ ⑭ ㉒ ㉓ ㉔ ㉕

TRUCK FACILITIES
P *with voucher*   **P** *only*
£14.00   £12.00
Coach parking available (13 spaces)

DRIVER FACILITIES
Accommodation on-site, Days Inn
Showers, 3 m, 1 f (free)
Phone top-ups/accessories
Truckers' accessories
Takeaway food
Euros changed/accepted
CB sales/repairs

All on-site facilities accessible 24 hours

108

Park Orpington Service Station, Orpington

FL1 ■

85-87 Sevenoaks Road, Orpington
Kent BR6 9JW
T 01689 835191

ON THE A223 From the M25 exit 4, follow the A21
towards London. Take the A223 towards Orpington and Park
Orpington is on the right-hand side just after you go over the
railway line.

CREDIT/DEBIT CARDS

FUEL CARDS (see key on page 9)
③ ⑦

TRUCK FACILITIES
Truck washing facilities

DRIVER FACILITIES
Truckers' accessories

All on-site facilities 24 hours

109

Pease Pottage Services

T3 ■

Moto Ltd
Pease Pottage, nr Crawley
East Sussex RH11 9YA
T 01293 535756 www.moto-way.com

M23 JUNCTION 11

CREDIT/DEBIT CARDS

FUEL CARDS (see key on page 9)
⑩ ㉔ ㉕

DRIVER FACILITIES
Takeaway food

*Full site details not available at time of going to
press. For more information please contact site.*

All on-site facilities accessible 24 hours

110

T4 ■ Portsmouth Truckstop & Lorry Park

C H Jones Ltd, Walton road
Railway Triangle Ind. Est., Farlington
Portsmouth, Hampshire PO6 1UJ
T 023 92376000

OFF THE A2030 From M27, head eastbound onto the A27 towards A3M and Chichester. Take the next exit, turn left onto A2030. Take the next immediate left. At the end of the road go left then next right. Truckstop is on the right before bridge.

FUEL CARDS (see key on page 9)
① ② ④ ㉘ ㉞

TRUCK FACILITIES

P with voucher	**P** only	Voucher value
£15.00	£12.00	£4.00

Coach parking available (10 spaces)
Quiet, Fridge lorry area, 24hr security
Manoeuvring room, Secure fence
Floodlights, CCTV, Adblue in containers,
Truck dealership/workshop

DRIVER FACILITIES
Accommodation, £14.00 pn
Showers, m 5, f 1 (£2), rest area, TV,
laundry, internet, phone top-ups/accessories, Takeaway food, Healthy menu, Evening entertainment, Arcade machines, Euros, Fax/copier

All on-site facilities accessible 24 hours | **111**

T3 ■ Reading Services eastbound

Moto Ltd
Burghfield, Reading
Berkshire RG30 3UQ
T 01189 566966 www.moto-way.com

M4 EASTBOUND BETWEEN JUNCTIONS 11 AND 12

CREDIT/DEBIT CARDS

FUEL CARDS (see key on page 9)
⑭ ㉒

DRIVER FACILITIES
Accommodation, Travelodge
Shower
Phone top-ups/accessories
Truckers' accessories
Takeaway food

Full site details not available at time of going to press. For more information please contact site.

All on-site facilities accessible 24 hours | **112**

T3 ■ Reading Services westbound

Moto Ltd
Burghfield, Reading
Berkshire RG30 3UQ
T 01189 566966 www.moto-way.com

M4 WESTBOUND BETWEEN JUNCTIONS 11 AND 12

CREDIT/DEBIT CARDS

FUEL CARDS (see key on page 9)
⑭

TRUCK FACILITIES
CCTV, Room for manoeuvre

DRIVER FACILITIES
Accommodation on-site, Travelodge
Shower, unisex(2), phone top-ups/accessories
Truckers' accessories
Takeaway food, Vegetarian/healthy meals
Clothing, Arcade machines, Internet

SITE COMMENTS/INFORMATION
Ritazza Coffee Bar and a Coffee Nation
self service machine also in the forecourt

BK, Ritazza and M&S 07:30-22:00, Uppercrust 08:00-18:00, WH Smith, Fresh Express and All other on-site facilities 24 hrs | **113**

ReD Fuel Cards (Europe) - Fuelserve, Calais   FL1 ●

Fuelserve Ltd, Rue des Goelands
Zone Industrielle Des Dunes
Calais, Nord Pas De Calais 62110, France
T 0033 (0) 321971194 www.redfuelcards.com

OFF THE E15 The Zone Industrielle Des Dunes is surrounded by the E15 to the north and east and the D119 to the south and west. Follow signs into the estate. Find the Rue des Gareness and turn onto the Rue des Oyats then onto Rue des Goelands.

CREDIT/DEBIT CARDS

FUEL CARDS (see key on page 9)
② ④

All on-site facilities 24 hours   **114**

Robo's Café and Diner   T2 ■

London Road South, Pycombe
Sussex BN45 7FJ
T 01273 844055

ON THE A23 Take the A23 south towards Brighton. Continue for half a mile past the junction with the A273 and Robo's is accessed via a lay-by on your left.

FUEL CARDS (see key on page 9)
㊷

TRUCK FACILITIES
Overnight **P** in access lay-by for LGVs
P free
Coach parking available, shared with LGV
Ample room for manoeuvring
Truck dealership/workshop nearby

DRIVER FACILITIES
Takeaway food

SITE COMMENTS/INFORMATION
Lorry parking in entrance lay-by only, cars can use car park next to café. Trucks please park considerately as this is also an access road. This site will accept payment by cheque

Parking and nearby shop and fuel 24 hours. All other on-site facilities 05:45-15:00 Mon-Fri, 05:45-12:00 Sat   **115**

Rownhams Services north-eastbound   T3 ■

Roadchef Ltd
Rownhams, Southampton
Hampshire SO16 8AP
T 02380 734480 Duty Manager 079132
14594 www.onyourway.com

M27 NORTH-EASTBOUND BETWEEN
JUNCTIONS 3 AND 4

CREDIT/DEBIT CARDS

FUEL CARDS (see key on page 9)
③ ㉓ ㉔ ㉖ ㉗

TRUCK FACILITIES
P with voucher   **P** only   Voucher value
£17.00   £10.00   £7.50
Coach parking available (22 spaces), Quiet area,
Truck washing, Abnormal bay on access road

DRIVER FACILITIES
Accommodation (£50.00 pn), Washroom, Free shower, male (1), female (1 westbound), TV, Internet access, Phone top-ups/ accessories, Truckers' accessories, Takeaway food, Vegetarian/ healthy meals, Arcade mach., Internet, Euros, Phone top-ups, Clothing.

SITE COMMENTS/INFORMATION
Ideal stop over site if delivering to Southampton Docks or Tesco Distribution centre.

Restbite and Wimpy open till 22:00. Costa, Shop, Forecourt and all other on-site facilities open 24hrs   **116**

T3 ■ Rownhams Services south-westbound

Roadchef Ltd
Rownhams, Southampton
Hampshire SO16 8AP
T 02380 734480 **Duty Manager** 07913
214594 www.onyourway.com

M27 SOUTH-WESTBOUND BETWEEN
JUNCTIONS 3 AND 4

CREDIT/DEBIT CARDS

FUEL CARDS (see key on page 9)
③ ㉔ ㉕ ㉖ ㉗

TRUCK FACILITIES
P *with voucher* **P** *only   Voucher value*
£17.00   £10.00   £7.50
Coach parking available (22 spaces)
Quiet area, Truck washing, Room for
manoeuvring, Abnormal load bay on
access road
DRIVER FACILITIES
Accommodation on-site (£50.00 pn)
Washroom, Showers, male (1) free with
parking, TV, Internet access, Phone top-
ups/accessories, Truckers' accessories
Takeaway food, Vegetarian/healthy meals
Arcade machines, Euros, Clothing

All on-site facilities accessible 24 hours   **117**

FL1 ■ Sandford Garage, Godshill

Sandford, Godshill
Isle of Wight, PO38 3AL
T 01983 840303

ON THE A3020 Take the A3020 from Newport to Shanklin.
Sandford Garage is on the left-hand side in the village of
Sandford, 1 mile east of Godshill.

CREDIT/DEBIT CARDS

FUEL CARDS (see key on page 9)
② ③ ㉓

TRUCK FACILITIES
Short-term coach parking (4 spaces)
Truck washing facilities

DRIVER FACILITIES
Clothing for sale
Phone top-ups

SITE COMMENTS/INFORMATION
'The only one like it on the Isle of
Wight!'

Parking and all other on-site facilities accessible 07:00-22:00.   **118**

FL1 ■ Shell Old Ford Road, Bow

445-453 Wick Lane, Bow, London,
Greater London E3 2TB
T 0208 9832500

OFF THE A12 Take the A11 north-eastbound out of central
London until the junction with the A12. Turn left onto this
towards Hackney. Take the next immediate slip road and turn
right across the carriageway into Wick Lane. Shell Old Ford is
50 yards on the right.

CREDIT/DEBIT CARDS

FUEL CARDS (see key on page 9)
㉕

TRUCK FACILITIES
Truck washing facilities

SITE COMMENTS/INFORMATION
Excellent customer service

Toilets accessible 06:00-23:00. All other on-site facilities 24 hours   **119**

Somerfield West Wellow

FL4 ◼

Ower, Romsey
Hampshire SO51 6AS
T 02380 817100

A36 ROUNDABOUT Exit the M27 at junction 2 and take the A36 towards Salisbury. Somerfield West Wellow is in 800 Yards at the roundabout with the A3090.

CREDIT/DEBIT CARDS

FUEL CARDS (see key on page 9)
① ③ ④ ⑦ ㉓

TRUCK FACILITIES
P free
Coach parking available, shared with LGV
Ample room for manoeuvring
Quiet area

DRIVER FACILITIES
Drivers' washroom
Premier Lodge 400 yards away
Takeaway

All on-site facilities 24 hours

120

Square Deal Café

FD2 ◼

Bath Road, Knowle Hill, Reading
Berkshire RG10 9YL
T 01628 822426

ON THE A4 Take the A4 from Maidenhead to Reading. Square Deal Café is on your left-hand side in the middle of Knowle Hill village, just before the Castle Royal Golf Club.

CREDIT/DEBIT CARDS

FUEL CARDS (see key on page 9)

TRUCK FACILITIES
Nearby overnight parking on request only
Ample room for manoeuvring
Quiet area nearby

DRIVER FACILITIES
Accommodation nearby, half mile, Bird In Hand Hotel

All on-site facilities opening times unknown

121

Staddlestones Nissan, Ryde

FL1 ◼

Brading Road, Ryde
PO33 1QG, Isle of Wight
T 01983 562705

ON THE A3055 Take the A3055 south out of Ryde towards Sandown. Staddlestones Nissan is on the left-hand side on the outskirts of the town, just beyond Tesco.

CREDIT/DEBIT CARDS

FUEL CARDS (see key on page 9)
③ ④

DRIVER FACILITIES
Takeaway food nearby

All on-site facilities 07:30-18:00

122

FL2 ● Watson Petroleum

**Watson Petroleum Ltd, Andes Road
Nursling Industrial Estate, Nursling
Southampton, Hampshire SO16 0AG**
T 02380 737330 www.watsonfuels.co.uk

OFF THE M271 Junction 1 off the M271. Follow the signs for the Nursling Industrial Estate. At the estate roundabout by B&Q, go straight across into Andes Rd. We are within 200 metres on the left hand side.

CREDIT/DEBIT CARDS

FUEL CARDS (see key on page 9)
① ② ④ ⑦ ③④

TRUCK FACILITIES
Overnight parking on roadside within estate, Coach parking available, Ample room for manoeuvring, Adblue at pump nearby
LGV sales/dealership/workshop nearby
LGV tyre repair/sales nearby
DRIVER FACILITIES
Accommodation nearby, 800 yards, Holiday Inn Express
SITE COMMENTS/INFORMATION
Assistance available for drivers between 08:00-17:00 only

Nearby parking and bunkering facilities 24 hours. **123**

T3 ■ Winchester Services northbound

**Roadchef Ltd
Shroner Wood, Martyr Worthy
nr Winchester, Hampshire SO21 1PP**
T 01962 791134

M3 NORTHBOUND BETWEEN JUNCTIONS 8 AND 9

CREDIT/DEBIT CARDS

FUEL CARDS (see key on page 9)
① ② ③ ④ ⑥ ㉓ ③④

TRUCK FACILITIES
P *with voucher* **P** *only* *Voucher value*
£12.00   £9.00   £4.00
Coaches overnight (12 spaces), Ample room for manoeuvre, Quiet, Floodlights
DRIVER FACILITIES
Showers, male (1), female (1), Phone top-ups/accessories, truckers' accessories, Takeaway food, Vegetarian/Healthy meals, Int. papers, Arcade machines, Internet, Euros
SITE COMMENTS/INFORMATION
Value for money food with great facilities for LGV drivers

All on-site facilities accessible 24 hours **124**

T3 ■ Winchester Services southbound

**Roadchef Ltd
Shroner Wood, Martyr Worthy
nr Winchester, Hampshire SO21 1PP**
T 01962 791140/791106

M3 SOUTHBOUND BETWEEN JUNCTIONS 8 AND 9

CREDIT/DEBIT CARDS

FUEL CARDS (see key on page 9)
① ② ③ ④ ⑦ ㉓ ③④

TRUCK FACILITIES
P *with voucher* **P** *only* *Voucher value*
£12.00   £9.00   £4.00
Coach parking available (12 spaces)
Ample manoeuvring, Quiet, Floodlights

DRIVER FACILITIES
Accommodation (£55) Showers, male (1), female (1), Phone top-ups/accessories, Truckers' accessories, Takeaway food, Vegetarian/Healthy meals, Int. Papers, Arcade machines

SITE COMMENTS/INFORMATION
Good LGV facilities

All on-site facilities accessible 24 hours **125**

Wrotham Heath Service Station, Wrotham Heath FL1 ■

London Road, Wrotham Heath
Kent TN15 7RY
T **01732 781113**

ON THE A20 Exit the M26 at junction 2A and take the A20 towards Maidstone for 600 yards. Wrotham Heath Services is on the right-hand side.

CREDIT/DEBIT CARDS

FUEL CARDS (see key on page 9)
① ㉓

DRIVER FACILITIES
Accommodation onsite, Travel Inn
Drivers' washroom
Phone top-ups/accessories
Takeaway food
Vegetarian meals

All on-site facilities 24 hours
126

STARTING OUT

An exciting series of novels by Wendy Glindon

Based on the author's own experiences behind the wheel, the stories centre around the enduring bond of friendship between the two main characters, vivacious lady trucker Carol Landers and her glamorous soul mate Gina, supporting each other without question, regardless of the situation, while giving the reader an insight into the lives of lady truckers on the roads of Europe where the only thing the women can ultimately rely on is their solid friendship and uncompromising trust in each other.

Both these books are on sale at all good bookshops, Amazon on-line or direct from the author's website: www.mothertrucker.co.uk

DRIVING ON

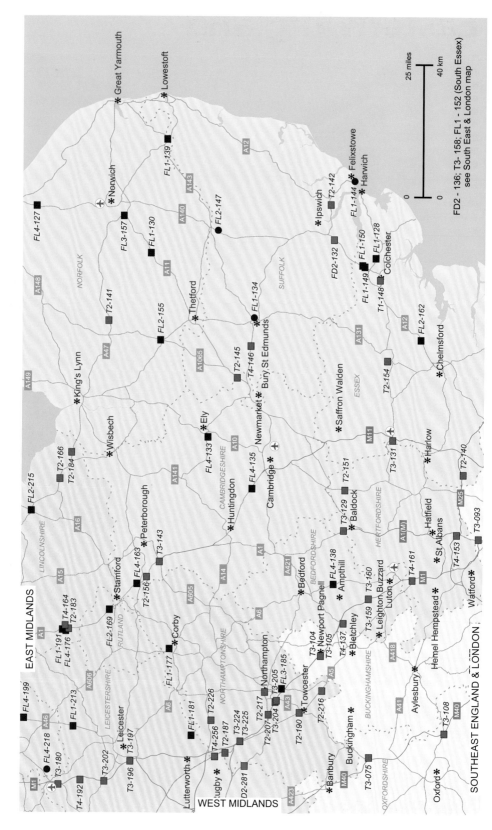

FD2 - 136; T3 - 158; FL1 - 152 (South Essex)
see South East & London map

Eastern England

■ *Cafe - Layby parking (FD1)*
■ *Cafe - No overnight parking (FD2)*
■ *Filling Station - No overnight parking/cafe (FL1)*
● *Bunkering Site - No overnight parking/cafe (FL1)*
■ *Filling Station - Nearby overnight parking no cafe (FL2)*
● *Bunkering Site - Nearby overnight parking no cafe (FL2)*
■ *Filling Station - Cafe no onsite overnight parking (FL3)*
■ *Filling Station - Onsite overnight parking (FL4)*
● *Bunkering Site - Onsite overnight parking (FL4)*
● *Bunkering Site - Cafe & onsite overnight parking (FL5)*
■ *Lorry Park - Onsite overnight parking no cafe or fuel (T1)*
■ *Truck Stop/Cafe - Onsite overnight parking (T2)*
■ *Motorway Service Station (T3)*
■ *Truck Stop - Bunker fuel/showers/cafe/onsite overnight parking (T4)*

For key to site symbols see page 8

FL4 ■   Alby Service Station

Cromer Road, Erpingham, Norwich
Norfolk NR11 7HA
T 01263 761393

ON THE A140 Alby Service Station is on the A140 between Aylsham and Cromer. If travelling to Cromer, Alby is on the right-hand side just after the left-hand side turnings for the village of Erpingham.

CREDIT/DEBIT CARDS

FUEL CARDS (see key on page 9)
❶ ❼

TRUCK FACILITIES
P Coach parking available, shared with LGV
Ample room for manoeuvring
Quiet area

DRIVER FACILITIES
B&B accommodation nearby
Post Office
Truckers' accessories nearby

SITE COMMENTS/INFORMATION
Video/DVD rental on-site
Helpful, friendly all female staff

Parking 24 hours. Other on-site facilities 07:00-20:00 Mon-Sat, 09:00-20:00 Sun   **127**

FL1 ■   Ardleigh South Services, Colchester

Harwich Road, Ardleigh, Colchester
Essex CO7 7SL
T 01206 231174

ON THE A120 Ardleigh is on the A120 Harwich to Colchester road, 3 miles before the interchange with the A12 and on the left-hand side of the carriageway if heading north-west.

CREDIT/DEBIT CARDS

FUEL CARDS (see key on page 9)
❶ ❷ ❸ ❹ ❼ ❿ ㉞

DRIVER FACILITIES
Truckers' accessories

All on-site facilities 24 hours   **128**

Baldock Services

T3

Extra MSA Forecourts Ltd
Radwell, Baldock, Hertfordshire SG7 5TR
T 01462 832810

A1M JUNCTION 10 Take the A507 to Baldock. Baldock services is 50 yards on the left.

CREDIT/DEBIT CARDS

FUEL CARDS (see key on page 9)
① ③ ④ ⑦ ㉞

TRUCK FACILITIES
Coach parking available (7 spaces)
P Overnight security patrol
Quiet area
Ample room for manoeuvring

DRIVER FACILITIES
Showers, 2 male, 1 female
Accommodation on-site
Internet access
Truckers' accessories
Takeaway food

Parking, showers, fuel and some food accessible 24 hours. Restaurant open 07:00-23:00

129

Besthorpe Filling Station, Attleborough

FL1

Besthorpe, Attleborough
Norfolk NR17 2LA
T 01953 452441

ON THE A11 SOUTHBOUND Besthorpe is on the A11 southbound carriageway between Wymondham and Attleborough, and 100 yards on from the Little Chef.

CREDIT/DEBIT CARDS

FUEL CARDS (see key on page 9)
③ ㉒ ㉓ ㉘ ㉝

DRIVER FACILITIES
Healthy menu available
Phone top-ups
Adblue in containers

All on-site facilities 06:00-21:00.

130

Birchanger Services

T3

Welcome Break Ltd
Bishops Stortford, Hertfordshire CM23 5QZ
T 01279 652364

M11 JUNCTION 8 Exit the M11 at junction 8 take turning for the A120.

CREDIT/DEBIT CARDS

FUEL CARDS (see key on page 9)
㉕

TRUCK FACILITIES
P *with voucher*   **P** *only*
£17.50   £15.00
Floodlighting, Plenty of room to manoeuvre

DRIVER FACILITIES
Takeaway food, Showers, male (3), Female (1) free, Washroom
Accommodation – Days Inn, £69.00
Vegetarian meals, Arcade machines, Euros accepted, Phone accessories, Phone top-ups, International papers

All on-site facilities accessible 24 hours

131

FD2 ■ Boss Hoggs Transport Café

**Old London Road, Copdock, Ipswich
Suffolk IP8 3JW
T 01473 730797**

OFF THE A12 If heading from Colchester to Ipswich, take the exit signposted to Copdock onto the London road. Boss Hogs is 400 yards along on the right.

CREDIT/DEBIT CARDS

FUEL CARDS (see key on page 9)

DRIVER FACILITIES
Drivers' washroom
Takeaway on-site
Plenty of room for manoeuvre in
lorry park

P SHORT-TERM

£1.80   50p   CR & HF £4.95

Monday-Friday 07:00-15:00   **132**

FL4 ■ BP Budgens

**Witchford Road Service Station
Witchford Road, Ely,
Cambridgeshire CB6 3NN
T 01353 669112**

ON THE A142 From the A10 northbound towards Ely turn left at the A142 Ely ring road. Staying on the A142, turn left at the next roundabout towards Wichford and BP Budgens is a few yards along on the right.

CREDIT/DEBIT CARDS
VISA

FUEL CARDS (see key on page 9)
22

TRUCK FACILITIES
P
Coach parking available, shared with LGV
Ample room for manoeuvring
Quiet area
Truck washing facilities

DRIVER FACILITIES
Travelodge on-site (£50 per night)
Takeaway food
Truckers' accessories

SITE COMMENTS/INFORMATION
Great food, clean friendly site with staff
who aim to please

4.2m   2 BP

P 5 OVERNIGHT

Parking 24 hours. Travelodge opening times unknown. Other on-site facilities 06:00-23:00   **133**

FL1 ● Bryan J Nunn Haulage Ltd

**Chapel Pond Hill, Bury St Edmunds,
Suffolk IP32 7HT
T 01284 705300**

OFF THE A143 From the roundabout with the A14 and A143, take the A143 towards Diss and Great Yarmouth. Continue over the next roundabout and turn right at the next, into Hollow Road. Take the next left and Bryan J Nunn is on the right.

CREDIT/DEBIT CARDS

FUEL CARDS (see key on page 9)
① ② ④ ⑤ ㉞

TRUCK FACILITIES
Truck washing facilities

Independent   AUTO BUNKER

Bunker fuel 24 hours   **134**

Cambridge Services, Extra MSA Services Ltd   FL4

Extra MSA Forecourts Ltd, Boxworth
Cambridge, Cambridgeshire CB3 8WU
T 01522 523737 www.extraservices.co.uk

ON THE A14 From the M11, take the A14 towards Godmanchester. Continue past the junction for Bar Hill and take the next junction signposted for Boxworth. Cambridge Services is on that junction on the left-hand side.

CREDIT/DEBIT CARDS

FUEL CARDS (see key on page 9)

TRUCK FACILITIES
P £13.00
Coach parking available (12 spaces)
Overnight security patrol
Ample room for manoeuvring
Quiet area

DRIVER FACILITIES
Showers, 3 male, 1 female (free)
Accommodation on-site (£55 per night)
Takeaway food
Truckers' accessories

SITE COMMENTS/INFORMATION
Easy access for LGVs

Parking, fuel, shop, showers and some food 24 hours. Amenity building open 06:00 and closes at 23:00   **135**

Carlton Transport Café   FD2

Arterial Road, Wickford
Essex SS12 9HZ
T 01268 727313

ON THE A127 From the A13, take the A130 towards Battlesbridge. After 1 mile turn left onto the A127 towards Basildon. Carlton Transport Café is 1 mile along on the right.

TRUCK FACILITIES
Ample room for manoeuvring
Short-term parking (20 spaces)

DRIVER FACILITIES
Washroom
Takeaway food

All on-site facilities accessible 07:00-13:30 Mon-Fri 07:30-11:30 Sat.   **136**

Crawley Crossing Bunker Stop   T4

C H Jones Ltd, Bedford Road
Husbourne Crawley, Bedfordshire MK43 0UT
T 01908 281084

OFF THE A507 From the M1, exit at junction 13 and head south on the A507 towards Woburn. Crawley Crossing is half a mile along on the right.

FUEL CARDS (see key on page 9)

TRUCK FACILITIES
P with voucher £6.00
Voucher value £1.00
Coach parking available, shared with LGV
Quiet area. Fridge lorry area sitated near exit road, Floodlights
Ample room for manoeuvring
Adblue at pump

DRIVER FACILITIES
Shower – 1 unisex (£1.50), washroom,
TV Euros changed/accepted
Truckers' accessories, CB repairs/sales
Takeaway food

Truckers shop accessible 08:00-16:00 Mon-Thurs, 08:00-14:00 Fri. Café and Showers accessible 07:00-22:00 Mon-Thurs, 07:00-20:00 Fri. 07:00-12:00 Sat. Bunker fuel and other on-site facilities accessible 24 Hours.   **137**

FL4 — Four Winds Service Station

Bedford Road, Haynes West End, Bedford Bedfordshire MK45 3QT
T 01234 743755

ON THE A6 If heading from Luton to Bedford on the A6, Four Winds is on the right-hand side about 2 miles past the intersection with the A507.

CREDIT/DEBIT CARDS

FUEL CARDS (see key on page 9)
① ④ ⑦ ⑧ ㉞

TRUCK FACILITIES
P
Coach parking available (4 spaces)
Quiet area
Fridge lorry area
Ample room for manoeuvring

DRIVER FACILITIES
Truckers' accessories
Takeaway food nearby

All on-site facilities 07:00 19:00 Mon-Fri, 08:00-16:00 Sat & Sun. On-site parking times unknown **138**

FL1 — Gillingham Service Station, Norfolk

Malthurst Ltd
Near Beccles, Norfolk NR34 0ED
T 01502 714400

A146 A143 INTERCHANGE Gillingham Service Station can be found at the Junction of the A146 Norwich to Lowestoft road and the A143 Great Yarmouth to Diss road.

CREDIT/DEBIT CARDS

FUEL CARDS (see key on page 9)
③ ⑭ ㉒ ㉓ ㉘

All on-site facilities 24 hours **139**

T2 — Junction 26 Truck Stop

Skillet Hill Farm, Honey Lane, Waltham Abbey, Essex EN9 3QU
T 07908 087072 www.junction26.org

OFF THE M25, JUNCTION 26 Sited between the two slip road roundabouts on the M25 at J26 across the road from the Marriot hotel (looks tight to turn in but you will fit).

TRUCK FACILITIES
P £15.00 Voucher value 1 Meal & Tea
Coaches overnight, shared with LGV
Secure fencing, Fridge lorry, Room to manoeuvre, Quiet parking, Floodlighting

DRIVER FACILITIES
Showers, male (2), female (1) (£2.00 if not parking), Internet, Healthy menu/vegetarian meals, Takeaway, TV, Euros

SITE COMMENTS/INFORMATION
Parking attendant 16:00-23:00. Fridge lorries switch off 22:00. Please do not park on the road to use our facilities.

Mon-Thur 06:00-21:00, Fri 06:00-20:00 Sat 06:00-14:00. Closed Sunday. Last food orders 1 hour before closing. **140**

Necton Diner   T2

Norwich Road, Necton
Norfolk PE37 8QH
T 01760 724180

ON THE A47 From Swaffham take the A47 towards
Norwich. Necton diner is about 3 miles from Swaffham at the
village of Necton and on the right-hand side if heading
towards Norwich.

TRUCK FACILITIES
P *with voucher* £10.00
Voucher value £5.25
Fridge lorry area, Overnight coaches
Ample room for manoeuvring, Quiet
parking area

DRIVER FACILITIES
Shower – 1 unisex (£1 or free with
parking), washroom, TV
Takeaway food, Arcade machines,
International papers

SITE COMMENTS/INFORMATION
Friendly chatty staff
Parking price includes hot meal and hot
drink with free refills. Drivers must ask
for key for showers.

Parking, toilets, showers and nearby fuel 24hrs. Other facilities open Mon-Thur 08:00-18:00,
Fri 08:00-17:00, Sat 08:00-15:00 or 16:00. Closed Sun till easter then open 7 days a week.

141

Orwell Crossing Lorry Park   T2

A14, Eastbound, Nacton, Ipswich, Suffolk,
IP10 0DD
T 01473 659 140

ON THE A14 IPSWICH BYPASS This site is situated on the
Eastbound Carriageway of the A14 Ipswich bypass and
halfway between the junctions with the A1189 and A12.

CREDIT/DEBIT CARDS

TRUCK FACILITIES
P £14.00 Voucher value £3.00
Coaches overnight, shared with LGV, 24
hour security, Floodlights, CCTV, Room to
manoeuvre, Fridge parking, Quiet parking

DRIVER FACILITIES
Showers, unisex (14), £2.50 or free if
parking, Washroom, Evening entertainment,
TV, Arcade machines, Games room, Internet,
Euros, Fax/copier, Truckers' accessories,
Vegetarian/Healthy meals, Takeaway

SITE COMMENTS
This site is 6 Miles from Felixstowe Port. All
food cooked fresh from local fresh produce.
A friendly welcome awaits all lorry drivers
and local customers.

All on-site facilities open 24 hours except for 1 week over Christmas

142

Peterborough Services   T3

Extra MSA Forecourts Ltd
Great North Road, Haddon, Peterborough
Cambridgeshire PE7 3UQ
T 01733 362950

A1M JUNCTION 17. Take A605 towards Warmington.
Peterborough Services is 100 yards on the left.

CREDIT/DEBIT CARDS

FUEL CARDS (see key on page 9)
① ③ ④ ⑦ ㉞

TRUCK FACILITIES
P
Coach parking available (19 spaces)
Overnight security patrol
Quiet area
Ample room for manoeuvring

DRIVER FACILITIES
Accommodation on-site
Showers, 2 m, 1 f, Internet access,
Truckers' accessories, Takeaway food

SITE COMMENTS/INFORMATION
Good LGV facilities

Parking, showers, shop, fuel and some food accessible 24 hours. Other on-site facilities 07:00-23.00

143

FL1 ReD Fuel Cards (Europe), Felixstowe

Fuelserve Ltd, Waterfront Services, Walton Ave, (Between Dock Gates 1 & 2), Felixstowe, Suffolk IP11 8HE
T 01394 674812 www.redfuelcards.com
OFF THE A14 From Ipswich, take the A14 to Felixstowe. At the junction with the A154 turn right continuing with the A14. At the next roundabout turn right into Walton Avenue. Site is 400 yards along on the right.

CREDIT/DEBIT CARDS

FUEL CARDS (see key on page 9)
① ② ④ ⑤ ⑥ ⑦ ㉙ ㉞

TRUCK FACILITIES
Truck dealership/workshop
Adblue at the pump

SITE COMMENTS/INFORMATION
HGV focused site in the centre of the Felixstowe port area

All on-site facilities open 24 hrs — **144**

T2 The Red Lodge Inn

70 Turnpike Road, Red Lodge
nr Bury St Edmunds, Suffolk IP28 8LB
T 01638 750529

ON THE OLD A11 (B1085) From the A14 Newmarket by-pass, take the A11 towards Norwich. After 1 mile take the B1085 towards Red Lodge village. The transport café is in the middle of the village on your left.

CREDIT/DEBIT CARDS

TRUCK FACILITIES
P
Coach parking available, shared with LGV
Ample room for manoeuvring
Quiet area. Floodlighting

DRIVER FACILITIES
Shower – 2 unisex, washroom, rest area, TV, internet access
Takeaway food

All on-site facilities 10:30-22:30 Mon-Sat, 10:30-12:00 Sun. Food available to 21:30 — **145**

T4 Risby's & ReD Fuel Cards Risby

Old Newmarket Road, Risby
nr Bury St Edmunds, Suffolk IP28 6QU/RU
T 01473 466790 01284 811772/01473 466666 www.risby.com
ON THE A14 Take the A14 westbound out of Bury St Edmunds for 4 miles. 1 mile after the junction with the B1106, take the sliproad for Risby. Cross the carriageway and turn left at the T-junction then right. Risby's and Red are on the left.

CREDIT/DEBIT CARDS

FUEL CARDS (see key on page 9)
① ② ④ ㉞

TRUCK FACILITIES
P *with voucher* £12.50
Voucher value 1 meal
Quiet area, Coach parking (shared with LGV), CCTV, Secure fencing, Floodlighting, Quiet parking, Adblue at pumps/in containers, Electric hook ups, Fridge lorries (switch off 22:00)

DRIVER FACILITIES
Shower – 3 m (£2.50 if voucher not used), Washroom, Rest area, TV, Clothing for sale, Truckers' accessories, Vegetarian/healthy meals, Takeaway, Phone top-ups, CB sales/repairs

Bunker fuel, AdBlue, Parking, Showers, Hot food & meeting rooms 24 hrs. Other on-site facilities accessible 07:00-22:00 Mon-Thu, 07:00-20:00 Fri. . — **146**

Roy Humphrey Car & Commercial FL2

Brome, Eye
Suffolk IP23 8AW
T 01379 870666

ON THE A140 SOUTHBOUND Take the A14 north west out of Ipswich, then the A140 northbound towards Norwich for 10 miles. Continue half a mile past the turnings for Eye and Roy Humphrey Car and Commercial is on your right.

CREDIT/DEBIT CARDS

FUEL CARDS (see key on page 9)
① ④ ⑦ ㉞

TRUCK FACILITIES
Coach parking available, shared with LGV
Security guard, Quiet area
Fridge lorry area, Ample room for manoeuvring, Truck dealership/workshop
Windscreen repair facility
Tyre repair/sales

DRIVER FACILITIES
Phone top-ups/accessories

SITE COMMENTS/INFORMATION
A large site with Renault Trucks dealership and a part-time snack van on-site

Parking and bunker fuel 24 hours. Part time on-site snack van 07:00-16:00   **147**

Sheepen Road Lorry & Coach Park T1 ■

Sheepen Road, Colchester, Essex CO1 1XQ
T 01206 282708 Colchester Borough Council
www.colchester.gov.uk
OFF THE A134 WESTWAY If heading from Chelmsford north on the A12, take the A133 (junction 27) on the outskirts of Colchester. Continue over first roundabout and turn right at the next, onto the A134 Westway. At the next roundabout take fourth (last) exit onto Sheepen Road. Lorry park is signposted from there.

 (?)

TRUCK FACILITIES
P LGV & PCV 6 hours daytime £5.00, overnight £8.50, Coach parking available, shared, also fridge lorry, Quiet area, Floodlighting, CCTV
Ample room for manoeuvring

DRIVER FACILITIES
Accommodation half a mile away at the George & Red Lion
Takeaway food nearby
Phone top-ups/accessories nearby
Clothing for sale nearby

SITE COMMENTS/INFORMATION
Access barrier height controlled to keep cars out, vehicles using lorry park must be at least van height. Lorry park has 7 large and 2 small parking bays. Drivers may require 2 shunts to park. Season ticket £230 for 3 months call 01206 282222

Parking 24 hours. Other nearby facilities opening times greatly varied   **148**

Shell Allstop, Colchester FL1 ■

Langham, Colchester
Essex CO4 5NQ
T 01206 233010

ON THE A12 NORTHBOUND From Colchester, take the A12 towards Ipswich. Shell Allstop is on the left-hand side, 1 mile beyond the intersection with the A120.

CREDIT/DEBIT CARDS

FUEL CARDS (see key on page 9)
③ ⑩ ㉔ ㉕

TRUCK FACILITIES
Short-term coach parking (1 space)

DRIVER FACILITIES
Hot drinks free to LGV drivers if buying fuel

SITE COMMENTS/INFORMATION
Friendly, helpful staff

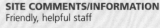
All on-site facilities 07:00-23:00. On-site short term parking times unknown   **149**

FL1 — Shell Birchwood, Colchester

Dedham, Colchester
Essex CO7 6HU
T 01206 321000

ON THE A12 SOUTHBOUND Take the A12 from Ipswich towards Colchester. Shell Birchwood is about 1 mile beyond the turning for Dedham and about 1 and a half miles north of the outskirts of Colchester on the left-hand side.

CREDIT/DEBIT CARDS

FUEL CARDS (see key on page 9)
③ ⑩ ㉔ ㉕

DRIVER FACILITIES
Hot drinks free to LGV drivers making other purchases

SITE COMMENTS/INFORMATION
This site is in an elevated position and is easily seen on approach

All on-site facilities 24 hours **150**

T2 — Silver Ball Café

London Road, Reed, nr Royston
Hertfordshire SG8 8BD
T 01763 848200

ON THE A10 Take the A10 from Royston towards Buntingford for 3 miles. Silver Ball Café is on the right at Reed, just past the turning for Therfield.

TRUCK FACILITIES
P
Coach parking (10 spaces). Quiet area
Ample room for manoeuvring

DRIVER FACILITIES
Accommodation on-site
Showers – m (charge), washroom, TV
Takeaway food

SITE COMMENTS/INFORMATION
Site easily accessible for LGVs

Parking and showers 24 hours. Other on-site facilities 06:00-22:00 **151**

FL1 — Silwood Depot (Team Fitwick Ltd)

Team Flitwick Ltd, Riverside Estate
Oliver Close, West Thurrock, Grays
Essex RM20 3EE T 01708 861122

OFF THE A126 From junction 30 of the M25 take the A13 Basildon. At the A126 turn right. Continue along the A126 to roundabout where A126 turns left. Go straight on, follow sharp right, across next roundabout and its on the left.

CREDIT/DEBIT CARDS

FUEL CARDS (see key on page 9)
① ② ④ ⑤ ㉞

TRUCK FACILITIES
Truck dealership/workshop
Ample room for manoeuvring
Adblue at the pumps

Bunker fuel 24 hours. Other on-site facilities 08:00-17:30 **152**

South Mimms Services & Truckstop   T4

Welcome Break Ltd
Old St Albans Road, South Mimms
Hertfordshire EN6 3NE
T 01707 649998 www.welcomebreak.co.uk

M25 JUNCTION 23 / A1(M) Junction 1 Intersection

CREDIT/DEBIT CARDS

FUEL CARDS (see key on page 9)
① ② ④ ⑤ ⑦ ⑫ ⑭ ㉒ ㉓ ㉕ ㉘
㉙ ㉝ ㉞

TRUCK FACILITIES
P with voucher   Voucher value
£20.00/17.50/10.00   £6.49/3.00
Overnight coach (59), 24hr security, Secure
fencing, Floodlights, Adblue in containers

DRIVER FACILITIES
Accommodation nearby, Days Inn, from
(£49.00) Showers, 1 m, 1 f, 8 unisex (£2,
free with parking), Washroom, Takeaway
food, Vegetarian/Healthy meals, TV, Arcade
mach., Euros, Phone top-ups, Clothing,
Truckers' accessories, CB sales/repairs

All on-site facilities accessible 24 hours   **153**

Springwood Grill   T2

Springwood Drive, Springwood Industrial
Estate, Braintree, Essex CM7 1YN
T 07885 306613

OFF THE M11 ON THE A120 From the M11 junction 8A,
take the A120 towards Braintree. Take 1st exit at the first
roundabout signposted Braintree. Continue for 1 mile,
Springwood road is on your left.

TRUCK FACILITIES
P free, Coach parking (30 spaces),
Floodlights, Room to manoeuvre, Fridge
parking, Quiet parking area, Truck
washing facilities

DRIVER FACILITIES
Showers, male 2, unisex 2 (£1),
Drivers' washroom, Healthy menu,
Takeaway, TV

Open Mon-Thurs 07:30-19:00, Fri 07:30-17:30, Sat 08.00-12:30.   **154**

Steamerpoint Service Station   FL2

Barry Walker & Sons, Swaffham Road
Ickburgh, Nr Mundford, Thetford, Norfolk
IP26 5HX
T 01842 878759

ON THE A1065 Take the A134 from Thetford to King's
Lynn. At the junction with the A1065, turn right towards
Ickburgh. Steamerpoint is 1 mile along on the right.

CREDIT/DEBIT CARDS

FUEL CARDS (see key on page 9)
① ② ③ ④

TRUCK FACILITIES
Nearby overnight parking
Short-term coach & LGV parking
available

DRIVER FACILITIES
Truckers' accessories
Accommodation at Crown Hotel,
Mundford, £43.50 per night

SITE COMMENTS/INFORMATION
Easy access for LGVs

All on-site facilities 06:30-20:00   **155**

T2
Stibbington Diner

2 Old Great North Road, Stibbington Peterborough, Cambridgeshire PE8 6LR
T 01780 782891

OFF THE A1 SOUTHBOUND Take the A1 south from Stamford and continue for 1 and a half miles beyond the junction with the A47. Stibbington Diner is on your left just before the railway line and 1 and a half miles before the turning for the village of Water Newton.

TRUCK FACILITIES
P £5.00
Coach parking available, shared with LGV
Ample room for manoeuvring
Quiet area. Floodlighting
Fridge lorry area

DRIVER FACILITIES
Showers – 4 m, 1 f (£1 or free if parking overnight), washroom
Takeaway food, TV, Vegetarian meals

SITE COMMENTS/INFORMATION
Fridge lorries must switch off after 21:00

All on-site facilities open 24 hours from Mon-Sat at 14:00, 08:00-22:00 Sun | **156**

FL2
Thickthorn Service Station & Little Chef

Norwich Road, Hethersett, Norwich Norfolk NR9 3AU
T 01603 508910

ON THE B1172 Take the A11 from Norwich to Thetford to the roundabout with the A47 and B1172. Take the B1172 towards Hethersett and Thickthorn Service Station is 200 yards on the left.

CREDIT/DEBIT CARDS

FUEL CARDS (see key on page 9)
③ ㉒ ㉕ ㉙ ⑩ ㉘

TRUCK FACILITIES
Short-term coach parking (2 spaces)
Overnight parking at Norwich cattle market

DRIVER FACILITIES
Accommodation available, Travelodge
Drivers' washroom

SITE COMMENTS/INFORMATION
This site also sells hot pasties

All on-site facilities 24 hours | **157**

T3
Thurrock Services

Moto Ltd, Arterial Road, West Thurrock, Grays, Essex RM16 3BG **T 01708 865487**
www.moto-way.com

M25 BETWEEN JUNCTIONS 30 AND 31 From the M25 clockwise, exit at junction 30. Keep to left and turn left at roundabout onto A1306 then left at next roundabout into services. From M25 anti-clockwise, exit at junction 31 and turn right onto A1306 then left at next roundabout into services.

CREDIT/DEBIT CARDS

FUEL CARDS (see key on page 9)
㉗

DRIVER FACILITIES
Shower
Accommodation, Travelodge
Takeaway food

Full site details not available at time of going to press. For more information please contact site.

All on-site facilities accessible 24 hours | **158**

Toddington Services northbound — T3

Moto Ltd
Toddington, Dunstable
Bedfordshire LU5 6HR
T 01525 878423 www.moto-way.com

M1 NORTHBOUND BETWEEN JUNCTIONS 11 AND 12

CREDIT/DEBIT CARDS

FUEL CARDS (see key on page 9)
10 14 22 24 25

DRIVER FACILITIES
Takeaway food
Phone top-ups/accessories
Truckers' accessories

Full site details not available at time of going to press. For more information please contact site.

All on-site facilities accessible 24 hours — **159**

Toddington South Services — T3

Moto Ltd
Toddington, Dunstable
Bedfordshire LU5 6HR
T 01525 878422 www.moto-way.com

M1 SOUTHBOUND BETWEEN JUNCTIONS 11 AND 12

CREDIT/DEBIT CARDS

FUEL CARDS (see key on page 9)
14

TRUCK FACILITIES
Coaches overnight, Floodlighting
Room for manoeuvre

DRIVER FACILITIES
Accommodation, Travelodge
Showers, male (10), female (15)
Takeaway food, Vegetarian/healthy meals
Phone top-ups/accessories, Internet
Truckers' accessories, Clothing,
International papers

All on-site facilities accessible 24 hours — **160**

Watling Street Café & Filling Station — T4

London Road, Flamstead, St Albans
Hertfordshire AL3 8HA
T 01582 840215/01582 840270

ON THE A5 CLOSE TO M1 From the M1, exit at junction 9 and take the A5 towards Dunstable. Watling Street Café is 500 yards on the right-hand side.

CREDIT/DEBIT CARDS

FUEL CARDS (see key on page 9)
1 2 4 5 34

TRUCK FACILITIES
P with voucher — **P** only — Voucher value
£10.00 — £5.00 — £5.00
Coach parking. Quiet area. Fridge lorry area
Manoeuvring room, Truck washing facilities/
dealership/ workshop, Floodlights, CCTV
Fridge parking (off 22:00)

DRIVER FACILITIES
Accommodation on-site, Showers m 4, f 1,
(£2), rest area, TV, CB repairs/sales, Takeaway
food, Vegetarian/Healthy meals, Arcade
machines, Euros, Fax/copier, Phone top-ups

Bunker fuel, parking and toilets 24 hours. Other on-site facilities accessible 06:00-21:00. Shop times unknown — **161**

FL2 — Witham Service Station

London Road, Witham
Essex CM8 1ED
T 01376 536030

ON THE B1389 From Chelmsford take the A12 towards Witham. On the outskirts of Witham take the sliproad for B1389. Witham Service Station is on the roundabout at the bottom of the sliproad.

CREDIT/DEBIT CARDS

FUEL CARDS (see key on page 9)
3 14 22 23 28 33

1,3 opposite/adjacent + 3 nearby
TRUCK FACILITIES
Overnight parking in lay-by
Floodlighting, on-site/nearby
CCTV, on-site/nearby
DRIVER FACILITIES
Phone top-ups
Train nearby
SITE COMMENTS/INFORMATION
This site was the winner of the 2004 'Food to Go' award!
LGVs need to use exit to enter this site

All on-site facilities 24 hours — **162**

FL4 — Woodview Café & Garage

Thornhaugh, Peterborough
Cambrigeshire PE8 6HA
T 01780 783410 (Garage)
01733 772030 (café)
ON THE A1 NORTHBOUND From the A1M, take the A1 towards Stamford. Woodview Café and Garage is on the left-hand side just past the village of Thornhaugh and about 1 mile north of the junction with the A47.

FUEL CARDS (see key on page 9)
7 Nearby

TRUCK FACILITIES
P
Ample room for manoeuvring
Truck dealership/workshop

DRIVER FACILITIES
Washroom, TV
Takeaway food

Toilets, parking, shop and fuel 24 hours. Other on-site facilities 07:00-20:00 Mon-Thurs, 07:00-17:00 Fri, 07:00-13:00 Sat — **163**

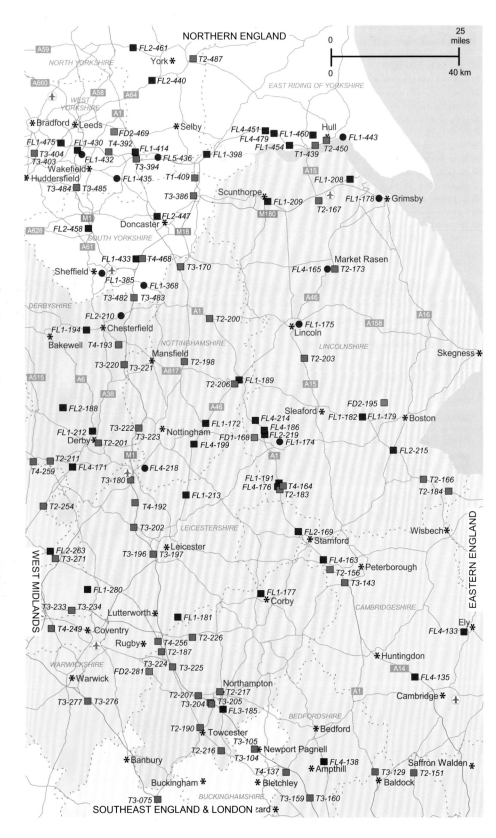

East Midlands

■ *Cafe - Layby parking (FD1)*
■ *Cafe - No overnight parking (FD2)*
■ *Filling Station - No overnight parking/cafe (FL1)*
● *Bunkering Site - No overnight parking/cafe (FL1)*
■ *Filling Station - Nearby overnight parking no cafe (FL2)*
● *Bunkering Site - Nearby overnight parking no cafe (FL2)*
■ *Filling Station - Cafe no onsite overnight parking (FL3)*
■ *Filling Station - Onsite overnight parking (FL4)*
● *Bunkering Site - Onsite overnight parking (FL4)*
● *Bunkering Site - Cafe & onsite overnight parking (FL5)*
■ *Lorry Park - Onsite overnight parking no cafe or fuel (T1)*
■ *Truck Stop/Cafe - Onsite overnight parking (T2)*
■ *Motorway Service Station (T3)*
■ *Truck Stop - Bunker fuel/showers/cafe/onsite overnight parking (T4)*

For key to site symbols see page 8

T4 ■   A1 Truck Stop & Stadium Diner

Bourne Road, Colsterworth, Grantham
Lincolnshire NG33 5JN
T 01476 861543/01476 860916

ON THE A151 From the A1 north or southbound, at Colsterworth Roundabout take the A151 towards Bourne. A1 Truck Stop & Stadium Diner is 400 metres on the right hand side.

CREDIT/DEBIT CARDS
VISA, MasterCard, Switch, Maestro, Delta

FUEL CARDS (see key on page 9)

① ② ④ ⑦ ㉞

TRUCK FACILITIES
P *with voucher*   P *only*
£10.00   £8.00
Coach parking available (10 spaces) shared with LGV, 24hr security, Secure fencing, Floodlights, Quiet, CCTV, Adblue at pump/in containers, Truck washing

DRIVER FACILITIES
Accommodation Travelodge, Showers, 5 m, 1 f (£1 if not parking), washroom, TV, truckers' accessories, CB repairs/sales, Takeaway food. Healthy menu, Euros, Fax/copier, Clothing

SITE COMMENTS/INFORMATION
Parking unattended at weekends.

Manned Secure Parking & Showers 24hr Mon-Fri. Bunker fuel/Toilet 24hr. Cafe 06:00-22:00 Mon-Fri, 07:00-14:00 Sat. CDC Truck Accessories Shop 07:00-19:00 Mon-Thurs, 07:00-14:00 Fri.   **164**

FL4 ●   A46 Truckstop

Gainsborough Road, Middle Rasen
Market Rasen, Lincolnshire LN8 3JU
T 01673 844994

A46 A631 INTERSECTION From Lincoln, take the A46 towards Market Rasen. At Middle Rasen turn right onto the A631 and the A46 Truckstop is 50 yards along on your right.

CREDIT/DEBIT CARDS

FUEL CARDS (see key on page 9)
① ② ⑦

TRUCK FACILITIES
P
Quiet area
Ample room for manoeuvring

DRIVER FACILITIES
Truckers' accessories
Takeaway food nearby
Clothing for sale nearby

SITE COMMENTS/INFORMATION
Fuel can be paid for in cash

Parking, fuel and standpipe 24 hours. Other on-site facilities opening times unknown   **165**

Anglia Motel — T2

**Washway Road, Fleet, nr Holbeach,
Spalding, Lincolnshire PE12 8LT
T 01406 422766**

ON THE A17 From Kings Lynn take the A17 towards
Sleaford. By-pass the village Fleet Hargate and continue for 1
mile. Anglia Motel is on the left-hand side 800 yards past the
turning for the B1515.

CREDIT/DEBIT CARDS

FUEL CARDS (see key on page 9)

TRUCK FACILITIES
P
Coach parking available (20 spaces)
Ample room for manoeuvring
Quiet area

DRIVER FACILITIES
Accommodation
Showers, 2 m, 2 f, washroom, rest area,
TV
Takeaway food

Parking and nearby fuel 24 hours. Showers 07:00-23:00 Mon-Sun. Other on-site facilities 07:00-21:00 Mon-Sun **166**

Barny's Café De Chauffeur — T2

**Melton Ross Road, Barnetby le Wold
Brigg, North East Lincolnshire DN38 6LB
T 01652 680966** www.barneyscafe.co.uk

ON THE A18 Come off junction 5 of the M180 interchange
before it becomes the A180. Follow signs for the A18 and
Humberside airport. Barney's is located 400 yards along on
the right.

CREDIT/DEBIT CARDS NEARBY

FUEL CARDS (see key on page 9)
① nearby
TRUCK FACILITIES
P with voucher £10.00 Voucher value
£2.00 (or free tea and shower)
Coach parking (4 spaces). Quiet area
Fridge parking (off 22:00), Truck dealership/
workshop nearby, Tyre repair/sales nearby,
Floodlights, Adblue at pump,
Windscreen/LGV tyre repairs nearby
DRIVER FACILITIES
Accommodation nearby, B&B, in village
Showers m 1, f 1, (£1 or free if parking), rest
area, TV, internet, Euros, truckers' accessories,
CB repairs/sales, takeaway food, Vegetarian
meals, Post Office nearby, Train nearby,
Loyalty cards

Parking, nearby fuel and shop accessible 24 Hours. Other on-site facilities including Clouds wifi internet,
Sky TV, upstairs function/meeting room, accessible 06:00-21:00 Mon-Fri, 06:00-14:00 Sat, 07.30-17.00 Sun **167**

Bistro Café — FD1

**Nottingham Road, Sedgebrook
nr Grantham, Lincolnshire NG32 2EP
T 01949 842164**

ON THE A52 If heading from Grantham to Nottingham on
the A52, the Bistro Café is on your right-hand side at the
village of Sedgebrook.

CREDIT/DEBIT CARDS

FUEL CARDS (see key on page 9)

TRUCK FACILITIES
P free
Parking in lay-by set close to road
Coach parking available, shared with LGV
Truck dealership/workshop nearby

DRIVER FACILITIES
Takeaway food

Parking 24 hours. Other on-site facilities 06:30-16:00 Mon-Fri, 06:30-13:00 Sat & Sun **168**

FL2 ■ Bloody Oaks Star Service Station, Tickencote

**Great North Road, Tickencote
Cambridgeshire PE9 4AD
T 01780 750850**

ON THE A1 Bloody Oaks is a few miles north of Stamford on the A1 northbound carriageway towards Grantham, just past the turning for the B1081.

CREDIT/DEBIT CARDS

FUEL CARDS (see key on page 9)

TRUCK FACILITIES
Overnight parking in lay-by

DRIVER FACILITIES
Clothing for sale
Takeaway food nearby

SITE COMMENTS/INFORMATION
Lovely site, wonderful staff

All on-site facilities 06:00-22:00. Nearby parking 24 hours in lay-by   **169**

T3 ■ Blyth Services

**Moto Ltd
Hilltop Roundabout, Blyth
Nottinghamshire S81 8HJ
T 01909 591841** www.moto-way.com

A1M A614 INTERCHANGE On the roundabout intersection with the A1M, A1, A164 and B6045.

CREDIT/DEBIT CARDS

FUEL CARDS (see key on page 9)

DRIVER FACILITIES
Accommodation on-site, Travelodge
Takeaway food

Full site details not available at time of going to press. For more information please contact site.

All on-site facilities accessible 24 hours   **170**

FL4 ■ Brobot A38 North, Brobot Petroleum Ltd

**Brobot Petroleum Ltd, Derby road
Egginton, Derby, Derbyshire DE65 6GY
T 01283 702565/703198**

ON THE A38 NORTHBOUND Brobot is on the northbound carriageway of the A38 between Burton upon Trent and Derby, and about half a mile before the junction with the A50.

CREDIT/DEBIT CARDS

FUEL CARDS (see key on page 9)

TRUCK FACILITIES
P free
Coach parking available, shared with LGV
Truck dealership/workshop nearby, room for manoeuver
Quiet area, Fridge parking

DRIVER FACILITIES
Drivers' rest area, Phone top-ups
Truckers accessories

SITE COMMENTS/INFORMATION
Popular, busy site

All on-site facilities 24 hours   **171**

Brobot East Bridgeford   FL1 ■

**Brobot Petroleum Ltd, Foss Way,
East Bridgeford, Nottinghamshire NG13 8LA
T 01949 21132**

ON THE A46 Brobot East Bridgeford is located on the A46 between Leicester and Newark. It is approximately 10 miles from Newark and is on the right-hand side of the A46 if heading towards Leicester.

CREDIT/DEBIT CARDS

FUEL CARDS (see key on page 9)
① ③ ⑦ ㉓

SITE COMMENTS/INFORMATION
Friendly, helpful staff

All on-site facilities accessible 24 hours   **172**

Caenby Corner Café   T2 ■

**Caenby Corner, Glentham, Market Rasen
Lincolnshire LN8 3AR
T 01673 878388**

ON THE A15 From Lincoln, take the A15 north towards the M180. Caenby Corner Café is near Glentham on the left-hand side at the junction with the A631.

CREDIT/DEBIT CARDS

FUEL CARDS (see key on page 9)
① ㉘ **nearby**

TRUCK FACILITIES
P Quiet area
Ample room for manoeuvring

DRIVER FACILITIES
Washroom, rest area
Takeaway food
Phone top-ups/accessories nearby

SITE COMMENTS/INFORMATION
Easy access for LGVs. This site is soon due for major redevelopment, to include Hotel, bar, filling station, restaurant and new parking area

Parking and nearby filling station accessible 24 hours. Other on-site facilities accessible 06:30-22:00   **173**

Chandlers Oil & Gas, Grantham   FL1 ●

**Chandlers Oil & Gas Ltd,
Warren Way, Alma Park Industrial Estate,
Grantham, Lincolnshire NG31 9SE
T 08456 20 20 10**

OFF THE A607 Take the A607 northbound out of Grantham. Continue past Texaco garage. Turn right into Belton Lane before hospital. Take 2nd right into Harrowby Lane for 1 mile. Left into Alma Park Road for half a mile then left into Warren Way.

CREDIT/DEBIT CARDS

FUEL CARDS (see key on page 9)
① ② ⑥ ㉞

TRUCK FACILITIES
Ample room for manoeuvring

Bunker fuel 24 hours. Site manned from 07:30-17:30 Mon-Fri. 09:00-12:00 Sat   **174**

FL1 ● Chandlers Oil & Gas, Lincoln

Chandlers Oil & Gas Ltd
Wrightsway, off Outer Circle Road
Lincoln, Lincolnshire LN2 4JY
T 01522 530505/532623

OFF THE B1308 From Horncastle take the A158 towards Lincoln. Turn left onto the B1308 and take the next left into Wrightsway. Chandlers is on the left at the bottom of the road.

CREDIT/DEBIT CARDS

FUEL CARDS (see key on page 9)
① ② ④ ㉞

DRIVER FACILITIES
Takeaway food nearby

All on-site facilities 24 hours   **175**

FL4 ■ Colsterworth Services

Travelodge Hotels Ltd, Colsterworth
Grantham, Lincolnshire NG33 5JR
T 01476 861077

ON THE A1 SOUTHBOUND If heading south from Grantham, Colsterworth services is on the A1 southbound carriageway, just beyond the roundabout with the A151.

CREDIT/DEBIT CARDS

FUEL CARDS (see key on page 9)
② ⑩ ㉗ ㉘

TRUCK FACILITIES
P with voucher
Coach parking available (6 spaces)
Ample room for manoeuvring

DRIVER FACILITIES
Showers, 1 male, 1 female (charge)
Drivers' washroom and rest area
Travelodge
Takeaway food
Phone top-ups/accessories

Parking and fuel 24 hours. Other on-site facilities 07:00-22:00   **176**

FL2 ■ Corby Service Station, Corby

Rockingham Road, Corby
Northamptonshire NN17 2AE
T 01536 2629044

ON THE A6116 If heading south from Uppingham on the A6003, turn left onto the A6116 towards Stanion and Brigstock. Corby Service Station is on the left at the next roundabout.

CREDIT/DEBIT CARDS

FUEL CARDS (see key on page 9)
③

DRIVER FACILITIES
Accommodation available nearby, half mile, Hotel Elizabeth, Rockingham
Takeaway food
Phone top-ups

On-site facilities 06:00-22:00   **177**

CPL Petroleum, Grimsby

FL1 ●

CPL Petroleum Ltd, Estate Road No 2
South Humberside Industrial Estate
Grimsby, North East Lincolnshire DN31 2TG
T 01472 350421

OFF THE A180 From Immingham take the A180 towards Grimsby. Go past the junction with the A1136 and turn right at the next roundabout. Continue for 150 yards, CPL is on the right.

CREDIT/DEBIT CARDS

FUEL CARDS (see key on page 9)

TRUCK FACILITIES
Ample room for manoeuvring

DRIVER FACILITIES
Accommodation nearby, half mile, Travel Inn

Bunker fuel 24 hours. Other on-site facilities 08:00-17:00

178

De Rodes Service Station, Boston

FL1 ■

East Heckington, Boston
Lincolnshire PE20 3QF
T 01205 821715

ON THE A17 EASTBOUND De Rodes is on the A17 at East Heckington, west of Boston on the left-hand side if heading east towards Boston and before the junction with the A1121.

CREDIT/DEBIT CARDS

FUEL CARDS (see key on page 9)

DRIVER FACILITIES
Truckers' accessories

All on-site facilities 07:00-22:00 Mon-Sat. 08:00-22:00 Sun

179

Donington Park Services

T3 ■

Disworth, Derby, Derbyshire DE74 2TN
T 01509 674951

M1 BETWEEN JUNCTIONS 23A AND 24 If heading south, exit M1 at junction 24 and take A453 towards Breedon on the Hill. Donington Park Services is at the next roundabout. If heading north, exit at junction 23A and it's on your left. From the A42 take 'other traffic' to roundabout not M1.

CREDIT/DEBIT CARDS

FUEL CARDS (see key on page 9)

DRIVER FACILITIES
Accommodation on-site, Holiday Inn
Takeaway food

Full site details not available at time of going to press. For more information please contact site.

All on-site facilities accessible 24 hours

180

FL1 ■   F Howkins & Son, Lutterworth

**Lutterworth Road North Kilworth,
Lutterworth, Leicestershire LE17 6EP
T 01858 880208**

ON THE A4304 NEAR M6/M1/A14 From Junction 20 of
the M1, take the A4304 towards Market Harborough. F
Howkins and Son is on the right before you reach Husbands
Bosworth, and near the junction with the B5414.

CREDIT/DEBIT CARDS

FUEL CARDS (see key on page 9)

③ ㉓ ㉖ ㉗

TRUCK FACILITIES
Truck washing facilities
CCTV on-site
Car MoT workshop

DRIVER FACILITIES
Phone top-ups
Post office

OTHER INFORMATION
No parking in front of locked yard gates
21.00 hours to 06.00 hours

All on-site facilities 06:30-21:00 Mon-Fri, 09:00-20:00 Sat & Sun   **181**

FL1 ■   Four Winds Service Station, Boston

**East Heckington, Boston
Lincolnshire PE20 3QF
T 01205 820600**

ON THE A17 Take the A17 from Sleaford to Boston. Four
Winds is on the right-hand side, 600 yards beyond the
turning with the B1395.

CREDIT/DEBIT CARDS

FUEL CARDS (see key on page 9)

③ ㉒

All on-site facilities 06:00-21:00 Mon-Sat, 07:00-21:00 Sun   **182**

T2 ■   The Fox Inn

**Great North Road, Colsterworth
Grantham, Lincolnshire NG33 5LN
T 01572 767697**

ON THE A1 The Fox Inn can be found on the A1
southbound carriageway about 2 miles south of Colsterworth
and the junction with the A151. Both north and southbound
carriageways are easily accessible upon exit from this site.

CREDIT/DEBIT CARDS

TRUCK FACILITIES
P with voucher £10.00
Voucher value: two free drinks
Short-term coach parking available (20+),
shared with LGV, Fridge parking
Ample room for manoeuvring
24 hour security, Floodlights, CCTV

DRIVER FACILITIES
Accommodation £40.00, Shower, male (1),
female (1), washroom, Take away, Healthy
menu, TV, Evening entertainment, Arcade
machines, Games room

SITE COMMENTS/INFORMATION
Pack up lunch available on request. Truckers
specials from £4.00, ask for more details.
Catering trailer coming soon 05:00-15:00.
Fridge lorries switch off 22:00

Parking and showers accessible 24 hours. Pub open from 17:00. Home cooked food from 18:00, last orders for kitchen at 21:45   **183**

Frankie's Café
T2 ■

**Bridge Road, Sutton Bridge, Spalding
Lincolnshire PE12 9SH
T 01406 350180**

ON THE OLD A17 From Kings Lynn, take A17 west for 10 miles. At Sutton Bridge take B1359 into the village. Frankie's is 1 mile on the right-hand side. From Holbeach take the A17, turn left at roundabout with A1101 for half mile then right at T-junction, continue for 2 miles.

CREDIT/DEBIT CARDS

FUEL CARDS (for nearby fuel)
25

TRUCK FACILITIES
Lorry park situated across road
P Coach parking
Ample room for manoeuvring
Quiet area nearby

DRIVER FACILITIES
Accommodation on-site, B&B
Showers – 1 unisex (charge)
Takeaway food

SITE COMMENTS/INFORMATION
Traditional transport café, operational for 50 years. Family run, all home made food from fresh produce

Parking and nearby filling station with shop and toilets 24 hours. Other on-site facilities 06:00-15:00 | **184**

Grange Farm Service Station, Northampton
FL1 ■

**Collingtree, Northampton
Northamptonshire NN4 0LY
T 01604 700498**

ON THE A508 SOUTHBOUND If heading from Northampton towards the M1 junction 15, Grange Farm is on the southbound carriageway immediately after the exit for the B526, a quarter of a mile from the motorway.

CREDIT/DEBIT CARDS

FUEL CARDS (see key on page 9)
2 3 4 7 8 22

DRIVER FACILITIES
Accommodation nearby, half mile, (Hilton Northampton & Innkeepers Lodge)
Internet access

SITE COMMENTS/INFORMATION
Bakery

Little Chef Restaurant opening times unknown. Other on-site facilities 24 hours | **185**

Grantham North Services
FL4 ■

**Moto Ltd, Gonerby Moor, nr Grantham
Lincolnshire NG32 2AB
T 01476 563451** www.moto-way.com

ON THE A1 Take the A1 bypassing Grantham, and Grantham North Services is on the right-hand side at the intersection with the B1174.

CREDIT/DEBIT CARDS

FUEL CARDS (see key on page 9)
14

DRIVER FACILITIES
Travelodge on-site
Takeaway food
Showers, unisex (1)
Phone top-ups
Vegetarian meals
Arcade machines
Internet

All on-site facilities 24 hours | **186**

T2 ■ Halfway House Public House

1 Watling Street, Kilsby, nr Rugby
Warwickshire CV23 8YE
T 01788 822888

ON THE A5 From the M1 exit 18, take the A5 towards Hinckley. Turn left at the next roundabout onto the A428, across next roundabout then left again at the next onto the A5 towards Kilsby. Halfway House is 400 yards along on the right.

CREDIT/DEBIT CARDS

FUEL CARDS NEARBY (see key on p 6)
㉒ ㉝

TRUCK FACILITIES
Parking and nearby layby, Coach parking , shared with LGV, Quiet

DRIVER FACILITIES
Accommodation £20.00 pn, Rest area Tea/coffee free with breakfast, Takeaway food, Vegetarian meals, Washroom, Showers, male (1) £3.00, TV, Clothing nearby, Arcade mach. Laundry nearby, Internet, Fax/copier, Post Office, Phone top-ups and Truckers accessories nearby

SITE COMMENTS/INFORMATION
Home made food in traditional pub, great atmosphere. Coach parties, welcome, showers subject to availability

Parking and some other facilities 24 hour. All other facilities 07:00-22:30 **187**

FL2 ■ Hulland General Store, Hulland Ward

Main Road, Hulland Ward, nr Ashbourne
Derbyshire DE6 3EA
T 01335 370721

ON THE A517 Hulland General Store Ltd is in the village of Hulland Ward on the A517 on the left-hand side if heading towards Ashbourne from Belper.

CREDIT/DEBIT CARDS

FUEL CARDS (see key on page 9)
① ② ③ ⑦

TRUCK FACILITIES
Overnight parking nearby
Ample room for manoeuvring
Quiet area nearby

DRIVER FACILITIES
Takeaway food
Truckers' accessories

Nearby parking 24 hours. Other on-site facilities 06:00-18:30 Mon-Sun **188**

FL1 ■ Interchange Filling Station, Newark

Lincoln Road, Winthorpe, Newark
Nottinghamshire NG24 2DF
T 01636 705130

ON THE A46 From Grantham take the A1 northbound around Newark, take the slip road signposted A46, turn left at the roundabout and head for Lincoln. At the next roundabout take the A17 towards Sleaford. Interchange Filling Station is 100 yards along on the left.

CREDIT/DEBIT CARDS

FUEL CARDS (see key on page 9)
① ② ④ ⑦ ㉞

DRIVER FACILITIES
Accommodation nearby, half mile, Travel Inn
Truckers' accessories

All on-site facilities 24 hours. **189**

Jacks Hill Café
T2 ■

**Watling Street, Towcester
Northamptonshire NN12 8ET
T 01327 350522**

ON THE A5 From M1 turn left at junction 15A onto the A43 towards Oxford. Continue until roundabout with the A5. Turn right onto the A5 towards Weedon and Jacks Hill Café is on the left-hand side.

TRUCK FACILITIES
P *with voucher* £10.00 *Voucher* £3.00
Coach parking (ring in advance), shared with LGV, Floodlights, Manoeuvring room, Quiet area

DRIVER FACILITIES
Accomm. on-site £15 pn, incl. parking
Showers – unisex 2 (free if parking overnight), washroom, rest area, TV, Euros changed/accepted, clothing for sale, truckers' accessories, CB repairs/sales, Takeaway food, Vegetarian meals, Arcade machines, Games room, Euros

SITE COMMENTS/INFORMATION
Extensive menu of great value homemade food, all-day breakfasts, friendly staff and clean air-conditioned site. Recently refurbished showers with seating, mirrors and lots of space.

Showers, toilets, parking and nearby fuel accessible 24 Hours. Cafe accessible 06:00- 21:30 Mon-Fri, 06:00-14:00 Sat, 07:00-14:30 Sun. TV room and bar accessible 18:00-23:00 Mon-Thurs.
190

Jubilee Garage (1980) Ltd, Grantham
FL1 ■

**A1, The Great North Road, Colsterworth
Grantham, Lincolnshire NG33 5JL
T 01476 860244**

ON THE A1 Jubilee Garage is on the A1 at Colsterworth, south of Grantham on the southbound carriageway, a few yards north of the junction with the A151.

CREDIT/DEBIT CARDS

FUEL CARDS (see key on page 9)

DRIVER FACILITIES
Accommodation nearby, 200 yards, Travelodge
Phone top-ups

All on-site facilities accessible 07:00-21:30.
191

Junction 23 Truckstop
T4 ■

**Ashby Road East, Shepshed, Leicester
Leicestershire LE12 9BS
T 01509 507480/507479**

ON THE A512 From the M1, exit at junction 23 and head west on the A512 towards Ashby de la Zouch. Junction 23 Truckstop is 200 yards on the right.

CREDIT/DEBIT CARDS

FUEL CARDS (see key on page 9)

TRUCK FACILITIES
P *with voucher* £14.00
Voucher value – £3.00
Coaches overnight, shared with LGV, Quiet area, Ample room for manoeuvring, 24hr security, Secure fencing, Floodlights, CCTV, Truck washing facilities, Adblue at pump/ container. Fridge parking, switch off 21:00.

DRIVER FACILITIES
Showers – m & f (£1.50), washroom, TV
Truckers' accessories, Takeaway food

Parking, bunker fuel, shop and showers 24 hours. Other on-site facilities 06:00-21:30 Mon-Fri, 06:00-11:00 Sat
192

T4 ■ Junction 29 Truckstop

**Hardwick View Road
Holmewood Industrial Estate, Holmewood
Chesterfield, Derbyshire S42 5SA
T 01246 856536**

OFF THE A6175 From junction 29 of the M1 take the A6175 towards Holmewood for 1 mile. At the next roundabout turn left into Holmewood Industrial Estate. Follow the road around and Junction 29 Truckstop is on the right.

CREDIT/DEBIT CARDS

FUEL CARDS (see key on page 9)

TRUCK FACILITIES
P with voucher £9.50 Voucher value – £2.50, Coach parking shared with LGV, Quiet, Ample room for manoeuvring, CCTV, Adblue at pump/in containers. Fridge parking, switch off 22:00-06:00

DRIVER FACILITIES
Showers – 6 m, 1 f (£1), washroom, rest area, TV, phone top-ups/accessories, clothing for sale, truckers' accessories, CB repairs/sales, Takeaway food, Vegetarian meals, evening ent. Arcade mach., Internet, Euros

All on-site facilities accessible 24 hours from monday 06.00 to Sat 12.00 noon **193**

FL1 ■ Ladywood Petrol Station, Chesterfield

**Chanderhill, Baslow Road, Chander Hill,
Near Holymoorside, Chesterfield
Derbyshire S42 7BN
T 01246 566312**

ON THE A619 Ladywood is on the A619 about 3 miles west of the centre of Chesterfield on the right-hand side if heading west and just past the turnings for Holymoorside.

CREDIT/DEBIT CARDS

FUEL CARDS (see key on page 9)

DRIVER FACILITIES
Hot drinks free to truckers
Takeaway

OTHER INFORMATION
High vehicles to use pump at barrier near to road

All on-site facilities accessible 07:00-18:00 **194**

FD2 ■ Langrick Station Café

**Main Road, Langrick, Boston
Lincolnshire PE22 7AH
T 01205 820023**

ON THE B1192 The Langrick Station Café can be found on the right-hand side of the B1192 if heading north between Brothertoft and New York, north-west of Boston.

CREDIT/DEBIT CARDS

FUEL CARDS (see key on page 9)

TRUCK FACILITIES
P free
Short-term coach parking available, shared with LGV
Quiet area
Ample room for manoeuvring

DRIVER FACILITIES
Takeaway food

All on-site facilities accessible 06:30-18:00 Mon- Fri, 06:30-12:00 Sat **195**

Leicester Forest East northbound   T3 ◼

Welcome Break Ltd
Hinckley Road, Leicester
Leicestershire LE3 3GB
T 0116 2386801

M1 NORTHBOUND BETWEEN
JUNCTIONS 21 AND 21A

CREDIT/DEBIT CARDS

FUEL CARDS (see key on page 9)

DRIVER FACILITIES
Accommodation, Days Inn
Takeaway food

Full site details not available at time of going to press. For more information please contact site.

All on-site facilities accessible 24 hours   **196**

Leicester Forest East southbound   T3 ◼

Welcome Break Ltd
Hinckley Road, Leicester
Leicestershire LE3 3GB
T 0116 2386801 www.welcomebreak.co.uk

M1 SOUTHBOUND BETWEEN
JUNCTIONS 21 AND 21A

CREDIT/DEBIT CARDS

FUEL CARDS (see key on page 9)

DRIVER FACILITIES
Accommodation, Travel Inn
Takeaway food

Full site details not available at time of going to press. For more information please contact site.

All on-site facilities accessible 24 hours   **197**

Limes Café   T2 ◼

Old Rufford Road, Bilsthorpe
nr Mansfield, Nottinghamshire NG22 8
T 01623 411254

ON THE A614 From Ollerton, take the A614 south towards Nottingham. Limes Café is 3 miles on the right-hand side, close to the village of Bilsthorpe and about 1 and a half miles before the roundabout with the A617.

TRUCK FACILITIES
P
Ample room for manoeuvring
Quiet area

DRIVER FACILITIES
Accommodation on-site
Washroom
Takeaway food

SITE COMMENTS/INFORMATION
This site has been established for more than 50 years providing home cooked food using fresh produce

Parking facilities accessible 24 hours. Other on-site facilities accessible 07:00-18:00   **198**

FL4 ■ — LMP Service Station Limited

**Stragglethorpe Crossroads
Radcliffe on Trent, Nottingham
Nottinghamshire NG12 2JU
T 0115 9893113**

ON THE A46 From Melton Mowbray, take the A606 to Nottingham. Turn right at the junction with the A46 towards Bingham. LMP Service Station is 5 miles on the right hand side, just past the village of cotgrave.

CREDIT/DEBIT CARDS

FUEL CARDS (see key on page 9)

㉕

TRUCK FACILITIES
P free
Coach parking available (2 spaces)
Ample room for manoeuvring

DRIVER FACILITIES
Drivers' rest area
Truckers' accessories
Phone top-ups/accessories nearby

Parking 24 Hours. Other on-site facilities opening times unknown **199**

T2 ■ — Markham Moor Truckstop

**Milton Road, Markham Moor, Retford
Nottinghamshire DN22 0QU
T 01777 838921**

ON THE A1 A638 INTERCHANGE From Newark take the A1 northbound for 15 miles. At the roundabout with the A638 take the turning for Milton. Markham Moor Truckstop is within 20 yards on the right-hand side.

FUEL CARDS (for nearby fuel)

㉘

TRUCK FACILITIES
P Coach parking available, shared with LGV, Ample room for manoeuvring
Fridge lorry area

DRIVER FACILITIES
Accommodation nearby, 50 yards, Travelodge, Showers – 3 m, 1 f, washroom, rest area, TV, phone top-ups/accessories

SITE COMMENTS/INFORMATION
This site has a very clean, large spacious restaurant serving home-made farmhouse food

Parking 24 hours. Restaurant 06:00-22:00 Mon, 05:30-22:00 Tues-Fri, 06:00-10:00 Sat. Showers 06:00-22:00 Mon-Sat **200**

T2 ■ — The Meadows Inn

**Derby Cattle Market Lorry Park
Chequers Road, West Meadows Ind. Estate
Derby, Derbyshire DE21 6
T 01332 361344**

ON THE A52 From the A601 Derby Inner Ring Road, take the A52 towards Nottingham. Continue past the roundabout with the A61, and Derby Cattle Market is 400 yards on the right.

CREDIT/DEBIT CARDS

FUEL CARDS (see key on page 9)

TRUCK FACILITIES
P
Coach parking available (20 spaces)
Quiet area
Ample room for manoeuvring

DRIVER FACILITIES
Showers, 3 m, washroom, TV
Takeaway food

SITE COMMENTS/INFORMATION
Home cooked food served in comfortable air-conditioned pub

Parking 24 hours. All other on-site facilities 10:00-14:30, 16:30-23:30. Nearby fuel 24 hours **201**

Moto Leicester, Moto Hospitality Ltd   T3 ■

Welcome Break Ltd
Little Shaw Lane, Markfield
Leicestershire LE67 9PP
T 01530 244777

M1 JUNCTION 22

Main Building not 24 Hours. Forecourt 24 Hours   **202**

CREDIT/DEBIT CARDS

FUEL CARDS (see key on page 9)
14

TRUCK FACILITIES
Overnight coach parking, Floodlighting

DRIVER FACILITIES
Accommodation, Travelodge
Takeaway food

Nocton Heath Truckstop & The kitchen   T2 ■

Sleaford Road, Nocton Heath, Lincoln
Lincolnshire LN4 2AR
T 01522 811299

ON THE A15 If heading along the A15 from Sleaford to Lincoln, Nocton Heath is on the right just after the turning for the B1202 and before the turning for the B1178.

Parking 24 hours. Restaurant weekends only. Café and all other on-site facilities 06:00-22:00 Mon-Fri, 06:00-17:00 Sat, 09:00-15:00 Sun   **203**

TRUCK FACILITIES
P Coach parking (3 spaces). Quiet area
Ample room for manoeuvring
Truck dealership/workshop

DRIVER FACILITIES
Showers – 1 m, 1 f (charge), washroom, rest area, TV
Takeaway food

SITE COMMENTS/INFORMATION
Meals prepared using fresh local produce. Recent refurbishment

Northampton Services northbound   T3 ■

Roadchef Ltd
Northampton
Northamptonshire NN4 9QY
T 01604 831888

M1 NORTHBOUND JUNCTION 15A

All on-site facilities accessible 24 hours   **204**

CREDIT/DEBIT CARDS

FUEL CARDS (see key on page 9)
14

TRUCK FACILITIES
P with voucher   **P** only   Voucher value
£15.00   £12.00   £7.00
Coach parking available (10 spaces)
Ample room for manoeuvring
Quiet area
Truck washing facilities
DRIVER FACILITIES
Showers, 2 m, 2 f, washroom, Internet access, Seating area, Phone top-ups/accessories, Truckers' accessories
Takeaway food. Clothing for sale
SITE COMMENTS/INFORMATION
New building with modern facilities

T3 ■ Northampton Services southbound

Roadchef Ltd
Northampton
Northamptonshire NN4 9QS
T 01604 831888

M1 SOUTHBOUND JUNCTION 15A

5.2m	BP	
P 20 OVERNIGHT		£*

CREDIT/DEBIT CARDS

FUEL CARDS (see key on page 9)
⑭

TRUCK FACILITIES
P *with voucher*   P *only*   *Voucher value*
£15.00   £12.00   £7.00
Coach parking available (10 spaces)
Ample room for manoeuvring
Quiet area
Truck washing facilities
DRIVER FACILITIES
Showers, 2 m, 2 f, Washroom, Internet access, Seating area, Phone top-ups/accessories, Truckers' accessories Takeaway food. Clothing for sale
SITE COMMENTS/INFORMATION
New building with modern facilities

All on-site facilities accessible 24 hours   **205**

T2 ■ The Ranch Café & Lorry Park

Old Great North Road
Newark, Nottinghamshire NG24 1BI
T 01636 611198

OFF THE B6326 From Leicester, take the A46 towards Newark and around the west side of the town. At the roundabout with the A617 and A616 take the B6326 towards the town. At the B6166, turn right and The Ranch Café is on your right.

Unknown NEARBY	NEARBY	
P 150 OVERNIGHT		NEARBY
	£1.95 50p	£3.75 NEARBY

TRUCK FACILITIES
P *with voucher*   P *only*   *Voucher value*
£9.00   £6.50   £2.50
Coach parking shared with LGV, Fridge lorries parking, Ample room for manoeuvring, CCTV, Quiet area. Floodlighting

DRIVER FACILITIES
Accommodation nearby, half mile, South Parade Hotel
Showers – 4 m, 2 f (free if paying to park), washroom, truckers' accessories Takeaway food

SITE COMMENTS/INFORMATION
Train nearby

Parking 24 hours. Other on-site facilities 06:00-21:00. Nearby fuel accessible 24 hours   **206**

T2 ■ Red Lion Pub and Cafe

Weedon Road, Upper Heyford,
Northampton
Northamptonshire NN7 4DE
T 01604 831914

OFF THE M1 JUNCTION 16 (ON THE A45) From the M1 exit at junction 16. At the roundabout take the A45 towards Northampton for 100 yards. The Red Lion Pub and Cafe will be on your right.

NEARBY Texaco	NEARBY	AUTO CD BUNKER NEARBY	Air NEARBY	NEARBY	NEARBY
P 100 OVERNIGHT	P-On-site F-Nearby				
		£1.25	60p	CR & LR + HF NEARBY £4.25	PB + OL NEARBY

CREDIT/DEBIT CARDS

TRUCK FACILITIES
P *with voucher* £12.00 *Voucher value*
2 x £2.00, Quiet area, Coaches overnight, 24hr security, Floodlights, CCTV, Fridge parking, Adblue at pump nearby, Windscreen repairs and LGV tyre repair/sales nearby, Ample room for manoeuvring
DRIVER FACILITIES
Showers, 4 m, 2 f (free), washroom, TV Takeaway food, Vegetarian/healthy meals, Accommodation, Premier Tavern Inn £40.00, Rest area, Evening ent., Arcade mach., Games room, Euros, Fax/copier, Post office nearby
SITE COMMENTS/INFORMATION
This site is set around a 300-year-old traditional pub. Food is cooked to order.

Parking and toilets accessible 24 hours. All other on-site facilities accessible 06:00-23:30, 7 days a week   **207**

Refinery Filling Station, South Killingholme

FL1 ■

**Humber Road, South Killingholme
North East Lincolnshire DN40 3DJ
T 01469 571564**

ON THE A160 From the M180, take the A180 towards Immingham. Turn left onto the A160 to South Killingholme for 2 miles. Refinery Service Station is on the right-hand side at the east end of the village.

CREDIT/DEBIT CARDS

FUEL CARDS (see key on page 9)
① ② ④ ⑦ ㉞

DRIVER FACILITIES
Truckers' accessories

All on-site facilities 24 hours

208

Rix Garage Scunthorpe (Jordons)

FL1 ■

**Rix Ltd, Grange Lane North
Scunthorpe, North Lincolnshire DN16 1BN
T 01724 841284**

ON THE B1501 From junction 4 of the M180 take the A18 towards Scunthorpe. Continue on the A18 for 800 yards beyond the junction with the A1029. Turn right onto the B1501 Grange Lane North and Rix is 600 yards on the left.

CREDIT/DEBIT CARDS

FUEL CARDS (see key on page 9)
① ⑦

DRIVER FACILITIES
Truckers' accessories

Fuel bunker times unknown. All other on-site facilities 07:00-22:00

209

RSL Distribution

FL2 ●

**Fan Road, Staveley, Chesterfield
Derbyshire S43 3PT
T 01246 280177**

OFF THE A619 Exit M1 at junction 30 and head for Barlborough and Clowne. At next roundabout take the A619 to Staveley and Chesterfield. Continue for 2 miles. Turn left after railway bridge into Fan Road and RSL is round the bend on the right.

CREDIT/DEBIT CARDS

FUEL CARDS (see key on page 9)
① ⑦

TRUCK FACILITIES
P free
Quiet area
Ample room for manoeuvring
Truck washing facilities
Truck dealership/workshop

DRIVER FACILITIES
Takeaway food nearby

All on-site facilities 07:00-18:00

210

T2 — The Salt Box Café

**Hatton, nr Derby
Derbyshire NG24 1BI
T 01283 813189**

ON THE A511 If heading east along the A50, exit at junction 6 onto the A511 for 1 mile. The Salt Box is on the right after the junction with the A516. If heading west, exit the A50 at junction 5 onto the A516 for 2 miles and The Salt Box is on the left

CREDIT/DEBIT CARDS

FUEL CARDS (for nearby fuel)
4 NEARBY

TRUCK FACILITIES
P with voucher £8.50 Voucher value £2.50
Coach parking (5 spaces), Quiet, Fridge lorry area, CCTV, Manoeuvring room, Floodlights, Truck dealership/workshop nearby

DRIVER FACILITIES
Showers – 3 m 2 f 3 unisex (£1.50), washroom, rest area, TV, takeaway food Vegetarian meals, Arcade machines, Euros, Post Office, internet access, phone top-ups/accessories nearby

SITE COMMENTS/INFORMATION
Family run cafe with home made food, friendly and welcoming atmosphere.

Parking 24 hours. Nearby fuel and shop 07:00-23:00. Other on-site facilities 07:00-19:00 Mon-Fri, 07:00-14:00 Sat **211**

FL1 — Shell Allestree, Derby

**Duffield Road, Allestree, Derby
Derbyshire DE22 2DG
T 01332 558330**

ON THE A6 Take the A6 north out of Derby. Shell Allestree is on the left-hand side, 400 yards north of the roundabout with the A38.

CREDIT/DEBIT CARDS

FUEL CARDS (see key on page 9)
3 10 24 25

All on-site facilities 24 hours **212**

FL1 — Six Hills Service Station, Six Hills

**Fosseway, Six Hills, nr Melton Mowbray
Leicestershire LE14 3PD
T 01509 880937**

ON THE A46 The Murco Station is on the A46 southbound towards Leicester, just before the turning for the B676 and after the A6006.

CREDIT/DEBIT CARDS

FUEL CARDS (see key on page 9)
2 3 23

TRUCK FACILITIES
NOT ACCESSIBLE FOR ARTICS

DRIVER FACILITIES
Truckers' accessories
Phone top-ups
Accommodation nearby
Vegetarian meals nearby
Healthy menu available nearby

SITE COMMENTS/INFORMATION
This site offers a warm and friendly service

All on-site facilities accessible 06:00-20:00 Mon-Fri, 07:00-20:00 Sat, 08:00-20:00 Sun **213**

Star Foston Service Station — FL4

**Long street, Foston, nr Grantham
Lincolnshire NG32 2LD
T 01400 283800**

ON THE A1 NORTHBOUND Star Foston is on the A1 northbound carriageway between Grantham and Long Bennington, close to the second turning for Allington if heading Northbound.

CREDIT/DEBIT CARDS

FUEL CARDS (see key on page 9)
① ② ③ ④ ⑦

TRUCK FACILITIES
P
Quiet area
Ample room for manoeuvring

DRIVER FACILITIES
Drivers' washroom

Parking 24 hours. Other on-site facilities 06:30-22:00 — **214**

Star Sutterton Service Station — FL2

**Holbeach Road, Sutterton, Boston
Lincolnshire PE20 9LG
T 01205 462800**

ON THE A17 Take the A16 from Spalding to Boston and turn right at the roundabout with the A17. Star Sutterton Service Station is 50 yards on the left.

CREDIT/DEBIT CARDS

FUEL CARDS (see key on page 9)
① ④ ⑦

TRUCK FACILITIES
Nearby overnight parking

DRIVER FACILITIES
Drivers' washroom
Drivers' rest area
Takeaway food nearby

SITE COMMENTS/INFORMATION
Friendly staff
Clean facilities and tidy, well stocked shop

All on-site facilities 24 hours except toilets — **215**

Super Sausage Café — T2

**Watling Street, Potterspury, nr Towcester
Northamptonshire NN12 7QX
T 01908 542964**

ON THE A5 If heading from Milton Keynes to Towcester on the A5, Super Sausage is on the left-hand side in the middle of the village of Potterspury.

CREDIT/DEBIT CARDS

FUEL CARDS (see key on page 9)

TRUCK FACILITIES
P
Quiet area
Ample room for manoeuvring

DRIVER FACILITIES
Washroom, rest area, clothing for sale
Takeaway food

SITE COMMENTS/INFORMATION
Large choice of meals to suit all diets and tastes. Fast efficient service from friendly staff

Parking 24 hours. Other on-site facilities 07:00-18:00 Mon-Fri, 08:00-16:00 Sat & Sun — **216**

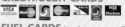

T2 — Super Sausage Café & Truckstop

**St Andrews Road, Northampton
Northamptonshire NN1 2SD
T 01604 636099**

ON THE A5059 Take the A508 northbound into city centre. At the junction with the A5123 turn left onto this road and across next roundabout. At junction with A45, continue ahead onto the A5095 towards Market Harborough. Super Sausage is a quarter of a mile on left.

TRUCK FACILITIES
P
Coach parking (22 spaces). Quiet area
Ample room for manoeuvring

DRIVER FACILITIES
Accommodation on-site
Showers – 2 m, washroom, rest area, TV, Internet access, takeaway food, phone top-ups/accessories, clothing nearby, Train nearby

SITE COMMENTS/INFORMATION
Situated in Northampton, close to town centre facilities. Train nearby

Parking 24 hours. Other on-site facilities 06:00-21:00 Mon-Thurs, 06:00-19:30 Fri, 06:00-15:00 Sat **217**

T4 — 'T Baden Hardstaff (South Notts Truckstop)

**South Notts Truckstop, Hillside
Gotham Road, Kingston on Soar
Nottingham, Nottinghamshire NG11 0DF
T 01159 831234**

OFF THE A453 From M1 junction 24, take A453 towards Nottingham. Continue for 3 miles then turn right towards West Leake and Gotham. Continue for half a mile then turn right towards Kingston on Soar. Truckstop is 200 yards on the left.

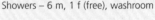

FUEL CARDS (see key on page 9)
❶

TRUCK FACILITIES
P £6.00
Ample room for manoeuvring
Quiet area. Fridge lorry area
Truck washing facilities

DRIVER FACILITIES
Showers – 6 m, 1 f (free), washroom

Parking accessible 24 hours. Other on-site facilities accessible 08:00-18:00 **218**

FL2 — Texaco Star Tollbar

**Gonerby Moor, Grantham
Lincolnshire NG32 2AD
T 01400 259400**

ON THE A1 SOUTHBOUND Texaco Star Tollbar is on the A1 southbound carriageway between Long Bennington and Grantham, on the left-hand side and on the corner of the turning for Marston.

CREDIT/DEBIT CARDS

FUEL CARDS (see key on page 9)
 ❶❷❸❹❼

TRUCK FACILITIES
Overnight parking at the Gonerby Moor roundabout A1 junction with B1174.

DRIVER FACILITIES
Accommodation available nearby at Gonerby Moor roundabout
Truckers' accessories

SITE COMMENTS/INFORMATION
Multi-lingual staff. Seven languages spoken! English, German, French, Spanish, Italian, Russian and Latvian

All on-site facilities 07:00-22:00 **219**

Tibshelf Services (formerly Chesterfield Services) Northbound T3 ■

**RoadChef Ltd, Tibshelf, Chesterfield
Derbyshire DE55 5TZ
T 01773 876600** www.roadchef.com

M1 JUNCTIONS 28–29

CREDIT/DEBIT CARDS

FUEL CARDS (see key on page 9)
① ② ③ ④ ⑨ ⑬ ㉗

TRUCK FACILITIES
P *with voucher* **P** *only* *Voucher value*
£17.00 £14.00 £7.50
Coach parking available, shared
Quiet area, fridge lorry area
Ample room for manoeuvring

DRIVER FACILITIES
Accommodation Premier Inn (£45 pn)
Showers, 1 male, 1 female (free),
washroom (combined), truckers'
accessories, Takeaway food

SITE COMMENTS/INFORMATION
Good LGV facilities

Showers, Premier Inn, ReStore & Costa 24hrs. Wimpey varies between 08:30-20:00. RestBite 07:00-22:00 **220**

Tibshelf Services (formerly Chesterfield Services) Southbound T3 ■

**RoadChef Ltd, Tibshelf,
Derbyshire DE55 5TZ
T 01773 876600** www.roadchef.com

M1 JUNCTIONS 28–29

CREDIT/DEBIT CARDS

FUEL CARDS (see key on page 9)
① ② ③ ④ ⑨ ⑬ ㉗

TRUCK FACILITIES
P *with voucher* **P** *only* *Voucher value*
£17.00 £14.00 £7.50
Coach parking available, shared
Quiet area, fridge lorry area
Ample room for manoeuvring

DRIVER FACILITIES
Showers, 1 male, 1 female (free),
washroom (combined), truckers'
accessories

SITE COMMENTS/INFORMATION
Good LGV facilities

Showers, Premier Inn, ReStore & Costa 24hrs. Wimpy varies between 08:30-20:00. RestBite 07:00-22:00 **221**

Trowell Services northbound T3 ■

**Moto Ltd
Trowell, Ilkeston
Nottinghamshire NG9 3PL
T 0115 9320291** www.moto-way.com

M1 NORTHBOUND BETWEEN JUNCTIONS 25 AND 26

CREDIT/DEBIT CARDS

FUEL CARDS (see key on page 9)
㉓ ㉗

TRUCK FACILITIES
P *with voucher* **P** *only* *Voucher value*
£15.00 £13.00 £6.00
Coach parking available (30 spaces)
CCTV. Quiet area
Fridge lorry area, shared with LGV

DRIVER FACILITIES
Accommodation, Travelodge
Showers, male (1), female (1),
washroom, rest area, TV, phone top-
ups/accessories, truckers' accessories
Takeaway food, Vegetarian meals,
Arcade machines

All on-site facilities accessible 24 hours **222**

T3 ■ Trowell Services southbound

Moto Ltd
Trowell, Ilkeston
Nottinghamshire NG9 3PL
T 0115 9320291 www.moto-way.com

M1 SOUTHBOUND BETWEEN JUNCTIONS 25 AND 26

CREDIT/DEBIT CARDS

FUEL CARDS (see key on page 9)
③ ㉓ ㉗

TRUCK FACILITIES
P *with voucher*   **P** *only*   *Voucher value*
£15.00   £13.00   £6.00
Coach parking spaces available, shared
with LGV, CCTV, Quiet area,
Fridge lorry area,

DRIVER FACILITIES
Accommodation, Travelodge
Showers, male (1), female (1),
washroom, rest area, TV, phone top-
ups/accessories, truckers' accessories
Takeaway food, Vegetarian meals,
Arcade machines

All on-site facilities accessible 24 hours   **223**

T3 ■ Watford Gap Services northbound

Roadchef Ltd
Watford, nr Northampton
Northamptonshire NN6 7UZ
T 01327 879001

M1 NORTHBOUND BETWEEN JUNCTIONS 16 AND 17

CREDIT/DEBIT CARDS

FUEL CARDS (see key on page 9)
⑬ ⑭ ㉒

TRUCK FACILITIES
P
Coach parking available (10 spaces)
Ample room for manoeuvring

DRIVER FACILITIES
Accommodation
Showers, 2 m, 2 f, washroom
Phone top-ups/accessories
Truckers' accessories
Takeaway food
Clothing for sale

All on-site facilities accessible 24 hours   **224**

T3 ■ Watford Gap Services southbound

Roadchef Ltd
Watford, nr Northampton
Northamptonshire NN6 7UZ
T 01327 879001

M1 SOUTHBOUND BETWEEN JUNCTIONS 16 AND 17

CREDIT/DEBIT CARDS

FUEL CARDS (see key on page 9)
⑬ ⑭ ㉒

TRUCK FACILITIES
P
Coach parking available (10 spaces)
Ample room for manoeuvring

DRIVER FACILITIES
Accommodation on-site
Showers, 2 m, 2 f, washroom, phone
top-ups/accessories, truckers'
accessories, takeaway food
Clothing for sale

All on-site facilities accessible 24 hours   **225**

Truckers' Handbook | **271**

Welford Truck Stop & Portly Ford Café   T2 ▦

**Northampton Road, Welford,
Northamtonshire NN6 6JF
T 01858 575120**

ON THE A14/A5199 INTERCHANGE Exit the M1 at
junction 19 and take the A14 towards Kettering. The site is
on your left hand side at the roundabout with the A5199.

TRUCK FACILITIES
P £8.00, Coaches overnight (5),
Floodlights, Room to manoeuvre,
Fridge parking, Quiet parking area

DRIVER FACILITIES
Showers, unisex (1), Vegetarian/Healthy
meals, Takeaway

Open Mon-Thurs 06:00-22:00, Friday 06:00-20:00   **226**

PRIESTLEY LGV

'WE CARE ABOUT OUR CUSTOMERS'

Class 1 and Class 2 : One to One Training
RIGID AND ARTIC
Sutton St James, Spalding, Lincolnshire, PE12 0EL.
Contact: 01945 440 726
www.priestleylgv.co.uk

Professional Training for Today's Haulage Industry

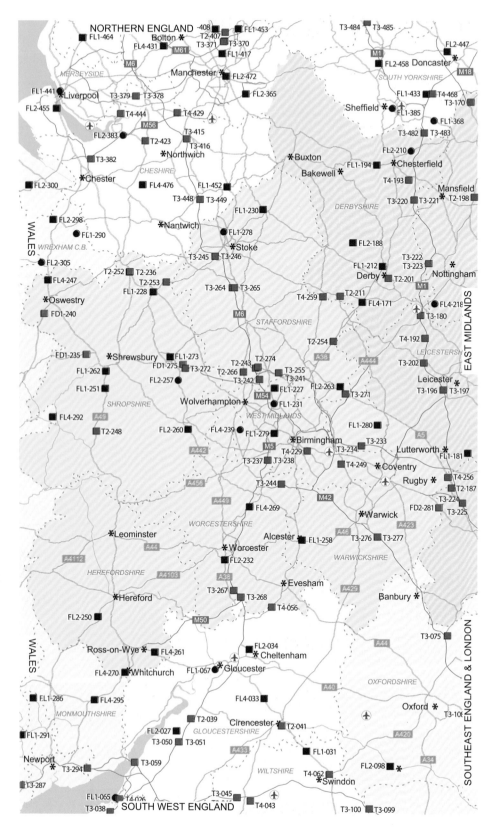

NORTHERN ENGLAND
-408 T3-484 T3-485
FL1-464 T2-407 FL1-453
Bolton ✳ T3-371 T3-370
M61 FL1-417
FL2-447
M1
FL2-458 Doncaster ✳
M18

MERSEYSIDE M6
SOUTH YORKSHIRE

Manchester ✳ FL2-472
FL2-365

FL1-441 Liverpool T3-379 T3-378
FL1-433 T4-468
Sheffield ✳ T3-170
FL2-455 FL1-385
FL1-368

T4-444 T4-429 T3-482 T3-483
M56 FL2-210
FL2-383 T3-415 ✳Chesterfield
T2-423 FL1-194 T3-416
T3-382 ✳Northwich ✳Buxton T4-193
Bakewell ✳ Mansfield
✳Chester T3-220 T3-221 T2-198 ✳
FL2-300 FL4-476 FL1-452
T3-448 T3-449 DERBYSHIRE
FL2-298 FL1-230 T3-222
WALES FL1-290 ✳Nantwich Derby ✳ T3-223
WREXHAM C.B. FL1-278 T2-201 Nottingham ✳
FL2-305 ✳Stoke FL1-212
FL4-247 T3-245 T3-246 M1
T2-252 T2-236 FL2-188 T3-180
T2-253 T4-259 T2-211 FL4-218
FL1-228 T3-264 T3-265 FL4-171
✳Oswestry STAFFORDSHIRE EAST MIDLANDS
FD1-240 M6 T4-192
T2-254 T4-192
FD1-235 A38 A444 T3-202
✳Shrewsbury FD1-275 T2-243 T2-274 LEICESTERSHIRE
FL1-273 T3-272 T2-266 T3-255 Leicester ✳
FL1-262 T3-242 T3-241 T3-196 T3-197
FL2-257 FL1-227 FL2-263
FL1-251 M54 T3-271
SHROPSHIRE Wolverhampton ✳ FL1-231 A5
FL4-292 A49 FL1-280 Lutterworth
T2-248 FL2-260 FL4-239 FL1-279 ✳Birmingham FL1-181
M5 T3-233
T4-229 T3-234 ✳Coventry T4-256
T3-237 T3-238 T4-249 Rugby ✳ T2-187
WEST MIDLANDS ✳ FD2-281 T3-224
A442 A456 T3-244 M42 T3-225
FL4-269 ✳Warwick A423
WORCESTERSHIRE ✳Leominster A46
A44 ✳Worcester Alcester FL1-258 T3-276 T3-277
A4112 FL2-232 WARWICKSHIRE
HEREFORDSHIRE A4103 A38
✳Evesham
✳Hereford T3-267 Banbury ✳
FL2-250 T3-268 A429
M50 T4-056 T3-075
Ross-on-Wye ✳ FL4-261 FL2-034
FL4-270 ✳Whitchurch FL1-067 ✳Cheltenham
✳Gloucester A44
FL1-286 FL4-295 FL4-033 Oxford ✳
MONMOUTHSHIRE T3-108
FL1-291 T2-039 Cirencester ✳ T2-041 OXFORDSHIRE
FL2-027 GLOUCESTERSHIRE A420
T3-050 T3-051 A433
Newport ✳ T3-059 FL1-031
WALES T3-294 A34
T3-287 WILTSHIRE FL2-098 ✳
T4-062
FL1-065 T4-026 ✳Swindon
T3-038 T3-045 SOUTHEAST ENGLAND & LONDON
SOUTH WEST ENGLAND T4-043
T3-100 T3-099

West Midlands

■ *Cafe - Layby parking (FD1)*
■ *Cafe - No overnight parking (FD2)*
■ *Filling Station - No overnight parking/cafe (FL1)*
● *Bunkering Site - No overnight parking/cafe (FL1)*
■ *Filling Station - Nearby overnight parking no cafe (FL2)*
● *Bunkering Site - Nearby overnight parking no cafe (FL2)*
■ *Filling Station - Cafe no onsite overnight parking (FL3)*
■ *Filling Station - Onsite overnight parking (FL4)*
● *Bunkering Site - Onsite overnight parking (FL4)*
● *Bunkering Site - Cafe & onsite overnight parking (FL5)*
■ *Lorry Park - Onsite overnight parking no cafe or fuel (T1)*
■ *Truck Stop/Cafe - Onsite overnight parking (T2)*
■ *Motorway Service Station (T3)*
■ *Truck Stop - Bunker fuel/showers/cafe/onsite overnight parking (T4)*

For key to site symbols see page 8

FL1 ■   A5 Service Station, Wallsall

Lime Lane, Pelsall, Walsall
West Midlands WS3 5AR
T 01543 373444

ON THE B4154 If Heading from Bloxwich on the A4124, turn left onto the B4154 and A5 Service Station is 1 mile along on the left. If heading from Brownhills, turn left onto the B4154 and it's 1 mile along on your right.

CREDIT/DEBIT CARDS

FUEL CARDS (see key on page 9)
① ② ④ ⑦ ⑧ ㉞

TRUCK FACILITIES
Truck washing facilities

DRIVER FACILITIES
Truckers' accessories

All on-site facilities 06:00-21:30 Mon-Fri, 07:00-17:00 Sat, 09:00-17:00 Sun.   **227**

FL1 ■   Adastra Service Station, Market Drayton

Chester Road, Ternhill, Market Drayton
Shropshire TF9 3QD
T 01630 638729

ON THE A41 Adastra is close to Market Drayton on the A41 Wolverhampton to Whitchurch road and is on the right-hand side just past the junction with the A53 if heading south.

CREDIT/DEBIT CARDS

FUEL CARDS (see key on page 9)
① ② ③ ④ ⑥ ⑦ ⑧ ㉒

TRUCK FACILITIES
Truck dealership nearby

DRIVER FACILITIES
Truckers' accessories

SITE COMMENTS/INFORMATION
Friendly staff

All on-site Facilities 07:00-22:00 Mon-Sun.   **228**

Birmingham Truckstop — T4

**The Wharf, Wharf Road, Tyseley
Birmingham, West Midlands B11 2DA
T 0121 6282339**

ON THE B1416 From the M42, exit at junction 6 and take the A45 towards Birmingham. At the junction with the A4040, turn left towards Tyseley. After 900 yards turn right onto B4146 Wharfdale Road. Continue into Wharf Road. Truckstop is on your left.

CREDIT/DEBIT CARDS

FUEL CARDS (see key on page 9)

TRUCK FACILITIES
P
Coach parking. Fridge lorry area
Ample room for manoeuvring
Truck dealership/workshop

DRIVER FACILITIES
Accommodation on-site, Showers – 3 m, washroom, rest area, TV, phone top-ups/accessories, Train nearby

SITE COMMENTS/INFORMATION
Home cooked and prepared food is of the highest quality at very affordable prices

Parking and showers accessible 24 hours. Restaurant accessible 06:00-21:00 Mon-Fri. 06:00-12:00 Sat **229**

Bridge End Garage, Leek — FL1

**Macclesfield Road, Leek
Staffordshire ST13 8LD
T 01538 384250**

ON THE A523 Bridge End Garage is on the outskirts of Leek and on your left-hand side if heading north on the A523.

CREDIT/DEBIT CARDS

FUEL CARDS (see key on page 9)

DRIVER FACILITIES
Phone top-ups

SITE COMMENTS/INFORMATION
Clean site with efficient, friendly and helpful staff

All on-site facilities 07:00-22:00 Mon-Fri, 08:00-22:00 Sat & Sun **230**

C H Jones Ltd Bunker Stop, Walsall — FL1

**C H Jones Ltd, Queen Street
Premier Business Park, Walsall
West Midlands WS2 9PB
T 01922 615231**

OFF THE A4148 From Junction 10 of the M6 take the A454 towards Walsall. After about half a mile turn right onto the A4148 towards West Bromwich. Take the next left then 2nd right and CH Jones is on the left.

CREDIT/DEBIT CARDS

FUEL CARDS (see key on page 9)

DRIVER FACILITIES
Takeaway food nearby
Train nearby

All on-site facilities 24 hours **231**

FL2 ■ Clerkenleap Service Station, Worcester

Bath Road, Broomhall, Worcester
Worcestershire WR5 3HR
T 01905 821898

ON THE A38 Exit the M5 at junction 7 and take the A44 for 500 yards. Turn left onto the A4440 for 2 miles then left onto the A38. Clerkenleap Services is 300 yards on the right-hand side.

CREDIT/DEBIT CARDS

FUEL CARDS (see key on page 9)
22

TRUCK FACILITIES
Overnight parking in Worcester city centre 2 miles away

DRIVER FACILITIES
Internet access
Truckers' accessories
Takeaway food

All on-site facilities 06:00-23:00   **232**

T3 ■ Corley Services North, Welcome Break Ltd

Welcome Break Ltd
Highfield Lane, Corley, Coventry
Warwickshire CV7 8NR
T 01676 540111

M6 NORTH-WESTBOUND BETWEEN JUNCTIONS 3 AND 4

CREDIT/DEBIT CARDS

FUEL CARDS (see key on page 9)
3 10 25

TRUCK FACILITIES
P *with voucher*   P *only*   *Voucher value*
£22.50   £20.00   £10.00
Room for manoeuvre

DRIVER FACILITIES
Takeaway food
Showers (southbound), male (1), Phone accessories/top-ups, Clothing, Truckers accessories, Vegetarian/healthy meals, Arcade machines, Euros accepted

SITE COMMENTS/INFORMATION
Left hand side of forecourt not accessible to LGVs due to canopy height

Selected catering and retail facilities accessible 24 hours. Forecourt open 24 hours.   **233**

T3 ■ Corley Services South

Welcome Break Ltd
Highfield Lane, Corley, Coventry
Warwickshire CV7 8NR
T 01676 540111

M6 SOUTH-EASTBOUND BETWEEN JUNCTIONS 3 AND 4

CREDIT/DEBIT CARDS

FUEL CARDS (see key on page 9)
3 25

TRUCK FACILITIES
P *with voucher*   P *only*   *Voucher value*
£22.50   £20.00   £10.00
Plenty of room to manoeuvre,
Quiet parking

DRIVER FACILITIES
Takeaway food, Showers, male (1), unisex (2), Vegetarian/healthy meals
Arcade machines, Internet, Euros
Fax/copier, Phone accessories/top-ups
Clothing, Truckers' accessories

Catering, Retail and forcourt facilities accessible 24 hours   **234**

Dinky's Dinah's FD1

Welshpool Road, Ford, nr Shrewsbury Shropshire SY5 9LG
T 01743 850070

ON THE A458 Dinky's Dinah's is a static portacabin café situated on the A458 Shrewsbury to Welshpool road in a large lay-by in the village of Ford. It's located on the left-hand side if heading towards Shrewsbury after Butt Lane on the left and before the BP garage.

CREDIT/DEBIT CARDS

FUEL CARDS (for nearby fuel)
5

TRUCK FACILITIES
P free
Parking in lay-by set back from road
Coach parking available (6 spaces)
Ample room for manoeuvring

DRIVER FACILITIES
Seating area
Truckers' accessories
Takeaway food. Clothing for sale

SITE COMMENTS/INFORMATION
Excellent service around the clock

All on-site facilities accessible 24 hours. Nearby fuel not accessible 24 hours **235**

The Famous Midway Truckstop T2 ■

Pree's Heath, Whitchurch Shropshire SY13 3JT
T 01948 663160

ON THE A41 This site is located on the Midway roundabout at the junction of the A41 and the A49, 4 miles south of Whitchurch.

CREDIT/DEBIT CARDS

TRUCK FACILITIES
P Lorry park situated across road
Ample room for manoeuvring
Quiet area nearby
Truck dealership/workshop nearby

DRIVER FACILITIES
Showers, rest area, TV, internet, truckers' accessories, takeaway food

SITE COMMENTS/INFORMATION
This site has won many awards and TV appearances and boasts free library access and a variety of special deals

Nearby parking 24 hours. Other on-site facilities 05:45-20:00 Mon-Fri, 05:45-18:00 Sat, 07:30-14:00 Sun **236**

Frankley Services northbound T3 ■

Moto Ltd Birmingham West Midlands B32 4AR
T 0121 5503131 www.moto-way.com

M5 NORTHBOUND BETWEEN JUNCTIONS 3 AND 4

CREDIT/DEBIT CARDS

FUEL CARDS (see key on page 9)
27

DRIVER FACILITIES
Drivers' rest area
Takeaway food
Truckers' accessories

Full site details not available at time of going to press. For more information please contact site.

All on-site facilities accessible 24 hours **237**

T3 ■   Frankley Services southbound

Moto Ltd
Birmingham
West Midlands B32 4AR
T 0121 5503131 www.moto-way.com

M5 SOUTHBOUND BETWEEN JUNCTIONS 3 AND 4

CREDIT/DEBIT CARDS

FUEL CARDS (see key on page 9)
㉗

DRIVER FACILITIES
Accommodation, Travelodge
Drivers' rest area
Takeaway food
Truckers' accessories

Full site details not available at time of going to press. For more information please contact site.

All on-site facilities accessible 24 hours   **238**

FL4 ●   Hawkins Transport Village

Stallings Lane, Kingswinford, Dudley,
West Midlands, DY6 7LL
T 01384 294949 www.aehawkins.co.uk
OFF THE A419 If heading north, exit M5 Junction 4 and take the A491 north towards Kingswinford. Stallings Lane is on the right, 200 yards past the junction with A4101. If heading south exit at junction 2 take A4123 and A461 to Dudley. Take A4101 to Kingswinford, turn right onto A491 then right into Stallings Lane.

FUEL CARDS (see key on page 9)
㉒ ㉓ ㉝   all opposite/adjacent

TRUCK FACILITIES
P £10.00
Coaches overnight, shared with LGV, 24 hour security, Secure fencing, Floodlights, CCTV, Room to manoeuvre, Fridge parking, Quiet parking, Truck washing, LGV sales/dealer/workshop/tyre repairs

DRIVER FACILITIES
Showers, male (1), unisex (1), Washroom

Open 24 Hour   **239**

FD1 ■   Heather's Kaf

Oswestry By-pass, Sweeney, nr Morda
Oswestry, Shropshire SY10 8

ON THE A483 If heading south towards Welshpool, by-pass Oswestry on the A483. Go past the roundabout with the A5 and Heather's Kaf is 1 mile on your right-hand side.

CREDIT/DEBIT CARDS

FUEL CARDS (see key on page 9)

TRUCK FACILITIES
P *free*, in lay-by set close to road
Truck dealership/workshop nearby
Tyre repair/sales nearby

DRIVER FACILITIES
Takeaway food

SITE COMMENTS/INFORMATION
Clean and tidy site with smiley, friendly staff

Parking, fuel and nearby shop accessible 24 hours. Other on-site facilities accessible 07:30-16:00   **240**

Hilton Park Services northbound   T3

Moto Ltd
Wolverhampton
West Midlands WV11 2AT
T 01922 701639 www.moto-way.com

M6 NORTHBOUND JUNCTION 10A

CREDIT/DEBIT CARDS

FUEL CARDS (see key on page 9)

10 14 22 24 25

DRIVER FACILITIES
Accommodation, Travelodge
Drivers' rest area
Takeaway food
Phone top-ups/accessories
Truckers' accessories

Full site details not available at time of going to press. For more information please contact site.

All on-site facilities accessible 24 hours   **241**

Hilton Park Services southbound   T3

Moto Ltd
Wolverhampton
West Midlands WV11 2AT
T 01922 701639 www.moto-way.com

M6 SOUTHBOUND BETWEEN JUNCTIONS 10 AND 11

CREDIT/DEBIT CARDS

FUEL CARDS (see key on page 9)

10 14 22 24 25

DRIVER FACILITIES
Accommodation, Travelodge
Drivers' rest area
Takeaway food
Phone top-ups/accessories
Truckers' accessories

Full site details not available at time of going to press. For more information please contact site.

All on-site facilities accessible 24 hours   **242**

The Hollies Transport Café   T2

Watling Street, Hatherton, Cannock
Staffordshire WS11 1SB
T 01543 503435

ON THE A5 From the M6, exit at junction 12 and take the A5 towards Cannock. The Hollies is 1 mile along on the left-hand side.

CREDIT/DEBIT CARDS

TRUCK FACILITIES
P
Ample room for manoeuvring

DRIVER FACILITIES
Accommodation
Showers – 1 m, 1 f (charge), washroom, TV, truckers' accessories
Takeaway food

All on-site facilities accessible 24 hours   **243**

T3 ■ Hopwood Park Services

Welcome Break Ltd
Alvechurch, Birmingham
West Midlands B48 7AU
T 0121 4474000 or 0121 4478418

M42 JUNCTION 2

CREDIT/DEBIT CARDS

FUEL CARDS (see key on page 9)
3 14 22 23 24 25 28 33

TRUCK FACILITIES

P *with voucher*	**P** *only*	*Voucher value*
£20.00	£17.50	£7.00

Overnight coach (14)
Room for manoeuvre, Fridge parking, Quiet

DRIVER FACILITIES
Takeaway food
Showers, male (2), female (1), unisex (1)
Vegetarian/healthy meals, Arcade machines, Euros, Phone accessories/top-ups, Clothing for sale

All on-site facilities accessible 24 hours **244**

T3 ■ Keele Services Northbound, Welcome Break Ltd

Welcome Break Ltd
Newcastle under Lyme
Staffordshire ST5 5HG
T 01782 626221

M6 NORTHBOUND
JUNCTIONS 15–16

CREDIT/DEBIT CARDS

FUEL CARDS (see key on page 9)
25

TRUCK FACILITIES

P *with voucher*	**P** *only*	*Voucher value*
£17.50	£15.00	£7.00

Overnight coach (13)
Room for manoeuvre, Fridge parking, Quiet, Pumps accessible to LGVs only one side

DRIVER FACILITIES
Takeaway food, Vegetarian/Healthy meals, Showers, male (3), female (1)
Arcade machines, Internet, Euros, Fax/copier, Phone accessories/top-ups
Clothing, Truckers' accessories

SITE COMMENTS/INFORMATION
Beautiful picturesque setting

All on-site facilities accessible 24 hours **245**

T3 ■ Keele Services Southbound, Welcome Break Ltd

Welcome Break Ltd
Newcastle under Lyme
Staffordshire ST5 5HG
T 01782 626221

M6 SOUTHBOUND
JUNCTIONS 15–16

CREDIT/DEBIT CARDS

FUEL CARDS (see key on page 9)
25

TRUCK FACILITIES

P *with voucher*	**P** *only*	*Voucher value*
£17.50	£15.00	£7.00

Overnight coach (14)
Room for manoeuvre, Fridge parking

DRIVER FACILITIES
Takeaway food

All on-site facilities accessible 24 hours **246**

e Lazy Kettle Transport Café   FL4 ■

**Gledrid Service Station, Oswestry By-pass
Oswestry, Shropshire SY11 3EN**
T **01691 770066**

A5/A483 INTERSECTION The Lazy Kettle is on the A483
Oswestry By-pass at the roundabout with the A5 and on the
right-hand side if heading north.

CREDIT/DEBIT CARDS

FUEL CARDS (see key on page 9)
28
TRUCK FACILITIES
Coach parking available
Quiet area. Fridge lorry area
Ample room for manoeuvring
Truck washing facilities
DRIVER FACILITIES
Showers, 4 male, 3 female
Travelodge on-site
Drivers' washroom, rest area, internet
access and phone top-ups/accessories
Truckers' accessories
Takeaway food nearby
SITE COMMENTS/INFORMATION
Plenty of room for parking, clean site

All on-site facilities 24 hours   247

The Lazy Trout Café   T2 ■

**Marshbrook, nr Church Stretton
Shropshire SY6 6RG**
T **01694 781336**

ON THE A49 Take the A49 from Ludlow to Shrewsbury. The
Lazy Trout is on the left-hand side, half a mile north of
Marshbrook and 1 mile south of Little Stretton.

TRUCK FACILITIES
P free. Quiet area
Ample room for manoeuvring
Truck dealership/workshop nearby

SITE COMMENTS/INFORMATION
Believed to be the oldest truckstop in the
country and world renowned (Corgi
have even made a model of it!). Set in
beautiful countryside. Proprietors
considering 24 hour, 7 days a week
opening in the near future

Parking 24 hours. All other on-site facilities 07:00-16:00   248

Lincoln Farm Café and Hotel   T4 ■

**Kenilworth Road, Hampton in Arden,
Solihull, West Midlands B92 0LS**
T **01675 442301/442769**

ON THE A452 From M42 exit at junction 6, take A45
towards Coventry then take A452 Kenilworth Road towards
Kenilworth, across junction with B4102 and Lincoln Farm
Café is about 2 miles further on the right-hand side.

FUEL CARDS (see key on page 9)
1
TRUCK FACILITIES
P with voucher £8.50 Voucher value £3.50
Ample room for manoeuvring
Quiet area. Night attendant
DRIVER FACILITIES
Accommodation on-site, £15 pn B&B
Showers – 9 m, 1 f (charge) – large and
spacious, Washroom, rest area, TV, Euros
changed/accepted, truckers' accessories,
Takeaway food, Vegetarian/Healthy
meals, Arcade mach.

SITE COMMENTS/INFORMATION
Large spacious shower rooms

Parking 24 hours. Nearby fuel and other on-site facilities 06:00-24:00 Monday, 04:00-24:00 Tues-Fri   249

FL2 ■ Locks Garage, Hereford

Allensmore, Hereford
Herefordshire HR2 9AS
T 01981 570206

A465 B348 INTERSECTION Locks Garage can be found on the A465 at the junction with the B4348 and on the left-hand side if heading towards Hereford.

CREDIT/DEBIT CARDS

FUEL CARDS (see key on page 9)
③ ④ ㉕

TRUCK FACILITIES
Overnight parking half mile away
Coach parking (shared with LGV) available
Truck washing facilities
Ample room for manoeuvring

DRIVER FACILITIES
Drivers' rest area
Truckers' accessories
Phone top-ups/accessories
Takeaway food nearby

Nearby parking 24 hours. All on-site facilities 05:00-22:00 Mon-Sun **250**

FL1 ■ Long Gardens, Shrewsbury

Dorrington, Shrewsbury
Shropshire SY5 7ER
T 01743 718275

ON THE A49 Take the A49 south from Shrewsbury. Continue for about 1 mile past the turnings for the village of Condover. Long Gardens is on the left-hand side, just before the turnings for Stapleton and about 1 mile before Dorrington.

CREDIT/DEBIT CARDS

FUEL CARDS (see key on page 9)
① ② ③ ④ ⑥ ⑦ ⑧ ㉞

SITE COMMENTS/INFORMATION
Fuel lane next to shop can be difficult to access for LGVs
Home made pies, pastries and cakes
Fresh fruit, veg and flowers on sale

All on-site facilities 07:30-18:30 Mon-Fri, 08:00-18:30 Sat, 09:00-17:00 Sun **251**

T2 ■ Lynn's Raven Café

Prees Heath, Whitchurch
Shropshire SY13 2AF
T 01948 665691

ON THE A41 A49 INTERSECTION If coming from Whitchurch, take the A41 south to the roundabout with the A49. Take the 3rd exit off the roundabout and follow the road as it bends to the right. Lynn's Raven Café is 100 yards on your left.

TRUCK FACILITIES
Coach parking shared with LGV
Ample room for manoeuvring
Quiet area. Floodlighting

DRIVER FACILITIES
Accommodation next door, Raven Pub
Showers – unisex, washroom, rest area, TV, internet access, Euros changed/accepted
Takeaway food

SITE COMMENTS/INFORMATION
Sunday carvery 12:00-14:00, snooker table, all day breakfasts available
Café being refurbished

Parking 24 hours. Other on-site facilities 07:00-20:00 Mon, 06:00-20:00 Tues, Wed, & Thurs, 06:00-19:00 Fri, 07:00-15:00 Sat & Sun **252**

Market Drayton Truck Stop — T2 ▪

**Adderley Road, Market Drayton,
Shropshire, TF9 3SW
T 01630 695831**

ON THE A53/A529 INTERSECTION Take the A53 around
the outskirts of Market Drayton. The site is at the intersection
of the A53 and A529.

TRUCK FACILITIES
P £5.00, Coaches overnight, shared with
LGV, Secure fencing, Floodlights, CCTV,
Room to manoeuvre, Fridge parking,
Quiet parking, Truck washing, LGV tyre
repair/sales

DRIVER FACILITIES
Showers, male (1), unisex (1),
Washroom, Vegetarian/Healthy meals,
Arcade machines, Euros

Open Mon-Thurs 07:00-17:00, Fri 08:00-15:00, Sat 08:00-Midday.   **253**

New Oak Moor Transport Café — T2 ▪

**304 Lichfield Road, Barton under Needwood,
nr Burton on Trent, Staffordshire DE13 8ED
T 01283 712712**

ON THE A38 From Lichfield take the A38 towards Burton
on Trent. Continue for three quarters of a mile past the
turning for Barton under Needwood, and New Oak Moor
Transport Café is on your left.

CREDIT/DEBIT CARDS

TRUCK FACILITIES
P Coach parking, by prior arrangement,
shared with LGV
Ample room for manoeuvring

DRIVER FACILITIES
Accomm. nearby, half a mile, Travelodge
Showers – 2 unisex, TV
Euros changed/accepted
Takeaway food

SITE COMMENTS/INFORMATION
This site is due for refurbishment,
internet access coming soon

Parking 24 hours. Other on-site facilities 06:00-20:00 Mon-Thurs, 06:00-18:00 Fri, 07:00-12:00 Sat   **254**

Norton Canes Services — T3 ▪

**Roadchef Ltd
Betty's Lane, Norton Canes, Cannock
Staffordshire WS11 9UX
T 01543 272540 Duty Mobile 07776 408987**

NEW M6 TOLL MOTORWAY BETWEEN TOLL 6 AND
TOLL 7. Can be accessed from east or westbound or from
the A5

CREDIT/DEBIT CARDS

FUEL CARDS (see key on page 9)
⑭

TRUCK FACILITIES
P with voucher P only Voucher value
£12.00   £9.00   £6.00
Coach parking available (25 spaces)
Ample room for manoeuvring
Quiet area, Floodlights, CCTV
Fridge parking, Quiet
DRIVER FACILITIES
Accommodation on-site (£49.50 pn)
Showers, 3 m, 1 f (free), Internet, Phone
top-ups/accessories, truckers' accessories
Takeaway food. Clothing for sale
SITE COMMENTS/INFORMATION
New site. Only service area on M6 toll

All on-site facilities accessible 24 hours   **255**

T4 ■ NT Truckstop, Rugby

(Previously BP Nightowl), Watling Street Clifton upon Dunsmore, Rugby Warwickshire CV23 0AE
T 01788 535115

ON THE A5 Exit at junction 18 of the M1 onto the A428 towards Rugby then take the A5 towards Hinckley. The Truckstop is about 3 miles along on the right-hand side.

CREDIT/DEBIT CARDS

FUEL CARDS (see key on page 9)
① ② ④ 34

TRUCK FACILITIES
P with voucher	**P** only	Voucher value
£13.00	£10.00	£3.00

Coaches overnight, shared with LGV, Full security on-site, Fridge parking in overflow lorry park, Quiet, Adblue

DRIVER FACILITIES
Showers – 8 unisex (£3.00 free with P), washroom, rest area, TV, laundry service, Clothing, Truckers' accessories, CB repairs/ sales, Takeaway food, Vegetarian/ healthy meals, Rest area, Arcade mach., Laundry, Internet, Euros, Fax/copier, Phone acc.,/top-ups

Bunker fuel accessible 24hrs. Restaurant open Mon-Fri 06.00-22.30, Sat 07.00-11.00, Sun 17.00-21.00. Shop open Sun 16.00 to Sat 11.30. Bar 06:00-23:00 Mon-Fri, 19:00-22:30 Sun. Site closed from noon Saturday to 16:00 Sun

256

FL2 ● Oakley Fuels Ltd

Halesfield 19, Telford Shropshire TF7 4QT
T 01952 684600

OFF THE A442 Take the A442 south from Telford towards Bridgnorth. Exit onto the sliproad for the A4169 towards Shifnal. At the next roundabout turn left into Halesfield 19. Continue to end of the road. Oakley Fuels is on the left.

CREDIT/DEBIT CARDS

FUEL CARDS (see key on page 9)
① ② ④ ⑤

TRUCK FACILITIES
Free overnight parking on road at end of estate
Coach parking available, shared with LGV
Quiet area
Ample room for manoeuvring
Truck dealership/workshop nearby
Windscreen repair facility nearby
Tyre repair/sales nearby

DRIVER FACILITIES
Takeaway food nearby

Bunker fuel, parking and water 24 hours. This site is manned from 08:00-17:00 Mon-Fri

257

FL1 ■ Oversley Mill Services, Alcester

Alcester By-pass, Alcester Warwickshire B49 6PQ
T 01789 400307/762684

ON THE A46 Oversley Mill Services is on the A46 at Alcester on the roundabout junction with the A435.

CREDIT/DEBIT CARDS

FUEL CARDS (see key on page 9)

① ② ③ ④ ⑧ ⑭ ㉒ ㉓ ㉔ ㉝ 34

DRIVER FACILITIES
Accommodation nearby, 50 yards, Travelodge
Truckers' accessories
Phone top-ups

All on-site facilities 24 hours

258

PJ's Transport Café   T4 ■

Lichfield Road, Draycott in the Clay, Ashbourne, Derbyshire DE6 5GX
T 01283 820669

ON THE A515, OFF THE A50 From the A50, take the A515 Lichfield road at the Sudbury roundabout. Continue for 1 mile and we are located at the rear of the 'Total' petrol station. We operate a one way system for safety.

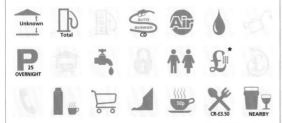

CREDIT/DEBIT CARDS

FUEL CARDS (see key on page 9)
① ③ ④ ㉓ ㉔ ㉕ ㉘ ㉞

TRUCK FACILITIES
P *with voucher* £11.00 Inc. meal and hot drink, Manoeuvring room, Quiet

DRIVER FACILITIES
Accommodation nearby, Boars Head Showers – 2 m, 2 unisex (free), washroom, rest area, TV, truckers' accessories, Takeaway food, Vegetarian/healthy meals, Internet, Fax/copier, Phone to ups, CB sales/repairs

SITE COMMENTS/INFORMATION
Site recently refurbished, Health & Safety 5 Star rated, Bottomless hot drink if parking overnight, Latecomers please call with ETA.

On-site parking 24hrs. Forecourt parking available 21.00-06.00. Fuel accessible 06:00-21:00. Other facilities accessible 07:00-21:00 Mon-Thurs, 07:00-16:00 Fri.   **259**

Quatford Service Station, Quatford   FL2 ■

Kidderminster Road, Quatford nr Bridgnorth, Shropshire WV15 6QJ
T 01746 763039

ON THE A442 Take the A442 south from Bridgnorth. Quatford Service Station is on the left-hand side at the south end of the village of Quatford.

CREDIT/DEBIT CARDS

FUEL CARDS (see key on page 9)
① ②

TRUCK FACILITIES
Overnight parking 2 miles away, Severn Street Car Park, Bridgnorth

DRIVER FACILITIES
Takeaway food
Truckers' accessories

All on-site facilities 07:00-19:00. Nearby parking PM only   **260**

Ross Spur Services southbound   FL4 ■

First Motorway Services Ltd Southbound Overcross, Ross on Wye Herefordshire HR9 7QJ
T 01989 565027

M50 JUNCTION 4 ON THE A449 Ross Spur is located at the end of M50 on the A449 southbound carriageway towards Ross on Wye.

CREDIT/DEBIT CARDS

FUEL CARDS (see key on page 9)
㉒

TRUCK FACILITIES
P
Coach parking available (2 spaces)
Quiet area
Ample room for manoeuvring

DRIVER FACILITIES
Accommodation 600 yards away at Travel Inn
Truckers' accessories

All on-site facilities 24 hours   **261**

FL1 ■ Shrewsbury Service Station, Shrewsbury

Hereford Road, Bayston Hill, Shrewsbury
Shropshire SY3 0DA
T 01743 874504

OFF THE A49 From Shrewsbury centre take the A49 south towards Hereford. Shrewsbury Services is situated on the roundabout with the A5.

Toilets 06:00-23:00. All other on-site facilities 24 hours

CREDIT/DEBIT CARDS

FUEL CARDS (see key on page 9)
③ ㉗

TRUCK FACILITIES
Short-term coach parking (6 spaces)

DRIVER FACILITIES
Accommodation nearby, 20 yards, Travelodge

262

FL2 ■ S R Tomson & Son, Tamworth

78 Glascote Road, Tamworth
Staffordshire B77 2AF
T 01827 50237/63137
www.tomscitroen.co.uk-
ON THE B5000 From M42 junction 10 take A5 towards Tamworth until junction with the A51. Turn right on to the A51. At next major junction turn left and follow signs for Glascote. S R Tomson is on the B5000 just by McGregor School.

Nearby parking times unknown. All other on-site facilities 24 hours

CREDIT/DEBIT CARDS

FUEL CARDS (see key on page 9)
③ ⑭ ㉒ ㉓ ㉘

TRUCK FACILITIES
Overnight parking in Castle grounds

DRIVER FACILITIES
Take away
Fax/copier, Phone top-ups

SITE COMMENTS/INFORMATION
Excellent service
Snack bar open AM only. Cold food available 24 hrs

263

T3 ■ Stafford Services Northbound

Moto Ltd
Stone
Staffordshire ST15 0EU
T 01785 811188 www.moto-way.com

M6 NORTHBOUND BETWEEN JUNCTIONS 14 AND 15

All on-site facilities accessible 24 hours

CREDIT/DEBIT CARDS

FUEL CARDS (see key on page 9)
⑭ ㉒

DRIVER FACILITIES
Accommodation, Travelodge
Takeaway food

Full site details not available at time of going to press. For more information please contact site.

264

Stafford Services southbound   T3

Roadchef Ltd
Stone
Staffordshire ST15 0EU
T 01785 826300 www.roadchef.com

M6 SOUTHBOUND BETWEEN JUNCTIONS 14 AND 15

CREDIT/DEBIT CARDS

FUEL CARDS (see key on page 9)
㉗

TRUCK FACILITIES
P *with voucher* **P** *only* *Voucher value*
£12.00   £9.00   £6.00
Coach parking available (15 spaces)
Ample room for manoeuvring
Quiet area

DRIVER FACILITIES
Accommodation (£46.95 pn)
Showers, 1 m, 1 f (free), washroom,
Internet access, phone top-ups/accessories,
truckers' accessories. Dog walking area
and kids play area. Takeaway food
Clothing for sale

All on-site facilities accessible 24 hours   **265**

Standeford Farm Café (Standeford Diner)   T2 ■

176 Stafford Road, Standeford
Wolverhampton, West Midlands WV10 7BN
T 01902 790389

ON THE A449 From junction 12 of the M6 follow the A5
towards Telford, turn left onto the A449 heading towards
Wolverhampton. Or from Junction 2 of the M54, turn right
towards Stafford. Standeford Farm Café is on the A449 in the
village of Standeford.

TRUCK FACILITIES
P *with voucher* **P** *only* *Voucher value*
£10.00   £5.00   £4.25
Ample room for manoeuvring
Coach parking. Quiet area, Floodlights,
CCTV, Truck washing, Fridge lorries
switch off at 22:00

DRIVER FACILITIES
Showers – 2 m, 1 f (£1 or free if parking
overnight), washroom, rest area, TV
Takeaway food, Vegetarian/Healthy
meals, Euros

SITE COMMENTS/INFORMATION
Customers can pay by cheque only with
bankers card.

Parking 24 hours. Other on-site facilities 05:30-20:00   **266**

Strensham Motorway Services northbound   T3 ■

Roadchef Ltd
Strensham, Worcester
Worcestershire WR8 0BZ
T 01684 293004

M5 NORTHBOUND BETWEEN JUNCTIONS 7 AND 8

CREDIT/DEBIT CARDS

FUEL CARDS (see key on page 9)
① ② ③ ④ ⑧ ㉓

TRUCK FACILITIES
P *with voucher* **P** *only* *Voucher value*
£20.00   £17.00   £10.00
Coach parking available (20 spaces)
Ample room for manoeuvring
Quiet area. Truck dealership/workshop
Secure fencing, Parking attendant on
duty daily from noon to 23:00
DRIVER FACILITIES
Accommodation, Premier Inn (£50.00)
Showers, 1 m, 2 f (free) Phone top-ups/
accessories, truckers' accessories. Takeaway
food. Vegetarian/ healthy meals, TV,
Arcade mach., Euros, Clothing for sale.

Restaurant, Retail shop & Costa Coffee open 24hrs. Wimpy open 09:00-22:00, Pizza Hut open 10:00-23:00   **267**

T3 ■ Strensham Motorway Services southbound

**Roadchef Ltd
Strensham, Worcester
Worcestershire WR8 9LJ
T 01684 290577**

M5 SOUTHBOUND BETWEEN JUNCTIONS 7 AND 8

CREDIT/DEBIT CARDS

FUEL CARDS (see key on page 9)
③ ⑧ ⑭ ㉓

TRUCK FACILITIES
P *with voucher* **P** *only* *Voucher value*
£20.00   £17.00   £10.00
Coach parking available (20 spaces)
Ample room for manoeuvring, Quiet
Truck washing facilities, Truck dealership/
workshop, Secure fencing, Floodlights,
Parking attendant noon to 23:00
DRIVER FACILITIES
Accommodation, Premier Inn (£50.00)
Showers, 2 m, 1 f (free) Phone top-
ups/accessories, truckers' accessories.
Takeaway food. Vegetarian/healthy meals
TV, Arcade machs., Clothing for sale

Restaurant, Retail shop & Costa Coffee open 24hrs. Wimpy open 09:00-22:00   **268**

FL4 ■ Swan Service Station

**Worcester Road, Wychbold, Bromsgrove
West Midlands B61 7ER
T 01527 861892**

ON THE A38 From M5 junction 5, take the A38 towards
Bromsgrove. Continue through Wychbold and Swan Service
Station is on the right before you get to Upton Warren.

CREDIT/DEBIT CARDS

FUEL CARDS (see key on page 9)
① ② ③ ④ ⑦ ㉞

TRUCK FACILITIES
P
CCTV. Quiet area
Ample room for manoeuvring
DRIVER FACILITIES
Hot drinks free with 100 litres
Drivers' washroom and rest area
Premier Lodge 400 yards away
Takeaway food
Phone top-ups/accessories
Good range of truckers' accessories
Train nearby

Café 07:00-19:00. Other on-site facilities 24 hours   **269**

FL4 ■ Symonds Yat Services northbound

**First Motorway Services Ltd
Symonds Yat, Whitchurch, Ross on Wye
Herefordshire HR9 6DP
T 01600 890219**

ON THE A40 NORTHBOUND This site is located at
Symonds Yat on the A40 northbound between Monmouth
and Ross on Wye just before the junction with the A4137.

CREDIT/DEBIT CARDS

FUEL CARDS (see key on page 9)
① ② ③ ④ ⑦ ㉒ ㉞

TRUCK FACILITIES
P
Coach parking available (3 spaces)
Ample room for manoeuvring
Quiet area

DRIVER FACILITIES
Shower, drivers' washroom
Rest area, TV
Truckers' accessories
Clothing for sale

Parking 24 hours. Other on-site facilities 06:00-21:00   **270**

Tamworth Services

T3 ■

Moto Ltd
Green Lane, Wilnecote, Tamworth
Staffordshire B77 5PS
T 01827 260120 www.moto-way.com

M42 JUNCTION 10

CREDIT/DEBIT CARDS

FUEL CARDS (see key on page 9)
③ ㉓ ㉗

TRUCK FACILITIES
P *with voucher*   **P** *only*   *Voucher value*
£16.00   £13.00   £6.00
Coaches overnight (12)
Plenty of room to manoeuvre in
lorry park

DRIVER FACILITIES
Showers, male (3), female (1)
Takeaway food, Vegetarian/healthy meals
Phone top-ups/accessories, TV, Arcade
machines, Truckers' accessories

All on-site facilities accessible 24 hours

271

Telford Services, Welcome Break Ltd

T3 ■

Priorslee Road, Shifnal, Telford,
Shropshire TF11 8TG
T 01952 238400 www.welcomebreak.co.uk

ON THE M54 JUNCTION 4 On the M54, exit at junction 4
and take the first exit, then first exit again.

CREDIT/DEBIT CARDS

FUEL CARDS (see key on page 9)
㉓ ㉔ ㉕ ㉗

TRUCK FACILITIES
P £13.00-15.00, Voucher–1 meal,
Coaches overnight, Floodlights, CCTV,
Manoeuvre room, Quiet area

DRIVER FACILITIES
Showers, male 1, female 1,
Accommodation, £40.00, Fax/copier,
Vegetarian/Healthy meals, Takeaway,
Arcade machines, Games room, Internet,
Euros, Phone accessories/top-ups,
Clothing, Truckers' accessories,
International papers

All on-site facilities open 24 Hours

272

Trench Lock 24-7, Telford

FL1 ■

Trench Lock, Telford
Shropshire TF1 6SZ
T 01952 243018

OFF THE A442 Exit M54 junction 5 and take the first exit
towards the A442. Turn left onto the A442 for 2 miles. At
the junction with the A518 turn left and Trench Lock is
immediately on your right.

CREDIT/DEBIT CARDS

FUEL CARDS (see key on page 9)
① ②

FUEL CARDS NEARBY
② ⑬ ㉑ ㉒

TRUCK FACILITIES
Short-term coach parking (3 spaces)

SITE COMMENTS/INFORMATION
Best LGV facilities in Telford!

All on-site facilities 24 hours. Short term on-site parking 24 hours

273

T2 ■ Truckers Rest

Watling Street, Four Crosses, Cannock
Staffordshire WS11 1SF
T 01543 469183

ON THE A5 From junction 12 of the M6 take the A5 towards Cannock. The Truckers Rest is about 2 miles along on the right. From junction 11 take the A460 towards Cannock, turn left at the junction with the A5 and the Truckers Rest is within a mile on your left.

CREDIT/DEBIT CARDS

TRUCK FACILITIES
P
Coach parking (10 spaces), shared with LGV. Quiet area, Floodlighting, Fridge parking in front of café
Ample room for manoeuvring

DRIVER FACILITIES
Accommodation nearby, 400 yards, Roman Way Hotel & Travel Inn
Showers m 2, unisex 2 (£1.00), Washroom, TV, Takeaway food, Vegetarian/Healthy meals, Arcade mach., Euros, Phone top-ups

SITE COMMENTS/INFORMATION
Excellent food and service

Cafe open Mon-Fri 06:00-23:30, Sat 06:00-15:00, Sun 07:00-17:30. **274**

FD1 ■ Val's Diner

Telford/Donnington Roundabout
Redhill, Telford, Shropshire TF2 9PA
07973 854798

ON THE A5 From M54 Junction 4 take the B5060 towards Oakengates. At the roundabout with the A5, turn left towards Cannock. Val's Diner is half a mile along on the right-hand side in a lay-by.

CREDIT/DEBIT CARDS

FUEL CARDS (see key on page 9)

TRUCK FACILITIES
P free
Parking in large lay-by set back from road
Truck washing facilities nearby

DRIVER FACILITIES
Accommodation nearby, Oaks at Redhill Hotel
Showers, 1 m, 1 f
Washroom, seating area
Takeaway food

SITE COMMENTS/INFORMATION
Home cooked food, friendly staff and a lovely cuppa. Nearby town centre facilities 1 mile away

Parking and showers accessible 24 hours. Other on-site facilities accessible 04:00-14:00 **275**

T3 ■ Warwick Services north-westbound

Welcome Break Ltd
Banbury Road, Ashore, Nr Warwick
Warwickshire CV35 0AA
T 01926 651681

M40 NORTH-WESTBOUND BETWEEN JUNCTIONS 12 AND 13

CREDIT/DEBIT CARDS

FUEL CARDS (see key on page 9)

TRUCK FACILITIES

P with voucher	**P** only	Voucher value
£20.00	£17.50	£7.00

Coaches overnight (10)
Floodlights, Room for manoeuvre, Adblue in containers

DRIVER FACILITIES
Accommodation, Days Inn (£52.95)
Takeaway food, Vegetarian/healthy meals, Showers, male (3), female (1), unisex (1) £10 ref. dep.
Phone top-ups, Arcade machines, Internet, Euros, Fax/copier

All on-site facilities accessible 24 hours **276**

Warwick Services south-eastbound   T3 ■

Welcome Break Ltd
Banbury Road, Ashore, Nr Warwick
Warwickshire CV35 0AA
T 01926 650168

M40 SOUTH-EASTBOUND BETWEEN
JUNCTIONS 12 AND 13

CREDIT/DEBIT CARDS

FUEL CARDS (see key on page 9)
(14) (22) (33)

TRUCK FACILITIES
P *with voucher*   P *only*   *Voucher value*
£20.00   £17.50   £7.00
Coaches overnight (10), Floodlights
Room for manoeuvre, Adblue in
containers

DRIVER FACILITIES
Accommodation, Days Inn (£52.95)
Takeaway food, Vegetarian/Healthy
meals, Showers, male (3), female (1),
unisex (1) £10 ref. dep.
Phone accessories/top-ups, Arcade
machines, Euros, Fax/copier

All on-site facilities accessible 24 hours   **277**

Watson Fuels   FL1 ●

Chemical Lane, Longbridge Hayes
Industrial Estate, Stoke on Trent,
Staffordshire ST6 4PB
T 01977 603313 www.watsonfuels.co.uk
OFF THE A500 From Junction 16 of M6 take the A500
towards Stoke on Trent. At the roundabout with the A527
turn left into Longbridge Hayes Road and continue into
Chemical Lane. Watson Fuels is on the left.

FUEL CARDS (see key on page 9)
(1) (2) (4)

All on-site facilities accessible 24 hour   **278**

West Cross Service Station, Smethwick   FL1 ■

166 Oldbury Road, Smethwick
West Midlands B66 1ND
T 0121 5556787

ON THE A457 From junction 1 M5 take the A4252 towards
Smethwick. At the roundabout with the A457 turn right.
Continue over roundabout with A4031 and West Cross is on
your left.

CREDIT/DEBIT CARDS

FUEL CARDS (see key on page 9)
(1) (3) (4) (34)

TRUCK FACILITIES
Ample room for manoeuvring

All on-site facilities 24 hours.   **279**

FL1 ■ Whittleford Service Station, Nuneaton

**Whittleford Road, Stockington, Nuneaton
Warwickshire CV10 9JD
T 02476 386327**

OFF THE B4114 Take the B4114 out of Nuneaton towards Hartshill. 500 yards after the junction with the B4111, turn left down Bucks Hill. Whittleford Service Station is 900 yards on the left.

CREDIT/DEBIT CARDS

FUEL CARDS (see key on page 9)

DRIVER FACILITIES
Truckers' accessories

All on-site facilities 06:00-21:00

280

T4 ■ Willoughby Café (formerly The Pantry Café)

**London Road, Willoughby, Nr Daventry
and Dunchurch
Warwickshire CV23 8BL
T 01788 890262**

ON THE A45 If heading from Daventry to Rugby on the A45, The Pantry Café is on the left-hand side in the middle of the village of Willoughby.

TRUCK FACILITIES
Parking nearby overnight (3)
Short-term coach parking on-site and nearby overnight (shared with LGV)
Ample room for manoeuvring
Fridge parking

DRIVER FACILITIES
Takeaway food
Vegetarian meals, TV

SITE COMMENTS/INFORMATION
Large parties please telephone in advance. Nearby parking situated in layby towards Daventry
Great home made food, warm friendly atmosphere. Real open log fire burning during winter months.

Mon-Fri 07:00-15:00, Sat 07:00-14:00

281

Holyhead ✳

ANGLESEY

Colwyn Bay ✳

Prestatyn ✳

Bangor ✳ *FL1-289*

A55

ABERCONWY & COLWYN

T2-284 ■

FLINTSHIRE

Caernarfon ✳

DENBIGHSHIRE

FL2-300 ■

FL1-441
Liverpool ●
■
FL2-455 ■ T4-444 ■
↑
FL2-383 ●
T2-4■
T3-382 ■
✳ Chester
CHESH

FL2-298 ■

A483 ● FL1-290

Porthmadog ✳

GWYNEDD

A487

A5

A494

FD1-308 ■

Bala ✳

FL2-305 ●
FL4-247 ■

T2-252 ■
T2-236 ■

✳ Oswestry
FD1-240 ■   A49

Dolgellau ✳

A458

Shrewsbury
FD1-235 ✳ ■
FL1-262 ■
FL1-251 ■

A470

FL4-292 ■
SHROPSHIRE

T2-248 ■

Aberystwyth ✳

✳ Llangurig

WEST MIDLANDS

A487

POWYS

FL4-302 ■

CEREDIGION

Llandrindod Wells ✳

A44

Leominster ✳

A49

Cardigan ✳

A483

HEREFORDSHIRE

A438

Fishguard ✳

Hereford ✳

PEMBROKESHIRE

CARMARTHENSHIRE

FL2-296 ■ ✳ Llandovery

A40

FL1-285 ■
Brecon

FL2-250 ■

Ross-on-Wye ✳
Whitchurch
FL4-270 ■

FL1-307 ■ ✳ Carmarthen
FL1-297 ■
FD1-282 ■
T3-299 ■

A40

A48

A465

*BLAENAU
GWENT*

MONMOUTHSHIRE

FL1-286 ■ FL4-295 ■

Haverfordwest ✳

A40

Pembroke ✳

A477

T3-306 ■
Swansea ✈

FL2-303 ■
FL1-283 ■

*NEATH PORT
TALBOT*

*RHONDDA
CYNON TAF*

FL1-291 ■

BRIDGEND

A470

CAERPHILLY

T3-294 ✳

T3-0■

T3-301 ■
FL4-293 ■ T3-288 ■

Newport ✳

FL1-304 ■   T3-287 ■

✳ Cardiff

FL1-■
T4-026 ●
T3-038 ■
FL1-0■
Bris

SOUTH WEST ENGLAND

M4

FL2-052 ■

VALE OF GLAMORGAN

✈

0
25
50 miles

0
40
80 kms

Weston-Super-Mare

T1-047 ■

A38

T3-057 ■
T3-058 ■

FL1-037 ■

Lynmouth ✳

Wales

■ Cafe - Layby parking (FD1)
■ Cafe - No overnight parking (FD2)
■ Filling Station - No overnight parking/cafe (FL1)
● Bunkering Site - No overnight parking/cafe (FL1)
■ Filling Station - Nearby overnight parking no cafe (FL2)
● Bunkering Site - Nearby overnight parking no cafe (FL2)
■ Filling Station - Cafe no onsite overnight parking (FL3)
■ Filling Station - Onsite overnight parking (FL4)
● Bunkering Site - Onsite overnight parking (FL4)
● Bunkering Site - Cafe & onsite overnight parking (FL5)
■ Lorry Park - Onsite overnight parking no cafe or fuel (T1)
■ Truck Stop/Cafe - Onsite overnight parking (T2)
■ Motorway Service Station (T3)
■ Truck Stop - Bunker fuel/showers/cafe/onsite overnight parking (T4)

For key to site symbols see page 8

FD1 ■ Al's Café (formerly Big Mike's Breakfast Bar)

**Near M4 Junction 49, Ammanford
Carmarthenshire SA40 0
0797 6074660**

ON THE A483 From the end of the M4, take the A483 towards Ammanford and continue for half a mile. Big Mike's is in a lay-by on the left.

  Unknown NEARBY / NEARBY

 6 OVERNIGHT

  £1.80 70p CR £2.75

CREDIT/DEBIT CARDS

FUEL CARDS (see key on page 9)

TRUCK FACILITIES
Parking in lay-by set close to road

DRIVER FACILITIES
Takeaway food

SITE COMMENTS/INFORMATION
This snack van is situated very close to Pont Abraham Services

Parking accessible 24 hours. Other on-site facilities accessible 06:00-15:00   282

FL1 ■ Baglan Service Station, Port Talbot

**Swan Road, Baglan, Port Talbot
Carmarthenshire SA12 8LA
T 01639 822898**

ON THE A48 If heading north-west, exit M4 at junction 41. Take A48 towards Briton Ferry and Baglan is on the right. If heading south-east, exit at junction 42 and take the A48 towards Port Talbot. Baglan is on the left.

 4.8m Texaco

   NEARBY

NEARBY / NEARBY / NEARBY

CREDIT/DEBIT CARDS

FUEL CARDS (see key on page 9)
① ② ③ ④

DRIVER FACILITIES
Takeaway food nearby

SITE COMMENTS/INFORMATION
Friendly staff

All on-site facilities 06:30-21:45 Mon-Fri, 08:00-21:45 Sat & Sun.   283

Billie Jeans Café

T2 ■

The Nant, Pentre Halkyn, Holywell
Flintshire CH8 8BD
T 01352 781118/712144

ON THE A55 If heading towards Chester on the A55, take the sliproad signposted for Pentre Halkyn and turn right at the T-junction. Billie Jeans Café is on the left-hand side of the re-entry sliproad, just before you go back onto the A5.

CREDIT/DEBIT CARDS

FUEL CARDS (see key on page 9)

TRUCK FACILITIES
P
Ample room for manoeuvring
Quiet area. Floodlighting
Truck dealership/workshop

DRIVER FACILITIES
Accommodation nearby, half a mile
Takeaway food

Bishops Meadow Filling Station, Brecon

FL1 ■

Hay Road, Brecon
Powys LD3 9WS
T 01874 614 927

ON THE B4602 Bishops Meadow can be found on the B4602, one mile north of Brecon and on the left-hand side if heading towards the A470.

CREDIT/DEBIT CARDS

FUEL CARDS (see key on page 9)
① ② ③ ④ ⑦ ⑧

DRIVER FACILITIES
Phone top-ups

Blaenavon Motor Company

FL1 ■

Cae White, Abergavenny Road
Blaenavon, Gwent NP4 9RG
T 01495 790235

ON THE B4246 From Abergavenny and Govilon take the B4246 towards Blaenavon. Blaenavon Motor Company is in the town and on your left just past the junction with the B4248.

CREDIT/DEBIT CARDS

FUEL CARDS (see key on page 9)
① ② ③ ④ ⑤

TRUCK FACILITIES
Quiet area
Ample room for manoeuvring
Truck dealership/workshop nearby

DRIVER FACILITIES
B&B accommodation nearby
Takeaway food nearby

SITE COMMENTS/INFORMATION
Welsh hospitality at its best! Extremely helpful and accommodating staff

T3 ■ Cardiff Gate Services

Cardiff Gate Business Park, Pontyclun, Cardiff, South Glamorgan CF23 8RA
T **029 20541122 www.** welcomebreak.co.uk

M4 JUNCTION 30

CREDIT/DEBIT CARDS

FUEL CARDS (see key on page 9)
28

TRUCK FACILITIES
P with voucher **P** only   Voucher value
£14.00   £12.00   £6.00
Coach overnight, shared with LGV
Floodlighting, CCTV, Plenty of room to manoeuvre
Quiet parking

DRIVER FACILITIES
Accommodation nearby, Ibis
Takeaway food, Showers, male (1), female (1), Accommodation nearby, Fax/copier, Internet nearby

All on-site facilities accessible 24 hours   **287**

T3 ■ Cardiff West Services

Moto Ltd
Pontyclun, Cardiff
South Glamorgan CF72 8SA
T **029 20891141** www.moto-way.com

M4 JUNCTION 33

CREDIT/DEBIT CARDS

FUEL CARDS (see key on page 9)
27

TRUCK FACILITIES
Quiet parking, Vegetarian/healthy meals
Arcade machines
Fax/copier, Phone top-ups

DRIVER FACILITIES
Accommodation, Travelodge
Takeaway food
Showers, male (2), female (2)

SITE COMMENTS/INFORMATION
Ask at restaurant for keys for showers.
Small refundable deposit required.

Restaurant facilities accessible 24 hours   **288**

FL1 ● CPL Petroleum, Bangor

CPL Petroleum Ltd, Llandygai Ind. Estate, Bangor, Gwynedd LL57 4YH
T **01248 352768**

OFF THE A5122 From the A55 take the A5122 towards Bangor. Go straight at the first and second roundabouts and left at the third one onto the Llandygai Industrial Estate. Follow the road to the right at the T-junction. Pumps are to the left.

CREDIT/DEBIT CARDS

FUEL CARDS (see key on page 9)
1 7 8

OTHER INFORMATION
A long hose is fitted to DERV pump for access across articulated vehicles

All on-site facilities 24 hours   **289**

CPL Petroleum, Wrexham — FL1 ●

CPL Petroleum Ltd, Bryn Lane
Wrexham Industrial Estate
Wrexham LL13 9UT
T 01978 661896

OFF THE A534 Take the A534 north eastbound out of Wrexham. At the village of Llan-y-Pwll turn right into Hugmore Lane for half a mile. At the roundabout turn left into Bryn Lane. CPL is 500 yards on the right.

CREDIT/DEBIT CARDS

FUEL CARDS (see key on page 9)
❶ ❼

TRUCK FACILITIES
Ample room for manoeuvring

DRIVER FACILITIES
Takeaway food nearby
Post Office
Euros changed/accepted

SITE COMMENTS/INFORMATION
Fuel can be paid for in cash during opening hours

Bunker fuel 24 hours. This site is manned 09:00-17:00 Mon-Fri when toilets/lubrication oil also available **290**

Enterprise Autos Ltd, Newport — FL1 ■

New Bridge By Pass, Crumlin, Newport
Gwent NP11 4QJ
T 01495 245713

ON THE A467 Exit the M4 at junction 28 and take the A4072 to the roundabout with the A468 and A467. Take the A467 for 15 miles. Pass Newbridge and Enterprise Autos is on the right just before Crumlin.

CREDIT/DEBIT CARDS

FUEL CARDS (see key on page 9)
❸ ㉓ ㉕ ㉗ ㉘

DRIVER FACILITIES
Phone top-ups

All on-site facilities 05:00-23:00 Mon-Sun **291**

Harry Tuffin Supermarket Ltd — FL4 ■

Church Stoke, Montgomery
Powys SY15 6AR
T 01588 620226 www.harrytuffin.co.uk

ON THE A489 From Newtown, take the A489 heading east towards Church Stoke. Harry Tuffins is on that road to the east of the village.

CREDIT/DEBIT CARDS

FUEL CARDS (see key on page 9)
❸ ❹

TRUCK FACILITIES
P free
Quiet area, Ample room for manoeuvring
Truck washing facilities, CCTV

DRIVER FACILITIES
Takeaway food, Vegetarian/healthy food
Post office, Laundry, Phone top-ups
Clothing

SITE COMMENTS/INFORMATION
Popular LGV site

Parking 24 hours. All other on-site facilities 07:00-20:00 **292**

FL4 ■ — Lalestone Service Station

Petrol Express Ltd, Lalestone
Bridgend, South Glamorgan CF32 0LY
T **01656 662910**

ON THE A48 NORTHBOUND From the M4, exit at junction 37 take the A4229 towards Pyle and North Cornelly. At the roundabout with the A48, turn right towards Lalestone. Continue for 3 miles, Lalestone Service Station is at the west end of the village on your left.

CREDIT/DEBIT CARDS

FUEL CARDS (see key on page 9)
① ③ ④ ⑦

TRUCK FACILITIES
P free
Coach parking available (4 spaces)
Overnight parking at rear of restaurant with permission

DRIVER FACILITIES
Accommodation half a mile away at Great House Hotel
Post Office and Phone top-ups nearby

SITE COMMENTS/INFORMATION
Easy access for LGVs

Parking 24 hours. Restaurant open evenings only. Other on-site facilities 06:00-09:00   **293**

T3 ■ — Magor Services

First Motorway Services Ltd
Magor, Caldicot
Monmouthshire NP26 3YL
T **01633 881887**

M4 JUNCTION 23A

CREDIT/DEBIT CARDS

FUEL CARDS (see key on page 9)
㉗

TRUCK FACILITIES
P with voucher **P** only   Voucher value
£15.00   £12.00   £7.00
Coach parking available (6 spaces), Ample room for manoeuvring, Quiet area, Floodlights, Truck dealership/workshop

DRIVER FACILITIES
Accommodation, Travelodge £55 pn
Showers, 1 m, 1 f, 1 unisex (free), washroom, rest area, TV, internet access, phone top-ups/accessories, truckers' accessories, Takeaway food, Vegetarian/healthy meals, Clothing, Arcade machines

Travelodge open 15:00-23:00 for check in. All other on-site facilities accessible 24 hours   **294**

FL4 ■ — Monmouth Services north-eastbound

Dingestow, Monmouth
Monmouthshire NP25 4BG
T **01600 740444**

ON THE A40 NORTH-EASTBOUND Monmouth Services is on the A40 Abergavenny to Monmouth road on the north-eastbound carriageway, just east of the A449 Raglan interchange.

CREDIT/DEBIT CARDS

FUEL CARDS (see key on page 9)
① ③ ⑦ ⑩ ⑭ ㉒ ㉘

TRUCK FACILITIES
P Coach parking available (10 spaces)
Fencing and floodlights
Quiet area
Ample room for manoeuvring

DRIVER FACILITIES
Travelodge on-site
Shower, drivers' washroom
Clothing for sale
Takeaway food
Truckers' accessories

Parking, showers and fuel 24 hours. Takeaway open 09:00-21:00. Travelodge 06:00-22:00   **295**

Morris Isaacs Garage, Llandovery — FL1 ■

**Queensway, Llandovery
Carmarthenshire SA20 0EG
T 01550 720176**

ON THE A40 Take the A40 from Llangadog to Llandovery, and Morris Isaacs Garage is in the town on the left-hand side, just before the junction with the A483.

CREDIT/DEBIT CARDS

FUEL CARDS (see key on page 9)

TRUCK FACILITIES
Overnight LGV parking nearby
Overnight coach parking nearby
CCTV nearby, Parking for fridge lorries nearby, LGV tyre repairs nearby

DRIVER FACILITIES
Accommodation nearby, 600 yards, Castle Hotel, Fax/copier, Phone top-ups, Post Office nearby, Clothing nearby, Truckers stuff nearby, Takeaway, Laundry, Train nearby

All on-site facilities 07:00-19:00. **296**

Nantycaws Filling Station, Carmarthen — FL1 ■

**Nantycaws, Carmarthen
Carmarthenshire SA32 8BE
T 01267 275955**

ON THE A48 Nantycaws Filling Station is to the east of Nantycaws village and about 5 miles east of Carmarthen on the A48. It is on your left-hand side if heading towards Cross Hands.

CREDIT/DEBIT CARDS

FUEL CARDS (see key on page 9)

TRUCK FACILITIES
Adblue in containers

DRIVER FACILITIES
Truckers' accessories
Phone top-ups
CB Sales/Accessories

SITE COMMENTS/INFORMATION
Friendly site with good access for trucks

Toilets and standpipe 24 hours. All on-site facilities 07:00-20:00 **297**

Parkwall Service Station, Wrexham — FL2 ■

**Mold Road, Gwersylt, Wrexham
Denbighshire LL11 4AH
T 01978 759020**

ON THE A541 Take the A541 from Wrexham towards Mold. Parkwall Service Station is at Gwersylt set back from the road on the left-hand side at the start of the dual carriageway. It is also about 600 yards on from the turning for the train station.

CREDIT/DEBIT CARDS

FUEL CARDS (see key on page 9)

TRUCK FACILITIES
NOT ACCESSIBLE FOR ARTICS
Overnight parking on road outside site
LGV sales/dealership/workshop

DRIVER FACILITIES
Take away, Phone accessories
Phone top-ups, Vegetarian meals
Healthy menu available

SITE COMMENTS/INFORMATION
Train nearby

Nearby parking 24 hours. All on-site facilities 06:30-22:00 **298**

T3 ▪ Pont Abraham Services, Roadchef

Roadchef Ltd
Llanedi, nr Pontardulais, Swansea
West Glamorgan SA4 0FU
T **01792 884663**

M4 JUNCTION 49 At the end of the M4 at the roundabout with the A48 and A483

CREDIT/DEBIT CARDS

FUEL CARDS (see key on page 9)
① ② ③ ④ ⑧ ⑭ ㉓

TRUCK FACILITIES
P *with voucher*   **P** *only*   *Voucher value*
£14.00   £17.00   £7.50
Coach parking shared with LGV
(6 spaces), Quiet area
Ample room for manoeuvring

DRIVER FACILITIES
Internet access, phone top-ups/accessories
Takeaway food
Clothing for sale

SITE COMMENTS/INFORMATION
Friendly staff and excellent service

All on-site facilities accessible 24 hours   **299**

FL2 ▪ Roundabout Service Station, Mold

Kings Street (Heol Y Brenin), Mold
Flintshire CH7 1LB
T **01352 757232**

ON THE A5119 From Wrexham take the A451 towards Mold. Continue through Mold on this road, past the roundabout with the A494 until the roundabout with the A5119. Roundabout Service Station will be right in front of you.

CREDIT/DEBIT CARDS

FUEL CARDS (see key on page 9)
① ② ③

TRUCK FACILITIES
Overnight parking opposite site

DRIVER FACILITIES
Accommodation available nearby,
600 Yards, Bryn Awel Hotel
Takeaway food nearby

OTHER INFORMATION
Tall LGVs should use pumps outside of canopy

All on-site facilities 24 hours   **300**

T3 ▪ Sarn Park Services

Welcome Break Ltd
Maestaeg, Nr Bridgend
South Glamorgan CF32 9RW
T **01656 768521** www.welcomebreak.co.uk

M4 JUNCTION 36 Follow the signs for Maestaeg & Services

CREDIT/DEBIT CARDS

FUEL CARDS (see key on page 9)
㉕

TRUCK FACILITIES
P *with voucher*   **P** *only*   *Voucher value*
£15.00   £13.00   £6.00
Coach overnight shared with LGV
Floodlights, Room for manoeuvre, Quiet parking, LGV tyre repair/ sales
DRIVER FACILITIES
Accommodation, Welcome Lodge
Takeaway food, Clothing for sale nearby
Showers, Washroom
SITE COMMENTS/INFORMATION
Drivers should provide proof of parking to access showers and washroom at hotel on-site

Forcourt and hotel open 24 hours. Other facilities opening times in main site may vary   **301**

Shell Service Station Llanrhyshyd | FL1 ■

Shell Service Station Llanrhyshyd & Welsh Cob Restaurant
Llanrhyshyd, Ceredigion SY23 5BT
T 01974 202903

ON THE A487 From Aberystwyth, take the A487 south for 10 miles. Shell Service Station Llanrhyshyd is on the south side of the village of Llanrhyshyd on the left-hand side.

 10ft 3in or 3.8m
 8 Shell
 Air

P 3 OVERNIGHT
 ♂♀
 £ NEARBY

 £1.95
 £1.00
 £4.00 B'FAST
PB

CREDIT/DEBIT CARDS

FUEL CARDS (see key on page 9)
② ③ ㉖ ㉗

TRUCK FACILITIES
NOT ACCESSIBLE FOR ARTICS

DRIVER FACILITIES
Takeaway food

OTHER INFORMATION
Drivers must ask permission to park overnight

All on-site facilities accessible 07:00-21:30 Mon-Sat, 08:00-21:30 Sun | **302**

Shell Swansea Bay | FL2 ■

Fabian Way, Neath
Carmarthenshire SA11 2JU
T 01792 326900

ON THE A483 From the M4, exit at junction 42 and take the A483 towards Swansea. Turn right around at the first roundabout and Shell Swansea will be on your left. To get back to Swansea, continue to and under the M4. Turn right around at the roundabout with the A48.

 2 Shell
 Air

P NEARBY
 ♂♀
 £

CREDIT/DEBIT CARDS

FUEL CARDS (see key on page 9)
③ ㉕

TRUCK FACILITIES
Overnight parking in lay-by half mile

SITE COMMENTS/INFORMATION
This is the only site on this road with LGV access. Staff are friendly, polite and willing to help in any situation. Staff and manager pride themselves on running a clean, well presented site

Toilets 05:00-23:00. All other on-site facilities 24 hours | **303**

Silvey Oils, Pontyclun | FL1 ●

Silvey Oils Ltd, Coed Cae Lane Ind. Estate
Talbot Green, Pontyclun, Mid Glamorgan
CF72 9EW T 0845 6644664

OFF THE A473 Exit M4 at junction 34 and take the A4119 towards Talbot Green for 2 miles. Turn left onto A473 for one mile, then then take 1st exit at roundabout, 2nd exit at next roundabout. After 500 yds turn left up concrete road by TNT. At T-junction at top turn right into site.

 3 Independent
 RED
 AUTO BUNKER

P SHORT-TERM

CREDIT/DEBIT CARDS

FUEL CARDS (see key on page 9)
① ② ④ ㉞

DRIVER FACILITIES
Train nearby

All on-site facilities 24 hours | **304**

FL2 ● Smithy Service Station

Carlton Fuels Ltd, Whitehurst, Chirk
Clwyd LL14 5AN
T **01691 778251**

OFF THE A5 From Llangollen take the A5 eastbound towards Newbridge. Continue to the junction with the B5605 signposted Newbridge. Turn left onto the B5605 for 10 yards. Smithy Service Station is immediately on your left.

CREDIT/DEBIT CARDS

FUEL CARDS (see key on page 9)

TRUCK FACILITIES
Coach parking available, shared with LGV
CCTV
Fridge lorry area
Ample room for manoeuvring
Truck dealership/workshop nearby
Tyre repair/sales

DRIVER FACILITIES
Takeaway food nearby

Bunker fuel and parking 24 hours. Lubrication oil, toilets and Red diesel 07:30-19:30 Mon-Sun **305**

T3 ■ Swansea Services, Moto Hospitality Ltd

Moto Ltd
Penllergaer, Swansea, SA4 9GT
T **01792 896222** www.moto-way.co.uk

M4 JUNCTION 47

CREDIT/DEBIT CARDS

FUEL CARDS (see key on page 9)

TRUCK FACILITIES
P with voucher   **P** only   Voucher value
£15.00   £13.00   £6.00
Coaches overnight, Room for manoeuvre, Fridge parking, Quiet parking
DRIVER FACILITIES
Accommodation, Travelodge
Takeaway food, Vegetarian/healthy meals, Showers, male (3), female (1), Washroom, Phone top-ups, Arcade machines, Clothing, Truckers accessories
SITE COMMENTS/INFORMATION
Dedicated commercial pumps under right hand side canopy

Forecourt, main facilities & Baristo Coffee Counter 24 hrs. Little Chef & WH Smith 07:00-22:00. BK 10:00-21:00 **306**

FL1 ■ Tenby Road Filling Station, Carmarthen

Llysonen Road, Carmarthen
Carmarthenshire SA33 5DT
T **01267 237854**

ON THE A40 Take the A40 out of Carmarthen towards St Clears. Tenby Road Filling Station is about 2 miles out of Carmarthen town centre on the right-hand side and about 1 mile past the village of Llanllwch.

CREDIT/DEBIT CARDS

FUEL CARDS (see key on page 9)

TRUCK FACILITIES
Short-term coach parking (2 spaces)

DRIVER FACILITIES
Truckers' accessories

SITE COMMENTS/INFORMATION
Easy access for LGVs

All on-site facilities 24 hours **307**

Tollgate Snack Bar   FD1 ■

Y Bwthyn, Glyndyfrwdy, nr Corwen
Denbighshire LL21 9HW
T 01490 430398

ON THE A5 If heading east towards Llangollen on the A5 from Betwys-Y-Coed continue through the villages of Corwen and Glyndyfrwdy. Tollgate Snack Bar is on the right hand side, half a mile east of the centre of the village of Glyndyfrwdy.

P
OVERNIGHT

£2.20   90p   HF-£3.00

TRUCK FACILITIES
P free. Quiet area,
Ample room for manoeuvring,
Parking only in on-site public lay-bys

DRIVER FACILITIES
Washroom
Takeaway food

SITE COMMENTS/INFORMATION
Site housed in a purpose built stone and slate building, with outstanding views of the Welsh mountains.

Parking accessible 24 hours. Other on-site facilities accessible 08:00-16:00 Mon-Sat. Sun 09:00-14:30   **308**

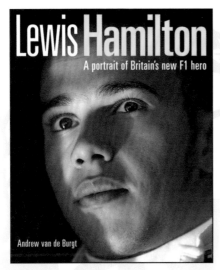

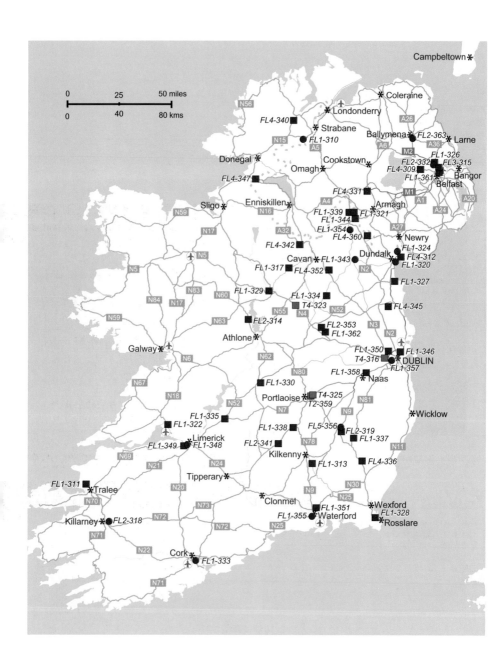

Ireland

■ Cafe - Layby parking (FD1)
■ Cafe - No overnight parking (FD2)
■ Filling Station - No overnight parking/cafe (FL1)
● Bunkering Site - No overnight parking/cafe (FL1)
■ Filling Station - Nearby overnight parking no cafe (FL2)
● Bunkering Site - Nearby overnight parking no cafe (FL2)
■ Filling Station - Cafe no onsite overnight parking (FL3)
■ Filling Station - Onsite overnight parking (FL4)
● Bunkering Site - Onsite overnight parking (FL4)
● Bunkering Site - Cafe & onsite overnight parking (FL5)
■ Lorry Park - Onsite overnight parking no cafe or fuel (T1)
■ Truck Stop/Cafe - Onsite overnight parking (T2)
■ Motorway Service Station (T3)
■ Truck Stop - Bunker fuel/showers/cafe/onsite overnight parking (T4)

For key to site symbols see page 8

FL4 — Airport Road Service Station

11 Tully Road, Nutts Corner, Crumlin County Antrim BT29 4SW, Northern Ireland
T 02890 825706

ON THE A26 Take the A52 westbound out of Belfast until the roundabout with the A26 and the B101. Turn right onto the A26 towards Antrim. Airport Road Service Station is 600 yards on the right.

CREDIT/DEBIT CARDS

FUEL CARDS (see key on page 9)
24 25

TRUCK FACILITIES
P
Coach parking available (4 spaces)
Overnight parking round back of site and in nearby lay-by
Adblue at pumps

DRIVER FACILITIES
Truckers' accessories

SITE COMMENTS/INFORMATION
Lots of space for LGVs, good facilities and helpful staff

Café, 08:00-17:00 Mon-Fri, 08:00-16:00 Sat. All other on-site facilities 07:00-22:00 Mon-Sat, 09:00-22:00 Sun
309

FL1 — Alt Border Trading Ltd

Alt Upper, Castlefin County Donegal, Ireland
T 00353 (0) 749146200

ON THE R235 From Castlefin take the R235 south towards Castlederg. Alt Border Trading is 4 miles on the left-hand side, just before the border.

CREDIT/DEBIT CARDS

FUEL CARDS (see key on page 9)
6 8 11 12 15 21

TRUCK FACILITIES
Short-term coach parking (3 spaces)
Truck dealership/workshop

All on-site facilities 07:30-22:30
310

Atlantic Oils Ltd, Tralee, County Kerry FL1

**Tralee Road, Ardfert, Tralee
County Kerry, Ireland
T 00353 (0) 667134 192/184/315**

ON THE R551 Take the R511 north-westbound out of
Tralee. Atlantic Oils is on that road in the middle of the town
of Ardfert, on the right-hand side.

CREDIT/DEBIT CARDS

FUEL CARDS (see key on page 9)
6 9 11 12

TRUCK FACILITIES
Truck washing facilities

DRIVER FACILITIES
Truckers' accessories

Bunker fuel and toilets 24 hours. Other on-site facilities 08:00-21:30 | **311**

Ballymac Service Station FL4

**Ballymascalan, Dundalk
County Louth, Ireland
T 00353 (0) 4293713311**

ON THE R173 Ballymac is about 2 miles north of Dundalk
centre, on the R173 and on the left-hand side if heading
away from the town. It is also about 800 yards on from the
roundabout with A1 and N52.

CREDIT/DEBIT CARDS

FUEL CARDS (see key on page 9)
5 8 9 11 12

TRUCK FACILITIES
Quiet area
Truck washing facilities

DRIVER FACILITIES
Takeaway food
Phone top-ups/accessories
Truckers' accessories

All on-site facilities 24 hours | **312**

Blackquarry Service Station, Kilkenny FL1

**Benettsbridge Road, Kilkenny
County Kilkenny, Ireland
T 00353 (0) 567761864**

ON THE R700 Take the R700 out of Kilkenny towards
Bennetsbridge. Blackquarry Service Station is on the right-
hand side just before you reach the N10 Kilkenny ring road.

CREDIT/DEBIT CARDS

FUEL CARDS (see key on page 9)
3 6 11 12 21

TRUCK FACILITIES
Truck washing facilities
Tyre repair/sales

DRIVER FACILITIES
Drivers' washroom
Takeaway food

All on-site facilities 08:00-22:00 | **313**

FL2 — Casey's Auto Centre Ltd, Rosscommon

**Athlone Road, Rosscommon
County Roscommon, Ireland
T 00353 (0) 906626101**

ON THE N61 Casey's Autocentre is on the roundabout junction of the N61 and N63 on the outskirts of the town of Roscommon.

CREDIT/DEBIT CARDS

FUEL CARDS (see key on page 9)
②⑥⑫㉗

TRUCK FACILITIES
Overnight parking available (6 spaces)
Coach parking available (4 spaces)
Truck dealership/workshop
Ample room for manoeuvring, CCTV

DRIVER FACILITIES
Drivers' washroom, rest area, quiet area
Accommodation available nearby, half mile, Royal Hotel & Abbey Hotel
Takeaway food
Phone top-ups/accessories
Truckers' accessories
Train nearby

Some facilities only 07:30-22:00. Fuel, parking, toilets, shop and other facilities 24 hours **314**

FL3 — Centra Quickstop

**Westbank Way, Duncrue Industrial Estate,
Liverpool Ferry Docks, Belfast, Co Antrim,
BT3 9LB, Northern Ireland
T 0289 0775863**

OFF THE M2 Exit M2 at junction 1. Turn right at roundabout onto the Dargan Road, continue for ½ mile then turn left at 2nd lights onto Westbank road. Site is ¼ on left hand side.

CREDIT/DEBIT CARDS

FUEL CARDS (see key on page 9)
③⑥⑫⑱

TRUCK FACILITIES
Manoeuvring room, LGV tyre repairs/sales

DRIVER FACILITIES
Phone top-ups

SITE COMMENTS
Great convenience store with hot food and instore bakery. Large stock of papers, groceries and general provisions.

Fuel bunkering accessible 24 hour. Food court 06:00-18:00 Mon-Fri, 06:00-13:00 Sat **315**

T4 ■ — Clondalkin Truck & Trailer Park

**Cloverhill Road
Clondalkin Commercial Park, Clondalkin
Dublin 22, County Dublin, Ireland
T '00353 (0) 14572161**

OFF THE R113 M50 junction 9, take N7 to junction with the R113, turn right onto Fonthill Road South. Right at next two roundabouts staying on the R113 New Nangor Road, then take next left, 2nd right and Clondalkin Park is 4th turning on left.

CREDIT/DEBIT CARDS

FUEL CARDS (see key on page 9)
⑥⑨⑫㉑

TRUCK FACILITIES
P
Coach parking (15 spaces)
Fridge lorry area
Ample room for manoeuvring
Truck dealership/workshop

DRIVER FACILITIES
Showers – 1 m, 1 f, washroom, TV
Takeaway, internet access and clothing for sale nearby, Train nearby

All on-site facilities accessible 24 Hours **316**

Corrigans Service Station, Moyne   FL1

Legga, Moyne, County Longford, Ireland
T 00353 (0) 494335333

ON THE R198 From Longford take the R198 to Arvagh. Corrigans is on that road in the village of Legga on the left-hand side.

CREDIT/DEBIT CARDS

FUEL CARDS (see key on page 9)
9 11 21

TRUCK FACILITIES
Short-term coach parking (1 space)
Truck washing facilities

All on-site facilities 08:30-22:00. Short time parking times unknown   **317**

Deros Coaches   FL2

Emo Oil Ltd, Killarney Bypass
Woodlands Industrial Estate
Killarney, County Kerry, Ireland
T 00353 (0) 876502111

OFF THE N22 Head north-west along the N22 towards Killarney from Cork. At the roundabout with the R876, continue ahead on the N22 Killarney Bypass. Take the next right and Deros is straight ahead at the bottom.

FUEL CARDS (see key on page 9)
6 9 11 12 21

TRUCK FACILITIES
Coach parking available (20 spaces, free)
Truck washing facilities
Truck dealership/workshop
Ample room for manoeuvring
Adblue at pump

DRIVER FACILITIES
Accommodation nearby, 500 yards,
Quality Hotel & Killarney Heights Hotels

SITE COMMENTS
Near to shopping centre and town centre facilities

All on-site facilities 24 hours   **318**

Devoys Gala, Carlow   FL2

Tullow Road, Carlow
County Carlow, Ireland
T 00353 (0) 599140400/599140705

ON THE N80 If heading from Carlow town centre to Tullow on the N80, Devoys can be found about 1 mile out of the town on the left-hand side before the R725 joins the N80.

CREDIT/DEBIT CARDS

FUEL CARDS (see key on page 9)
1 2 3 6 9 11 12 19 21

TRUCK FACILITIES
Overnight LGV parking at nearby church and shopping centre
Short-term coach and LGV parking available on-site (2 spaces)
Truck washing facilities nearby
Tyre repair/sales nearby

DRIVER FACILITIES
Takeaway food nearby
Phone top-ups, Laundry, Fax/copier, and Post Office nearby, Train nearby

SITE COMMENTS/INFORMATION
1 mile from town centre

Nearby parking PM hours only. Bunkering 24 hours, all other on-site facilities 07:30-22:00 Mon-Sun   **319**

FL1 — Dundalk Truckstop

**Emo Oil Ltd, Coes Road Industrial Estate
Dundalk, County Louth, Ireland
T 00353 (0) 429338977/429333833/429334815**

OFF THE N52 From the M1 take the N52 around the east side of Dundalk. Continue past the roundabout with the R172 for half a mile. Turn left onto the Coes Road Ind. Est. and Dundalk Truckstop is a few yards on the left.

CREDIT/DEBIT CARDS

FUEL CARDS (see key on page 9)
⑥⑧⑨⑪⑫⑰⑱㉑

All on-site facilities 24 hours

320

FL1 — Dunmoran Service Station, Emyvale

**Mullinderg, Emyvale
County Monaghan
T 00353 (0) 4786108**

ON THE N2 Take the N2 northbound from Monaghan towards Aughnacloy. Dunmoran Service Station is in the village of Emyvale, just past the river and on the right-hand side.

CREDIT/DEBIT CARDS

FUEL CARDS (see key on page 9)
②⑤⑫

SITE COMMENTS/INFORMATION
Good quality low priced food
Breakfasts include free tea and toast
Takeaway breakfasts available

Bunker fuel 24 hours. Other on-site facilities 07:30-23:00 Mon-Sat, 08:30-23:00 Sun

321

FL1 — Emerald Service Station, County Clare

**Ennis Road, Newmarket on Fergus
County Clare, Ireland
T 00353 (0) 61368449/862447150**

ON THE R458 From the N18 take the R458 into Newmarket on Fergus. Emerald Service Station is at the north end of the town on the left-hand side if heading north.

CREDIT/DEBIT CARDS

FUEL CARDS (see key on page 9)
⑫㉑

TRUCK FACILITIES
Truck washing facilities

DRIVER FACILITIES
Truckers' accessories

SITE COMMENTS/INFORMATION
Friendly, efficient service

All on-site facilities 07:00-21:00

322

Feericks Hotel   T4 ■

Rathowen, Nr Mullingar, County Westmeath, Ireland
T 00353 (0) 4376025 00353 (0) 4376960
www.feericks.ie

ON THE N4 This site is at Rathowen on the main N4 road between Mulingar & Longford.

CREDIT/DEBIT CARDS

FUEL CARDS (see key on page 9)
① to **㉝**

TRUCK FACILITIES
P Free, Coaches overnight, shared with LGV, Floodlights, CCTV, Room to manoeuvre, Quiet parking

DRIVER FACILITIES
Showers, unisex (2), Washroom, Accommodation €40-90, Rest area, Vegetarian/Healthy meals, Takeaway, TV, Laundry, Internet, Fax/copier, Post Office,

SITE COMMENTS
Famous for good food and steakhouse

323

Four Counties Oil, Dundalk   FL1

Four Counties Oil Ltd, Newry Road
Dundalk, County Louth, Ireland
T 00353 (0) 429332299/862523170

ON THE N1 Head north on the M1 to the end and the junction with the N52. Turn right, then left onto the N1. Follow this through Dundalk centre heading for Newry. Four Counties is 500 yards past the river and on the right.

CREDIT/DEBIT CARDS

FUEL CARDS (see key on page 9)
①②③⑥⑨⑪⑫⑭⑮⑱⑲

TRUCK FACILITIES
Truck washing facilities

DRIVER FACILITIES
Truckers' accessories

SITE COMMENTS/INFORMATION
Loyalty cards available with redeemable points system for every litre of fuel that can be used to purchase items in the shop

All on-site facilities opening times unknown   **324**

The Gandon Inn   T4 ■

Emo, Portlaoise
County Laois, Ireland
T 00353 (0) 578626622/578626686

ON THE N7 From the M7 take exit 15 signposted Mountmellick and Portarlington. The Gandon Inn is in a few yards on your left.

CREDIT/DEBIT CARDS

FUEL CARDS (see key on page 9)
②⑫㉞

TRUCK FACILITIES
P free
Coach parking available (2 spaces)
Ample room for manoeuvring
Quiet area

DRIVER FACILITIES
Accommodation €50.00 B&B
Shower, rest area, TV, internet access
Phone top-ups/accessories
Takeaway food. CB repairs/sales nearby

SITE COMMENTS/INFORMATION
This site is very close to the motorway with good access for LGVs

Parking and DCI bunker fuel accessible 24 hours. Other on-site facilities accessible 07:00-23:00   **325**

FL1 Glen Service Station, Glengormley

**88 Ballyclare Road, Glengormley
County Antrim BT36 8HH
T 02890 842576**

ON THE B56 From the M2 A8M intersection take the A6 towards Newtownabbey for 1 mile. At the B56 turn left for 500 yards. Glen Service Station is on the left near the Northcott Shopping Centre.

CREDIT/DEBIT CARDS

FUEL CARDS (see key on page 9)

SITE COMMENTS/INFORMATION
This site is next to the Northcott Shopping Centre and within a few metres of a park and ride bus service

All on-site facilities 07:00-23:00. **326**

FL1 Green Mount Filling Station, Castlebellingham

**Four Counties Oil Ltd, Greenmount, Castlebellingham, County Louth, Ireland
T 00353 (0) 429382429**

ON THE N1 If heading north on the M1, take the R170 and N1 exit and head north on N1 to Castlebellingham for 2 miles and it's on the right. If heading south, take the R116 exit and head into Castlebellingham. Turn right at the N1 for 2 miles and it's on the left.

CREDIT/DEBIT CARDS

FUEL CARDS (see key on page 9)

TRUCK FACILITIES
Truck washing facilities

DRIVER FACILITIES
Internet access
Truckers' accessories

SITE COMMENTS/INFORMATION
Good access for LGVs

Parking and fuel bunker times unknown. All other on-site facilities 07:00-21:00 **327**

FL1 Kielys Centra, Killinick Service Station

**Rosslare Road, Nr Rosslare Harbour, Killinick, County Wexford, Ireland
T 00353 (0) 539158862**

ON THE N25 From Rosslare harbour take the N25 towards Wexford. Killinick Service Station is at Killinick on the left-hand side, 1 mile after the turning for the R740 Rosslare road.

CREDIT/DEBIT CARDS

FUEL CARDS (see key on page 9)

TRUCK FACILITIES
CCTV

DRIVER FACILITIES
Accommodation nearby, half a mile, Danby Lodge Hotel
Post Office, Phone top-ups
Takeaway nearby

SITE COMMENTS/INFORMATION
This site is close to the port

All on-site facilities 07:00-22:00. Short term parking times unknown **328**

Longford Motors, Longford FL1

Strokestown Road, Longford
County Longford, Ireland
T 00353 (0) 4346055

ON THE N5 Take the N5 eastbound out of Longford. Longfold Motors is on the left-hand side, 500 yards beyond the junction with the R198.

CREDIT/DEBIT CARDS

FUEL CARDS (see key on page 9)

DRIVER FACILITIES
Accommodation nearby, 600 yards, Longford Arms Hotel

SITE COMMENTS/INFORMATION
Easy access for LGVs
Huge forecourt

All on-site facilities 08:00-22:00.   **329**

Loughnanes Service Station, Birr FL1

Tullamore Road, Birr
County Offaly, Ireland
T 00353 (0) 5791 20066

ON THE N52 Take the N52 out of Birr towards Tullamore. Loughnanes Service Station is just outside of the village on the right-hand side.

CREDIT/DEBIT CARDS

FUEL CARDS (see key on page 9)

TRUCK FACILITIES
Truck dealership nearby

DRIVER FACILITIES
Truckers' accessories

All on-site facilities 07:00-22:30.   **330**

M1 Service Area FL4

Drumgormal, Dungannon
County Tyrone BT71 7PG, Northern Ireland
T 02887 724541

ON THE A4 From Belfast, head west to Dungannon along M1. At Dungannon junction (junction 15) on motorway continue straight for 1 and a half miles to Enniskillen along the A4. M1 Service Area is on your left hand side before Granville.

CREDIT/DEBIT CARDS

FUEL CARDS (see key on page 9)

TRUCK FACILITIES
P free
Coach parking available (4 spaces)
Quiet area, Ample room for manoeuvring

DRIVER FACILITIES
Showers, 1 male, 1 female (free)
Takeaway food, Vegetarian/healthy food
Phone top-ups/accessories
Truckers' accessories

SITE COMMENTS/INFORMATION
LGV diesel pump at back of shop

Parking 24 hrs. Fuel/shop Mon-Sat 06:30-22:00. Sun 07:30-22:00. Subway access 08:00-18:00 Mon-Sat   **331**

FL2 — Maxol Direct

**Maxol Ltd, 48 Trench Road, Mallusk
Newtownabbey, County Antrim BT36 4TY
Northern Ireland
T 02890 848586**

OFF THE M2 JUNCTION 4 M2 junction 4, take A6 towards Templepatrick/Antrim for 1 mile. Take 3rd turning on left to Park Road. At the end turn left onto Mallusk Road, then next left and left again to Trench Road. Maxol is 200 yards on the left.

CREDIT/DEBIT CARDS

FUEL CARDS (see key on page 9) 6 17

TRUCK FACILITIES
Coach parking available, shared with LGV
P free
Ample room for manoeuvring

DRIVER FACILITIES
Accommodation nearby, half mile, Chimney Corner Hotel
Takeaway food nearby
Euros changed/accepted

SITE COMMENTS/INFORMATION
Parking on nearby industrial estate car park permitted from 18:00-07:00 only

All on-site facilities 24 hours. This site is manned between 09:00-17:00 Mon-Fri **332**

FL1 — McDonalds Oil Ltd

**Top Oil Ltd, Kinsale Road
Kinsale Road Industrial Estate
Cork, County Cork, Ireland
T 00353 (0) 214316300 www.top.ie**

OFF THE N27 From the N25 that runs east to west along the south of Cork, head for the roundabout junction with the N27. At that roundabout turn northbound into Kinsale Road Industrial Estate. McDonalds Oil is 300 yards on the left-hand side.

CREDIT/DEBIT CARDS

FUEL CARDS (see key on page 9) 1 2 4 6 8 9 11 12 19 21

TRUCK FACILITIES
Truck dealership/workshop

DRIVER FACILITIES
Accommodation nearby, half mile, Travelodge

All on-site facilities 24 hours **333**

FL1 — Millbrook Service Station, Oldcastle

**Oldcastle, County Meath, Ireland
T 00353 (0) 498541300**

ON THE R195 Take the R195 south-westbound from Virginia to Castlepollard. Millbrook Service Station is on that road, 1 mile past the junction with the R154.

CREDIT/DEBIT CARDS

FUEL CARDS (see key on page 9) 6 9 11 21

TRUCK FACILITIES
Short-term coach parking
Truck washing facilities

DRIVER FACILITIES
Truckers' accessories

All on-site facilities 08:00-22:00. Short term parking times unknown **334**

Mulrooney's Service Station, Nenagh — FL1

Ballywilliam, Nenagh, County Tipperary Ireland
T 00353 (0) 6742881

ON THE N7 From Nenagh take the N7 towards Limerick. Mulrooney's is on the right-hand side about 3 miles from Nenagh town centre.

CREDIT/DEBIT CARDS

FUEL CARDS (see key on page 9)
6 9 11 12

DRIVER FACILITIES
Truckers' accessories

Bunker fuel 24 hours. Other on-site facilities 07:00-21:00

335

Nolans Service Station — FL4

Ryland Road, Bunclody
County Wexford, Ireland
T 00353 (0) 539376231

ON THE N80 Gavin Row is on the N80 at the south side of the village of Bunclody. It is on your right if heading south-east.

CREDIT/DEBIT CARDS

FUEL CARDS (see key on page 9)
6 8 9 11 21

TRUCK FACILITIES
P
Coach parking available (8 spaces)
Quiet area
Ample room for manoeuvring
Truck washing facilities

DRIVER FACILITIES
Drivers' washroom
Truckers' accessories
Takeaway food, clothing, CB repairs/sales and phone top-ups/accessories nearby

SITE COMMENTS/INFORMATION
Lots of space for parking on-site

All on-site facilities 24 hours

336

Nolan's Service Station, Nolans Tyres — FL4

Main Street, Ballon
County Carlow, Ireland
T 00353 (0) 599159219/599159020

ON THE N80 Nolans Service Station is at Ballon on the N80. 8 miles from Carlow and on the right-hand side if heading for Bunclody.

CREDIT/DEBIT CARDS

FUEL CARDS (see key on page 9)
3 12

TRUCK FACILITIES
Ample room for manoeuvring
Truck washing facilities
Tyre repair/sales

DRIVER FACILITIES
Takeaway food

Short term parking times unknown. All other on-site facilities 06:30-22:00

337

FL1 · Oliver Stanley Motors Ltd, Durrow

**Cork Road, Durrow
County Laois, Ireland
T 00353 (0) 578736404**

ON THE N8 Oliver Stanley Motors is on the N8 in the village of Durrow on the left-hand side if heading towards Urlingford. It is situated at the south-west end of the village.

CREDIT/DEBIT CARDS

FUEL CARDS (see key on page 9)
① ② ③ ⑥ ⑧ ⑨ ⑪ ⑫ ⑭ ⑳

DRIVER FACILITIES
Post Office nearby
Phone top-ups nearby

SITE COMMENTS/INFORMATION
Cashback facility available for Laser Card holders

All on-site facilities 08:00-21:00 Mon-Fri, 08:00-20:00 Sat, 09:30-20:00 Sun Bunker fuel accessible 24 hours **338**

FL1 · Paddy Mcquaid's, Emyvale

**Knockafubble, Glaslough, Emyvale,
County Monaghan, Ireland
T 00353 (0) 4788108**

BETWEEN THE N2 AND R185 Take the N2 northbound from Monaghan to Emyvale. At Emyvale turn right towards Glaslough. Paddy Mcquaids is 2 miles along on the left-hand side.

CREDIT/DEBIT CARDS

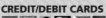

FUEL CARDS (see key on page 9)
② ⑥ ⑨ ⑫

DRIVER FACILITIES
Fax/copier
Phone top-ups

Bunker fuel 24 hours. Other on-site facilities 08:30-21:30 **339**

FL4 · Parkside Service Station

**Trentaboy, Drumkeen, Ballybofey
County Donegal, Ireland
T 00353 (0) 749134149**

ON THE N13 Take the N14 from Letterkenny towards Lifford for 1 mile, then turn right and follow the N13 southbound towards Ballybofey for 3 miles. Parkside Services is on the left-hand side.

CREDIT/DEBIT CARDS

FUEL CARDS (see key on page 9)
⑨ ㉑

TRUCK FACILITIES
P free
Coach parking available (12 spaces)
Truck dealership/workshop

DRIVER FACILITIES
Takeaway food

SITE COMMENTS/INFORMATION
Friendly service and value for money

Parking 24 hours. All on-site facilities 07:00-22:00 Mon-Thurs, 07:00-23:00 Fri, 08:00-22:00 Sat & Sun **340**

Pierce Kavanagh Properties Ltd, Urlingford — FL2

Church View, Urlingford
County Kilkenny, Ireland
T 00353 (0) 568831213/568831234
www.kavanahcoaches.com

ON THE N8 If heading north-eastbound on the N8, Pierce Kavanagh Properties is in Urlingford on the left-hand side, 200 yards before the junction with the R693.

CREDIT/DEBIT CARDS

FUEL CARDS (see key on page 9)
5 12

TRUCK FACILITIES
Short-term coach parking available (10 spaces), shared with LGV
Nearby overnight parking

DRIVER FACILITIES
Truckers' accessories
Vegetarian meals
Healthy menu available
Takeaway
Phone top-ups

Toilets 24 hours. All other on-site facilities 06:00-23:00 — **341**

Rakeelan Service Station — FL4

Emo Oil Ltd, Derrylin Road, Rakeelan
Ballyconnell, County Cavan, Ireland
T 00353 (0) 499526614

ON THE R205 Take the road that runs from Ballyconnell to the A509. Rakeelan Service Station is at Rakeelan on the right-hand side just before the border.

CREDIT/DEBIT CARDS

FUEL CARDS (see key on page 9)
8 20

TRUCK FACILITIES
Coach parking available (5 spaces)
Overnight parking at rear of filling station
Truck washing facilities
Truck dealership/workshop nearby

DRIVER FACILITIES
Shower
Truckers' accessories

Bunker fuel 24 hours. Other on-site facilities 07:00-22:00. Overnight parking times unknown — **342**

Roe Oils Ltd, Shercock — FL1

Roe Oils Ltd, Lisdrumskeagh
Near Carrickmacross, Shercock
County Cavan, Ireland
T 00353 (0) 429669229

ON THE R178 From Bailieborough take the R178 towards Shercock. Once in the main street take left at T junction, first right and continue for 100 yards, turn right again for 200 yards. Right again and Roe Oils is on the right.

CREDIT/DEBIT CARDS

FUEL CARDS (see key on page 9)
2 4 6 12

TRUCK FACILITIES
Adblue at the pumps

SITE COMMENTS/INFORMATION
Credit/Debit cards accepted during office hours. Toilets and Adblue only accessible during opening hours

All on-site facilities 24 hours. Oil accessible 08:00-17:00 Mon-Fri 08:00-12.30 Sat — **343**

FL1 Silverstream Service Station Ltd, Silverstream

Tamlet, Silverstream
County Monaghan, Ireland
T 00353 (0) 4785550

ON THE R213 From Casleblaney take the N2 north through Clontibret, past the junction with the R214 and turn right onto the R213. Continue for 3 miles, Silverstream is on the right, 200 yards from the border.

CREDIT/DEBIT CARDS

FUEL CARDS (see key on page 9)
6 9 11 12 15 19 21

TRUCK FACILITIES
Short-term coach parking (3 spaces)

DRIVER FACILITIES
Truckers' accessories

All on-site facilities 24 hours   **344**

FL4 Smyths Service Station

Emo Oil Ltd, Derry Road, Slane
County Meath, Ireland
T 00353 (0) 419824555

ON THE N2 Take the N2 northbound out of Slane and head for Collon. Smyths Service Station is 600 yards on the right.

CREDIT/DEBIT CARDS

FUEL CARDS (see key on page 9)
6 9 11 21

TRUCK FACILITIES
P
Coach parking available, shared with LGV
Overnight parking in car park
Truck washing facilities

DRIVER FACILITIES
Truckers' accessories

SITE COMMENTS/INFORMATION
Good service
Easy access for LGVs

Bunker fuel 24 hours. Other on-site facilities 06:00-22:00   **345**

FL1 Stat Oil Omni Park, Dublin

Stat Oil Ltd, off Swords Road
Omni Park Shopping Centre, Santry
County Dublin 9, Dublin, Ireland
T 00353 (0) 18621329/18869500

OFF THE R132 M1 towards Dublin and exit junction for R104 towards Santry. Continue for 300 yards to junction with R132. Turn left onto it for 600 yards. Turn right towards Omni Park Shopping Centre and Stat Oil is 50 yards on your right.

CREDIT/DEBIT CARDS

FUEL CARDS (see key on page 9)
3 4 6 12 14 15 23

TRUCK FACILITIES
NOT ACCESSIBLE FOR ARTICS

SITE COMMENTS/INFORMATION
Clean site with good food. Friendly, helpful staff

All on-site facilities 07:00-00:00.   **346**

Straddle Service Station FL2

**Cloghore, Ballyshannon
County Donegal, Ireland
T 00353 (0) 719852555**

ON THE N15 From Ballyshannon, Head for Enniskillen on N3. Station on left about 5 miles out. Take A46 for Donegal. Upon entering Belleeks' 40mph limit the station is about 300 yards up on the right hand side.

CREDIT/DEBIT CARDS

① ② ③ ④ ⑥ ⑨ ⑪ ⑫ ⑭ ⑮ ⑰ ⑱ ⑲ ⑳ ㉒ ㉓ ㉔ ㉕

FUEL CARDS (see key on page 9)

TRUCK FACILITIES
Truck dealership/workshop nearby
Overnight coach parking shared with LGV, Floodlighting, CCTV, Plenty of room to manoeuvre, Fridge, quiet parking, Adblue in containers

DRIVER FACILITIES
Internet access, Bureau de change
Truckers' accessories, Fax/copier, Phone acccessories, Phone top-ups
Accommodation Carlton Hotel
Hoohans, Fiddlestone, nearby

Fuel bunker 24 hours. All other on-site facilities 07:00-23:00. Nearby overnight parking **347**

Suttons Oil, Limerick FL1

**Suttons Oil Ltd, Courtbrack Avenue
off Dock Road, Limerick,County Limerick,
Ireland T 00353 (0) 61227333**

OFF THE N69 From Cork, take the N20 then the R526 towards Limerick. At the Raheen Business Park roundabout, turn left onto N18, then N69 towards Limerick. After 1 and a half miles turn right into Courtbrack Ave after Motorzone dealership. Suttons is 150 yards on left

CREDIT/DEBIT CARDS

FUEL CARDS (see key on page 9)

⑦ ㉑

TRUCK FACILITIES
Truck dealership/workshop
Adblue in containers
LGV tyre repairs/sales nearby

DRIVER FACILITIES
Takeaway, Evening entertainment, Post Office, Phone top-ups and Truckers accessories nearby, Truckers' accessories

SITE COMMENTS/INFORMATION
LGVs permitted access to site in spite of Courtbrack Avenue weight limit.

All on-site facilities 08:00-12:30, 14:00-16:30 **348**

Tara Service Station, Limerick FL1

**Dock Road, Limerick
County Limerick, Ireland
T 00353 (0) 61301818/61302102**

ON THE N69 From the N20 if heading north east, exit at St Patrickswell and follow the R526 towards Limerick. At Raheen Business Park roundabout turn left onto N18. Keep heading for Limerick Town centre and the Tara Service Station is 1 mile along on the left.

CREDIT/DEBIT CARDS

FUEL CARDS (see key on page 9)
② ④ ⑤ ⑥ ⑧ ⑨ ⑪ ⑫ ⑮ ⑳ ㉑ ㉞

All cards using auto bunker must be on the UK Fuels network

TRUCK FACILITIES
Additonal parking nearby
Short term coach parking

DRIVER FACILITIES
Truckers' accessories

Bunker fuel 24 hours. Other on-site facilities 7:00-23:00 Mon-Fri, 07:00-22:00 Sat, 09:00-22:00 Sun **349**

FL1   Texaco Service Station, Blanchardstown

Blanchardstown Corporate Park
Blanchardstown, County Dublin 15, Dublin
Ireland T 00353 (0) 18606520

OFF THE R121 Exit the M50 at junction 6 and take the N3 towards Dunshaughlin. Take the slip for the R121and turn right for Blanchardstown Industrial Park. Continue through Industrial Park to roundabout with Ballycoolin Road. Texaco Blanchardstown is on that roundabout.

CREDIT/DEBIT CARDS

FUEL CARDS (see key on page 9)
3 **12**

TRUCK FACILITIES
Truck washing facilities

DRIVER FACILITIES
Hot deli food available all day

SITE COMMENTS/INFORMATION
Great service, friendly staff

All on-site facilities 06:30-22:00   **350**

FL1   Texaco Service Station, Newrath

Dublin Road, Newrath, Waterford
County Waterford, Ireland
T 00353 (0) 51844509

ON THE N9 Take the N9 out of Waterford towards Carlow. Texaco Service Station Waterford is on the left-hand side, 400 yards before the junction with the N24.

CREDIT/DEBIT CARDS

FUEL CARDS (see key on page 9)
6 **9** **11** **12** **15**

TRUCK FACILITIES
Short-term coach parking (6 spaces)

Bunker fuel 24 hours. Other on-site facilities 07:00-21:00. Short-term parking times unknown   **351**

FL4   Texaco Spar Service Station, Cavan

Dublin Road, Cavan
County Cavan, Ireland
T 00353 (0) 494332515

ON THE N3 Take the N3 southbound around the east side of Cavan until you reach the roundabout with the N55. Turn right, continuing on the N3 for 200 yards and Texaco Spar is on the right.

CREDIT/DEBIT CARDS

FUEL CARDS (see key on page 9)
2 **3** **6** **11** **12** **22** **23**

TRUCK FACILITIES
Coach parking available
Ample room for manoeuvring
Truck washing facilities

DRIVER FACILITIES
Drivers' washroom, phone top-ups
Accommodation half a mile away at Hotel Kilmore
Takeaway food and truckers' accessories
Post Office

SITE COMMENTS/INFORMATION
Award winning deli. counter food

All on-site facilities 05:30-00:30. Short term on-site and nearby overnight parking times unknown   **352**

Thomas Flynn & Sons Ltd — FL2

**The Downs, Mullingar
County Westmeath, Ireland
T 00353 (0) 449374148**

ON THE N4 Take the N4 out of Mullingar towards Dublin. Thomas Flynn & Sons is on the dual carriageway on the left-hand side, 1 mile after the turning for the R156 to Killucan.

CREDIT/DEBIT CARDS

FUEL CARDS (see key on page 9)
6 9 11 12 21

TRUCK FACILITIES
Short-term coach parking (7 spaces)
Nearby overnight LGV parking

DRIVER FACILITIES
Internet access
Truckers' accessories

SITE COMMENTS/INFORMATION
Low cost fuel. Excellent location

All on-site facilities 08:30-18:00. Short-term on-site and nearby overnight parking times unknown — **353**

T Martin Fuels — FL1

**Ballybay Road, Killyvane, Monaghan
County Monaghan, Ireland
T 00353 (0) 4782279**

ON THE R162 Take the R162 out of Monaghan towards Ballybay. T Martin Fuels is on the right-hand side, half a mile beyond the turning for the R188 to Rockcorry.

CREDIT/DEBIT CARDS

FUEL CARDS (see key on page 9)
12

TRUCK FACILITIES
Short-term coach parking (10 spaces)
Truck dealership/workshop

SITE COMMENTS/INFORMATION
Easy access for LGVs

Short-term parking times unknown. All other on-site facilities 07:30-19:30 — **354**

Top Oil, Waterford — FL1

**Top Oil Ltd, Butlers Town, Holy Cross
Cork Road, Waterford
County Waterford, Ireland
T 00353 (0) 51871555**

ON THE N25 Take the N25 out of Waterford towards Cork. Top Oil is on that road on the left, 800 yards past Waterford Industrial Estate and 300 yards before the Gaa Football Club.

CREDIT/DEBIT CARDS

FUEL CARDS (see key on page 9)
6 9 11 12 21

TRUCK FACILITIES
Ample room for manoeuvring

SITE COMMENTS/INFORMATION
Air only available during opening hours

Bunker fuel 24 hours. Other on-site facilities 09:00-21:00 Mon-Fri. 09:00-17:00 Sat & Sun — **355**

FL1 — Tougher Oil, Carlow

**Tougher Oil Ltd, Dublin Road, Carlow
County Carlow, Ireland
T 00353 (0) 599143443**

OFF THE N9 From the M9 take the N9 towards Carlow. Remain on the N9 beyond the roundabout with the N80 on the outskirts of Carlow. At the next roundabout take the N9 again then take the next immediate right onto Dublin Road. Tougher Oil is 400 yards on the right.

CREDIT/DEBIT CARDS

FUEL CARDS (see key on page 9)
5 6 12

TRUCK FACILITIES
Overnight parking with permission only
Coach parking available, shared with LGV
P free
Floodlighting
Fridge lorry area
Ample room for manoeuvring

DRIVER FACILITIES
Accommodation nearby, half a mile, Seven Oaks Hotel

Bunker fuel and parking 24 hours. Toilets 08:00-18:00. Restaurant from 07:00-22:00 **356**

FL1 — Tougher Oil, Dublin

**Tougher Oil Ltd, J F K Drive
J F K Industrial Estate,
Bluebell, Dublin 12, County Dublin, Ireland
T 00353 (0)14569977**

OFF THE R110 From the M50, exit at junction 9 and take the R110 towards Dublin. Continue past junction with Long Mile Road and Killeen Road. Take next left and left again into J F K Drive. Follow round to the right and Tougher Oil is on the right.

CREDIT/DEBIT CARDS

FUEL CARDS (see key on page 9)
5 12

All on-site facilities 24 hours **357**

FL1 — Tougher Oil, Naas

**Tougher Oil Ltd, Newhall, Naas
County Kildare, Ireland
T 00353 (0) 45433143**

ON THE R445 From the M7, exit at junction 8 and take the R445 towards Newbridge for 1 and a half miles. Tougher Oil is on the left-hand side.

CREDIT/DEBIT CARDS

FUEL CARDS (see key on page 9)
5 6 8 11 12 21

DRIVER FACILITIES
Truckers' accessories

All on-site facilities 24 hours **358**

Treacy's
T2 ■

The Heath, Portlaoise
County Laois, Ireland
T 00353 (0) 578646539
www.gandoninn.com

OFF THE N7 From Cork or Limerick take exit 16 off the M7.
From Dublin take exit 15 off the M7

CREDIT/DEBIT CARDS

TRUCK FACILITIES
P free to customers
Coach parking (2 spaces) shared with
LGV. Quiet area
Ample room for manoeuvring, Nearby
fuel facilities at the Gandon Inn

DRIVER FACILITIES
Showers, TV
CB sales/repairs nearby,
Vegetarian/Healthy meals, Fax/copier

SITE COMMENTS/INFORMATION
Well known and much loved truckstop in
beautiful old thatched roof building. Has
been serving food to truckers for over
20 years!

Mon-Sat 07:00-22:00. Sun 12:00-21:00
359

Tullynagrow Fuelserve
FL4

Stat Oil Service Station, Tullynagrow
Creighanroe, Castleblayney to Keady Border
Castleblayney, County Monaghan, Ireland
T 00353 (0) 429751784

ON THE R181 From the centre of Castleblaney take the
R181 signposted toward Keady. Tullynagrow Fuelserve is left-
hand side, half a mile from the town centre.

CREDIT/DEBIT CARDS

FUEL CARDS (see key on page 9)
3 8 9 12 18 19 20 21

TRUCK FACILITIES
P
Coach parking available
Quiet area
Ample room for manoeuvring

DRIVER FACILITIES
Drivers' washroom
Glencarn Hotel on-site
Takeaway food and clothing for sale nearby
Phone top-ups/accessories nearby

Bunker fuel and parking 24 hours. Other on-site facilities 07:30-22:00
360

Westbank Service Station, Belfast
FL1

Nicholls Fuel Oils Ltd, Westbank Road
Cuncrue Industrial Estate
Belfast, Ulster BT3 9JL, Northern Ireland
T 02890 775863

OFF THE M2 JUNCTION 1 Exit the M2 at junction 1 and
head east for the Docks onto Dargan Road. Continue for 1 mile
then turn left into Westbank Road. Continue for half a mile and
go past ferry terminal. Westbank Service Station is on the left.

CREDIT/DEBIT CARDS

FUEL CARDS (see key on page 9)
1 2 4 7 34

SITE COMMENTS/INFORMATION
This site is 600 yards from the ferry
terminal

All on-site facilities 06:00-18:00. Short term on-site parking times unknown
361

FL1 — The Western Gem, Mullingar

Top Oil Ltd, Ballinalack, Mullingar
County Westmeath, Ireland
T 00353 (0) 449371160

ON THE N4 Take the N4 north-west out of Mullingar towards Longford. The Western Gem is in the middle of the village of Ballinalack on the right-hand side.

CREDIT/DEBIT CARDS

VISA MasterCard Maestro

FUEL CARDS (see key on page 9)
9 11 12

TRUCK FACILITIES
Short-term coach parking

All on-site facilities 07:30-00:00. Short term parking times unknown

362

FL2 — W R Kennedy

Pennybridge Ind Est, Ballymena
County Antrim BT42 3HB
Northern Ireland
T 028 25656616/25656833

ON THE A36 From the south end of the M2, take the A36 towards Ballymena town centre. W R Kennedy is 500 yards on the left.

CREDIT/DEBIT CARDS

FUEL CARDS (see key on page 9)
1 2 4 6 12 20 34

TRUCK FACILITIES
Overnight parking on car park at edge of estate, plus short-term LGV parking on-site
Truck dealership/workshop

Parking, toilets and bunker fuel 24 hours. Breakdown repair centre opening times unknown

363

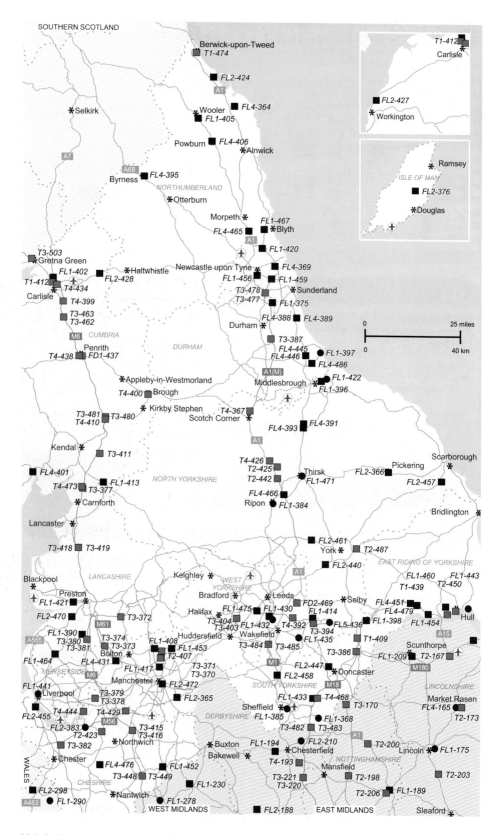

Northern England

■ *Cafe - Layby parking (FD1)*
■ *Cafe - No overnight parking (FD2)*
■ *Filling Station - No overnight parking/cafe (FL1)*
● *Bunkering Site - No overnight parking/cafe (FL1)*
■ *Filling Station - Nearby overnight parking no cafe (FL2)*
● *Bunkering Site - Nearby overnight parking no cafe (FL2)*
■ *Filling Station - Cafe no onsite overnight parking (FL3)*
■ *Filling Station - Onsite overnight parking (FL4)*
● *Bunkering Site - Onsite overnight parking (FL4)*
● *Bunkering Site - Cafe & onsite overnight parking (FL5)*
■ *Lorry Park - Onsite overnight parking no cafe or fuel (T1)*
■ *Truck Stop/Cafe - Onsite overnight parking (T2)*
■ *Motorway Service Station (T3)*
■ *Truck Stop - Bunker fuel/showers/cafe/onsite overnight parking (T4)*

For key to site symbols see page 8

FL4 ■ Adderstone Services (WJ Davidson & Sons)& Purdy lodge

W J Davidson & Son, Belford
Northumberland NE70 7JU
T 01668 213440 www.purdylodge.co.uk

ON THE A1 Adderstone Services can be found on the A1 north of Warenford at the junction with the B1341 and on the right-hand side if heading north.

CREDIT/DEBIT CARDS

FUEL CARDS (see key on page 9)

① ② ③ ④ ⑦ ㉓ ㉞

TRUCK FACILITIES
P with voucher, £10.00 (voucher = £5)
P only £5.00
Coach parking available, shared with LGV
Quiet area, Ample room for manoeuvring
Adblue at the pumps

DRIVER FACILITIES
Male shower (1) female (1) Unisex (1) and drivers' washroom, Accommodation (£54.95 pn), TV, Arcade machines, Phone top-ups, Euros changed/accepted Takeaway food, Truckers' accessories

On-site accommodation opening times unknown. All other on-site facilities 24 hours **364**

FL2 ■ Ashton Road Service Station, Stockport

Ashton Road, Bredbury, Stockport
Cheshire SK6 2QN
T 01614 4300279

M60 JUNCTION 25 ON THE A6017 From the M60 junction 25, take the A6017 towards Denton. Ashton Road Services is about 100 yards along on the left.

CREDIT/DEBIT CARDS

FUEL CARDS (see key on page 9)

① ③ ⑦

TRUCK FACILITIES
Overnight parking nearby

DRIVER FACILITIES
Truckers' accessories
Takeaway food nearby

All on-site facilities 24 hours **365**

B & M Harland Ltd, Pickering FL2

Malton Road Garage, Malton Road
Pickering, North Yorkshire YO18 7JL
T 01751 472673

ON THE A169 Malton Road Garage can be found on the A169 Pickering to Malton road, 200 yards south of the junction with the A170.

1 BP

P NEARBY

£1.65 70p NEARBY

CREDIT/DEBIT CARDS

FUEL CARDS (see key on page 9)
3 14 23 28 33

TRUCK FACILITIES
Overnight parking in town centre nearby

DRIVER FACILITIES
Accommodation available nearby, 500 yards, 3 hotels
Truckers' accessories
Vegetarian meals
Post Office

SITE COMMENTS/INFORMATION
Excellent range of quality food products
Easy access for LGVs

All on-site facilities 06:30-22:00 **366**

Barton Park Services/Poplar 2000 (Barton Lorry Park) T4

Moto Ltd, A1 Great North Road
Barton, nr Richmond
North Yorkshire DL10 6NA
T 01325 377777

OFF THE A1 Exit A1M at junction 56 and head towards Barton. Barton Park Services is immediately on your right.

5 BP RED AUTO BUNKER

P 50 OVERNIGHT P & F *

£2.50 £1.20 CR & LR £4.00

CREDIT/DEBIT CARDS

FUEL CARDS (see key on page 9)
1 2 6 14 22 23 25 28 29 33

TRUCK FACILITIES

P *with voucher*	**P** *only*	*Voucher value*
£9.00	£7.00	£3.00

Ample room for manoeuvring
Quiet parking, Adblue in containers

DRIVER FACILITIES
Showers – 3 m (20ps or £1 coins), washroom, rest area, Takeaway, Vegetarian/Healthy meals, TV, phone top-ups/accessories, clothing for sale, truckers' accessories,Arcade machines, Fax/copier

SITE COMMENTS/INFORMATION
Fridge lorry area at top of lorry park. BP cards use pumps 10/11, Keyfuels & Red 1/5

Shop, parking, fuel and some food accessible 24 hours. Other facilities accessible 06:00-22:00 **367**

Bayford & Co Sheffield (M1 Dervstop) FL1

Bayford & Co Ltd, Houghton Road
North Anston Trading Est., North Anston,
Sheffield, South Yorkshire S25 4JJ
T 01909 567131

OFF THE B6463 From the M1, exit at junction 31 and take the A57 to Worksop. After 1 mile turn left onto the B6463 Todwick road then take the 2nd right into Houghton Road. Bayford & Co is 200 yards along on the right.

Unknown Independent RED

CREDIT/DEBIT CARDS

FUEL CARDS (see key on page 9)
1 2 4 7 34

All on-site facilities 06:00-17:15 **368**

FL4   Bewicke Service Station

**Bewicke Road, Willington Quay, Wallsend
Tyne and Wear NE28 6LX
T 0191 2625809**

OFF THE A187 From the A194M continue along the A194 to the A19. Turn left towards Jarrow and the Tyne Tunnel. Once through the tunnel, follow signs for the A187 Newcastle upon Tyne. Continue for half a mile then turn right up Bewicke Road. The site is in front of you.

CREDIT/DEBIT CARDS

FUEL CARDS (see key on page 9)
① ② ③ ④ ㉞

TRUCK FACILITIES
P free
Quiet area, Floodlighting, CCTV
Ample room for manoeuvring

DRIVER FACILITIES
Unisex shower (1)
Drivers' washroom
Phone top-ups
Train nearby

On-site and nearby parking not 24 hours. All other on-site facilities 24 hours   **369**

T3   Birch Services eastbound

**Moto Ltd
Birch, Heywood
Greater Manchester OL10 2QH
T 0161 6430911** www.moto-way.com

M62 EASTBOUND BETWEEN JUNCTIONS 18 AND 19

CREDIT/DEBIT CARDS

FUEL CARDS (see key on page 9)
③ ㉓ ㉖ ㉗

TRUCK FACILITIES
Overnight coach parking (10)
P with voucher   **P** only   Voucher value
£16.00   £18.00   £7.50
Floodlighting, Fridge parking, Abnormal loads area adjacent to lorry park

DRIVER FACILITIES
Accommodation £50.00, Travelodge
Takeaway food, Vegetarian/Healthy meals, Showers, male (2), female (1)
Arcade mach., Phone accessories, Phone top-ups, Truckers' accessories

Burger King open 10:00-22:00. All other on-site facilities accessible 24 hours   **370**

T3   Birch Services westbound

**Moto Ltd
Birch, Heywood
Greater Manchester OL10 2RB
T 0161 6430911** www.moto-way.com

M62 WESTBOUND BETWEEN JUNCTIONS 18 AND 19

CREDIT/DEBIT CARDS

FUEL CARDS (see key on page 9)
③ ㉓ ㉖ ㉗

TRUCK FACILITIES
P with voucher   **P** only   Voucher value
£16.00   £18.00   £7.50
Overnight coach parking, Floodlighting

DRIVER FACILITIES
Takeaway food, Showers, male (1), female (1), Accommodation –
Travelodge, £50.00
Vegetarian/Healthy menu, Arcade machines, Phone top-ups, Truckers' accessories

Burger King open 10:00-22:00. All other on-site facilities accessible 24 hours   **371**

Blackburn Services
T3

Extra MSA Forecourts Ltd
Darwen, Blackburn, Lancashire BB3 0AT
T 01254 870360

M65 JUNCTION 4

CREDIT/DEBIT CARDS

FUEL CARDS (see key on page 9)
① ③ ④ ⑦ ⑧ ⑩ ⑭ ㉒ ㉕ ㉗ ㉞

TRUCK FACILITIES
P
Overnight security patrol
Quiet area
Ample room for manoeuvring
DRIVER FACILITIES
Showers, 1 male, 1 female
Accommodation, Travelodge
Truckers' accessories
Takeaway food
SITE COMMENTS/INFORMATION
Good LGV facilities

Parking, fuel, showers, shop and some food accessible 24 hours. Restaurant open 07:00-22:00

372

Bolton West Services northbound
T3

First Motorway Services Ltd
nr Horwich, Bolton, Lancashire BL6 5UZ
T 01204 468641

M61 NORTHBOUND BETWEEN JUNCTIONS 6 AND 8

CREDIT/DEBIT CARDS

FUEL CARDS (see key on page 9)
⑭

TRUCK FACILITIES
P with voucher   P only   Voucher value
£11.00   £8.00   £5.00
Coach parking available (12 spaces)
Quiet area, Ample room for
manoeuvring, Truckwash 09:00-16:00
Floodlights

DRIVER FACILITIES
Shower unisex (1) free, washroom, rest
area, TV
Accommodation, Travelodge (£55 pn)
Takeaway food, Arcade machines
Truckers' accessories, Clothing for sale

Parking, showers, fuel and restaurant 24 hours. Shop 07:00-19:00. Travelodge opening times unknown

373

Bolton West Services southbound
T3

First Motorway Services Ltd
nr Horwich, Bolton, Lancashire BL6 5UZ
T 01204 468641

M61 SOUTHBOUND BETWEEN JUNCTIONS 6 AND 8

CREDIT/DEBIT CARDS

FUEL CARDS (see key on page 9)
⑭

TRUCK FACILITIES
P with voucher   P only   Voucher value
£11.00   £8.00   £5.00
Coach parking available (10 spaces)
Quiet area, Ample room for manoeuvring
Truckwash 09:00-16:00, Floodlights
DRIVER FACILITIES
Unisex shower (2) free, washroom, rest
area, TV Accommodation on-site,
Travelodge (£55 pn)
Truckers' accessories, Clothing for sale
Takeaway food nearby, TV,
Arcade machines

Travelodge open 15:00-23:00 for check in. All other on-site facilities accessible 24 Hours

374

FL1 ■ Bournmoor Filling Station, Houghton le Spring

**Chester Road, Bournmoor,
Houghton le Spring
Tyne and Wear DH4 6EY
T 01913 852514**

ON THE A183 From junction 63 of the A1M, take the A183 towards Sunderland. Bournmoor Filling Station is on the right-hand side just past the turning for the A1052.

CREDIT/DEBIT CARDS

FUEL CARDS (see key on page 9)
① ② ③ ④ ⑦ ⑧ ㉘ ㉞

DRIVER FACILITIES
Truckers' accessories
Fax/copier

SITE COMMENTS/INFORMATION
Very popular with lorry drivers.
Also has a 'Dog Wash' on-site!

All on-site facilities 24 hours **375**

FL2 ■ Bray Hill Service Station, Douglas

**Bray Hill, Douglas IM4 4LL
Isle of Man
T 01624 621181**

ON THE A2 From the ferry terminal, take the A1 north-west out of Douglas town centre towards Peel. At the junction with the A5 and A2 turn right onto the A2 towards the TT Grandstand. Bray Hill is 1 mile on the left next to the A22.

CREDIT/DEBIT CARDS

FUEL CARDS (see key on page 9)
③ ㉔ ㉕ ㉘

TRUCK FACILITIES
Overnight parking at TT Grandstand Park

DRIVER FACILITIES
Accommodation available nearby, half mile, Wellbeck Hotel & Castle Mona

All on-site facilities accessible 07:00-22:30 **376**

T3 Burton in Kendal Services northbound

**Moto Ltd
Burton West, Carnforth
Lancashire LA6 1JF
T 01524 781234** www.moto-way.com

M6 NORTHBOUND BETWEEN JUNCTIONS 35 AND 36

CREDIT/DEBIT CARDS

FUEL CARDS (see key on page 9)
⑭

DRIVER FACILITIES
Accommodation on-site, Travelodge
Takeaway food
Shower (male)
Vegetarian/healthy meals
Arcade machines
Phone top-ups

All on-site facilities accessible 24 hours **377**

Burtonwood Services eastbound — T3

Welcome Break Ltd
Great Sankey, Warrington
Cheshire WA5 3AX
T 01925 651656 www.welcomebreak.co.uk

M62 EASTBOUND JUNCTION 8

CREDIT/DEBIT CARDS

FUEL CARDS (see key on page 9)
25

TRUCK FACILITIES
Overnight coach park (29)
Floodlighting, Plenty of room to
manoeuvre, Quiet parking

DRIVER FACILITIES
Takeaway food, Vegetarian/healthy
meals, TV, Arcade machines, internet,
Euros, Fax/copier, Phone top-ups
Showers (1 unisex)

SITE COMMENTS/INFORMATION
Abnormal loads area is situated along
the perimeter of lorry park

Forecourt accessible 24 hours. Main building hours vary seasonally, normall 06:30-21:30 — **378**

Burtonwood Services westbound — T3

Welcome Break Ltd
Warrington
Cheshire WA5 3AX
T 01925 651656

M62 WESTBOUND BETWEEN JUNCTIONS 8 AND 9

CREDIT/DEBIT CARDS

FUEL CARDS (see key on page 9)
10 24 25 27

DRIVER FACILITIES
Accommodation, Welcome Lodge
Takeaway food

*Full site details not available at time of going to
press. For more information please contact site.*

All on-site facilities accessible 24 hours — **379**

Charnock Richard Services northbound — T3

Welcome Break Ltd
nr Coppul, nr Chorley,
Lancashire PR7 5LR
T 01257 791746

M6 NORTHBOUND BETWEEN JUNCTIONS 27 AND 28

CREDIT/DEBIT CARDS

FUEL CARDS (see key on page 9)
25

DRIVER FACILITIES
Accommodation, Welcome Lodge
Takeaway food

*Full site details not available at time of going to
press. For more information please contact site.*

All on-site facilities accessible 24 hours — **380**

T3 — Charnock Richard Services southbound

Welcome Break Ltd
nr Coppul, nr Chorley,
Lancashire PR7 5LR
T 01257 791746

M6 SOUTHBOUND BETWEEN JUNCTIONS 27 AND 28

All on-site facilities accessible 24 hours

CREDIT/DEBIT CARDS

FUEL CARDS (see key on page 9)
10 24 25 27

DRIVER FACILITIES
Accommodation, Welcome Lodge
Takeaway food

Full site details not available at time of going to press. For more information please contact site.

381

T3 — Chester Services (Hapsford)

Roadchef Ltd
Hapsford
Cheshire CH2 4QZ
T 01928 728500

M56 JUNCTION 14

Costa & Restore Shop 24 hrs. Restaurant open 07:00-21:30. Wimpy seasonal variable hours

CREDIT/DEBIT CARDS

FUEL CARDS (see key on page 9)
25

TRUCK FACILITIES
P *with voucher*   **P** *only*   *Voucher value*
£20.00   £17.00   £10.00
Coach parking available (20 spaces)
Quiet area, Room for manoeuvring
Truck dealership/workshop

DRIVER FACILITIES
Accommodation on-site, Premier Inn
£55.00, Showers, 1 m, 1 f (free),
Internet access. Truckers' accessories,
Takeaway food, Vegetarian/healthy meals,
Arcade machines, Euros, Fax/copier,
Clothing for sale, Phone top-ups

382

FL2 ● — County Oil Group Runcorn (M56 Derv Stop)

County Oil Group Ltd, Beca House
Ashville Way, Ashville Ind Est
Sutton Weaver, Runcorn, Cheshire WA7 3EL
T 01928 718000 www.countyoil.co.uk

OFF THE A557 M56 south-west, exit at junction 12 and take left-hand A557 towards Frodsham. After a few yards take the next right into Clifton Lane, then the 2nd left into Ashville Way. County Oil is half-way down on the right.

All on-site facilities 24 hours

CREDIT/DEBIT CARDS

FUEL CARDS (see key on page 9)
1 2 4 5 7 34

TRUCK FACILITIES
P £5.00
Quiet area, Truck washing facilities
Truck dealership/workshop
Ample room for manoeuvring
Secure fencing, CCTV, Quiet parking
area, Adblue at pumps and in containers

DRIVER FACILITIES
Accommodation available Holiday Inn
Drivers washroom, Internet nearby
Euros accepted nearby, Fax/copier,
Sauna, Jaccuzi and Gym nearby

383

CPL Petroleum, Ripon

FL1 ●

**CPL Petroleum Ltd
Dallamires Lane Industrial Estate
Ripon, North Yorkshire HG4 1TT
T 01765 607606 www.cplpetroleum.co.uk**

OFF THE A61 From the A1 if heading south, take the A61 Ripon ring road to Harrogate. Continue across the roundabout with the B6265 and take a right at the next immediate roundabout. CPL is a couple of yards along on the right.

CREDIT/DEBIT CARDS

FUEL CARDS (see key on page 9)
① ② ④ ⑪

DRIVER FACILITIES
Takeaway nearby
Phone accessories
Phone top-ups nearby
Clothing nearby
Adblue in containers
LGV tyre repairs nearby

SITE COMMENTS/INFORMATION
This site only accepts chip and pin (smart) fuel cards

All on-site facilities 08:00–17:00

384

CPL Petroleum, Sheffield

FL1 ●

**CPL Petroleum Ltd, Parkway Avenue
Broadoaks, Sheffield, South Yorkshire S9 3BJ
T 0114 2440537**

OFF THE A57 From M1 junction 33, follow the A630 towards Sheffield. Continue onto the A57 and across the junction with the A6102. At the next exit turn right crossing the carriageway, then left at the next roundabout. CPL is 200 yards along on the right.

CREDIT/DEBIT CARDS

FUEL CARDS (see key on page 9)
① ④ ㉞

TRUCK FACILITIES
Truck dealership/workshop

DRIVER FACILITIES
Train nearby

Toilets and bunker fuel accessible 24 hours. Truck Dealership/Workshop 08:00–18:00

385

Doncaster North Services

T3

**Moto Ltd
Doncaster
South Yorkshire DN8 5GS
T 01302 847700 www.moto-way.com**

M18 / M180 INTERCHANGE JUNCTION 5

CREDIT/DEBIT CARDS

FUEL CARDS (see key on page 9)
② ③ ④ ⑭ ㉒

TRUCK FACILITIES
P *with voucher*   P *only*   *Voucher value*
£16.00   £14.00   £6.00
Overnight coach parking (10)
Room for manoeuvre, Adblue at pump

DRIVER FACILITIES
Accommodation on-site, Travelodge
Drivers' rest area, Takeaway food,
Vegetarian/healthy meals, TV, Arcade
machines, Internet, Fax/copier, Phone
top-ups/accessories, Clothing
Showers, male (2), female (1) free,
Washroom, Truckers' accessories

All on-site facilities accessible 24 hours

386

T3 — Durham Services

Roadchef Ltd
Tursdale Road, Bowburn
County Durham DH6 5NP
T 0191 3779222

A1M JUNCTION 61
On the A1M at junction 61, Durham Services is a couple of yards along on the A688.

All on-site facilities accessible 24 hours

CREDIT/DEBIT CARDS

FUEL CARDS (see key on page 9)
1 2 3 7 8 10 13 14 25 28

TRUCK FACILITIES
P *with voucher*   P *only*
£17.00   £14.00
Coach parking available (9 spaces)
Quiet area
Ample room for manoeuvring

DRIVER FACILITIES
Accommodation on-site, Premier Inn £55 & £50, Showers, unisex (1), rest area, internet access, truckers' accessories Takeaway food, Healthy menu, Arcade machines, Games room, Euros, Fax/copier, Phone top-ups

387

FL4 — Easington East

Hawthorn, Nr Easington, Peterlee,
Co Durham SR7 8SS
T 0191 5274100/0191 5274110

ON THE A19 This site is situated on the A19 Halfway between the exits for Easington and Cold Heseldon.

24 hrs

CREDIT/DEBIT CARDS

FUEL CARDS (see key on page 9)
3 24 25 26 28

TRUCK FACILITIES
P free, Coaches overnight (10)
Secure fencing, Floodlights, Room to manoeuvre, Fridge parking

DRIVER FACILITIES
Vegetarian/Healthy meals, Takeaway, Phone top-ups, Truckers' accessories

388

FL4 — Easington West

Hawthorn, Nr Easington, Peterlee,
Co Durham SR7 8SS
T 0191 5274100/0191 5274110

ON THE A19 This site is situated on the A19 Halfway between the exits for Easington and Cold Heseldon.

24 hrs

CREDIT/DEBIT CARDS

FUEL CARDS (see key on page 9)
3 24 25 26 28

TRUCK FACILITIES
P free, Coaches overnight (1) Secure fencing, Floodlights, Room to manouvre, Fridge parking

DRIVER FACILITIES
Takeaway, Phone top-ups, Truckers' accessories, Healthy/vegetarian meals

389

Eccleston Green Filling Station, Chorley · FL1 ■

**218 The Green, Eccleston, Chorley
Lancashire PR7 5SU
T 01257 452593**

ON THE B5250 From the A581, take the B5250 towards Eccleston. Eccleston Green Filling Station is in the middle of the village on the left-hand side.

CREDIT/DEBIT CARDS

FUEL CARDS (see key on page 9)
① ⑦ ⑧

DRIVER FACILITIES
Truckers' accessories

All on-site facilities 06:00-22:30.

390

Exelby Services A19 South Ltd · FL4 ■

**Exelby Services Ltd, Ingleby Arncliffe
Northallerton, North Yorkshire DL6 3JX
T 01609 882662**

ON THE A19 SOUTHBOUND Exelby Services A19 Southbound is located 12 miles south of Teesside, 1 mile north of the A19/A172 junction.

CREDIT/DEBIT CARDS

FUEL CARDS (see key on page 9)
① ③ ④ ⑤ ⑦ ⑧ ⑬ ⑭ ⑮ ⑯ ㉒ ㉓
㉘ ㉝ ㉞

TRUCK FACILITIES
P £2.50
Quiet area, Floodlighting, CCTV
Fridge parking, Adblue at pump/in container, Ample room for manoeuvring

DRIVER FACILITIES
Drivers' washroom, Drivers' rest area
Takeaway food
Phone top-ups/accessories
Truckers' accessories

All on-site facilities 24 hours

391

Exelby Services Castleford · T4

**California Drive, Whitwood, Castleford,
West Yorkshire WF10 5QH
T 01977 603313**

OFF THE M62 If heading west, exit M62 at junction 31, turn right at roundabout, go under motorway then 1st exit at next roundabout. Exelby is 500 Yds on the left.

CREDIT/DEBIT CARDS

FUEL CARDS (see key on page 9)
① ② ③ ④ ⑤ ⑥ ⑦ ⑧ ⑭ ⑮ ⑯ ㉒
㉝

TRUCK FACILITIES
P £9.50, Coaches overnight, Secure fencing, CCTV, Truck washing, Room to manoeuvre, Fridge parking, Adblue at pump/in containers, Night time security

DRIVER FACILITIES
Showers, male 4, female 2(£1),
Vegetarian/Healthy meals, Evening entertainment, TV, Euros, Phone top-ups, Clothing, Truckers' accessories, CB sales/repairs

All on-site facilities open 24 hours.

392

FL4 ■ Exelby Services Ltd

**Exelby Services Ltd, Ingleby Arncliffe
Northallerton, North Yorkshire DL6 3JT
T 01609 882280** www.exelbyservices.co.uk

ON THE A19 NORTHBOUND This site is located on the A19, 12 miles south of Teeside, 1 mile north of the A19/A172 junction.

CREDIT/DEBIT CARDS

FUEL CARDS (see key on page 9)

① ② ③ ④ ⑥ ⑦ ⑧ ⑬ ⑭ ⑮ ⑯ ㉒
㉓ ㉘ ㉝ ㉞

TRUCK FACILITIES
P £2.50
Quiet area, Floodlighting, CCTV
Ample room to manoeuvre
Overnight coach shared with LGV
Room for manoeuver, Fridge parking
Adblue at pump/in container

DRIVER FACILITIES
Drivers' washroom, Drivers' rest area
Takeaway food,
Phone top-ups/accessories
Truckers' accessories

Parking 24 hours. All other on-site facilities 06:00-22:00 Mon-Fri, 08:00-21:00 Sat & Sun **393**

T3 ■ Ferrybridge Services

**Moto Ltd
nr Knottingley, Wakefield
West Yorkshire WF11 0AF
T 01977 672767 www.moto-way.com**

M62 JUNCTION 33

CREDIT/DEBIT CARDS

FUEL CARDS (see key on page 9)
㉗

TRUCK FACILITIES
P with voucher   **P** only   Voucher value
£18.00   £16.00   £7.50
Coach overnight (6), Floodlights, Quiet
Room for manoeuvre, Fridge parking

DRIVER FACILITIES
Accommodation on-site, Travelodge
£55.00, Takeaway food, Phone top-ups/accessories , Truckers' accessories
Showers, male (2), female (1), Washroom
Vegetarian/healthy meals, Arcade machines

SITE COMMENTS/INFORMATION
Fridge lorries should use bottom of lorry park.

All on-site facilities accessible 24 hours **394**

FL4 ■ The Filling Station (Border Park Services)

**Byrness, Newcastle upon Tyne
Tyne and Wear NE19 1TR
T 01830 520525**

ON THE A68 The Filling Station is on the south east side of the village of Byrness on the A68 Rochester to Jedburgh road, and on the left-hand side if heading towards Jedburgh.

CREDIT/DEBIT CARDS

FUEL CARDS (see key on page 9)
③

TRUCK FACILITIES
P
Quiet area
Ample room for manoeuvring

DRIVER FACILITIES
Takeaway food
Truckers' accessories

Parking 24 hours. Other on-site facilities 08:00-07:00 in summer, 07:30-08:00 in winter **395**

Fleet Point Service Station, Middlesbrough   FL1 ■

Cambridge Rd, Middlesbrough
Redcar and Cleveland TS3 8AG
T 01642 219300/219301

A66 A171 INTERCHANGE Take the A66 out of
Middlesbrough towards South Bank. Fleetpoint is situated at
the roundabout with the A171 signposted towards
Guisborough and the B1513.

CREDIT/DEBIT CARDS

FUEL CARDS (see key on page 9)
3 14 28

DRIVER FACILITIES
Takeaway food nearby

Toilets 06:00-22:00. All other on-site facilities 24 hours   **396**

F Peart & Co Ltd   FL1 ●

Baltic Street, Hartlepool
County Durham TS25 1PW
T 01429 263331/852100 www.fpeart.co.uk

OFF THE A689 From Stockton on Tees take the A689
towards Hartlepool. Continue on this road past the junction
with the B1277. Turn right at the next roundabout. Take next
right after Tesco into Baltic St. F Peart is 200 yards on the left.

CREDIT/DEBIT CARDS

FUEL CARDS (see key on page 9)
1 4 34

TRUCK FACILITIES
Ample room for manoeuvring

DRIVER FACILITIES
Takeaway food nearby
Phone top-ups/accessories nearby
Clothing for sale nearby

SITE COMMENTS/INFORMATION
Oil can be paid for in cash during office
hours

All on-site facilities 06:00-22:00. This site is manned from 08:00-17:00 Mon-Fri   **397**

Glews Garage & Country Kitchen   FL1 ■

Rawcliffe Road, Goole
East Yorkshire DN14 8JS
T 01405 764525

ON THE A614 From the M62, exit at junction 36 and take
the A614 towards Rawcliffe. Glews garage is 50 yards on
your left.

CREDIT/DEBIT CARDS

FUEL CARDS (see key on page 9)
3 23 24 25 26 27 28

DRIVER FACILITIES
Accommodation on-site
Takeaway food
Phone top-ups

SITE COMMENTS/INFORMATION
Clean tidy and welcoming site
Car dealership also on-site

All on-site facilities 24 hours   **398**

Golden Fleece & Thistle Café

T4

**Exelby Services Ltd, Carleton, Carlisle
Cumbria CA4 0AN
T 01228 542766**

M6 JUNCTION 42 ON THE A6 From the M6 exit at junction 42 and take the A6 towards Penrith. Golden Fleece is a couple of yards along on the left-hand side.

CREDIT/DEBIT CARDS

FUEL CARDS (see key on page 9)
① ② ③ ④ ⑤ ⑥ ⑦ ⑧ ⑨ ⑫ ⑬ ⑭
⑮ ㉒ ㉓ ㉝ ㉞

TRUCK FACILITIES
Quiet area, Ample room for manoeuvring, Adblue at pumps/in containers

DRIVER FACILITIES
Showers – 2 unisex (charge), washroom, clothing for sale, truckers' accessories, Internet wi-fi only, Phone accessories/top-ups

Parking and fuel accessible 24 hours. Other on-site facilities opening times unknown **399**

Grand Prix Services (Brough Lorry Park)

T4

**Grand Prix Services, Main Street
Brough, Cumbria CA17 4AY
T 01768 341328**

ON THE B6276 The village of Brough is off the A66 at the junction with the A685. If heading from Penrith on the A66 exit for Brough onto the B6276 and the Lorry Park is 400 yards along on your left.

CREDIT/DEBIT CARDS

FUEL CARDS (see key on page 9)

TRUCK FACILITIES
Coach parking shared with LGV
CCTV. Quiet area on-site. Fridge lorry area
Ample room for manoeuvring
Truck dealership/workshop nearby

DRIVER FACILITIES
Showers – 3 unisex (free), washroom, TV
Takeaway food, Post Office nearby

SITE COMMENTS/INFORMATION
On-site fuel can be purchased for cash only

Parking 24 hours. All other on-site facilities 06:15-22:00 Mon-Fri. Nearby cashpoint machine until 20:00 **400**

Greenodd Service Station

FL4

**Greenodd, nr Ulverston
Cumbria LA12 7RE
T 01229 861434**

A5092 / A590 INTERSECTION From the A590 between Ulverston and Newby Bridge, take the A5092 towards Grizebeck. Greenodd Service Station is a few yards along on the left.

CREDIT/DEBIT CARDS

FUEL CARDS (see key on page 9)
③ ㉗

TRUCK FACILITIES
P
Coach parking available, shared with LGV
Ample room for manoeuvring
Quiet area

DRIVER FACILITIES
Truckers' accessories

SITE COMMENTS/INFORMATION
Good location, most accessible LGV site for many miles

Parking 24 hours. Other on-site facilities 07:30-08:00 **401**

Harker Service Station, Carlisle

FL1 ■

Harker, Nr Carlisle, Cumbria CA6 4DT
T 01228 674274

ON THE 97 Exit [illegible] At the M6 and take the A7 north towards Longtown. Harker Service Station is about half a mile along on the left-hand side.

CREDIT/DEBIT CARDS

FUEL CARDS (see key on page 9)
① ② ④ ㉞

DRIVER FACILITIES
Truckers' accommodation

Toilets 24 hours, other quality facilities 07.00-23.00

402

Hartshead Moor Services north-eastbound

T3

Welcome Break Ltd
Brighouse, West Yorkshire HD6 4JX
T 01274 876584
www.welcomebreak.co.uk

M62 NORTH-EASTBOUND BETWEEN
JUNCTIONS 25 AND 26

CREDIT/DEBIT CARDS

FUEL CARDS (see key on page 9)
㉓ ㉔ ㉕ ㉘

TRUCK FACILITIES
P with voucher   **P** only   Voucher value
£17.50   £15.00   £7.00
Overnight coach park shared with LGV
Room for manoeuvre, Fridge parking
Truck washing, Security 17:00-06:00

DRIVER FACILITIES
Accommodation, Days Inn from £35.00,
Showers, male (2), Takeaway food,
Vegetarian/healthy meals, TV, Arcade
machines, Euros, Fax/copier, Phone top-ups
Toilets & Showers in both forecourt and
main building. Parking discount schemes
available on request.

All on-site facilities accessible 24 hours

403

Hartshead Moor Services south-westbound

T3

Welcome Break Ltd
Brighouse, West Yorkshire HD6 4JX
T 01274 876584
www.welcomebreak.co.uk

M62 SOUTH-WESTBOUND BETWEEN
JUNCTIONS 25 AND 26

CREDIT/DEBIT CARDS

FUEL CARDS (see key on page 9)
㉔ ㉕ ㉖ ㉗ ㉘

TRUCK FACILITIES
P with voucher   **P** only   Voucher value
£17.50   £15.00   £7.00
Overnight coach shared with LGV
Room for manoeuvre, Fridge parking
Security guards 17:00-06:00
Truck washing

DRIVER FACILITIES
Takeaway food, Vegetarian/healthy meals
TV, Euros, Fax/copier, Phone top-ups
Showers, male (2), Accommodation, Days
Inn, from £35 Toilet/showers in both
forecourt and main building. Parking
discount schemes available on request.

All on-site facilities accessible 24 hours

404

FL1 ■ Haugh Head Garage, Wooler

Haugh Head, Wooler
Northumberland NE71 6QP
T 01668 281316

ON THE A697 Haugh Head Garage is on the A697, on the left hand side if heading towards Morpeth and about 1 mile south of Wooler.

CREDIT/DEBIT CARDS

FUEL CARDS (see key on page 9)
①②③④⑥⑦

TRUCK FACILITIES
Short-term coach parking (3 spaces)

DRIVER FACILITIES
Truckers' accessories
Phone top-ups

OTHER INFORMATION
LGVs please use 2nd entrance when heading south, 1st entrance when heading north to avoid forecourt canopy

All on-site facilities 07:00-20:00 Mon-Sat, 08:00-20:00 Sun | **405**

FL4 ■ Hedgeley Services

Powburn, Alnwick
Northumberland NN66 4HU
T 01665 578214

ON THE A697 Hedgeley Services is situated on the A697 at Powburn approximately 18 miles north of Morpeth and on the right-hand side if heading north.

CREDIT/DEBIT CARDS

FUEL CARDS (see key on page 9)
①②③④⑦㉞

TRUCK FACILITIES
P free with fuel purchased
Coach parking available (6 spaces)
Quiet area, CCTV
Ample room for manoeuvring

DRIVER FACILITIES
Vegetarian meals, Arcade machines
Fax/copier, Post Office, Phone top-ups

SITE COMMENTS/INFORMATION
Popular LGV site

Parking 24 hours. Restaurant open 08:00-22:00. Other on-site facilities 06:00-22:00 (22:30 in summer) | **406**

T4 ■ Heywood Distribution Park

Estate Office, Pilsworth Road, Heywood
Lancashire OL10 2TT
T 01706 368645
www.heywooddistributionpark.com

OFF THE A58 From the M66, exit at junction 3 and head towards Heywood. At the T-junction turn right and follow the road left as it bears left into Pilsworth Road. Heywood Distribution Park is within 1 mile.

FUEL CARDS (see key on page 9)
TRUCK FACILITIES
P
Coach parking (20 spaces)
24 hour guards with dogs
Secure fencing, CCTV and floodlighting
Quiet area. Fridge lorry area
Ample room for manoeuvring
Truck washing facilities
Tyre repair/sales nearby

DRIVER FACILITIES
Accommodation nearby,
see Birch Motorway Services Eastbound
Washroom, rest area, TV. Takeaway nearby

SITE COMMENTS/INFORMATION
Police Secured Car Park Award

Parking and showers 06:00-00:00. Some facilities open 08:00-14:00. Other on-site facilities times vary | **407**

Hooley Bridge Service Station, Bury FI 1

003/021 Rochdale Old Road, Bury
Lancashire BL9 7TL
T 0101 7812890

ON THE B6222 From Rochdale take the B0222 towards Bury. Hooley Bridge Services is on the right-hand side about 1 mile away from the motorway bridge.

All on-site facilities 06:00-22:00

400

CREDIT/DEBIT CARDS

FUEL CARDS (see key on page 9)

DRIVER FACILITIES
Truckers' accessories

Jones and Jones Transport Services T1

Goole Road, Moorends, Doncaster
South Yorkshire DN8 4JR
T 01405 812413

OFF THE A614 From the M18, exit at junction 6 and take the A614 towards Rawcliffe. After 1 mile, turn right into North Common Road for 1 mile. At the T-junction turn left and Jones and Jones Transport is a few yards along on the right.

All on-site facilities 24 hours

409

TRUCK FACILITIES
P £7.00
Quiet area
Ample room for manoeuvring
Truck dealership/workshop on-site
Floodlighting, CCTV

DRIVER FACILITIES
Showers on-site (free)
Unisex showers (2)
Drivers' washroom
Takeaway food nearby
Phone top-ups/accessories

Junction 38 Truckstop, (Tebay Truckstop) M6 Diesel & Westmorland Ltd T4

Old Tebay, Penrith, Cumbria CA10 3SS
T 015396 24505 www.westmorland.com
M6 JUNCTION 38 Exit the M6 at Junction 38 and take the B6260 to Orton. The truckstop is on the left.

CREDIT/DEBIT CARDS

FUEL CARDS (see key on page 9)

TRUCK FACILITIES
P *with voucher* £8.00 **P** *only* – 2 hours £1.00, £3.50 overnight *Voucher value* £2.00, Manoeuvring room, Coaches–shared with LGV, Quiet, Truck washing, Floodlights, CCTV, Fridge parking, Quiet, Adblue at pumps/in containers, Changeover bays

DRIVER FACILITIES
Hot drinks free, Washroom, Showers – 3 m, 1 f (free with overnight P), TV, Truckers' accessories, Accommodation nearby, Vegetarian/ Healthy meals, Takeaway, TV, Arcade mach., Euros, Phone access./top-ups, Clothing, CB

Café: Mon-Fri 06.30-22.30, Sat 06.30-19.30, Sun 06.30-22.30. Village Shop: Mon-Fri 07.00-22.30, Sat 07.00-19.30, Sun 07.00-22.30. Petrol Forecourt & shop: Open 24 hours

410

T3   Killington Lake Services southbou

**Roadchef Ltd
Killington Lake, Kendal
Cumbria LA8 0NW
T 01539 620739**

M6 SOUTHBOUND BETWEEN JUNCTIONS 37 AND 36

CREDIT/DEBIT CARDS

FUEL CARDS (see key on page 9)
③ ⑧ ⑭ ㉓ ㉘

TRUCK FACILITIES
P *with voucher* **P** *only* *Voucher value*
£12.00   £9.00 £6.00
Coach parking available (3 spaces)
Ample room for manoeuvring
Quiet area
Truck dealership/workshop
DRIVER FACILITIES
Accommodation (£48.95 pn), internet
access, truckers' accessories
Takeaway food. Clothing for sale
SITE COMMENTS/INFORMATION
Killington Lake is in a peaceful, picturesque
setting with friendly staff always on hand

All on-site facilities accessible 24 hours   **411**

T1   Kingstown Truck Park

**Millbrook Road, Kingstown Industrial
Estate, Carlisle, Cumbria CA3 0EU
T 07775 770 973**

OFF M6 JUNCTION 44 From Juction 44 M6, take A7
Towards Carlisle. Turn right at 2nd light, 2nd right at Mini
dealership and site is behind.

TRUCK FACILITIES
P £7.00, Coaches overnight, shared with
LGV, LGV sales/dealer/tyre repairs
nearby, Secure fencing, Floodlights,
CCTV, Room to manoeuvre, Fridge
parking, Quiet area

DRIVER FACILITIES
Showers, male 2, unisex 2, Takeaway
nearby, Post Office nearby, Phone
accessories/to ups nearby, Truckers'
accessories nearby, Vegetarian/Healthy
meals nearby

SITE COMMENTS/INFORMATION
Change-over price £9.00. (Contracts
available) Parking not allowed on estate
roads (patrols in force.) Nearby fuel
facilities 1/4 mile away.

All on-site facilities 24 hrs. Manned from Mon-Fri 05:00-22:30. "Pay and Display" otherwise **412**

FL1   Kirkby Lonsdale Motors, Kirkby Lonsdale

**Kendal Road, Kirkby Lonsdale
Cumbria LA6 2HH
T 01524 271778**

ON THE A65 Kirkby Lonsdale Motors can be found on the
A65. Just before the village of Kirkby Lonsdale and on the
right-hand side if heading from junction 36 of the M6.

CREDIT/DEBIT CARDS

FUEL CARDS (see key on page 9)
③ ⑭ ㉕

DRIVER FACILITIES
Truckers' accessories

All on-site facilities 07:00 19:30   **413**

Knottingley Star Service Station, Knottingley FL1

**14 Pontefract Road, Knottingley
West Yorkshire WF11 0DJ
T 01977 636600**

ON THE A645 Exit the M62 at junction 33 and take the A1 toward Knottingley the M62 turn right and Knottingley Star Services is 300 yards along on the right.

CREDIT/DEBIT CARDS

FUEL CARDS (see key on page 9)

TRUCK FACILITIES
Truck dealer/stop/workshop

DRIVER FACILITIES
Accommodation nearby, 500 yards, Travel Inn
Internet access
Truckers' accessories
Takeaway food nearby
Train nearby

SITE COMMENTS/INFORMATION
Very friendly staff

All on-site facilities 24 hours.   414

Knutsford Services northbound   13

**Moto Ltd
Northwich Road, Knutsford
Cheshire WA16 0TL
T 01565 634167** www.moto-way.com

M6 NORTHBOUND BETWEEN JUNCTIONS 18 AND 19

CREDIT/DEBIT CARDS

FUEL CARDS (see key on page 9)

TRUCK FACILITIES
Overnight coach park (10)
DRIVER FACILITIES
Takeaway food, Showers, male (2)
Accommodation
Vegetarian/Healthy meals
Arcade machines, Fax/copier, Phone accessories/top-ups
Clothing, Truckers' accessories
SITE COMMENTS/INFORMATION
Limited parking and manouvring space for LGVs on Northbound, drivers encouraged to use Lymm truckstop or Southbound side of Knutsford Services.

All on-site facilities accessible 24 hours   415

Knutsford Services southbound   T3

**Moto Ltd
Northwich Road, Knutsford
Cheshire WA16 0TL
T 01565 634167** www.moto-way.com

M6 SOUTHBOUND BETWEEN JUNCTIONS 18 AND 19

CREDIT/DEBIT CARDS

FUEL CARDS (see key on page 9)

DRIVER FACILITIES
Takeaway food, Vegetarian/healthy meals
Showers, female (1)
Accommodation
Arcade machines, fax/copier, phone accessories/top-ups
Clothing, Truckers' accessories

Full site details not available at time of going to press. For more information please contact site.

All on-site facilities accessible 24 hours   416

FL1 ■ K P Hill Service Station, Higher Blackley

355 Victoria Avenue, Higher Blackley
Greater Manchester M9 8WQ
T 0161 7403959

ON THE A6104 Exit the M60 at junction 19 and follow the
A576 towards Manchester city centre. After about a quarter of
a mile turn left onto the A6104 Victoria Road. K P Hill Service
Station is on the right-hand side after about a quarter of a mile.

CREDIT/DEBIT CARDS

FUEL CARDS (see key on page 9)
① ② ④ ⑦ ㉞

DRIVER FACILITIES
Phone top-ups/accessories

All on-site facilities 07:00-21:00 Mon-Fri   **417**

T3 ■ Lancaster Services northbound

Moto Ltd
Lancaster
Lancashire LA2 9DU
T 01565 634167 www.moto-way.com

M6 NORTHBOUND BETWEEN JUNCTIONS 32 AND 33

CREDIT/DEBIT CARDS

FUEL CARDS (see key on page 9)
⑩ ⑭ ㉒ ㉔ ㉕

DRIVER FACILITIES
Accommodation, Travelodge
Drivers' rest area
Takeaway food

*Full site details not available at time of going to
press. For more information please contact site.*

All on-site facilities accessible 24 hours   **418**

T3 ■ Lancaster Services southbound

Moto Ltd
Lancaster
Lancashire LA2 9DU
T 01524 791775 www.moto-way.com

M6 SOUTHBOUND BETWEEN JUNCTIONS 32 AND 33

CREDIT/DEBIT CARDS

FUEL CARDS (see key on page 9)
⑩ ⑭ ㉒ ㉔ ㉕

DRIVER FACILITIES
Accommodation, Travelodge
Drivers' rest area
Takeaway food

*Full site details not available at time of going to
press. For more information please contact site.*

All on-site facilities accessible 24 hours   **419**

Lane End Garage, Cramlington — FL1

**Burradon Road, Annitsford, Cramlington
Northumberland NE23 7BD
T 0191 2500260**

ON THE B1505 From the A1, take the A19 towards Wallsend. At the roundabout with the A189 and A1171, turn right onto the B1505 Front Street. Lane End Garage is 800 yards on the left-hand side before the roundabout with the B1321.

CREDIT/DEBIT CARDS

FUEL CARDS (see key on page 9)
22

TRUCK FACILITIES
Truck dealership nearby

DRIVER FACILITIES
Takeaway food nearby

SITE COMMENTS/INFORMATION
Coach hire also available on-site

All on-site facilities 07:00-20:30. **420**

Leagate Texaco Service Station, Preston — FL1

**Blackpool Road, Lea, Preston
Lancashire PR4 0XB
T 01772 732321**

ON THE A583 From Preston, take the A583 towards Blackpool. Leagate is on the outskirts of Preston on your left, 900 yards before the junction with the A584 and the village of Clifton.

CREDIT/DEBIT CARDS

FUEL CARDS (see key on page 9)
1 2 3 4

DRIVER FACILITIES
Accommodation nearby, 50 yards, Travel Inn, £53.00 per night

All on-site facilities 07:00-21:00 Mon-Fri, 09:00-19:00 Sat & Sun **421**

Les Woolston Haulage Ltd (Butler Fuels) — FL1

**1-4 Puddlers Road, Southbank
Middlesbrough TS6 6TX
T 01642 430704**

OFF THE A66 Take the A66 out of Middlesbrough city centre towards Redcar. At the roundabout with the B1513, continue on the A66 to the next roundabout where you turn left into Normanby Road. Take next right into Puddlers Road, Les Woolston is 200 yards on right.

CREDIT/DEBIT CARDS

FUEL CARDS (see key on page 9)
1 2 4 7 34

TRUCK FACILITIES
Truck washing facilities
Truck dealership/workshop

DRIVER FACILITIES
Train nearby

All on-site facilities 24 hours **422**

T2 — Let's Eat Café

**Tarporley Road, Lower Whitley
Warrington, Cheshire WA4 4EZ
T 01928 717322**

ON THE A49 From the M56, exit at junction 10 and take the A49 south towards Whitchurch. Let's Eat Café is 3 miles further on the right-hand side, 800 yards before the junction with the A533.

CREDIT/DEBIT CARDS

TRUCK FACILITIES
P
Coach parking (10 spaces)
Quiet area
Ample room for manoeuvring

DRIVER FACILITIES
Showers – 2 m, 2 f, TV
Phone top-ups/accessories
Takeaway food

SITE COMMENTS/INFORMATION
Clean friendly, newly refurbished café
seating 50

Parking 24 hours. Other on-site facilities 07:00-19:00 Mon-Thurs, 07:00-15:00 Fri, 08:00-13:00 Sat & Sun **423**

FL2 — Lindisfarne Service Station, Beal

**Beal, Berwick upon Tweed
Northumberland TD15 2PD
T 01289 381232**

ON THE A1 SOUTHBOUND Lindisfarne is on the A1 on the right-hand side if heading north, at the junction for the road to Holy Island. Six miles south of Berwick upon Tweed.

CREDIT/DEBIT CARDS

FUEL CARDS (see key on page 9)
① ② ③ ④ ⑦ ㉞

TRUCK FACILITIES
Overnight parking in lay-by

DRIVER FACILITIES
Takeaway food
Truckers' accessories
Phone top-ups

SITE COMMENTS/INFORMATION
Truckers made very welcome
Showers being installed in 2008

Nearby parking 24 hours. All on-site facilities 06:00-23:00 Mon-Sun **424**

T2 — Little Bistro

**Burneston, Bedale
North Yorkshire DL8 2JJ
T 01845 567990**

ON THE A1 SOUTHBOUND Little Bistro is set back from the road on the A1 southbound carriageway, 4 miles south of Leeming Bar, 1 mile after the turning for Gatenby but before the turning for Pickhill.

CREDIT/DEBIT CARDS

TRUCK FACILITIES
P
Coach parking (10 spaces)
Ample room for manoeuvring

DRIVER FACILITIES
Showers – 3 m, 3 f, washroom, rest area, TV, clothing shop, truckers' accessories, takeaway food

SITE COMMENTS/INFORMATION
All food freshly cooked. Friendly staff, quick service and high standards. Good atmosphere and a pleasant environment

Parking accessible 24 hours. Other on-site facilities accessible 07:00-21:00 **425**

Londonderry Lodge Truckstop & Exelby Services Ltd T4

**Londonderry, Northallerton
North Yorkshire DL7 9ND/B
T 01677 422143/422185**
www.exelbyservices.co.uk

ON THE OLD A1 If heading north on A1 take the exit before the A684 signposted for Exelby and Leeming and turn across the carriageway. Londonderry Lodge and Exelby Services will be in front of you to the right.

CREDIT/DEBIT CARDS

FUEL CARDS (see key on page 9)
① ② ③ ④ ⑤ ⑥ ⑦ ⑧ ⑨ ⑭ ㉒ ㉓ ㉞

TRUCK FACILITIES
P £3.50 and £3.70
Ample room for manoeuvring, Quiet, Truck dealership/workshop, Adblue at pumps/in containers, LGV sales/dealership/ workshop

DRIVER FACILITIES
Accommodation, £18 pn, Showers – 1 m, 1 f (free), washroom, rest area, TV, truckers' accessories Takeaway food, Phone top-ups

SITE COMMENTS/INFORMATION
Although 2 separate companies, they are next door to each other

Showers 05:00-00:00 weekdays. Bunker fuel 24 hrs between 09:00 Sun and 18:00 Sat. All other facilities 24 hrs | **426**

Long & Small Service Station, Maryport FL2

**Main Road, Flimby, Maryport
Cumbria CA15 8RB
T 01900 602742**

ON THE A596 Long and Small is on the A596 on the left-hand side if heading north about 800 yards past the village of Flimby and two-and-a-half miles south of the town of Maryport.

CREDIT/DEBIT CARDS

① ② ③ ④ ⑦ ㉕ ㉞
FUEL CARDS (see key on page 9)

TRUCK FACILITIES
Nearby overnight parking

DRIVER FACILITIES
Truckers' accessories

All on-site facilities 07:00-19:00 Mon-Fri | **427**

Low Row Service Station, Brampton FL2

**Low Row, Brampton
Cumbria CA8 2JE
T 01697 746344**

ON THE A69 Exit the M6 at junction 44 and take the A69 eastbound. Go around Brampton and continue for 2 more miles. Low Row Service Station is on the left-hand side.

CREDIT/DEBIT CARDS

FUEL CARDS (see key on page 9)
① ② ③ ④ ⑥ ⑭ ⑮ ㉒ ㉓ ㉗ ㉝ ㉞

TRUCK FACILITIES
Nearby overnight parking

DRIVER FACILITIES
Truckers' accessories
Hot drink free with 100 litres of fuel
Takeaway food
Phone top-ups

All on-site facilities 24 hours | **428**

T4 — Lymm Services & Truckstop (Poplar 2000)

**Cliff Lane, Lymm
Cheshire WA13 0SP
T 01925 757777**

OFF THE A50 From junction 20 M6 northbound or junction 9 M56 in either direction exit onto the sliproad and turn right at 3 consecutive roundabouts. From junction 20 M6 southbound, exit onto sliproad, across 1st roundabout and right at the next.

CREDIT/DEBIT CARDS

FUEL CARDS (see key on page 9)
② ④ ⑦ ㉒ ㉘

TRUCK FACILITIES
P
Coach parking (13 spaces)
Quiet area. Fridge lorry area
Ample room for manoeuvring
Truck washing facilities
Truck dealership/workshop

DRIVER FACILITIES
Accommodation, Travelodge
Showers, rest area, TV, phone top-ups/accessories, clothing for sale, truckers' accessories, CB repairs/sales
Takeaway food

Travelodge opening times unknown. All other on-site facilities accessible 24 hours — **429**

FL1 ■ — Manor Service Station, Wakefield

**Bradford Road, East Ardsley
Wakefield, West Yorkshire WF3 2HE
T 01924 872543**

ON THE A650 (Off M1 Junction 41) take the A650 towards Morley. Manor Service Station is 400 yards on the left.

CREDIT/DEBIT CARDS

FUEL CARDS (see key on page 9)
③ ⑭ ㉒ ㉓ ㉘ ㉝

DRIVER FACILITIES
Takeaway, Post Office, Phone top-ups, and Off licence nearby

OTHER INFORMATION
This site is also a Paypoint agent

All on-site facilities 24 hours. — **430**

FL4 ■ — Merlin Service Station

**254 Bolton Road, Westhoughton
Bolton, Lancashire BL5 3EF
T 01942 793547**

ON THE A6 From the M61, exit at junction 5 and take the A58 towards Westhoughton. Turn right at next roundabout onto the A6 heading for Wingates and Merlin is 600 yards on the left-hand side.

CREDIT/DEBIT CARDS

FUEL CARDS (see key on page 9)
⑦ ㉞

TRUCK FACILITIES
P
Quiet area
Ample room for manoeuvring
Truck washing facilities

DRIVER FACILITIES
Takeaway food nearby

SITE COMMENTS/INFORMATION
Friendly service and car showroom on-site

Parking 24 hours. Other on-site facilities 07:00-20:30 — **431**

Morrisons HGV, Wakefield

FL1 ●

Morrisons Supermarkets Ltd, Kenmore Road, Wakefield Industrial Estate, Carr Gate, Wakefield, West Yorkshire WF2 0XF
T 01924 870000

M1 JUNCTION 41 OFF THE A650 Exit M1 at junction 41 and take A650 signposted Wakefield. At next roundabout, turn left into Kenmore Road and across next roundabout. Morrisons HGV is a few yards on the left.

CREDIT/DEBIT CARDS

FUEL CARDS (see key on page 9)
① ② ④ ㉞

DRIVER FACILITIES
Train nearby

All on-site facilities 24 hours

432

Morrisons, Rotherham

FL1 ▪

Morrisons Supermarkets Ltd
Bawtry Road, Bramley, Rotherham
South Yorkshire S66 1YZ
T 01709 709064

OFF THE A361 Exit the M18 at Junction 1 and take the A361 to Rotherham for 200 yards. Turn left at the next sliproad with the traffic lights and Morrisons is on the left.

CREDIT/DEBIT CARDS

FUEL CARDS (see key on page 9)
① ② ③ ④ ⑦ ㉞

DRIVER FACILITIES
Accommodation nearby, 100 yards, Ibis, £33 per night

DRIVER FACILITIES
Phone top-ups/accessories nearby Clothing for sale, Takeaway and Cashpoint nearby

All on-site facilities accessible 06:30-22:00 Mon-Fri, 07:00-21:00 Sat, 08:00-22:00 Sun

433

NT Truckstop, Carlisle

T4 ▪

(Previously BP Nightowl), Parkhouse Road Kingstown Industrial Estate, Carlisle Cumbria CA3 0JR
T 01228 534192

OFF THE A7 From junction 44 of the M6, take the A7 towards Kingstown. Take the next right across the carriageway and follow signs for the industrial estate. You will see the Truckstop on your left.

CREDIT/DEBIT CARDS

FUEL CARDS (see key on page 9)
① ② ④ ㉞

TRUCK FACILITIES
P *with voucher*   **P** *only*   *Voucher value*
£15.00   £13.50   £3.00
CCTV, anticlimb fencing, security guards Ample room for manoeuvring, Quiet area. Fridge lorry area, Floodlights, Adblue in containers

DRIVER FACILITIES
Accommodation on-site, £27.99-£39.99 pn Showers – 6 unisex (free), washroom, rest area, TV, clothing shop, truckers' accessories, CB repairs/sales, Takeaway food, Fax/copier

Restaurant accessible 06:00-23:00 Mon, 05:00-23:00 Tue-Fri, 05:00-12:00 Sat, 05:00-22:00 Sun. Bar accessible 18:00-23:00 Mon, Tue,Thurs, Fri. 16:00-23:00 Wed. Bunker fuel and all other on-site facilities accessible 24 Hours.

434

FL1 ● Onward Refinishing Services Ltd

Onward Business Park, Ackworth
Pontefract, West Yorkshire WF7 7BE
T 01977 614007

OFF THE A638 From the end of the A1M, take the A638 towards South Elmsall. Past South Elmsall to Ackworth Moor Top across junction with A628 staying on A638 for half a mile. Turn right into Onward Business Park and Onward Refinishing is 20 yards ahead of you.

CREDIT/DEBIT CARDS

FUEL CARDS (see key on page 9)

All on-site facilities 24 hours | **435**

FL1 ● Pallet Yard Truckstop

Doncaster Road, The Maltings Ind. Est.
Whitley Bridge, Goole
East Yorkshire DN14 0HH
T 01977 662881

OFF M62 JUNCTION 34 Exit at Junction 34 M62 and follow signs for local traffic along Selby Road towards Eggborough. Go over canal bridge and turn left before level crossing, continue to end of the road. Pallet Yard Truckstop is at the dead end.

CREDIT/DEBIT CARDS

FUEL CARDS (see key on page 9)

TRUCK FACILITIES
Coach parking available, shared with LGV
Fridge lorry area
Ample room for manoeuvring

DRIVER FACILITIES
Takeaway food
Showers in nearby pub

SITE COMMENTS/INFORMATION
Friendly, helpful site manager

On-site café open until 15:00. Other on-site facilities 24 hours. Nearby restaurant, bar and showers 16:00- 20:00 | **436**

FD1 ◻ Penrith Country Cuisine

Penrith, Cumbria CA11 8
07779 630331

ON THE A66 EASTBOUND From the M6, exit at junction 40 and take the A66 Eastbound. Penrith Country Cuisine is in 100 yards in a big lay-by on your left. To get back to the M6, continue east for 400 yards and turn around at the roundabout.

CREDIT/DEBIT CARDS

FUEL CARDS (see key on page 9)

TRUCK FACILITIES
Parking in large lay-by
Coach parking available, shared with LGV
Ample room for manoeuvring
Truck dealership/workshop nearby

DRIVER FACILITIES
Accommodation nearby, 500 yards,
North Lakes Shire Inns Hotel
Takeaway food. CB sales/repairs nearby

SITE COMMENTS/INFORMATION
This site has very quick and easy access from, and back, to the M6
Breakfast price includes tea or coffee

Parking 24 hours in lay-by. All other on-site facilities 07:30-14:30 Mon-Fri, 08:30-14:00 Sat | **437**

Penrith Truckstop   T4

**Penrith Ind. Est., Penrith
Cumbria CA11 9EH
T 01768 866995** www.awjtruckstop.co.uk

M6 JUNCTION 40 OFF A592 Signposted from junction 40 of the M6. Take A592 into Ullswater Road then left into Hawsater Road. Penrith Truckstop will be on your right.

CREDIT/DEBIT CARDS

FUEL CARDS (see key on page 9)

TRUCK FACILITIES
P *with voucher* £12.00 *Voucher value –* £2.00 and free shower, Quiet, Fridge lorry area, 24hr security, Secure fencing, Floodlts, Manoeuvring room, CCTV, Adblue in containers, Truck dealership/ workshop
DRIVER FACILITIES
Accommodation, single £20.00, twin £32.00, Showers m 10, f 1 (free to overnight patrons), rest area, TV, internet, phone top-ups/accessories, clothing for sale, truckers' accessories, CB repairs/ sales, Takeaway (healthy avail.) food. Train nearby, Games room, Fax/copier

Parking and fuel 24 hours. All other facilities 24 hours from between 06:00 Mon-13:00 Sat, 12:00-22:00 Sun **438**

Priory Way Lorry Park   T1

**Henry Boot Way, off Priory Way, Kingston Upon Hull, East Yorkshire, HU4 7DY
T 01482 331895**

OFF THE A63 From M62, follow A63 into Hull. Go past Humber Bridge on right and into Clive Sullivan Way. After 1 mile turn left into Priory way then next right.

TRUCK FACILITIES
P £10.00 (includes £2 refundable deposit), Fridge parking, Electric hook up Quiet area, 24 hours security, Secure fencing, Floodlights, CCTV

DRIVER FACILITIES
Showers, unisex 2, free with parking Drivers' washroom

SITE COMMENTS/INFORMATION
Security barrier at entrance. Hazardous loads parking area available.

All on-site facilities accessible 24 hours. **439**

Q8 Bilborough Top Services, York   FL2

**York/Leeds Road, Bilborough, York
North Yorkshire YO23 3PP
T 01937 832720**

ON THE A64 This site can be found at Bilborough on the A64 between Leeds and York on the south-west bound carriageway, one and a half miles west of the interchange with the A1237.

CREDIT/DEBIT CARDS

FUEL CARDS (see key on page 9)

TRUCK FACILITIES
Truck dealership/workshop
Nearby overnight parking

DRIVER FACILITIES
Accommodation available nearby, 400 yards, Travel Inn

Toilets 07:00-22:00. Other on-site facilities 24 hours **440**

FL1 ● Quay Fuels

157 Regent Road, Kirkdale, Liverpool
Merseyside L5 9ZA
T 0151 2075155

ON THE A5036 From the M57 take A580 exit towards Bootle. Continue ahead at the A580 until the A59. Turn left onto this. Turn right onto A5054 Boundary Street then right at the Mersey Estuary onto A5036 Regent Road. Quay fuels is 400 yards on the right.

CREDIT/DEBIT CARDS

FUEL CARDS (see key on page 9)

TRUCK FACILITIES
Truck washing facilities
Adblue at the pumps and in containers

DRIVER FACILITIES
Train nearby

All on-site facilities 06:00-18:00   441

T2 Quernhow Transport Café & Caravan Site

And CB Truck & Accessories.
Baldersby, Thirsk, North Yorkshire YO7 4LG
T 01845 567221

ON THE A1 NORTHBOUND From Harrogate take the A1M towards Darlington. Continue past Ripon onto the A1 for 5 miles. Quernhow Transport Café is on the left hand side 3 miles after the junction with the A61, and 400 yards before the junction with the B6267. 18 miles from Scotch Corner.

TRUCK FACILITIES
P *with voucher* £6.50 **P** *only* £6.00
Voucher value – shower and breakfast
Coach parking (10 spaces). Quiet area
Ample room for manoeuvring, Fridge
parking

DRIVER FACILITIES
Accommodation on-site, £39.95 en-suite room, B&B and evening meal
Showers – 4 m, 6 f (£1.50), washroom, TV, laundry service, Euros changed/accepted, phone top-ups/accessories, clothing for sale, truckers' accessories, CB repairs/sales, takeaway food, Healthy menu

SITE COMMENTS/INFORMATION
This site is opposite A1 Diesel Ltd. Credit and debit card facility coming soon

All on-site facilities accessible 24 hours. For nearby fuel times see A1 Diesel Ltd   442

FL1 ● Rix Shipping Dervstop

Rix Ltd, King George Dock, Hull
East Riding of Yorkshire HU9 5PR
T 01482 838383

OFF THE A1033 From the A15 bridge over the Humber heading northbound, turn right onto the A63. Stay on it into Hull and out the other side, heading towards the King George Dock. Turn right at Ferry Terminal junction, left at roundabout. Rix is on the left.

CREDIT/DEBIT CARDS

FUEL CARDS (see key on page 9)

SITE COMMENTS/INFORMATION
This site is within half a mile of the ferry terminal

All on-site facilities 24 hours   443

Roll Inn Motel & Truckstop · T4

**10 Tan House Lane, Widnes
Cheshire WA8 0RR
T 0151 4246355**

OFF THE A562 Exit the M62 at junction 7 and take the A557 towards Widnes for 2 miles. At the junction with the A562, turn left into it for 400 yards. At the next roundabout turn right into Tan House Lane and then immediately left. Roll Inn is on your left.

CREDIT/DEBIT CARDS

FUEL CARDS (see key on page 9)
① ③ ④ ⑤ ⑦ ㉞

TRUCK FACILITIES
P
Ample room for manoeuvring
Quiet area
Truck washing facilities
Truck dealership/workshop

DRIVER FACILITIES
Accommodation on-site,
Showers, washroom, rest area, TV,
phone top-ups/accessories

All on-site facilities accessible 24 hours — **444**

Ron Perry & Son · FL4 ■

**Elwick, Hartlepool
Cleveland TS27 3HH
T 01740 644223**

ON THE A19 SOUTHBOUND Take the A19 from Peterlee towards Middlesborough. Ron Perry & Son is on the southbound carriageway, 2 miles south of Elwick, 2 miles north of Wolviston, and just south of the turning for Dalton Piercy.

CREDIT/DEBIT CARDS

FUEL CARDS (see key on page 9)
① ② ④ ⑦ ⑩ ㉘ ㉞

DRIVER FACILITIES
Takeaway food nearby

SITE COMMENTS/INFORMATION
Excellent staff!

All on-site facilities 06:00-22:00 — **445**

Ron Perry & Son & Café A19 · FL4 ■

**Elwick, Hartlepool
Cleveland TS27 3HH
T 01740 644223**

ON THE A19 NORTHBOUND Take the A19 from Middlesborough towards Peterlee. Ron Perry & Son and Café A19 is on the northbound carriageway, 2 miles south of Elwick, 2 miles north of Wolviston, and just south of the turning for Dalton Piercy.

CREDIT/DEBIT CARDS

FUEL CARDS (see key on page 9)
① ② ⑦ ⑩ ㉘ ㉞

TRUCK FACILITIES
P
Quiet area
Ample room for manoeuvring

DRIVER FACILITIES
Takeaway food nearby

SITE COMMENTS/INFORMATION
Excellent staff!

Parking 24 hours. Other on-site facilities 06:00-22:00 — **446**

FL2 ▣ Royal Blue Service Station, Doncaster

Royal Blue Service Station, York Road, Doncaster, South Yorkshire DN5 8LY
T 01302 390157

ON THE A638 From the centre of Doncaster, take the A630 around the north-west side of the town, then take the A19 for half a mile to the roundabout with the A638. Take the A638 for 400 yards and it's on your left opposite Morrisons.

CREDIT/DEBIT CARDS

FUEL CARDS (see key on page 9)
① ③ ④ ⑦

TRUCK FACILITIES
Coach parking available, shared with LGV
Ample room for manoeuvring
Nearby overnight parking on roadside,
4 spaces, free of charge

DRIVER FACILITIES
Phone top-ups

All on-site facilities 24 hours   **447**

T3 ▢ Sandbach Services northbound

Roadchef Ltd
Sandbach
Cheshire CW11 2FZ
T 01270 767134

M6 NORTHBOUND BETWEEN JUNCTIONS 16 AND 17

CREDIT/DEBIT CARDS

FUEL CARDS (see key on page 9)
① ③ ㉓ ㉖ ㉗

TRUCK FACILITIES
P *with voucher*   **P** *only*   *Voucher value*
£20.00   £15.00   £10.00
Coach parking spaces available, Quiet
Ample room for manoeuvring
Truck dealership/workshop

DRIVER FACILITIES
Showers, 1 m, 1 f, TV. Truckers'
accessories, Takeaway food, Vegetarian
meals, Arcade machines, Euros, Fax/
copier, Post Office nearby, Phone top-ups,
Clothing, Truckers' accessories, Int. papers,
CB sales/repairs nearby, Train nearby

Esso Petrol Forecourt, Costa Coffee and Restore Retail shop all accessible 24 hours   **448**

T3 ▢ Sandbach Services southbound

Roadchef Ltd
Sandbach
Cheshire CW11 2FZ
T 01270 767134

M6 SOUTHBOUND BETWEEN JUNCTIONS 16 AND 17

CREDIT/DEBIT CARDS

FUEL CARDS (see key on page 9)
① ③ ㉔ ㉖ ㉗

TRUCK FACILITIES
P *with voucher*   **P** *only*   *Voucher value*
£20.00   £15.00   £10.00
Coach parking spaces available
Quiet area
Ample room for manoeuvring
Truck dealership/workshop

DRIVER FACILITIES
Showers, 1 m, 1 f, TV
Truckers' accessories, Takeaway food
Clothing for sale, Vegetarian meals,
Arcade machines, Euros

Esso Petrol Forecourt, Costa Coffee and Restore Retail Shop open 24 hours   **449**

Scoffalot Café T2

186 Hessle Road, Hull
East Riding of Yorkshire HU3 3AD
T 01482 323289

OFF THE A63 From the M62, take the A63 into Hull. Continue past the junction with the A1166 for 1 mile. At next roundabout (a weird shaped one) take the 2nd exit onto Hessle Road. Scoffalot is 50 yards opposite the Total garage.

FUEL CARDS (for nearby fuel)
28

TRUCK FACILITIES
P Overnight parking on the road and in nearby garage car park.
Coach parking available, shared with LGV
Ample room for manoeuvring
Tyre repair/sales, tank cleaning, windscreen repair and quiet area nearby

DRIVER FACILITIES
Washroom, takeaway food
Laundry, phone top-ups/accessories, truckers' accessories, Post Office and Euros accepted/changed nearby

SITE COMMENTS/INFORMATION
Close to Leisure Land. Roast dinner every day. Abnormal loads park on road only

All on-site facilities 06:30-14:00 Mon-Sun **450**

Shell Beacon FL4 ■

Brough
North Humberside HU15 1SA
T 01430 426110

ON THE A63 EASTBOUND Beacon services is situated beyond the end of the M62 a few 100 yards further on after it becomes the A63. This site is located on the left-hand side if heading east and is situated next to the Travelodge.

CREDIT/DEBIT CARDS

FUEL CARDS (see key on page 9)
3 25 26

TRUCK FACILITIES
P free
Coach parking available, shared with LGV
Ample room for manoeuvring
Quiet area

DRIVER FACILITIES
Hot drinks free with 100 litres of fuel
Drivers' washroom on-site
Travelodge nearby

SITE COMMENTS/INFORMATION
Friendly staff

All on-site facilities 24 hours except Little Chef Restaurant. Nearby Travelodge opening times unknown **451**

Shell Congleton, Congleton FL1 ■

Clayton By-pass, Congleton
Cheshire CW12 1LR
T 01260 291610

ON THE A34 Exit the M6 at junction 17 and take the A534 towards Congleton. At the junction with the A34 turn left onto it and continue on it for half a mile. Shell Congleton is on your left between Tesco and Macdonalds.

CREDIT/DEBIT CARDS

FUEL CARDS (see key on page 9)
3 23 25 26 27

DRIVER FACILITIES
Accommodation nearby, half a mile, Lion and Swan
Takeaway nearby

All on-site facilities 24 hours. **452**

FL1 ■ Shell Eagle, Rochdale

**Queensway, Rochdale
Lancashire OL11 1TJ
T 01706 716960**

ON THE A664 Take the A627M into Rochdale. Turn right at the end, then left at the roundabout onto the A664. Continue for 800 yards and Shell Eagle is on the right.

CREDIT/DEBIT CARDS

FUEL CARDS (see key on page 9)
10 24 25

All on-site facilities 24 hours
453

FL1 ■ Shell Grand Dale, Molton

**Main Road, Molton, Hull
East Yorkshire HU14 3HG
T 01482 635900**

ON THE A63 Shell Grand Dale is on the A63 westbound carriageway between North Ferriby and Brough. Six miles from the centre of Hull and 6 miles from the start of the M62.

CREDIT/DEBIT CARDS

FUEL CARDS (see key on page 9)
3 25 27

DRIVER FACILITIES
Truckers' accessories

All on-site facilities 24 hours
454

FL2 ■ Shell Lairds

**117 New Chester Road, Birkenhead
Wirral CH41 9BW T 0151 6660940**
ON THE A41 From the M53, exit at junction 5 and take the A41 towards Birkenhead for 7 miles. Continue for 400 yards beyond the junction with the B5136 and Shell Lairds is on the right-hand side. Or from Liverpool city centre, take tunnel through to Birkenhead exit onto the A41. Shell Lairds is the first service station on the left.

CREDIT/DEBIT CARDS

FUEL CARDS (see key on page 9)
25

TRUCK FACILITIES
Overnight parking on Cambell Town Road, Ample room for manoeuvring Windscreen repairs/sales and tyre repairs nearby

DRIVER FACILITIES
Truckers' accessories
Takeaway food nearby
Phone accessories nearby, phone top-ups

SITE COMMENTS/INFORMATION
Train nearby

All on-site facilities 24 hours
455

Shell Redheugh Bridge — FL1

**Askew Road West, Gateshead
Tyne and Wear NE8 2JX
T 0191 4903950**

OFF THE A1 & A184 From the A1M, take the A1 around Gateshead for 4 miles. Turn right at the junction with the A184 onto this road heading towards Gateshead centre. Take the sliproad signposted A189 onto the roundabout. Turn left and Shell Redheugh is on your immediate left

CREDIT/DEBIT CARDS

FUEL CARDS (see key on page 9)
③ ㉔ ㉕ ㉖ ㉙

DRIVER FACILITIES
Vegetarian meals
Healthy menu available
Phone top-ups
Truckers' accessories

All on-site facilities 24 hours. **456**

Shell Staxton — FL2

**Spittal Corner, Old Malton Road, Staxton, Scarborough
North Yorkshire YO12 4NW
T 01944 712900**

ON THE A64 Shell Staxton is on the A64 south of Scarborough, just west of the roundabout with the A1039.

CREDIT/DEBIT CARDS

FUEL CARDS (see key on page 9)
㉕

TRUCK FACILITIES
Overnight parking 1 mile away in lay-by

DRIVER FACILITIES
Healthy menu available
Phone top-ups

SITE COMMENTS/INFORMATION
Friendly site, easy access site for LGVs

All on-site facilities and nearby parking 24 hours **457**

Shell Wentworth Park Service Station — FL2

**Maple Road, Tankersley, Barnsley
South Yorkshire S75 3DL
T 01226 350479**

OFF THE A61 From junction 35 of the M1, take the A61 heading west towards Chapeltown. At the roundabout with the A616 take the 4th exit onto the industrial estate and Maple Road. Follow the road around and Shell Wentworth is on your right.

CREDIT/DEBIT CARDS

FUEL CARDS (see key on page 9)
① ② ③ ④ ⑦ ⑭ ㉓ ㉕

TRUCK FACILITIES
Overnight parking on industrial estate road (10 spaces)
Coach parking available (5 spaces)

DRIVER FACILITIES
Accommodation available 100 yards, Travel Inn
Truckers' accessories
Vegetarian meals available
Healthy menu available
Takeaway nearby

Nearby parking and all on-site facilities 24 hours **458**

FL1 ■   Shell Whitemarepool

Newcastle Road, Wardley, Southshields, Gateshead, Tyne & Wear NE10 8YB
T 01914 954820

ON THE A194 Shell Whitemarepool is at the roundabout at the end of the A194(M) and on the left hand side if heading north.

CREDIT/DEBIT CARDS

FUEL CARDS (see key on page 9)
3 24 25 26 28

TRUCK FACILITIES
Floodlighting, CCTV

DRIVER FACILITIES
Vegetarian/Healthy meals, Takeaway, Phone top-ups, Truckers' accessories

All on-site facilities open 24 Hours   **459**

FL1 ■   Shell Willerby

Beverley Road, Willerby, Hull, East Yorkshire HU10 6NT
T 01482 672890

ON THE A165 On the A165 Between Humber Bridge and Beverly (on the left hand side side if going towards Beverly.)

CREDIT/DEBIT CARDS

FUEL CARDS (see key on page 9)
3 22 23 24 25 26

DRIVER FACILITIES
Takeaway nearby

All site Facilities open 24 hours   **460**

FL2 ■   Skipbridge Service Station

Green Hammerton, York North Yorkshire YO26 8EQ
T 01423 330365

ON THE A59 From junction 47 of the A1M take the A59 towards York. Skipbridge Services is about 5 miles along on the right-hand side, past the village of Kirk Hammerton.

CREDIT/DEBIT CARDS
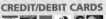

FUEL CARDS (see key on page 9)
27

TRUCK FACILITIES
Overnight parking half a mile away (15 spaces)
Coach parking available (10 spaces)
Ample room for manoeuvring
Fridge lorry area

DRIVER FACILITIES
Truckers' accessories
Takeaway food, Train nearby

SITE COMMENTS/INFORMATION
Access for larger loads can be a little tight

Nearby parking 24 hours. Other on-site facilities 06:30-21:00   **461**

Southwaite Services northbound — T3

Moto Ltd
Southwaite, nr Carlisle
Cumbria CA4 0NT
T 01697 473476 www.moto-way.com

M6 NORTHBOUND BETWEEN JUNCTIONS 41 AND 42

CREDIT/DEBIT CARDS

FUEL CARDS (see key on page 9)
27

DRIVER FACILITIES
Takeaway food
Phone top-ups/accessories
Truckers' accessories

Full site details not available at time of going to press. For more information please contact site.

All on-site facilities accessible 24 hours — **462**

Southwaite Services southbound — T3

Moto Ltd
Southwaite, nr Carlisle
Cumbria CA4 0NT
T 01697 473476 www.moto-way.com

M6 SOUTHBOUND BETWEEN JUNCTIONS 41 AND 42

CREDIT/DEBIT CARDS

FUEL CARDS (see key on page 9)
27

DRIVER FACILITIES
Accommodation, Travelodge
Takeaway food
Phone top-ups/accessories
Truckers' accessories

Full site details not available at time of going to press. For more information please contact site.

All on-site facilities accessible 24 hours — **463**

Spar Total, Alfred Jones Ltd — FL1

Spar Total, Alfred Jones Ltd, 242
Southport Road
Ormskirk, Lancashire L39 1LZ
T 01695 580550
ON THE A570 From junction 3 of the M58, follow the A570 into Ormskirk. Stay on A570 and continue through the town towards Southport. Spar Total is on the right on the outskirts of Ormskirk.

CREDIT/DEBIT CARDS

FUEL CARDS (see key on page 9)
1 3 4 7

DRIVER FACILITIES
Phone top-ups

All on-site facilities 24 hours — **464**

FL4 ■ Stannington Services

North Road, Stannington, Morpeth
Northumberland NE61 6ED
T 01670 789386

OFF THE A1 Take the A1 from Morpeth to Newcastle upon Tyne. Continue past the junction with the A197 and the turning for the village of Clifton. Within 500 yards take the next sliproad. Stannington Services is on your left at the staggered junction.

CREDIT/DEBIT CARDS

FUEL CARDS (see key on page 9)
① ② ④ ⑦ ③④

TRUCK FACILITIES
P
Quiet area
Ample room for manoeuvring

DRIVER FACILITIES
Drivers' washroom
Truckers' accessories

All on-site facilities 24 hours   **465**

FL4 ■ Star Rainton

Rainton, Thirsk
North Yorkshire YO7 3QA
T 01765 641100

ON THE A1 Take the A1M north past junction 49 and onto the A1. Star Rainton is half a mile on the left.

CREDIT/DEBIT CARDS

FUEL CARDS (see key on page 9)
④ ⑦

TRUCK FACILITIES
P
Ample room for manoeuvring

DRIVER FACILITIES
Drivers' washroom and rest area
Takeaway food
Phone top-ups/accessories

SITE COMMENTS/INFORMATION
Easy access for LGVs
Only LGV site for 50 miles

All on-site facilities 24 hours   **466**

FL1 ■ Station Garage, Blyth

Front Street, Bebside, Blyth
Northumberland NE24 4JD
T 01670 352325/352419

ON THE A193 Take the A193 north-westbound out of Blyth until you reach the roundabout with the A189. Go straight across towards Bebside. Station Garage is a few yards on the left.

CREDIT/DEBIT CARDS

FUEL CARDS (see key on page 9)
①

TRUCK FACILITIES
NOT ACCESSIBLE FOR ARTICS

All on-site facilities 07:00-22:00 Mon-Fri, 07:00-21:00 Sat, 08:00-20:00 Sun   **467**

The Stockyard — T4

Hellaby Industrial Estate, Hellaby
South Yorkshire S66 8HN
T 01709 730083

M18 JUNCTION 1 OFF THE A631 Exit the M18 at junction 1 and take the A631 towards Maltby for 200 yards. At next roundabout turn left into Denby Way. Follow road around and The Stockyard is on the left.

CREDIT/DEBIT CARDS

FUEL CARDS (see key on page 9)
❸ ㉘

TRUCK FACILITIES
P with voucher £9.50, voucher = £1.50
Quiet. Fridge lorry area (end of park)
Ample room for manoeuvring
Truck dealership/workshop

DRIVER FACILITIES
Accommodation nearby, half mile, Campanile & Hellaby Hall, Showers 5 m, 1f, (free if parking), Rest area, TV, Clothing, truckers' accessories, takeaway food, Arcade machines, Euros

SITE COMMENTS/INFORMATION
Dedicated heated smoking area, friendly atmosphere and great evening entertainment including live music and Karaoke in Harry's Bar.

Facilities 05:00-23:00 Tues-Thurs, 06:00-23:00 Mon, 07:00-23:00 Sat, (closed 10:30-16:00 Sat) — 468

Sue's Pitstop — FD2

(formerly the Redwood Café)
Ledston Luck Enterprise Park
Garforth, Leeds, West Yorkshire LS25 7BD
T 0113 2863307

OFF THE A656 From M1 junction 47 head to Castleford on the A656. Straight over at roundabout and the cafe is 400m on the Left. From the A1 at junction 42 head towards Leeds on the A63. Take a Left at the A63/A656 roundabout, cafe 400m on the Left.

CREDIT/DEBIT CARDS

FUEL CARDS (see key on page 9)

TRUCK FACILITIES
P free
Short-term coach parking available
Ample room for manoeuvring
Truck dealership/workshop nearby

DRIVER FACILITIES
Drivers' washroom
Takeaway food

All on-site facilities accessible. 07:00-15:00 Mon-Fri, 07:00-11:00 Sat — 469

Suthers Star Garage — FL2

Liverpool Road, Walmer Bridge, Preston
Lancashire PR4 5JS
T 01772 612281

OFF THE A59 Take the A59 from Ormskirk to Preston, past Tarleton and the B5247 for Leyland. Continue to Much Hoole. At the roundabout with the Fox Cub pub, take 2nd exit to Walmer Bridge and keep to the left fork. Suthers Star Garage is 200 yards on the right.

CREDIT/DEBIT CARDS

FUEL CARDS (see key on page 9)
㉗

TRUCK FACILITIES
Overnight parking in Longton
Business Park
Tyre repair/sales

DRIVER FACILITIES
Takeaway food
Post Office nearby

SITE COMMENTS/INFORMATION
Family run business established in 1930!

All on-site facilities 07:00-22:00 — 470

FL1 ● Total Butler, Thirsk

**Total Butler Ltd, Energy House
Thirsk Industrial Park, Thirsk
North Yorkshire YO7 3BX
T 01845 525414**

OFF THE A170 Exit A1M at junction 49 and take A168 to Thirsk. After 5 miles turn left onto A170 and after 400 yards right into Thirsk Industrial Park. Take 2nd left and Total Butler is round the bend on the left.

CREDIT/DEBIT CARDS

FUEL CARDS (see key on page 9)
① ② ④ ⑦ ㉞

All on-site facilities 08:00-17:00   471

FL2 ■ Total Service Station, Ardwick

**Chancellor Lane, Ardwick, Manchester
Greater Manchester M12 6JZ
T 0161 2731030**

ON THE A665 Take the A75M east through Manchester to the end. Merge onto the A365 and follow signs for the A665. Turn south on the A665 towards the Longsight District. Total Service Station Ardwick is 200 yards on the left.

CREDIT/DEBIT CARDS

FUEL CARDS (see key on page 9)
③ ㉘

TRUCK FACILITIES
Overnight parking just around the corner

DRIVER FACILITIES
Truckers' accessories, Takeaway food nearby, Healthy menu available Phone top-ups

SITE COMMENTS/INFORMATION
This site is close to all routes in and out of the city centre

All on-site facilities 24 hours   472

T4 ■ Truckhaven (Carnforth) Ltd

**Carnforth Truckstop, Scotland Road
Warton, Carnforth, Lancashire LA5 9RQ
T 01524 736699**

ON THE A6 From the M6 junction 35, join the A601M towards Carnforth and Morcambe. At the first roundabout turn left onto the A6. Continue for 200 yards and Truckhaven is on your right.

CREDIT/DEBIT CARDS

FUEL CARDS (see key on page 9)
① ② ③ ⑧ ㉓ ㉗

TRUCK FACILITIES
P with voucher £8.00 inc. eve. meal Voucher value £1.50 Ample room for manoeuvring, Overnight coach, CCTV. Quiet area, Secure fencing, Floodlights, Fridge parking (directed) , P-T security

DRIVER FACILITIES
Accomm. £22 single, £32 twin Showers – 8 m, 1 f (free), washroom, rest area, TV, truckers' accessories Takeaway food, Vegetarian meals, Arcade machines, Internet, Euros, Fax/copier, Phone top-ups, Clothing

We are open 24 hours at the Forecourt, Parking, Reception and Shop. Restaurant open 24 hours except Sat & Sun (closes at 22:00 Sat to 07:00 Sun then opens 05:00 Mon.)   473

Tweed Dock Lorry Park — T1

Tweed Dock, Berwick upon Tweed
Northumberland TD15 2AB
T 01289 307404 www.portofberwick.co.uk

OFF THE A1167 From the A1, take the A698 or A1167 into Berwick upon Tweed and follow signs for Tweedmouth and then Tweed Dock. Please note that the lorry park is on the south-west bank of the river Tweed where it joins the North Sea.

CREDIT/DEBIT CARDS NEARBY

TRUCK FACILITIES
P £7.00 without voucher
CCTV

DRIVER FACILITIES
Unisex shower (2)
Drivers' washroom
Accommodation 600 yards away at the Queens Head
Takeaway food nearby
Fax/copier, phone top-ups nearby

SITE COMMENTS
This site is situated on a working dock and is very limited on spaces

All on-site facilities 16:00-07:00 — **474**

Victoria Filling Station, Morley — FL1

Bruntcliffe Road, Morley, Leeds
West Yorkshire LS27 OJZ
T 0113 2527538

ON THE A650 Can be accessed from north or southbound carriageway of M621 or westbound carriageway of M62 at Junctions 27. Take A650 towards Wakefield for half a mile and it's on the left. Or from M62 junction 28, take A650 towards Bradford for 2 miles, it's on the right.

CREDIT/DEBIT CARDS

FUEL CARDS (see key on page 9)
① ④ ⑦ ㉕ ㉞

TRUCK FACILITIES
Truck washing facilities

DRIVER FACILITIES
Accommodation nearby, 500 yards, Old Vicarage & Innkeepers Lodge
Truckers' accessories

All on-site facilities 24 hours. — **475**

Wardle Services — FL4

Nantwich Road, Wardle, nr Taporley
Cheshire CW6 9JS
T 01829 260304

ON THE A51 Take the A51 from Nantwich towards Chester. Wardle Services is on the right, 3 miles beyond the junction with the A534, north west of the village of Wardle and before the village of Caveley.

CREDIT/DEBIT CARDS

FUEL CARDS (see key on page 9)
① ② ③ ④ ⑦ ㉗ ㉞

TRUCK FACILITIES
P £6.00
Coach parking available, shared with LGV
Ample room for manoeuvring
Quiet area, Secure fencing
Floodlighting, CCTV
Truck washing facilities

DRIVER FACILITIES
Drivers' washroom, Takeaway food nearby, Clothing for sale nearby
CB sales/repairs nearby

Parking 24 hours. Other on-site facilities 07:00-19:00 — **476**

T3 — Washington Services northbound

Moto Ltd
Portobello, Birtley, Durham
County Durham DH3 2SJ
T 0191 4103436 www.moto-way.com

A1M NORTHBOUND JUNCTION 64

All on-site facilities accessible 24 hours

CREDIT/DEBIT CARDS

FUEL CARDS (see key on page 9)
27

TRUCK FACILITIES
Coach parking available (3 spaces)

DRIVER FACILITIES
Accommodation, Travelodge
Phone top-ups/accessories
Truckers' accessories
Takeaway food
Shower, washroom and rest area nearby

477

T3 — Washington Services southbound

Moto Ltd
Portobello, Birtley, Durham
County Durham DH3 2SJ
T 0191 4103436 www.moto-way.com

A1M SOUTHBOUND JUNCTION 64

All on-site facilities accessible 24 hours

CREDIT/DEBIT CARDS

FUEL CARDS (see key on page 9)
27

TRUCK FACILITIES
Coach parking available (3 spaces)

DRIVER FACILITIES
Accommodation, Travelodge
Shower, rest area, TV
Phone top-ups/accessories
Truckers' accessories
Takeaway food

478

FL4 — West Cave Services

Triple 8, Brough
East Yorkshire HU15 1RZ
T 01430 422127

ON THE A63 WESTBOUND From Hull take the A63 westbound out of the city. West Cave Services is on the A63 westbound carriageway, half a mile before the M62.

Restaurant 07:00-22:00. Travelodge opening times unknown. Parking, shop and fuel 24 hours

CREDIT/DEBIT CARDS

FUEL CARDS (see key on page 9)
14 22

TRUCK FACILITIES
P
Coach parking available, shared with LGV
Ample room for manoeuvring

DRIVER FACILITIES
Travelodge 400 yards away
Truckers' accessories

SITE COMMENTS/INFORMATION
Friendly staff, good service.
Truckers' facilities due to be upgraded soon

479

Westmorland Services–Northbound, Tebay Services T3

Westmorland Ltd
Orton, Nr Tebay, Cumbria CA10 3SB
T 015396 24511 www.westomorland.com

M6 NORTHBOUND BETWEEN JUNCTIONS 38 AND 39

Farm shop on-site selling local produce including ice-cream and fair trade goods. During summer months we have an outside BBQ area during selling home made food cooked on-site.

CREDIT/DEBIT CARDS

FUEL CARDS (see key on page 9)

③ ⑩ ⑭ ㉓ ㉘

TRUCK FACILITIES

P with voucher   **P** only   Voucher value
£10.00   £13.00   £3.00
Coaches overnight, Quiet parking

DRIVER FACILITIES

Accommodation on-site, Westmorland Hotel, Takeaway food, Vegetarian/Healthy meals, Showers, male (1), female (1) refund. dep., Phone top-ups, Arcade machines, Fax/copier, Clothing, Truckers' accessories

SITE COMMENTS/INFORMATION

Farm shop on-site, outdoor BBQ facilities during summer

All on-site facilities accessible 24 hours

480

Westmorland Services–Southbound, Tebay Services T3

Westmorland Ltd
Orton, Nr Tebay, Cumbria CA10 3SB
T 01539 624511 www.westmorland.com

M6 SOUTHBOUND BETWEEN JUNCTIONS 38 AND 39

Farm shop on-site selling local produce including ice-cream and fair trade goods. During summer months we have an outside BBQ area selling home made food cooked on-site.

CREDIT/DEBIT CARDS

FUEL CARDS (see key on page 9)

③ ⑩ ⑭ ㉒ ㉓ ㉕

TRUCK FACILITIES

P with voucher   **P** only   Voucher value
£10.00   £13.00   £3.00
Coaches overnight, Room for manoeuvre
Abnormal loads should not use pumps 11, 12 & 14

DRIVER FACILITIES

Takeaway food, Vegetarian/Healthy meals, Showers, m (1), f (1) refund. dep, Accom., Westmorland Hotel, Phone top-ups, Arcade mach., Fax/copier, Truckers' accessories

SITE COMMENTS/INFORMATION

Farm shop on-site, outdoor BBQ facilities during summer

All on-site facilities accessible 24 hours

481

Woodall Services northbound T3

Welcome Break Ltd
nr Killamarsh, nr Sheffield
South Yorkshire S26 7XR
T 0114 2486434 www.wwelcomebreak.co.uk

M1 NORTHBOUND BETWEEN JUNCTIONS 30 AND 31

CREDIT/DEBIT CARDS

FUEL CARDS (see key on page 9)

① ㉔ ㉕ ㉖ ㉗

TRUCK FACILITIES

P with voucher   **P** only   (Discounts
£8.50   £10.00   available)
Coaches overnight, shared with LGVs
24hr security, Secure fencing, Floodlights
Room for manoeuvre, Fridge parking, Quiet, Adblue at pumps/in containers

DRIVER FACILITIES

Takeaway food, Vegetarian/Healthy meals, Showers, male (2), female (2), unisex (1), Washroom, Accommodation £39.00, Arcade machines, Games room, Internet, Euros, Fax/copier, Phone accessories/top-ups, Clothing, Truckers' accessories

All on-site facilities accessible 24 hours

482

T3 | Woodall Services southbound

Welcome Break Ltd
nr Killamarsh, nr Sheffield
South Yorkshire S26 7XR
T 0114 2486434 www.welcomebreak.co.uk

M1 SOUTHBOUND BETWEEN JUNCTIONS 30 AND 31

CREDIT/DEBIT CARDS

FUEL CARDS (see key on page 9)
⑩ ㉔ ㉕

TRUCK FACILITIES
P with voucher   **P** only   (Discounts
£8.50   £10.00   available)
Coaches overnight (6), 24hr security, Secure
fencing, Room for manoeuvre, Fridge
parking, Quiet, Adblue at pump/in
container

DRIVER FACILITIES
Accommodation, Days Inn (39.00)
Takeaway food, Vegetarian/Healthy meals,
Showers, male (2), female (2), Washrooms,
Arcade mach., Games room, Internet,
Euros, Fax/copier, Phone accessories/top-
ups, Clothing, Truckers' accessories

All on-site facilities accessible 24 hours   **483**

T3 | Woolley Edge Services northbound

Moto Ltd
West Bretton, Wakefield
West Yorkshire WF4 4LQ
T 01924 830371 www.moto-way.com

M1 NORTHBOUND BETWEEN JUNCTIONS 38 AND 39

CREDIT/DEBIT CARDS

FUEL CARDS (see key on page 9)
③ ㉔ ㉖ ㉗ ㉙

TRUCK FACILITIES
P with voucher   **P** only   Voucher value
£16.00   £10.00   £6.00
Coaches overnight, shared with LGV
Room for manoeuvre, Quiet, Abnormal
load parking area opposite HGV parking

DRIVER FACILITIES
Takeaway food, Showers, male (1),
female (1), Phone top-ups/accessories

Main Site operates 24 Hours (excluding Christmas Day)   **484**

T3 | Woolley Edge Services southbound

Moto Ltd
West Bretton, Wakefield
West Yorkshire WF4 4LQ
T 01924 830371 www.moto-way.com

M1 SOUTHBOUND BETWEEN JUNCTIONS 38 AND 39

CREDIT/DEBIT CARDS

FUEL CARDS (see key on page 9)
㉗

DRIVER FACILITIES
Accommodation, Travelodge
Takeaway food
Phone top-ups/accessories

*Full site details not available at time of going to
press. For more information please contact site.*

All on-site facilities accessible 24 hours   **485**

Wynyard Park Service Area

FL4 ■

**Coal Lane, Wolviston, Billingham
Cleveland TS22 5PZ
T 01740 644875**

A19 A689 INTERCHANGE Exit the A19 southbound at the junction with the A689 and turn right on the A689 towards Wolviston and Billingham. Turn left at the next roundabout into the service area complex. The filling station is on the left.

CREDIT/DEBIT CARDS

FUEL CARDS (see key on page 9)
① ② ③ ⑭ ㉓ ㉔ ㉕ ㉖ ㉗ ㉘

TRUCK FACILITIES
P with voucher – £5.00
Coach parking available, shared with LGV
Ample room for manoeuvring,
Floodlighting, Fridge parking, Quiet

DRIVER FACILITIES
Hot drinks free with 100 litres
Accommodation nearby
Takeaway, Arcade machines and Post
Office nearby, Phone top-ups

SITE COMMENTS/INFORMATION
Helpful friendly staff available round the clock

Holiday Inn opening times unknown. All other on-site facilities 24 hours

486

York Lorry Park

T2

**York Auction Centre, Bridlington Road,
Murton, York, North Yorkshire, YO19 5GF
T 01904 489731 or 01904 486720 at night
www.ylc.co.uk**
OFF THE A64 YORK BYPASS Take the A64 around the outskirts of York At the roundabout with the A1079 and A166 take the A166 Bridlington road and follow signposts for Auction Centre.

TRUCK FACILITIES
P £10.00 with voucher, £8.00 without,
Voucher value £2.50
Coaches overnight, shared with LGV
24 hour security, Secure fencing,
Floodlights, CCTV, Room to manoeuvre,
Quiet parking area, Fridge lorries banned
from site

DRIVER FACILITIES
Showers, male (3), female (1),
Washroom, Healthy menu, Takeaway, TV

Open to LGV Parking 17:00-09:00 daily

487

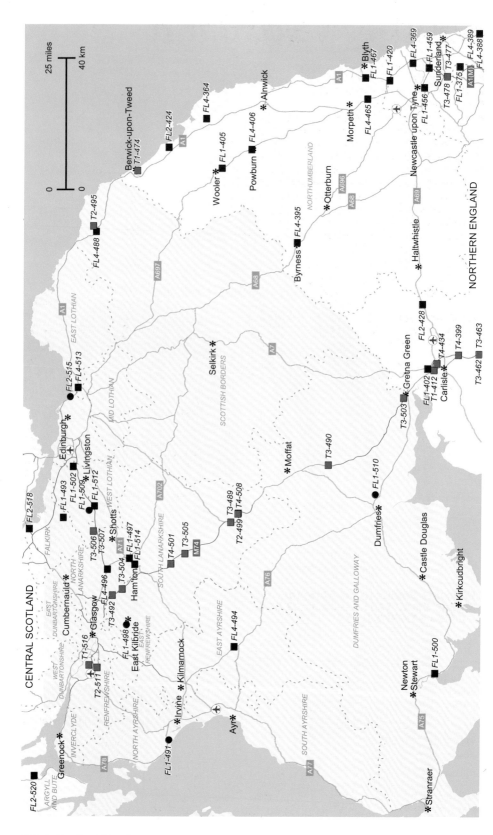

Southern Scotland

■ *Cafe - Layby parking (FD1)*
■ *Cafe - No overnight parking (FD2)*
■ *Filling Station - No overnight parking/cafe (FL1)*
● *Bunkering Site - No overnight parking/cafe (FL1)*
■ *Filling Station - Nearby overnight parking no cafe (FL2)*
● *Bunkering Site - Nearby overnight parking no cafe (FL2)*
■ *Filling Station - Cafe no onsite overnight parking (FL3)*
■ *Filling Station - Onsite overnight parking (FL4)*
● *Bunkering Site - Onsite overnight parking (FL4)*
● *Bunkering Site - Cafe & onsite overnight parking (FL5)*
■ *Lorry Park - Onsite overnight parking no cafe or fuel (T1)*
■ *Truck Stop/Cafe - Onsite overnight parking (T2)*
■ *Motorway Service Station (T3)*
■ *Truck Stop - Bunker fuel/showers/cafe/onsite overnight parking (T4)*

For key to site symbols see page 8

FL4 ■   3D Garages Ltd

**A1 Grantshouse Services, Grantshouse
Duns, Berwickshire TD11 3RW
T 01361 850206**

ON THE A1 On the A1 between Dunbar and Berwick upon Tweed. 3D Garages is located at Grantshouse opposite the junction with the A6112.

CREDIT/DEBIT CARDS

FUEL CARDS (see key on page 9)

TRUCK FACILITIES
P
Quiet area
Ample room for manoeuvring

DRIVER FACILITIES
Drivers' washroom
Takeaway food
Phone top-ups/accessories

SITE COMMENTS/INFORMATION
Site recently refurbished
No fridge lorries overnight

Parking 24 hours. Other on-site facilities 06:00-22:00 Mon-Fri, 07:00-22:00 Sat, 07:00-21:00 Sun   **488**

T3 ■   Abington Services

**Welcome Break Ltd, nr Abington
Biggar, South Lanarkshire ML12 6RG
T 01864 502637/502835**

A74M JUNCTION 13

CREDIT/DEBIT CARDS

FUEL CARDS (see key on page 9)

DRIVER FACILITIES
Accommodation on-site, Welcome Lodge, From £49.00 per night
Takeaway food
Showers, unisex (2)
Accommodation from £49.00 per night
Truckers' accessories
Vegetarian/healthy meals
TV, Arcade machines, Euros accepted
Fax/copier, Phone accessories
Phone top-ups

All on-site facilities accessible 24 hours   **489**

Annandale Water Services

T3 ▪

**Roadchef Ltd
Johnstonebridge, nr Lockerbie
Dumfries and Galloway DG11 1HD
T 01576 470870** www.roadchef.com

A74M JUNCTION 16 Accessible from Northbound and Southbound carriageways.

All on-site facilities accessible 24 hours

CREDIT/DEBIT CARDS

FUEL CARDS (see key on page 9)
① ③ ⑭ ㉒ ㉓ ㉘ ㉝

TRUCK FACILITIES
P *with voucher*   **P** *only   Voucher value*
£17.00   £14.00   £7.50
Coach parking available (15 spaces)
Quiet area. Truck dealership/workshop
Ample room for manoeuvring,
Floodlighting, Fridge
DRIVER FACILITIES
Accommodation £53.00, showers, 1 m, 1 f free, internet access, phone top-ups/accessories, truckers' accessories Takeaway food, vegetarian, healthy, TV, arcade mach. Euros accepted, Clothing for sale
SITE COMMENTS/INFORMATION
Parking facilities are beside forecourt

490

B Brogan, Stevenson

FL1 ●

**B Brogan Ltd, Old Quarry Road
off New Street, Stevenson, Ayrshire
KA20 3HS
T 01294 468511**
OFF THE B752 Take A78 dual carriageway west around Kilwinning. At roundabout with A738 turn left along the A78. Go past Safeway. At roundabout with A738 Townhead Street, take that road for 500 yards. Left into New Street B752 then 2nd left.

All on-site facilities 07:00-17:00 Mon-Fri. 08:00-12:00 Sat.

CREDIT/DEBIT CARDS

FUEL CARDS (see key on page 9)
① ② ④ ⑦ ⑧ ㉞

TRUCK FACILITIES
Truck washing facilities
Ample room for manoeuvring
Short-term parking only with permission

DRIVER FACILITIES
Post Office nearby
Takeaway food nearby
Train nearby

SITE COMMENTS/INFORMATION
Fuel can be paid for in cash
Internet access coming soon to this site

491

Bothwell Services southbound

T3 ▪

**Roadchef Ltd
nr Bothwell, Glasgow
South Lanarkshire G71 8BG
T 01698 854123**

M74 SOUTHBOUND BETWEEN JUNCTIONS 4 AND 5

Cost Coffee, restaurant, parking, fuel, shop and shower accessible 24 hrs

CREDIT/DEBIT CARDS

FUEL CARDS (see key on page 9)
③ ⑧ ⑭ ㉒ ㉓

TRUCK FACILITIES
P *with voucher*   **P** *only   Voucher value*
£20.00   £17.00   £10.00
Coach parking available (14 spaces)
Ample room for manoeuvring
DRIVER FACILITIES
Shower, 1 unisex (free), TV, Internet access, Arcade machines, Takeaway food, Vegetarian/healthy meals
Truckers' accessories, Phone top-ups
Clothing, Accommodation, Premier Inn Hamilton, £56.00
SITE COMMENTS/INFORMATION
Abnormal load area at top end of lorry park next to Forecourt

492

FL1 ■   Bowhouse Service Station, Falkirk

Echobank, Maddison, Falkirk
Central Region FK2 0BX
T 01324 711789 or site office 01324 712669

ON THE A801 From the M9, exit at junction 4 and take the A801 south. Bowhouse is on the A801 on the left, just after the junction with the B825. From Junction 4 of the M8, take the A801 north and Bowhouse is on the right just before Maddison.

CREDIT/DEBIT CARDS

FUEL CARDS (see key on page 9)
① ② ④ ⑤ ㉕ ㉞

All on-site facilities 24 hours   **493**

FL4 ■   Bridgend Garage Ltd

1 Main Street, Auchinleck
East Ayrshire KA18 2AB
T 01290 421224

ON THE B7083 OFF THE A76 Head south from Kilmarnock on the A76 and take the B7083 into Auchinleck village. Continue for half a mile and Bridgend Garage is on the right-hand side at the far end of the village.

CREDIT/DEBIT CARDS

FUEL CARDS (see key on page 9)
① ② ③ ④ ㉓ ㉖ ㉗ ㉞

TRUCK FACILITIES
P free, 4 on-site 2 opposite, Fridge parking, Coach parking available (1), shared with LGV, Ample room for manoeuvring, Quiet area, Truck dealership/workshop nearby, Adblue in containers

DRIVER FACILITIES
Shower, Phone top-ups/accessories Takeaway food, Train nearby

SITE COMMENTS/INFORMATION
LGVs must use pumps outside
12ft high canopy

All on-site facilities 24 hours   **494**

T2 ■   Cedar Transport Café

Harelawside, Grantshouse, Duns
Berwickshire TD11 3RP
T 01361 850371

OFF THE A1 From Dunbar, take the A1 to Berwick upon Tweed. Continue for 200 yards past the turning for the A6112 and take the next left into a 'crescent'. The Cedar Café will be on your left-hand side.

CREDIT/DEBIT CARDS

FUEL CARDS (see key on page 9)

TRUCK FACILITIES
P free
Coach parking available (6 spaces)
Quiet area
Ample room for manoeuvring

DRIVER FACILITIES
Showers – 1 m, 1 f (charge), washroom, TV
Takeaway food

SITE COMMENTS/INFORMATION
Varied menu. Winner of *Commercial Motor*'s best truckstop and best breakfast awards

08:00-20:00 Sun-Fri, 08:00-17:00 Sat. Parking accessible 24 hours   **495**

Circular Services   FL4 ■

Glasgow/Edinburgh Road, Newhouse
Near Motherwell, Strathclyde
Lanarkshire ML1 5SY
T 01698 860236

ON THE A775 From junction 6 of the M8 take the A73
heading south towards Newhouse. At the next roundabout,
turn right onto the B7066 towards Belshill. Circular Services is
a few yards along on the left.

CREDIT/DEBIT CARDS

FUEL CARDS (see key on page 9)
①②③④⑥⑦㉞

TRUCK FACILITIES
P free
Quiet area
Truck dealership/workshop nearby

DRIVER FACILITIES
Travel Inn on-site (£35 per night)
Takeaway food
Truckers' accessories

SITE COMMENTS/INFORMATION
Happy, cheerful staff. Welcoming site

Parking 24 hours. Travelodge times unknown. All other on-site facilities 05:00-16:00   **496**

Cooper Brothers, Winshaw   FL1 ■

Overtown Road, Newmains, Winshaw
Lanarkshire ML2 8HF
T 01698 385477

ON THE A71 From M74 northbound exit at junction 8 and
take the A71 towards Livingstone. Cooper Brothers is at the
junction with the A73. From the A8, exit junction 6 onto A73
to Carluke and Cooper Brothers is at the junction with the A71.

CREDIT/DEBIT CARDS

FUEL CARDS (see key on page 9)
⑦

DRIVER FACILITIES
Truckers' accessories
Phone top-ups/accessories
Takeaway food

SITE COMMENTS/INFORMATION
Easy access for LGVs

On-site facilities 07:30-22:00 Mon-Fri, 07:30-21:00 Sat, 09:00-21:00 Sun   **497**

CPL Petroleum, East Kilbride   FL1 ●

CPL Petroleum Ltd, 22 Hawkbank Road
College Milton North, East Kilbride
Glasgow, South Lanarkshire G74 5HA
T 01355 243692

OFF THE A726 Take the A726 towards East Kilbride from
Glasgow. Continue 1 mile past roundabout with the B766. At next
roundabout, turn left onto Stewartfield Way. Right at roundabout
into Castleglen Road then left at roundabout into Hawkbank Road.

CREDIT/DEBIT CARDS

FUEL CARDS (see key on page 9)
①

TRUCK FACILITIES
Ample room for manoeuvring

DRIVER FACILITIES
Accommodation nearby, half mile,
Stakis East Kilbride
Takeaway food nearby
Post Office nearby

SITE COMMENTS/INFORMATION
This site is 2 miles from all town centre
facilities

Fuel 24 hours. Site is manned from 08.30-17:00 Mon-Fri, when red diesel/lubrication oil are available   **498**

T2 ■ — Crawford Arms Hotel

**111 Carlisle Road, Crawford, Biggar
South Lanarkshire ML2 6TP
T 01864 502267**

OFF THE A702 Come off the A74M at junction 14 and follow signs for Crawford village. The Crawford Arms is located in the middle of the village on your left, just past the turning for Belstane Avenue.

CREDIT/DEBIT CARDS

FUEL CARDS (see key on page 9)

TRUCK FACILITIES
P
Quiet area
CCTV
Ample room for manoeuvring

DRIVER FACILITIES
Accommodation £27 B&B and evening meal
Showers, male (2), female (1) unisex (1)
(free), washroom, TV, Takeaway,
Vegetarian/Healthy meals, Arcade
machines, Fax/copier

SITE COMMENTS/INFORMATION
Good home cooked food
Easy access to motorway

Parking and nearby fuel 24 Hours. Other on-site facilities 06:00-01:00 Mon-Fri, 08:00-01:00 Sat & Sun   **499**

FL1 ■ — Creetown Service Station, Creetown

**Castle Douglas Road, Creetown
Near Newtown Stewart
Dumfries and Galloway DG8 7DA
T 01671 820233**

ON THE A75 Creetown Service Station is on the A75 at the south end of the village of Creetown, 7 miles south-east of Newton Stewart.

CREDIT/DEBIT CARDS

FUEL CARDS (see key on page 9)
① ② ④ ⑦ ⑧ ㉞

All on-site facilities 08:00-19:00 Mon-Fri, 08:00-18:00 Sat, 09:00-17:00 Sun   **500**

T4 ■ — Europa Truckstop

**Wellburn Interchange, Lanark, Nr Glasgow
Strathclyde ML11 0HY
T 01555 894889** www.europatruckstop.com

AT THE M74 JUNCTION 10 If heading south, exit at junction 9 and take B7086 to Kirkmuirhill for 600 yards. Turn right onto B7078 for 2 miles. Turn right at roundabout with Junction 10, go under motorway and Europa is ahead of you at the next roundabout.

CREDIT/DEBIT CARDS

FUEL CARDS (see key on page 9)
① ② ③ ④ ⑤ ⑥ ⑦ ⑧ ⑪ ⑫ ⑭

TRUCK FACILITIES
P with voucher £10.00, Voucher = £2.00
Coach parking available (20 spaces)
Quiet area. Fridge parking, Truck washing
facilities, Full on-site security

DRIVER FACILITIES
Accommodation on-site, £12 single, £25
twin, Showers, 7m, 2f, rest area, TV,
internet, Euros, phone top-
ups/accessories, clothing for sale,
truckers' accessories, CB repairs/sales
Takeaway food, Vegetarian meals,
Evening entertainment, Games Room,
Laundry

All on-site facilities accessible 24 hours   **501**

Fairfield Service Station, Broxburn   FL1 ■

Edinburgh Road, Broxburn
West Lothian EH52 5BQ
T 01506 852567

ON THE A89 From the M9 exit at junction 1 and take the A89 towards Broxburn. Fairfield Service Station is about 1 and a half miles along on the right.

CREDIT/DEBIT CARDS

FUEL CARDS (see key on page 9)
① ② ③ ④ ⑤ ㉞

DRIVER FACILITIES
Takeaway food

OTHER INFORMATION
All LGVs must follow signs to bunkering pumps. Retail canopy is only 3.9 metres in height. Bunkering canopy is 5.6 metres in height

On-site Greggs Bakers Shop open early until 16.30. All other facilities open 24 hours   **502**

Gretna Green Services   T3 ■

Welcome Break Ltd
Gretna
Dumfries and Galloway DG16 5HQ
T 01461 337567

A74M BETWEEN JUNCTION 21 AND THE A74

CREDIT/DEBIT CARDS

FUEL CARDS (see key on page 9)
⑭

DRIVER FACILITIES
Accommodation, Welcome Lodge
Takeaway food

Full site details not available at time of going to press. For more information please contact site.

All on-site facilities accessible 24 hours   **503**

Hamilton Services   T3 ■

Roadchef Ltd
Hamilton
Lanarkshire ML3 6JW
T 01698 282176

M74 NORTHBOUND BETWEEN JUNCTIONS 5 AND 6

CREDIT/DEBIT CARDS

FUEL CARDS (see key on page 9)
③ ⑧ ⑭ ⑫ ㉒ ㉓

TRUCK FACILITIES
P *with voucher*   **P** *only*   *Voucher value*
£20.00   £17.00   £10.00
Coach parking available (14 spaces)
Quiet area, Ample room for manoeuvring
Abnormal load area located on left stand alone bay behind lorry park

DRIVER FACILITIES
Accommodation on-site (£56 pn)
Shower, 1 unisex (free), TV, internet access, truckers' accessories, Takeaway food, Vegetarian/healthy meals, Clothing, Phone top-ups/ accessories, Arcade machines, Internet, Euros

Costa Coffee, restaurant, shop, forecourt, toilets and shower facilities accessible 24 hours   **504**

T3 ■ Happendon Services (Cairn Lodge)

Cairn Lodge Ltd
Carlisle Road, Douglas, Strathclyde ML11 0JU
T 01555 850260 (filling station) 851880 (office)

M74 JUNCTION 12-11 If heading northbound, exit at junction 12, at end of sliproad, turn right at the roundabout then left at the next. If heading southbound, exit at junction 11 and go straight across the roundabout. Happendon Services is about half a mile on from there.

CREDIT/DEBIT CARDS
VISA · EUROCARD/MasterCard · Diners Club International · JCB · Maestro · Delta · Solo · VISA Electron

FUEL CARDS (see key on page 9)
① ③ ④ ⑦ ⑩ ㉔ ㉕ ㉞

TRUCK FACILITIES
P
Coach parking available (40 spaces)
Evening security guard. Quiet area
Ample room for manoeuvring
Truck dealership/workshop nearby

DRIVER FACILITIES
Shower
Truckers' accessories. Takeaway food
Clothing for sale

SITE COMMENTS/INFORMATION
This site is soon to be refurbished

Restaurant and shop opening times unknown. All other on-site facilities accessible 24 hours   **505**

T3 ■ Harthill Services north-eastbound

BP Ltd
Harthill, Shotts
Lanarkshire ML7 5TT
T 01501 750820

M8 NORTH-EASTBOUND BETWEEN
JUNCTIONS 4 AND 5

CREDIT/DEBIT CARDS
VISA · EUROCARD/MasterCard · JCB · Maestro · Delta

FUEL CARDS (see key on page 9)
⑭ ㉒ ㉗

DRIVER FACILITIES
Takeaway food

Full site details not available at time of going to press. For more information please contact site.

All on-site facilities accessible 24 hours   **506**

T3 ■ Harthill Services south-westbound

BP Ltd
Harthill, Shotts
Lanarkshire ML7 5TT
T 01501 751830

M8 SOUTH-WESTBOUND BETWEEN
JUNCTIONS 4 AND 5

CREDIT/DEBIT CARDS
VISA · EUROCARD/MasterCard · JCB · Maestro · Delta

FUEL CARDS (see key on page 9)
⑭ ㉒ ㉗

DRIVER FACILITIES
Takeaway food

Full site details not available at time of going to press. For more information please contact site.

All on-site facilities accessible 24 hours   **507**

Heatherghyll Truckstop & Hungry Trucker Café T4 ∎

Carlisle Road, Crawford
South Lanarkshire ML12 6
T 01864 502641

OFF THE A702 If heading north, exit the A74M at junction 14 and follow the A702. Turn right at the roundabout near the entrance slip road for the A74M and Heatherghyll is on the left. If heading south, Exit A74 at junction 14, go across roundabout and it's on the left

CREDIT/DEBIT CARDS

FUEL CARDS (see key on page 9)
TRUCK FACILITIES
P *with voucher* £10.00 **P** *only* £6.00
Coach parking (2 spaces) shared with LGV
Ample room for manoeuvring
Truck dealership/workshop, Quiet area
Adblue in containers,Windscreen/LGV
tyre repairs/sales nearby

DRIVER FACILITIES
Showers – 2 m, 1 f (£1), washroom, rest area, TV, internet access, Euros, Phone top-ups/accessories, Takeaway food, Vegetarian/Healthy meals

SITE COMMENTS/INFORMATION
Great veiws over lovely countryside.
Fridge lorries switch off at 21:00

Parking and nearby fuel accessible 24 hours. Other on-site facilities accessible 06:00-23:00   **508**

Johnstone Oils Ltd FL1 ●

Standhill, Whitburn Industrial Estate
Bathgate, West Lothian EH48 2HR
T 01506 656535

OFF THE A7066 From the M8, exit at junction 4. Take the A801 towards Armdale and Bathgate. Continue to roundabout with A706, A7066 and B702. Turn right onto A7066 for 600 yards. Turn left and left again into Inchcross Steadings, then 3rd left. Johnstone is on right.

CREDIT/DEBIT CARDS

FUEL CARDS (see key on page 9)
❶

TRUCK FACILITIES
Ample room for manoeuvring

DRIVER FACILITIES
Takeaway food nearby

SITE COMMENTS/INFORMATION
Red diesel and lubrication oil can be paid for in cash only

All on-site facilities 08:00-17:00 Mon-Fri   **509**

Johnstone Wallace Fuels FL1 ●

Dargavel Stores, Lockerbie Road
Dumfries, Dumfries and Galloway DG1 3PG
T 01387 750747

ON THE A709 From Dumfries take the A709 towards Lockerbie. Johnstone Wallace Fuels is on the right-hand side 1 mile beyond the junction with the A75.

CREDIT/DEBIT CARDS

FUEL CARDS (see key on page 9)
❶ ❷ ❹ ㉞

All on-site facilities 24 hours   **510**

T2 ■ Junction 27 (formerly Travellers Rest Truckstop)

Wallneuk Road, Paisley, nr Glasgow
Renfrewshire PA3 4BT
T 0141 5872448

OFF THE A741 From the M8, exit at junction 27 and take the A741 towards Paisley town centre for 1 mile. Opposite the right-hand turning for the A726, take the left turning into Wallneuk Road signposted for the Superbowl, and Travellers Rest is opposite the Superbowl.

TRUCK FACILITIES
P
Coach parking (40 spaces). Quiet area
Ample room for manoeuvring
Fencing and CCTV. Truckwash nearby
Truck dealership/workshop nearby

DRIVER FACILITIES
Accommodation nearby, half mile,
Watermill Hotel
Showers – 2 m, washroom, TV
Takeaway food. CB sales/repairs nearby,
Train nearby

SITE COMMENTS/INFORMATION
Walking distance of town centre

Parking 24 hours. Other on-site facilities 06:20-23:00 Mon-Fri, 06:20-02:00 Sat & Sun — **511**

FL1 ■ MossHall Service Station

55 West Main Street, Blackburn
West Lothian EH47 7LX
T 01506 634215/01506 634214

ON THE A705 If heading east on the M8, exit at junction 4 and turn right onto the A801 towards Livingston. At the T-junction with the A705 turn left towards Livingston and MossHall is a few yards along on the right.

CREDIT/DEBIT CARDS

FUEL CARDS (see key on page 9)
① ② ③ ④ ⑤ ⑦ ㉞

DRIVER FACILITIES
Euro's changed/accepted
Phone top-ups

OTHER INFORMATION
Drivers with smart bunker fuel cards must fuel at rear of forecourt due to height restrictions

All on-site facilities accessible 24 hours. Toilets are closed between 22:00 and 06:00 — **512**

FL4 ■ Musselburgh Services & Little Chef

Old Craighall, Musselburgh
East Lothian EH21 8RE
T 0131 6536070

OFF THE A1 BY-PASS From the A1 Mussleburgh by-pass, take the exit signposted B6415 and A702 Edinburgh City by-pass. Take the B6415 towards Mussleburgh. Mussleburgh Services is 100 yards on the right.

CREDIT/DEBIT CARDS

FUEL CARDS (see key on page 9)
㉔ ㉗

TRUCK FACILITIES
P Coach parking available
Quiet area
Ample room for manoeuvring

DRIVER FACILITIES
Accommodation on-site
Shower
Drivers' washroom
Takeaway food
Clothing for sale

Fuel, parking, shop and showers 24 hours. All other on-site facilities 07:00-22:00 — **513**

Old Toll Garage, Overtown

FL1 ■

**128 Main Street, Overtown
North Lanarkshire ML2 0QP
T 01698 374094**

ON THE A71 From the M74 exit junction 8 and take the A71 towards Shotts. Or from the M74 junction 7 take the A72, then turn left onto the A71 for Shotts. Old Toll Garage is in the town of Overtown next to the junction with the B754 to Craigneuk.

CREDIT/DEBIT CARDS

FUEL CARDS (see key on page 9)

TRUCK FACILITIES
Short-term coach parking (1 space)

DRIVER FACILITIES
Truckers' accessories

All on-site facilities 06:00-20:00. On-site short term parking times unknown

514

Secure Coach Parks Ltd

FL2 ●

**Freightliner Terminal, Sir Harry Lauder Road
Portobello, Edinburgh EH15 2QA
T 0131 6691911**

OFF THE A199 Exit the M8 at junction 1 and turn right onto the A720. Continue round the city to the A1. Turn left onto the A1 towards Portobello. At the roundabout with the A199, go straight across, follow around to the left and take the first left turn into the site.

CREDIT/DEBIT CARDS

FUEL CARDS (see key on page 9)

TRUCK FACILITIES
Ample room for manoeuvring
Truck washing facilities

DRIVER FACILITIES
Takeaway food nearby
Internet access nearby
Phone top-ups/accessories

SITE COMMENTS/INFORMATION
This site also has a chemical toilet drop for coaches

All on-site facilities 24 hours

515

Westway Lorry park

T1 ■

**Porterfield Road, Renfrew, Renfrewshire
PA4 8DJ T 0141 8866373/8867356**
www.westway-park.com

OFF THE A741 From the M8 junction 27 take the A741 towards Renfrew. The turning for Porterfield Road is about half a mile along on your left just before the park. Continue on Porterfield road for 400 yards. Westway Lorry Park is on your left.

TRUCK FACILITIES
P £5.00
Quiet area
Ample room for manoeuvring
Fridge lorries parking
24 hour security, Secure fencing
CCTV

DRIVER FACILITIES
Shower, 1 male (free)
Drivers' washroom
Takeaway food nearby
Accommodation nearby

All on-site facilities 24 hours

516

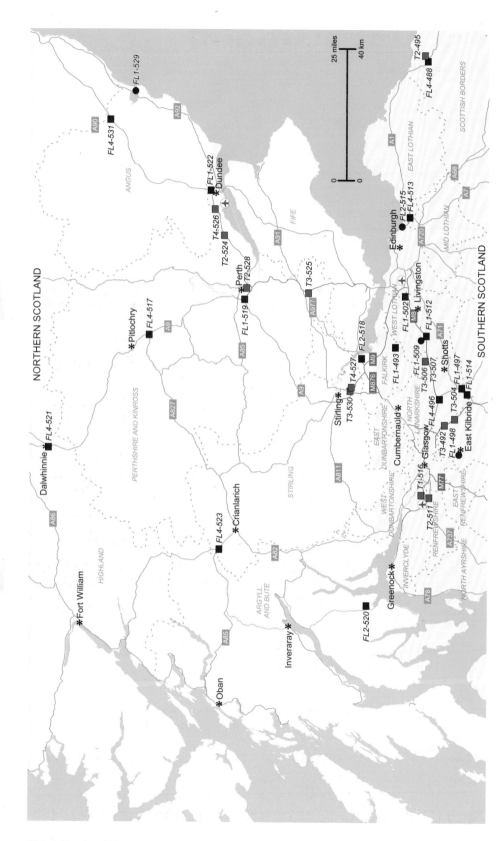

Central Scotland

■ *Cafe - Layby parking (FD1)*
■ *Cafe - No overnight parking (FD2)*
■ *Filling Station - No overnight parking/cafe (FL1)*
● *Bunkering Site - No overnight parking/cafe (FL1)*
■ *Filling Station - Nearby overnight parking no cafe (FL2)*
● *Bunkering Site - Nearby overnight parking no cafe (FL2)*
■ *Filling Station - Cafe no onsite overnight parking (FL3)*
■ *Filling Station - Onsite overnight parking (FL4)*
● *Bunkering Site - Onsite overnight parking (FL4)*
● *Bunkering Site - Cafe & onsite overnight parking (FL5)*
■ *Lorry Park - Onsite overnight parking no cafe or fuel (T1)*
■ *Truck Stop/Cafe - Onsite overnight parking (T2)*
■ *Motorway Service Station (T3)*
■ *Truck Stop - Bunker fuel/showers/cafe/onsite overnight parking (T4)*

For key to site symbols see page 8

FL4 ■   Ballinluig Services

**Ballinluig, Pitlochry
Perth and Kinross PH9 0LG
T 01796 482212**

ON THE OLD A9 Ballinluig Services can be found at Ballinluig on the A9. 20 miles north of Perth, 5 miles south of Pitlochry. Between Pitlochry and Birnam and on the right-hand side if heading north.

CREDIT/DEBIT CARDS

FUEL CARDS (see key on page 9)
① ② ③ ④ ⑤ ⑥ ⑦ ⑧ ⑭ ㉒ ㉓ ㉘ ㉝ ㉞

TRUCK FACILITIES
P free, Coach parking available, shared with LGV, Ample room for manoeuvring, Fridge parking, Quiet area

DRIVER FACILITIES
Showers, 1 male, 1 female (free) Takeaway food, Vegetarian/healthy meals, Fax/copier, Phone top-ups/accessories, Truckers' accessories, Clothing for sale, Post Office nearby

SITE COMMENTS/INFORMATION
Fridge Lorries switch off at 22:00

Parking 24 hours. Shop and other facilities 08:00-20:30. Fuel 07:00-22:00   **517**

FL2 ■   BP Spar Kincardine

**Kincardine Bridge Road, Falkirk
Stirlingshire FK2 8PH
T 01324 831066**

ON THE A876 Take the M9 exit 7 onto the M876 and follow it to the roundabout at the end. Continue on the A876 for 1 mile. Viewforth Services is on the left.

CREDIT/DEBIT CARDS

FUEL CARDS (see key on page 9)
① ③ ④ ⑦ ⑭ ㉒ ㉞

TRUCK FACILITIES
Overnight parking on lane close to the site

DRIVER FACILITIES
Takeaway food

SITE COMMENTS/INFORMATION
This site is close to all major motorways in the area

Nearby parking 24 hours. All on-site facilities 06:00-22:00   **518**

Broxden Services, Perth   FL1 ■

2 Broxden Avenue, Perth
Perth and Kinross PH2 0PX
T 01738 626332

OFF THE A93 From the roundabout at the end of the M90, take the A93 towards Perth, turn right at the next roundabout and Broxden Services is on the same site as McDonald's and the Park and Ride.

CREDIT/DEBIT CARDS

FUEL CARDS (see key on page 9)
③ ㉓ ㉖ ㉗

TRUCK FACILITIES
Short-term coach parking (6 spaces)
Floodlighting, CCTV, plenty of room, quiet parking area, Adblue in containers

DRIVER FACILITIES
Takeaway food nearby, phone top-ups

SITE COMMENTS/INFORMATION
New site. Clean facilities
Accomodation nearby, Travelodge

All on-site facilities 24 hours.   **519**

Cot House Services, Argyll   FL2 ■

Cot House, Dunoon, Argyll
Argyll and Bute PA23 8QT
T 01369 840333

ON THE A815 Cot House Services is on the A815 between the villages of Ardbeg and Inverchapel approximately 6 miles north of Dunoon on the left-hand side if heading north.

CREDIT/DEBIT CARDS

FUEL CARDS (see key on page 9)
① ③

TRUCK FACILITIES
Overnight local parking nearby

SITE COMMENTS/INFORMATION
Regular special offers and sales, large variety of stock in shop

All on-site facilities 06:30-22:00   **520**

Dalwhinnie Service Station   FL4 ■

Dalwhinnie, Inverness
Highland PH19 1AF
T 01528 522311

ON THE A889 Dalwhinnie is a few miles south of Newtonmore at the A9 end of the A889 which is the road that joins the A86 to the A9.

CREDIT/DEBIT CARDS

FUEL CARDS (see key on page 9)
① ② ③ ④ ⑦ ㉞

TRUCK FACILITIES
P Free
Coach parking available, shared with LGV
Ample room for manoeuvring

DRIVER FACILITIES
Accommodation nearby
TV, showers, internet access
Takeaway food
Train nearby

Parking 24 hours. Fuel/shop 07:00-20:00 Mon-Fri, 08:00-18:00 Sat, 10:00-18:00 Sun.   **521**

FL1  Forfar Road Service Station, Dundee

Forfar Road, Dundee
Angus DD4 9BT
T 01382 507534 www.forfarroad.co.uk

ON THE A90 From Perth, follow A90 towards Dundee and around north side of the town. At junction with the A929 and A972 stay on the A90 as it turns left. Continue across next roundabout and Forfar Station is 200 yards on the left.

CREDIT/DEBIT CARDS

FUEL CARDS (see key on page 9)

TRUCK FACILITIES
Ample room for manoeuvring

DRIVER FACILITIES
Phone top-ups

Toilets until 22:00. Other on-site facilities 24 hours

522

FL4  The Green Welly Stop

Tyndrum, Perth and Kinross FK20 8RY
T 01301 702088 www.thegreenwellystop.co.uk

ON THE A82 The Green Welly is located on the A82 between the villages of Clifton and Tyndrum on the right-hand side if heading north-west.

CREDIT/DEBIT CARDS

FUEL CARDS (see key on page 9)

TRUCK FACILITIES
P free Coach parking available (4 spaces)
Ample room for manoeuvring
Quiet area, CCTV

DRIVER FACILITIES
Takeaway food, Phone accessories/top-ups, Truckers' accessories, Train nearby

SITE COMMENTS/INFORMATION
Please have your fuel cards checked before fuelling.

Parking 24 hours. Other on-site facilities 07:00-22:00 in summer, 08:00-21:00 in winter

523

T2  Horse Shoe Café

Abernyte Road, Inchture, Nr Dundee
Perth and Kinross PH14 9
T 01828 686283

ON THE A90 If heading to Dundee from Perth, exit at the Inchture interchange and turn left onto the B953 towards Abernyte and the Horse Shoe Café is about half a mile along on the left.

TRUCK FACILITIES
P free
Ample room for manoeuvring
Quiet area, Truck dealership/workshop

DRIVER FACILITIES
Washroom
Takeaway food, Vegetarian/Healthy meals

SITE COMMENTS/INFORMATION
Plans to build shower block and more parking spaces underway
Refurbishment planned soon

Parking and nearby fuel accessible 24 hours. Other on-site facilities accessible 07:30-21:00

524

Kinross Services | T3

Moto Ltd
nr Kinross
Perth and Kinross KY13 0NQ
T 01577 863123 www.moto-way.com

M90 AT JUNCTION 6. On the A977.

CREDIT/DEBIT CARDS

FUEL CARDS (see key on page 9)
27

TRUCK FACILITIES
Coach parking available (6 spaces)

DRIVER FACILITIES
Accommodation on-site, Travelodge
Shower, washroom, TV, truckers'
accessories
Takeaway food

All on-site facilities accessible 24 hours | **525**

'The Last Drop' (Tayside Truckstop) | T4

Tayside Truckstop, Smeaton Road
West Gourdie Ind. Est., Dundee
Angus DD2 4UT
OFF THE A90 From Perth, take the A90 to Dundee and
around the north side of the town. Turn left into Myrekirk
Road at the roundabout signposted to Gourdie Industrial
Estate. Continue to the end of the road then turn right and
right again and it's on your right.

CREDIT/DEBIT CARDS

FUEL CARDS (see key on page 9)
1 2 4 7 34

TRUCK FACILITIES
P Overnight (charge)
Coach parking (4 spaces). CCTV
Ample room for manoeuvring
Quiet area. Fridge lorry area
Truck washing facilities
Truck dealership/workshop

DRIVER FACILITIES
Accomm. nearby, half a mile, Travelodge
Showers – 3 unisex (free), washroom,
rest area, TV, Euros changed/accepted
Takeaway food

Parking & bunker fuel 24 hours. Bar 12:00-23:00 Mon-Thu, 12:00-00:00 Fri, 11:00-00:00 Sat, 12:30-23:00 Sun
Restaurant 07:30-20:45 Mon, 06:30-20:45 Tue-Fri, 07:30-23:45 Sat. Other on-site facilities accessible 06:30-21:00 | **526**

Muirpark Truckstop & Garage | T4

Bannockburn Road, Bannockburn,
Nr Stirling, Stirlingshire FK7 8AL
T 07785 970444 www.muirparktruckstop.co.uk

ON THE A9 From junction 9 of the M9 or junction 9 of the
M80, take the A91 towards Bannockburn. At the roundabout
with the A9, turn right onto the A9 towards Falkirk. Muirpark
is a few yards along on the left-hand side.

CREDIT/DEBIT CARDS

FUEL CARDS (see key on page 9)
1 2 4 34

TRUCK FACILITIES
P free
Quiet area, Overnight coach, Floodlights
Ample room for manoeuvring, CCTV

DRIVER FACILITIES
Showers – 3 m, 1 f (£1.00),
Accommodation nearby, Washroom,
rest area, TV, Takeaway food, Vegetarian
meals, Clothing and CB sales/repairs
nearby, Euros

SITE COMMENTS/INFORMATION
Family run business, home cooked food,
friendly service and helpful staff

Parking and fuel accessible 24 hours. Other on-site facilities accessible 07:00-21:00 Mon-Thurs, 07:00-14:00 Fri | **527**

T2 — Nancy's Harbour Restaurant

**Shore Road, Perth Harbour, Perth
Perth and Kinross PH2 8BD
T 01738 625788**

OFF THE A912 If heading south, exit at junction 9 of M90 and re-enter the carriageway heading north. Exit at junction 10 onto the A192 towards Perth. In three quarters of a mile turn right into Friarton Road. Harbour Restaurant is half a mile on the right.

TRUCK FACILITIES
P Quiet area
Ample room for manoeuvring

DRIVER FACILITIES
Accommodation on-site
Shower – 1 m, (charge), washroom

SITE COMMENTS/INFORMATION
Please note that there is considerably more parking available around this site in the evening and throughout the night than is available during the day. Phone for more details

Parking 24 hours. All other on-site facilities 06:30-18:00 Mon-Thurs, 06:30-16:00 Fri, 08:00-13:00 Sat
Nearby shop and fuel 24 hours

528

FL1 ● — Rix Derv Stop

**Rix Ltd, North Quay, Montrose
Angus DD10 8DS
T 01674 673562**

OFF THE B9133 From the A92 heading north into Montrose, take your first right onto the B9133 Wharf Street. Keep right as the road bears right into River Street. Rix is near the bottom, on the left just before the tight left-hand bend.

CREDIT/DEBIT CARDS

FUEL CARDS (see key on page 9)
7

TRUCK FACILITIES
Ample room for manoeuvring

DRIVER FACILITIES
Accommodation nearby, half mile, Links Hotel

All on-site facilities 24 hours

529

T 3 — Stirling Services

**Moto Ltd
Pirnhall interchange, Stirling
Stirlingshire FK7 8EU
T 01786 813614** www.moto-way.com

M9 M80 INTERCHANGE Exit at junction 9 from either the M9 or the M80 and Stirling Services is on the roundabout at the bottom of either sliproad.

CREDIT/DEBIT CARDS

FUEL CARDS (see key on page 9)
3 **27**

TRUCK FACILITIES
P *with voucher*   **P** *only*   *Voucher value*
£15.00   £13.00   £6.00
Coach parking available (4 spaces)
Fridge parking, Quiet parking
Room to manoeuvre

DRIVER FACILITIES
Accommodation on-site, Travelodge
Shower, female (1) (free)
TV, Takeaway food, Vegetarian meals
Post Office, Arcade machines, Phone top-ups, Clothing

Forecourt & Fresh Express Restaurant open 24 hours. WH Smith open 07:00-22:30, BK open 11:00-21:00

530

Stracathro Service Area   FL4 ■

Stracathro, nr Brechin, Angus DD9 7PX
T 01674 840048

ON THE A90 By-pass Brechin on the A90 heading for Stonehaven. Two miles past the turning for the B966 you will see signs for Stracathro Services. Stracathro Services are accessible both north and south-bound with a slip road for north-bound traffic and a fly-over for southbound traffic.

CREDIT/DEBIT CARDS

FUEL CARDS (see key on page 9)
① ② ③ ④ ⑦ ㉓ ㉞

TRUCK FACILITIES
P with voucher, £9.50 (voucher = £8.00)
Coach parking available, shared with LGV
Ample room for manoeuvring
Quiet area
Fridge lorries welcome, no separate area
Adblue in containers

DRIVER FACILITIES
Shower, 1 unisex (£2.00)
TV
Takeaway food, Vegetarian meals
Truckers' accessories, Phone top-ups

Fuel, shop and toilets 24 hours. Other on-site facilities 06:00-21:00 Mon-Fri, 06:00-20:00 Sat, 07:00-21:00 Sun   **531**

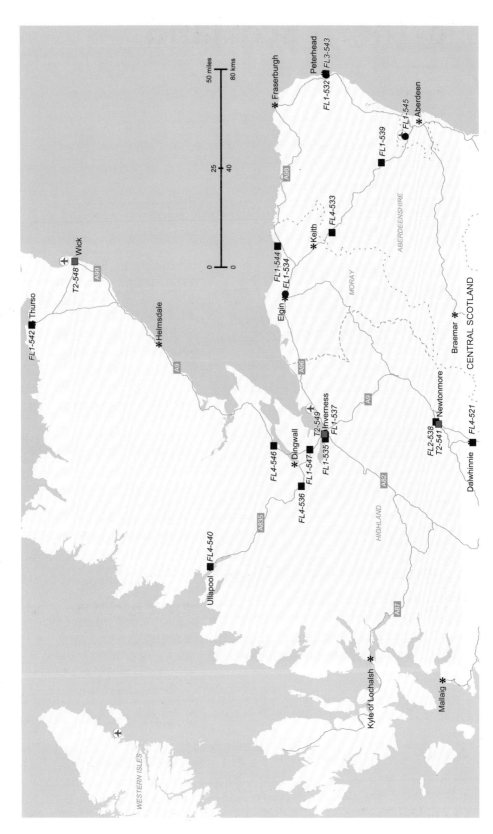

Northern Scotland

■ *Cafe - Layby parking (FD1)*
■ *Cafe - No overnight parking (FD2)*
■ *Filling Station - No overnight parking/cafe (FL1)*
● *Bunkering Site - No overnight parking/cafe (FL1)*
■ *Filling Station - Nearby overnight parking no cafe (FL2)*
● *Bunkering Site - Nearby overnight parking no cafe (FL2)*
■ *Filling Station - Cafe no onsite overnight parking (FL3)*
■ *Filling Station - Onsite overnight parking (FL4)*
● *Bunkering Site - Onsite overnight parking (FL4)*
● *Bunkering Site - Cafe & onsite overnight parking (FL5)*
■ *Lorry Park - Onsite overnight parking no cafe or fuel (T1)*
■ *Truck Stop/Cafe - Onsite overnight parking (T2)*
■ *Motorway Service Station (T3)*
■ *Truck Stop - Bunker fuel/showers/cafe/onsite overnight parking (T4)*

For key to site symbols see page 8

FL1 ●   Asco UK, Peterhead

Asco Oils Ltd, Upperton Yard, Damhead Peterhead, Aberdeenshire AB42 2PF
T 01779 873014

OFF THE A90 From Ellon, take the A90 north-eastbound towards Peterhead. At the roundabout with the A982, turn left staying on the A90. Take the next small turning on the left and left again into Asco UK.

CREDIT/DEBIT CARDS

FUEL CARDS (see key on page 9)
❶

TRUCK FACILITIES
Ample room for manoeuvring

Bunker fuel 24 hours. Manned by security guard   **532**

FL4 ■   Ashgrove

Cairnie, Huntly
Aberdeenshire AB54 4TL
T 01466 760223

ON THE A96 Ashgrove is on the A96 at the village of Cairnie on the left-hand side. Halfway between Keith and Huntly.

CREDIT/DEBIT CARDS

FUEL CARDS (see key on page 9)
❶❷❸㉕㉞

TRUCK FACILITIES
Coach parking available (2 spaces)
Quiet area
Ample room for manoeuvring
Overnight parking on roadside within the complex
Truck washing facilities

DRIVER FACILITIES
Takeaway food
Phone top-ups/accessories

Fuel, shop and toilets 06:00-22:00 Mon-Sat, 08:00-20:00 Sun. Parking 24 hours
All other on-site facilities 07:00-18:30 Mon-Fri, 08:00-17:00 Sat & Sun   **533**

Ballie Brothers Ltd

FL1 ●

**Linkwood Place, Linkwood Ind. Est.
Elgin, Moray IV30 1HZ
T 01343 555312**

OFF THE A96 Take the A96 Elgin to Lhanbryde Road, following the signs for Linkwood Industrial Estate on the outskirts of Elgin. Take the first right after turning into the estate and Ballie Brothers is on the left.

CREDIT/DEBIT CARDS

FUEL CARDS (see key on page 9)
①②④⑦㉞

TRUCK FACILITIES
Short-term coach parking (14 spaces)
Truck washing facilities
Truck dealership/workshop
Tyre repair/sales nearby

DRIVER FACILITIES
Accommodation nearby, half mile, Travel Inn
Takeaway food

Short-term parking and bunker fuel 24 hours. Other on-site facilities 06:30-02:00 **534**

Blackpark Filling Station, Inverness

FL1 ■

**Clachnaharry Road, Inverness
Highland IV3 8QH
T 01463 233632**

ON THE A862 (The old A9) If heading north-westbound out of Inverness on the A862 towards Beauly, Blackpark Filling Station is on your left opposite the West side of the Carse Industrial Estate, past B&Q and the canal bridge.

CREDIT/DEBIT CARDS

FUEL CARDS (see key on page 9)
①②③⑦⑧㉗

DRIVER FACILITIES
Clothing for sale
Takeaway food nearby

All on-site facilities 06:30-22:00 Mon-Sun. **535**

Contin Filling Station

FL1 ■

**Main Road, Contin, Near Strathpeffer,
Ross-shire, Highland IV14 6ES
T 01997 421948**

ON THE A835 Take the A9 north-west out of Inverness. At Tore turn left onto the A835. Contin Filling Station is in the middle of the village of Contin on your right-hand side, 500 yards past the turning for the A834.

CREDIT/DEBIT CARDS

FUEL CARDS (see key on page 9)
①②③④⑦⑧⑬㉓㉕㉞

TRUCK FACILITIES
Short-term coach parking
Floodlighting
CCTV
Plenty of room for manoeuvre in lorry park

DRIVER FACILITIES
Accommodation nearby, 100 yards, Coul House
Phone top-ups
Post Office nearby

All on-site facilities 07:30-20:00 **536**

FL1 • CPL Petroleum, Inverness

CPL Petroleum Ltd, 33 Harbour Road
Longman Industrial Estate
Inverness, Highland IV1 1UA
T 01463 238989

OFF THE A82 From the A9 heading north, by-pass Inverness and continue past junction with the B865. Left at next round-about and take A82 towards town. Left at next roundabout then second turning on the right. CPL is at the end of the road.

CREDIT/DEBIT CARDS NEARBY

FUEL CARDS (see key on page 9)
❶

DRIVER FACILITIES
Accommodation nearby, half mile, Braemore Hotel & Travel Inn
Takeaway food nearby
International papers nearby

Red diesel 08:30-17:00. All other on-site facilities 24 hours

537

FL2 ■ Grants Filling Station (Sinclairs), Newtownmore

Perth Road, Newtownmore
Highland PH20 1AP
T 01540 673217

ON THE B9150 From the A9, take the B9150 into Newtonmore and Grants is on your left-hand side in the village before you reach the A86.

CREDIT/DEBIT CARDS

FUEL CARDS (see key on page 9)
❶❷❸❹❼❽㉗

TRUCK FACILITIES
Overnight parking next door at Chefs Grill

DRIVER FACILITIES
Accommodation available nearby, 500 yards, The Pines
Train nearby

SITE COMMENTS/INFORMATION
Large forecourt area
Easy access for LGVs

Parking 24 hours at nearby Chefs Grill. All on-site facilities 07:00-22:00 Mon-Sun

538

FL1 ■ Inverurie Service Station, Inverurie

North Street, Inverurie
Aberdeenshire AB51 4DJ
T 01467 620443

OFF THE A96 If heading south on the A96, take the first turning into Inverurie and head towards the town centre. The service station is on the main road and on the right-hand side, just after the junction with the B9001.

CREDIT/DEBIT CARDS

FUEL CARDS (see key on page 9)
❸㉗

DRIVER FACILITIES
Accommodation nearby, half a mile, Strathburn Hotel
Showers nearby
Post Office nearby

SITE COMMENTS/INFORMATION
Good location on main road

All on-site facilities 24 hours.

539

Lochbroom Filling Station, Ullapool — FL2 ■

Garve Road, Ullapool
Ross-shire IV27 2SX
T 01854 612298 W www.lochbroom.com

ON THE A835 Take the A9 north-west out of Inverness. At Tore, turn left onto the A835 and continue to Ullapool. Lochbroom Filling Station is on the right-hand side just before the junction with the A835.

CREDIT/DEBIT CARDS

FUEL CARDS (see key on page 9)
① ② ③ ④ ⑥ ⑧ ⑬ ㉕

TRUCK FACILITIES
Quiet area nearby
Overnight coach shared with LGV
Electric hook up nearby
Plenty of room for manoeuvre

DRIVER FACILITIES
Accommodation available nearby, Riverside Hotel, £30.00
Takeaway, Evening ent., Laundry, Internet, and Post Office nearby, Phone top-ups

SITE COMMENTS/INFORMATION
Site very close to the ferry terminal
Fridge lorries switch off pm

All on-site facilities 07:30-21:00 — **540**

Newtonmore Grill (formerly The Chef's Grill Diner) — T2 ■

Perth Road, Newtonmore, nr Inverness
Highland PH20 1BB
T 01540 673702

OFF THE A9 ON THE B9150 From Perth, take the A9 towards Inverness. Take the B9150 into Newtonmore and The Chef's Grill Diner is 1 mile on your left before you reach the A86.

CREDIT/DEBIT CARDS

TRUCK FACILITIES
Addional parking on local roads.
Coach parking shared with LGV
Quiet area. Fridge lorry area
Fridges must switched off by 23:00
Ample room for manoeuvring
Truck dealership/workshop nearby

DRIVER FACILITIES
Accommodation nearby, various hotels
Shower – 1 unisex, TV, laundry service, truckers' accessories, takeaway food

SITE COMMENTS/INFORMATION
Staff will arrange accommodation for you and deliver you to the hotel personally

Parking 24 hours. Restaurant and other facilities 06:30-22:00 Mon-Fri. 06:30-20:00 Sat. 08:00-20:00 Sun.
Bar until Midnight Sun, Mon, Tues & Wed and until 01:00 Thurs — **541**

Pennyland Service Station, Caithness — FL1 ■

Scrabster Road, Thurso, Caithness
Highland KW14 7JU
T 01847 892029

ON THE A9 Follow the A9 through Thurso towards Scrabster. Pennyland is on the left-hand side as you are leaving the town.

CREDIT/DEBIT CARDS

FUEL CARDS (see key on page 9)
③ ㉗

TRUCK FACILITIES
Truck dealership/workshop
Plenty of room to manoeuvre

DRIVER FACILITIES
Accommodation nearby, half a mile, Murray House & Pentland Hotel
Phone top-ups/accessories

All on-site facilities 07:00-22:00. — **542**

FL2 ■ Peterhead Motors & Pit-stop Cafe, Peterhead

**South Road, Peterhead
Aberdeenshire AB42 2XX
T 01779 475171**

ON THE A982 If heading northbound into the town along the A982, Peterhead Motors is on the left-hand side, a few yards south of the junction with the A950.

CREDIT/DEBIT CARDS

FUEL CARDS (see key on page 9)
① ② ③ ④ ⑤ ⑭ ㉒ ㉓ ㉗ ㉞

TRUCK FACILITIES
Truck washing facilities
Tank cleaning facilities
Nearby overnight parking + 2 short-term on-site parking spaces
LGV tyre repairs/sales

DRIVER FACILITIES
Truckers' accessories
Takeaway food

SITE COMMENTS/INFORMATION
Well stocked Spar Shop on-site

Nearby parking times unknown. Toilets 06:30-22:00. Other on-site facilities 24 hours **543**

FL1 ■ Regency Oils, Buckie

**Regency Oils Ltd, 15 Marine Parade
Buckie, Aberdeenshire AB56 1UT
T 01542 832327**

OFF THE A942 From the A98 Fochabers to Cullen road, take the A942 into Buckie. Continue on that road around the tight right-hand bend so that the sea is on your left. From there Regency Oils will be 200 yards on your right.

CREDIT/DEBIT CARDS

FUEL CARDS (see key on page 9)
③ ④ ⑦ ㉞

TRUCK FACILITIES
Adblue available at pumps

All on-site facilities 08:00-20:00. **544**

FL1 ● Regency Oils, Dyce

**Regency Oils Ltd, Kirkhill Place
Kirkhill Industrial Estate, Dyce, Aberdeen
Aberdeenshire AB21 0GU
T 01542 832327**

OFF THE A96 From Aberdeen take A96 to Inverurie. Continue for 2 miles beyond junction with the A947. Turn right to Kirkhill Industrial Estate. After half a mile turn right for 400 yards then left. Take next right into Kirkhill Place and it's on the left.

CREDIT/DEBIT CARDS

FUEL CARDS (see key on page 9)
① ② ④ ⑦ ㉞

TRUCK FACILITIES
Adblue at the pumps

DRIVER FACILITIES
Accommodation nearby, half mile, Aberdeen Airport Thistle & Speedbird Inn

SITE COMMENTS/INFORMATION
This site is within half a mile of an airport

All on-site facilities 24 hours **545**

Skiach Services   FL4 ∎

**Unit 4D, Evanton Industrial Estate
Evanton, Rosshire IV16 9XH
T 01349 830182** www.gleaner.co.uk

OFF THE A9 Take the A9 from Inverness to Alness, by-passing Evanton on your left. Skiach Services is on your left, just before the turning for the B9176 towards Bonar Bridge and Sittenham.

CREDIT/DEBIT CARDS

FUEL CARDS (see key on page 9)
② ③ ④ ㉔ ㉕ ㉞

TRUCK FACILITIES
P free
Coach parking available (10 spaces)
Ample room for manoeuvring
Floodlighting, CCTV, Fridge parking
Quiet parking
DRIVER FACILITIES
Showers – 1 unisex, £1.00
Drivers' washroom
TV, Arcade machines
Takeaway food, Vegetarian meals
Phone top-ups/accessories
Fax/copier, Truckers' accessories

Café open until 22:00. All other on-site facilities 24 hours   **546**

Tore Service Station, Tore   FL1 ∎

**Main Road, Tore, nr Inverness
Rosshire IV6 7RZ
T 01463 811622**

ON THE A832 From Inverness, take the A9 north-west for 7 miles. At the roundabout with the A832 and A835 turn right onto the A832 towards Munlochy. Tore Service Station is 400 yards on the left-hand side.

CREDIT/DEBIT CARDS

FUEL CARDS (see key on page 9)
① ② ④ ⑦ ㉞

TRUCK FACILITIES
Short-term coach parking

DRIVER FACILITIES
Hot drinks free to LGV drivers
buying fuel

All on-site facilities 06:00-22:00 Mon-Thu, 06:00-21:00 Fri, 07:00-21:00 Sat, 09:00-19:00 Sun   **547**

Wick Harbour Café   T2 ∎

**21 Harbour Quay, Wick, Caithness
Highland KW1 5EP
T 01955 602433**

ON THE A99 From the A882 follow signs for Wick town centre. Turn left at the junction with the A99 into Cliff Road, continue for a few yards. Turn right into River Street and follow it around along Martha Terrace, then sharp left into Harbour Quay.

TRUCK FACILITIES
Lorry park opposite at harbour front
P free. Coach parking
Ample room for manoeuvring
Truck dealership/workshop nearby

DRIVER FACILITIES
Accommodation on-site, £25
Takeaway food
Clothing for sale nearby
Train nearby

SITE COMMENTS/INFORMATION
Close to town centre facilities

Nearby parking accessible 24 hours at harbour front. Current opening hours are Mon-Sat 09.00-17:00   **548**

T2 ■

Woody's Truckstop

**12 Henderson Road, Longman Ind. Est.
Inverness, Invernesshire IV1 1SN
T 01463 715815/239162**

OFF THE A82 Take the A9 along the east side of Inverness. At the roundabout with A82, turn towards town along Longman Road. At the next roundabout turn around heading back out of the town, take next left. Woody's is 400 yards on the right.

TRUCK FACILITIES
P
Quiet area
Coach parking available, shared with LGV
Ample room for manoeuvring
CCTV, security guard
Fridge lorry area at bottom of lorry park
Truck dealership/workshop nearby
Tyre repair/sales, truckwash and windscreen repairs nearby

DRIVER FACILITIES
Showers – 2 m, 1 f, washroom, TV
Euros changed/accepted Takeaway food
CB sales/repairs nearby

Parking 24 hours. All other on-site facilities 05:45-21:00 Mon-Fri, 05:45-18:00 Sat, 08:00-14:00 Sun   **549**

Acknowledgements

AUTHOR ACKNOWLEDGEMENTS

- The Melbournes, Alliers and 'Paddy' Searle for keeping me fed.
- Gary Russell, Colin Turner, Wendy Glindon and Dave Seager for their wisdom, information and financial assistance.
- Everyone at BBC Radio 4 and Alicia, Ben and Emily at BBC3 (a great time had by all!).
- Future Publishing, *Trucking* magazine, *Truck and Driver*, *Motoring and Leisure*, *Fast Forward* and *Transport News*.
- *The Daily Mirror*, *Birmingham Post*, *Coventry Telegraph*, *Western Morning News*, *Warwickshire Evening Telegraph*, *Coventry Citizen*, *Coventry Observer*, *Western Gazette* and Emma at *The Sunday Times*.
- Sam and Doug (happy snappers!).
- Capital Trucking, Colin Barge at VBG, Tom Brown at Acasia Software.
- Keltruck West Bromwich and Steve Philpot at Royal Mail Bristol.
- The FTA, RHA, AA, CWU, RAC, Air One, G&G Vitamins, Birmingham Org, St John Ambulance and Skills for logistics.
- All my translators the world over!
- Everyone at Pertemps Bristol and Financial Solutions for keeping me in the black (most of the time).
- All at Business Post, British Bakeries, Royal Mail, Sainsbury's and Chris at Gist for photographs and employment!
- Volvo Trucks for some great images.
- All fuel card companies for sending me their directories.
- All Bristol's truck dealerships for their time and advice.
- Amazon, Yell.com, DVLA, DSA, Microsoft and Google (for invaluable information).
- All the sites that took the time and made the effort to be included in this publication.
- Everyone at Haynes Publishing (for their patience and hard work).
- All those who I haven't already mentioned who contributed in some way to help make this book a reality (you know who you are).

I thank you from the bottom of my steel toe-cap boots!

Author:	**Lisa Marie Melbourne**
Project Manager:	**Louise McIntyre**
Page build:	**Chris Fayers**
Design:	**Lee Parsons**
Illustrations:	**Matthew Marke**
Copy editor:	**Ian Heath**
Maps:	**Customised Mapping**